Entrepreneurship

BICENTENNIAL
1807
WILEY
2007
BICENTENNIAL

THE WILEY BICENTENNIAL–KNOWLEDGE FOR GENERATIONS

Each generation has its unique needs and aspirations. When Charles Wiley first opened his small printing shop in lower Manhattan in 1807, it was a generation of boundless potential searching for an identity. And we were there, helping to define a new American literary tradition. Over half a century later, in the midst of the Second Industrial Revolution, it was a generation focused on building the future. Once again, we were there, supplying the critical scientific, technical, and engineering knowledge that helped frame the world. Throughout the 20th Century, and into the new millennium, nations began to reach out beyond their own borders and a new international community was born. Wiley was there, expanding its operations around the world to enable a global exchange of ideas, opinions, and know-how.

For 200 years, Wiley has been an integral part of each generation's journey, enabling the flow of information and understanding necessary to meet their needs and fulfill their aspirations. Today, bold new technologies are changing the way we live and learn. Wiley will be there, providing you the must-have knowledge you need to imagine new worlds, new possibilities, and new opportunities.

Generations come and go, but you can always count on Wiley to provide you the knowledge you need, when and where you need it!

WILLIAM J. PESCE
PRESIDENT AND CHIEF EXECUTIVE OFFICER

PETER BOOTH WILEY
CHAIRMAN OF THE BOARD

Entrepreneurship

William Bygrave

Babson College

Andrew Zacharakis

Babson College

BICENTENNIAL
1807
WILEY
2007
BICENTENNIAL

John Wiley & Sons, Inc.

ASSOCIATE PUBLISHER	Judith Joseph
SENIOR ACQUISITIONS EDITOR	Jayme Heffler
ASSOCIATE EDITOR	Jennifer Conklin
EDITORIAL ASSISTANT	Carissa Marker
EXECUTIVE MARKETING MANAGER	Christopher Ruel
PRODUCTION SERVICES MANAGER	Dorothy Sinclair
SENIOR PRODUCTION EDITOR	Sandra Dumas
DESIGN DIRECTOR	Harry Nolan
DESIGNER	Michael St. Martine
SENIOR MEDIA EDITOR	Allison Morris
SENIOR PHOTO EDITOR	Hilary Newman
PRODUCTION MANAGEMENT SERVICES	PineTree Composition
COVER PHOTO CREDIT	©Oleg Prikhodko/Stockphoto
BICENTENNIAL LOGO DESIGN	Richard J. Pacifico

This book was set in 10.5/12pt Adobe Garamond by Laserwords Private Limited, Chennai, India and printed and bound by R.R. Donnelley/Willard. The cover was printed by Phoenix color.

The book is printed on acid-free paper. ∞

To order books or for customer service please call 1-800-CALL WILEY (225-5945).

Library of Congress Cataloging-in-Publication Data:

Bygrave, William D., 1937–
   Entrepreneurship / William Bygrave, Andrew Zacharakis.
      p. cm.
   ISBN-13: 978-0-471-75545-6
   ISBN-10: 0-471-75545-1
  1. New business enterprises. 2. Entrepreneurship. 3. Small business—Management. I. Zacharakis, Andrew. II. Title.
   HD62.5.B938 2008
   658.4′21—dc22

                        2007001283

ISBN 13 978-0-471-75545-6

Printed in the United States of America

10 9 8 7 6 5 4 3 2 1

To Frederic C. Hamilton and John H. Muller, Jr., pioneers, entrepreneurs, and benefactors of Babson College.

CONTENTS IN BRIEF

CONTENTS

x | **Contents**

PREFACE

The green shoots of entrepreneurship give an economy its vitality. They give rise to new products and services, fresh applications for existing products and services, and new ways of doing business. Entrepreneurship stirs up the existing economic order and prunes out the dead wood. Established companies that fail to adapt to the changes cease to be competitive in the marketplace and go out of business.

Within the broadest definition, entrepreneurs are found throughout the world of business because any firm, big or small, must have its share of entrepreneurial drive if it is to survive and prosper. This textbook focuses on starting and growing independent new ventures. It is based on entrepreneurship courses taught at Babson College and at universities around the world.

One of the most common questions that entrepreneurship educators are asked is, Can entrepreneurship be taught? Our response is that anyone with a desire to become an entrepreneur will be more successful if he or she has taken a course on how to start and grow a new venture. About 40% of the students who have taken the new-venture course at Babson College since 1985 have gone on to start full-time businesses at some time in their careers. Many have started more than one.

While this textbook empowers would-be entrepreneurs to start and grow their new ventures, it's not only for them. Any student who reads this book will learn about the entrepreneurial process and the role of entrepreneurship in the economy. We believe that all business students, whether or not they start a new business, will benefit from learning about entrepreneurship. After all, entrepreneurship and small business create most of the jobs in the U.S. economy and account for almost half the GDP. They are ubiquitous, and so integral to the economy that almost every student will work in one way or another with entrepreneurs and small businesses after graduation. This textbook will stand students in good stead—not only for starting their own firms, but also for dealing with startups as investors, bankers, accountants, lawyers, customers, vendors, employees, landlords, and in any other capacity.

An entrepreneurial revolution has transformed the economy since the mid 1970s. Central to that revolution is information technology, especially personal computers and the Internet. Information technology has profoundly changed the way companies do business, none more so than startup companies. Today's students were born after the personal computer came into common use, and they came of age in the era of the Web. We believe they need an entrepreneurship text in which information technology is completely integrated all the way through.

This book combines concepts and cases to present the latest theory about entrepreneurship and relate actual experiences. The concepts cover what would-be entrepreneurs need to know to start and grow their businesses, and the cases illustrate how real entrepreneurs have gone out and done it. They cover all stages of the entrepreneurial process, from searching for an opportunity to shaping it into a commercially attractive product or service, launching the new venture, building it into a viable business, and eventually harvesting it.

Chapter 1 discusses the role of entrepreneurship in the U.S. economy and looks at the entrepreneurial competitiveness of nations throughout the world. Chapter 2 is an overview of the factors critical for starting a new enterprise and building it into a successful business.

Chapters 3 through 8 look in detail at what budding entrepreneurs need to do before they open their doors for business. The section starts with searching for opportunities and evaluating them. It explains how to build a workable business model and covers marketing, strategy, team building, financial projections, and business planning. At the end of this section students know how to write a business plan and how much startup capital they need to start their ventures.

The next section, Chapter 9 through 11, deals with financing businesses. Chapter 9 reviews the sources of financing for starting and growing businesses, both in the United States and worldwide. Chapter 10 discusses the nuts and bolts of raising money, particularly equity, to start and grow a business. And Chapter 11 examines debt and other sources of financing.

Entrepreneurs need to understand the legal and tax issues associated with organizing a new business. They also need to know how to protect their intellectual capital. Chapters 12 and 13 explore these topics.

Anyone can start a new venture, but very few new businesses grow into substantial enterprises. Chapter 14 discusses what it takes to grow a business into a healthy company that provides financial rewards for the entrepreneur and good jobs for employees.

Each chapter is accompanied by a case study of entrepreneurs in action. We chose the cases carefully, using these criteria:

- The entrepreneurs and their companies represent a spectrum of situations and industries that is as broad as we could make it.
- The judgment point in most cases occurs in the twenty-first century—some as recently as 2005 and 2006.
- All stages of the entrepreneurial process are covered, from pre-startup through harvest.
- Almost all the entrepreneurs in the cases are in their 20s and 30s; some are recent graduates.

There's no substitute for the experience gained from actually starting a business, but we believe that by completing the case studies in this book students will gain wisdom that would take years to pick up by trial and error as entrepreneurs starting and building businesses from scratch.

Each chapter ends with a unique Opportunity Journal. Here students can reflect on the lessons learned and think about how to apply them to their own entrepreneurial ventures, or to managing their careers. Finally, a Web exercise builds upon key concepts covered in each chapter.

Teaching Supplements

Instructor's Manual

The Instructor's Manual has been designed to facilitate convenient lesson planning and includes the following:

- **Sample Syllabi.** Suggestions are given on dividing up the chapter material based on the frequency and duration of your class period.
- **General Chapter Outline.** The main headers provide a quick snapshot of all of the chapter content.

- *Case Teaching Notes.* Detailed teaching notes go into depth on the material covered in each chapter's accompanying case. They include discussion questions, classroom activities, and additional information on the businesses and entrepreneurs from the cases.

This comprehensive resource can be found on the Instructor Companion Site at www.wiley.com/college/bygrave.

PowerPoint Slides

A robust set of PowerPoint slides gives you the ability to completely integrate your classroom lecture with a powerful visual statement of chapter material. The entire collection of roughly 150 slides is available for downloading from the Instructor Companion Site at www.wiley.com/college/bygrave.

Test Bank

With 60 questions per chapter, the test bank consists of multiple choice, true/false, and short answer questions of varying difficulty. A computerized version of this test bank is also available on the Instructor Companion Site so that you can customize your quizzes and exams. Access these resources at www.wiley.com/college/bygrave.

Additional Cases

In addition to the 14 cases included in the book, 14 additional cases, available on the book's companion site, give instructors more choices and give students more real-life examples. Cases available online include:

Andres Galindo
Alexander Norman and Toni Randolph-Norman
College Coach
Matt Grant
Enox
CardSmith
Makers Mark
Vayusa (the *Ajay Bam* second case)
Beautiful Legs by Post
Neverfail
Matt Coffin
SolidWorks (the *Jon Hirschtick* second case)
David Pearlman
StudentCity.com

Video Cases (DVD)

Eleven videos accompany cases from the book, engaging students and giving them the opportunity to hear first-hand accounts from the entrepreneurs themselves. Available on DVD for instructors, these videos are ideal lecture launchers and a great way to grab a class's attention. Ask your local Wiley representative for more information. Video cases include:

Malincho
Alison Barnard
Jim Poss
Adam Aircraft
ClearVue
Ajay Bam
P'kolino
DayOne
SolidWorks (the *Jon Hirschtick* case)
BetterLiving Patio Rooms
Nancy's Coffee

Acknowledgments

A comprehensive textbook on entrepreneurship covers a very wide range of disciplines that require specialized knowledge, so we invited leading experts to write some of the chapters.

- Entrepreneurial marketing is an emerging academic discipline; two of its leading experts are Abdul Ali at Babson College and Kathleen Seiders at Boston College, who wrote Chapter 6, "Entrepreneurial Marketing."

- Joel Shulman, Babson College, who specializes in entrepreneurial finance, contributed Chapter 11, "Debt and Other Forms of Financing."

- Legal and tax issues go hand in hand when setting up a new business; Richard Mandel, who is a Babson professor and a partner with the law firm Bowditch and Dewey that specializes in small business, wrote Chapter 12.

- Businesses increasingly depend on intellectual know-how, which must be safeguarded just as carefully as physical assets. Chapter 13, "Intellectual Property," was authored by Joseph Iandorio and Kirk Teska, who are patent attorneys in the firm that bears their names.

- Babson professors Donna Kelley and Edward Marram wrote Chapter 14, "Entrepreneurial Growth." Kelley is an expert on innovation, and Marram specializes in growing businesses.

We thank all the contributing authors for their commitment and dedication to making this book as valuable as it can be for students.

We are forever indebted to everyone involved in the entrepreneurial process who has shared experience and wisdom with us. They include entrepreneurs from novices to old hands, informal investors, business angels, venture capitalists, bankers, lawyers, and landlords—indeed, anyone involved with entrepreneurs. We have learned so much from them. We're especially thankful for all the students and alumni we have worked with over the years. Their feedback has helped us shape what we teach, and how we teach it.

We believe that entrepreneurs who successfully build businesses are inherently good coaches and teachers; they have to be if they are to develop and encourage employees. This generosity is borne out by their willingness to share their know-how with budding entrepreneurs. One important way in which entrepreneurs have done that is by allowing us to write cases about them and their companies, and then by coming to class when the cases are discussed. We make a video of each entrepreneur in a question-and-answer session with students immediately after the case is taught for the first time. Those videos, which are an integral part of the case study, are available to instructors using this textbook.

A huge "thank you" to the principals featured in the case studies in this book and on its companion Web site. They are Kalin Pentchev, Andres Galindo, Alison Barnard, Matt Grant, Stephen Kramer, Michael London, Jim Poss, Voislav Damevski, Rick Adam, John Hamilton, Taran Lent, Brooks O'Kane, Bill Samuels, Jr., Ajay Bam, Elizabeth Preis, Andrew Zenoff, Matt Coffin, Axel Bichara, Jon Hirschtick, John Esler, Beth Wood-Leidt, Mario Ricciardelli, Steve Duplessie, Alexander Norman, Antonio Turco-Rivas, J.B. Schneider, and Toni Randolph Norman.

We thank all the case writers who researched and wrote the cases in this book and on its companion Web site. Carl Hedberg, who wrote many of the cases, deserves special recognition.

We'd also like to thank our student research assistants, who helped track down relevant examples in the popular press, acted as our first-draft readers, and worked hard on the instructional support materials; they are current and former Babson MBA students Rich Enos, Richard Raeke, Alexey Amerikov, and Ge Song.

It is a pleasure to be members of the Arthur M. Blank Center for Entrepreneurship at Babson College. Our Babson colleagues are an inspiration. They are pioneers of entrepreneurship education who are continually coming up with new ways of teaching. The Babson faculty comprises a marvelous mix of academics and what we call "pracademics"—practicing academics—who are entrepreneurs, venture capitalists, angel investors, lawyers, and others associated day-to-day with starting and running businesses. Jeffry Timmons, who we affectionately call the Johnny Appleseed of entrepreneurship education, is a mentor on the art and science of teaching entrepreneurship. Steve Spinelli, vice-provost at Babson and himself a graduate of Babson's MBA entrepreneurship program and co-founder of Jiffy Lube, is a pillar of support. Candida Brush, chairperson of the entrepreneurship department, is always encouraging us. Edward Marram, director of the Babson Arthur M. Blank Center for Entrepreneurship and the founder and CEO of GEO-CENTERS, is a valuable sounding board for anything to do with teaching, especially writing cases. We have benefited from discussions with Brian Abraham, Fred Alper, Jean-Luc Boulnois, Mike Caslin, Les Charm, Alan Cohen, Mike Gordon, Len Green, Tim Habbershon, Neal Harris, Bill Johnston, Glenn Kaplus, Donna Kelley, Julian Lange, Nan Langowitz, Maria Minniti, Kevin Mulvaney, Heidi Neck, Ernie Parizeau, Elizabeth Riley, Joel Shulman, and Natalie Taylor, all of whom teach at Babson College.

The Babson administration and staff have supported our efforts: Michael Fetters, formerly provost, encouraged us to write this book and gave us permission to include the cases in the book. Fritz Fleischmann, dean of faculty, eased our labor by supporting sabbatical leaves for both of us. Patricia Greene, the present provost, and Mark Rice, the dean of the graduate school, are steadfast champions of entrepreneurship. William Lawler, associate dean of the graduate school, provided financial support for the writing of some of the cases; David Wylie edited some of them; and Valerie Duffy made sure that the case collection was up to date. Frances Nilsson was always resourceful in helping us with our library and online research. Jim McKellar dealt efficiently with administrative matters.

We are thankful for the financial support we received from the benefactors of the Frederic C. Hamilton Chair for Free Enterprise and the John H. Muller, Jr. Chair for Entrepreneurship—chairs that we are privileged to hold.

We greatly appreciate all the help that we received from the staff at Wiley and its affiliates. Jayme Heffler, senior acquisitions editor, was a continual source of inspiration and encouragement. Carissa Marker's always prompt administrative support kept us on schedule—never an easy task for authors. Hilary Newman organized the selection of pictures. Elisa Adams did a fine job of line editing our manuscript. Christopher Ruel, as marketing manager at Wiley, is making sure the book is disseminated to a wide audience. We are indebted to Sandra Dumas (Senior Production Editor) and John Shannon and

Patty Donovan (Production Coordinators) at Pine Tree Composition for transforming the manuscript into a beautiful finished textbook.

Many reviewers offered thoughtful suggestions that have improved this book. We are indebted to every one of them:

Richard Benedetto, *Merrimack College*
Lowell Busenitz, *University of Oklahoma*
Pat H. Dickson, *Georgia Institute of Technology*
Hung-bin Ding, *Loyola University*
William Gartner, *Clemson University*
Todd A. Finkle, *University of Akron*
Jeffrey June, *Miami University of Ohio*
Heidi Neck, *Babson College*
William R. Sandberg, *University of South Carolina*

Finally, we are both indebted to our families, our patient and supportive wives, and our beautiful and talented children. Thank you for being understanding when we were pushing hard to meet our deadlines.

Bill Gates (bottom left) and Paul Allen (bottom right) with the Microsoft team in December 1978. The company, then almost 4 years old, had revenue of $1.4 million for the 1978 calendar year. For the fiscal year ended June 30, 2005, Microsoft's revenue was almost $40 billion and it had 63,564 employees! (*Source*: Courtesy Microsoft) Bill Gates and Warren Buffet, the two richest men in the world—both self-made—together with Melinda Gates discuss how they will donate most of their fortunes to charity, New York City, June 2006. (*Source*: Spencer Platt/Getty Images News and Sports Services)

THE POWER OF ENTREPRENEURSHIP

This is the entrepreneurial age: In 2006, about half a billion people worldwide were either actively involved in trying to start a new venture or were owner-managers of a new business.[1] More than fifteen hundred new businesses are born every hour of every working day in the United States. Entrepreneurs are driving a revolution that is transforming and renewing economies worldwide. Entrepreneurship is the essence of free enterprise, because the birth of new businesses gives a market economy its vitality. New and emerging businesses create a very large proportion of innovative products and services that transform the way we work and live, such as personal computers, software, the Internet and the Web, biotechnology drugs, overnight package deliveries, and big-box stores. They generate most new jobs. For example, from 1990 to 1994, small, growing firms with 100 or fewer workers generated 7–8 million new jobs in the U.S. economy, whereas firms with more than 100 workers destroyed 3.6 million. In 1998–1999, small business accounted for two-thirds of the 2.6 million net new jobs. And according to the most recent data, small business created *all* the net new jobs in the period 2000–2001.[2]

There has never been a better time to practice the art and science of entrepreneurship. But what is entrepreneurship? Early in the twentieth century, Joseph Schumpeter, the Moravian-born economist writing in Vienna, gave us the modern definition of an entrepreneur—the person who destroys the existing economic order by introducing new products and services, by introducing new methods of production, by creating new forms of organization, or by exploiting new raw materials. According to Schumpeter, that person is most likely to accomplish this destruction by founding a new business but may also do it within an existing one.

Schumpeter was explaining how entrepreneurs had suddenly increased the standard of living of a few industrialized nations.[3] When the industrial revolution began in England around 1760, no nation had enjoyed a standard of living equal to that of Imperial Rome 2,000 years earlier. But from 1870 to 1979, for example, the standard of living of sixteen nations jumped seven-fold on average.[4]

Very few new businesses have the potential to initiate a Schumpeterian "gale" of creation-destruction, as Apple Computer did in the computer industry. The vast

This chapter written by William D. Bygrave.

majority enter existing markets. So in this textbook, we take a broader definition of entrepreneurship than Schumpeter's. Ours encompasses everyone who starts a new business. Our entrepreneur is the person who perceives an opportunity and creates an organization to pursue it. And the entrepreneurial process includes all the functions, activities, and actions associated with perceiving opportunities and creating organizations to pursue them. Our entrepreneur's new business may, in a few rare instances, be the revolutionary sort that rearranges the global economic order, as Wal-Mart, FedEx, and Microsoft have done, and Amazon.com, eBay, and Orbitz.com are now doing. But it is much more likely to be of the incremental kind that enters an existing market.

The Changing Economy

General Motors was founded in 1908 as a holding company for Buick. On December 31, 1955, General Motors became the first American corporation to make over one billion dollars in a year. At one point it was the largest corporation in the United States in terms of its revenues as a percent of GDP. In 1979, its employment in the U.S. peaked at 600,000. In April 2005, General Motors posted a $1.1 billion loss for the first quarter of the year. Its debt was downgraded to junk bond status, and it announced plans to cut 25,000 jobs in the U.S. Once the job cuts have been executed, General Motors will employ 125,000 Americans.

Wal-Mart was founded by Sam Walton in 1962. For the year ended January 31, 2006, Wal-Mart had record sales of $312.4 billion and record earnings of $11.2 billion. Sales increased 9.5% and net income 9.4%. More than 175 million customers visited Wal-Mart stores worldwide every week. During 2004, Wal-Mart added 117 stores in the U.S., and another 248 in Canada, Mexico, Brazil, Argentina, England, Germany, China, and Japan. Wal-Mart created 125,000 new jobs globally in 2004. Wal-Mart was the world's largest corporation in 2006 with 1.3 million associates in the U.S. and a total of 1.8 million globally. It was estimated that more than 3 million American jobs were supported by Wal-Mart.

"We're all working together; that's the secret. And we'll lower the cost of living for everyone, not just in America, but we'll give the world an opportunity to see what it's like to save and have a better lifestyle, a better life for all. We're proud of what we've accomplished; we've just begun.
—*Sam Walton (1918–1992).*

In this chapter we will look at the importance of entrepreneurship and small business to the U.S. and the global economy, describe the entrepreneurial revolution, present a conceptual model for the entrepreneurial sector of the economy and use it to explain major factors in the revolution, and compare and contrast entrepreneurial activity among nations within the context of the conceptual model.

Entrepreneurship and Small Business in the U.S.

In the U.S. there are 24 million or so businesses, of which approximately 99.5% are small businesses.[5] In general, businesses with 500 or fewer employees are classified as small.[6] They account for half the private sector workers and 44.3% of the private payroll, and they generate approximately half the nonfarm private gross domestic product (GDP). If the small business sector of the U.S. economy were a nation, its GDP would rank second in the world: right behind the U.S. medium- and big-business sector, ahead of the entire economy of Japan, and far ahead of the economies of Germany, the U.K, France, and Italy.[7]

Not only are small businesses the engine for job creation, they are also a powerful force for innovation. They employ 39% of all high-tech workers and produce approximately

14 times more patents per employee than large firms.[8] Their share of U.S. research and development (R&D) grew from 5.9% in 1984 to an estimated 20.7% in 2003, with the dollar value growing from $4.4 billion in 1984 to an estimated $40.1 billion in 2003—a nine-fold increase.[9]

Half of the 24 million small businesses are part-time and half are full-time undertakings. Of 12 million full-time businesses, approximately 6 million have only 1 employee (the self-employed owner).[10] Approximately two-thirds of the 12 million full-time businesses are unincorporated and one-third of them are incorporated.

At any one time, approximately 7 million *nascent entrepreneurs* in the U.S. are trying to create a new business; each has conceived an idea for a new venture and taken at least one step toward implementing his or her idea. Many of them abandon their ventures during the gestation period and never actually open their businesses; nonetheless, each year at least 3 million new ventures are born, of which about 75% start from scratch. Most of the others are purchases of existing businesses.[11] Two in every 3 businesses are started in the owner's home. Most remain tiny because they are part-time businesses, but around 600,000 have at least 1 full-time employee.

Survival rates for new businesses were the focus of several different studies.[13] One of the most thorough was done by Alfred Nucci at the U.S. Census Bureau, who calculated the 10-year survival rates of business establishments.[14] He found that 81% survive at least one year, 65% two years, 40% five years, and 25% ten years. The survival rate for independent startups was slightly lower. For example, the one-year rate was 79% instead of 81%. The chance of survival increased with age and size. Survival rates also varied somewhat with industry, but not as strongly as with age and size.

Of course, survival does not necessarily spell success. In general, the median income of small business owners is almost the same as that of wage and salary earners. However, the income distribution is much broader for small business owners, which means that they are more likely to have significantly less income or significantly more income than wage and salaried workers.[15] But small business owners are also building equity in their companies as well as taking income from them, so it is possible that small business owners are better off overall than their wage-earning cohorts. However, a study of business owners disposing of their businesses through sale, closure, passing it on, and other methods found that comparatively few saw their standard of living changed by their business. Only 17% reported that their business had raised their standard of living, while 6% reported the opposite.[16]

Small businesses are distributed throughout the U.S., but not uniformly. The proportion of full-time self-employed by state in 1999 ranged from a high of 14.9% for Alaska to a low of 7.3% for Missouri. In rural areas 10.0% were self-employed, which was almost one percentage point higher than the national average.[17] In 1997, 40% of small businesses were in service industries, 20% in retail, 12% in construction, 8% in wholesale, 8% in finance, 6% in manufacturing, 4% in transportation and communications, and 2% in agricultural services.[18]

The new business formation index was stable through the 1950s and most of the 1960s; there was virtually no growth. By 1970, net new business formation was growing and the growth continued through the 1970s, 1980s, and into the 1990s.[19] No one noticed the change at the time. One of the first documented references to what was taking

A survey by ACNielsen International Research in July 2005 found the following:[12]

- 58% of Americans say they've dreamed of starting a business and becoming their own boss.

- The most common reason for wanting to start a business is to increase one's personal income (66% of respondents), followed by increased independence (63%).

- The primary barriers to starting a business are insufficient financial resources (cited by 49% of respondents) and satisfaction with their current situation (29%).

place was an article called "The coming entrepreneurial revolution" in *The Economist* in December 1976.[20] In this article, Norman Macrae argued that the era of big business was drawing to an end and future increases in employment would come mainly from either smaller firms or small units of big firms. The following year, David Birch published his book *Job Creation in America: How Our Smallest Companies Put the Most People to Work*.[21] The title says it all: It captures the important finding from Birch's comprehensive study of business establishments.

No issue gets the attention of politicians more than job creation. Birch's findings and the stream of research that ensued[22] forever changed the attitude of policy makers to small business. Until then most of their focus had been on big business. After all, in 1953 Charles Erwin Wilson, then GM's president, is reported to have said during the hearings before the Senate Armed Services Committee, "What's good for General Motors is good for the country." At the time, GM was one of the largest employers in the world—only Soviet state industries employed more people.[23]

Entrepreneurial Revolution

On November 1, 1999, Chevron, Goodyear Tire & Rubber Company, Sears Roebuck, and Union Carbide were removed from the Dow Jones Industrial Average (DJIA) and replaced by Intel, Microsoft, Home Depot, and SBC Communications. Intel and Microsoft became the first two companies traded on the NASDAQ exchange to be listed in the DJIA.

This event symbolized what is now called the *entrepreneurship revolution* that transformed the U.S. economy in the last quarter of the twentieth century. Intel and Microsoft are the two major entrepreneurial driving forces in the information technology revolution that has fundamentally changed the way in which we live, work, and play. SBC (formerly Southwestern Bell Corporation) was one of the original "Baby Bells" formed after the U.S. Department of Justice antitrust action resulted in the breakup of AT&T. It is an excellent example of how breaking up a monopoly leads to entrepreneurial opportunities. And Home Depot exemplifies the big-box stores that have transformed much of the retail industry.

Intel was founded in Silicon Valley by Gordon Moore and Robert Noyce and funded by Arthur Rock, the legendary venture capitalist. Gordon Moore, the inventor of Moore's Law,[24] and Robert Noyce, one of the two inventors of the integrated circuit,[25] had been at the birth of Silicon Valley with William Shockley, the co-inventor of the transistor, when Shockley Semiconductor Laboratory was founded in Mountain View in 1956. They left Shockley in 1957 to found Fairchild Semiconductor, which in 1961 introduced the first commercial integrated circuit. In 1968, they left Fairchild to start Intel.

Ted Hoff, employee number 12 at Intel, invented the microprocessor in 1968. In 1971 Intel launched the first commercial microprocessor, heralding a new era in integrated electronics. Then in 1974 it launched the first general-purpose microprocessor, the Intel 8080, which was the brain of the first personal computer,[26] the Altair 8800—a $439 hobbyist's kit—announced by MITS (Micro Instrumentation and Telemetry Systems of Albuquerque) on the front cover of the January 1, 1975, edition of *Popular Electronics*.

According to personal computer folklore, Paul Allen, then working at the minicomputer division of Honeywell in Massachusetts, hurried to his childhood friend and fellow computer enthusiast, Bill Gates, who was a Harvard sophomore, and waving *Popular Electronics* with a mock-up of the Altair 8800 on its front cover, exclaimed, "This is it! It's about to begin!" Within a month or so, Gates had a version of BASIC to run on the Altair. He and Allen joined together in an informal partnership called Micro-Soft and moved to Albuquerque.

"When I was 19, I caught sight of the future and based my career on what I saw. I turned out to have been right."

— *Bill Gates*

Microsoft grew steadily by developing software for personal computers. By 1979 it had moved to Bellevue, Washington, near Seattle where Gates and Allen had grown up. It then had revenue of more than $2 million and 28 employees. It got its big break in 1980–81 when, building on the core of a product acquired from Seattle Computer Products, Microsoft introduced MS-DOS for IBM's first PC. Fourteen years later when Microsoft released Windows 95 in 1995, it sold 4 million copies in 4 days. Its success helped to move the personal computer into 250 million homes, businesses, and schools worldwide. In the early 1990s, Microsoft committed itself to adding Internet capabilities to its products. When Microsoft joined the DJIA in 1999, there were more than 200 million Internet users, up from 3 million just 5 years earlier.

SBC came about in 1984 because of the breakup of AT&T. SBC's growth has come mainly through acquisitions, so we are not making the case that SBC itself is especially entrepreneurial. However, the breakup of AT&T did unleash a wave of entrepreneurship that produced the explosive growth of the telecommunications industry in the last 20 years. According to a recent survey, the top 5 innovations since 1980 are the Internet, cell phones, personal computers, fiber optics, and e-mail.[27] No doubt about it, the phenomenal growth of wireless communications and the Internet would not have happened if AT&T had been allowed to keep its pre-1983 stranglehold on the telecom industry. (AT&T floundered after it was broken up. In 2004, it was dropped from the DJIA, and in 2005 it was acquired by SBC, which then adopted AT&T, Inc. as its corporate name; as a result, AT&T's legendary "T" ticker symbol on the New York Stock Exchange returned to the DJIA.)

Bernard Marcus and Arthur Blank founders of Home Depot, posing with TV set showing them in video teaching employees how to sell in a slump.

Home Depot was founded in 1979 by Bernie Marcus and Arthur Blank. The chain of hardware and do-it-yourself (DIY) stores holds the record for the fastest time for a retailer to pass the $30 billion, $40 billion, $50 billion, $60 billion, and $70 billion annual revenue milestones. It is the second largest retailer in the U.S., surpassed only by Wal-Mart. And it almost set the record for the fastest time from starting up to joining the DJIA when it was only 20 years old. By comparison, Wal-Mart was 35 years old when it displaced F. W. Woolworth in the DJIA. Along with Wal-Mart, Home Depot has set the pace for the retail industry in the last two decades. Together, the two account for about 3% of the nation's GDP and 1.6 million jobs.

At the turn of the twentieth century, about 50% of the U.S. workers were employed in agriculture and domestic service. Less than 100 years later, the number was about 4%. Much of this transformation came about because innovations, many of them introduced by entrepreneurs, made agriculture a shining example of increasing productivity, and labor-saving products such as the vacuum cleaner, gas and electric ranges, washing machines and clothes dryers, dishwashers, automobiles, lawn mowers, floor polishers, processed foods, microwave ovens, and services increased the productivity of household labor. The proportion of the workforce in manufacturing grew from 19% in 1900 to 27% in 1950, thereby providing alternative employment opportunities for farm laborers and domestic workers.

By the turn of the twenty-first century, only 15% of the jobs were in manufacturing and about 40% were in service industries; the proportion of knowledge-based jobs was estimated to be more than 50%. The DJIA reflects the changing face of the U.S. economy: In 1896 the 12 companies comprising the DJIA reflected the dominance of agriculture and basic commodities; in 1928—the first time the DJIA comprised 30 companies—the members reflected the importance of manufacturing, retailing, and the emerging radio industry; and in 1999 the shift was toward knowledge-based industries.

DJIA Companies

1896	1928	1999
American Cotton Oil	Allied Can	Alcoa
American Sugar	Allied Chemical	American Express
American Tobacco	American Smelting & Refining	AT&T Corp.
Chicago Gas	American Sugar	Boeing
Distilling & Cattle Feeding	American Tobacco	Caterpillar
General Electric	Atlantic Refining	Citigroup
Laclede Gas Light	Bethlehem Steel	Coca-Cola
National Lead	Chrysler	Disney
North American	General Electric	DuPont
Tennessee Coal, Iron & Railroad	General Motors	Eastman Kodak
U.S. Leather	General Railway	Exxon-Mobil
U.S. Rubber	Goodrich	General Electric
	International Harvester	General Motors
	International Nickel	Hewlett-Packard
	Mack Trucks	Home Depot
	Nash Motors	Honeywell
	North American	IBM
	Paramount Publix	Intel
	Postum	International Paper
	Radio Corporation	Johnson & Johnson
	Sears, Roebuck	McDonald's
	Standard Oil (NJ)	Merck
	Texas Corporation	Microsoft
	Texas Gulf Sulphur	Morgan JP
	Union Carbide	Philip Morris
	U.S. Steel	Procter & Gamble
	Victor Talking Machines	SBC Communications
	Westinghouse	3M
	Woolworth	United Technologies
	Wright	Walmart

On April 8, 2004, International Paper, AT&T, and Eastman Kodak were replaced with Pfizer, Verizon, and AIG.

Of course, only a few of the entrepreneurial giants ever get into the DJIA, which is composed of only 30 of the most widely held stocks. The following are some of the other legendary entrepreneurs and their companies that featured in the entrepreneurship revolution of the last 30 years.

Perhaps one of the most revolutionary entrepreneurial ideas outside of high-tech industries was Fred Smith's notion to deliver packages overnight anywhere in the U.S. Smith identified a need for shippers to have a system designed specifically for airfreight that could accommodate time-sensitive shipments such as medicines, computer parts, and electronics in a term paper that he wrote as a Yale undergraduate. Smith's professor did not think much of the idea and gave it a C. After tours of duty in Vietnam, Smith founded his company, Federal Express (FedEx) in 1971 and it began operating in 1973 out of Memphis International Airport. In the mid-1970s, Federal Express had taken a leading role in lobbying for air cargo deregulation that finally came in 1977. These changes allowed Federal Express to use larger aircraft and spurred the company's rapid growth. Today FedEx has the world's largest all-cargo air fleet, including McDonnell-Douglass MD-11s and Airbus A-300s and A-310s.[28]

In 1971 when Southwest Airlines began operations, *inter*state airline travel was highly regulated by the federal government, which had set up the Civil Aeronautics Board (CAB) in 1938 to regulate all domestic air transport as a public utility, setting fares, routes, and schedules. The CAB was required to ensure that the airlines had a reasonable rate of return. Most of the major airlines, whose profits were virtually guaranteed, favored the system. Not surprisingly, competition was stifled and almost no new airlines attempted to enter the market. However, *intra*state passenger travel was not regulated by the CAB, so Southwest, following the pioneering path of Pacific Southwest Airline's (PSA) service within California, initiated passenger service within Texas. The success of PSA and Southwest in providing cheap airline travel within California and Texas provided powerful ammunition for the deregulation of *inter*state travel, which came about in 1981 as a consequence of the airline deregulation act of 1978.[29] Since deregulation, more than one hundred startup airlines inaugurated interstate scheduled passenger service with jet aircraft.[30] Herb Kelleher, the charismatic co-founder of Southwest Airlines, is often credited with triggering airline deregulation by persevering with his legal battle to get Southwest airborne in the face of fierce legal opposition from Braniff, Trans-Texas, and Continental Airlines. Two of those airlines took their legal battle all the way to the U.S. Supreme Court, which ruled in Southwest's favor at the end of 1970.[31]

Robert Swanson was 27 when he hit upon the idea that a company could be formed to commercialize biotechnology. At that time he knew almost nothing about the field. By reading the scientific literature, Swanson identified the leading biotechnology scientists and contacted them. "Everybody said I was too early—it would take ten years to turn out the first microorganism from a human hormone or maybe twenty years to have a commercial product—everybody except Herb Boyer."[32] Swanson was referring to Professor Herbert Boyer at the University of California at San Francisco, co-inventor of the patents that, according to some observers, now form the basis of the biotechnology industry. When Swanson and Boyer met in early 1976, they almost immediately agreed to become partners in an endeavor to explore the commercial possibilities of recombinant DNA. Boyer named their venture Genentech, an acronym for genetic engineering technology. Just seven months later, Genentech announced its first success, a genetically engineered human brain hormone, somatosin. According to Swanson, they accomplished ten years of development in seven months. Most observers say it was Swanson's entrepreneurial vision that brought about the founding of the biotech industry. Today, there are about 1,500 U.S. biotech companies with combined revenues of more than $50 billion.

At almost the same time that Swanson was starting Genentech in southern San Francisco, not many miles away Steve Jobs and Stephen Wozniak were starting Apple Computer in Silicon Valley. Their computer, the Apple I in kit form, was an instant hit with hobbyists. The Byte Shop—the first full-time computer store anywhere in the world, which opened in Silicon Valley in December 1975—ordered 25 of them in June 1976. The owner of The Byte Shop asked Jobs to put the Apple I computer board in a case because his customers were asking for complete units, not just kits. When they did so, both Apple and The Byte Shop had a hot product on their hands. The Byte Shop grew to a chain of 75 stores. "Without intending to so, Wozniak and Jobs had launched the microcomputer by responding to consumer demand."[33]

Genentech's IPO in October 1980, followed by Apple's IPO only two months later, signaled that something magical was stirring in the biotech and personal computer industries. It triggered a wave of venture capital investment and IPOs in both industries.

A tipping point in the infant personal computer industry was the introduction of the VisiCalc spreadsheet. Dan Bricklin conceived it when he was sitting in an MBA class at Harvard in 1978, daydreaming about how he could make it easier to do repetitive calculations. Bricklin designed the prototype software to run on an Apple II. Together with Bob Frankston he formed a company, Software Arts, to develop the VisiCalc spreadsheet. When they introduced their first version in May 1979, it turbocharged the sale of Apple computers. Subsequently, sales of IBM PCs were rocketed into the stratosphere by Mitch Kapor's Lotus 1-2-3 worksheet.

The late 1970s and the early 1980s were miraculous years for entrepreneurial ventures in the computer industry. Miniaturization of hard-disk drives, a vital component in the information technology revolution, was pioneered by Al Shugart, first at Shugart Associates, then at Seagate Technology. Dick Eagan and Roger Marino started EMC Corporation in 1979, initially selling computer furniture, and with the seed money from that they launched into selling Intel-compatible memory. From that beginning, Eagan and Marino built EMC into a company that during the 1990s achieved the highest single-decade performance of any listed stock in the history of the New York Stock Exchange. Today it is the dominant company in the data storage industry.

Robert Metcalfe, the inventor of Ethernet, founded 3Com in 1979 to manufacture computer network products. 3Com built its business around Ethernet plug-in cards for personal computers. Today Ethernet is so widely used that it is usually built into most PC motherboards.

Michael Dell, while still a student at the University of Texas, Austin, in 1984, began selling IBM-compatible computers built from stock components that he marketed directly to customers. By concentrating on direct sales of customized products, Dell became the largest manufacturer of personal computers in the world, and Michael Dell was CEO longer than any other executive in the PC hardware industry.

Entrepreneurs were at the conception and birth of new products and services that have transformed the global economy in the last 35 years. However, what is turning out to be the biggest of them all began in 1989 when Tim (now Sir Timothy) Berners-Lee conceived the World Wide Web (WWW). We are in the midst of a revolution that is changing our lives more profoundly and faster than anyone could have imagined before the Web became operational in 1992. No major new product has been adopted as quickly by such a large percentage of the U.S. population as the Web.

Time for new technologies to reach 25% of the U.S. population	
Household electricity (1873)	46 years
Telephone (1875)	35 years
Automobile (1885)	55 years
Airplane travel (1903)	54 years
Radio (1906)	22 years
Television (1925)	26 years
VCR (1952)	34 years
PC (1975)	15 years
Cellular phone	13 years
World Wide Web	**7 years**

Source: The *Wall Street Journal*, June 1997

Web: Three Revolutions Converge

In 1989 when Tim Berners-Lee wrote a proposal to develop software that resulted in the World Wide Web, he was not the first to conceive of the idea. As far back as 1945, Vannevar Bush, proposed a "memex" machine with which users could create information "trails" linking related text and illustrations and store the trails for future reference.[34]

As it turned out, he was 50 years ahead of the technologies that were needed to implement his idea. After all, the first digital computer was then only a couple of years old. Fifteen years later, Ted Nelson, inspired by Bush's "memex," was the first person to develop the modern version of hypertext. He wrote—prophetically, as it turned out—in 1960:

> . . . the future of humanity is at the interactive computer screen. . .the new writing and movies will be interactive and interlinked. . . . we need a world-wide network to deliver it. . .[35]

But Nelson too was far ahead of the technology. In 1962 there were fewer than ten thousand computers in the world. They cost hundreds of thousands of dollars and were primitive machines with only a few thousand bytes of magnetic core memory, and programming them was complicated and tedious. AT&T had a monopoly over the phone lines that were used for data communication. And the ARPANET, which was the forerunner of the Internet, had not yet been conceived.[36]

Berners-Lee was a 25-year-old physics graduate of Oxford University working as a consultant at CERN, the European Particle Physics Laboratory in Geneva, Switzerland in 1980, when he wrote his own private program for storing information using the random associations the brain makes. His "Enquire" program, which was never published, formed the conceptual basis for his future development of the Web.[37] In 1980, the technology existed for implementing Berners-Lee's concept, but the power of the technology was low and the installed base of computers was tiny compared to what it would be 10 years later. By 1989 when he revived his idea, three revolutions were ready for it. They were in *Digital Technology*, *Information Technology (IT)*, and *Entrepreneurship*. The semiconductor revolution enabled the digital revolution, which in turn enabled the IT revolution. By 1992, when the Web was released by CERN, the Internet had one million hosts, computers were 1,000 million times faster, and network bandwidth was 20 million times greater than 20 years earlier. The entrepreneurship revolution meant that there was an army of entrepreneurs and would-be entrepreneurs, especially in the U.S., with the vision and capacity to seize the commercial opportunities presented by the Web.

Development of the Web

In September 1990 Berners-Lee, then back at CERN, was given the go-ahead to write a global hypertext system. He began demonstrating prototypes of his line browser (which he called the World Wide Web) early in 1991. In mid-1992 the Web was made available by CERN. In February 1993, the National Center for Supercomputing Applications (NCSA) released the first alpha version of Marc Andreessen's "Mosaic for X." On April 30, 1993, CERN's directors made a declaration that WWW technology would be freely usable by anyone, with no fees payable to CERN. By December 1994 the Web was growing at approximately 1% a day—with a doubling period of less than 10 weeks.[38]

In the next 10 years, Internet usage exploded.* By 2005 the number of users was approaching one billion, which was almost 15% of the entire population of the world.

---

* The Internet and the World Wide Web (now usually called the Web) are two separate but related entities. However, most people use the terms interchangeably. The Internet is a vast network of networks, *a* networking infrastructure. The Web is a way of accessing information over the Internet. It is an information-sharing model that is built on top of the Internet.

Internet Users Worldwide, 2005

	Country or Region	Internet Users Latest Data	Population (2005 Est.)	Internet Penetration	% Users of World
1	United States	202,888,307	296,208,476	68.50%	21.60%
2	China	103,000,000	1,282,198,289	7.90%	11.00%
3	Japan	78,050,000	128,137,485	60.90%	8.30%
4	Germany	47,127,725	82,726,188	57.00%	5.00%
5	India	39,200,000	1,094,870,677	3.60%	4.20%
6	United Kingdom	35,807,929	59,889,407	59.80%	3.80%
7	South Korea	31,600,000	49,929,293	63.30%	3.40%
8	Italy	28,610,000	58,608,565	48.80%	3.00%
9	France	25,614,899	60,619,718	42.30%	2.70%
10	Brazil	22,320,000	181,823,645	12.30%	2.40%
11	Russia	22,300,000	144,003,901	15.50%	2.40%
12	Canada	20,450,000	32,050,369	63.80%	2.20%
13	Spain	15,565,138	43,435,136	35.80%	1.70%
14	Indonesia	15,300,000	219,307,147	7.00%	1.60%
15	Mexico	14,901,687	103,872,328	14.30%	1.60%
16	Taiwan	13,800,000	22,794,795	60.50%	1.50%
17	Australia	13,784,966	20,507,264	67.20%	1.50%
18	Netherlands	10,806,328	16,316,019	66.20%	1.20%
19	Poland	10,600,000	38,133,891	27.80%	1.10%
20	Malaysia	9,513,100	26,500,699	37.90%	1.10%
	Top 20 Countries	761,766,979	3,975,852,010	19.20%	81.20%
	Rest of the World	176,943,950	2,444,250,712	7.20%	18.80%
	Total World Users	938,710,929	6,420,102,722	14.60%	100.00%

Source: http://www.internetworldstats.com/top20.htm

Entrepreneurship Revolution Strikes Gold

Marc Andreessen moved to Silicon Valley in 1994, teamed up with veteran IT entrepreneur Jim Clark, and incorporated Mosaic Communications (later renamed Netscape Communications). Clark put $6 million of his own money into Mosaic, and venture capitalists added another $6 million.[39] Their intent was to create a browser that would surpass the original Mosaic. It was a classic Silicon Valley startup with programmers working 18-hour days, 7 days a week, sometimes even working 48 hours at one stretch just coding. In October 1994, the Netscape browser was posted as a download on the Internet. In no time at all, it was the browser of choice for the majority of Web users; in December 1994 Netscape Communications began shipping Netscape Navigator, which started to produce income.

Netscape Navigator was an instant success, gaining 75% of the browser market within four months of its introduction. Netscape Communications was only 16 months old when it went public in August 1995. Its IPO was one of the most spectacular in history and made Jim Clark the first Internet billionaire. According to an article in *Fortune Magazine*, "It was the spark that touched off the Internet boom."[40]

A gold rush was underway. "Netscape mesmerized investors and captured America's imagination. More than any other company, it set the technological, social, and financial tone of the Internet age."[41] A generation of would-be entrepreneurs was inspired by Netscape's success. What's more, corporate executives from established businesses wanted to emulate Jim Barksdale, the former president of McCaw Communications, who joined Netscape's board in October 1994, became CEO in January 1995, and made a huge fortune in just eight months. Investors—both angels and venture capitalists—hustled to invest in Internet-related startups. It seemed as if everyone was panning for Internet gold, not only in Silicon Valley but throughout the U.S., and a couple of years later throughout the rest of the world.

Netscape is a superb example of American venture capital at its best, accelerating the commercialization of innovations especially at the start of revolutionary new industries driven by technology. Venture capital was in at the start of the semiconductor and the minicomputer industries in the late 1950s and early 1960s, the biotech and personal computer industries in the late 1970s, and now it was eager to invest in what promised to be the biggest of them all, the Internet and the Web.

Venture capital is not invested exclusively in technology companies. It was in at the beginning of the overnight package delivery industry with its investment in Federal Express, at the start of major big-box retailers such as Home Depot and Staples, and the creation of new airlines including JetBlue. No wonder Jiro Tokuyama, then dean of the Nomura School of Advanced Management in Japan and a highly influential economist, stated that entrepreneurial firms and venture capital are the great advantages that you [Americans] have.[42] By 2003 venture-capital-backed companies accounted for approximately 8.5% of jobs in the U.S. and 16% of its GDP.

The Web presented numerous opportunities that were soon being exploited by entrepreneurs. It created a huge demand for more and more capacity on the Internet, which in turn presented opportunities for hardware and software entrepreneurs. They were fortunate to find venture capitalists eager to invest in their startups. Figure 1.1 shows the number of venture capital investments in Internet-related companies and the total amount invested between 1994 and 2004; it also shows the landmark events of the IPOs of Netscape, Yahoo, Amazon.com, and eBay. The period 1996 through 2000 was a golden era for classic[43] venture capitalists and the entrepreneurial companies they invested in. Golden both metaphorically and literally, as more and more venture capitalists and entrepreneurs seemed to have acquired the Midas touch. Some of the financial gains from

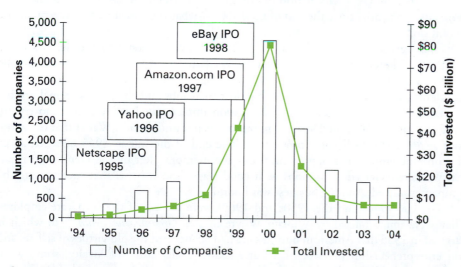

Source: Venture Economics

Figure 1.1

Venture capital investments in Internet-related companies

venture-capital-backed companies were indeed of mythological proportions. For instance, Benchmark Capital's investment of $5 million in eBay multiplied 1,500-fold in just two years.[44] True, Benchmark's investment in eBay set the all-time record for Silicon Valley, but there were plenty of instances when investments increased at least a hundred-fold and in some cases a thousand-fold. With investments such as those, overall returns on U.S. classic venture capital soared, with the one-year return peaking at 143% at the end of the third quarter in 2000, compared with average annual returns in the mid-teens prior to the golden era.

During a 1999 news conference at the World Economic Forum in Davos, Switzerland, reporters pestered Bill Gates again and again with variations of the same question: "These Internet stocks, they're a bubble?" An irritated Bill Gates finally confronted the reporters, "Look, you bozos, of course they're a bubble, but you're all missing the point. This bubble is attracting so much new capital to the Internet industry, it is going to drive innovation faster and faster."[45]

But the gold rush came to an end in 2000. The Internet bubble burst. Many companies failed, others were forced into fire-sale mergers, investors were hammered, many jobs were lost, and doom and gloom was pervasive. There was much hand-wringing about the incredible wastefulness of the U.S. method of financing new industries. However, by August 9, 2005—the tenth anniversary of Netscape's IPO—some companies founded during the gold rush were thriving. The market capitalization of just four of them—Google, eBay, Yahoo, and Amazon.com—was about $200 billion, which handily exceeded all the venture capital invested in all the Internet-related companies through 2000; what's more, it even topped the combined amount raised from venture capital and IPOs. Granted, there were many more losers than winners, but five years after the bust, it was clear that the U.S. society as a whole had already benefited mightily and the best was yet to come. No doubt about it, entrepreneurs and their financial backers had put the U.S. in a dominant position globally when it came to Internet-related products and services.

Causes of the Entrepreneurial Revolution

The U.S. has always been a nation of entrepreneurs. But why has it become more and more entrepreneurial since the end of the 1960s—what is now called the entrepreneurial revolution?

First we need to step back and look at the U.S. economy in the decades before the 1970s. The Great Depression that followed the stock market collapse of October 1929 had an enormous effect on society. By 1932, when Franklin Roosevelt was elected president, over 13 million Americans had lost their jobs and the gross national product had fallen 31%. The Roosevelt administration implemented many policies to try and bring the nation out of the Depression, but it was not until World War II that the nation once again started to become prosperous. The end of the war in 1945 heralded an era of economic growth and opportunity. But the memories left by the Depression meant that workers preferred secure jobs with good wages and benefits that medium and big companies offered. And big business was booming.

The late 1940s and the 1950s and 1960s were the era of the corporate employee. They were immortalized by William Whyte in *The Organization Man*,[46] in which he "argued in 1956 that American business life had abandoned the old virtues of self-reliance and entrepreneurship in favor of a bureaucratic 'social ethic' of loyalty, security and 'belongingness.' With the rise of the postwar corporation, American individualism had disappeared from the mainstream of middle-class life."[47] The key to a successful career was: "Be loyal to the company and the company will be loyal to you." Whyte's writing assumed the change was permanent and it favored the large corporation.

Big American businesses were seen as the way of the future, not just in the U.S. but worldwide. John Kenneth Galbraith's seminal book *The New Industrial State*[48] and Jean-Jacques Servan-Schreiber's *Le Défi Américain* (The American Challenge)[49] both "became the bible to advocates of industrial policies"[50] supporting big business. Both books were instant best sellers. *Le Défi Américain* sold 600,000 copies in France alone and was translated into 15 languages. Galbraith wrote in 1967, "By all but the pathologically romantic, it is now recognized that this is not the age of the small man." He believed that the best economic size for corporations was "very, very large."

The works of Whyte, Galbraith, and Servan-Schreiber were required reading in universities through the 1970s. Schumpeter's work was hardly ever mentioned,[51] and when it was, it was his book *Capitalism, Socialism, and Democracy* published in 1942,[52] in which he was very pessimistic that capitalism would survive. Unlike Karl Marx, who believed the proletariat would bring about the downfall of capitalism, Schumpeter reasoned that the very success of free enterprise would create a class of elites who would favor central control of the economy and thereby curb free enterprise. His first book, *The Theory of Economic Development*,[53] originally published in German in 1911, in which he endorsed entrepreneurship, was hardly ever mentioned. What's more, in the 1970s there was an abundance of university courses dealing with Karl Marx and almost none dealing with entrepreneurship. It's not surprising that the world was first alerted to the entrepreneurial revolution by a journalist, Norman Macrae, rather than by an academic scholar. About a decade later, researchers confirmed retrospectively that entrepreneurial activity had indeed been on the increase in the U.S. in the 1970s.[54]

Entrepreneurship did not disappear in the 1930s, 1940s, 1950s, and 1960s; it simply did not grow very much. What brought about the change in the economy that stirred up entrepreneurship around 1970? To try to understand what changes were taking place we need to look at the social, cultural, and political context of an economy. A framework for this perspective is presented in Figure 1.2, the Global Entrepreneurship Monitor (GEM) model for the economy.[55]

The central argument[56] of the GEM model is that national economic growth is a function of two sets of interrelated activities: those associated with established firms and those related directly to the entrepreneurial process. Activity among established firms explains only part of the story behind variations in economic growth. The entrepreneurial process may also account for a significant proportion of the differences in economic prosperity among countries and among regions within countries.

When looking at the nature of the relationship between entrepreneurship and economic growth, it is important to distinguish between entrepreneurial opportunities and entrepreneurial capacity. What drives entrepreneurial activity is that people perceive opportunities and have the skills and motivation to exploit them. The outcome is the creation of new firms and, inevitably, the destruction of inefficient or outmoded existing firms. Schumpeter's process of creative destruction is captured in the model by business churning. Despite its negative connotation, creative destruction actually has a positive impact on economic growth—declining businesses are phased out as startups maneuver their way into the market. These dynamic transactions occur within a particular context, which the GEM model calls *Entrepreneurial Framework Conditions* and which include factors such as availability of finance, government policies and programs designed to support startups, R&D transfer, physical and human infrastructure, education in general, education and training for entrepreneurship, social and cultural norms, and internal market openness.

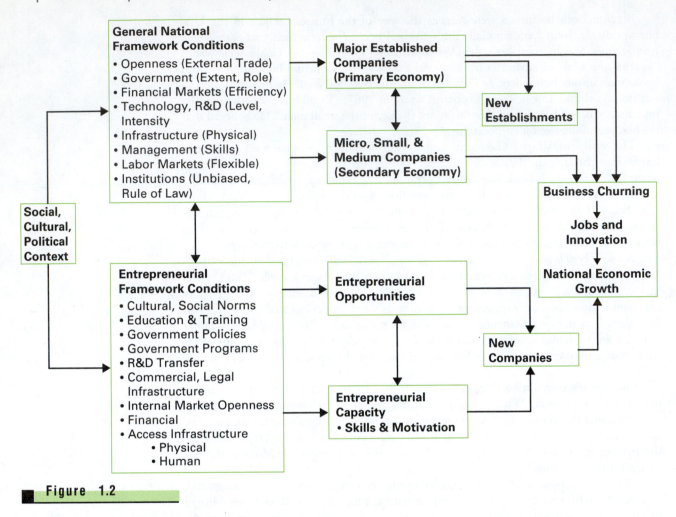

Figure 1.2

GEM model of economic growth

Changes in the Entrepreneurial Framework Conditions

Now let's look at some of the major changes in the framework conditions that have fueled the entrepreneurial revolution.

Cultural and Social Norms. First let's consider the most important components, the entrepreneurs themselves. In the 1960s a generation of Americans born in the late 1930s and the 1940s—including the first baby boomers—came of age. They had no first-hand memory of the Great Depression. When they were growing up, the economy was doing well most of the time, so they really had not experienced hard times like their parents had endured. Hence, they were not as concerned about job security. Many were even rebelling against large corporations, some of which were seen as members of the military-industrial complex that was supporting the very unpopular war in Vietnam; some companies were trading with South Africa where apartheid still prevailed; and others were under attack by consumer activists such as Ralph Nader.[57] It was a generation of Americans who were better educated than their parents, and for them starting a new business was a credible career.

The Fortune 500 employed 20% of the workforce in the 1960s. That percentage began to decline in 1980 and has declined every year since then, down to about 10% by 2005. Hence, jobs in big companies became scarcer. Many companies downsized, and according to George Gendron, who was the publisher of *Inc. Magazine* during the 1980s and 1990s, 20% of downsized executives started businesses. Gendron also suggested that some of the executives who were retained—often the "best and the brightest"—became disillusioned by their career prospects in stagnant companies, and that led to a "second exodus" that produced more entrepreneurial activity.[58]

Other important social changes boosted entrepreneurship in the 1990s. More women became business owners, and the proportion of Asian-owned firms increased, as did Hispanic-owned and African-American-owned firms. According to Gendron, for people with limited options in employment, entrepreneurship represents the "last meritocracy."

Government.
The 1970s was the decade when Washington bailed out Penn Central Railroad, Lockheed, and Chrysler. Washington seemed more concerned with big business than with small. But it did recognize the need to pay attention to startups with high potential, especially the ones funded by venture capitalists. There had been a burst of venture-capital-backed startups in the last half of the 1960s. But in the early 1970s venture capital dried up to a trickle. Looking back from the perspective of the late 1990s, when $10 billion of new money flowing into the industry seemed routine, it is scarcely believable that only $10 million of new money was committed in 1975. Congress took urgent steps in 1978 to stimulate the venture capital industry, including reducing the capital gains tax and easing the ERISA prudent man rule, which had inhibited pension funds from investing in venture capital funds. The pension floodgates opened and the inflow of venture capital increased to $4.9 billion by 1987. Likewise, venture capital invested in portfolio companies increased from a low of $250 million in 1975 to 3.9 billion in 1987—a 16-fold increase.[59]

The government asserted its role of ensuring *market openness* by minimizing anti-competitive behavior. We've already mentioned that legislation toward the end of the 1970s deregulated the airfreight and airline passenger industries. That was followed in the early 1980s by the Justice Department's move to break up AT&T's monopoly.

The government deserves immense credit for its funding of R&D in government, universities, and corporations, both directly and indirectly through purchases of products. Its support was vital in the development of the computer, communications, biotech, and many other industries. Washington initiated the Small Business Innovation Research (SBIR) program in 1983 to ensure that small businesses shared some of the federal R&D dollars for new technology-based developments. In 2002, a total of 5,820 awards totaling $1.43 billion went to small businesses as a result of the SBIR program. In general, funds awarded under the SBIR program go to develop new technologies that are high-risk and high-reward. Some might say it is pre-venture capital money. From that viewpoint, $1.43 billion is a big sum when compared with just $352 million that venture capitalists invested in seed-stage technology companies in 2002. A total of $13.6 billion has been awarded over the 19 years of the SBIR program through 2002.[60]

R&D transfer.
Commercial development of intellectual property resulting from federally funded research is a major benefit to the U.S. economy. It was given a major boost by the passage of the Bayh-Dole Act, implemented in 1980. The primary intent of that law was to foster the growth of technology-based small businesses by allowing them to own the patents that arose from federally sponsored research. Under Bayh-Dole, universities were allowed to grant exclusive licenses—a feature that was regarded as crucial if small businesses were to commercialize high technologies that were inherently risky propositions.[61]

Before 1980, U.S. universities were granted about 300 patents a year. In 2003, they applied for about 10,000. In 1980, 25 to 30 universities had offices for technology transfer. Today more than 1,200 do.[62] *The Economist* magazine hailed Bayh-Dole as "the most inspired piece of legislation to be enacted in America over the past half-century." *The Economist* estimated that Bayh-Dole had created 2,000 new companies, 260,000 new jobs, and contributed $40 billion annually to the U.S. economy.[63] That assessment was made in 1998 and more progress has been made since then.[64]

The government itself has technology transfer offices at most of its research laboratories,[65] and many large companies have licensing offices. IBM, for example, which annually spends about $5 billion on R&D, was granted 3,248 patents in 2004. It generates about $1 billion annually from licensing intellectual property, which comprises both patents and copyrights.

Fruits of Federally Funded R&D

The success of Bayh-Dole goes far beyond the efforts of Bob Dole and Birch Bayh. This legislation combined the ingenuity and innovation from our university laboratories with the entrepreneurial skills of America's small businesses. Most importantly, this combination created the incentive necessary for private investment to invest in bringing new ideas to the marketplace. The delicate balance of ingenuity, entrepreneurship, and incentive upon which the success of Bayh-Dole has depended must not be disrupted.

A few of the products which have been produced in the last six years are:

- Taxol, the most important cancer drug in 15 years, according to the National Cancer Institution.
- DNA sequencer, the basis of the entire Human Genome Project.
- StormVision, which airport traffic and safety managers use to predict the motion of storms.
- Prostate-specific antigen test, now a routine component of cancer screening.
- V-Chip, which allows families to control access to television programming.

Statement of Senator Birch Bayh to the National Institutes of Health, May 25, 2004

Physical Infrastructure. The biggest change in entrepreneurship in the last ten years is due to the Web, the great equalizer. Small businesses now have at their fingertips a tool so powerful that it is leveling the playing field. Big businesses no longer enjoy as many scale economies as they did before the Internet. Information that could have been gathered only by a multitude of market researchers can now be found with a search engine and a couple of clicks of a mouse. Entrepreneurs don't have to spend a fortune to reach customers with print, radio, and television advertising; they can target their potential customers via the Web. When they want to find a vendor, the Web is there to help them; likewise when they are seeking employees, bankers, and investors. Furthermore, the cost of communications of all kinds (except snail mail) has plummeted since AT&T was broken up. A long-distance telephone call that cost 40 cents a minute in 1980 now can be made for as little as 1 cent. And if small-business persons need to travel by air, they can shop the Web to find the cheapest ticket, automobile rental, and hotel room.

The worldwide distribution of goods and services is now open to everyone. Just consider what eBay has already done to change the entrepreneurial landscape. According to a 2005 study by ACNielsen International Research, 724,000 Americans report that selling on eBay is their primary or secondary source of income.[66] An American entrepreneur can sell merchandise to a customer anywhere in the world; PayPal (founded in 1998 and now part of eBay) can ensure that the entrepreneur receives payment speedily and securely online; the merchandise can be delivered to the buyer within a day or so via FedEx; and buyer and seller can track the shipment online at each step of its journey.

David Mcnew/Getty Images News and Sports Services

Meg Whitman, president and CEO of eBay, speaks at Comdex 2001 in Las Vegas.

Outsourcing of services and goods makes companies more efficient and effective. Entrepreneurs can now focus on their company's core competency and let vendors take care of noncore items such as payroll, Web hosting, telemarketing, manufacturing, and distribution. There are even companies that will help entrepreneurs find outsource partners. Outsourcing enables small businesses to act like big ones, and some small companies are even called *virtual companies* because they outsource so much of their work.

For some entrepreneurs, business incubators combine many of the advantages of outsourcing. Incubators provide not only physical space but also shared services. Many incubators also provide ready access to human infrastructure. In 1980 there were only 12 business incubators in the U.S.; over the period between 1985 and 1995 the number of incubators in the U.S. grew 15-fold, from 40 to nearly 600—and by 2003 there were some 850 incubators.[67] The National Business Incubation Association (NBIA) estimated that North American incubator resident and graduate companies had created about half a million jobs since 1980. (A "resident company" is one that is still in an incubator; a "graduate company" is one that has left it.) In 2001 alone, North American incubators assisted more than 35,000 startup companies that provided full-time employment for nearly 82,000 workers and generated annual revenue of more than $7 billion.[68]

Human Infrastructure. Access to human infrastructure is as important as access to physical infrastructure—maybe more so. The human infrastructure for entrepreneurs grew rapidly in the last twenty years or so, and gaining access to it has never been easier. Thirty years ago, starting a new venture was a lonely pursuit, fraught with pitfalls that would have been avoided by someone with prior entrepreneurial experience. Today, numerous entrepreneurship experts gladly help people who are starting or growing companies. There are support networks, both informal and formal, of professionals who know a lot about the entrepreneurial process. Just search the Web for "entrepreneur AND assistance AND your town," and you might be astonished by the number of hits.

Education, Training, and Professionalization. Entrepreneurship education and training is now readily available, part of the professionalization of entrepreneurship that has taken place over the last 20 years.[69] According to Gendron, a body of knowledge and skills has developed over the last 20 years to enhance the chances of entrepreneurial success. A good illustration is the widely dispensed advice that would-be entrepreneurs should write a business plan before they launch their new ventures. The world of entrepreneurship is awash with information about business plans. The field has come a long way since the pioneers of entrepreneurship training put writing a business plan at the core of their programs in the 1970s.[70]

When Babson College and the University of Texas started their internal business plan competitions in 1985, only a few schools had entrepreneurship courses. Today more than 60% of four-year colleges and universities have at least one entrepreneurship course, and many have entrepreneurship centers. Today, entrepreneurship training courses are readily available to all sectors of the population.

The Accidental Entrepreneur

Like many other scientists and engineers who have ended up founding companies, I didn't leave Caltech as an entrepreneur. I had no training in business; after my sophomore year of college I didn't take any courses outside of chemistry, math, and physics. My career as an entrepreneur happened quite by accident.

There is such a thing as a natural-born entrepreneur ... But the accidental entrepreneur like me has to fall into the opportunity or be pushed into it. Most of what I learned as an entrepreneur was by trial and error, but I think a lot of this really could have been learned more efficiently.

— *Gordon Moore (Co-founded Fairchild Semiconductor in 1957 and Intel in 1968).*[71]

Financial. Raising money for a new business is seldom easy, but the process of raising startup and expansion capital has become more efficient in the last 20 years or so. In 1982, for instance, an economist at the National Science Foundation stated that venture capital was shrouded in empirical secrecy and an aura of beliefs.[72] The same held true for angel investing. In contrast, today there is an abundance of help. The amount of venture capital under management has grown from $3.7 billion in 1980 to more than $250 billion in 2005.[73] We do not have reliable numbers for business angel investors, but we do know that informal investors—everyone from parents to external business angels—now invest about $100 billion annually in startup and baby businesses. Furthermore, informal investors are ubiquitous. Five percent of American adults report they "invested" in someone else's venture in the last three years.[74] It is impossible to claim that the availability of financing has driven the entrepreneurial revolution, but it does appear that sufficient financing has been available to fuel it.

Churning and Economic Growth

Technological change, deregulation, competition, and globalization presented countless opportunities, which American entrepreneurs seized and commercialized. It caused a lot of *churning*, or Schumpeter's creative destruction. But 11 new businesses with employees were started for every 10 that died over the decade 1990–2000.[75] It is this churning that gives the economy its vitality: only a society that willingly adapts to change can have a dynamic economy.

We can find examples of churning in every industry that is not a monopoly or a regulated oligopoly. Who can recall VisiCalc or for that matter Lotus 1-2-3? At the height of their fame they were two of the most widely used software packages for PCs. Today, Excel is the spreadsheet of choice. In one week alone in May 1982, when Digital Equipment Corporation (DEC) introduced its ill-fated Rainbow PC, four other companies introduced PCs.[76] At the peak of the PC industry frenzy in the early 1980s, more than 200 companies had either introduced PCs or were planning to do so. Only a handful of PC manufacturers exist today. DEC, which in 1982 was the second-largest computer manufacturer in the world, was eventually bought by Compaq, which in turn merged with Hewlett-Packard. In 2004, IBM sold its PC division to Lenovo, a company founded in 1984 by a group of academics at the government-backed Chinese Academy of Sciences in Beijing.

Not only did the advent of the PC churn up the entire computer industry, it virtually wiped out the typewriter industry. And it changed the way office work is organized. Secretaries had to learn computer skills or they were out of work.

More examples of churning: Southwest Airlines is now the most successful U.S. airline; two of its giant rivals in 1971 no longer exist, and the third, Continental, has been bankrupt twice, in 1983 and 1990. In August 2005, United Airlines, US Airways, Hawaiian Airlines, ATA Airlines (also known as American Trans Air), and Aloha Airlines were all in Chapter 11 bankruptcy, and only a handful of the 100 or so passenger airlines started up since deregulation are still around. Who goes to a travel agent to get a regular airline ticket or book a hotel room today? Where is the fax machine headed? Likewise video stores and CD retailers? Why are newspapers laying off workers? Who is buying a film camera? And even entrepreneurship academics should watch out. Donald Trump, building on his TV success with *The Apprentice,* has started Trump University to teach—what else?—entrepreneurship.

> Entrepreneurial competition, according to Schumpeter, "strikes not at the margins of the profits . . . of the existing firms but at their foundations and very lives." Established companies that stick with their old ways of doing business self-destruct as their customers turn to new competitors with better business models.

Granted, churning causes a lot of disruption, and nowhere more than in the lives of those who lose their jobs as a result. But overall, society is the beneficiary. Entrepreneurship produces new products and services, it increases productivity, it generates employment, and in some cases it keeps inflation in check. Economists estimate that Wal-Mart alone knocked 20%—perhaps as much as 25%—off the rate of inflation in the 1990s.[77] According to Alfred Kahn, the father of airline deregulation, airline passengers are now saving $20 billion a year.[78] And with Skype and the Internet, you can ". . . talk to anyone, anywhere in the world for free. Forever."[79]

In August 2005, the U.S. economy was robust. The GDP was growing at 3.5% and unemployment was about 5%. Much of its vigor was the result of churning in the economy. The *Times* of London observed, "There are global lessons in the discomfiting success of the U.S. economy. Creative destruction not only produces winners and losers; it makes even the winners nervous. The natural human instinct is to want to shelter from such turmoil. But the real winners will be the ones who embrace it."[80] However, not everyone thought that the U.S. model was the desirable way to economic growth. President Jacques Chirac and his Prime Minister, Dominique de Villepin, struggling to invigorate France's stagnant economy, didn't much care for the "Anglo-Saxon" model of unfettered competition. Villepin, on taking office in mid-2005, said, "I am profoundly attached to

> The power of Wal-Mart is such, it's reversed a 100-year history in which the manufacturer was powerful and the retailer was sort of the vassal. . . . It turned that around entirely.
>
> — *Nelson Lichtenstein,*
> *University of California, Santa Barbara*

the French social model."[81] Less than six months later, rioting broke out in poor neighborhoods populated largely by North Africans where youth unemployment was often 40% or higher; it spread throughout France and continued for two weeks. The protests caused a three-month, nationwide state of emergency.[82]

Next we will look at how other nations as well as the U.S are faring with entrepreneurship.

Global Entrepreneurship Monitor

The Global Entrepreneurship Monitor was conceived in 1997* to study the economic impact and the determinants of national-level entrepreneurial activity. With its coverage of more than 50 countries worldwide, GEM is the largest coordinated research effort ever undertaken to study population-level entrepreneurial activity. Member nations comprise approximately 95% of the world's GDP and two-thirds of its population. Because of its worldwide reach and rigorous scientific method, GEM has become the world's most influential and authoritative source of empirical data and expertise on the entrepreneurial potential of nations.[83]

The main objectives of GEM are to gather data that measure the entrepreneurial activity of nations and other data related to entrepreneurial activity; to examine what national characteristics are related to levels of entrepreneurial activity; and to explain how differences in entrepreneurial activity are related to different levels of economic growth among nations.

GEM distinguishes between two types of entrepreneurial activity.[84]

◉ *Nascent entrepreneurs* are individuals who are actively trying to start a new business but who have not yet done so.

◉ *Baby business managers* are owner-managers of a new business that is no more than 42 months old.

There are three main measures of entrepreneurial activity.

◉ TEA (total entrepreneurial activity) is the percent of the adult population that are either nascent entrepreneurs or baby businesses owner-managers or both. It measures the overall entrepreneurial activity of a nation.

◉ TEA (opportunity) is the percent of the adult population that are trying to start or have started a baby business to exploit a perceived opportunity.

◉ TEA (necessity) is the percent of adults who are trying to start or have started a baby business because all other options for work are either absent or unsatisfactory.

---

* GEM in itself is an example of not-for-profit (social) entrepreneurship. It was conceived in 1997 by Babson College and London Business School professors. It was prototyped with bootstrap funding and volunteers, and was officially launched in 1998 with research teams from 10 nations and supported with funding raised by each team from national sponsors. By 2006 it has evolved into an international consortium of more than 200 researchers from more than 50 nations with a combined annual budget of about $4 million. It produces annual global reports on the overall state of entrepreneurship in those nations, country-specific reports, reports on special topics such as women entrepreneurship, financing, and job creation. More than 100 global and regional reports can be read and downloaded at www.gemconsortium.org.

GEM countries are Argentina, Australia, Austria, Belgium, Brazil, Canada, Chile, China, Colombia, Croatia, Czech Republic, Denmark, Ecuador, England, Finland, France, Germany, Greece, Hong Kong, Hungary, Iceland, Ireland, Israel, Italy, Jamaica, Japan, Jordan, Korea, Latvia, Malaysia, Mexico, Netherlands, New Zealand, Northern Ireland, Norway, Peru, Philippines, Poland, Portugal, Russia, Scotland, Singapore, Slovenia, South Africa, Spain, Sweden, Switzerland, Taiwan, Thailand, Uganda, United Kingdom, United States, Venezuela, and Wales.

Principal Findings from GEM

The total entrepreneurial activity by country in 2004 is shown in Figure 1.3. The total entrepreneurial activity varied from a low of 2.5% to a high of 40% for adults 18 to 64 years old. The average level was 9.3% or one adult in eleven.

The vertical bars in Figure 1.3 are 95% confidence intervals. The error bars are wide for some countries and narrow for others because of different sample sizes. Germany, Spain, Sweden, and the United Kingdom have narrow bars because the samples were very large. Where bars overlap there is no statistical difference among those nations. For example, among countries with lower TEA rates, Slovenia, Hong Kong, and Belgium have comparable levels of entrepreneurial activity; among the more active countries, the United States, Argentina, Australia, Brazil, Iceland, and New Zealand have comparable TEA rates.

GEM defines two types of entrepreneurship: opportunity based and necessity based. In general, nations with high per capita income have proportionately less necessity-pushed entrepreneurial activity and more opportunity-pulled, and vice versa for nations with low income, as shown in Figure 1.4. People in higher-income nations tend to have more opportunities for employment and stronger safety nets like social welfare programs, especially for the out-of-work; hence, proportionately fewer are pushed into entrepreneurship to support themselves and their families. The relatively high R-squared of 57% confirms that much of the variation in the ratio of opportunity-to-necessity entrepreneurship among nations is accounted for by differences in per capita income.

The relationship between the TEA rate and per capita income (see Figure 1.5) is U-shaped, indicating that as nations become more prosperous, entrepreneurial activity declines, bottoms out at around $22,000 per capita with GDP converted to Purchasing Power Parity (PPP) rather than raw GDP, and then increases. A possible explanation is that as a nation makes the transition from a less-developed nation to a developing nation,

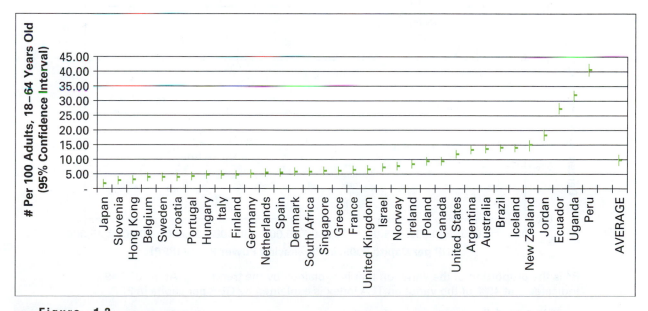

Figure 1.3

Total Entrepreneurial Activity (TEA prevalence) 2004: By country

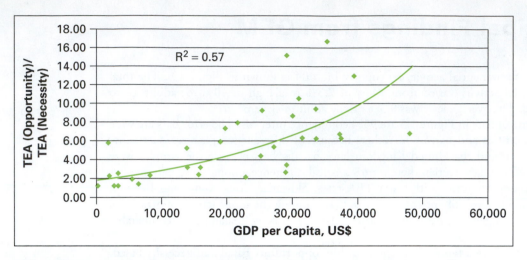

R^2 is the proportion of the variation that is explained by the trend line. An R^2 of 0.57 indicates that 57% of the variation TEA (Opportunity)/Tea (Necessity) ratio is explained by GDP per capita.

Figure 1.4

TEA (opportunity)/TEA (necessity)—2004

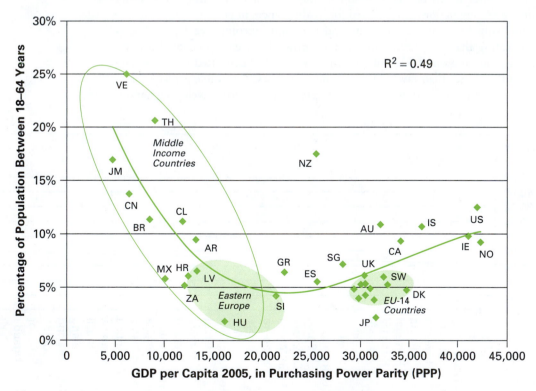

R^2 is the proportion of the variation that is explained by the trend line. An R^2 of 0.49 indicates that 49% of the variation TEA index is explained by GDP per capita in PPP.

Figure 1.5

TEA vs. GDP per capita in PPP—2005

there are more opportunities for employment with established businesses, hence entrepreneurship, especially necessity-driven, declines. Entrepreneurial activity bottoms out and then increases again as more and more opportunities, particularly in service and knowledge-based industries, are spotted by entrepreneurs with the skills and motivation to develop them. Note that 14 European Union (EU) countries, including France, Germany, and Italy, are clustered very close together below the trend line, whereas 6 countries with Anglo-Saxon economic systems—Australia, Canada, Ireland, New Zealand, U.K., and the United States—are either above the trend or fall right on it.

Age[85]

Young people between 25 and 34 years of age are the most entrepreneurially active group of the population regardless of the wealth of the country (see Figure 1.6). After the age of 35, all populations show a steady decline in entrepreneurial activity. This indicates that age is an important factor in the decision to become an entrepreneur. A nation's demographic structure has a significant impact on the immediate level of entrepreneurial activity in the short term, and demographic change has a significant impact on entrepreneurial activity in the long term.

Different income groups* have markedly different entrepreneurship activity levels across all age groups. Low-income countries have the highest activity levels across all age groups, ranging from 1 person in every 5 (for the 25–34-year-old group), down to 1 person in 10 among 55–64 year olds. However, the level of necessity entrepreneurship is higher in low-income countries and is also very high among the younger age groups in those countries, where better opportunities for employment are scarcer.

Among the three income categories, low-and high-income nations have higher levels of entrepreneurial activity across all age groups than middle-income nations have. Low-income countries experience roughly three times the level of activity across all age groups

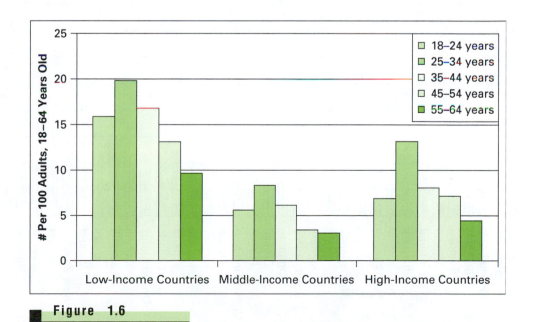

Figure 1.6

TEA 2004 by age categories and country income group

* Low-income ≤$10,000 per capita annually; middle income>$10,000 ≤$25,000; high income>$25,000.

as do middle-income countries; the difference between high-and middle-income countries is less.

The difference between the level of activity of the 25–34-year-old group and that of the 35–44-year-old group in high income nations is notable (a TEA of 12.45 compared with 7.9 for the older group). This result is consistent with the observation that an entrepreneurial revolution has been taking place in the United States, and perhaps in other high-income countries where the 1990s witnessed an ever-increasing number of 25–34 year olds actively engaged in starting businesses.[86]

Gender[87]

Almost 50% more men than women are entrepreneurially active. These differences are consistent across age groups and across most countries. In no country are women more entrepreneurially active than men, but there is wide variation among countries.

In 2004, France, Greece, Hong Kong, and Spain all showed large gender gaps in entrepreneurial activity, while in Ecuador, Finland, Hungary, Japan, Peru, South Africa, and the United States participation rates were statistically identical (see Figure 1.7). The narrower gaps in this last group of countries may be the result of two different sets of circumstances. First, the ratio of female to male entrepreneurs is higher in the case of necessity-based entrepreneurship, which constitutes a high proportion of activity in the low-income countries (Ecuador, Hungary, Peru, and South Africa). Second, for high-income countries such as Finland and the U.S., the closing gender gap may be the result of targeted programs, cultural changes, and more emphasis on entrepreneurial

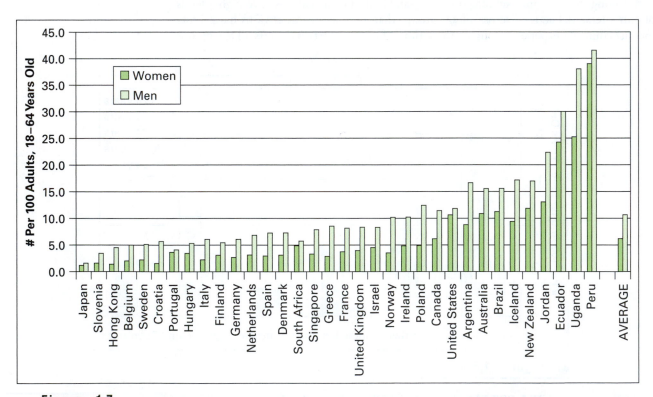

Figure 1.7

TEA 2004 for men and women

education leading to more equal opportunities for women.* The largest gender division occurs in the middle-income nations, where men are 75% more likely than women to be entrepreneurially active. The smallest gap appears in the high-income countries, where the percentage difference falls to 33%.

Education[88]

It's widely believed that levels of educational attainment have implications for entrepreneurial behavior. Figure 1.8 shows the relationship between entrepreneurship and less than secondary education, secondary education, and post-secondary education for each of the three income groups. Secondary education refers to young people roughly between the ages of 12 and 18.[89]

The wide differential between the educational profiles of entrepreneurs in low and high-income countries is obvious. In high-income countries, 57% of entrepreneurs have a post-secondary education, suggesting that in these countries the education systems are tending to build skills for entrepreneurs. In the poorest countries, only 23% of entrepreneurs have a post-secondary education. On the other hand, almost half of entrepreneurs in low-income nations have not completed secondary education; this is the case for only 13% of their high-income counterparts. In the middle-income countries, the best and least-educated fall between these two extremes and exhibit a slight tendency toward the better-educated end of the continuum.

Financing

Entrepreneurial activity and financing go hand in glove, so it is no surprise that in general they are correlated. There are two main types of financing for new ventures: equity and debt. As a general rule, equity financing has to come before debt, particularly borrowing from a bank. Hence, GEM focuses on equity financing, which is informal investments from the

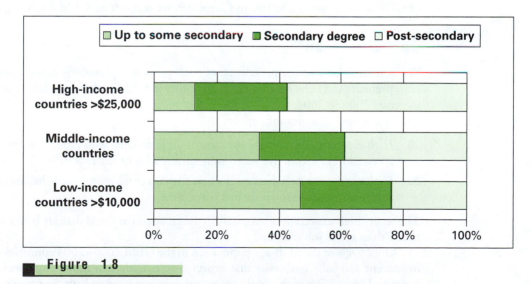

Figure 1.8

TEA 2004: Education by country income group (GDP per capita)

---

* What appears to be a closing gender gap may possibly be the result of sample bias. For example, in Japan the overall level of activity is very low, resulting in large standard errors, which make statistically significant gender differences hard to capture.

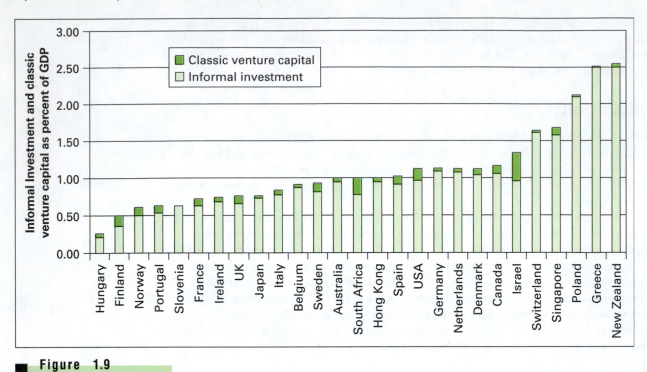

Figure 1.9

Informal investment and classic venture capital, percent of GDP

entrepreneurs' families and friends, business angels, and, on rare occasions, formal venture capitalists. The combined amount of informal investment and venture capital as a percent of GDP is shown in Figure 1.9. In Chapter 9, we will discuss GEM financing in detail.

Job Creation[90]

We will now look at the prevalence of high-growth expectations among both nascent entrepreneurs and baby businesses, as identified in GEM's adult population surveys from the years 2000 to 2004.

The following definitions apply:

- *High-expectation nascent entrepreneur* is an individual who expects to employ at least 20 employees within five years' time through his or her new firm.

- *High-expectation baby business* is a new firm up to 42 months old that aims to employ at least 20 employees within five years' time.

The term "high-expectation" emphasizes the fact that the GEM data are based on expected rather than actual job creation.

Only 5.4% of the adult-age population in the GEM 2000–2004 countries were active in nascent and baby businesses that expected to employ 2 or more employees in 5 years' time; and only 2.7% of the adult-age population expected to have 5 or more employees. For the growth expectations of 10+, 20+, and 50+ employees, the percentages drop to 1.6, 0.8, and 0.4. In other words, fewer than 1 person in every 100 is involved with a nascent or baby business that expects to create 20 or more jobs in 5 years. And only 4 of 1,000 expect to create 50 or more jobs. Hence, expectations of rapid growth are rare.

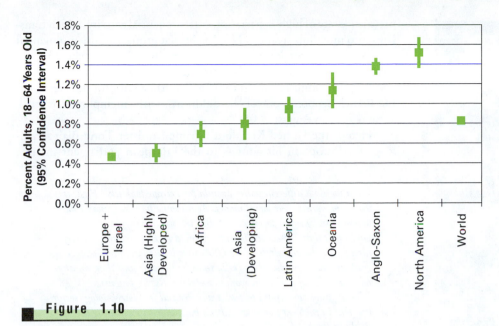

Figure 1.10

TEA by growth expectation in different world regions: High-expectation nascent and baby businesses that expect at least 20 jobs in 5 years

The rate of high-expectation entrepreneurial activity varies significantly among world regions and individual countries. The regions with the highest participation rate in high-expectation entrepreneurial activity (see Figure 1.10) are North America (Canada and the U.S.) and Oceania (Australia and New Zealand). For those regions, the rate of high-growth entrepreneurial activity ranges from approximately 1.1% to 1.6%. The lowest rate of high-expectation activity is observed for European and highly developed Asian countries (Hong Kong, Korea, Japan, and Singapore), where it is approximately 0.5%.

The prevalence rate of high-expectation entrepreneurial activity is worryingly low in Europe and highly developed Asia. There are no differences among European country groups (large EU countries, small European countries, new EU member countries), even though there are differences between individual countries. The United Kingdom and Germany's participation rates are approximately 0.7%, which is about half the U.S. level. Sweden's participation rate of 0.5% is lower than in the United Kingdom or Germany, but double that of Spain (0.2%), which has the lowest participation rate.

Although GEM data are for expected job creation, they are consistent with empirical studies of actual job creation. For instance, one study found that 4% of new firms in the United Kingdom created 50% of all jobs created by all new firms.[91] Another study reported that more than 70% of the employment growth in the United States came from only 3% of all firms.[92]

Twenty-First Century Economies: Anglo-Saxon or Social Models?

It is very interesting that a group of nations with so-called Anglo-Saxon economic systems (Australia, Canada, Ireland, New Zealand, the United Kingdom, and the U.S.) has a high

Michael Kappelie/Getty Images News and Sports Services

British Prime Minister Tony Blair and French President Jacques Chirac.

prevalence rate of high-expectation entrepreneurial activity, which translates into more job creation. Nations in that group had unemployment rates around 5% or lower in 2005, except for Canada, where unemployment was above 6%. It is a finding that President Jacques Chirac and his prime minister might chew over as they hunt for policies to get the French economy out of the doldrums, with unemployment stuck around 10% in August 2005.[93]

Here is the United Kingdom's Prime Minister Tony Blair's challenge for Europe in his address to the European parliament in June 2005.[94]

What would a different policy agenda for Europe look like? First, it would modernize our social model. Again some have suggested I want to abandon Europe's social model. But tell me: what type of social model is it that has 20 million unemployed in Europe, productivity rates falling behind those of the USA; that is allowing more science graduates to be produced by India than by Europe; and that, on any relative index of a modern economy—skills, R&D, patents, IT—is going down not up? India will expand its biotechnology sector five-fold in the next five years. China has trebled its spending on R&D in the last five.

Of the top 20 universities in the world today, only 2 are now in Europe.[95] The purpose of our social model should be to enhance our ability to compete, to help our people cope with globalization, to let them embrace its opportunities and avoid its dangers. Of course we need a social Europe. But it must be a social Europe that works.

And we've been told how to do it. The Kok report[96] in 2004 shows the way. Investment in knowledge, in skills, in active labor market policies, in science parks and innovation, in higher education, in urban regeneration, in help for small businesses. This is modern social policy, not regulation and job protection that may save some jobs for a time at the expense of many jobs in the future.

Early in 2006, Dominique de Villepin, France's prime minister, proposed legislation aimed at cutting chronic youth unemployment by easing rigid labor laws that make it very difficult to fire employees. Students rose up all over France to protest the proposed changes and shut down classes at half of France's 84 state-run universities in the biggest student uprising since 1968 (when student riots forced the de Gaulle government to hold an election). The students' attitude in 2006 was summed up by these comments.[97]

Elodie, 21, a sociology student, said, "The issues are different from those our parents were protesting about. We are marching for the right to proper jobs."

Romain, 20, a communications student, said, "We don't want the Anglo-Saxon economic model here."

A survey discovered that the top career goal of three-quarters of young French people was to be a civil servant.[98] This is in stark contrast to the U.S., where the majority of young people want to be an entrepreneur at some time during their careers.[99]

CONCLUSION

Entrepreneurial activity in the United States now accounts for much of the nation's prosperity and its competitiveness in the global economy. The disappearance of "old" jobs, particularly in mature manufacturing industries, and their replacement by "new" jobs, especially in service and knowledge-based industries, is disconcerting to workers whose jobs are threatened. But society has to accept *churning*—the creation of new enterprises and the destruction of obsolete ones—because it gives the U.S. economy its vitality.

The entrepreneurial framework includes factors such as availability of finance, government policies and programs designed to support startups, R&D transfer, physical and human infrastructure, education in general, education and training for entrepreneurship, social and cultural norms, and internal market openness. All of these factors combined determine the degree of entrepreneurial activity in a nation, or for that matter in a region within a nation. Among the large developed nations, the U.S. sets the entrepreneurial benchmark. What's more, the so-called Anglo-Saxon economic systems seem to engender more entrepreneurial activity than systems dominated by the social model, which is the prevalent system in most of continental Europe—and especially in France. The question remains: How do non-Anglo-Saxon economies find an entrepreneurial path that leads them out of the economic doldrums?

In this chapter, we have looked at the importance of entrepreneurship to national economies. In the following chapters we will look at the specifics of how entrepreneurs start and grow their new ventures.

YOUR OPPORTUNITY JOURNAL

We are excited that you are exploring an entrepreneurial journey, one that may lead you to launch a business while in college, after graduation, or at some future point in your life. We know that all great entrepreneurs are avid readers and thinkers, and as such we encourage you to capture some of your thoughts as you read this book. These thoughts may focus on a new venture that you are interested in creating, or they may focus more on your entrepreneurial career plan. In either event, we will close each chapter with space for you to reflect on what it means to you and your potential venture.

Reflection Point	Your Thoughts...
1. What world-changing industries or opportunities do you see developing over the next five to ten years?	
2. What innovations or new technologies will drive these world-changing opportunities?	
3. Which regions of the world have the greatest potential for developing these opportunities? Which are you most interested in?	
4. What skills do you need to develop to take advantage of these opportunities?	

WEB EXERCISE

What do you think will be the next major innovation (e.g., the Internet) that changes the way we work and play? Search the Web to identify trends, statistics, and other evidence to support your insight.

NOTES

1 Reynolds, P. D., Bygrave, W. D., Autio, E., and Hay, M. *Global Entrepreneurship Monitor—2002 Summary Report.* www.gemconsortium.org. Estimate for 2006 is based on GEM 2006 data.

2 Firms with fewer than 500 employees saw a net increase in employment of 1,150,875 over the period 2000–2001; however, large business employment decreased on net by 150,905. Overall net employment increased 999,970. The small business share varies from year to year and reflects economic trends. Over the decade of the 1990s, small business share of net job creation fluctuated between 60% and 80%. Small businesses accounting for all of the net new jobs is not unique to 2000–2001. During the economic downturn in the early 1990s, a similar result occurred.

Sources: U.S. Bureau of the Census; advocacy-funded research by Joel Popkin and Company (Research Summary #211); Federal Procurement Data System; advocacy-funded research by CHI Research, Inc. (Research Summary #225); Bureau of Labor Statistics, Current Population Survey; U.S. Department of Commerce, International Trade Administration.

3 Schumpeter, J. A. *The Theory of Economic Development.* Cambridge, MA: Harvard University Press. 1934. (This book was originally published in German in 1911.)

4 Maddison, A. *Phases of Capitalist Development.* New York, N Y: Oxford University Press. 1989. W. J. Baumol. Entrepreneurship and a century of growth. *Journal of Business Venturing.* 1 (2): 141–145. 1986.

5 Small Business Administration FAQs. http://app1.sba.gov/faqs/faqindex .cfm?areaID=2. *The Shape of Small Business.* www.nfib.com/object/Policy Guide2.html.

6 For the Small Business Administration definitions of small business, refer to www.sba.gov/gopher/Financial -Assistance/Defin/defi4.txt.

7 This is based on GDPs and actual currency exchange rates in 2004.

8 Small Business Administration FAQs. http://app1.sba.gov/faqs/faqindex .cfm?areaID=2.

9 Source: www.nvca.org/pdf/Venture Impact2004.pdf based on data from NSF, R&D in Industry: 1991–2000, Tables A3 and A4; NSF, Preliminary Release, 2001 and 2002, Tables A3 and A4; NSF, Infobrief, "U.S. R&D Projected to Have Grown Marginally in 2003."

10 *The Shape of Small Business.* www. nfib.com/object/PolicyGuide2.html.

11 Ibid. The estimate of new business startups ranges from 3 million to 4.5 million. It is impossible to make a precise upper limit because may new ventures are abandoned very soon after they are started and never get entered into any data set that tracks startups.

12 www.forbes.com/businesswirc/feeds/ businesswire/2005/07/21/

businesswire20050721005296r1. html.

[13] Kirchhoff, Bruce A. *Entrepreneurship and Dynamic Capitalism*. Westport, CT: Praeger. 1994.

[14] Nucci, A. The demography of business closings. *Small Business Economics*. 12, 25–39. 1999.

[15] *The Shape of Small Business*. www. nfib.com/object/PolicyGuide2.html.

[16] Dennis, W. J., Jr. and Fernald, L. W., Jr. The Chances of Financial Success (and Loss) from Small Business Ownership. *Entrepreneurship Theory and Practice*. 1:75–83. 2002.

[17] Reported in *The Shape of Small Business*. www.nfib.com/object/Policy Guide2.html.

Source: Current Population Survey, Bureau of the Census, March 1999, special run for the NFIB Education Foundation prepared by Carolyn Looff Associates, Lexington, KY, 2000.

[18] Reported in *The Shape of Small Business*. www.nfib.com/object/Policy Guide2.html.

Source: Special Tabulation of Business Information Tracking System, Census Bureau, prepared for the NFIB Education Foundation by the Census Bureau, 2000.

[19] *The Shape of Small Business*. www.nfib. com/object/PolicyGuide2.html.

The net business formation index was discontinued in 1995 when one of its two components was no longer available.

[20] Macrae, N. The coming entrepreneurial revolution. *The Economist*. December 15, 1976.

[21] Birch, David L. *Job Creation in America: How Our Smallest Companies Put the Most People to Work*. New York, NY: The Free Press. 1978.

[22] For example: Acs, Z. *The New American Evolution*. U.S. Small Business Administration Office of Economic Research, June, 1998.

Kirchhoff, Bruce A. *Entrepreneurship and Dynamic Capitalism*. Westport, CT: Praeger. 1994.

[23] At one point General Motors was the largest corporation in the United States ever, in terms of its revenues as a percent of GDP. In 1953 Charles Erwin Wilson, then GM's president, was named by President Eisenhower as secretary of defense. When he was asked, during the hearings before the Senate Armed Services Committee, if as secretary of defense he could make a decision adverse to the interests of General Motors, Wilson answered affirmatively but added that he could not conceive of such a situation, "because for years I thought what was good for the country was good for General Motors and vice versa." Later this statement was often garbled when quoted, suggesting that Wilson had said simply, "What's good for General Motors is good for the country." At the time, GM was the one of the largest employers in the world—only Soviet state industries employed more people. http://en.wikipedia.org/wiki/ Charles_Erwin_Wilson.

[24] "The observation made in 1965 by Gordon Moore, co-founder of Intel, that the number of transistors per square inch on integrated circuits had doubled every year since the integrated circuit was invented. Moore predicted that this trend would continue for the foreseeable future. In subsequent years, the pace slowed down a bit, but density has doubled approximately every 18 months, and this is the current definition of Moore's Law. Most experts, including Moore himself, expect Moore's Law to hold for at least another two decades." Source: www.webopedia.com/TERM/M/ Moores_Law.html0.

[25] Working independently and unaware of each other's activity, Jack Kilby at Texas Instruments and Robert Noyce at Fairchild Semiconductor Corporation invented almost identical

integrated circuits at the same time. "In 1959 both parties applied for patents. Jack Kilby and Texas Instruments received U.S. patent #3,138,743 for miniaturized electronic circuits. Robert Noyce and the Fairchild Semiconductor Corporation received U.S. patent #2,981,877 for a silicon-based integrated circuit. The two companies wisely decided to cross license their technologies after several years of legal battles, creating a global market now worth about $1 trillion a year." Source: http://inventors.about.com/library/weekly/aa080498.htm.

26 The first personal computers were actually called microcomputers. The phrase "personal computer" was common currency before 1981, and was used as early as 1972 to characterize Xerox PARC's Alto. However, due to the success of the IBM PC, what had been a generic term came to mean specifically a microcomputer compatible with IBM's specification. Source: http://en.wikipedia.org/wiki/Ibm 5150.

27 The top 25 in descending order are the Internet, cell phone, personal computer, fiber optics, e-mail, commercialized GPS, portable computers, memory storage disks, consumer-level digital cameras, radio frequency ID tags, MEMS, DNA fingerprinting, air bags, ATMs, advanced batteries, hybrid cars, OLEDs, display panels, HDTVs, space shuttles, nanotechnology, flash memory, voice mail, modern hearing aids, and short-range high-frequency radio. Source: www.cnn.com/2005/TECH/01/03/cnn25.top25.innovations/.

28 www.fedex.com/us/about/today/history/.

29 http://en.wikipedia.org/wiki/Airline_Deregulation_Act.

30 Jordan, W. A. Airline Entry Following U.S. Deregulation: The Definitive List of Startup Passenger Airlines, 1979–2003.

www.trforum.org/forum/getpaper.php?id=22&PHPSESSID=119446d6d13ce93d6c6aea3df05010ce.

31 www.tsha.utexas.edu/handbook/online/articles/SS/eps1_print.html.

32 Bygrave, W.D. and Timmons, J.A. *Venture Capital at the Crossroads*. Boston, MA: Harvard Business School Press, 1992.

33 Rogers, E. M. and Larsen, J. K. *Silicon Valley Fever: Growth of High-Technology Culture*. New York, NY: Basic Books. 1984.

34 Bush, Vannevar. As we may think. *The Atlantic Monthly*, July 1945.

35 Nelson, Ted. The story so far. *Ted Nelson Newsletter*, Number 3, October 1994.

36 www.computerhistory.org/exhibits/internet_history/internet_history_80s.shtml.

37 "Tim Berners-Lee, Inventor of the World Wide Web, Knighted by Her Majesty Queen Elizabeth II. www.w3.org/2004/07/timbl_knighted.

38 *New Scientist Magazine*. December 17, 1994.

39 www.smartcomputing.com/editorial/dictionary/detail.asp?DicID=17855.

40 Lashinsky, Adam. Remembering Netscape: The Birth of the Web. www.fortune.com/fortune/print/0,15935,1081456,00.html.

41 Ibid.

42 Gevirtz, D. *The Entrepreneurs: Innovation in American Business*. New York, NY: Penguin Books. 1985. p. 30.

43 Classic venture capital is money invested privately in seed, startup, expansion, and late-stage companies. The term "classic" is used to distinguish it from money invested privately in acquisitions, buyouts, mergers, and reorganizations.

44 www.forbes.com/2001/02/06/0207VC.html.

45 Friedman, T. L. *The World Is Flat*. New York, NY: Farrar, Straus and Giroux. 2005.

46 Whyte, W. *The Organization Man*. New York, NY: Simon & Schuster. 1956.

47 Postrel, V. How has "The Organization Man" changed? *The New York Times*, January 17, 1999.

48 Galbraith, J. K. *The New Industrial State*. Boston, MA: Houghton Mifflin. 1967.

49 Servan-Schreiber, J. J. *The American Challenge*. New York, NY: Scribner. 1968.

50 McCrae, Norman. We're all entrepreneurial now—17 April 1982. www.normanmacrae.com/intrapreneur.html.

51 For example, a mid-1980s study by Calvin Kent of the content of popular principles of economics "revealed that entrepreneurship was either neglected, improperly presented, or only partially covered." Kent, C. A. and Rushing, F. W. Coverage of entrepreneurship in principles of economics textbooks: An update. *Journal of Economics Education*, Spring 1999, pp. 184–189.

52 Schumpeter, J. A. *Capitalism, Socialism, and Democracy*. Third edition. New York, NY: Harper Torchbooks. 1950. First published in 1942.

53 Schumpeter, J. A. *The Theory of Economic Development*. Cambridge, MA: Harvard University Press. 1934. Reprinted edition, Cambridge, MA: Harvard University Press, 1949.

54 Blau, D. M. A Time-Series Analysis of Self-Employment in the United States. *Journal of Political Economy*, 95, 445–467. 1987. Evans, D. and Leighton L. S. The Determinants of Changes in U. S. Self-Employment. *Small Business Economics*, 1(2) 11989, 111–120. 1987.

55 Acs, Z. J., Arenius, P., Hay, M., and Minniti, M. *The Global Entrepreneurship Monitor: 2004 Executive Report*. www.gemconsortium.org.

56 This is excerpted from Reynolds, P. D., Hay, M., Bygrave, W. D., Camp, S. M., and Autio, E. *Global Entrepreneurship Monitor: 2000 Executive Report*. www.gemconsortium.org.

57 Ralph Nader's best-selling book *Unsafe at Any Speed: The Designed-In Dangers of the American Automobile* published in 1965 claimed that automobile manufacturers were ignoring safety features, like seat belts, and were reluctant to spend money on improving safety.

58 George Gendron on the State of Entrepreneurship. December 2002.
www.pioneerentrepreneurs.net/bigidea_gendron.php.

59 Bygrave, W. D. and Timmons, J. A. *Venture Capital at the Crossroads*. Boston, MA: Harvard Business School Press. 1992.

60 2002–2003 The Small Business Economy: A Report to the President. United States Printing Office, Washington, D.C. 2004. www.sba.gov/advo/stats/sb_econ02-03.pdf.

61 Nelson, L. 1998. The Rise of Intellectual Property Protection in the American University. *Science*, Vol. 279, Issue 5356, 1460–1461. www.sciencemag.org/cgi/content/full/279/5356/1460.

62 Morris. D. Who gets the fruits of public R&D? *Minneapolis Star Tribune*, November 28, 2004.
www.ilsr.org/columns/2004/112804.html.

63 Innovation's golden goose. *The Economist*, December 12, 2002.

64 Statement of Senator Birch Bayh to the National Institutes of Health, May 25, 2004. http://ott.od.nih.gov/Meeting/Senator-Birch-Bayh.pdf.

65 www.nal.usda.gov/ttic/guide.htm.

66 Singletary, M. How to get the most bang from eBay. *Maine Sunday Telegram.* August 7, 2005.

67 Wiggins, J. and Gibson, D. V. Overview of US incubators and the case of the Austin Technology Incubator. *Int. J. Entrepreneurship and Innovation Management*, Vol. 3, Nos. 1/2, 2003.

www.ic2.org/publications/Incubator%20Paper%20with%20Joel.pdf.

68 Business Incubation FAQ. www.nbia.org/resource_center/bus_inc_facts/index.php.

69 George Gendron on the State of Entrepreneurship. December 2002.

www.pioneerentrepreneurs.net/bigidea_gendron.php.

70 Lange, J., Mollov, A., Pearlmuttter, M., Singh, S., and Bygrave, W. Pre-startup formal business plans and post-startup performance: A study of 116 new ventures. Presented at the Babson Kauffman Entrepreneurship Research Conference. Babson College, June 2005.

71 Moore, G. E. The Accidental Entrepreneur. Originally published in *Engineering & Science,* Summer 1994, vol. LVII, no. 4, California Institute of Technology.

http://nobelprize.org/physics/articles/moore/.

72 Boylan, M. What we know and don't know about venture capital. American Economic Association Meeting, December 28, 1981, and National Economist Club, January 19, 1982.

73 National Venture Capital Association.

74 Bygrave, W. D. *Global Entrepreneurship Monitor: 2004 Financing Report* (with Steve Hunt). www.gemconsortium.org.

75 www.sba.gov/advo/research/dyn_b_d8902.pdf.

76 Rifkin, G. and Harrar, G. *The Ultimate Entrepreneur: The Story of Ken Olsen and Digital Equipment Corporation.* Chicago, IL: Contemporary Books. 1998.

77 Lichtenstein, N. Is Wal-Mart good for America? *PBS Frontline.* June 9, 2004. www.pbs.org/wgbh/pages/frontline/shows/walmart/interviews/lichtenstein.html.

78 http://www.news.cornell.edu/stories/April05/HEC.05.cover.html.

79 www.skype.com/.

80 Baker, G. Everything in the American garden is lovely. So why the long face, buddy? Timesonline, August 5, 2005. www.timesonline.co.uk/article/0,19269−1721814,00.html.

81 *Time*, July 18, 2005. www.time.com/time/globalbusiness/printout/0,8816,1083940,00.html.

82 Harriss, Joseph A. Riots? What Riots? *The American Spectator*, 39:1, p. 58. February 2006.

83 Autio, E. 2005. Global Entrepreneurship Monitor: GEM-Mazars Special Report on High-Expectation Entrepreneurship. www.gemconsortium.org.

84 Excerpted from GEM global reports and special reports. www.gemconsortium.org.

85 Excerpted from the *Global Entrepreneurship Monitor 2004 Executive Report.*

86 Acs, Z. J. and D. Storey. 2004 Entrepreneurship and Economic Development. *Regional Studies*, 38, 1−12.

87 Excerpted from the *Global Entrepreneurship Monitor 2004 Executive Report.*

88 Ibid.

89 Note: Education data were standardized across all countries in order to make this comparison possible.

90 Excerpted from Autio, E. Global Entrepreneurship Monitor: GEM-Mazars Special Report on High-Expectation Entrepreneurship. 2005. www.gemconsortium.org.

91 Storey, D. *Understanding the Small Business Sector*. London: Routledge. 1994.

92 Birch, D. *Who Is Creating Jobs?* Cambridge, MA: Cognetics. 1995.

93 *Time*, July 18, 2005. www.time.com/time/globalbusiness/printout/0,8816,1083940,00.html.

94 Address to the EU Parliament, Prime Minister Blair, June 23, 2005.

http://news.bbc.co.uk/1/hi/uk_politics/4122288.stm.

95 *The Economist*, September 8, 2005.

America rules
The world's top universities*

<table>
<tr><td>1</td><td>Harvard University</td><td>America</td></tr>
<tr><td>2</td><td>Stanford University</td><td>America</td></tr>
<tr><td>3</td><td>University of Cambridge</td><td>Britain</td></tr>
<tr><td>4</td><td>University of California (Berkeley)</td><td>America</td></tr>
<tr><td>5</td><td>Massachusetts Institute of Technology</td><td>America</td></tr>
<tr><td>6</td><td>California Institute of Technology</td><td>America</td></tr>
<tr><td>7</td><td>Princeton University</td><td>America</td></tr>
<tr><td>8</td><td>University of Oxford</td><td>Britain</td></tr>
<tr><td>9</td><td>Columbia University</td><td>America</td></tr>
<tr><td>10</td><td>University of Chicago</td><td>America</td></tr>
<tr><td>11</td><td>Yale University</td><td>America</td></tr>
<tr><td>12</td><td>Cornell University</td><td>America</td></tr>
<tr><td>13</td><td>University of California (San Diego)</td><td>America</td></tr>
<tr><td>14</td><td>Tokyo University</td><td>Japan</td></tr>
<tr><td>15</td><td>University of Pennsylvania</td><td>America</td></tr>
<tr><td>16</td><td>University of California (Los Angeles)</td><td>America</td></tr>
<tr><td>17</td><td>University of California (San Francisco)</td><td>America</td></tr>
<tr><td>18</td><td>University of Wisconsin (Madison)</td><td>America</td></tr>
<tr><td>19</td><td>University of Michigan (Ann Arbor)</td><td>America</td></tr>
<tr><td>20</td><td>University of Washington (Seattle)</td><td>America</td></tr>
</table>

* Ranked by a mixture of indicators of academic and research performance, including Nobel prizes and articles in respected publications

Source: Jiao Tong University, Shanghai

96 Kok, Wim. Facing the Challenge: The Lisbon Strategy for Growth and Employment. Report from the High Level Group chaired by Wim Kok, November 2004. http://europa.eu.int/growthandjobs/pdf/kok_report_en.pdf.

97 "Students march in Paris as the unrest spreads" by Colin Randall in Paris. March 15, 2006. www.telegraph.co.uk/news/main.jhtml?xml=/news/2006/03/15/wparis15.xml&sSheet=/news/2006/03/15/ixworld.html.

98 Harriss, J.A. Celebrating 70 years of socialism. *The American Spectator*, April, 39(3): 53. 2006.

99 Several studies have been done on the interests that young people have in entrepreneurship. For example, in their book *The E Generation: Prepared for the Entrepreneurial Economy*, Marilyn Kourilsky and William Walstad explain that youth are overwhelmingly interested in entrepreneurship. In fact, they found that six out of ten young people aspire to start a business of their own. The Gallup Organization, in conjunction with the Kauffman Foundation, conducted the first national poll on entrepreneurship. What they found was that 70% of students polled wanted to start their own business. www.entre-ed.org/testimony.htm.

Malincho

Bulgarian Kalin Pentchev leaned into his cell phone conversation as he scribbled numbers on the top flap of a shipping box. Speaking quickly in his native tongue, the big man jabbed the air in front of him for emphasis.

"Look, I will tell you this. If you come down on your price, I will sign a contract to guarantee that my company will purchase one hundred thousand pounds of your cheese in the coming year."

He drew circles and blocks around the numbers as he listened to the impassioned response from a feta cheese producer 3,500 miles away.

"You need to think about that?" Kalin said at last with a fair amount of exasperation. "Well, don't think too long; it's already April and this year 2003 isn't getting any younger. You're not the only producer in Bulgaria, my friend, and you must understand that I will be signing a favorable volume agreement with someone, and soon. Right. Okay, you get back to me."

Kalin smiled as he clicked off. No matter that he had no idea how he could possibly sell that much cheese in a year, or that he was playing hardball with one of the only producers he felt he could trust back in his homeland. As was his nature, Kalin was moving forward like a tightrope walker performing daring feats without a net, protected only by a supreme faith in his own ability to overcome whatever challenge he encountered or set for himself.

As he resumed packing orders of East European food products to be shipped to his customers all over the United States, Kalin shook off concerns about the pile of neglected tasks back at his apartment; paperwork for a sizable UPS shipping credit, his U.S. tax return, and a few applications for debt-consolidation loans.

With his New Jersey–based import business, Malincho.com, growing exponentially during a slump in the economy, Kalin wasn't going to let those pressing tasks slow him down. After all, to someone who had grown up under a communist regime, this business of capitalism in America seemed almost like child's play.

Coming to America

In the spring of 1998, Kalin was awarded a small scholarship from Stockton College in New Jersey. Eager to get to the United States in advance of classes that would begin in September, Kalin joined a few friends who were headed for work with a summer camp in Maine. After discovering that his employer asked much and paid little, Kalin journeyed south:

> I left the camp because I had some disagreements with the boss; they were paying way too low . . . He treated us like we were white slave labor from Eastern Europe. I mean, we might be poor, but we are not slaves. . . . I went to Atlantic City where I had a friend in the university where I was going to study accounting. We lived in a community of about twenty people from Bulgaria . . . So we found work pushing chairs on the boardwalk.

This case was prepared by Carl Hedberg under the direction of Professor William Bygrave.

Kalin graduated in 2001 with a degree in finance and accounting. Soon after, he appeared to have landed a job with a financial accounting firm. In a twist of fate, he instead found himself at a wedding in the Czech Republic, discussing the import/export business:

> *A financial accounting firm almost hired me. They showed me the office, everything. They asked if I wanted to take the summer off before starting work like Americans usually do when they finish school. But I said, I need some money here now. I stopped sending resumes, because I considered myself hired. I don't know what happened. I called them two weeks later to ask for advice on a place I could rent in their area, and they said, you know, we found somebody else. I said, why didn't you call me? I mean it was ridiculous. I was very upset.*
>
> *Right after this I went to the Czech Republic. I have two cousins there and one was getting married. A dear friend of mine from Bulgaria had come over for this wedding, and on the day we would talk . . . We started talking about exporting damaged European-made cars from America back to Europe. So he said, when you go back to the United States find out how we can transport these cars . . .*

Back in the States, it didn't take Kalin long to learn that the high transport fees would make it nearly impossible to build a profitable damaged-auto export business. His research, however, led him to the idea of importing feta cheese and selling it to fellow Bulgarians on the East Coast—a growing, tight-knit community that he knew was hungry for a taste of home (see Exhibit 1.1).

Having decided to forgo looking for a job in favor of building an enterprise from scratch, Kalin held onto a part-time job he had all through school as a breakfast waiter at a popular Greek restaurant along the board walk. In July 2001, Kalin took the ferry to New York to meet with a former school classmate whose father owned a high-profile Bulgarian winery:

> *They own one of the best wineries in Bulgaria and have been in the import-export business a long time. They sell wine all over the world and have offices in Switzerland and England. So this guy told me, "Look, I am exporting cheese now from Bulgaria to Switzerland. If you are thinking about the cheese we can go ahead and do it."*
>
> *He tells me it works like this. Everything is on the phone. You just call the producer and you order the cheese. You say this has to come here, this has to go there. You pay this guy this, you pay this guy that. You stay home on the phone. The container comes to you, somebody unloads it, and then you have to sell it. That's it.*
>
> *Then he says, you know, you will have to buy a whole container of cheese; not just one pallet, and a shipping container is like a whole room full of cheese . . . And so, I started thinking about the cheese.*

Research and the Wine Guy

Kalin already knew that the style of cheese known as "feta" was invented in the Trakia peninsula in southern Bulgaria. The Bulgarians called their version "white cheese," while the Greeks created a mystique by using the word "feta." Although the Greeks were now trying to legally prevent other countries from using the term feta, most cheese connoisseurs agreed that by any name, the Bulgarian product—especially that made from sheep's milk—was the best in the world. Kalin learned that wholesalers sold the cheese

EXHIBIT 1.1	Bulgarian Immigration and U.S. Population		
Immigration Period	Reason for Travel	Estimated Numbers	Characteristics
1920–WWII	Work as temporary field and construction workers	10,000	Most stayed and were assimilated into the U.S. culture.
Post WWII– 1989	Asylum seekers escaping the communist regime	Minimal	During the Cold War, many qualified asylum candidates in the U.S. were regarded as potential spies.
Post-Communism	Tourism, education, work-visa lottery winners	The U.S. Bulgarian community is estimated at 300,000, with 60,000 in Chicago, 30,000 in New York, and 3,000 in the Boston area.	Ease of travel and established ethnic communities have diminished the need for temporary visitors to assimilate fully into the U.S. culture.

Data and analysis: Silvia Zaharinova, Babson College MBA '03

The 2000 United States Census listed 55,489 U.S. citizens of Bulgarian heritage. The states with the large Bulgarian-American communities included:

California - 7,845
Illinois - 6,000
New York - 5,937
Florida - 3,310
Ohio - 2,937

2000 Census Bulgarian-American population, by state:

Alabama 217
Alaska 106
Arizona 1,052
Arkansas 114
California 7,845
Colorado 1,495
Connecticut 722
DC 207
Delaware 113
Florida 3,310
Georgia 967
Hawaii 100
Idaho 288
Illinois 6,000
Indiana 1,053
Iowa 563
Kansas 237
Kentucky 226

Louisiana 261
Maine 221
Maryland 1,160
Massachusetts 1,140
Michigan 2,522
Minnesota 963
Mississippi 97
Missouri 804
Montana 245
Nebraska 161
Nevada 1,014
New Hampshire 118
New Jersey 1,511
New Mexico 228
New York 5,937
North Carolina 609
North Dakota 142

Ohio 2,937
Oklahoma 429
Oregon 904
Pennsylvania 1,469
Rhode Island 144
South Carolina 363
South Dakota 33
Tennessee 317
Texas 2,140
Utah 434
Vermont 52
Virginia 1,168
Washington 2,248
West Virginia 203
Wisconsin 766
Wyoming 134

either vacuum-packed in various retail sizes, or as loose portions stacked between sheets of special paper inside sealed tin buckets of salty brine.

During the summer of 2001, Kalin spent a good deal of his time searching through the vast resources of the U.S. Customs Department—both online and at their ground-floor offices in the World Trade Center complex in New York City. A young customs clerk, intrigued with Kalin's enthusiastic quest for information, saved Kalin time and money by offering her help in sorting through the myriad of import regulations, restrictions, and fees associated with food imports.

Kalin had always assumed that he would be importing an excellent grade of cow's milk feta, since it was nearly as good as sheep's feta—and less than half the price. The clerk, however, pointed out that the U.S. Government levied significant tariffs on imported dairy cow products as a way of protecting domestic producers. The best-quality sheep feta was duty-free, and would therefore be a cheaper import.

All the while, Kalin continued to brainstorm with his Bulgarian winery contact about developing a business where Kalin would receive, sell, and distribute containers of cheese that were funded and exported by this well-heeled and experienced professional. Since a minimum shipment of about 28,000 pounds of cheese would cost $40,000, Kalin figured that this arrangement would work well until he was able to save some money and gain more experience. After that, he imagined that he would make an offer to buy his partner out. He never got that chance. As the summer dragged on, Kalin began to suspect that this businessman was more style than substance:

> I was doing my research about the cheese; how we can sell this cheese and so on and so forth. But it took this guy with the wine very much time to finish everything. He said he had a producer, he had the connections, so all we had to do was to agree on what to order and send. But he kept saying he was busy with other things, so at some point I got fed up. I said, "Look, we have to do something. Time is going." The cheese business is seasonal since you can only milk the sheep from April to August. The rest of the year I don't know. A short time later I was disappointed to find out that he was not actually exporting cheese to Switzerland like he had said. He was only helping a friend do it. He didn't even know the price of the cheese.

As Kalin began to press his would-be partner hard for substantive action, he got a warning call from his trusted friend who had been investigating the auto-export opportunity. Bulgarian newspapers were reporting that the father of Kalin's "wine guy" was not only millions of dollars in debt, he was also about to be indicated on charges relating to a host of questionable business practices. Kalin acted fast:

> So I called the wine guy and said, "Look, why didn't you tell me you are in deep trouble?" He said, "I have nothing to do with the winery. We have sixteen other firms that do different kinds of things." He said they had a scheme where they can take the money out of the winery and put the cash in through other firms so they end up with the money in the end. He says they are fine, very fine. I mean no problem. So I said, you are what your father is, and I don't buy any of this. And he said, oh, you doubt me? I am a big business man, and you are nobody.

With no savings and precious little knowledge of the import business, Kalin tried one last time to force the man into action:

> I gave him three options. First, you can pay for the whole container since you are a big business man, and I'm going to sell that cheese here and we are still in business together. Second option was a fifty-fifty split where I would raise half the money. Or third, I would cover his expenses up to that point.

I told him that all this money, this forty-thousand dollars, I have to raise from somewhere. I don't have it in my pocket. I just graduated school and I'm in debt already. He said, "Look, I am going to give you a chance. You pay for the first container as a test. If you can sell this container, this means that you are a good businessman. Anyway, for a second container you're going to need the same amount of money because you have to overlap the containers. By January, if you sell everything I'm going to join in with the big money. Okay?"

Not okay. Kalin hung up on him and began calling everyone he knew.

The First Container

Kalin had been talking to people in his community about his import business for some time, so many of the calls he made were to friends who had expressed interest and encouragement. He explained that he needed to raise $40,000 in cash, since, as many of his Bulgarian compatriots already understood, credit cards and bank drafts would not be accepted. Cash meant cash. Kalin described his pitch to raise money.

All my friends were students, working hard—some working two jobs. They have money in the bank, but it is for tuition. I told them, look guys, together me and my girlfriend have over forty-thousand dollars as a line available on our credit cards. What we are going to do if this thing screws up is take cash from those cards—never mind about the big interest that they will charge us—and at least we are going to pay your tuitions with those credit cards. I mean, I never lied to anybody that I have money on the side, or that my father is rich or something.

In one hour Kalin had exhausted his contacts and had raised six individual investments of $5,000 each—all interest free. Still, he was $10,000 shy of the cash he would need to order a shipment of cheese. Then he had an idea:

I called up a friend of my family in Bulgaria. Tania was a businessperson for real. She operated one of the best restaurants in the second biggest city, and she was like an aunt to me. She said, "Okay, I am going to put ten grand into this." Now, I knew that I couldn't send all this money to the producer because I didn't know the producer. So I told Tania that all money goes through you, you pay him and make sure you see the things loaded on the container. She said fine.

On the fifteenth of August, my friends gave me the money—five days later I sent thirty-thousand dollars to Tania in Bulgaria. So she paid the guy; one third when we placed the order, one third when they began packaging our order, and the last third when they loaded it into the container. After the producer has his money, he forgets about you right away.

Lose Your Job? Buy a New Car

On the last morning of August, Kalin reported for his waitstaff job at the restaurant as usual, but discovered that he had been taken off the schedule. Earlier that summer, Kalin had mentioned his business idea to the owner of the establishment (a wealthy Greek gentleman who at the time was the largest landowner in Atlantic City) in the hope that the businessman might offer some helpful advice. He didn't, and when he learned that Kalin had gone ahead with ordering the cheese, he had him terminated because he was afraid that Kalin would become distracted and unreliable. Kalin recalled that his initial anger at this latest curveball was almost immediately overtaken by a desire to hit a homerun:

> I had been working there nearly four years; I brought them so many Bulgarian customers and workers! I got so upset I wrote the Greek guy a letter. I said that he should have at least warned me. So he called me, and says that his aunt is running the place, and she had a bad moment and decided to take me off the schedule. He said it was okay; that I could come back. I said forget about it.
>
> Then I said to myself, "Look, probably this is good, because I will never stop working at the restaurant because it is cash on the side." I was going to be importing-exporting, so I had to forget about that job as a waiter.
>
> My car had just broken down, and my girlfriend and I were fed up with buying old cars that get broken all the time—with dealers and mechanics always screwing you and never fixing in right. Also, when you run a business, you have to have a decent car. So on the fourth of September we ended up buying a brand new Maxima—the perfect car. My container is at sea, and I buy a brand-new car.

Having virtually no cash on hand, Kalin put the $3,000 down payment for the Maxima on his credit card. With no further payments due for 45 days, Kalin was determined to make the most of this grace period. His first journey in the new car was to a large refrigerated warehouse 30 miles away in North Jersey, since he understood that the would need an established storage facility to accept delivery of his cheese after it cleared customs. Knowing also that these businesses typically would not work with startups or inexperienced clients, he wore a suit and tie. Dressing for success might have had some impact, but, he recalled, it was his new set of wheels that really made the difference:

> My car helped me to get the storage, because the owner, Tony, was from a rural area and he judged people by their cars. So I come there with a brand-new car. I am young—his age—and I had a better car than he did. He had some truck, and his sister—who owned the storage place with him—was driving a Nissan Sentra. And I drive up in a Maxima with almost no miles on it.
>
> So I told him that I had started doing the cheese, and that it was a good business. He showed me the storage, and we started talking about the cheese. He was thinking we are big; he didn't know it was only me. Then he said look you're not dealing drugs, right? I said, come on now, I am not dealing drugs. He was thinking I am Russian.[1] I said no, I speak Russian very good, but I am not Russian, and we are not dealing drugs. After that he said he wanted us to go there. I told him the container was already on its way.

Kalin contracted with a customs broker whose job it was to expedite the paperwork and procedures necessary for the cheese to clear customs. She explained to Kalin that since this was a first-time import, the container would likely be thoroughly checked before it was released. As nervous as an expectant father, Kalin made it clear to her that he wanted to be notified the moment the container passed customs so that he could be at the storage facility when it arrived. Then, on September 11, 2001, while Kalin's container of cheese

---

[1] In 2002, the Narcotics and Organized Crime Bureau division of the New Jersey State Police indicated that political, economic, and social changes occurring in the former Soviet Union and Eastern Bloc countries had provided significant opportunities for Russian organized crime groups to expand their influence in and around the state. In April of that year, federal authorities announced a sweeping racketeering indictment against ten suspected Russian émigré mobsters operating in Philadelphia and in Northern New Jersey. Sources: The New Jersey State Police, the U. S. Department of Justice, and *The Philadelphia Inquirer* (*Charges reveal new-look mob of Russian émigré*, April 26, 2002).

was still somewhere out in the middle of the Atlantic Ocean, terrorists flew a pair of passenger planes into the World Trade Center buildings in New York City.

Welcomes to the Business

In the confusion following the attacks, Kalin's broker had been able to get his container released without delay. The bad news was that she never called to give Kalin the good news. On September 25th, Kalin got a heart-stopping call from Tony, the owner of the storage business. The container had been delivered to his facility, but when he opened it (to check for drugs), he discovered a smelly mess of leaking buckets of cheese. Kalin jumped in his Maxima for the long, nerve-racking drive. What he found when he got there was not good:

> The producer [in Bulgaria] had packed eighty square metal buckets—they weigh forty-four pounds apiece—one over another in eight rows. Now they are not using perfect metal because they want to keep the packaging cheap—and the salt kills the metal. You can imagine the bottom two rows; these big cans were cracked, and the white salty brine was all over the floor. It smelled, and Tony wanted to know what I was going to do about it. And I was thinking, on my god, what am I going to do now?

Kalin rolled up his sleeves and went to work. Hours later he was relieved to find that less than 5% of the order had been damaged in transit. Once this tally—just under 1,000 pounds—was confirmed, Tony directed his workers to help Kalin toss the broken containers into the dumpster. Kalin took Tony aside:

> I asked him to allow me to repack this cheese. There was a lot of money there, and also, I was brought up that you can't throw away food. I told him that when I was young, I used to starve, and my father used to starve. You always ate everything on your plate. As an American person, Tony was thinking that because the insurance will pay, why bother repacking, just throw it out because you will get the money anyway. I was thinking that since it was insured in Bulgaria, there is no guarantee that I am going to get this two-thousand dollars. So I told him I can't throw the food away; I cannot afford to do that.

Despite a state law prohibiting nonemployees from entering a transfer-warehouse facility, Kalin prevailed. He rushed home to recruit some friends to help him out, and to give the producer in Bulgaria a call:

> I called up the producer and said, how did you load this? I pay you for cheese that is supposed to be in a package good for sale, not for repack. Also, out of six different kinds of cheese just one of them was matching the invoice number. Most of them were less, some of them were more. This is ridiculous. I said, come on! I paid you everything; you send me less, and then we have damage because you arranged the cans like this. All he said was, "Welcomes to the business." Can you imagine this? But he did give me the recipe for brine—water, salt and lemon extract. With two friends helping, it took us a week to repack those broken cans piece by piece.

On the Road

Now that he had his inventory organized and secure, Kalin began to sell the quality cheese locally at very low prices. A short while later, he received some important advice from a Bulgarian feta producer:

I was doing anything to sell, because I had to sell the cheese, but this guy from Bulgaria reminded me that the milking season was over for the year. He said that to be in this business, you have to sell the cheese slower, and at a higher price. If I sell at 5% margins, he said that you are going to end up getting no more merchandise from us.

So I said okay. I make a brochure, I rent a truck, and I went down to a Bulgarian church in [Washington] D.C. where people were getting together. A lot of friends were helping me because they spread out the word to the community, and I was delivering the cheese to people's houses with the truck—no matter the gas.

Realizing that Bulgarian feta was prized throughout the Middle East and Eastern Europe, Kalin cruised the ethnic neighborhoods around D.C. in search of restaurants, delis, and grocery stores. Since his mobile method of distribution and sales seemed to invite a type of street-side haggling common in open-air marketplaces around the world, Kalin found himself struggling to maintain his pricing structure. At one stop, a Lebanese storekeeper drove a particularly hard bargain for a sizable bulk order. After Kalin had unloaded and packed the order neatly in the shop's cooler, he found the man wasn't finished haggling:

He looks in his drawer, and he says, "You know, this price too much, I'm going to give you less, because you never called me, you never sent me samples, you never did anything. So come on, come on, I'm going to be buying only from you from now on." I got back in my truck after and I said I have to be out of my mind. I mean, if for the rest of my life I'm going to deal with people like this, I'm going to go mad.

Worse than the constant haggling was the realization that while these retailer were selling his product for at least double their cost, Kalin sensed that the truck rental alone would eat up most of the 20% margins he was struggling to uphold. for all his hard work, he suddenly feared that he might even end up with less money than what he had started out with.

Desperate and determined, he started calling large-volume cheese buyers along the East Coast—intent on pre-selling some orders before he set out again. Kalin explained that it was in late October of 2001 when he had a major breakthrough:

So, I call this one big company in Florida—I think they were importing from Greece—but the guy wanted to see the cheese. He asked me to UPS him one small round can. Oh my gosh, I thought. I immediately called a friend and told him that I sold all of my cheese. He said, really? You sold the cheese? I said no, but if I can send samples on the ground with UPS, then I knew that I am going to sell everything I have—through the mail and online.

Kalin moved quickly. After UPS and Federal Express both assured him that they had no restrictions against shipping cheese products, he established a Web site named *Malincho*—a playful Bulgarian nickname for a little boy. Then he set about to find a source of economical shipping containers:

I didn't want to spend money on boxes, so I go to all my friends to see if they had recently bought a TV, a microwave, or had other boxes around. My first two orders I sent to a friend who works in a pizza place in Boston . . . I just put the can in the box—no cushion; nothing else. I figure this can is very tough so I'll just put the label on the box. I just dropped it at UPS, and it was perfect. My friend called and said the can got here—with no damage, thank you very much.

Three weeks after Kalin mailed out that first package, a UPS representative paid a visit to the world headquarters of Malincho.com—the small apartment Kalin shared with his girlfriend and two other friends. Kalin explained to the young salesman that every few days he would fill up the Maxima at the cold storage facility, and then store and ship the product on the back porch because it stayed cold out there. The rep—who had been sent there to open a business account with Malincho before their competitor FedEx moved in—seemed surprised and a bit amused by the meager surroundings. Confident that he would be wiping that smile off the lad's face soon enough, Kalin served up strong coffee and laughed right along with him.

Credit Sales

By November, Kalin was driving customers to Malincho.com by world-of-mouth and with small advertisements in Bulgarian newspapers. He set up the site to accept major credit cards, but discovered that many of his fellow countrymen were reluctant to place orders online:

> The holidays were coming, and people were visiting online. But many of these Bulgarians had won the "green card lottery" and they came here not knowing English or anything about America. In Bulgaria there is a lot of credit-card fraud, and people had heard that some of the criminals were using Web sites to get credit-card numbers. And they think that my site smells like I'm going to get their credit card and start charging for this and that. And if that happens, they think, "how am I going to dispute the charges if I can't even speak English?" So then, they don't buy.

To overcome this obstacle, Kalin decided for a time to build his business on trust. Customers would receive a Malincho invoice with their delivered order, along with a note requesting prompt payment for the cheese plus shipping charges. Kalin carefully tracked his receivables and found that if it had not been for one woman in Ohio and a shopkeeper in New Hampshire, his bad debt account would have been zero. Many of his friends were shocked to learn that he was shipping orders, some of which totaled hundreds of dollars, on faith. Kalin was not as surprised, though, since Malincho.com was fast becoming an online community of people who literally spoke the same language; and back home, stiffing a vendor was a serious offense:

> My buyers were thinking; here is this Bulgarian guy importing cheese. He should be big, or if he's not big, he has somebody powerful behind him. And if I don't pay him, he can get to my relatives in Bulgaria and beat them up for the money.
>
> So I figure, why pay over 2% to Visa or MasterCard when with this cash payment method customers appeared to be coming, and paying? And besides, it was helping me build the business.

Expansion

The early part of 2002 was a very busy time for Kalin, who was doing deals all over the board. In January he purchased several pallets of Lutenica, a Bulgarian condiment, from a woman in D.C. who had given up trying to sell off a container that she had imported a couple of years earlier. Kalin added the spread product to Malincho.com at a high markup, and when it sold very well, he rolled his cash on hand into a container of 20 pallets of other assorted dry-storage items like marmalade, roasted red peppers, and thin wafers. With the help of a $5,000 sale from Florida and a similar sale to an import group in Chicago, by April, Kalin had nearly sold out his inventory of cheese.

As the weather warmed up, the Maxima—splattered throughout with cheese and brine—began to reek. Not wanting to degrade the car any further, and needing a larger transport vehicle anyway, Kalin took out his credit card once again to purchase a Chevy van.

The changing season also meant that the back porch of his apartment would no longer work as a refrigerated shipping area, but Kalin had not been able to convince Tony to rent Malincho refrigerated repacking space. After Kalin had placed an order for a third container—all cheese, like the first—he approached an established importer who was leasing a cold-room from Tony:

> *This one French guy was renting one of the rooms but it was too big from him. So I suggested to the French guy that we split the room—and I would pay Tony extra money. I told him I didn't need much space; just enough so I can pack and ship. But Tony got very offended because to him it looked like I was trying to work out a side deal with the French guy. I said no, no, I am willing to pay you extra to do this so I can get my business going. He refused, and then he said, it's time for you to find another storage place.*

Out on the street with another 28,000 pounds of cheese chugging toward New York, Kalin went to see a Russian sausage maker in his neighborhood that he had heard had more refrigeration and dry-space than he was using. They came to an arrangement that Kalin explained was far from ideal:

> *The Russian guy said, okay, you can use my place here for six-hundred a month—cash under the table—off the books. But that's it—no key, because, he said, look, I make sausages here; you can come here only when I am here. That's it, end of story. He doesn't know me, and I don't know him, and now I am going to put my product inside his place. I was thinking that once I get all my cheese in there, he could lock the door and say get off my property—I don't want to see you. Sometimes, though, you have no choice—you just have to make decisions on trust.*

Even with the shipping department moved off the back porch, the steadily increasing sales had begun to strain life in the small apartment. Kalin and his girlfriend soon moved to an apartment of their own—complete with enough space to run the business side of Malincho.

In advance of the summer months, Kalin set out to devise an insulated shipping container. After much research and running around, Kalin purchased a bulk order of boxes and pre-cut styrofoam inserts. Realizing that the sausage maker would never agree to accept numerous pallets of packaging materials, Kalin convinced the box seller to inventory the supplies. Kalin was pleasantly surprised to discover that once he switched from used appliance boxes to insulated containers with ice parks, sales spiked by more than enough to cover the added shipping costs.

By the fall of 2002, Kalin had negotiated volume-customer pricing with UPS and with his corrugated box supplier. He had also convinced his Bulgarian suppliers to properly shrink-wrap all of his orders onto pallets that conformed to U.S. standards for size and construction. Most importantly, those suppliers had agreed to help Kalin control his inventory flow by shipping mixed orders containing a variety of different products.

A reporter from *USA Today* called in the middle of the busy Christmas season. Kalin was at the sausage plant, and Vladimir—Malincho's self-taught (and volunteer) Webmaster who had studied accounting with Kalin back in Bulgaria—answered the

EXHIBIT 1.2

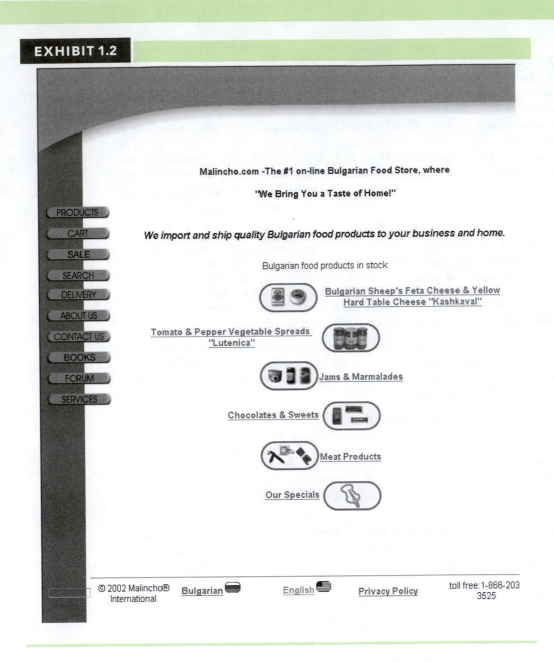

phone in his native tongue. The reporter didn't call back, but he did visit Malincho.com (see Exhibit 1.2). Kalin recalled the thrill of having his young enterprise mentioned in the national press:

> *People called me from Bulgaria because one newspaper in Bulgaria literally translates everything from USA Today. I couldn't image that we had been in business for just one year and a half and here we are being written up in that newspaper,* Newsweek *magazine did an article and quoted me, and then there was another article in a Bulgarian newspaper called* Capital—*that reporter didn't even call. He found us online. It was amazing.*

Funding Challenges

Bolstered by press coverage and the strategic use of search-engine tags, Malincho continued to add customers to its core base of about 2,000 loyal regulars. Since many of those customers still were not willing or able to shop online, Kalin produced a simple inventory printout that was sent with each order.

By February of 2003, Kalin had his own key to the factory, and online sales of his landlord's sausages—listed under "Meat Products" on Malincho.com—were more than covering the rent for the shared space. Sales were averaging $16,000 a month, inventory on hand was just under $60,000, and the fifth and sixth containers were on their way. Kalin was packing and shipping more than 100 orders per week to customers who were now required to prepay by check or credit card.

All of this activity had ballooned his need for short-term capital, and although Kalin had paid back half of the people who had extended him funding for the first container, he had found it necessary to borrow more cash in order to keep his inventory current. Kalin summarized his financial situation:

> Right now I owe about forty-thousand to credit cards, and sixty-thousand to people. I also have a ten grand personal loan from Fleet Bank. A while back I went to them and said that I wanted to consolidate the debt on my credit cards. When they gave me money, I put it into the business. Now I want to consolidate for real this time, but the banks say I need three years' tax returns—I haven't been here that long. I figure I need about one-hundred grand to consolidate my debts, and another fifty-thousand dollars so that I can get my own place for storage and packing. Then I could hire people to work for me so we could grow faster.

Kalin was in that enviable yet difficult point on the new venture curve where his growing business was too small to financially support even one full-time employee, but was large enough to require his every waking hour. He described a typical day:

> In the morning I'm taking orders, making labels, calling people, and playing big businessman. In the afternoon I am just a worker who has to check the orders and pack all the packages. It's not easy, but it's worth it. Physical labor is healthy labor. I am not ashamed of doing anything because it's what you have to do to grow.

Not Going to Go Down

Kalin sealed up and labeled the last box for that day. Grabbing a chocolate-coated Mura wafer bar from inventory, he hopped up onto a pallet of Lutenica for a short break before heading home. Long days. Precarious finances. It was time to make some decisions as to how best to move forward.

Although Malincho.com had become his main source of sales, Kalin was weighing other options as well. Retail margins, for example, were so much higher than wholesale that he was considering opening a storefront location. Wholesaling, on the other hand, was a no-frills business model that worked well with Kalin's need to meet with a variety of key wholesalers, retailers, and suppliers. Although Kalin knew that getting better control over his finances was critical to the survival of his growing venture, he had discovered that it takes more than money to grow a business:

I know that a small business can go down for three reasons. First, if you give up, that's it. You have to refuse to give up. The second big reason is the money. If you don't have the cash flow to pay your bills, you die. But the most important thing is you. Because if you believe in something, and you can find other people who believe in the same thing, you're going to be able to do it, no matter what.

Preparation Questions

1. Apply the Timmons entrepreneurship framework (entrepreneur-opportunity-resources) to analyze this case. Pay particular attention to Kalin's traits and how he gathered resources for his venture.

2. What business models are open to a food-product importer? What steps should Kalin take to position his company for the next phase of early-stage growth?

3. Imagine you are a potential investor and Kalin has just given you his rocket pitch. What are your concerns? Would you help him out?

Anita Roddick standing in front of one of her Body Shop cosmetic stores. The store was started in 1976 by Anita and Gordon Roddick in Brighton, England to sell cosmetic, skin care, and bath products made from all natural ingredients. In 2006, Body Shop with about 2,000 stores in 53 countries was sold for $1.1 billion to L'Oreal, the French cosmetics giant. (*Source*: Ian Cook/Getty Images News and Sports Services)

THE ENTREPRENEURIAL PROCESS

An **entrepreneur** is someone who perceives an opportunity and creates an organization to pursue it, and the **entrepreneurial process** includes all the functions, activities, and actions that are part of perceiving opportunities and creating organizations to pursue them. But is the birth of a new enterprise just happenstance, and its subsequent success or failure a chance process? Or can the art and science of entrepreneurship be taught? Clearly, professors and their students believe that it can be taught and learned, because entrepreneurship is one of the fastest growing new fields of study in American higher education. A study by the Kauffman Foundation in 2002 found that 61% of U.S. colleges and universities have at least one course in entrepreneurship.[1] It is possible to study entrepreneurship in certificate, associates, bachelors, masters, and PhD programs.

That transformation in higher education—itself a wonderful example of entrepreneurial change—has come about because a whole body of knowledge about entrepreneurship has developed during the past two decades or so. The process of creating a new business is well understood. Yes, entrepreneurship can be taught. No one is guaranteed

> An entrepreneur is someone who perceives an opportunity and creates an organization to pursue it.

> The entrepreneurial process includes all the functions, activities, and actions that are part of perceiving opportunities and creating organizations to pursue them.

This chapter written by William D. Bygrave.

A model of the entrepreneurial process

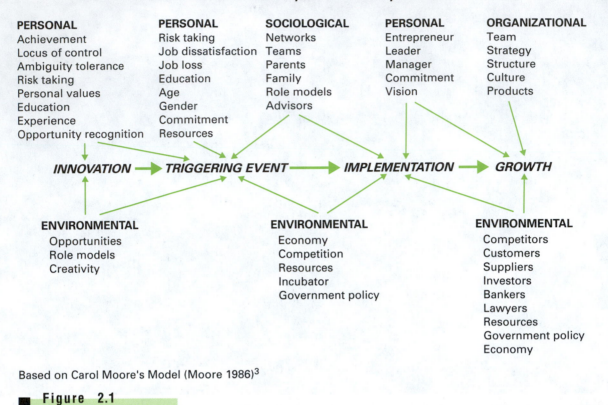

Based on Carol Moore's Model (Moore 1986)[3]

Figure 2.1

to become a Bill Gates or Donna Karan, any more than a physics professor can guarantee to produce an Albert Einstein or a tennis coach can guarantee a Venus Williams. But students with the aptitude to start a business can become better entrepreneurs.

Critical Factors for Starting a New Enterprise

We will begin by examining the entrepreneurial process (see Figure 2.1). These are the factors—personal, sociological, organizational, and environmental—that give birth to a new enterprise and influence how it develops from an idea to a viable enterprise. A person gets an idea for a new business, either through a deliberate search or a chance encounter. Whether or not he or she decides to pursue that idea depends on factors such as alternative career prospects, family, friends, role models, the state of the economy, and the availability of resources.

Origins of Home Depot[2]

Bernie Marcus was president of the now-defunct Handy Dan home improvement chain, based in California, when he and Arthur Blank were abruptly fired by new management. That day and the months that followed were the most pivotal period in his career, he says. "I was 49 years old at the time and

I was pretty devastated by being fired. Still, I think it's a question of believing in yourself. Soon after, we [Blank and Marcus] started to realize that this was our opportunity to start over," says Marcus.

Marcus and Blank then happened upon a 120,000-square-foot store called Homeco, operating in Long Beach, California. The two instantly realized that the concept—an oversized store packed with merchandise tagged with low prices—had a magical quality. They wanted to buy the business, but it was essentially bankrupt. Marcus and Blank talked Homeco owner Pat Farah into joining them in Atlanta, and the trio, along with Ron Brill, began sketching the blueprint for Home Depot.

There is almost always a *triggering event* that gives birth to a new organization. Perhaps the entrepreneur has no better career prospects. For example, Melanie Stevens was a high school dropout who, after working a number of minor jobs, had run out of career options. She decided that making canvas bags in her own tiny business was better than earning low wages working for someone else. Within a few years she had built a chain of retail stores throughout Canada.

Sometimes the person has been passed over for a promotion, or even laid off or fired. Howard Rose had been laid off four times as a result of mergers and consolidations in the pharmaceutical industry, and he had had enough of it. So he started his own drug packaging business, Waverly Pharmaceutical. Tim Waterstone founded Waterstone's bookstores after he was fired by W. H. Smith. Ann Gloag quit her nursing job and used her bus-driver father's $40,000 severance pay to set up Stagecoach bus company with her brother, exploiting legislation deregulating the U.K.'s bus industry. Jordan Rubin was debilitated by Crohn's disease when he invented a diet supplement that restored his health; he founded a company, Garden of Life, to sell that diet. Noreen Kenny was working for a semiconductor company and could not find a supplier to do precision mechanical work, so she launched her own company, Evolve Manufacturing Technologies, to fill that void. The Baby Einstein Company was started by Julie Aigner-Clark when she discovered that there were no age-appropriate products available to help her share her love of art, classical music, language, and poetry with her newborn daughter.

For some people, entrepreneurship is a deliberate career choice. Sandra Kurtzig was a software engineer with General Electric who wanted to start a family and work at home. She started ASK Computer Systems Inc., which became a $400 million-a-year business.

Where do would-be entrepreneurs get their ideas? More often than not it is through their present line of employment or experience. A 2002 study of the *Inc.* 500—"America's [500] fastest growing companies"—found that 57% of the founders got the idea for their new venture in the industry they worked in, and a further 23% in a related industry. Hence, 80% of all new high-potential businesses are founded in industries that are the same as, or closely related to, the one in which the entrepreneur has previous experience. That is not surprising, because it is in their present employment that entrepreneurs will get most of their viable business ideas. Some habitual entrepreneurs do it over and over again in the same industry. Joey Crugnale, himself an *Inc.* 500 Hall of Famer and an *Inc.* Entrepreneur of the Year, became a partner in Steve's Ice Cream in his early 20s. He eventually took over Steve's Ice Cream and created a national franchise of some 26 units, and a new food niche, gourmet ice creams. In 1982, Crugnale started Bertucci's, where gourmet pizza was cooked in wood-fired brickovens, and built it into a nationwide chain of 90 restaurants. Then he founded Naked Restaurants as an incubator to launch his innovative dining concepts. The first one, the Naked Fish, opened in 1999 and brought his wood-fired grill approach to a new niche: fresh fish and meats with a touch of Cubanismo. The second, Red Sauce, opened in 2002 and serves moderately priced authentic Italian food somewhat along the lines of Bertucci's.

Others start businesses over and over again in related industries. In 1981, James Clark, then a Stanford University computer science professor, founded Silicon Graphics, a computer manufacturer with 1996 sales of $3 billion. In April 1994, he teamed up with Marc Andreessen to found Netscape Communications. Within 12 months, its browser software, Navigator, dominated the Internet's World Wide Web. Netscape went public in August 1995. Then in June 1996 Clark launched another company, Healtheon (subsequently merged with WebMD), to enable doctors, insurers, and patients to exchange data and do business over the Internet with software incorporating Netscape's Navigator.

Much rarer is the serial entrepreneur such as Wayne Huizenga, who ventures into unrelated industries: first in garbage disposal with Waste Management, next in entertainment with Blockbuster Video, then in automobile sales with AutoNation. Along the way he was the original owner of the Florida Marlins baseball team, which won the World Series in 1997.

What factors influence someone to embark on an entrepreneurial career? Like most human behavior, entrepreneurial traits are shaped by *personal attributes* and *environment*.

Personal Attributes

Twenty-five years ago, at the start of the entrepreneurial 1980s, there was a spate of magazine and newspaper articles that were entitled "Do you have the right stuff to be an entrepreneur?" or words to that effect. The articles described the most important characteristics of entrepreneurs and, more often than not, included a self-evaluation exercise to enable readers to determine if they had the right stuff. Those articles were based on flimsy behavioral research into the differences between entrepreneurs and nonentrepreneurs. The basis for those exercises was the belief, first developed by David McClelland in his book *The Achieving Society*, that entrepreneurs had *a higher need for achievement* than nonentrepreneurs, and that they were moderate risk takers. One engineer almost abandoned his entrepreneurial ambitions after completing one of those exercises. He asked his professor at the start of an MBA entrepreneurship course if he should take the class because he had scored very low on an entrepreneurship test in a magazine. He took the course, however, and wrote an award-winning plan for a business that was a success from the very beginning.

There is no neat set of behavioral attributes that allows us to separate entrepreneurs from nonentrepreneurs. A person who rises to the top of any occupation, whether an entrepreneur or an administrator, is an achiever. Granted, any would-be entrepreneur must have a need to achieve, but so must anyone else with ambitions to be successful.

It does appear that entrepreneurs have a *higher internal locus of control* than nonentrepreneurs, which means that they have a stronger desire to be in control of their own fate.[4] This has been confirmed by many surveys in which entrepreneurs say independence is a very important reason for starting their businesses. The main reasons they gave were independence, financial success, self-realization, recognition, innovation, and roles (to continue a family tradition, to follow the example of an admired person, to be respected by friends). Men rated financial success and innovation higher than women did. Interestingly, the reasons that nascent entrepreneurs gave for starting a business were similar to the reasons given by nonentrepreneurs for choosing jobs.[5]

The most important characteristics of successful entrepreneurs are shown in Figure 2.2.

Environmental Factors

Perhaps as important as personal attributes are the external influences on a would-be entrepreneur. It's no accident that some parts of the world are more entrepreneurial than

Dream	Entrepreneurs have a vision of what the future could be like for them and their businesses. And, more important, they have the ability to implement their dreams.
Decisiveness	They don't procrastinate. They make decisions swiftly. Their swiftness is a key factor in their success.
Doers	Once they decide on a course of action, they implement it as quickly as possible.
Determination	They implement their ventures with total commitment. They seldom give up, even when confronted by obstacles that seem insurmountable.
Dedication	They are totally dedicated to their businesses, sometimes at considerable cost to their relationships with friends and families. They work tirelessly. Twelve-hour days and seven-day work weeks are not uncommon when an entrepreneur is striving to get a business off the ground.
Devotion	Entrepreneurs love what they do. It is that love that sustains them when the going gets tough. And it is love of their product or service that makes them so effective at selling it.
Details	It is said that the devil resides in the details. That is never more true than in starting and growing a business. The entrepreneur must be on top of the critical details.
Destiny	They want to be in charge of their own destiny rather than dependent on an employer.
Dollars	Getting rich is not the prime motivator of entrepreneurs. Money is more a measure of success. Entrepreneurs assume that if they are successful they will be rewarded.
Distribute	Entrepreneurs distribute the ownership of their businesses with key employees who are critical to the success of the business.

Figure 2.2

The 10 Ds—The most important characteristics of a successful entrepreneur

others. The most famous region of high-tech entrepreneurship is Silicon Valley. Because everyone in Silicon Valley knows someone who has made it big as an entrepreneur, role models abound. This situation produces what Stanford University sociologist Everett Rogers called *Silicon Valley fever.*[6] It seems as if everyone in the valley catches that bug sooner or later and wants to start a business. To facilitate the process, there are venture capitalists who understand how to select and nurture high-tech entrepreneurs, bankers who specialize in lending to them, lawyers who understand the importance of intellectual property and how to protect it, landlords who are experienced in renting real estate to fledgling companies, suppliers who are willing to sell goods on credit to companies with no credit history, and even politicians who are supportive.

Knowing successful entrepreneurs at work or in your personal life makes becoming one yourself seem much more achievable. Indeed, if a close relative is an entrepreneur, you are more likely to want to become an entrepreneur yourself, especially if that relative is your mother or father. At Babson College, more than half of the undergraduates studying entrepreneurship come from families that own businesses, and half of the *Inc. 500* entrepreneurs in 2005 have a parent who was an entrepreneur.[7] But you don't have to be from a business-owning family to become an entrepreneur. Bill Gates, for example, was following the family tradition of becoming a lawyer when he dropped out of Harvard and founded Microsoft. He was in the fledgling microcomputer industry, which was being built by entrepreneurs, so he had plenty of role models among his friends and acquaintances. The U.S. has an abundance of high-tech entrepreneurs who are household names. One of them, Ross Perot, is so well known that he was the presidential candidate preferred by one in five American voters in 1992.

Some universities are hotbeds of entrepreneurship. For example, Massachusetts Institute of Technology has produced numerous entrepreneurs among its faculty and alumni. Companies with an MIT connection transformed the Massachusetts economy from one based on decaying shoe and textile industries into one based on high technology. According to a 1997 study by the Bank of Boston, 125,000 jobs in Massachusetts were MIT-related.[8] Nationwide in 1996, 733,000 people working in more than 8,500 plants and offices held jobs that originated with companies founded by MIT graduates. The 4,000 or so firms that MIT graduates founded accounted for at least 1.1 million employees worldwide and generated $232 billion of world revenues. If MIT-related companies were a nation, it would be the 24th largest economy in the world. The neighborhood of East Cambridge, which is adjacent to MIT, was termed "The Most Entrepreneurial Place on Earth"[9] by *Inc.* magazine. Roughly 10% of Massachusetts' software companies and approximately 20% of the state's 280 biotechnology companies are headquartered in that square mile.

It is not only in high tech that we see role models. Consider these examples:

- It has been estimated that half of all the convenience stores in New York City are owned by Koreans.

- It was the visibility of successful role models that spread catfish farming in the Mississippi Delta as a more profitable alternative to cotton.

- The Pacific Northwest has more microbreweries than any other region of the United States.

- Hay-on-Wye—a tiny town in Wales with 1,500 inhabitants—has 39 second-hand bookstores. It claims to be the "largest used and antiquarian bookshop in the world." It all began in 1961 when Richard Booth, an Oxford graduate, opened his first bookstore.

African-Americans make up 12% of the U.S. population, but owned only 4% of the nation's businesses in 1997.[10] One of the major reasons for that low number is the lack of role models. A similar problem exists among Native Americans. Fortunately, this situation is rapidly improving. Between the 1992 and 1997 censuses, the number of minority-owned businesses grew more than four times as fast as U.S. firms overall, increasing from 2.1 million to about 2.8 million firms.[11] According to the 2002 census, Hispanics/Latinos owned 6.9% of the nation's businesses, African-Americans owned 5.2%, Asians owned 4.8%, and American Indians and Alaskan Natives owned 0.9%.[12]

Other Sociological Factors

Besides role models, entrepreneurs are influenced by other sociological factors. *Family responsibilities* play an important role in the decision to start a company. It is a relatively easy career decision to start a business when you are 25 years old, single, and without many personal assets and dependents. It is a much harder decision when you are 45 and married, with teenage children preparing to go to college, a hefty mortgage, car payments, and a secure, well-paying job. A 1992 survey of European high-potential entrepreneurs, for instance, found that on average they had 50% of their net worth at risk because it was tied up in their businesses. And at 45+, if you fail as an entrepreneur, it will not be easy to rebuild a career working for another company. But despite the risks, plenty of 45-year-olds are taking the plunge; in fact, the median age of the CEOs of the 500 fastest-growing small companies, the *Inc.* 500 in 2004, was 43 (range 26–54) and the median age of their companies was six years.[13]

Another factor that determines the age at which entrepreneurs start businesses is the trade-off between the *experience* that comes with age and the *optimism* and *energy* of youth.

As you grow older you gain experience, but sometimes when you have been in an industry a long time, you know so many pitfalls that you are pessimistic about the chance of succeeding if you decide to go out on your own. Someone who has just enough experience to feel confident as a manager is more likely to feel optimistic about an entrepreneurial career. Perhaps the ideal combination is a beginner's mind with the experience of an industry veteran. A beginner's mind looks at situations from a new perspective, with a can-do spirit.

Twenty-seven-year-old Robert Swanson was a complete novice at biotechnology but was convinced that it had great commercial potential. His enthusiasm combined with Professor Herbert Boyer's unsurpassed knowledge about the use of recombinant DNA to produce human protein. The two just assumed that Boyer's laboratory bench work could be scaled up to industrial levels. Looking back Boyer said, "I think we were so naïve, we never thought it couldn't be done." Together they succeeded and started a new industry.

Marc Andreessen had a beginner's mind in 1993 when, as a student and part-time assistant at the National Center for Supercomputing Applications at the University of Illinois, he developed the Mosaic browser and produced a vision for the Internet that until then had eluded many computer industry veterans, including Bill Gates. When Andreessen's youthful creativity was joined with James Clark's entrepreneurial wisdom, earned over a dozen years as founder and chairman of Silicon Graphics, it turned out to be an awesome combination. Their company, Netscape, distributed 38 million copies of Navigator in just two years, making it the most successful new software introduction ever.

Before leaving secure, well-paying, satisfying jobs, would-be entrepreneurs should make a *careful estimate of how much sales revenue* their new businesses must generate before they will be able to match the income they presently earn. It usually comes as quite a shock when they realize that if they are opening a retail establishment, they will need annual sales revenue of at least $600,000 to pay themselves a salary of $70,000 plus fringe benefits such as health care coverage, retirement pension benefits, and long-term disability insurance. Six hundred thousand dollars a year is about $12,000 per week, or about $2,000 per day, or about $200 per hour, or $3 per minute if they are open 6 days a week, 10 hours a day. Also, they will be working much longer hours and bearing much more responsibility if they become self-employed. A sure way to test the strength of a marriage is to start a company that is the sole means of support for your family. For example, 22.5% of the CEOs of the Inc. 500 got divorced while growing their businesses. On a brighter note, 59.2% got married, and 18.3% of divorced CEOs remarried.[14]

When they actually start a business, entrepreneurs need a host of *contacts,* including customers, suppliers, investors, bankers, accountants, and lawyers. So it is important to understand where to find help before embarking on a new venture. A network of friends and business associates can be of immeasurable help in building the contacts an entrepreneur will need. They can also provide human contact, which is important because opening a business can be a lonely experience for anyone who has worked in an organization with many fellow employees.

Fortunately, today there are more organizations than ever before to help fledgling entrepreneurs. Often that help is free or costs very little. The Small Business Administration (SBA) has Small Business Development Centers in every state; it funds Small Business Institutes; and its Service Core of Retired Executives provides free assistance to entrepreneurs. Many colleges and universities also provide help. Some are particularly good at writing business plans, usually at no charge to the entrepreneur. There are hundreds of incubators in the United States where fledgling businesses can rent space, usually at a very reasonable price, and spread some of their overhead by sharing facilities such as copying and FAX machines, secretarial help, answering services, and so on. Incubators are often associated with universities, which provide free or inexpensive counseling. There are numerous associations where entrepreneurs can meet and exchange ideas.

Evaluating Opportunities for New Businesses

Let's assume you believe that you have found a great opportunity for starting a new business. How should you evaluate its prospects? Or, perhaps more importantly, how will an independent person such as a potential investor or a banker rate your chances of success? The odds of succeeding appear to be stacked against you, because according to small business folklore, only one business in ten will ever reach its tenth birthday. This doesn't mean that 90% of the estimated three million businesses that are started every year go bankrupt.[15] We know that even in a severe recession, the number of businesses filing for bankruptcy in the United States has never surpassed 100,000 in any year. In an average year, the number is about 50,000. In 2001, for instance, there were slightly fewer than 40,000. So what happens to the vast majority of the ones that do not survive 10 years? Most just fade away: They are started as part-time pursuits and are never intended to become full-time businesses. Some are sold. Others are liquidated. Only 700,000 of the three million are legally registered as corporations or partnerships, which is a sure sign that many of the remaining 2.3 million never intended to grow, because, in general, an entrepreneur will go the bother and expense of registering a new venture as a separate legal entity only if it is expected to become a full-time business with employees. Hence, the odds that your new business will survive may not be as long as they first appear to be. If you intend to start a full-time, incorporated business, the odds that the business will survive at least eight years with you as the owner are better than one in four, and the odds of its surviving at least eight years with a new owner are another one in four. So the eight-year survival rate for incorporated startups is about 50%.[16]

But survival may not spell success. Too many entrepreneurs find that they can neither earn a satisfactory living in their businesses nor get out of them easily because they have too much of their personal assets tied up in them. The happiest day in an entrepreneur's life is the day doors are opened for business. For unsuccessful entrepreneurs, an even happier day may be the day the business is sold—especially if most personal assets remain intact. What George Bernard Shaw said about a love affair is also apt for a business: Any fool can start one, but it takes a genius to end one successfully.

How can you stack the odds in your favor so that your new business is a success? Professional investors, such as venture capitalists, have a talent for picking winners. True, they also pick losers, but a startup company funded by venture capital has, on average, a four in five chance of surviving five years—better odds than for the population of startup companies as a whole. Very few businesses—perhaps no more than one in a thousand—will ever be suitable candidates for investments from professional venture capitalists. But would-be entrepreneurs can learn a lot by following the evaluation process used by professional investors.

There are three crucial components for a successful new business: the opportunity, the entrepreneur (and the management team, if it's a high-potential venture), and the resources needed to start the company and make it grow. These are shown schematically in Figure 2.3 in the basic Timmons framework. At the center of the framework is a business plan, in which the three basic ingredients are integrated into a complete strategic plan for the new business. The parts must fit together well. It's no good having a first-rate idea for a new business if you have a second-rate management team. Nor are ideas and management any good without the appropriate resources.

The crucial driving force of any new venture is the lead entrepreneur and the funding management team. Georges Doriot, the founder of modern venture capital, used to say something like this: "Always consider investing in a grade-A man with a grade-B idea. Never invest in a grade B-man with a grade-A idea." He knew what he was talking about. Over the years he invested in about 150 companies, including Digital Equipment Corporation (DEC), and watched over them as they struggled to grow. But Doriot made his statement about business in the 1950s and 1960s. During that period there were far fewer startups; U.S. firms dominated the marketplace, markets were growing quickly, there was almost no competition from overseas, and most entrepreneurs were male. Today, in the global marketplace with ever-shortening product life cycles, and low growth or even no growth for some of the world's leading industrial nations, *the crucial ingredients for entrepreneurial success are a superb entrepreneur with a first-rate management team and an excellent market opportunity.*

It's often said that entrepreneurship is largely a matter of luck. That's not so. We do not say that becoming a great quarterback, a great scientist, or a great musician is a matter of luck. There is no more luck in becoming successful at entrepreneurship than in becoming successful at anything else. In entrepreneurship, it is a question of recognizing a good opportunity when you see one and having the skills to convert that opportunity into a thriving business. To do that, you must be prepared. So in entrepreneurship, as in any other profession, *luck is where preparation and opportunity meet.*

In 1982, when Rod Canion proposed to start Compaq to make personal computers, there were already formidable established competitors, including IBM and Apple, and literally hundreds of companies were considering entering the market or had already done so. Despite the competition, Ben Rosen of the venture capital firm Sevin Rosen Management Company invested in Compaq. Started initially to make transportable PCs, Compaq quickly added a complete range of high-performance PCs and grew so fast that it soon broke Apple's record for the fastest time from founding to listing on the *Fortune* 500.

What did Ben Rosen see in the Compaq proposal that made it stand out from all the other personal computer startups? The difference was Rod Canion and his team. Rod Canion had earned a reputation as an excellent manager at Texas Instruments. Furthermore, the market for personal computers topped $5 billion and was growing at a torrid pace. So Rosen had found a superb team with a product targeted at an undeveloped niche, transportable PCs, in a large market that was growing explosively. By 1994, Compaq was the leading PC manufacturer with 13% of the market.

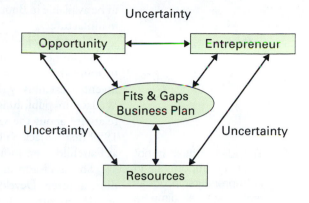

Based on Jeffry Timmons' framework[17]

Figure 2.3

Three driving forces

> The crucial ingredients for entrepreneurial success are a superb entrepreneur with a first-rate management team and an excellent market opportunity.

> In entrepreneurship, as in any other profession, luck is where preparation and opportunity meet.

The Opportunity

Perhaps the biggest misconception about an idea for a new business is that it must be unique. Too many would-be entrepreneurs are almost obsessed with finding a unique idea. Then, when they believe they have it, they are haunted by the thought that someone is just waiting to steal it from them. So they become super-secretive, reluctant to discuss it with anyone who doesn't sign a nondisclosure agreement. That makes it almost impossible to evaluate the idea, and many counselors who provide free advice to entrepreneurs refuse to sign nondisclosure agreements. Generally speaking, these super-secret, unique ideas are big letdowns when the entrepreneur reveals them. Some notable recent examples were "drive-through pizza by the slice," "a combination toothbrush and toothpaste gadget," and "a Mexican restaurant in Boston." One computer programmer said he had a fantastic new piece of software for managing hairdressing salons. He was completely floored when he found that less than a month previously another entrepreneur had demonstrated a software package for exactly the same purpose. Another entrepreneur had an idea for fluoride-impregnated dental floss. Not three months later, the identical product turned out to be available in Boots—Britain's largest chain of drug stores and a major pharmaceutical manufacturer.

Almost any idea a would-be entrepreneur might have will also have occurred to others. In fact, some of the most revolutionary thoughts in the history of humankind occurred to more than one person almost simultaneously. Newton and Leibnitz independently invented calculus within a few years of each other; Darwin was almost preempted by Wallace in publishing his theory of evolution; Poincaré formulated a valid theory of relativity about the same time Einstein did; and the integrated circuit was invented in 1959 first by Jack Kilby at Texas Instruments, and then independently by Robert Noyce at Fairchild a few months later.

So the idea in itself is not what is important. In entrepreneurship, ideas really are a dime a dozen. Developing the idea, implementing it, and building a successful business are the important things. Alexander Fleming discovered penicillin by chance but never developed it as a useful drug. About 10 years later Ernst Chain and Howard Florey unearthed Fleming's mold and immediately saw its potential. They soon were treating patients in England with it, and before the end of World War II, penicillin was saving countless lives. It was a most dramatic pharmaceutical advance and heralded a revolution in that industry.

> The idea in itself is not what is important. In entrepreneurship, ideas really are a dime a dozen. Developing the idea, implementing it, and building a success-ful business are the important things.

> Would-be entrepreneurs who are unable to name a customer are not ready to start a business. They have found an idea but have not yet identified a market need.

The Customer

Many would-be entrepreneurs fail to think carefully enough about who makes up the market for their product or service. They should have a very specific answer to this question: "Can you give me the names of prospective customers?" If they have a consumer product—let's say it's a new shampoo—they should be able to name the buyers at different chains of drug stores in their area. If they are unable to name several customers immediately, they simply have an idea, not a market. There is no market unless customers have a real need for the product—a proven need rather than a hypothetical need in the mind of a would-be entrepreneur. A few rare cases may be revolutionary new products with markets waiting to be formed, but most entrepreneurial ideas are for existing products with improved performance, price, distribution, quality, or service. Simply put, customers must perceive that the new business will be giving them better value for their money than existing businesses.

The Timing

Time plays a crucial role in many potential opportunities. In some emerging industries, there is a definite window of opportunity that opens only once. For instance, about 25 years ago, when VCRs were first coming into household use in the United States, there was a need for video stores in convenient locations where viewers could pick up movies on the way home from work. Lots of video retail stores opened up on main streets and in shopping centers. They were usually run by independent store owners. Then the distribution of videos changed. National chains of video stores emerged. Supermarket and drug store chains entered the market. Today, the window of opportunity for starting an independent video store is closed. There are simply too many big competitors in convenient locations.

In other markets, high-quality restaurants, for example, there is a steady demand that does not change much from year to year, so the window of opportunity is always open. Nevertheless, timing can still be important, because when the economy turns down, those kinds of restaurants are usually hit harder than lower-quality ones, so the time to open one is during a recovering or booming economy.

If the window of opportunity appears to be very brief, it may be that the idea is a consumer fad that will quickly pass away. It takes a very skilled entrepreneur indeed to make money out of a fad. When Lucy's Have A Heart Canvas of Faneuil Hall Marketplace in Boston introduced shoelaces with hearts on them, they flew off the shelves. Children and teenagers could not get enough of them for their sneakers. The store ordered more and more of them. Then demand suddenly dropped precipitously. The store and the manufacturer were left holding huge inventories that could not be sold. As a result, the store almost went under.

Slimming Fad Fades Fast, Inventories Balloon

The late Dr. Robert C. Atkins built a business around the low-carbohydrate, high-protein diet that bears his name. The 1992 and 1999 editions of his book *Dr. Atkins' New Diet Revolution* sold more than 10 million copies worldwide. The book is among of the top 50 best-selling books ever published and was on *The New York Times* bestseller list for 5 years. Atkins' company Atkins Nutritionals, Inc. expanded into 250 food products (nutrition bars, shakes, bake mixes, breads) and nearly 100 nutritional supplements (antioxidants, essential oils) in more than 30,000 outlets. Sales ramped up rapidly at the beginning of the 2000s. Demand was boosted in 2003 by a widely publicized article in the May edition of the influential *New England Journal of Medicine*, reporting that subjects on a low-carb, high-protein diet not only lost weight but also—and perhaps more importantly—had an increase in good cholesterol levels

and a decrease in triglycerides, which was contrary to expectations. In October 2003, Goldman Sachs & Company and Boston-based Parthenon Capital LLC bought a majority stake in the firm for an estimated $700 million.

At the peak of the low-carb "get-thin-quick" craze in January 2004, 9.1 percent of the U.S. population claimed to be on the diet. There were 16 national distributors of low-carb products. National supermarkets introduced low-carb products. Food manufacturers rushed to promote low carbohydrate products. The diet was so popular that it was partially blamed for the bankruptcy of Interstate Bakeries, the producer of Twinkies and Wonderbread. Then the fad faded fast. By 2005 only 2.2 percent of Americans were on low-carb diets. The fall was so precipitous that manufacturers were caught with bloated inventories. Surplus low-carb products were being shipped to Appalachian food banks. For the year ended 2004, Atkins Nutritionals lost $341 million. In August 2005, it filed for Chapter 11 with liabilities of $325 million.

Most entrepreneurs should avoid fads or any window of opportunity they believe will be open for a very brief time, because it inevitably means they will rush to open their business, sometimes before they have time to gather the resources they will need. That can lead to costly mistakes.

The Entrepreneur and the Management Team

Regardless of how right the opportunity may seem to be, it will not become a successful business unless it is developed by a person with strong entrepreneurial and management skills. What are the important skills?

First and foremost, entrepreneurs should have experience in the same industry or a similar one. Starting a business is a very demanding undertaking indeed. It is no time for on-the-job training. If would-be entrepreneurs do not have the right experience, they should either get it before starting their new venture or find partners who have it.

Some investors say the ideal entrepreneur is one who has a track record as a successful entrepreneur in the same industry and who can attract a seasoned team. Half the CEOs of the *Inc.* 500 high-growth small companies had started at least one other business before they founded their present firms. When Joey Crugnale acquired his first ice cream shop in 1977, he already had almost 10 years in the food service industry. By 1991, when Bertucci's brick-oven pizzeria went public, he and his management team had a total of more than 100 years experience in the food industry. They had built Bertucci's into a rapidly growing chain with sales of $30 million and net income of $2 million.

Without relevant experience, the odds are stacked against the neophyte in any industry. An electronics engineer had a great idea for a chain of fast-food stores. When asked if he had ever worked in a fast-food restaurant, he replied, "Work in one? I wouldn't even eat in one. I can't stand fast food!" Clearly, he would have been as miscast as a fast-food entrepreneur as Crugnale would have been as an electronics engineer.

True, there are entrepreneurs who have succeeded spectacularly with no prior industry experience. Anita Roddick of The Body Shop and Ely Callaway of Callaway Golf are two notable examples. But they are the exceptions that definitely do not prove the rule.

Second to industry know-how is *management experience*, preferably with responsibility for budgets or, better yet, accountability for profit and loss. It is even better if a would-be entrepreneur has a record of increasing sales and profits. Of course, we are talking about the *ideal* entrepreneur. Very few people measure up to the ideal. That does not mean they should not start a new venture. But it does mean they should be realistic about the size of the business they should start. Eighteen years ago, two 19-year-old students wanted to start a travel agency business in Boston. When asked what they knew about the industry, one replied, "I live in California. I love to travel." The other was silent. Neither of them had worked in the travel industry, nor had anyone in either of their families. They were advised to get experience. One joined a training program for airline ticket agents; the other took a course for travel agents. They became friends with the owner of a local Uniglobe travel agency who helped them with advice. Six months after they first had the idea, they opened a part-time campus travel agency. In the first six months they had about $100,000 of revenue and made $6,000 of profit but were unable to pay themselves any salary. In that way, they acquired experience at no expense and at low risk. Upon graduation, one of them, Mario Ricciardelli, made the business his full-time job and continued building it and gaining experience at the same time. In 2004, after many bumps in the road, the business had sales revenue of $23 million and was one of the largest student travel businesses in the world.

Resources

> Entrepreneurial frugality requires
>
> - Low overhead
> - High productivity, and
> - Minimal ownership of capital assets.

It's hard to believe that Olsen and Anderson started DEC with only $70,000 of startup capital and built a company that at its peak ranked in the top 25 of the *Fortune* 500 companies. "The nice thing about $70,000 is that there are so few of them, you can watch every one," Olsen said. And watch them he did. Olsen and Anderson moved into a 100-year-old building that had been a nineteenth-century woolen mill. They furnished it with second-hand furniture, purchased tools from the Sears catalog, and built much of their own equipment as cheaply as possible. They sold $94,000 worth of goods in their first year and made a profit at the same time—a very rare feat indeed for a high-tech startup.

Successful entrepreneurs are frugal with their scarce resources. They keep overheads low, productivity high, and ownership of capital assets to a minimum. By so doing they minimize the amount of capital they need to start their business and make it grow.

Determining Resource Needs and Acquiring Resources

In order to determine the amount of capital that a company needs to get started, an entrepreneur should first assess what resources are crucial for the company's success in the marketplace. Some resources are more critical than others. What does the company expect to do better than any of its competitors? That is where it should put a disproportionate share of its very scarce resources. If the company is making a new high-tech product, technological know-how will be vital, and the most important resource will be engineers and the designs they produce. Therefore, the company must concentrate on recruiting and keeping excellent engineers, and safeguarding the intellectual property they produce, such as engineering designs and patents. If the company is doing retail selling, the critical factor will most likely be location. Choosing the wrong initial location for a retail store just because the rent is cheap can be a fatal mistake, because it's unlikely there will be enough resources to relocate.

When Southwest Airlines started up in 1971, its strategy was to provide frequent, on-time service at a competitive price between Dallas, Houston, Austin, and San Antonio. To meet its objectives, Southwest needed planes that it could operate reliably at low cost. It was able to purchase four brand-new Boeing 737s—very efficient planes for shorter routes—for only $4 million each, because the recession had hit the airlines particularly hard and Boeing had an inventory of unsold 737s. From the outset, Southwest provided good, reliable service and had one of the lowest costs per mile in the industry.

Items that are not critical should be obtained as thriftily as possible. The founder of Burlington Coat Factory, Monroe Milstein, likes to tell the story of how he obtained estimates for gutting the building he had just leased for his second store. His lowest bid was several thousand dollars. One day he was at the building when a sudden thunderstorm sent a crew of laborers working at a nearby site to his building for shelter from the rain. Milstein asked the crew's foreman what they would charge for knocking down the internal structures that needed to be removed. The foreman said, "Five." Milstein asked, "Five what?" The foreman replied, "Cases of beer."

A complete set of resources includes everything the business will need, but a business does not have to do all of its work in-house with its own employees. It is often more effective to subcontract the work. That way it need not own or lease its own manufacturing plant and equipment, nor worry about recruiting and training production workers. Often, it can keep overhead lower by using outside firms to do work such as payroll, accounting, advertising, mailing promotions, janitorial services, and so on.

Google founders Larry Page and Sergey Brin bought a terabyte of disks at bargain prices and built their own computer housings in Larry's dorm room, which became Google's first data center. Unable to interest the major portal players of the day, Larry and Sergey decided to make a go of it on their own. All they needed was a little cash to move out of the dorm—and to pay off the credit cards they had maxed out buying a terabyte of memory. So they wrote up a business plan, put their PhD plans on hold, and went looking for an angel investor. Their first visit was with a friend of a faculty member.

Andy Bechtolsheim, one of the founders of Sun Microsystems, was used to taking the long view. One look at their demo and he knew Google had potential—a lot of potential. But though his interest had been piqued, he was pressed for time. As Sergey tells it, "We met him very early one morning on the porch of a Stanford faculty member's home in Palo Alto. We gave him a quick demo. He had to run off somewhere,

Ralph Orlowski/Getty Images News and Sports Services

Google founders Sergey Brin (L) and Larry Page (R) smile prior to a news conference during the opening of the Frankfurt bookfair on October 7, 2004, in Frankfurt, Germany.

so he said, 'Instead of us discussing all the details, why don't I just write you a check?' It was made out to Google Inc. and was for $100,000."

The investment created a small dilemma. Since there was no legal entity known as "Google Inc.," there was no way to deposit the check. It sat in Larry's desk drawer for a couple of weeks while he and Sergey scrambled to set up a corporation and locate other funders among family, friends, and acquaintances. Ultimately they brought in a total initial investment of almost $1 million.

On September 7, 1998, more than two years after they began work on their search engine, Google Inc. opened its door in Menlo Park, California. The door came with a remote control, as it was attached to the garage of a friend who sublet space to the new corporation's staff of three. The office offered several big advantages, including a washer and dryer and a hot tub. It also provided a parking space for the first employee hired by the new company: Craig Silverstein, now Google's director of technology.

Excerpted from "Google History."[18]

Even startup companies can get amazingly good terms from outside suppliers. An entrepreneur should try to understand the potential suppliers' marginal costs. *Marginal cost* is the cost of producing one extra unit beyond what is presently produced. The marginal cost of the laborers who gutted Milstein's building while sheltering from the rain was virtually zero. They were being paid by another firm, and they didn't have to buy materials or tools.

A small electronics company was acquired by a much larger competitor. The large company took over the manufacturing of the small company's products. Production costs shot up. An analysis revealed that much of the increase was due to a rise in the cost of purchased components. In one instance, the large company was paying 50% more than the small company had been paying for the same item. It turned out that the supplier had priced the item for the small company on the basis of marginal costs and for the large company on the basis of total costs.

Smart entrepreneurs find ways of controlling critical resources without owning them. A startup business never has enough money, so it must be resourceful. It should not buy what it can lease. Except when the economy is red hot, there is almost always an excess of capacity of office and industrial space. Sometimes a landlord will be willing to offer a special deal to attract even a small startup company into a building. Such deals may include reduced rent, deferral of rent payments for a period of time, and building improvements made at low or even no cost. In some high-tech regions, landlords will exchange rent for equity in a high-potential startup.

When equipment is in excess supply, new businesses can lease it on very favorable terms. A young database company was negotiating a lease with IBM for a new minicomputer when its chief engineer discovered that a leasing company had identical secondhand units standing idle in its warehouse. The young company was able to lease one of the idle units for one-third of IBM's price. About 18 months later, the database company ran out of cash. Nevertheless, it was able to persuade the leasing company to defer payments, because by then there were even more minicomputers standing idle in the warehouse, and it made little economic sense to repossess one and add it to the idle stock.

Startup Capital

You've developed your idea; you've carefully assessed what resources you will need to open your business and make it grow; you've pulled all your strategies together into a business plan; and now you know how much startup capital you need to get you to the point where your business will generate a positive cash flow. How are you going to raise that startup capital?

There are two types of startup capital: **debt** and **equity**. Simply put, with debt you don't have to give up any ownership of the business, but you have to pay current interest and eventually repay the principal you borrow; with equity you have to give up some of the ownership to get it, but you may never have to repay it or even pay a dividend. So you must choose between paying interest and giving up some of the ownership.

In practice, your choice usually depends on how much of each type of capital you can raise. Most startup entrepreneurs do not have much flexibility in their choice of financing. If it is a very risky business without any assets, it will be impossible to get any bank debt without putting up some collateral other than the business's assets—and most likely that collateral will be personal assets. Even if entrepreneurs are willing to guarantee the whole loan with their personal assets, the bank will expect them to put some equity into the business, probably equal to 25% of the amount of the loan. If your personal assets are less than the amount of the loan, the bank might recommend an SBA-guaranteed loan, in which case you would have to put in more equity.

The vast majority of entrepreneurs start their businesses by leveraging their own savings and labor. Consider how Apple, one of the most spectacular startups of all time, was funded. Steve Jobs and Stephen Wozniak had been friends since their school days in Silicon Valley. Wozniak was an authentic computer nerd. He had tinkered with computers from childhood, and he built a computer that won first prize in a science fair. His SAT math score was a perfect 800, but after stints at the University of Colorado, De Anza College, and Berkeley, he dropped out of school and went to work for Hewlett-Packard. His partner, Jobs, had an even briefer encounter with higher education: After one semester at Reed College, he left to look for a swami in India. When he and Wozniak began working on their microcomputer, Jobs was employed at Atari, the leading video game company.

Apple soon outgrew its manufacturing facility in the garage of Jobs' parents' house. Their company, financed initially with $1,300 raised by selling Jobs' Volkswagen and Wozniak's calculator, needed capital for expansion. They looked to their employers for help. Wozniak proposed to his supervisor that Hewlett-Packard should produce what later became the Apple II. Perhaps not surprisingly, Hewlett-Packard declined. After all, Wozniak had no formal qualification in computer design; indeed, he did not even have a college degree. At Atari, Jobs tried to convince founder Nolan Bushnell to manufacture Apples. He too was rejected.

However, on the suggestion of Bushnell and Regis McKenna, a Silicon Valley marketing ace, the two partners contacted Don Valentine, a venture capitalist, in the fall of 1976. In those days, Jobs' appearance was a holdover from his swami days; he definitely did not project the image of Doriot's grade-A man, even by Silicon Valley's casual standards. Valentine did not invest. But he did put them in touch with Armas Markkula, Jr., who had recently retired from Intel a wealthy man. Markkula saw the potential in Apple, and he knew how to raise money. He personally invested $91,000, secured a line of credit from Bank of America, put together a business plan, and raised $600,000 of venture capital.

The Apple II was formally introduced in April 1977. Sales took off almost at once. Apple's sales grew rapidly to $2.5 million in 1977 and $15 million in 1978. In 1978, Dan Bricklin, a Harvard business student and former programmer at DEC, introduced the first electronic spreadsheet, VisiCalc, designed for the Apple II. In minutes it could do tasks that had previously taken days. The microcomputer now had the power to liberate managers from the data guardians in the computer departments. According to one source, "Armed with VisiCalc, the Apple II's sales took off, and the personal computer industry was created." Apple's sales jumped to $70 million in 1979 and $117 million in 1980.

In 1980, Apple sold some of its stock to the public with an initial public offering (IPO) and raised more than $80 million. The paper value of their Apple stock made instant millionaires of Jobs ($165 million), Markkula ($154 million), Wozniak ($88 million), and Mike Scott ($62 million), who together owned 40% of Apple. Arthur Rock's venture capital investment of $57,000 in 1978 was suddenly worth $14 million, an astronomical compound return of more than 500% per year, or 17% per month.

By 1982, Apple IIs were selling at the rate of more than 33,000 units a month. With 1982 sales of $583 million, Apple hit the *Fortune* 500 list. It was a record. At five years of age, it was at that time the youngest company ever to join that exclusive list.

> I was very lucky to have grown up in this industry. I did everything coming up — shipping, supply chain, sweeping floors, buying chips, you name it. I put computers together with my own hands. As the industry grew up, I kept on doing it.
>
> — *Steve Jobs, 2000*[19]

	All Nations	U.S.
Close family member	40%	44%
Other relative	11%	6%
Work colleague	10%	9%
Friend/Neighbor	28%	28%
Stranger	9%	7%
Other	2%	6%
	100%	100%

Source: Global Entrepreneurship Monitor 2002[21]

Figure 2.4

Relationship of investor to entrepreneur

Success as spectacular as Apple's has seldom been equaled. Nonetheless, its financing is a typical example of how successful high-tech companies are funded. First, the entrepreneurs develop a prototype with personal savings and **sweat equity**, or ownership earned in lieu of wages. Then a wealthy investor—sometimes called an *informal investor* or *business angel*, who knows something about the entrepreneurs, or the industry, or both—invests some personal money in return for equity. When the company is selling product, it may be able to get a bank line of credit secured by its inventory and accounts receivable. If the company is growing quickly in a large market, it may be able to raise capital from a formal venture capital firm in return for equity. Further expansion capital may come from venture capital firms or from a public stock offering.

Would-be entrepreneurs sometimes don't start their ventures because they feel they can't raise sufficient money to get started. More often than not, they were unrealistic about the amount of money they could reasonably have expected to raise for their startup. Many of the best companies started with very little capital. For example, 42% of the *Inc.* 500 companies had initial capital of less than $10,000, 58% less than $20,000, and 68% less than $50,000. Only 21% started with more than $100,000.[20] Only a few percent of this cream of the crop of entrepreneurs started their companies with venture capital, which is by far the rarest source of seed investment. It is estimated that at most only 1 in 10,000 of all new ventures in the U.S. have venture capital in hand at the outset.

The vast majority of new firms will never be candidates for formal venture capital or a public stock offering. Nevertheless, they will have to find some equity capital. In most cases, after they have exhausted their personal savings, entrepreneurs will turn to family, friends, and acquaintances (see Figure 2.4). It can be a scary business. Entrepreneurs often find themselves with all their personal net worth tied up in the same business that provides all their income. That is double jeopardy, because if their businesses fail, they lose both their savings and their means of support. Risk of that sort can be justified only if the profit potential is high enough to yield a commensurate rate of return.

Profit Potential

The level of profit that is reasonable depends on the type of business. On average, U.S. companies make about 5% net income. Hence, on one dollar of revenue, the average company makes five cents profit after paying all expenses and taxes. A company that consistently makes 10% is doing very well, and one that makes 15% is truly exceptional. Approximately 50% of the *Inc.* 500 companies make 5% or less; 13% of them make 16% or more. Profit margins in a wide variety of industries for companies both large and small are published by Robert Morris Associates, so entrepreneurs can compare their forecasts with the actual performance of similar-sized companies in the same industry.

Any business must make enough profit to recompense its investors (in most cases that is the entrepreneur) for their investment. This must be the profit after all normal business expenses have been accounted for, including a fair salary for the entrepreneur and any family members who are working in the business. A common error in assessing the profitability of a new venture is to ignore the owner's salary. Suppose someone leaves a secure job paying $50,000 per year plus fringe benefits and invests $100,000 of personal savings to start a new venture. That person should expect to take a $50,000 salary plus fringe benefits out of the new business. Perhaps in the first year or two, when the business is being built, it may not be possible to pay $50,000 in actual cash; in that case, the pay that is not actually received should be treated as deferred compensation to be paid in the future. In addition to an adequate salary, the entrepreneur must also earn a reasonable return on the $100,000 investment. A professional investor putting money into a new, risky business would expect to earn an annual rate of return of at least 40%, which would be $40,000 annually on a $100,000 investment. That return may come as a capital gain when the business is sold, or as a dividend, or as a combination of the two. But remember that $100,000 compounding annually at 40% grows to almost $2.9 million in 10 years. When such large capital gains are needed to produce acceptable returns, big capital investments held for a long time do not make any sense unless very substantial value can be created, as occasionally happens in the case of high-flying companies, especially high-tech ones. In most cases, instead of a capital gain, the investor's return will be a dividend, which must be paid out of the cash flow from the business.

The cash flow that a business generates is not to be confused with profit. It is possible, indeed very likely, that a rapidly growing business will have a negative cash flow from operations in its early years even though it may be profitable. That may happen because the business may not be able to generate enough cash flow internally to sustain its ever-growing needs for working capital and the purchase of long-term assets such as plant and equipment. Hence, it will have to borrow or raise new equity capital. So it is very important that a high-potential business intending to grow rapidly make careful cash-flow projections so as to predict its needs for future outside investments. Future equity investments will dilute the percentage ownership of the founders, and if the dilution becomes excessive, there may be little reward remaining for the entrepreneurs.

Biotechnology companies are examples of this problem: they have a seemingly insatiable need for cash infusions to sustain their R&D costs in their early years. Their negative cash flow, or *burn rate*, sometimes runs at $1 million per month. A biotechnology company can easily burn up $50 million before it generates a meaningful profit, let alone a positive cash flow. The expected future capital gain from a public stock offering or sale to a large pharmaceutical company has to run into hundreds of millions of dollars, maybe into the billion-dollar range, for investors to realize an annual return of 50% or higher, which is what they expect to earn on money invested in a seed-stage biotechnology company. Not surprisingly, to finance their ventures biotechnology entrepreneurs as a group have to give up most of the ownership. A study of venture-capital-backed biotechnology companies found that after they had gone public, the entrepreneurs and management were left with less than 18% of the equity, compared with 32% for a comparable group of computer software companies.[22]

> For entrepreneurs, happiness is a positive cash flow.

We've said that most businesses will never have the potential to go public. Nor will the owners ever intend to sell their businesses and thereby realize a capital gain. In that case, how can those owners get a satisfactory return on the money they have invested in their businesses? The two ingredients that determine return on investment are (1) the amount invested, and (2) the annual amount earned on that investment. Hence, entrepreneurs should invest as little as possible to start their businesses and make sure that their firms will be able to pay them a "dividend" big enough to yield an appropriate annual rate of return. For income tax purposes, that "dividend" may be in the form of a salary, bonus, or fringe benefits rather than an actual dividend paid out of retained earnings. Of course, the company must be generating cash from its own operations before that dividend can be paid. For entrepreneurs, happiness is a positive cash flow. And the day a company begins to generate **free cash**—that is, more cash than needed to sustain operations and purchase assets to keep the company on its growth trajectory—is a very happy day in the life of a successful entrepreneur. In 2002, Microsoft was generating $1 billion of free cash flow per month. That was about $100,000 per minute on the basis of a five-day working week, eight hours per day. No wonder Bill Gates was smiling a lot.

Awash with Cash

Microsoft is an awesome money machine. Its annual cash flow from operations kept increasing in the early 2000s to $15.8 billion in 2003. That was more than $2,000 per second based on a five-day work week, eight hours per day. Microsoft's stash of cash kept piling up so that by 2004 its cash and short-term investments stood at $60.6 billion—slightly topping the value of all the gold stored in Fort Knox at 2004 prices. It was enough money to give each family in the U.S. $760.

In July 2004, Microsoft's directors approved a plan to buy back up to $30 billion of common shares over four years. By June 30, 2005, it had repurchased $8 billion of its shares. (Data from Microsoft's 2005 annual report)

Ingredients for a Successful New Business

The great day has arrived. You found an idea, wrote a business plan, and gathered your resources. Now you are opening the doors of your new business for the first time, and the really hard work is about to begin. What are the factors that distinguish winning entrepreneurial businesses from the also-rans? Rosabeth Kanter prescribed Four Fs for a

Founders	Every startup company must have a first-class entrepreneur.
Focused	Entrepreneurial companies focus on niche markets. They specialize.
Fast	They make decisions quickly and implement them swiftly.
Flexible	They keep an open mind. They respond to change.
Forever-innovating	They are tireless innovators.
Flat	Entrepreneurial organizations have as few layers of management as possible.
Frugal	By keeping overhead low and productivity high, entrepreneurial companies keep costs down.
Friendly	Entrepreneurial companies are friendly to their customers, suppliers, and employees.
Fun	It's fun to be associated with an entrepreneurial company.

Figure 2.5

The Nine Fs for entrepreneurial success

successful business,[23] a list that has been expanded into the Nine Fs for entrepreneurial success (see Figure 2.5).

First and foremost, the founding entrepreneur is the most important factor. Next comes the market. This is the "era of the other," in which, as Regis McKenna observed, the fastest-growing companies in an industry will be in a segment labeled "others" in a market-share pie chart. By and large, they will be newer entrepreneurial firms rather than large firms with household names; hence, specialization is the key. A successful business should focus on niche markets.

The rate of change in business gets ever faster. The advanced industrial economies are knowledge based. Product life cycles are getting shorter. Technological innovation progresses at a relentless pace. Government rules and regulations keep changing. Communications and travel around the globe keep getting easier and cheaper. And consumers are better informed about their choices. To survive, let alone succeed, a company has to be quick and nimble. It must be fast and flexible. It cannot allow inertia to build up. Look at retailing: The historical giants such as Kmart are on the ropes, while nimble competitors dance around them. Four of the biggest retailing successes are Les Wexner's The Limited, the late Sam Walton's Wal-Mart, Bernie Marcus and Arthur Blank's Home Depot, and Anita Roddick's The Body Shop. Entrepreneurs such as these know that they can keep inertia low by keeping the layers of management as few as possible. Tom Peters, an authority on business strategy, liked to point out that Wal-Mart had three layers of management, whereas Sears had ten a few years back when Wal-Mart displaced Sears as the nation's top chain of department stores. "A company with three layers of management can't lose against a company with ten. You could try, but you couldn't do it!" says Peters. So keep your organization flat. It will facilitate quick decisions and flexibility, and keep overhead low.

Small entrepreneurial firms are great innovators. Big firms are relying increasingly on strategic partnerships with entrepreneurial firms in order to get access to desirable R&D. The trend is well under way. Hoffmann-La Roche, hurting for new blockbuster prescription drugs, purchased a majority interest in Genentech and bought the highly regarded biotechnology called PCR (polymerase chain reaction) from Cetus for $300 million. Eli Lilly purchased Hybritech. In the 1980s, IBM spent $9 billion a year on research and development, but even that astronomical amount of money could not sustain Big Blue's commercial leadership. As its market share was remorselessly eaten away by thousands of upstarts, IBM entered into strategic agreements with Apple, Borland, Go,

Lotus, Intel, Metaphor, Microsoft, Novell, Stratus, Thinking Machines, and other entrepreneurial firms for the purpose of gaining computer technologies.

When it introduced the first personal computer in 1981, IBM stood astride the computer industry like a big blue giant. Two suppliers of its personal computer division were Intel and Microsoft. Compared with IBM, Intel was small and Microsoft was a midget. By 2002, Intel's revenue was $26.8 billion and Microsoft's was $28.4 billion. Between 1998 and 2002 Microsoft's revenue increased 86% while IBM's stood still. In 2002, IBM — the company that invented the PC — had only 6% of the worldwide market for PCs. In December 2004, IBM announced that it was selling its PC division to Lenovo, the leading Chinese manufacturer of PCs. Today, it is Microsoft's Windows operating system and Intel's microprocessors — the so-called WINTEL — that are shaping the future of information technology.

When it comes to productivity, the best entrepreneurial companies leave the giant corporations behind in the dust. According to 2004 computer industry statistics, Dell's revenue per employee was $891,139, Microsoft's was $646,228 while Hewlett-Packard's was $527,172 and IBM's was $302,278. Of course, Dell subcontracts more for its manufacturing, but this does not explain all the difference. Whether you hope to build a big company or a small one, the message is the same: Strive tirelessly to keep productivity high.

But no matter what you do, you probably won't be able to attain much success unless you have happy customers, happy workers, and happy suppliers. That means you must have a friendly company. It means that everyone must be friendly, especially anyone who deals with customers. "The most fun six-month period I've had since the start of Microsoft" is how Bill Gates described his astonishing accomplishment in reinventing his 20-year-old company to meet the threat posed by Internet upstarts in the mid-1990s. In not much more than six months of Herculean effort, Microsoft had developed an impressive array of new products to match those of Netscape. Having fun is one of the keys to keeping a company entrepreneurial. If Microsoft's product developers had not been having fun, they would not have put in 12-hour days and sometimes overnighters to catch up with the Netscape.

Most new companies have the Nine Fs at the outset. Those that become successful and grow pay attention to keeping them and nurturing them. The key to sustaining success is to remain an entrepreneurial gazelle and never turn into a lumbering elephant and finally a dinosaur, doomed to extinction.

□ CONCLUSION

It is easy to start a business in the U.S.; anyone can do it. What distinguishes successful entrepreneurs from less successful ones is the ability to spot opportunities for high-potential businesses and then to develop their new venture into a thriving business. As the business grows, the successful entrepreneur is able to attract key management team members, to motivate employees, to find more and more customers and keep them coming back, and to develop increasingly sophisticated relationships with financiers.

Reflection Point	Your Thoughts...	

YOUR OPPORTUNITY JOURNAL ☐

1. What life events might trigger your entrepreneurial career?

2. What ideas do you have for a new business?
   a. What ideas can you draw from your past work experience?
   b. What ideas can you draw from your family's work experience?

3. Which of your personal attributes will most help you succeed as an entrepreneur?

4. Which attributes do you think you need to further develop?

5. Who are your entrepreneurial role models? Can you foster any of them into mentors?

6. Is your idea an opportunity? Explain.

7. Is the timing right to launch your venture?

8. What are some cost-effective ways for you to get started?

NOTES ☐

[1] According to the Kauffman study, 1,992 two- and four-year colleges and universities offer at least one course in entrepreneurship, up from about 300 in the 1984–85 school year. http://money.cnn.com/magazines/fsb/fsb_archive/2006/03/01/8370301/index.htm.

[2] www.stores.org/archives/jan99cover.asp.

[3] Moore, Carol. "Understanding entrepreneurial behavior." In J. A. Pearce II and R. B. Robinson, Jr., eds., *Academy of Management Best Paper Proceedings*, Forty-sixth Annual Meeting of the Academy of Management, Chicago, 1986.

[4] Brockhuas, R. Risk-taking propensity of entrepreneurs. *Academy of Management Journal*, 23, 509–520, 1980.

[5] Carter, N. M., Gartner, W. B., Shaver, K. G., and Gatewood, E. J. The career reasons for nascent entrepreneurs. *Journal of Business Venturing*, 19 (2003), 13–39.

[6] Rogers, E. M. and Larsen, J. K. *Silicon Valley Fever: Growth of High-Technology Culture*. New York, NY: Basic Books. 1984.

[7] *Inc. 500*, 2005, September 2005.

[8] MIT: The impact of innovation. Bank of Boston, 1997.

[9] *Inc. Magazine*. March 1, 1990.

[10] www.census.gov/Press-Release/www/2001/cb01-54.html.

[11] www.census.gov/Press-Release/www/2001/cb01-115.html.

[12] www.census.gov/Press-Release/www/releases/archives/cb05_108_table.xls.

[13] *Inc. 500*, 2004. Vol. 25, Issue 12.

[14] *Inc. 500*, 2000. Vol. 22, Issue 15.

[15] For more information on startups and failures, refer to William Dennis, "The shape of small business." NFIB foundation. www.nfib.com/object/PolicyGuide2.html.

[16] Detailed information on survival rates can be found in the following articles:

Boden, R. J. Jr. Analysis of business dissolution by demographic category of business ownership. 2000. www.sba.gov/advo/research/rs204tot.pdf

Kirchhoff, Bruce A. and Phillips, Bruce D. "Innovation and Growth Among New Firms in the U.S. Economy," Frontiers of Entrepreneurship Research, Babson College, Wellesley, MA. pp. 173–188, 1989.

Kirchhoff, Bruce A., *Entrepreneurship and Dynamic Capitalism*. Westport, CT: Praeger, 1994.

Phillips, Bruce D., and Kirchhoff, Bruce A. "Formation, Growth, and Survival: Small Firm Dynamics in the U.S. Economy," Small Business Economics, 1: pp. 65–74, 1989.

[17] Timmons, Jeffry A. *New Venture Creation*. Homewood, IL: Richard D. Irwin, 2001.

[18] www.google.com/corporate/history.html.

[19] *Business Week*, February 6, 2006, p. 66.

[20] *Inc. 500*, 2000. Vol. 22, Issue 15.

[21] The information in Figure 2.4 was extracted from the Global Entrepreneurship Monitor 2002 data set. www.gemsonsortium.org.

[22] Bygrave, William D. and Timmons, Jeffry A. *Venture Capital at the Crossroads*. Boston, MA: Harvard Business School Press, 1992.

[23] Kanter, Rosabeth Moss. *Change Masters: Innovation and Entrepreneurship in the American Corporation*. New York: Simon and Schuster, 1985.

Alison Barnard

Having spent her Saturday morning redesigning window displays, folding inventory, and following up with a supplier who seemed disinclined to take back an entire shipment she felt was unacceptable, Alison Barnard, 27, was finally settled at her desk in the corner—fully intending to make some progress on her growing management task list. Chief among those neglected missions was getting up to speed on her software system for monitoring sales and inventory.

In-jean-ius, her upscale "jeans and t-shirt" boutique in Boston's North End, was attracting professional and wealthy women from Maine to Rhode Island. As one of many satisfied customers wrote, "Alison has an uncanny ability to match up the right person with the perfect pair of jeans. If you have ever gone 'jean shopping' you know that that is not an easy thing to do! Experience In-jean-ius for yourself. You won't shop for jeans anywhere else again."

March, 2006. Alison looked up from her work with weary smile.

Open just over six months, and actuals are tracking nearly twice my projections...

As it had from the very beginning, running her hit venture continued to consume nearly every waking hour. The creative, high-energy founder was far less concerned with burning out than with having the day-to-day concerns usurp her ability to plan and manage for growth. And with only one full-time employee—not yet fully trained—Alison couldn't expect much relief anytime soon.

Her attention was suddenly drawn to an exchange between her salesperson and a well-dressed, middle-aged woman who was favoring a sleek pair of low rises. From where she sat, Alison could see that the woman was built for something a bit less daring. When the associate began fishing for the correct size in that style, Alison left her desk (and her task list) to steer the sale toward a more conservative brand that would ultimately prove to offer the best fit. Another satisfied customer...

Alison Barnard: Shopper

Like many rural-suburban American teens, young Alison Barnard had been an avid shopper. But there was something more. The daughter of a serial entrepreneur and an enterprising mother, she had developed an eye for opportunity and value-add that she ceaselessly trained on the business of creating a unique upscale shopping experience; trends, service, selection, presentation, decor. Despite her keen interest in retailing, she headed off for college with a more conservative career track in mind:

I really thought I wanted to be in brand management, marketing, or retail consulting. I figured that someday I would have a store, but thought it might be something I'd do when I retired, like you kind of hung out in your store.

But I had all of these ideas. I like clothing, I like the shopping experience, and I like dealing with people. One idea was to have an all-black store, because black apparel is such a staple for any woman's wardrobe.

This case was prepared by Carl Hedberg under the direction of William Bygrave. Copyright © Babson College, 2006.

In May of 2002, Alison received her undergraduate degree in business from the University of Richmond. Back in the Boston area, her first job was with a dot-com startup. She left there for an interesting opportunity with another high-potential venture. While the work environment there was most definitely not for her, that "mistake" would have a major impact on her career trajectory.

Catalysts

Hired as part of the seminar development team at a medical device company in Cambridge, Massachusetts, Alison quickly discovered that her talents weren't exactly appreciated:

> They were part of this old boy network that really looked down on females. They told me, for example, that I needed to cover on Thursdays for the receptionist when she went to lunch. Swell. I hated that place, and I immediately began interviewing for something better.
>
> At one point I went on a job interview, and since my boss approved of higher education, I told her I had gone to Babson College to investigate their MBA program. When I checked into it in order to support my little lie, I found out that Babson had a one-year program that looked really interesting; you're there, you're focused and doing it, and then you're out.

Alison began the One-Year MBA at Babson in the spring of 2003. Since she was still brainstorming retail store concepts with anyone who would engage, her mom's hairdresser suggested that as a next step she ought to get some floor time in the real world. That summer, Alison started work as a part-timer at an upscale boutique near Boston. Although she still had no immediate plans to develop a new venture, her MBA studies melded well with her exposure to retailing:

> I quickly realized that my first concept about an all-black store was a bad idea. Women buy black, but they don't shop for it. They'll even go into a store and say they want anything but black—because they have too much black in their wardrobe. But then in the end, they'll buy something black.
>
> At the time I was really getting into jeans myself. At Babson I wore jeans and a t-shirt every day. My first pair were Sevens, one of the early entrants into what I would call the premium denim revolution. Jeans are no longer just weekend wear; they are worn in the workplace and for going out. Premium denim has become a fashion staple, and women now have an average of about eight pairs of jeans in their wardrobe.
>
> So an all-jeans store became sort of my fun idea—something I thought would be just another idea that would be passed by. Still, my concept was interesting enough to attract a team in class to do the business plan.

Realizations

Nothing Alison and her team members discovered in their research surprised her in the least (see Exhibit 2.1). When asked what pain point she expected her store to relieve, she didn't hesitate a moment:

> Women's point of pain is themselves. The reality is that every female hates themselves in some sort of way. And if she doesn't like something about her body, jeans can bring out the worst qualities. But they can also make you look great if they fit right.
>
> There are some decent stores in the area that sell premium jeans (see Exhibit 2.2), but they all forget to mention the fact that fit is by far a woman's number one concern when searching for jeans. Women are not brand loyal; they are fit loyal.

EXHIBIT 2.1 Research Findings

What Woman Want: Survey Results

We conducted primary research through a survey of 90 woman in the Boston area to find out their jean buying habits, including number of jeans owned, where they purchase their jeans, brands they are loyal to, and what they would like to see in a jean store. The complete results can be found in Exhibit 2.2.

The survey conducted to extract the jean-purchasing behaviors of 90 females aged 21–35 reveals:

- Woman are willing to spend money for jeans
    - 30% $51–$75
    - 17.8% $76–85
    - 18.9% $101–$130
    - 17.8% $130+

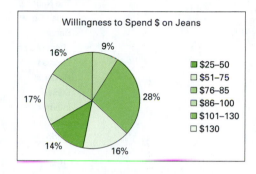

- Fit matters and influences where and which brands they purchase
    - 86.7% of woman said their #1 reason for shopping at certain stores was stores carrying jeans that fit them
    - Brand preference based on fit
    - 82% of woman say they are not loyal to one brand of jean
- Woman need more . . .
    - More selection→ 49.4% want more options
    - More information→ so many jean brands and styles and so little time
    - More help→ make the process less time consuming, less of a hassle

In addition, open-ended questions regarding what they dislike about the jean-buying process and what they would like to see in a new jean store environment revealed the following:

- Overall, woman dislike the jean-buying process, even though they enjoy buying a new pair of jeans.
- Disorganization of the store and inconsistency of jean sizes by brands made woman want to see more sales help, which was lacking in the stores they currently frequent for jean buying.

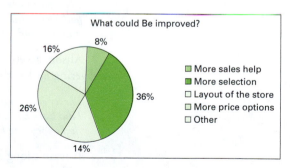

EXHIBIT 2.2		Premium Jean Stores in Eastern Massachusetts				
Store	Private Label	Trendy Jean Brands	Jean Expertise	Knowledgeable Customer Service	Welcome Atmosphere	Large Selection of Brands
Jean Therapy		X	X	X		
The National Jean Co.		X		X		X
Banana Republic	X					
Express	X					
Riccardi		X				X
Diesel	X		X	X		
Intermix		X			X	
Gap	X					
Mudo		X	X	X		
Lucky Brand	X					
Jasmine Sola*		X			X	X
Jeans Addiction		X		X		X

*Luciano Manganella, who founded this upscale boutique in Harvard Square in 1970, four years after emigrating from Italy, sold Jasmine Sola in the summer of 2005 to the nearly national 500-store New York & Co. This move, Manganella said, was the only way he could expand beyond his present 15 stores to an expected 25 stores—all on the East Coast—by the end of 2006. The undisclosed amount of the sal was estimated to be in excess of $20 million.

When she graduated in the spring of 2004, Alison was offered an opportunity to learn even more:

The woman who was managing the boutique was going on maternity leave starting in the fall. The partners knew I wanted to open a store someday and they said that they would train me, and help me out until she returned in the spring of 2005.

Alison accepted their offer. She soon discovered, however, that they would be delivering far less than they promised:

I never got anything we had agreed to, including health insurance or training of any kind. I did learn how to handle receivables, pricing, dating, and ordering, but I figured out that stuff on my own by examining the invoices and checking in the orders.

It wasn't long before Alison was certain that she could run a shop of her own. She was still drawn to the $6.3 billion women's denim market, a highly fragmented space with hundreds of manufacturers and inconsistent retail offerings, from boutiques, chain stores, and department stores. Still, she felt that she "would have to jump on it right away before anyone else did"—it was now or never:

I had been keeping my idea secret from the store owners because I didn't trust them at all. Sure, they liked me, but they also had money and resources. That summer, I was attending a fashion show with one of the owners. He said that he had always wanted to open a jeans and t-shirt store, but that his business partner—a woman—wasn't interested in the concept. At that point I told him about my idea, and before you know it, we were talking about going into business together.

He called a few times after the trip to talk it over. We never touched on details like money or ownership breakdown, but we did go to look at a spot in Wellesley [Massachusetts]. But then he just dropped it; never talked about it again. It was as if we had never had a conversation about it! That's the sort of thing you get from a lot of people in this industry.

But how was I going to do it alone? Where was I going to get the money?

Commitments

Based on her projections (see Exhibit 2.3), Alison expected her retail store would have first year sales of just over $375,000. She had also calculated that startup costs, including build out and inventory, would be in the range of $125,000. She was confident that she could attract investors, but first she wanted to secure a location that would be acceptable to what she was sure would be her toughest constituency:

Fashion denim manufactures are represented by showrooms in New York City and in LA [Los Angeles]. They are very committed to their brands, and very particular about who they will sell to. To avoid saturation, they won't sell to a store that is too close to another client, and they will even shut off an established shop that locates a new store too close to another buyer. Territory protection is a great asset for existing stores, but it makes it very hard to find locations that have the right customer traffic and are not in conflict with existing vendors.

Alison's boyfriend, Bryan, was active in the Boston real estate market. On weekends, Alison often accompanied him as he made the rounds to various properties he was managing. One icy morning in early 2005, Alison fell for a corner location in the North End:

This place was a bit removed from the busiest section of Hanover Street, but the outside was SO nice; all dark wood, newly redone. I had Bryan call the number because as a real estate agent, I knew they would take him seriously. He set up a meeting with the landlord—a top neurosurgeon who owned the building as an investment. He had already denied seven previous proposals, but said he liked mine a lot.

Soon, they were talking hard numbers:

I learned a lot in negotiating with him because he had a huge ego—just like a lot of good surgeons do. I had to figure out how to make him feel he was still getting something out of it. He was also getting stuck on little details. For example, he wanted to control my window displays, and be able to go to arbitration over it.

And the space may have been beautiful on the outside, but the inside was unbelievably awful. It was scary. It needed new floors, new ceilings, new walls, and a new heating system.

In late February, Alison signed a three-year lease that included a few months free rent—she now had until September. All along, her father had felt strongly that she should have lined up the capital first:

My dad was saying, "What are you thinking?" He totally disagreed with what I was doing, but I told him I'd find the money. He loaned me the deposit on the location, and he called up my uncle, who is an accountant. The three of us sat down and came up with an investment offering.

EXHIBIT 2.3	Five Year Projections, Income Statement				
Sales	**Year 1**	**Year 2**	**Year 3**	**Year 4**	**Year 5**
Jeans					
Unit Sales	1,635	1,962	2,315	2,547	2,801
Average Price	135	142	149	156	164
	220,725	278,604	344,935	397,332	459,364
Tops					
Unit Sales	2,453	3,434	4,120	4,862	5,737
Average Price	54	40	42	45	48
	132,462	137,360	173,040	218,790	275,376
Accessories					
Unit Sales	550	633	791	988	1,235
Average Price	45	45	50	50	55
	24,750	28,485	39,550	49,400	67,925
Total Sales	**377,937**	**444,449**	**557,525**	**665,522**	**802,665**
Cost of Sales					
Jeans	94,912	119,589	148,171	171,137	197,663
Tops	58,860	61,803	79,108	97,237	126,313
Accessories	11,550	13,283	12,452	15,565	19,457
Total Cost of Sales	165,322	194,675	239,731	283,939	343,433
Sales Expenses					
Credit Card Commissions	10,222	12,000	14,737	17,482	21,186
Discounts & Promos	2,759	3,476	4,307	4,975	5,746
Returns	14,031	16,470	20,228	23,995	29,078
Damage & Theft	12,026	14,117	17,338	20,567	24,924
Total Sales Expenses	39,038	46,063	56,610	67,019	80,934
Gross Margin	**173,577**	**203,711**	**261,184**	**314,564**	**378,298**
Buying Expenses Incl Travel	2,400	3,600	4,000	4,200	4,400
Administration					
Rent	17,500	31,200	32,400	33,600	34,800
Staff Salaries & Benefits	24,960	31,200	33,600	33,600	33,600
Staff Payroll taxes	7,488	9,360	10,080	10,080	10,080
Management Salaries	51,996	52,800	55,000	60,000	65,000
Management Payroll taxes	15,439	15,840	15,840	15,840	15,840
Health Insurance	3,000	3,000	3,000	3,000	3,000
Interest	900	1,200	1,040	880	720
Communications & Media	3,300	3,300	3,300	3,300	3,300
Professional fees	4,308	4,308	4,308	4,308	4,308
Depreciation	12,266	13,381	13,381	13,381	13,381
Insurance	2,880	2,880	2,880	2,880	2,880
Utilities (electric & gas)	4,200	4,200	4,200	4,200	4,200
	148,237	172,669	179,029	185,069	191,109
Total Expenses	**150,637**	**176,269**	**183,029**	**189,269**	**195,509**
Pre-Tax Profit	22,940	27,442	78,155	125,295	182,789
Net Profit	**14,844**	**17,425**	**47,914**	**76,265**	**110,825**

EXHIBIT 2.3   (Continued)

	Year 1	Year 2	Year 3	Year 4	Year 5
Beginning Cash	125,000	19,077	47,883	125,561	235,571
Inflows					
Sales	377,937	444,449	557,525	665,522	802,665
Depreciations	12,233	13,381	13,381	13,381	13,381
Outflows					
Cost of Sales	(165,322)	(194,675)	(239,731)	(283,939)	(343,333)
Sales Expenses	(39,038)	(46,063)	(56,610)	(67,018)	(80,934)
Marketing Expenses	(2,400)	(3,600)	(4,000)	(4,200)	(4,400)
Admin. Expenses	(148,237)	(172,669)	(179,029)	(185,069)	(191,109)
Note Payment	(20)	(2,000)	(2,000)	(2,000)	(2,000)
Taxes	(8,096)	(10,017)	(30,798)	(49,030)	(71,964)
Pre-Opening & build-out	(58,000)				
Opening Inventory	(75,000)				
Increase in A/P			18,940	22,364	26,990
Net (Outflow) Inflow	(105,923)	28,806	77,678	110,010	149,296
Ending Cash Balance	19,077	47,883	125,561	235,571	384,867

Finding the Money

Before she went the equity route, Alison wanted to investigate other avenues. The news was not good:

> My dad referred me to some people he knew at Boston Private Bank—very conservative. Talks went fine until they became insistent that if they were going to do anything, they would have to have a guarantor for the loan—a co-signer. Well, I wasn't going to do that; I wanted this to be my responsibility.
>
> I tried to get an SBA loan through a small bank on the North Shore, but I had no collateral, and I was paying off student loans. They said no way, because even though the SBA would be backing it, a bad loan would give them a worse rating through the SBA. I looked into grants, but the process was too long. I also tried to get startup funding through the Hatchery Program at Babson. They said no as well; that really surprised me.

With the clock ticking on her lease, Alison went ahead with the investor plan she had crafted with her closest advisors:

> We were not going to give people the option of deciding how much money they could invest. Instead, we said this is the deal: there are six slots of $25,000 each, and your options are full equity, debt/equity, or you can do full debt.[1]

---

[1] The valuation for the offer was based on her Year One sales projections. Each $25,000 investment would be worth 6.25% in equity. Debt/equity investors could choose either 10,000/15,000 debt/equity ratio or 15,000/10,000 debt/equity ratio. The all-debt interest rate was originally 10%, but when a wealthy investor from Denver offered an all-debt loan at 8%, the terms were adjusted to maintain parity.

I sent an e-mail to all my contacts saying this is where I am, and that I was looking for investors. A lot of people responded to me; I was shocked.

A former classmate at Babson (who had started a men's skin-care line), e-mailed to say that he was very upset with me because he thought I was giving up way too much equity. But I didn't look at it that way at all. It was a different business model; he was going to the masses, and I was very local.

Her father was in for one share; all equity. He uncle let her choose, so she set him up as a debt/equity investor. She had a Babson woman (who had always liked her idea) in for all equity, and a private investor in Denver for all debt. The final two shares were to be all equity:

A guy I used to work with told me he wanted to do $50,000, but he wanted to do it for 15% equity instead of 12.5%. I quickly said no. I had deals in place with other people; those are the terms. He said that's fine, he'd still like to do it.

Armed with a bit of cash and some solid commitments, Alison charged forward to make her vision a bricks and mortar reality.

Building Momentum (and Shelving)

Having initially envisioned a space in the range of 1,800 square feet, Alison found the 600 square foot shell to be a significant creative challenge—so much so, that she hired an expert:

I needed to accommodate a starting inventory of around 600 pairs of jeans and a selection of tops (see Exhibit 2.4). My biggest concern was we had to have wide enough aisles to walk around.

I thought I could do it myself, but against my better judgment I hired an interior designer. I worked with him and came up with a compact shelving system that started almost at the floor and went up only as high as I could reach. I am 5' 5", and that is about the average. If someone was shorter, I could get it for them. I really wanted my store to feel very comfortable and warm—like you're in a good friend's closet. But the designer never quite got the need to maximize the space.

She added with a smile that she had been able to attract effective talent to the task of building out her vision:

Bryan built all of the shelving with his father, an engineer. I showed them my drawings, gave them the measurements, and they did it. He actually project managed the build-out, and we did a lot of the work together. I saved so much money because of him. We painted it ourselves, and did other little things here and there. The contractors knew him well, and since he gives them so much business, they were willing to cut us breaks here and there.

I went around and found furniture pieces for practical use that would make it feel more homey, like an armoire, a big dining room table, and a couple of benches. The furniture is all white, so the store has a shabby-chic feeling to it.

To monitor her sales and margins, Alison invested in a high-end software inventory system. The trouble was, the salesperson had yet to train her, and he wasn't returning her calls. But that challenge would have to wait; it was time to buy.

EXHIBIT 2.4	Opening Inventory; Brand selection

Denim Vendors	T-Shirt/Tops Vendors
ABS	ABS
AG	C & C California
Bella Dahl	Central Park West
Big Star	Custo
Blu Jeanious	Ella Moss
Cambio	Hale Bob
Chip and Pepper	Jakes
Christopher Blue	James Perse
Citizens of Humanity	Juicy Couture
Habitual	Lilla P.
Hudson	Michael Stars
IT Jeans	Mimi & Coco
James Jeans	Muchacha
Juicy Couture	Notice
Kasil	Rebecca Beeson
Notify	Splendid
Paper Denim & Cloth	Susana Monaco
Parasuco	Three Dots
Red Engine	Troo
Rock & Republic	Velvet
Sacred Blue	
Saddelite	
Salt Works	
Seven for All Mankind	
Tacto	
True Religion	
Tylerskye	
Womyn	
Yanuk	

Learning Curves

With investors in place and the build-out moving along, Alison flew to Los Angeles and New York to haggle (and sashay), for "permission" to play:

> I had a list of brands that I wanted, based on my experience at the boutique. I was very concerned about fit and consistency. I was constantly looking at other girl's butts, so I knew that there was a core group of "in fashion" trendy jeans that I needed to have, and that people liked. I also had to have some Mom jeans: higher-waisted, not young, but still sophisticated and nice looking.
>
> From there it was about attending big trade shows in New York to touch the material and examine the styles. That doesn't tell you much about fit, and unfortunately you can't try on the floor samples.

Buying is always stressful. There are times when my head is pounding and everything looks the same. The sellers are really snobby, and I had to dress totally trendified so they could look me up and down and say, "Okay, you can buy from us." Great, thanks. If I'm a good businessperson, does the way I'm dressed matter at all? No, of course not; but that's what it's like.

Although I had a pretty good idea of what I needed for my opening inventory, I did make some mistakes. I also bought some jeans that I would not have normally, but I couldn't get some of the brands that I wanted to start with—they wouldn't sell to a new store.

The denim reps that did sell to her demanded full payment up front. Using bank cards secured with her mother's credit, Alison pulled together a $75,000 inventory of jeans, tops, and accessories like trendy shoes and jewelry. That's when she was given a bit of a scare:

A month before I opened, my last investor calls to say he's going to knock his investment down because he didn't want to be an aggressive shareholder. I panicked; I was in the final phases of my build-out, I had done all my buying, and here he was telling me I was going to be $25,000 short!

Despite her angst, Alison decided to sit tight. Things were moving along nicely, and it wasn't long before she realized that she'd be able to open her store without the additional capital.

In-jean-ius

A week before her opening in July 2005, Alison hired a friend of a friend as her first employee. Her mom was there to help out, along with her 17-year-old sister. The plan was to be open from around lunchtime to just past dinnertime, six days a week, and stay open a bit later on Sundays. Alison explained that it was soon evident that the location required a flexible approach:

The North End is interesting because in the summer they have a variety of feasts and festivals. I was often staying open until nearly midnight. I was working all the time—anything that would make a sale. I immediately surpassed my business plan estimates, and it kept building.

As a new retailer in town, she attracted a few of the usual suspects who thought they might be able to take advantage of the young proprietor. They thought wrong:

The area is safe, but like any city neighborhood, it has its share of drug addicts. The first week I was open, two junkies came in. The guy was distracting me while the girl was stealing. I knew what was going on, but I didn't see her take anything. The general idea is that unless you see them do it, you can't do anything.

When they left, a girl walks in and says, "Excuse me, those two just walked out with a pair of jeans." Well, I am not a very tough person—I grew up in the suburbs—and I don't know what I was thinking or what came over me, but I ran after them. I took the jeans out of the guy's hand and the bag off of her shoulder. I told her that I knew she had jewelry of mine, and I found it in there. I walked away from them to call the police. They ran away and my neighbors got in their car to go find them. They took my younger sister with them because she knew what they looked like.

They found them and brought them back to the store so I could positively ID them. They were arrested and taken away. From then on, everyone in the North End thought hey, she's tough—and the druggies, who all talk, stayed away.

Soon after that, Alison was in hot pursuit again:

I chased another girl down the street, and when I wouldn't let her get in her car, she tried to punch me. Bryan tells me all the time I have to stop doing that; someday I could get hurt.

Of course, I tell my employees not to do anything like that; just call the police. But I take it so personally; that's mine, you're stealing from me! How can you do that? Don't you know I'm a new business?

Over the next few months, Alison's total loss to theft was a single pair of shoes and a pair of earrings. The other good news was that sales continued to track far ahead of her estimates. In the first six months, the store had generated a net income of $20,307 on sales of $294,061. Alison explained that although word of mouth was an important factor in her early success, attracting the imagination of the local press had been key:

I'm not the only one who has had this idea, and other trendy jeans stores have definitely gotten their share of press, but people are really taking to my message: "You're going to get help, and we're going to work with you to find jeans that fit. We have jeans for everybody." Nobody else is saying that this is all about fit, and that's the message that I relay in every piece of PR that I send out. And they keep coming to talk to me.

While the young entrepreneur was thrilled with how things were going, she was ready to start spending less time on the sales floor and more time with strategic and management challenges. Easier said than done.

Fold or Finance?

Since the local press always seemed to focus on *her* skills and *her* story, Alison wondered how that might impact her ability to replicate her concept:

How do you grow when the store is about you? People come here because they like dealing with me. How do I duplicate myself? That's not to say that someone can't do what I'm doing and do it well, but employees are never going to treat people exactly the way you do. I have a lot of learning to do in terms of managing my employees, delegating, and sharing my knowledge.

One of her many priorities was to develop a training manual that, in addition to describing the particular fit characteristics of various brands, would clearly articulate her vision for customer service. She thought of contacting the Ritz-Carlton in Boston—to her mind a master of customer service—to see if they might let her review their training materials. Until she did have some documentation in place, though, she'd have to communicate her philosophy on the fly:

I sort of torture my employees when they're hired. They have to come in and spend a few hours trying on everything in the store—like a restaurant that requires their servers to try everything on the menu so they can talk about it.

I am also pretty strict about keeping the store neat and organized. I think that is so important in a small space like this. Whenever I come into the store, I can immediately see items that are unfolded or out of place.

My office is a desk in the corner, so I'm right there to offer help or teach them the little tricks I've learned. I also try to stay at my desk and let them take care of whoever comes in, but I can't just keep quiet if they are not saying the right thing. I always have to get my two cents in.

Now that she had a full-time employee nearly up to speed, and a sharp former classmate from Babson working on weekends as a fun job, Alison had begun to carve out some time each week to recharge:

I have had to give up spending much time with Bryan, and that has been a huge problem. My taking Sundays has become so important because we get to spend time together. Despite the fact that he is also an entrepreneur, he has had a really big struggle with the idea that he is number two to this business. That's been hard and it's something we're working on.

Her other challenging relationship was with the numbers:

Nailing down the actuals is a big issue for me, and I am in the process of doing that. I'm not bad with financials, but they are a bit intimidating; I am really just much more into customer service and marketing. There are so many other things that I could be doing to bring in sales, so I'd rather do those things first.

It's true; I would rather have my store neat and folded than work on my financials. That is always my first priority. If the store looks good, then I can do other things. The problem is, I am constantly rearranging the store, and that is my way of being creative; putting different things together, doing the windows over every week.

My uncle does my accounting, and I am paying close enough attention to know I'm doing much better than my projections, but I need to focus on it more. And I need to find a training course for that inventory software so I can run those reports and coordinate things the right way.

Down by One

It had been one of the best-selling days to date. Alison closed her shop at 8:30 that night and returned to her desk with the absurd idea that she might have some energy left for paperwork. It wasn't just that she was tired; she now had a brand-new challenge on her plate: that day, her one full-time employee had given her two-week notice.

Preparation Questions

1. Is this business scalable? Discuss the limitations and challenges.
2. What tasks and goals should Alison be focusing on at this stage of her venture?
3. Discuss the signing of a lease prior to having the money. What was the risk?
4. Discuss her fundraising and valuation. If you were an equity investor, what return expectations would you have?
5. If women are coming to Alison's store from all over, how important is location? Discuss the implications on growth.

Stacy Madison, founder of Stacy's Pita Chips which has grown to $60M in sales was sold to Frito Lay in January 2006. (*Source*: Courtesy Frito/Lay, Inc.)

OPPORTUNITY RECOGNITION, SHAPING, AND RESHAPING

Would-be entrepreneurs often have one of two things on their minds: "How do I come up with a good business idea?" (see Chapter 2) or "I have a great idea for a new business."

Belief in your idea is a great thing. But first step back and ask a more important question: "Is this idea an *attractive* opportunity?" Moving from an idea to a viable opportunity is an iterative process. Entrepreneurs need to conduct a series of tests—what we refer to as **market tests**—to identify interesting ideas and then see whether they are viable opportunities. Each test is an escalation of commitment, an important step to successfully launching the venture. So the process of recognizing, shaping, and reshaping an opportunity combines thought and action to take the idea from formulation to execution. Both are critical as you embark on your entrepreneurial adventure. In this chapter, we will lay out the process from the very beginning—the idea—and move through opportunity shaping and reshaping.

This chapter written by Andrew Zacharakis.

From Glimmer to Action: How Do I Come Up with a Good Idea?

We said in the preceding chapter that most successful ideas are driven by the entrepreneur's personal experience. Entrepreneurs gain exposure to their fields through their jobs and use this experience to identify possible opportunities for a new venture. Considering that many students have limited work experience, you may not have the knowledge base to generate a new idea. So how, then, does a student find a worthy idea?

Start by looking inside yourself and deciding what you really enjoy. What gives you energy? What can you be passionate about for the many years it will take to start and grow a successful company? For those who lack this professional experience or who find they haven't enjoyed their professional life to date, it takes effort to find the answers to these questions.

Finding Your Passion

Think long term. What are your goals for your degree, and where would you like to be five years and ten years down the road? Most students have difficulty envisioning the future. They know they want an exciting job with lots of potential (and, of course, above-average pay), but they haven't really thought about their careers in detail. Students often have a general idea of which industries and types of jobs are interesting to them (say, "something in finance"), but lack a clear sense of what type of company they want to work for after college (culture, customers, and so forth). After all, school is a time of self-discovery, and this self-discovery is critical for both undergraduates and MBAs. In fact, many people enroll in MBA programs with the express goal of switching careers or industries and use the graduate program as a stepping-stone toward a field they are more passionate about. It can thus pay dividends to spend time thinking beyond the next exam, semester, or year.

Launching an entrepreneurial venture takes a tremendous amount of time and energy, and you will have difficulty sustaining that level of energy if you aren't passionate about the business. How do you go about finding your passion? There are two primary ways. First, think deeply about all the things that give you joy. What do you do in your spare time? What are your hobbies? What types of newspaper and magazine articles or Internet blogs do you read? The reality of our capitalistic society is that all those things you enjoy likely have ancillary businesses around them. Some are obvious. Many students have a passion for investment finance. They have been tracking stocks for a number of years and trade them for their personal portfolio. There are many viable businesses associated with personal finance, ranging from directly trading stocks to providing analysis of the industry through a blog, for instance.

Other passions may not have as many clear-cut examples of ancillary businesses. You may have a passion for hiking. On the surface, hiking seems like a free endeavor, yet there are numerous ancillary businesses that support this activity, ranging from designing, manufacturing, and distributing hiking gear and clothing to providing specialty tours for the extreme hiker. Take World Class Teams,[1] for example. This company was founded by Robyn Benincasa, a former tri-athlete and adventure racer. After winning the Eco-Challenge she decided to turn her passion for adventure and the out-of-doors into a business. Today World Class Teams provides team building and experiential education programs to all kinds of clients. Or take one of the best-known examples in this industry—Yvon Chouinard. One of the pioneers of mountaineering and rock climbing, Chouinard turned his knack for creating useful climbing tools into a small business that served most of his friends in the California climbing community. Today his company, Patagonia, is a world leader in outdoor sporting clothes and equipment and continues to pioneer as a model for socially responsible businesses.

The world is full of examples of enterprising individuals who turned their passions into a lifetime of fulfilling work. After your initial search of "self," you may still have a fuzzy sense of what you're passionate about. To help refine your self-analysis, talk to people in your "sphere of influence."

While it is often difficult for people to be introspective about what they love, your strengths may be clearer to those who know you well. The first place to start is your family. They have watched you grow and seen what you excel at and enjoy. Ask your parents what they see as your greatest strengths. What weaknesses do they think you are blind to? What activities over the years have given you the greatest joy? Just keep in mind that while your parents and other family members clearly know you best, their perspective may be somewhat biased. Mike Bellobuono[2] started a successful chain of bagel shops called Bagelz, but if he had followed the advice of his parents, he would have taken a job at Aetna, the insurance company. In your search, also go outside your family and ask your friends, teachers, and former work associates (even if the latter group is limited to your old manager at McDonald's). How do they perceive you? The insight others provide is usually surprising. We all have blind spots that prevent us from seeing ourselves in a clear light. Seeking the opinions of others can help us overcome those blind spots and better understand our true passions.

During your search of "self," you may realize that you are passionate about something, but haven't yet developed the skill set to successfully translate that passion into a viable business. For example, you may fall in love with a new restaurant idea, say fast-casual Thai, but never have worked in a restaurant. Opening a restaurant is a worthy goal, but many students don't want to put in the effort to learn about the business. Instead of going to work as a waiter in a restaurant upon graduation, they will take a corporate job with a life insurance company. They rationalize that the pay is better and this will give them the nest egg needed to launch their restaurant. While we don't want to downplay the importance of cash flow, if you or others on your team haven't earned some deep experience in the operations of a restaurant, you will burn through your nest egg quickly and likely fail. Instead of taking the bigger paycheck, go work at a restaurant. You'll learn what customers like and how to deliver it cost effectively while also earning a bit of money. More importantly, you'll have an "apprenticeship" at a successfully run restaurant and will learn many of the major areas that you need to watch out for when the time comes to launch your own restaurant. This apprenticeship won't make you rich in the short term, but it will provide a platform for greater personal wealth and fulfillment in the long run. If you truly want to be an entrepreneur, you will need to make countless sacrifices. One of the first may be bypassing a higher-paying job for the opportunity to roll up your sleeves and gain hands-on experience in your field of choice. Just remember that the knowledge you gain will be far more valuable than the salary you give up.

Once you identify your passions, you have a strong base to start to identify ideas for business opportunities. Today's business environment is intensely competitive, and simple replication (another bagel shop) is often a recipe for failure. You will need to work on developing ideas that are unique and have something in them that can be a source of sustainable competitive advantage. This process is the focus of the next section, and it will help you understand how to take a basic idea and turn it into a great opportunity.

Idea Multiplication

All great ideas start with a seed of an idea. The trick is moving from that seed to something that is robust, exciting, and powerful. Doing so requires input from others, such as your fellow co-founders, trusted mentors, friends, and family. Spend as much time as possible brainstorming your idea with this group. These informal conversations help you think through the idea and flesh it out. You will learn more about some of the shortcomings or challenges of the business idea, and you will also gain new insights on how it might grow beyond that first product or service.

We offer one caution, however: Avoid becoming a "cocktail-party entrepreneur." This is the individual who always talks of becoming an entrepreneur, or brags of the ideas he or she thought of that others turned into exciting, profitable ventures. In other words, a cocktail entrepreneur is all talk and no action. Anybody can be a cocktail entrepreneur because it doesn't require any effort or commitment, just a few people who are willing to listen. To become a true entrepreneur requires effort beyond that first conversation. It requires continual escalation of commitment.

We have found a few useful processes that help move you beyond the simple initial idea. The first is called **idea multiplication** and is best exemplified by IDEO, the idea think tank responsible for many of the product innovations we take for granted. For instance, that thick, gripable toothbrush you use every morning was developed by IDEO, as was the design of your computer monitor and any number of other products you use everyday. Figure 3.1 highlights the top 20 IDEO innovations. IDEO, founded by Stanford engineering professor David Kelley, is hired by leading corporations worldwide to develop and design new products. We can learn a lot by observing its process.[3] There are four basic steps: (1) Gather stimuli, (2) multiply stimuli, (3) create customer concepts, and (4) optimize practicality. Let's talk about each.

John Harding/Time Life pictures/Getty Images News and Sports Services

David Kelly, Stanford Engineering Professor who founded IDEO, an innovative design firm.

Gather Stimuli. All good ideas start with the customer. Most often, entrepreneurs come across ideas by noting that there is some product or service they would like but can't find. This is your first interaction with a customer—yourself. To validate this idea, you need to go further by gathering stimuli.[5] IDEO does this through a process called *customer anthropology*, in which the IDEO team goes out and observes the customer in action in their natural environment and identifies their pain points.[6] For example, in an ABC *Nightline* segment about IDEO, the team went to a grocery store to better understand how customers shop and, more specifically, how they use a shopping basket. The team's mission was to observe, ask questions, and record information. They did not ask leading questions in hopes that the customer would validate a preconceived notion of what that shopping cart should be. Instead, the questions were open ended.

Beware the leading question. As an entrepreneur who is excited about your concept, you may find it all too easy to ask, "Wouldn't your life be better if you had concept X?" or "Don't you think my product/service idea is better than what exists?" While this might be a direct way to validate your idea, it requires that people answer honestly and understand exactly what they need. Most people like to be nice and they want to be supportive of new ideas—until they actually have to pay money for them. Second, many times people can't envision your product/service until it actually exists, so their feedback may be biased.

Product	Year	Description
Computer mouse	1981	A computer mouse for navigating a computer desktop.
Compass	1982	The precursor to the modern day laptop.
Microsoft mouse	1987	An ergonomically designed mouse for use with Windows.
Ford car audio system	1989	Audio system design for Ford automobiles.
Aerobie football	1992	Foam football with fins to stabilize the ball in air.
ATM wall surround	1993	ATMs designed with walls to provide privacy for transactions.
4000 & 7000 series LAN extender	1995	Cisco router series for controlling traffic on local-area computer networks.
Nike V12 sunglasses	1996	Breakthrough in style and functionality in sunglass design.
ForeRunner	1997	Portable electronic heart defibrillator.
Yeoman XP-1	1997	GPS system for map plotting.
Humalog/humulin insulin pen	1998	Redesigned insulin pen injector for diabetes patients.
Palm V	1999	Stylish and technologically enhanced redesign of Palm's signature product.
Leap	2000	Scientifically designed desk chair for enhanced comfort and back support.
i-Zone	2000	Disposable instant camera intended for children's market.
Acela	2000	Helped design customer-centric features of Amtrak's high-speed train.
Eyemodule2	2001	Digital camera for use with Handspring PDAs.
Apollo booster	2001	Redesign of children's car seats for Evenflo.
Muji CD player	2002	Wall-mounted CD player with simple, artistic design.
MoneyMaker Deep Lift Pump	2003	Human-powered irrigation pump for use in impoverished regions.
Windows home computing concept	2005	Computer interface linking personal entertainment and home computing units.

Figure 3.1[4]

Top 20 IDEO innovations

During the "gathering stimuli" phase, act as if you were Dian Fossey observing mountain gorillas in Africa—just *observe*. Ideally, you'll gather stimuli as a team so that you have multiple interpretations of what you have learned.

Multiply Stimuli. The next phase in the IDEO process is to multiply stimuli. Here, the team reports back on their findings and then starts brainstorming on the concept and how to improve upon the solution. One of our colleagues shared with us the trick of comedy improv for facilitating this process. A group of actors (usually three to four) pose a situation to the audience and then lets the audience shout out the next situation or reply that one actor is to give to another. From these audience suggestions, the actors build a hilarious skit. The key to success is to always say, "Yes, and..." Doing so allows the skit to build upon itself and create a seamless and comical whole. Likewise, multiplying stimuli requires that the team takes the input of others and builds upon it. Be a bit wild-eyed in this process. Let all ideas, no matter how far-fetched, be heard and built upon, because even if you don't incorporate them into the final concept, they might lead to new insights that are ultimately important to the product's competitive advantage.

Remember that "Yes, and..." means that you build upon the input of your colleagues. All too often in a group setting it is easy to say, "That won't work because..." These kinds of devil's advocate debates, while important in the later phases of business development, can prematurely kill off creative extensions in this early phase. Also beware of "Yes, but..." statements that are really just another way of saying, "Your idea won't work and here's why..." The key to this phase of development is to generate as many diverse ideas as possible.

As you go through this multiplication stage, *brain-writing* is a useful technique to avoid prematurely squashing interesting extensions. The process is like brainstorming, but the focus is on written rather than on verbal communication. The biggest shortcoming of brainstorming is that it opens up the opportunity for the most vocal or opinionated members of the group to dominate the conversation and idea-generation process. In contrast, brain-writing ensures that everyone has a chance to contribute ideas. To start, the team identifies a number of core alternative variations to the central idea (or if you have a disparate team, as you might for an entrepreneurship class, use each member's favored idea). Put the core ideas onto separate flip-chart sheets and attach them to the wall. Then the team and trusted friends, or classmates, go around and add "Yes, and..." enhancements to each idea. Keep circulating among the flip-chart sheets until everyone has had an opportunity to think about and add to each idea. At the end of that cycle, you'll have several interesting enhancements to consider. Instead of publicly discussing the ideas, have everybody vote on the three to five they like best by placing different color sticky notes on the sheets. In essence, this is another "market test" in which your team and other interested parties are gauging the viability of the idea.[7]

Create Customer Concepts.

Once you've narrowed the field to the idea and features you think have the most potential, the next step is to create customer concepts. In other words, build a simple mock-up of what the product will look like. This helps the team visualize the final product and see which features/attributes are appealing, which are detrimental, and which are nice to have but not necessary. Keep in mind that this mock-up doesn't need to be functional; it is just a tool to solidify what everybody is visualizing and to help the team think through how the product should be modified.

When your team is developing a service, your mock-up won't necessarily be a physical representation, but some kind of abstract modeling of what you hope to achieve. For example, the initial mock-up for a restaurant is often just a menu. Students who want to take the research process even further will often prepare a few sample plates that the proposed restaurant will serve. One of our former students catered a student club meeting with Argentinean beef dishes he hoped to offer. This allowed him to get a reaction to the recipes and think through how to modify them to better suit customer expectations and tastes.

Optimize Practicality.

Quite often at this stage people "over-develop" the product and incorporate every bell and whistle that the team has come up with during the brainstorming process. This is fine—the next and last step is to optimize practicality, when the team will identify those features that are either unnecessary, impractical, or simply too expensive.

This is the phase in which it is important to play devil's advocate. As the IDEO developers state, it is a time for the "grown-ups" to decide which features are the most important to optimize. If the previous steps have gone well, the team has learned a tremendous amount about what the customer may want, and that means they have a deeper understanding of the features/attributes that create the greatest value for the customer. Referring to the Jim Poss case[8] presented at the end of this chapter, Jim and his team found that the most important attributes of his solar-powered trash receptacles were

(1) durability—the bins were in public places and rough treatment or vandalism was a real threat, (2) size—the receptacle couldn't be overly large or it wouldn't fit in the public places intended, and the bags couldn't weigh too much when filled, and (3) price—the higher up-front purchase cost had to be offset by the reduced trips to collect trash, so the receptacle would pay for itself within a year. Understanding these basic parameters helped Jim's team refine its original design. For durability, they found that sheet metal was a cost-effective casing, that a Lexan plastic cover on the solar panel prevented vandalism and accidental chipping, and so forth. They went through a similar process to determine the right size. These steps helped them design a product that the customer would want, at a price the customer was willing to pay.

The entire idea-generation process is iterative. At each of the four steps we've presented, you learn, adjust, and refine. You start to understand the critical criteria that customers use in their purchasing decision and the pain points in building your product or delivering your service. This process allows you to identify and refine your idea with relatively little cost, compared to the costs you'd incur if you immediately opened your doors for business with what you believed to be the most important attributes. Nonetheless, up to this point you still don't know whether your idea, which is now very robust and well thought out, is a viable opportunity.

Is Your Idea an Opportunity?

While the idea-generation process helps you shape your idea so that it is clearer and more robust, it is only part of the process. The difference between venture success and failure is a function of whether your idea is truly an opportunity. Before quitting your job and investing your own resources (as well as those of your family and friends), spend some time studying the viability of your idea. There are five major areas you need to fully understand prior to your launch: (1) customers, (2) competitors, (3) suppliers and vendors, (4) the government, and (5) the broader global environment (see Figure 3.2). We'll discuss each of these areas in turn.

The Customer

Who is your customer? This broad question, the first you must answer, can be problematic. For instance, you might be tempted to think, if you're hoping to open a restaurant, that anyone who would want to eat in a restaurant is your customer. In other words, just about everyone in the world except for the few hundred hermits spread out across the country. But you need to narrow down your customer base so that you can optimize the features most important to your customer. So a better question is, "Who is your *core* customer?" Understanding who your primary customer is lets you better direct your efforts and resources to reach that customer. You can further refine your definition.

Starting with your initial definition, break your customers down into three categories: (1) Primary Target Audience (PTA), (2) Secondary Target Audience (STA), and (3) Tertiary Target Audience (TTA). Most of your attention should focus on the PTA. These are the customers you believe are most likely to buy at a price that preserves your margins, and with a frequency that reaches your target revenues. Let's consider our fast-casual Thai restaurant example. Fast-casual restaurants usually have larger footprints (more square feet) than fast-food restaurants and food-court outlets. Thus, you want a customer willing to pay a bit more than a fast-food customer for perceived higher quality. A wise location might be a destination mall with outlets like Barnes & Noble, Pottery Barn, and other stores that attract middle-income and higher-income shoppers. Your PTA, in this

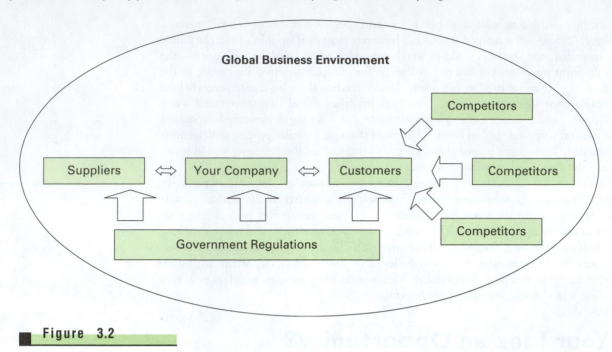

Figure 3.2

The opportunity space

situation, might be soccer moms (30 to 45 years old, with household incomes ranging from $50,000 to $150,000). These women tend to shop, watch what they eat, and enjoy ethnic food.

During the investigation stage, you would focus your attention on better understanding your PTA. How often do they shop? How often to they eat out? What meals are they more likely to eat outside the home? What other activities do they participate in besides shopping and dining out? What you are collecting is information about things like income and ethnicity (demographics), and on personality traits and values (psychographics[9]). Both categories help you design and market your product or service. During the launch phase, you would design the decor in a manner that most appeals to the PTA. You would create a menu that addresses their dietary concerns and appeals to their palette. During operations, you would market toward your PTA and train your employees to interact with them in an appropriate and effective manner. Note that the efforts across the three stages of your venture (investigation, launch, and operations) are different than they would be if you were launching a fast-food restaurant or a fancy sit-down French restaurant because your target audience is different.

While you should focus most of your attention on your PTA, the STA group also deserves attention. The PTA may be your most frequent, loyal customers, but to increase your revenues you'll want to bring in some of your STA as well. In the restaurant example, your STA may be men with similar demographics as your PTA, older couples who are active and near retirement age, and younger yuppie post-college working professionals (see the box describing the demographics of fast-casual customers). These groups are likely to find your restaurant appealing, but may not attend with the same frequency (possibly more on weekends or during the dinner hour versus lunch). Your STA may also be part of your growth strategy. For instance, after you get past your first two to three restaurants, you may choose to expand your menu or your location profile (urban centers, for instance). Understanding which STA is the most lucrative helps you make better growth decisions.

Fast-Casual Demographics

The most often cited reason for the growth in the fast-casual segment is the generation of consumers who grew up on fast food and won't eat it anymore. Add the aging baby boomers looking for healthier alternatives and who can afford to pay a little more for better quality. The price of a meal in a moderately priced restaurant has dropped; it's now only 25% more than the price of a meal purchased in a grocery store and prepared at home ... making dining out an economically viable alternative. Other fast-casual demos:

- The 18–34 age group is most likely to opt for fast-casual and makes up 37% of the traffic at such outlets
- 15% of fast-casual customers were under 18
- 28% were 35–49
- Casual dining is too slow for kids ... parents don't want to eat fast food
- Fast-casual restaurants offer teens on dates a destination their parents are comfortable with that does not serve alcohol
- Casual dining companies are responding to the fast-casual trend by aggressively marketing take-out business
- Casual dining has now become an event ... not a spur-of-the-moment dining decision

Excerpted from *E-Business Trends (Food and Beverage)*, August 21, 2002.
www.army.mil/cfsc/documents/business/trends/E-TRENDS-8-21-02.doc.

Finally, your TTA requires a little attention. During the investigation and launch stage, you shouldn't spend much time on the TTA. However, once you begin operating, a TTA may emerge that has more potential then you originally realized. Keeping your eyes and ears open during operations helps you adjust and refine your opportunity to better capture the most lucrative customers. In our restaurant example, you might find that soccer moms aren't your PTA, but that some unforeseen group emerges, such as university students. If you segment your customer groups throughout the three stages as we have outlined, you'll be better prepared to adapt your business model if some of your preconceptions turn out to be incorrect.

We've said that it's important to understand your audience's demographics and psychographics. Part of your investigation phase should include creating customer profiles. Figure 3.3 provides a sampling of the types of demographics and psychographics that might be used in describing your customer.

Trends. Customers aren't static groups that remain the same over time. They evolve, they change, they move from one profile to another. In order to best capture customers, you need to spot trends that are currently influencing their buying behavior and that might influence it in the future. When considering trends, look at broader macro trends and then funnel down to a more narrow focus on how those trends affect your customer groups. Trends might also occur within customer groups that don't affect the broader population.

One of the most influential trends in the macro environment within the U.S. over the last 50 years has been the life cycle of the baby boom generation. Born between 1946 and 1964, the country's 77.6 million baby boomers are usually married (69.4%), well educated (college graduation rates hit 19.1% at the end of the boomer generation, compared to just 6% for prior generations), and active (46% of boomers exercise regularly).[10] What links them as a generation is the experience of growing up in post-World War II America, a time of tremendous growth and change in this nation's history. Since they represent such

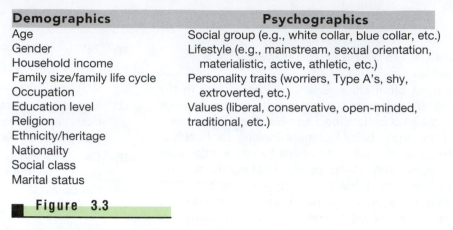

Demographics	Psychographics
Age	Social group (e.g., white collar, blue collar, etc.)
Gender	Lifestyle (e.g., mainstream, sexual orientation,
Household income	materialistic, active, athletic, etc.)
Family size/family life cycle	Personality traits (worriers, Type A's, shy,
Occupation	extroverted, etc.)
Education level	Values (liberal, conservative, open-minded,
Religion	traditional, etc.)
Ethnicity/heritage	
Nationality	
Social class	
Marital status	

Figure 3.3

Common demographic/psychographic categories

a large percentage of the U.S. population, it is no wonder that they have created numerous new categories of products and services. For example, in the 1950s the disposable diaper industry emerged and then exploded to the point where today it has $4.32 billion in sales. In the late 1950s and through the 1960s, the rapidly growing population created a need for large numbers of new schools, which in turn led to a building frenzy. (Now you know why so many schools were named after former President John F. Kennedy.) In the late 1960s and the 1970s, the rock-and-roll industry exploded. Then in the 1980s, as these baby boomers became parents, a new car category was created (the minivan) which saved Chrysler from bankruptcy. In the 1990s the boomers were in their prime working years, and new investment categories emerged to help them plan for their retirement and their children's college educations. Today, as the boomers age, we see growth in pharmaceuticals and other industries related to the more mature segment. According to one market research firm, "boomers are expected to change America's concepts of aging, just as they have about every previous life stage they have passed through."[11] How does this macro trend influence your idea?

Numerous macro trends affect the potential demand for your product or service. Trends create new product/service categories, or emerging markets, that can be especially fruitful places to find strong entrepreneurial opportunities. The convergence of multiple trends enhances the power of an opportunity like the Internet boom. First, the PC was common in the workplace, and as a result many Americans grew comfortable using it. That led to a proliferation of PCs in the home, especially for children and teenagers who used it for school, work, and video games. While the Internet had been available for decades, the development by Tim Berners-Lee of the WWW system of hyperlinks connecting remote computers, followed by the development of the Mosaic Web browser (the precursor to Netscape and Explorer), and the proliferation of Internet service providers like Prodigy and AOL, created huge opportunities for commerce online. From the very first domain name—symbolics.com—assigned in 1985, the Web has evolved into an integral component of the modern economy. Even though many dot-coms failed, others have established themselves as profitable household names, like eBay and Amazon. com. That many of these successful businesses have become multi-*billion* dollar companies in less than a decade speaks to the incredible power of convergent trends.

Trends also occur in smaller market segments and may be just as powerful as macro trends; in fact, they may be precursors to larger macro trends. For example, according to Packaged Facts, a market-research consultancy, the market for religious products (including blockbuster movies, pop music, clothing, books, and even games and toys) is expected to top $8.6 billion in annual sales by 2008. This is up from $5.6 billion in 1999, and reflects a growing trend in Christian goods and services.[12] Indeed, major companies are capitalizing on this market. At the end of 2005 Starbucks announced it would be featuring a quotation on its coffee cups from Rick Warren, pastor and best-selling author of *The Purpose-Driven Life,* which includes the line, "You were made by God and for God, and until you understand that, life will never make sense."[13] While the quote is just one of many that the company featured on its coffee cups, you can rest assured that the decision to include it was a calculated move to make the company's products more appealing to the growing Christian market.

Another important trend is the changing demographics of the U.S. population. By many estimates, in 2030 nearly 1 in 4 U.S residents will be Hispanic if current trends hold.[14] With the incredible growth in both size and purchasing power of this untapped market, it's no wonder that companies are scrambling to serve emerging opportunities. The past decade has seen a proliferation of media outlets targeting the Spanish-speaking U.S. population, and since some pundits believe the Hispanic population could emerge as the next middle class, it's likely more and more companies will find ways to capture this enormous demographic.

Trends often foretell emerging markets and suggest when the window of opportunity for an industry is about to open. Figure 3.4 lists some influential trends over the last 50 years. However, it is the underlying convergence of trends that helps us measure the power of our ideas and whether they are truly opportunities.

How Big Is the Market?
Trends suggest increasing market demand. Thus, one of the questions that distinguish ideas from opportunities asks whether there is sufficient market demand to generate the level of revenues necessary to make this an exciting career option. As we pointed out in Chapter 2, an entrepreneur typically needs the new venture to generate a minimum of $600,000 per year in revenue to meet market rates on his or her forgone salary. While this level might make a nice "mom and pop" store, many students are interested in creating something bigger. The larger your goals, the more important are your market-demand forecasts. To accurately gauge your demand, start at the larger macro market and funnel demand down to your segment and your geographic location. Granted, as you expand, you'll likely move beyond your segment and your geographic origins, but the most critical years for any venture are its first two. You need to be certain that you can survive the startup, and that means you need to be confident of your base demand.

Trend	Impact
Baby Boom generation	Pampers, rock 'n' roll, television, minivans, real estate, McMansions, etc.
Personal computing	Internet, media on-demand, electronic publishing, spreadsheets, electronic communication
Obesity	Drain on healthcare system, growth of diet industry, changes in food industry, health clubs, home gyms
Dual-income households	Child care, home services — landscaping, house cleaning, prepared foods

Figure 3.4

Important trends over the last 50 years

Overall Amount Spent on Dining Out in 2004	$325.5 billion[15]
Size of Market Segments	
Full-service restaurants	$157 billion[16]
Quick-service restaurants (including fast casual)	$128.2 billion
Cafeterias, grills, & buffets	$5.1 billion
Social caterers	$5.0 billion
Snack and non-alcoholic beverage bars	$15.5 billion
Bars and taverns	$14.7 billion
Market Share for Ethnic Restaurants	$107 billion[17]
Market Share by Region	
New England	$19.1 billion[18]
Middle Atlantic	$42.5 billion
South Atlantic	$59.1 billion
East North Central	$49.7 billion
East South Central	$17.2 billion
West North Central	$20.2 billion
West South Central	$35.9 billion
Mountain	$22 billion
Pacific	$59.9 billion
Massachusetts	
Fast-casual	$9.7 billion[19]
Ethnic	$209 million[20]
Natick (we are opening in the Natick shopping district)	$194 million[21]
Massachusetts population_____6.4 million	
Natick population_____32 thousand	
Framingham population_____67 thousand	
Wellesley population_____29 thousand	
Soccer Moms (women between 30–45)_____14 thousand	$19 million

■ Figure 3.5

Market size for Thai fast-casual restaurant

Let's go back to our Thai fast-casual restaurant example to begin to understand how large our market demand might be. Figure 3.5 steps through the demand forecast. It is best to start with the overall market size—in this case, the size of the entire restaurant industry in the U.S. Next, segment the industry into relevant categories. We are interested in both the relative size of the fast-casual segment as well as the size of the ethnic segment. It would be ideal to find the size of the fast-casual-ethnic (or better yet, Thai) segment, but as you narrow down to your opportunity there is likely to be less information because you may be riding new trends that suggest future demand that has yet to materialize. Finally, during your initial launch, you'll likely have some geographic focus. Extrapolate your overall market data so that it captures your geographic market. In this case, we took the population of the towns within a five-mile drive along the major thoroughfare on which our restaurant would be located and multiplied that percentage of the state population by the total spent in the state (Massachusetts). Basically, for this last step you should try to assess the number of soccer moms in your geographic reach. The U.S. census makes this very easy as it breaks out demographics by town. Thus, it appears that there are roughly 14,000 soccer moms in this target market.

Market Size Today and into the Future. While it is important to size your market today, you'll also need to know how big it will be in the future. If you are taking advantage of trends, your market is likely growing. Attractive opportunities open up in growing markets because there is more demand than supply, and a new firm doesn't need to compete on price. In the early years when the firm is going through a rapid learning curve, operational expenses will be proportionately higher than in later years when the firm has established efficient procedures and systems. Second, market growth means that your competitors are seeking all the new customers entering the market rather than trying to steal customers away from you.

Projecting growth is notoriously difficult, but you can make some educated guesses by looking at trends and determining overall market size as described earlier. Then make some estimates of what type of market penetration you might be able to achieve and how long it will take you to get there. If all else fails, the easiest thing to do is to verify past growth. As trend analysis tells us, past growth is usually correlated with future growth, which means you can make reasonable estimates based on historical numbers. The **S-curve** is a powerful concept that highlights the diffusion of product acceptance over time.[22] When a product or innovation is first introduced, few people are aware of it. Typically, the firm has to educate consumers about why they need this product and the value it offers. Hence, the firm concentrates its effort on early adopters. It is expensive to develop the right concept and educate the consumer, but the firm can offset this cost somewhat by charging a high price.

As customers react to the concept, the company and other new entrants learn and modify the original product to better meet customer needs. At a certain point (designated on the vertical line 1 in Figure 3.6), customer awareness and demand exceeds supply and the market enters a fast growth phase. During this time (designated between points 2 and 3 in Figure 3.6), a dominant design emerges and new competitors enter to capture the "emerging market." Typically, demand exceeds supply during this phase, meaning that competitors are primarily concerned with capturing new customers entering the market. After point 3, market demand and supply equalize, putting price pressure on the companies as they fight to capture market share from each other. Finally, innovations push the product toward obsolescence and overall demand declines.

While it is hard to say what market size indicates the window is opening and what size indicates it is closing, research suggests that markets become attractive around $20 million in revenue. Demand and supply tend to equalize around $1 billion.

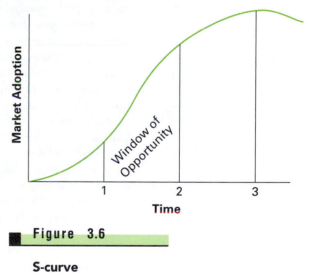

Figure 3.6

S-curve

Frequency and Price. Market size and growth are important, but we also need to think about how often our average customer buys our product or service and how much he or she is willing to pay. Ideally, our product or service would have perfectly inelastic demand; the customer would pay any price to have it. For a product with elastic demand, the quantity demanded will go down if the price goes up, and vice versa. Inelasticity results in the opposite—whether prices increase or decrease, the demand for the product stays stable. Consider front row seats for your favorite baseball team or theater production. Nearly everyone would like to sit in the front row, but most of us can't or don't because the price is too high. However, if the price were lowered by a certain amount we might be more than happy to buy the tickets. This is an example of elastic demand—as the price decreases demand for that product increases.

In contrast, consider gasoline. People who rely on a car to get to work have little choice but to pay the prices charged at the pump. If prices go down they are unlikely to buy more gas, and if prices go up they will still need to buy enough gas to get to work and run errands. While not perfectly inelastic, the demand for gasoline is relatively inelastic. In reality, there will almost always be elasticity in customer demand, and our price will be a function of that elasticity. We need to determine the optimal price that encourages regular purchases, accounts for the value inherent in our product, and allows us to earn an attractive margin on the sale. These three variables are highly correlated, and an imbalance would hurt the profitability and even the viability of the firm.

In a classic mistake, some entrepreneurs use a penetration-pricing strategy. They reason that in order to pull customers from existing alternatives, the firm needs to price lower than the competition. Then, once the product is able to gain acceptance and market share, the company can raise prices to increase gross margins and better reflect underlying value. There are a number of flaws in this logic. First, as we've noted, attractive ventures are often launched in emerging markets where demand exceeds supply. This means that price is relatively inelastic. Consumers want the product and are willing to pay a premium for it. Second, many new products are designed to be better than existing alternatives. These products offer greater value than competitive products and the price should reflect this greater value, especially since it usually costs more to add the features that led to it. Third, price sends a signal to the customer. If a product with greater value is priced lower than or at the same price as competing products, customers will interpret that signal to mean it isn't as good, despite claims that it has greater value.

Fourth, even if customers flock to the low-priced product, this rapid increase in demand can sometimes cause serious problems for a startup. Demand at that price may exceed your ability to supply, resulting in stock-outs. Consumers are notoriously fickle and are just as likely to go to a competitor as wait for your backlog to catch up.[23] Finally, these same customers may resist when you try to recapture value by raising prices in the future. They will have developed an internal sense of the value of your product, and they may take this opportunity to try other alternatives. The last thing you want is a business built around customers who are always searching for the lowest price. These will be the first people to leave you when a competitor finds a way to offer a lower price.

The Internet boom and bust saw many poor pricing decisions. Internet firms entered the market at very low price points. Take kozmo.com, for example. Many thought the company's revolutionary approach to delivering things like groceries and videos would change the way people shopped, but in the end, the value proposition was too good to be true. The company was delivering goods at a cost higher than it was charging. The total ticket for a simple order of a few sodas, a bag of chips, and a candy bar might be only $7, but kozmo.com was paying as much as $10 to the person who had to find those items and then deliver them. The venture-capital-backed company burned through almost all its cash before it finally recognized the flaw of its pricing logic, but by then it was too late.[24]

Webvan is an eerily similar example. In its attempt to deliver groceries directly to consumers, the company failed to adapt its business model to the extremely thin gross profit margins of the grocery business. Webvan offered to deliver groceries free of charge, but the labor costs of deliveries, along with the warehousing needs of a large-scale grocery delivery operation, were such that the company was losing money on almost every order. Webvan burned through $1 billion in cash before failing.[25] This is one of the primary rules of economics—you shut down the business if the price you are charging can't cover the direct costs of the good or service.

The argument many Internet entrepreneurs made at the time was that the "number of eyeballs" looking at a site was more important than profitability, which firms figured would come later as they developed a critical mass of customers. These firms reasoned that they could charge lower prices than "brick-and-mortar" outlets (traditional stores that the customer had to physically visit) because they didn't have the overhead costs of renting or buying so many store locations. Furthermore, Internet companies could serve a larger volume of customers via a single Web site than a chain of stores could serve in thousands of physical locations. For the most part, these strategies failed due to a number of reasons.

First, the Internet firms continued reducing prices to the point where they weren't generating a positive gross margin. The continued decrease in price was a function of competition. New online firms that were basically identical started to appear. For instance, do you remember the difference between pets.com and petopia.com? Traditional retailers responded by adding Web sites as an additional channel of distribution. Toys "R" Us was able to enter and secure new customers at one-tenth the cost of Toys.com due to higher name recognition.

Finding the right price to charge is difficult. It requires understanding your cost structure. You cannot price under your costs of goods sold (COGS) for an extended period of time unless you have lots of financing (and are certain that access to financing will continue into the future). Thus, your minimum price should be above your COGS. Some firms look at their costs to produce a unit of the product, and then add a set percentage on top of that cost to arrive at the price. This is called **cost-plus pricing**, and the problem is that it may set your price lower or higher than the underlying value in your product or service. For example, if you price at 40% above marginal cost, that may result in your product being a great value (software usually has gross margins of 70% or better) or drastically overpriced (groceries often have gross margins in the 20% range).

A better approach is to assess market prices for competing products. For instance, consider GMAT test-preparation courses that help students strengthen their business school applications. At the time of this writing, a quick scan of Kaplan and Princeton Review reveals that prices for their classroom GMAT programs are $1,349 and $1,249, respectively. Given the similarities of the content, structure, and results of these programs, it is no surprise that their prices are comparable. The slight difference reflects the differences in marketing and operational strategy as well as the value customers perceive in the services. Over the years, Kaplan and Princeton Review have gained deep insight into what parents will pay. For an entrepreneur entering this marketplace, Kaplan and Princeton Review provide a starting point in deciding what price can be charged. The entrepreneur would adjust his or her price based on the perceived difference in value of the offering.

Many entrepreneurs claim that they have no direct competition so it is impossible to determine how much customers might pay. In such cases, which are very rare, it is essential to understand how customers are currently meeting the need that you propose to fill. Assess how much it costs them to fulfill this need and then determine a price that reflects the new process plus a premium for the added value your product delivers.

Margins. For new ventures, research suggests that gross margins of 40% are a good benchmark that distinguishes more attractive from less attractive opportunities. It is important to have higher gross margins early in the venture's life, because operating costs during the early years are disproportionately high due to learning curve effects. For instance, no matter how experienced they are in the industry, your team will incur costs as you train yourselves and new hires. Over time, the team will become more efficient and the associated costs of operations will reach a stability point. Another reason for keeping margins high is that the new venture will incur costs prior to generating sales associated with those costs. For instance, well before you are able to generate any leads or sales, you will need to hire salespeople and invest time and money training them. Even if you are a sole proprietorship, you will incur costs associated with selling your product or service before you receive any cash associated with the sale. For instance, you may have travel expenses like airline tickets or gasoline for your car, and infrastructure expenses like a new computer and office furniture. This lag between spending and earning creates a strain on cash flows, whether you are a one-person shop or a growing enterprise, and if your margins are thin to begin with, it will be harder to attract the investment needed to launch.

It typically takes three to five years for a firm to reach stability and for operating costs to stabilize. At this point strong firms hope to achieve net income as a percentage of sales of 10% or better. If the net income margin is lower, it will be hard to generate internal cash for growth or to attract outside investors, to say nothing about generating returns for the founding team.

The exceptions to this rule are businesses that can generate high volumes. During the 1980s and 1990s, many new ventures sought to replicate the Wal-Mart concept. Staples, Office Max, Home Depot, and Lowe's are good examples. Gross margins on these businesses range from as low as 10% to 33%, and net income margins from 1.8% to 6.5%. However, the stores do such enormous volumes that they are still able to generate huge profits. For example, in the 12-month period ending on January 31, 2006, Wal-Mart posted profits of $11.2 *billion*, which is more in profits than the vast majority of all U.S. companies had in sales, and it was able to do so because it generated $287 billion in sales during the same period. While Wal-Mart's net profit margin of 3.5% is small by most measures, its sales and profit numbers are clear indicators that its business strategy is working.

The performance of these big companies suggests another kind of industry structure that can be very attractive—fragmented industries. Prior to the launch of Staples and Home Depot, people filled their office supply and hardware needs through "mom and pop" companies. These small enterprises served small geographic regions and rarely expanded beyond them. The "big box" stores entered these markets and offered similar goods at much lower prices against which "mom and pop" firms couldn't compete.

While entering a fragmented industry and attempting to consolidate it, as big box stores do, can create huge opportunities, the financial and time investments required are substantial. For instance, Arthur Blank and Bernard Marcus founded Home Depot in 1978 in the Atlanta area. While its individual stores had enormous sales and profit potential, the company needed significant upfront capital for the initial building costs and inventory, and it raised venture capital followed by $7.2 million from its 1981 public offering (which translates to $14 million in 2005 dollars). Almost 10 years later, Thomas Stemberg founded Staples and followed a nearly identical path in office supplies. Here again, the startup costs were enormous and the company relied heavily on its founders' experience in retailing. Staples raised $33.83 million in venture capital before it went public in April 1989, raising $51.3 million.[26] The bottom line is that such opportunities are rarer than in emerging markets, and they require a team with extensive industry experience and access to venture capital or other large institutional financing resources.

Reaching the Customer. Reaching the customer can be very difficult, even for the most experienced entrepreneur. Take the example of the founder of Gourmet Chili.[27] After completing his MBA, he spent many years with one of the top three food producers in the country, where he gained a deeper understanding about the industry. In the 1980s he joined a small food startup company that developed a new drink concept that became widely successful and was ultimately acquired by Kraft Foods. Still a young man, he cashed out and started his own venture, Gourmet Chili. Its first product was chili in a jar, like Ragú spaghetti sauce. The product tasted better than competitors like Hormel Chili (in a can). Despite his extensive entrepreneurial and industry experience and even though his product tasted better, the entrepreneur couldn't overcome one obstacle: how to reach the customer.

Chili in a jar is usually distributed in grocery stores, but this is a very difficult market to enter on a large scale. The industry is consolidated and mature, with only 19 chains throughout the entire country. Large product and food companies like Procter & Gamble and General Mills control much of the available shelf space, due to their power and ability to pay the required slotting fees.[28] Grocery stores also have an incentive to deal with fewer rather than more suppliers because it improves their internal efficiency.

Given that, companies that sell only a few products, such as Gourmet Chili, have a more difficult time accessing large chain stores. And even though smaller chains may find a unique product like Gourmet Chili appealing, it costs one-product companies more to distribute through these channels, since they have to deal with multiple vendors instead of sealing a few large distribution agreements. Alternatively, Gourmet Chili could work with a large food brokerage company, but that would mean giving a portion of its margins to the brokerage. With all these options, the economics of distribution make it almost impossible to generate a decent margin on this type of company.

One of the most overlooked keys to entrepreneurial success is distribution. How *do* you reach the customer? While Gourmet Chili might have been able to reach the customer through alternative distribution channels, like the Internet, these are likely to generate lower sales volume and higher marketing expenses, because you have to educate the customer not only about what your product is, but also about where to find it.

It is important to understand the entire value chain for the industry you are competing in. You need to lay out the distribution of your product from raw materials all the way to the end consumer. Figure 3.7 captures the value chain for Gourmet Chili.[29] From the figure, you can see the respective gross margins of the players—note that their net income margins would be much lower based on their operating costs. The higher gross margins of the grocery stores indicate their relative power. Consider whether there is a variation on your business idea that would allow you to enter the portion of the value chain where greater margins are available. In sum, you must understand the entire value chain in order to determine where opportunities to make a profit might exist.

While Gourmet Chili wasn't successful gaining distribution, the following excerpt shows how a small food company, Stacy's Pita Chips, can slowly gain distribution and build momentum to the point where it achieves a successful harvest for the entrepreneurs.

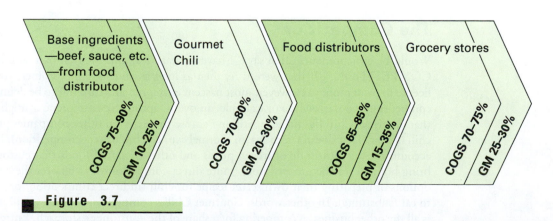

Figure 3.7

Value chain of Gourmet Chili

Stacy's Pita Chips Gaining Widespread Distribution

Stacy's Pita Chips didn't start out as a snack food maker. Instead, Stacy Madison, a social worker by training, and Mark Andrus, a psychologist, wanted to open a restaurant. Their first venture was a small food cart that sold pita bread wraps in downtown Boston. They were instantly successful and soon had long lines of hungry customers waiting for their freshly made wraps. Some of these potential customers tired of waiting in line and would give up before placing an order. To minimize the number of lost customers, Stacy and Mark started serving seasoned pita chips, baked from the bread they had left at the end of each day. The pita chips were a hit. In addition to great rollup sandwiches, customers had a delicious incentive while they waited in line. Eventually, the couple were running two businesses and had to make a choice. They chose the pita chips, figuring they'd be able to gain national growth more rapidly. A new venture was born.

Even though Stacy and Mark had a great product, the question was, how could they reach the end consumer en masse? Most people buy chips in the grocery store, but getting space in the snack aisle is nearly impossible. Large distributors sell to grocery stores, and they are only interested in products that their buyers (the grocery stores) want. Recognizing this problem, Stacy decided that there was another way into this channel; Stacy's would place its chips in the natural food aisle and the in-store delis.

Stacy and Mark attended trade shows and made direct contact with grocery stores, sold them on their product, and secured trial placements in the stores. Stacy supplied display racks for her chips to each store and worked hard to increase consumer awareness by giving sample chips to shoppers. Without a distributor, Stacy's Pita Chips often shipped their product via UPS, but once they secured 10 or more stores in a particular geographic region, they went to the stores and asked who distributed snacks to them. The stores often contacted the distributors on Stacy's behalf, asking them to handle the product for them. Stacy noted, "Having customers that the distributor sold to gave us leverage. They wanted to carry our products because we created customer demand for them." Once Stacy's had a few large distributors in line, the company had gained momentum and other stores and distributors wanted to carry the product. In 2005, Stacy's hit $60 million* in sales and Frito-Lay, the largest snack food maker in the world, finalized the acquisition of the company in January 2006.

Compiled from a personal interview with Stacy Madison, March 22, 2006.
*"Frito-Lay is extending its healthy snack offerings with the acquisition of Stacy's Pita Chip, Randolph, Mass., for an undisclosed sum." *Brandweek* 46.43 (Nov 28, 2005): 5(1).

The Competition

Would-be entrepreneurs often say, "I have a great idea, and the best part is, there's NO COMPETITION." If that were true, then as long as you have a customer, you have a license to print money. However, most nascent entrepreneurs turn out to be defining their competition too narrowly. For example, an overly optimistic entrepreneur might suggest that Gourmet Chili has no competition because there are no other companies producing chili in a jar. That doesn't account for Hormel canned chili (direct competition). It doesn't account for the multitude of frozen pizzas and other prepared foods that customers can bring home from the grocery store (more direct competition). It ignores the customers' options of preparing their own secret recipe for chili (indirect competition) or going out to eat (substitute). In other words, Gourmet Chili's competition isn't just chili in a jar; it is all the other businesses competing for a share of the consumer's stomach. Entrepreneurs ignore these competitors and substitutes at their peril.

To fully identify the competition, start with the customer. How is the customer currently fulfilling the need or want you intend to fill? You must identify direct competitors, indirect competitors, and substitutes. The number and strength of your competition mirrors the market structure. In a mature market, the industry is likely consolidated and the power of existing competitors is strong. From the Gourmet Chili example, the industry is highly consolidated. Five major prepared-food companies control 57% of the market: Nestle S.A., Kraft Foods Inc., Unilever, Frito-Lay, Inc., and Cargill, Inc.[30] Entering this market is difficult, as we saw earlier, because the major competitors control the primary channel of distribution.

Even if you successfully enter the market, the strength of the competition enables them to retaliate. Competitors can lower prices to a point that makes it difficult for new ventures to compete due to economies of scale and scope. They can spend more on their advertising campaign and other marketing expenditures and increase their visibility due to greater resource reserves or easier access to capital. The good news is that many times strong competitors won't bother with new startups, because they're so small that they aren't noticeable, or because they don't feel threatened either in the short or medium term. However, entrepreneurs should plan for contingencies just in case the larger competitors retaliate earlier than expected.

When markets are emerging, like the market for MP3 players, fewer products compete for customers primarily because the demand exceeds the supply. The main struggle within these markets is trying to find and own the dominant design that will become the customer favorite. The classic example of convergence toward a dominant design is the personal computer operating system. In the early years, there were a multitude of potential operating systems that ran computers ranging from Apple to Tandy/Radio Shack. In the 1970s, Digital Research Inc.'s CP/M system looked to be the dominant system, until the company's founder, Gary Kildall, blew off a meeting with IBM officials looking for an operating system for the company's new personal computer. IBM then approached Microsoft, which had bought QDOS from Seattle Computer Co. for the foundation of its MS-DOS system. Tandy Radio Shack, meanwhile, created a proprietary system, TRS-DOS, for its own computers. Figure 3.8 shows some of the competing systems, when they were designed, and when they went out of business. Note that by the late 1980s DOS controlled 85% of the marketplace, Apple had 7%, and all others were also-rans.[31] What this means is that firms in emerging markets have to work feverishly to design a better product and to communicate its benefits to customers, because your competition is doing the same. MS-DOS became the dominant operating system primarily because it was included in the most popular PC at the time, the IBM PC. As PC design converged toward the IBM design, existing PC manufacturers and new manufacturers alike adopted

Operating System	Year Introduced	Year It Failed
Tandy/Radio Shack TRS-DOS	1977	1987
Apple DOS	1978	1983
Digital Research Inc. CP/M	1976	1983
Seattle Computer Co. QDOS	1980	1981
Microsoft MS-DOS	1981	1995
Microsoft Windows	1983	
Apple Macintosh OS	1984	

Figure 3.8

Operating system move to dominant design

the Microsoft DOS platform. This example highlights the evolution of most marketplaces. Once a dominant design is in place, the market moves rapidly to maturity.

Emerging markets are characterized by "stealth" competitors. Entrepreneurs often believe their idea is so unique that they will have a significant lead over would-be competitors. But just as your venture will operate "under the radar" as it designs its products, builds its infrastructure, and tests the product with a few early beta customers, so will a number of other new ventures likely be at similar stages of development. While it is relatively easy to conduct due diligence on identifiable competition, it is extremely difficult to learn about competition that isn't yet in the marketplace. Thus, it is imperative for new ventures to scan the environment to identify and learn about "stealth" competition.

There are several sources of intelligence you can tap. It is probable that your competition is using similar inputs, and thus similar suppliers, as you are. As you interview your potential suppliers, make sure to query them about similar companies with whom they are working. While the suppliers may not divulge this information, more often than not they don't see it as a conflict of interest to do so. Outside professional equity capital can also help you determine competitors. Angels and venture capitalists see many deals and have knowledge about how an industry is developing even if they haven't funded one of your "stealth" competitors. Again, you can talk to professional investors about who they see as strong emerging competitors. Furthermore, a number of widely available databases track and identify companies that receive equity financing. Price Waterhouse Coopers publishes MoneyTree,[32] which allows you to screen new investments by industry, region, and venture capitalists making the investment. VentureWire is one of many daily e-mail newsletters published by Dow Jones that tracks current deals—and the best part is that VentureWire Alert is free.[33] The smart entrepreneur will diligently monitor his or her industry and use these resources, as well as many others, to avoid being surprised by unforeseen competition. An excellent source of industry gossip is trade shows.

While your direct competition is most relevant to your success, you also should spend some time understanding why your target customer is interested in your indirect competitors and substitutes. As you increase your knowledge of the total marketplace, you will start to understand the key success factors (KSFs) that distinguish those firms that win and those that lose. KSFs are the attributes that influence where the customer spends money. If we think once again about Gourmet Chili, customers base their food purchasing decisions on a number of factors, including taste, price, convenience (time to prepare and serve), availability (the distribution channel issue discussed earlier), and healthy attributes of the food, among other factors. As you gather data on these factors, constructing a competitive profile matrix to identify the relative strength of each will help you decide how to position your venture into the marketplace (see Figure 3.9). Gauge how well each of your competitors is doing by tracking their revenues, gross margins, net income margins, and net profits. Note that we don't yet know what the figures are for Gourmet Chili because it has yet to hit the marketplace. Likewise, "homemade chili" in the figure is the creation of the consumer, who buys all the ingredients separately at the grocery store.

As you examine the competitive profile matrix, you understand the competitors' strategy and which customers they are targeting. Hormel, for example, is targeting price-sensitive, convenience-minded consumers. Typical customers might include a male living on his own, college students, or others who don't have the time or desire to cook but are living on a budget. Homemade chili, on the other hand, falls in the domain of the person who enjoys cooking and has more time. The stay-at-home parent may have the time to shop for all the ingredients and to cook the chili from scratch, or weekend gourmets might like to have something special for guests or family. Gourmet Chili might appeal to families where both parents work outside the home. They want quality food but don't have the

	Gourmet Chili	Hormel	Homemade	DiGiorno Pizza
Taste	Good	Fair	Excellent	Fair
Price	High $3.50	Medium $1.89	Low	Very High $6.50
Convenience	High	High	Low	High
Availability	Low	High	High	High
Healthy	Medium	Low	High	Medium
Revenues		<$135million*		$500 million*
Gross Margins		23.7%*		34.9%*
Net Income Margins		16.5%*		loss*
Net Profit		22.3 million*		

*Financial figures for Hormel and DiGiorno are for the whole company, not just the product.

■ Figure 3.9

Competitive profile matrix

time to cook it from scratch and are not as sensitive to prices. Lastly, DiGiorno pizza (a higher-quality pizza) is targeting families who want something in the freezer for those nights that they just don't have time to cook. While there are many more competitors than we have highlighted in the matrix, it is often best to pick representative competitors rather than to highlight every potential company. The matrix is a tool to help you understand the competitive landscape by drilling down deep on a few key competitors. Although you'll want to be aware of every potential competitor and substitute, focusing on a few in depth will help you devise a successful strategy.

From this information, you can start to get the broad guidelines of the competitors' strategies—Hormel is pursuing a low-cost strategy—and of what might be an appropriate strategy for Gourmet Chili. It might pursue a differentiation strategy of better quality at a higher price. Moreover, considering the difficulties of entering the distribution channels, it might focus on a niche strategy. Maybe Gourmet Chili could access health-oriented grocery stores like Whole Foods. Understanding the marketplace helps you formulate a strategy that can help you succeed.

Suppliers and Vendors

Understanding the customers and competition is critical to determining whether your idea is indeed an opportunity, but other factors also need consideration. Referring back to the value chain we created for Gourmet Chili (see Figure 3.7), you'll notice that suppliers are providing commodity goods such as beef, vegetables, and other food products. These types of vendors usually have limited power, which means that more of the ultimate gross margin in the chain goes to Gourmet Chili. However, in some instances, your suppliers can have tremendous power and that will directly affect your margins. For example, Microsoft as the dominant operating system and core software provider, and Intel as the dominant microprocessor supplier, have considerable power over PC manufacturers. Microsoft has gross margins of 85% and Intel has gross margins of 70%,[34] whereas average gross margins for PC manufacturers are between 8% and 25%.[35] Putting aside the strong competition in the mature PC market for a moment, the fact that suppliers have so much power lessens the opportunity potential for entrepreneurs entering the PC market—unless they find an innovation to supplant the Intel chip or the Microsoft operating system.

The Government

For the most part, the U.S. government is supportive of entrepreneurship. Taxes are lower than in most nations in the world, the time required to register a new business is shorter, and the level of regulations is generally lower. However, in certain industries, government regulation and involvement are significantly higher, such as in pharmaceuticals and medical devices. Gloria Ro Kolb founded Fossa Medical, which invented a stent that more quickly and effectively removes kidney stones. In order to bring her product to market, Kolb had to guide her product through FDA approval. The approval process is often lengthy, taking on average 20 months before the product can be brought to market.[36] During this time the startup company is incurring costs with no revenue to offset the negative cash flow, increasing the time to break even, and also increasing the amount of money at risk if the venture fails. While the upfront time and expense is an entry barrier that reduces potential future competition, Fossa benefits only if the product proves successful in gaining both FDA approval and adoption by doctors. Thus, as an entrepreneur, you need to be aware of government requirements and their impact on your business. If the requirements are stringent, such as getting FDA approval, and the potential margins you can earn are relatively low, it is probably not a good opportunity. In the case of Fossa, the stents command a very high margin, so the company can more than recoup its investment if it successfully navigates FDA approval and secures wide doctor adoption.

The Global Environment

As the world marketplace becomes global, your opportunity is increasingly strengthened by looking overseas. What international customers fit within your PTA, STA, and TTA? How easy is it to reach them? When might you go international? On the flip side, you also need to be aware of your international competitors. Have they entered your market yet? When might they? It is increasingly common for entrepreneurial firms to use an outsourcing strategy, which means you may need to evaluate international vendors and their relative power. In Chapter 4, we go into much greater detail on global strategies, but for now let's see whether the global environment makes your idea a stronger or weaker opportunity.

The Opportunity Checklist

Figure 3.10 summarizes the concepts we have covered in this chapter. Use it to evaluate whether your idea is a strong opportunity, or evaluate several ideas simultaneously to see which one has greater promise. While your opportunity would ideally fit entirely in the middle column under "Better Opportunities," there will be some aspects where it is weak. Examine the weak aspects and see how you can modify your business model to strengthen them. In the end, of course, the goal is to be strong in more areas than you are weak.

"I Don't Have an Opportunity"

After doing a thorough analysis, some entrepreneurs conclude that the marketplace isn't as large or accessible, or competition is much greater than they expected and they quickly reach the conclusion that they should abandon their dreams. But in fact if you analyze

Customer	Better Opportunities	Weaker Opportunities
Identifiable	PTA	STA
Demographics	Clearly defined and focused	Fuzzy definition and unfocused
Psychographics	Clearly defined and focused	Fuzzy definition and unfocused
Trends		
Macro market	Multiple and converging	Few and disparate
Target market	Multiple and converging	Few and disparate
Window of opportunity	Opening	Closing
Market structure	Emerging/fragmented	Mature/decline
Market size		
How many	PTA	STA
Demand	Greater than supply	Less than supply
Market growth		
Rate	20% or greater	Less than 20%
Price/Frequency/Value		
Price	GM > 40%	GM < 40%
Frequency	Often and repeated	One time
Value	Fully reflected in price	Penetration pricing
Operating expenses	Large and fixed	Low and variable
NI Margin	>10%	<10%
Volume	Moderate	Very high
Distribution		
Where are you in the value chain?	High margin, high power	Low margin, low power
Competition		
Market structure	Emerging	Mature
Number of direct competitors	Few	Many
Number of indirect competitors	Few	Many
Number of substitutes	Few	Many
Stealth competitors	Unlikely	Likely
Key success factors		
Relative position	Strong	Weak
Vendors		
Relative power	Weak	Strong
Gross margins they control in the value chain	Low	High
Government		
Regulations	Low	High
Taxes	Low	High
Global environment		
Customers	Interested and accessible	Not interested or accessible
Competition	Nonexistent or weak	Existing and strong
Vendors	Eager	Unavailable

Figure 3.10

Opportunity checklist

every aspect of the business, and if you do your assessment completely, you'll always find a reason for the business to fail. There is no perfect business. There will be areas of weakness in any business model, and it is human nature to amplify those weaknesses until they seem insurmountable. Step back, take a second look, and ask yourself two questions: First, how can you modify your business model so that it isn't as weak in those aspects? Second, what can go right as you launch your business?

> "Analysis and criticism are of no interest to me unless they are a path to constructive, action-bent thinking. Critical type intelligence is boring and destructive and only satisfactory to those who indulge in it. Most new projects—I can even say every one of them—can be analyzed to destruction."
>
> — Georges Doriot,
> *Founder of the modern venture
> capital industry*

The entrepreneurial process is one of continuous adjustment. Many times entrepreneurs stick stubbornly to an idea as it was originally conceived. After a thorough customer and competitive analysis, you need to find ways to modify the business concept so that it better matches the needs of your customer and so that it has advantages over your competitors. The more you learn about the opportunities that exist for your product, the more you must refine your business plan. For instance, as you open your doors and customers come in and provide feedback, you'll find more ways to improve your business model. If you ignore feedback and remain stuck to your initial concept as you originally visualized it (and possibly as you wrote it in your plan), you are more likely to fail. The business planning process is ongoing, and you'll learn more about your opportunity every step along the way. Therefore, to prematurely abandon your concept after some negative feedback from your analysis is a mistake unless the negatives far outweigh the positives in Figure 3.10.

It is also natural to assume the worst possible outcomes, fixating on the weak aspects of the business model and failing to recognize what can go right. For example, Ruth Owades, who founded Calyx & Corolla (a direct flower-delivery service from the growers to your home), persisted in launching a mail order catalog called *Gardener's Eden* for unique gardening tools even though the initial analysis suggested it would be difficult to break even in the first year.[37] While Owades envisioned her business as seasonal—customers would order gardening supplies during the spring planting season—she found that she had two seasons: people also used the catalog during the Christmas season for gifts. She found too that the amount people would spend per order was higher than expected, making the dynamics of the business much more robust than she initially imagined.

Your pre-launch analysis is just a starting point. You need to understand the variables in your business model, how they might be greater or less than you initially imagine, and what that might mean for your business. In the next chapter we will define and examine business models—how you make money and what it costs to generate revenues.

☐ CONCLUSION

All opportunities start with an idea. We find the ideas that most often lead to successful businesses have two key characteristics. First, they are something that the entrepreneur is truly passionate about. Second, the idea is a strong opportunity as measured on the opportunity checklist. To be sure of having a strong opportunity, entrepreneurs need a deep understanding of their customer, preferably knowing the customer by name. Better opportunities will have lots of customers currently (market size) with the potential for even more customers in the future (market is growing). Furthermore, these customers will buy the product frequently and pay a premium price for it (strong margins). Thus, entrepreneurs need to be students of the marketplace. What trends are converging, and how do these shape customer demand today and into the future?

Savvy entrepreneurs also recognize that competitors, both direct and indirect, are vying for the customers' attention. Understanding competitive dynamics helps entrepreneurs shape their opportunities to reach the customer better than the competition can. As this chapter points out, the entrepreneurial environment is holistic and fluid. In addition to the customer and competition, entrepreneurs need to understand how they source their raw materials (suppliers) and what government regulations mean to their business. If all these elements—customers, competitors, suppliers and government—are favorable, the entrepreneur has identified a strong opportunity. The next step is successfully launching and implementing your vision.

YOUR OPPORTUNITY JOURNAL

Reflection Point

Your Thoughts...

1. What do you really enjoy doing? What is your passion? Can your passion be a platform for a viable opportunity?

2. What do your friends and family envision you doing? What strengths and weaknesses do they observe? How do their insights help lead you to an opportunity that is right for you?

3. What ideas do you have for a new business? How can you multiply the stimuli around these ideas to enhance them and identify attractive opportunities?

4. Put several of your ideas through the opportunity checklist in Figure 3.10. Which ideas seem to have the highest potential?

5. How can you shape, reshape, and refine your opportunities so that they have a greater chance to succeed and thrive?

6. Identify some early, low-cost market tests that you can use to refine your opportunity. Create a schedule of escalating market tests to iterate to the strongest opportunity.

WEB EXERCISE

Subscribe to the free list serve VentureAlert (www.djnewsletters@dowjones.com). Track the stories on a daily basis. Which companies are receiving venture capital? What trends does this flow of money suggest? How might these trends converge to create new opportunities?

NOTES

1 www.worldclassteams.com/welcome.htm.

2 Spinelli, S., Alyse, A., & D'Heilly, D. Mike Bellobuono Case. Wellesley, MA: Babson College. 1996.

3 See the ABC *Nightline* segment "The Deep Dive" aired on July 13, 1999.

4 Compiled from IDEO Web site at http://ideo.com/portfolio/ and from Edmondson, Amy C. "Phase Zero: Introducing New Services at IDEO." Boston, MA: Harvard Business School Publishing. December 14, 2005, p. 13.

5 The four-step process outlined in this chapter—gather stimuli, multiply stimuli, create customer concepts, and optimize practicality—come from a process outlined by Doug Hall. See Hall, D. *Jump Start Your Brain*. New York: Warner Books. 1996.

6 *Pain points* are those aspects about a current product or service that are suboptimal or ineffective from the customer's point of view. Improving on these factors or coming up with an entirely new product or service that eliminates these points or pain can be a source of competitive advantage.

7 For those of you are interested in learning more about brain-writing, visit www.usabilitybok.org/methods/p314?section=basic-description.

8 Bygrave, W., and Hedberg, C. Jim Poss case. Babson College. 2004.

9 Psychographic information categorizes customers based on their personality and psychological traits, lifestyles, values, and social group membership. It helps you understand what motivates customers to act in the ways they do, and is important because members of a specific demographic category can have dramatically different psychographic profiles. Marketing strictly based on demographic information will be ineffective because it ignores these differences. Our use of soccer moms captures both the demographic and psychographic attributes of a broad customer profile.

10 Packaged Facts. "The U.S. Baby Boomer Market: From the Beatles to Botox." 3rd Edition: November 2002. Pp. 8–10.

11 Packaged Facts. "The U.S. Baby Boomer Market: From the Beatles to Botox." 3rd Edition: November 2002. P. 7.

12 Packaged Facts. "The U.S. Market for Religious Publishing and Products." August 2004. P. 6.

13 Grossman, Cathy Lynn. "Starbucks stirs things up with a God quote on cups." *USA Today*. October 19, 2005. www.usatoday.com/life/2005-10-19-starbucks-quote_x.htm.

14 Rives, Karen. "U.S. Hispanics Expected to Fill Baby Boomer Labor Gap." Hispanic Business.com: March 3, 2006. www.hispanicbusiness.com/news/newsbyid.asp?id=29151&cat=Headlines&more=/news/more-news.asp.

15 Ebbin, R., Grindy, B., Riehle, H., Roach, D., and Smith, T. "Restaurant Industry Sales

Trends in Recent Years." 2005 Restaurant Industry Forecast. National Restaurant Association, 2005: 44.

16 Ibid.

17 Anonymous. Fullservice Steams Ahead. *Restaurants USA*, October 2001. This article estimates that ethnic food accounts for one-third of total restaurant sales, so we multiplied the total industry size by one-third.

18 Ebbin, R., Grindy, B., Riehle, H., Roach, D., and Smith, T. "Projected Growth in State & Regional Economic Indicators." 2005 Restaurant Industry Forecast. National Restaurant Association, 2005: 34.

19 Ibid.

20 Based on 2.1% fast-casual market share estimate from Think-Equity Partners, LLC. Company Note: Chipotle Mexican Grill. Think-Equity Partners LLC. February 16, 2006. Investext Plus. Babson College Horn Library, Babson Park, MA. March 4, 2005. http://web3 .infotrac.galegroup.com/itw/.

21 http://quickfacts.census.gov/qfd/ states/25000.html.

22 Brown, R. Managing the "S" Curves of Innovation. *The Journal of Consumer Marketing*, 9(1): 61–72. 1992.

23 *Backlog* is the sales that have been made but not fulfilled due to lack of inventory to finalize the sale.

24 Slaton, Joyce. "Webvan, Kozmo— RIP. Money Lessons We've Learned from the Last Mile Failures." SFGate.com: 21 July, 2001.

25 Maney, K. Founder of Webvan Grocery Store Tries Again with Online Newsstand. *USA Today*, July 23, 2003, pgs. B1, B3.

26 VentureXpert.

27 The name of the company and entrepreneur are disguised.

28 Slotting fees are fees that supermarket chains charge suppliers for providing shelf space in their stores.

29 Information for this value chain was gathered from financial data on sample industry companies found at http://biz.yahoo.com/ic/340.html and linked pages.

30 General rankings for food sales found at http://biz.yahoo.com/ic/profile/ 340_1349.html.

31 Reimer, Jeremy. "Total Share: 30 Years of Personal Computer Market Share Figures." http://arstechnica .com/articles/culture/total-share.ars. December 14, 2005.

32 www.pwcmoneytree.com/moneytree/ index.jsp.

33 www.djnewsletters@dowjones.com.

34 Hoovers Online.

35 http://biz.yahoo.com/ic/ind_index. html.

36 www.fda.gov/cder/reports/ reviewtimes/default.htm.

37 Stevenson, H., Von Werssowetz, R., and Kent, R. Ruth Owades. Harvard Business School Publishing Case 383051. 1982.

□ **CASE** **Jim Poss**

On his way through Logan Airport, Jim Poss stopped at a newsstand to flip through the June 2004 *National Geographic* cover story that declared, "The End of Cheap Oil." Inside was a two-page spread of an American family sitting amongst a vast array of household possessions that were derived, at least in part, from petroleum-based products: laptops, cell phones, clothing, footwear, sports equipment, cookware, and containers of all shapes and sizes. Without oil, the world will be a very different place. Jim shook his head.

> *. . . and here we are burning this finite, imported, irreplaceable resource to power three-ton suburban gas-guzzlers with "these colors don't run" bumper stickers!*

Jim's enterprise, Seahorse Power Company (SPC), was an engineering startup that encouraged the adoption of environmentally friendly methods of power generation by designing products that were cheaper and more efficient that twentieth-century technologies. Jim was sure that his first product, a patent-pending solar-powered trash compactor, could make a real difference.

> *In the United States alone, 180,000 garbage trucks consume over a billion gallons of diesel fuel a year. . .*

By compacting trash on-site and off-grid, the mailbox-sized "BigBelly" could cut pick-ups by 400%. The prototype—designed on the fly at a cost of $10,000—had been sold to Vail Ski Resorts in Colorado for $5,500. The green technology had been working as promised since February, saving the resort lots of time and money on round-trips to a remote lodge accessible only by snow machine.

Jim viewed the $4,500 loss on the sale as an extremely worthwhile marketing and proof-of-concept expense. Now that they were taking the business to the next level with a run of 20 machines, Jim and his SPC team had to find a way to reduce component costs and increase production efficiencies.

Jim returned the magazine to the rack and made his way to the New York Shuttle gate. An investor group in New York City had called another meeting, and Jim felt that it was time for him to start asking the hard questions about the deal they were proposing. These investors in socially responsible businesses had to be given a choice: either write him the check they had been promising—and let him run SPC the way he saw fit—or decline to invest altogether so he could concentrate on locating other sources of funding to close this $250,000 seed round. So far, all Jim had received from this group were voices of concern and requests for better terms—it was time to do the deal or move on.

Green Roots

As a kid, Jim Poss was always playing with motors, batteries, and electronics. He especially enjoyed fashioning new gadgets from components he had amassed by dismantling all

Carl Hedberg prepared this case under the supervision of Professor William Bygrave, Babson College, as a basis for class discussion rather than to illustrate either effective or ineffective handling of an administrative situation. Funding provided by the F.W. Olin Graduate School of Business and a gift from the class of 2003. Copyright © by Babson College 2004.

manner of appliances and electronic devices. He also spent a lot of time out of doors cross-country skiing with his father. Jim said that by his senior year in high school, he knew where he was headed:

I had read Silent Spring[1] *and that got me thinking about the damage we are doing to the earth. And once I started learning about the severity of our problems—that was it. By the end of my first semester at Duke University, I had taken enough environmental science to see that helping businesses to go green was going to be a huge growth industry.*

Jim felt that the best way to get businesses to invest in superior energy systems was to make it profitable for them to do so. In order to prepare himself for this path, Jim set up a double major in Environmental Science and Policy, and Geology—with a minor degree in engineering. He graduated in 1996 and found work as a hydrologist, analyzing soil and rock samples for a company that engineered stable parking lots for shopping malls. He didn't stay long:

That certainly wasn't my higher calling. I poked around, and within six months I found a fun job redesigning the production capabilities at a small electronics firm. Soon after that, I started working for this company called Solectria; that was right up my alley.

As a sales engineer at Solectria—a Massachusetts-based designer and manufacturer of sustainable transportation and energy solutions—Jim helped clients configure electric drive systems for a wide range of vehicles. He loved the work, and developed an expertise in using spreadsheets to calculate the most efficient layout of motors, controllers, power converters, and other hardware. By 1999, though, he decided that it was once again time to move on:

Solectria had a great group of people, but my boss was a micro-manager and I wasn't going to be able to grow. I found an interesting job in San Francisco as a production manager for a boat manufacturing company—coordinating the flow of parts from seven or eight subcontractors. When the [Internet] bubble burst, the boat company wasn't able to raise capital to expand. My work soon became relatively mundane, so I left.

This time, though, Jim decided to head back to school:

I had now worked for a bunch of different businesses and I had seen some things done well but a lot of things done wrong. I knew that I could run a good company—something in renewable energy, and maybe something with gadgets. I still had a lot to learn, so I applied to the MBA program at Babson College. I figured that I could use the second-year EIT[2] module to incubate something.

---

[1] *Silent Spring*, written in 1962 by Rachel Carson, exposed the hazards of the pesticide DDT, eloquently questioned humanity's faith in technological progress, and helped set the stage for the environmental movement. Appearing on a CBS documentary shortly before her death from breast cancer in 1964, the author remarked, "Man's attitude toward nature is today critically important simply because we have now acquired a fateful power to alter and destroy nature. But man is a part of nature, and his war against nature is inevitably a war against himself . . . [We are] challenged as mankind has never been challenged before to prove our maturity and our mastery, not of nature, but of ourselves."

[2] The Entrepreneurship Intensity Track (EIT) was a compressed and highly focused entrepreneurship curriculum for graduate students at Babson College. The program provided a select group of MBAs who intended to become full-time entrepreneurs as soon as they graduated with the necessary skills to take their new venture ideas through the critical stages of exploration, investigation, and refinement, so they could launch their businesses during the spring of their second year.

Opportunity Exploration

Between his first and second year at Babson, Jim applied for a summer internship through the Kauffman Program. He sent a proposal to the Spire Corporation—a publicly traded manufacturer of highly engineered solar electric equipment—about investigating the market and feasibility of solar-powered trash compactors. Jim had copied his idea to someone he knew on the board, and the same week that the HR department informed him that there were no openings, he got a call from the president of the company:

> *Roger Little had talked with the board member I knew and said that while they weren't interested in having me write a case study on some solar whatever-it-was, he said they'd like me to write some business plans for Spire—based on their existing opportunities and existing operations. I said sure, I'll take it.*

That summer, Jim worked with the executive team to complete three business plans. When they asked him to stay on, Jim agreed to work 15 hours per week—on top of his full-time MBA classes. He mentioned that every month or so he would bring up his idea for a solar-powered trash compactor with the Spire executives, but their answer was always the same:

> *I was trying to get them to invest in my idea or partner with me in some way, and these guys kept saying, "It'll never work." So I just kept working on them. I did the calculations to show them that with solar we could do ten compactions a day and have plenty [of electric charge] on reserve for a run of cloudy weather. Finally, they just said that they don't get into end-user applications.*

Early in his second year, Jim attended a product design fair featuring young engineers from Babson's new sister school, the Franklin W. Olin School of Engineering. He connected with Jeff Satwicz, an engineering student with extensive experience in remote vehicle testing for the Department of Defense. When Jim got involved with a project that required engineering capabilities, he knew who to call:

> *I went up the hill to Olin to ask Jeff if he'd like to help design a folding grill for tailgating—he said sure. It's funny, the two schools are always talking about working together like that, but it doesn't happen until the students sit in the Café together and exchange ideas. That's how it works; the faculty wasn't involved—and they didn't really need to be.*

Although Jim didn't stay with the grill team, the project had forged a link with an engineer with a penchant for entrepreneurship. Now certain of his trajectory, Jim incorporated the Seahorse Power Company (SPC)—a nod to his ultimate aspiration of developing power systems that could harness the enormous energy of ocean waves and currents.

Understanding that sea-powered generators were a long way off, Jim began to investigate ways to serve well-capitalized ventures that were developing alternative-energy solutions. One idea was to lease abandoned oil wells in California for the purpose of collecting and selling deep-well data to geothermal energy businesses that were prospecting in the area. When Jim sought feedback, he found that even people who liked his concept invariably pointed him in a different direction:

> *Everybody kept telling me that wind was where it's at—and they were right; it's the fastest growing energy source in the world. All the venture capitalists are looking at wind power. I realized, though, that if I was going to make wind plants, I'd have to raise two to five*

hundred million dollars—with no industry experience. Impossible. So instead, I started looking at what these [wind-plant ventures] needed.

The DAQ Buoy

Jim discovered that The Cape Wind Project, a company working to build a wind farm on Nantucket Sound, had erected a $2.5 million, 200-foot monitoring tower to collect wind and weather data in the targeted area. Jim felt that there was a better way:

Meteorological testing is a critical first step for these wind businesses. I thought, whoa, they've just spent a lot of money to construct a static tower that probably won't accurately portray the wind activity in that 25-square-mile area. And without good data, it's going to be really hard for them to get funding.

My idea was to deploy data buoys that could be moved around a site to capture a full range of data points. I spent about six months writing a business plan on my data acquisition buoy—the DAQ. I figured that to get to the prototype stage I'd need between $5 and $10 million. This would be a pretty sophisticated piece of equipment, and a lot of people worried that if a storm came up and did what storms typically do to buoys, we'd be all done. I was having a hard time getting much traction with investors.

Finding the Waste

Even while he was casting about for a big-concept opportunity, Jim had never lost sight of his solar compactor idea. With the spring semester upon him, he decided to see if that business would work as an EIT endeavor. Although he was sure that such a device would be feasible—even easy—to produce, he didn't start to get excited about the project until he took a closer look at the industry:

I did an independent study to examine the trash industry. I was about a week into that when I looked at the market size and realized that I had been messing around with expensive, sophisticated business models that didn't offer close to the payback as this compactor would.

U.S. companies spent $12 billion on trash receptacles in 2000, and $1.2 billion on compaction equipment in 2001. The average trash truck gets less than three miles to the gallon and costs over $100 an hour to operate. There are lots of off-grid sites [3] that have high trash volumes—resorts, amusement parks, and beaches—and many are getting multiple pick-ups a day. That's a tremendous waste of labor and energy resources.

Joining him in the EIT module was first-year MBA candidate, Alexander Perera. Alex had an undergraduate degree in Environmental Science from Boston University, as well as industry experience in renewable energy use and energy-efficiency measures. The pair reasoned that if a solar compactor could offer significant savings as a trash collection device, then the market could extend beyond the off-grid adopters to include retail and food establishments, city sidewalks, and hotels (see Exhibit 3.1).

---

[3] Sites without electrical power.

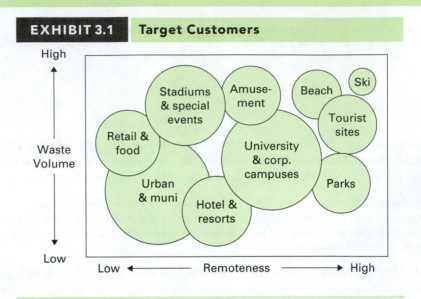

EXHIBIT 3.1 Target Customers

Gearing Up

By the time the spring semester drew to a close, they had a clear sense of the market and the nature of the opportunity—in addition to seed funding of $22,500: $10,000 from Jim's savings, and $12,500 through the Hatchery Program at Babson College. Since solar power was widely perceived as a more expensive, more complex, and less-efficient energy source than grid-power, it was not surprising to discover that the competition—dumpster and compaction equipment manufacturers—had never introduced a system like this. Nevertheless, Jim and Alex were certain that if they could devise a reliable, solar-powered compactor that could offer end users significant cost savings, established industry players could be counted on to aggressively seek to replicate or acquire that technology.

Understanding that patent protections were often only as good as the legal minds that drafted them, Jim had sought out the best. The challenge was that most of the talented patent attorneys he met with were far outside his meager budget. In May of 2003, Jim got a break when he presented his idea at an investor forum:

> I won $1,500 in patent services from Brown and Rudnick.[4] That might not have taken me too far, but they have a very entrepreneurial mindset. They gave me a flat rate for the patent—which is not something many firms will do. I paid the $7,800 upfront, we filed a provisional patent in June, and they agreed to work with me as I continued to develop and modify the machine.

Jim's efforts had again attracted the interest of Olin engineer Jeff Satwicz, who in turn brought in Bret Richmond, a fellow student with experience in product design, welding, and fabrication. When the team conducted some reverse-engineering to see if the vision was even feasible, Jim said they were pleasantly surprised:

> I found a couple of kitchen trash compactors in the Want Ads and bought them both for about 125 bucks. We took them apart, and that's when I realized how easy this was going to be . . . of course, nothing is ever as you think it's going to be.

---

[4] Brown Rudnick Berlack Israels, LLP, Boston, Massachusetts.

Pitching Without Product

Figuring that it was time to conduct some hard field research, they decided to call on businesses that would be the most likely early adopters of an off-grid compactor. Alex smiled as he described an unexpected turn of events:

> We had a pretty simple client-targeting formula: remoteness, trash volume, financial stability, and an appreciation for the environmental cachet that could come with a product like this. Literally the first place I called was the ski resort in Vail, Colorado. Some eco-terrorists had recently burned down one of their lodges to protest their expansion on the mountain, and they were also dealing with four environmental lawsuits related to some kind of noncompliance.
>
> This guy Luke Cartin at the resort just jumped at the solar compactor concept. He said, "Oh, this is cool. We have a lodge at Blue Sky Basin that is an hour and a half round trip on a snow cat. We pick up the trash out there three or four times a week; sometimes every day. We could really use a product like that . . ." That's when you put the phone to your chest and think, Oh my gosh . . .

Jim added that after a couple of conference calls, they were suddenly in business without a product:

> I explained that we were students and that we had not actually built one of these things yet (sort of). Luke asked me to work up a quote for three machines. They had been very open about their costs for trash pick-up, and I figured that they'd be willing to pay six grand apiece. I also had a rough idea that our cost of materials would fall somewhat less than that.
>
> Luke called back and said that they didn't have the budget for three, but they'd take one. I was actually really happy about that, because I knew by then that making just one of these was going to be a real challenge.

In September, SPC received a purchase order from Vail Ski Resorts. When Jim called the company to work out a payment plan with 25% upfront, Luke surprised them again:

> He said, 'We'll just send you a check for the full amount, minus shipping, and you get the machine here by Christmas.' That was great, but now we were in real trouble because we had to figure out how to build this thing quickly, from scratch—and on a tight budget.

Learning by Doing

The team set out to design the system and develop the engineering plans for the machine that SPC had now trademarked as the "BigBelly Solar-Powered Trash Compactor." Although his Olin team was not yet versant with computer-aided design (CAD) software, Jim saw that as an opportunity:

> These guys were doing engineering diagrams on paper with pens and pencils—but now we were going to need professional stuff. I said that we could all learn CAD together, and if they made mistakes, great, that's fine; we'd work through it.

Concurrent to this effort was the task of crunching the numbers to design a machine that would work as promised. As they began to source out the internal components, they searched for a design, fabrication, and manufacturing subcontractor that could produce the steel cabinet on a tight schedule. Although the team had explained that SPC would be overseeing the entire process from design to assembly, quotes for the first box still ranged from $80,000 to $400,000. Jim noted that SPC had an even bigger problem to deal with:

On top of the price, the lead times that they were giving me were not going to cut it; I had to get this thing to Colorado for the ski season!

So, we decided to build it ourselves. I went to a local fabricator trade show, and discovered that although they all have internal engineering groups, some were willing to take a loss on the research and development side in order to get the manufacturing contract.

We chose Boston Engineering since they are very interested in developing a relationship with Olin engineers. They gave me a hard quote of $2,400 for the engineering assistance, and $2,400 for the cabinet. By this time we had sourced all the components we needed, and we began working with their engineer to size everything up. Bob Treiber, the president, was great. He made us do the work ourselves out at his facility in Hudson (Massachusetts), but he also mentored us, and his firm did a ton of work pro bono.

Fulfillment and Feedback

As the Christmas season deadline came and went, the days grew longer. By late January 2004, Jim was working through both of the shifts they had set up: from four in the morning to nearly eleven at night. In February, they fired up the device, tested it for three hours, and shipped it off to Colorado (see Exhibit 3.2). Jim met the device at their shipping dock, helped unwrap it, met the staff, and put a few finishing touches on the machine. Although it worked, even at zero degree temperatures, it had never been tested in the field. Jim left after a few days, and for two weeks, he endured a deafening silence.

Jim wrestled with how he could check in with SPC's first customer without betraying his acute inventor's angst about whether the machine was still working, and if it was, what Vail thought about it. Finally, when he could stand it no longer, he placed the call under

EXHIBIT 3.2 **The BigBelly Arrives in Vail**

a.

b.

the guise of soliciting satisfied-customer feedback. The news from Vail nearly stopped his heart:

> They said that they had dropped the machine off a forklift and it fell on its face. Oh man, I thought; if it had fallen on its back, that would have been okay, but this was bad—real bad. And then Luke tells me that it was a bit scratched—but it worked fine. He told me how happy they were that we had made it so robust. When I asked how heavy the bags were that they were pulling out of the thing, he said, "I don't know; we haven't emptied it yet . . ." I was astounded.

As it turned out, the Vail crew discovered that the single collection bag was indeed too heavy—a two-bin system would be more user-friendly. The resort also suggested that the inside cart be on wheels, that the access door be in the back, and that there be some sort of wireless notification when the compactor was full.

As the SPC team got to work incorporating these ideas into their next generation of "SunPack" compactors, they were also engineering a second product that they hoped would expand their market reach to include manufactures of standard compaction dumpsters. The "SunPack Hippo" would be a solar generator designed to replace the 220-volt AC-power units that were used to run industrial compactors. The waste-hauling industry had estimated that among commercial customers that would benefit from compaction, between 5% and 20% were dissuaded from adopting such systems because of the set-up cost of electrical wiring. SPC planned to market the system through manufacturing and/or distribution partnerships.

Protecting the Property

While the interstate shipment of the BigBelly had given SPC a legal claim to the name and the technology, Jim made sure to keep his able patent attorneys apprised of new developments and modifications. SPC had applied for a provisional patent in June of 2003, and they had one year to broaden and strengthen those protections prior to the formal filing. As that date approached, the attorneys worked to craft a document that protected the inventors from infringement, without being so broad that it could be successfully challenged in court.

The SPC patents covered as many aspects of Sun Pack products as possible, including energy storage, battery charging, energy-draw cycle time, sensor controls, and wireless communication. The filling also specified other off-grid power sources for trash compaction, such as foot pedals, windmills, and waterwheels.

Even without these intellectual property protections, though, Jim felt that they had a good head start in an industry segment that SPC had created. Now they had to prove the business model.

The Next Generation

While the first machine had cost far more to build than the selling price, the unit had proven the concept and had been a conduit for useful feedback. A production run of 20 machines, however, would have to demonstrate that the business opportunity was as robust as the prototype appeared to be. That would mean cutting the cost of materials by more than 75% to around $2,500 per unit. SPC estimated that although the delivered price of $5,000 was far more expensive than the cost of a traditional trash receptacle, the system could pay for itself by trimming the ongoing cost of collection (see Exhibit 3.3).

The team had determined that developing a lease option for the BigBelly would alleviate new-buyer jitters by having SPC retain the risk of machine ownership—a move that could increase margins by 10%. Over the next five years SPC expected to expand its potential customer pool by reducing the selling price to around $3,000—along with a corresponding drop in materials costs (see Exhibit 3.4).

EXHIBIT 3.3   Customer Economics

Remote Locations (e.g., Ski Resorts)

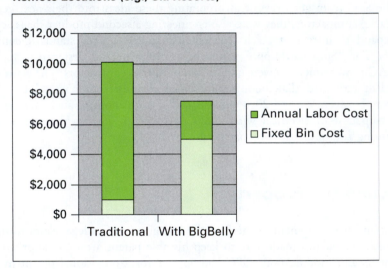

Urban Locations

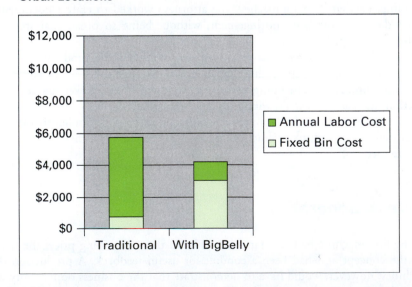

EXHIBIT 3.4   BigBelly Economics

Near Term

In Five Years

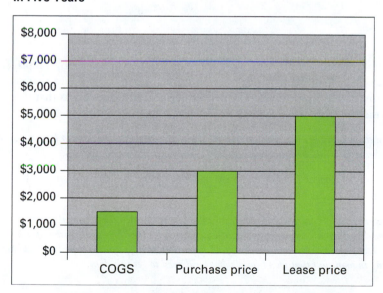

With steel prices escalating, the SPC team designed their new machines with 30% fewer steel parts. They also cut the size of the solar panel and the two-week battery storage capacity in half, and replaced the expensive screw system of compaction with a simpler, cheaper, and more efficient sprocket-and-chain mechanism (see Exhibit 3.5).

In order to offer an effective service response capability, the team tried to restrict their selling efforts to the New England area, although "a sale was a sale." One concern that kept cropping up was that this unique device would be a tempting target for vandals.

EXHIBIT 3.5   **BigBelly CAD Schematic**

a.   b.

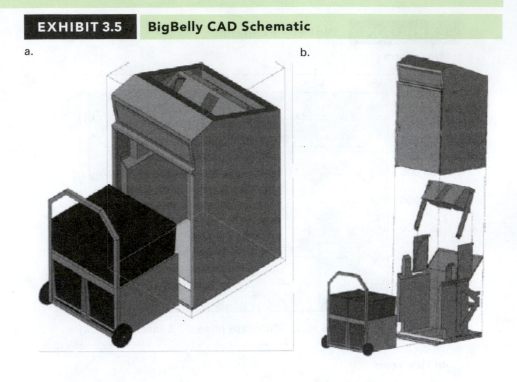

Team members explained that the solar panel on top was protected by a replaceable sheet of Lexan,[5] that all mechanical parts were entirely out of reach, and that the unit had already proven to be quite solid. The general feeling, Jim noted, was that if the machine could be messed with, people would find a way:

> One state park ranger was worried that it would get tossed into the lake, so I assured him that the units would be very heavy. He said, "So they'll sink really fast..."

Jim added that the overall response had been very favorable—so much so that once again, there was a real need for speed:

> We have pre-sold nearly half of our next run to places like Acadia National Park in Maine, Six Flags amusement park in Massachusetts, Harbor Lights in Boston, beaches on Nantucket, and to Harvard University. Fifty percent down-payment deposits should be coming in soon, but that won't cover what we'll need to get this done.

Projections and Funding

During this "early commercialization period," Jim was committed to moderating investor risk by leveraging on-campus and contractor facilities as much as possible. The company was hoping to close on an A-round of $250,000 with a pre-money valuation of $2.5 million by early summer to pay for cost-reduction engineering, sales and marketing, and working

---

[5] A clear, high-impact-strength plastic used in many security applications.

EXHIBIT 3.6	SPC Financial Projections				
	2004	**2005**	**2006**	**2007**	**2008**
BigBelly Unit Sales	50	300	1,200	3,600	9,000
BigBelly Revenues	$225,000	$1,200,000	$4,200,000	$10,800,000	$22,500,000
Hippo Royalty Revenues	0	120,000	525,000	1,620,000	3,937,500
Total Income	225,000	1,320,000	4,725,000	12,420,000	26,437,500
COGS	146,250	660,000	2,100,000	4,860,000	9,000,000
Gross Income	78,750	660,000	2,625,000	7,560,000	17,437,500
SG&A	400,000	1,600,000	2,600,000	5,000,000	11,000,000
EBIT	($321,250)	($940,000)	$25,000	$2,560,000	$6,437,500

EXHIBIT 3.7	Market Size and Penetration				
	2004	**2005**	**2006**	**2007**	**2008**
Top-Down					
SunPack Market* (Billion)	$1.0	$1.0	$1.0	$1.0	$1.0
SunPack % Penetration	0.0%	0.1%	0.5%	1.2%	2.6%
Bottom-UP					
Total Potential Customer**	30, 000	30,000	30,000	30,000	30,000
Potential units/customer	20	20	20	20	20
Total potential units	600,000	600,000	600,000	600,000	600,000
Cumulative units sold	50	350	1,550	5,150	14,150
Cumulative % penetration	0.0%	0.1%	0.3%	0.9%	2.4%

*Assume $600,000,000 BigBelly market (5% of $12 billion waste receptacles sold to target segments), plus a $400,000,000 power unit market ($1.2 billion compacting dumpsters sold/$12,000 average price x $4,000 per power unit).

**Assume 400 resorts, 600 amusement parks, 2,000 university campuses, 5,000 commercial campuses, 2,200 hotels, 4,000 municipalities, 57 national parks, 2,500 state parks and forests, 3,700 RV parks and campgrounds, and 17,000 fast-food and retail outlets.

capital. The following year the company expected to raise a B-round of between $700K and $1 million.

SPC was projecting a positive cash flow in 2006 on total revenues of just over $4.7 million (see Exhibit 3.6). The team felt that if their products continued to perform well, their market penetration estimates would be highly achievable (see Exhibit 3.7). Jim estimated that by 2008, SPC would become an attractive merger or acquisition candidate.

In January of 2004, as Jim began work on drafting an SBIR[6] grant proposal, his parents helped out by investing $12,500 in the venture. That same month, while attending a wind energy conference sponsored by Brown and Rudnick, Jim overheard an investor saying that he was interested in putting a recent entrepreneurial windfall to work in socially responsible ventures. Jim decided it was worth a try:

---

[6] The Small Business Innovation Research (SBIR) program was a source of government grant funding driven by ten federal departments and agencies that allocated a portion of their research and development capital for awards to innovative small businesses in the U.S.

I gave him my three-minute spiel on the compactor. He said that it sounded interesting, but that he was into wind power—after all; this was a wind-power conference. "Well then," I said, "have I got a business plan for you!"

That afternoon Jim sent the investor the most recent version of the data acquisition buoy business plan. That led to a three-hour meeting where the investor ended up explaining to Jim why the DAQ was such a good idea. Jim said that the investor also understood how difficult it would be to get the venture fully funded:

[The investor] said, "Well, I sure wish you were doing the Data Acquisition Buoy, but I can also see why you're not." I assured him that my passion was, of course, off-shore wind, and that it was something I was planning to do in the future. So he agreed to invest $12,500 in the compactor—but only because he wanted to keep his foot in the door for what SPC was going to do later on.

In February, after the folks at Vail had come back with their favorable review, Jim called on his former internship boss at the Spire Corporation. Roger Little was impressed with Jim's progress, and his company was in for $25,000. In April, the team earned top honors in the 2004 Douglas Foundation Graduate Business Plan Competition at Babson College. The prize—$20,000 cash plus $40,000 worth of services—came with a good deal of favorable press as well. The cash, which Jim distributed evenly among the team members, was their first monetary compensation since they had begun working on the project.

Although SPC could now begin to move ahead on the construction of the next 20 cabinets, Jim was still focused on the search for a rather uncommon breed of investor:

This is not a venture capital deal, and selling this idea to angels can be a challenge because many are not sophisticated enough to understand what we are doing. I had one group, for example, saying that this wouldn't work because most trash receptacles are located in alleys—out of the sun.

Here we have a practical, common-sense business, but since it is a new technology, many investors are unsure of how to value it. How scalable is it? Will our patent filings hold up? Who will fix them when they break?

Earlier that spring Jim had presented his case in Boston to a gathering of angels interested in socially responsible enterprises. Of the six presenters that day, SPC was the only one offering products that were designed to lower direct costs. During the networking session that followed, Jim said that one group in particular seemed eager to move ahead:

They liked that Spire had invested, and they seemed satisfied with our projections. When I told them that we had a $25,000 minimum, they said not to worry—they were interested in putting in $50K now, and $200 K later. In fact, they started talking about setting up funding milestones so that they could be our primary backers as we grew. They wanted me to stop fundraising, focus on the business, and depend on them for all my near-term financing needs.

At this point I felt like I needed to play hardball with these guys; show them where the line was. My answer was that I wasn't at all comfortable with that, and that I would be comfortable when I had $200 K in the bank—my bank. They backed off that idea, and by the end of the meeting, they agreed to put in the $50,000; but first they said they had to do some more due diligence.

Momentum

By May of 2004, the Seahorse Power Company had a total of six team members.[7] All SPC workers had been given an equity stake in exchange for their part-time services. The investor group expressed deep concern with this arrangement, saying that the team could walk away when the going got tough—and maybe right when SPC needed them most. Jim explained that it wasn't a negotiable point:

> They wanted my people to have "skin in the game" because they might get cold feet and choose to get regular jobs. I told them that SPC workers are putting in 20 hours a week for free when they could be out charging consulting rates of $200 an hour. They have plenty of skin in this game, and I'm not going to ask them for cash. Besides, if we could put up the cash, we wouldn't need investors, right?

As Jim settled into his seat for the flight to New York, he thought some more about the investors' other primary contention—his pre-money valuation was high by a million:

> These investors—who still haven't given us a dime—are saying they can give me as much early-stage capital as SPC would need, but at a pre-money of $1.5 million, and dependent on us hitting our milestones. With an immediate funding gap of about $50,000, it's tempting to move forward with these guys so we can fill current orders on time and maintain our momentum. On the other hand, I have already raised some money on the higher valuation, and maybe we can find the rest before the need becomes really critical.

Preparation Questions

1. Apply the Timmons entrepreneurship framework (entrepreneur-opportunity-resources) to analyze this case.
2. Discuss Jim Poss's fund raising strategies. What other options might be considered for raising the funds SPC needs? Is this a good investment?
3. Discuss the growth strategy. What additional market(s) should Poss pursue?

---

[7] Three of the most recent equity partners were Richard Kennelly, a former Director at Conservation Law Foundation where he concentrated on electric utility deregulation, renewable energy, energy efficiency, air quality, and global warming; Kevin Dutt, an M.B.A in Operations Management and Quantitative Methods from Boston University with extensive work experience in improving manufacturing and operational practices in a range of companies; and Steve Delaney, an MBA from The Tuck Schook at Dartmouth College with a successful track record in fundraising, business development, market strategy, finance, and operations.

JetBlue CEO David Neeleman passes out snacks to passengers. (*Source*: Landon Nordeman/Getty Images/News and Sports Services)

UNDERSTANDING YOUR BUSINESS MODEL AND DEVELOPING YOUR STRATEGY

Once you've identified your opportunity, the next step is to devise a strategy to execute that opportunity. While you're probably familiar with the basic strategy categories from previous coursework—differentiation, low cost, niche—many would-be entrepreneurs fail to grasp the intricacies of devising and implementing their strategy. All strategies are driven by the company's business model. So before you state that your firm is going to pursue a differentiation strategy or a niche strategy, first you need to understand exactly what your business model is.

This chapter written by Andrew Zacharakis.

The Business Model

Every firm's business model consists of two components: a revenue model and a cost model. The **revenue model** breaks down all the sources of revenue that your business will generate. For instance, if you own a restaurant, your basic revenue model would separate food and beverage into two main sources of revenue. You may take that further and break down the revenue model by meals (breakfast, lunch, and dinner), categories of food (Italian, American, etc.) or even food item (pizzas, hamburgers, etc.). The more detailed your categories, the more information you can glean about how certain aspects of your business are performing.

The **cost model** identifies how you are spending your resources to make money. It includes your costs of goods sold (COGS) and your operating expenses. Basically, the business model is represented by your company's income statement. Understanding the business model enables entrepreneurs to make decisions that lead to greater revenue for lower costs.

The Revenue Model

All businesses must generate revenue if they are to survive. Even nonprofit organizations need revenue, whether from donations or a combination of donations, government grants, and income generated from sales of a product or service. Without this revenue nonprofits would be unable to achieve their missions. Breaking down the revenue sources into categories helps an entrepreneur understand how the firm can increase each.

Different revenue categories often require variations on the firm's central strategy to achieve the highest possible outcomes. For instance, Amazon.com's revenue model consists of a number of categories according to the products it sells online. On its Web site customers can find everything from books and music to toys, computers, and electronics. In addition, the company breaks out sales by geographic region (see Figure 4.1). Amazon's strategy is to become the Wal-Mart of the Web, moving well beyond marketing books to selling items in a diverse array of product categories.[1] While Amazon markets its site heavily, spending close to $200 million annually to draw customers to it, Amazon varies its strategy based on the product categories. For example, Amazon initially touted itself as "The Earth's Biggest Bookstore," which meant it had to carry (or have access to) more titles than its competitors. For toys, on the other hand, it outsourced marketing and fulfillment to Toys "R" Us. The agreement gave Toys "R" Us access to Amazon's order fulfillment system and gave Amazon a wider selection of products. In this category, Amazon was merely a portal for another company to sell its goods, although the co-branding strategy drew more people to the site and increased revenues for both firms. However, co-branding can bring difficulties. Amazon and Toys "R" Us have been unhappy with each other. In the spring of 2006 the relationship was dissolved, and it now appears that Toys "R" Us will launch its own branded site to compete against Amazon.[2]

Different revenue categories for a firm are influenced by "drivers" that are directly correlated with the level of revenues the company earns. Using Amazon again, we see that the number of customers buying products from the site has the greatest influence on the revenues generated. Digging deeper, we find that other drivers influence revenue as well. For instance, it isn't just how many customers buy, but how much they spend per purchase and how often they buy (once a year, six times a year, etc.). The picture is still incomplete, because not every person who visits Amazon will buy. Some people visit Amazon to comparison shop, while others use it to research books on a particular topic, which they then borrow from the local library. Thus, other revenue drivers include the percentage of visitors to the site who make a purchase, as well as the number of times those customers will visit before actually completing a transaction.

	2001	2002	2003	2004	2005
Total Revenue	**$3,122,433**	**$3,932,936**	**$5,263,699**	**$6,921,124**	**$8,489,923**
Media	2,455,628	3,098,614	4,048,948	5,102,349	5,931,000
Electronics	593,658	746,918	1,103,125	1,686,244	2,329,000
Other	73,147	87,404	111,626	132,531	229,923
North America	**2,460,366**	**2,761,457**	**3,258,413**	**3,847,344**	**4,711,000**
Media	1,810,175	1,994,949	2,269,472	2,589,438	3,045,000
Electronics	577,524	681,041	878,519	1,127,754	1,444,000
Other	72,637	85,467	110,422	130,152	222,000
International	**662,097**	**1,171,479**	**2,005,286**	**3,073,780**	**3,778,923**
Media	645,453	1,103,665	1,779,476	2,512,911	2,886,000
Electronics	16,134	65,877	224,606	558,490	885,000
Other	510	1,937	1,204	2,379	7,923
Cost of Revenue	**2,323,875**	**2,940,318**	**4,006,531**	**5,319,127**	**6,451,923**
North America	1,803,107	2,020,473	2,391,749	2,823,792	3,444,000
International	520,768	919,845	1,614,782	2,495,335	3,007,923
Gross Profit	**$798,558**	**$992,618**	**$1,257,168**	**$1,601,997**	**$2,038,000**
Operating Expenses					
Marketing	138,481	125,383	122,787	158,022	193,000
Fulfillment	374,052	392,467	477,032	590,397	727,000
Technology and content	241,165	215,617	207,809	251,195	406,000
General and administrative	89,862	79,049	88,302	112,220	153,000
Total stock compensation exp	4,637	68,927	87,751	57,702	87,000
Total Operating Expenses	**$848,197**	**$881,443**	**$983,681**	**$1,169,536**	**$1,566,000**
Operating Income	**($49,639)**	**$111,175**	**$273,487**	**$432,461**	**$472,000**

Source: Morgan Stanley Research
U.S. $ in thousands

■ **Figure 4.1**

Amazon.com's business model

While consumer awareness of the Amazon brand influences all the drivers, Amazon can pursue any number of tactics to move the drivers in its favor. For example, advertising enhances Amazon's overall brand image. In addition, Amazon uses tactics such as bundling to increase the average order size (if you buy this book, we will offer this one at a discount). Many other tactics, such as co-branding with Toys "R" Us and offering affiliates a percentage of sales for referrals, help to increase the number of visits to the site as well as the number of times a year that people visit. All these drivers influence the revenues that Amazon achieves. Entrepreneurs can formulate strategies to achieve their goals if they understand the central drivers and how they can influence them. If you don't fully understand your revenue drivers, you won't achieve the highest success.

The Cost Model

Typically, a firm needs to spend money to influence the revenue drivers. Thus, entrepreneurs also need to understand the cost model, which includes two primary categories: COGS (costs of goods sold) and operating costs. Referring to Figure 4.1, we can identify the cost model for Amazon. COGS represent those costs directly associated with the revenue source. For a product company, COGS generally include the raw materials and direct labor needed to make the product. For a retailer like Amazon, COGS are the costs of purchasing the products from various manufacturers that Amazon then sells.[3]

Some products have very small COGS. For example, software is very cheap to produce after it has been developed. COGS may include only the cost of buying and burning a CD, packaging it, and shipping it to a retailer or customer.[4] The COGS may be even lower if the software can be downloaded from the Web. For service firms, COGS is mostly composed of the direct labor in delivering the service. For instance, at a consulting firm the COGS would be the salary costs of the consultants working on the project, and at a tutoring company the COGS would be the hourly wages paid to the tutors for every hour worked.

As with revenues, we categorize COGS by product categories. For Amazon, strong control would suggest that it break out COGS for books, toys, and so on and directly tie those COGS to the revenue generated by each product category. However, in its publicly available financials Amazon only breaks out COGS by geographic region. We suspect its internal reporting is more detailed, but since business is highly competitive companies usually reveal as little detail as they can in public reports. Those internal details help entrepreneurs understand which products have strong gross margins and which products don't.

By understanding how sales drive COGS, entrepreneurs can achieve higher margins as well as increase revenues. For example, many firms now outsource production to more efficient producers in order to increase gross margins. P'kolino, a playroom furniture company founded by Antonio Turco-Rivas and JB Schneider, has been investigating manufacturing companies in different countries from the United States to Brazil and China. Moving production offshore can greatly reduce the manufacturing costs and thereby increase gross margins, but there may be other tradeoffs to consider. To start, what other costs will P'kolino incur from outsourcing? Transportation costs will be much higher from China and travel costs will increase as P'kolino founders periodically visit the production sites to monitor quality and manage relationships. Do the savings from less expensive overseas manufacturing offset these increased transportation and travel costs? The answer is usually yes, given the high cost of manufacturing in the United States, but there are yet more factors to consider. Lead times for overseas outsourcing will have to be higher. If P'kolino is slow in moving its designs to the manufacturer, it may miss the critical holiday selling season. If the company has some proprietary components, outsourcing may cause manufacturing details to leak and seriously damage the firm's competitive advantage.

Along with influencing gross margins, outsourcing can powerfully reduce the upfront fixed costs the firm would incur if it produced its products itself. New ventures require more time to break even due to high upfront fixed costs. Outsourcing production means the firm is moving from fixed expenses to variable expenses, because it is paying the subcontractor based on the number of units it produces. In May 2003, the founders of startup Keen Footwear decided to use subcontractors in China to make the company's line of shoes and sandals. Within two months the Chinese subcontractor began production, and Keen sold 700,000 pairs of shoes for revenues of $30 million in 2004.[5] Designers at Kidrobot use Adobe Illustrator to design their toys. Once completed, the plans are sent to China where workers build prototypes. The designers then hone the prototypes and send the models back to China for production. As a result, Kidrobot can turn around a new toy in four months, as opposed to the industry average of one year for larger toymakers. The 11-member firm was expected to achieve revenues of $5.5 million in 2005.[6] Avoiding the huge upfront costs of building a factory decreases the time to break even. But as we noted earlier, firms do not want to outsource their competitive advantage. Outsourcing production rarely jeopardizes firms' competitive advantage, because their advantage usually isn't in the production process. Nonetheless, entrepreneurs must remain careful.

Operating costs provide the other main component of the cost model. Referring to Figure 4.1, we find that Amazon incurs large marketing expenses (12% of operating costs in 2005) to ensure that its brand continues to be at the forefront of consumers' minds. Rapid delivery is also important for the company's strategy. Fulfillment costs accounted for 46% of operating costs in 2005. By examining Amazon's cost model, we get a sense of the key elements of its strategy: brand recognition through marketing, world class Web technologies and content (ensuring that customers have a pleasant experience when they visit the site), and quick delivery through high-tech fulfillment operations.

To create a viable business model, Amazon must develop and sustain clear competitive advantages. For instance, the company spends a considerable amount of money marketing the brand. This is essential for an Internet company that has little or no brick-and-mortar-retail presence. In addition, we see that the company's cost of sales is 76% of revenues, which suggests that Amazon is pursuing a high-volume, low-cost strategy. This is related to the high marketing costs already mentioned, because generating high volume takes significant marketing and advertising investments.

We also see that Amazon's competitive advantage stems from keeping an enormous selection of products available at competitive prices. At the time of Amazon's founding, the average book superstore carried 150,000 titles in stock. Amazon started with one million titles. Again, the strategies are interdependent. By having a far greater selection than local stores, the company increases the likelihood of customer purchases, and also increases the chances that a customer purchasing a unique title will purchase another book he or she has been meaning to buy. This availability strategy enables Amazon to meet the needs of customers who want their purchases quickly, but it leads to high inventory and fulfillment expenses. All these expenses lead to lower net income margins, but this is offset in turn by high volumes. Consider Wal-Mart—it may average net margins in the low single digits, but when it is achieving those margins on *hundreds of billions* of dollars in revenue, the end result is billions of dollars of profit. Amazon is pursuing a similar strategy, and it is an expensive one. The company needed significant upfront capital while establishing itself. Prior to going public in May 1997, Amazon raised 10.6 million from private equity sources. Although it raised $54 million in public offerings, the company didn't become profitable until 2003.[7]

Once entrepreneurs understand their basic business model, they can build a strategy to compete and win in the marketplace. The strategy and business model are interrelated: Entrepreneurs can have a broad sense of what overall strategy they want to pursue, but until they have a full understanding of their business model it is difficult to move on to tactics to implement that strategy.

The First-Mover Myth

Beware entrepreneurs who claim they have a "first-mover's advantage." This claim is part and parcel of the "we don't have any competition" claim discussed in the previous chapter. Most entrepreneurs who make these claims don't truly understand the nature of their business and what a first-mover's advantage really is. Elizabeth Preis, founder of Beautiful Legs by Post (BLBP), a mail-order firm that delivered quality panty hose to professional women in the U.K., claimed that her firm had a first-mover advantage because no other specialty mail catalog had yet tapped into this market.[8] Preis said she would capture these women before other firms had the chance to enter. This would create loyalty to BLBP, she claimed, that would not only ensure her company would beat the competition, but also dissuade potential competitors from entering the market. Let's ignore the fact that "other specialty mail catalogs" is an overly narrow definition of her competition and focus instead on how Preis intended to execute this "first-mover advantage." Her three-year pro-forma financials show that she expected to capture 1.17% of her target market of up-scale professional women. Such low penetration over three years isn't necessarily bad, but clearly it is not a first-mover's advantage. At that level, BLBP wouldn't preempt competition from entering; there are too many women who haven't bought from, let alone heard of, BLBP to have any sense of loyalty or switching costs.

This example illustrates several key aspects about capturing a first mover's advantage.

- You have to be first (or very early) into the market.
- You need to capture a large percentage of the market quickly (which means fast growth).
- You need to create switching costs so the customer will stick with you (even in today's Internet world where searching for competing brands is easy and low cost).

Gaining a first-mover's advantage isn't impossible, but it is very difficult and expensive. For instance, it is fair to say that Amazon successfully executed a first-mover's advantage, although technically it wasn't the first online bookseller. Amazon went from a startup company out of Seattle in July 1995 to a global firm with sales of $8.49 billion in 2005. It introduced Internet retailing to many customers and educated them on the benefits. But even with that first-mover advantage, other firms came into the marketplace and have succeeded. For instance, barnesandnoble.com seems to be doing well. For all goods sold online, Amazon had the largest market share at 2.8%, and barnesandnoble.com had the fourth largest at 0.4%. While Amazon expanded into selling other goods, barnesandnoble.com, the book retailer's independent Web site, had stayed with selling books and other media. Its revenues were $424.8 million in 2004. As the following callout box illustrates, eBay is another example of a successfully executed first-mover's advantage. You'll notice that eBay sustains its position with an active acquisition strategy.

Executing a First-Mover Advantage at eBay

Since its inception, eBay focused on viral marketing (any advertising that encourages or facilitates people to pass along a marketing message, such as when people use free e-mail that tags the e-mail company's name in every message sent) rather than a large advertising budget to build its network of users. With this strategy, eBay has created a largely organically grown, self-policing, and self-regulating market, for which it receives a cut of every transaction. It started in 1995 and raised $6.55 million in venture capital before raising $63 million in its 1998 initial public offering. Given that size is one of eBay's key advantages, the company has decided to expand its global presence, buying local upstarts in the process rather than adding services.

As of 2006, eBay commands 90% of the online auction market. Its revenues have grown from $32 million in 1996 to $224 million in 1999 to $700 million in 2002 to more than $1.7 billion in 2005. In September 2005, eBay announced that it would purchase the voice-over-Internet company Skype for $2.6 billion. eBay president and CEO Meg Whitman cited Skype's growing network of users, leadership position, and competitive advantage as reasons for the acquisition.

"eBay, PayPal, and Skype are the leading brands for three of the most important areas on the net: e-commerce, online payment, and voice communications," Whitman said. "By combining Skype with eBay and PayPal, we can create an unparalleled e-commerce and communications engine for buyers and sellers around the world."[9]

A first-mover's advantage is expensive because firms have to quickly capture a large part of the available market. As we have discussed, Amazon and eBay both raised over $60 million to execute their first-mover strategies. That money was used to build organizational infrastructure and reach new customers. At the time of Amazon's initial public offering, company officials said, "Amazon will invest heavily in promotion and marketing, site development, and technology and operating infrastructure development. In addition, Amazon intends to offer attractive discounts that will reduce its already slim gross margins."[10] The company's formula for success depended on its ability to extend its brand position, provide customers with outstanding value and a superior shopping experience, and achieve sufficient sales volume to realize economies of scale.

The stage of the marketplace also contributes to the high costs of a first-mover's advantage. Referring back the industry S-curve in Figure 3.6, you'll see that a new market emerges slowly. Rather than investing marketing dollars to educate customers on why their product is better, in a new market companies find themselves educating customers on why they need the product in the first place. This can take a lot of time and money, and it is a unique challenge of emerging markets.

There is an added danger to being a first mover: you may get it wrong. The history of business is littered with first movers supplanted by offerings that better met the customer's needs. Figure 4.2 lists some first movers and the firms that eventually gained dominance in those markets.

Figure 4.2 and the success of Amazon and eBay tell us that being first does not by itself lead to success. For a first mover, a winning strategy is complemented by other components that lead to a sustainable, bundled competitive advantage. In Amazon's case, its heavy bet on brand awareness led firms such as Toys "R" Us to partner with it, further enhancing the brand. Amazon has coupled this strategy with a rapid fulfillment infrastructure that allows the company to gain a cost advantage on efficiently delivering products to customers on a timely basis. In contrast, eBay's success combined being first to the market with installing a strong seller base. All the mini-stores on eBay use the platform because of its ubiquitous name. These sellers know that they will have strong customer traffic because of the eBay brand. Even if a more attractive technology is introduced, it will be difficult to get buyers and sellers to switch to that platform.

Considering the high costs, it is nearly impossible to achieve a first-mover advantage without significant outside financing, most often venture capital financing. Fewer than 0.1% of all firms receive venture capital. Since most firms aren't attractive to VCs or other large sources of capital, the first-mover advantage is often too expensive a strategy to pursue. Relax. As we have tried to illustrate, the first-mover's advantage often fails anyway. Most successful firms win not because of some inherent, large competitive advantage; instead, they win because they execute better than the competition. These firms are flexible and adapt to the customer so that they continue to add value long after the initial launch.

Industry	First Mover	Current Leader
Online stock trading	K. Aufhauser	Charles Schwab[11]
Presentation software	Harvard Graphics	PowerPoint[12]
Personal digital assistants	Amstrad PenPad/Apple Newton	Palm Pilot[13]
Free e-mail	Juno	Hotmail/Yahoo
Automatic teller machines	Docutel	Diebold[14]
Online bookseller	Book Stacks Unlimited[15]	Amazon.com
Diet soda	Royal Crown	Coca-Cola[16]

Figure 4.2

Supplanting the first mover advantage

Winning is more about implementation of your strategy than about formulating some grand strategy that nobody has ever thought of before. Don't get us wrong—you absolutely need a well-thought-out strategy—but in the end execution of that strategy will determine your success or failure.

Formulating a Winning Strategy

Winning strategies include some combination of the following attributes: better, cheaper, and faster. Your business needs to create some value for which people are willing to pay. P'kolino, the children's playroom furniture company mentioned earlier, is pursuing customers with better design. The company expects parents and grandparents to pay more for a unique product that encourages creative play. Ferrate Solutions, a company that has developed a new process to create a water-treatment compound, expects municipalities to buy its products because they treat water faster and cheaper than existing treatment methods. That advantage, combined with a well-established process, should help the company gain market share.

We would expect to see their competitive advantages reflected in the business models of both these firms. P'kolino should achieve high gross margins because parents—and more specifically, financially well-off parents—are willing to pay a premium for well-designed children's furniture. Its margins may be offset somewhat by the distribution channels the firm uses. If, for example, it uses Pottery Barn, the prestigious and powerful retailer may appropriate more of those gross margins. While P'kolino might be able to retain stronger gross margins by selling directly to parents, it would incur higher operating costs such as marketing and fulfillment infrastructure costs. Entrepreneurs can capture the tradeoffs between different approaches by examining their relative impacts on the net income margin. Ferrate, on the other hand, produces its compound at a very low cost. Even though it sells the compound cheaper than the competing bundle of chemicals, it still earns higher margins due to its lower cost of production. Just like P'kolino, however, Ferrate will likely need strong distribution partners and may have to relinquish a large portion of its gross margins to gain access to sales channels.

We can summarize P'kolino's competitive advantage as better designs and Ferrate's as a patent-protected production process. Other companies may have a branding advantage or just execute better than the competition. Whatever the company's competitive advantages, it needs to take steps to protect them. There are numerous paths for doing so. If you have a unique product that includes significant intellectual property, you may file for patent protection or choose to maintain trade secrets. Ferrate, for example, has patents on its process for producing the ferrate compound. (Chapter 13 covers intellectual property issues in greater detail.)

The People Are What Matters

Students often think that their company needs to have an explicit, identifiable, and patentable competitive advantage. However, more often than not, your competitive advantage will be complemented by the tacit knowledge held by the people within your company. Southwest Airlines, for example, is the most profitable airline partially due to its direct route strategy (rather than the hub-and-spoke system of the old-line airlines). Southwest employees also work more efficiently than their counterparts at traditional airlines. Existing airlines have tried and failed to imitate their friendly customer interactions and motivation to get airplanes quickly serviced and back into the air. In other words, Southwest's competitive advantage is inherent in the tacit knowledge of its employees. The most difficult aspects of a firm's strategy to imitate are the people and the execution of the strategy. From the very beginning of your company's life, you need to create a culture that is conducive to fostering the human elements of your business.

Probably the most important thing founders do is to create the organization's culture. While the original culture will evolve, companies tend to be replications of what they were in the past, so it is critical that you get the culture right at the beginning. You need to create an atmosphere that encourages people to bond to the company. Yes, your people believe in the mission; yes, they believe in the product; but more importantly, your team needs to believe in each other and want to continue to be part of the organization. Let's break building and maintaining a culture into three main categories: values, selection, and structure.

Values. As the founder, you need to identify what values you want to drive your organization. Values are beliefs shared by all members. For example, JetBlue based its organization building on five core values:[17]

- Safety
- Caring
- Integrity
- Fun
- Passion

Values communicate what kind of work environment founders want to create and what guidelines they use in hiring future employees. For JetBlue, safety is a central value, and without question this is a critical value for the airline industry. The other values communicate that JetBlue treats its employees the way it expects its employees to treat the customers. The values put into place at the company's founding will flow through to formulating and implementing the strategy. More importantly, values create the foundation on which your company will grow.

Selection. It's important to hire the right person the first time. Communicating the values you've identified to new team members goes a long way to making sure there is a fit between the employee and the company. Every new person added to the company will reinforce the values you've put in place, thereby helping to sustain the company's culture. JetBlue focuses on its five core values when interviewing job candidates and structures its interview questions around these values.[18] Canadian entrepreneur Peter Armstrong earned success with his first business, Spotlight Tours, by focusing on customer relationships. In order to build those relationships with customers, he hired graduating theater students as tour directors. He pursued the same strategy after buying the failing Rocky Mountaineer tours from VIA Rail and turned it into Canada's first profitable passenger rail line in 40 years by pursuing the luxury vacation market at a premium fare.[19]

Structure. The structure of a new venture changes as it matures. Early on, it is very informal as the founders and a few early hires do a wide variety of tasks. There are a couple of things to keep in mind as you build your early organization. First, you need to hire people who can "wear many hats," who can work on a prototype, contact vendors, create budgets, and talk to customers as the need arises. It can often be a mistake to hire a corporate lifer who is used to working in one functional area and having expensive administrative support. Such employees, while talented, may not operate well in the informal startup environment.

Second, as team-building expert Elizabeth Riley[20] says: "over-hire." That is, find team members and early-stage employees who are overqualified for the tasks they will initially be doing. While you might save some money by hiring someone else with fewer skills, as a young and resource-constrained new venture, you won't have the time and money to help that person learn on the job.

Finally, you need to create a flexible organizational structure. While you may have an organizational chart, reporting and communications need to be free to flow throughout the organization. That means that any employee during this startup phase can freely talk to any other. This loose structure facilitates learning about your business model, about processes that do and don't work, about customers needs, and so forth. It fosters and promotes flexibility. The universal truth about strategy formulation and business planning as a whole is that it needs to change and adjust during implementation based on your customers' reactions. If you build a flexible organization, you will be in a better position to adjust your strategy. As the organization matures, the structure will necessarily become more formalized. While it is easy to be informal with 5, 10, or even 20 employees, it is inefficient when you have 150.

In sum, an organization's culture starts at its founding and determines your strategy—and ultimately your success—for the life of the organization. Take time to think about what kind of culture you want, and create a plan to make sure it is implemented.

Entry Strategy

Successful launches are iterative. Southwest Airlines didn't start with a nationwide route plan, but instead serviced routes between Dallas, Houston, and San Antonio. After this initial market test in Texas, the company adjusted its processes, improved upon its customer interactions, and then added more routes. Over time the carrier has continued to add routes and today flies to 60 cities nationwide. Since its inception, Southwest has flown one type of airplane—the Boeing 737—which helps streamline its operation. In addition, the company has focused on using less congested airports and flying point-to-point, rather than using the hub-and-spoke system of traditional airlines. Each new route proved the Southwest business model and created an opportunity to reevaluate and improve the product. Raising millions in advance of a national route structure and then launching nationwide from day one would have surely led to failure for Southwest, considering the high startup costs of creating an airline. By advancing step by step, the company learned a lot of lessons that it otherwise would have missed. Likewise, you should devise an entry strategy for your firm that allows you to test your concept in the market at a relatively low cost.

Benchmarking. Before you raise a dime of outside capital, first learn from others. Benchmark competitors and learn "best practices" from firms that operate inside and outside your industry of interest. Create a simple matrix that identifies the firm, its strategy, core customers, sources of competitive advantage, basic revenue model (including margins), major cost categories, and any other elements that you think might be useful. JetBlue followed much of Southwest's formula during its startup phase. Its founder and CEO, David Neeleman, worked for six months as an executive vice president at Southwest Airlines before he was fired. At JetBlue, Neeleman places a high priority on a cooperative company culture and hiring the right people to fit that model. Until recently, JetBlue flew only one type of jet. The flight attendants help clean up the plane for quicker turnarounds at the gate, and Neeleman, when flying, will lend a hand with these chores.[21]

Figure 4.3 compares JetBlue during its launch phase to some of its competition. It highlights a gap in the marketplace where JetBlue could enter (geographic opening for a low-cost carrier out of New York), as well as the ways different firms are competing. You can see that a low-cost, point-to-point system focusing on leisure travel makes sense, and it appears that JetBlue should pursue this strategy. Gathering this initial information puts you in the position to do an initial, ideally low-cost, market test.

	JetBlue	Southwest	UAL	AA	FedEx
Strategy	Low cost	Low cost	Geographic coverage (national and international)	Geographic coverage	International, overnight package delivery
Core Customer	Leisure traveler	Leisure traveler	Business and leisure	Business and leisure	Business
Competitive Advantage	Cost structure (non-union, no hubs, smaller airports)	Cost structure (no hubs, smaller airports)	Size of fleet, geographic coverage	Size of fleet, geographic coverage	Size of fleet, geographic coverage, entry barriers
Revenue Model	Airfare, freight	Airfare, freight	Airfare, freight	Airfare, freight	Package
Cost Model	Labor, fuel, aircraft, landing fees, and infrastructure	Same	Same plus higher costs associated with "hub" system	Same plus higher costs associated with "hub" system	Same plus higher costs associated with "hub" system
Other	Investment in IT, customer focus, employee focus, hands-on CEO	Standardized aircraft, customer and employee focus, hands-on CEO			Investment in IT, employee focus, hands-on CEO

■ **Figure 4.3**

Benchmarking comparison for JetBlue

We included FedEx in the matrix because entrepreneurs should look outside their immediate industry and identify "best practice" companies there. From FedEx, JetBlue can learn the power of a state-of-the-art information technology infrastructure, as well as lessons on creating an effective corporate culture.

Initial Market Test. You can devise your initial market test once you have a strong understanding of the competition. For JetBlue, the initial market test entailed operating one route and then expanding routes based upon what it had learned. If you are planning to open a restaurant and believe you will compete based on unique recipes and cuisine, preparing your menu for family and friends would be a simple, low-cost test. Do they like the food? What other items might they like to see on the menu? Note that you can do this test without spending any money on an actual location. Next, you might see about catering one or two events. Here, you can test whether people will pay for your cuisine and further refine your menu. The next step might be to offer your food on a mall cart that sells smaller items in common areas at shopping malls. Are people drawn to your cart? Do they buy? This test helps you determine location. What kind of traffic patterns does the business need? Which demographic group is most drawn to the cuisine? Based upon your learning during this market test, you might be ready to open your first restaurant. Figure 4.4 illustrates a market test schedule. Developing this schedule not only guides your learning, but helps you understand when, how, and how much it will cost to achieve the next milestone.

The concept of escalating market tests is powerful. While you can visualize and plan for your business in great detail over a long period of time, you never truly learn whether it is a viable business until you make a sale. Too many entrepreneurs make the mistake of spending $1 million or more to open up that first restaurant only to find that customers

Market Test	What You Expect to Learn	Timing
Prepare dinner for family and friends	Do they like the menu? What else would they add? When would they eat this food? How often?	2–3 events over the next month.
Try to sell a catering event	Can you actually sell the concept? Can you prepare larger quantities in an efficient manner? How does preparing large quantities impact taste?	1–2 events one month after the initial test.
Rent a mall cart	What kind of people (demographics) are attracted to your concept? When do they buy (lunch, dinner)? How much do they buy? How often do they buy? What kind of traffic patterns seem to be most conducive to the business?	Operate for 1–2 months. Do this by month 3 of business.
Open first restaurant	What preparation processes are most effective? What kind of staffing do you need? What hours of operation capture the largest percentage of customers?	6 months after launch.
Open second restaurant	Can the processes be replicated? Do the same types of customers come into this location? What attributes seem to define the best location?	Open 1 year after first restaurant.
Open restaurants 3–5	Can you replicate processes? What processes need to be established at the central level to oversee all the restaurants?	Open in years 2–5.
Franchise the concept	Are potential franchisees interested in your concept? Are your processes sound so that a franchisee can replicate your company-owned restaurants?	Franchise in years 5–8.

■ **Figure 4.4**

Market test schedule

don't like the basic concept. Adapting your concept at that point is more costly than it would have been if you had completed some earlier market tests. If you adapt your menu and cuisine at every step in Figure 4.4, you'll be much closer to a winning concept when you open your first restaurant.

It is important to remember that successful new venture creation is an iterative process. Regardless of how large your company grows, you will continually adapt your business based on what you learn at each market test. At a company like Microsoft, for instance, new software products go through an alpha test, during which the company uses the software internally. After the software is debugged, it goes to a beta site. In beta, a handful of customers use the product and report back problems as well as additional functions that they would like to see. Based upon the feedback, the company might continue with more beta tests. Once they feel that the product is close to their goal, managers release it to the larger market. As any company that has been through a product recall can attest, prematurely releasing a product is an incredibly expensive proposition. The costs include the possibility of having to distribute replacements for defective units, the opportunity costs of disgruntled customers who choose not to buy from you again, and the broader costs of damage to your reputation in the market as customers spread the word that your product is inferior. A controlled launch plan will help you manage the process and avoid these potentially debilitating costs.

Creating a Platform. Figure 4.4 shows the concept of creating a platform on which to grow your business. Opening the first restaurant is the platform, whereas opening successive restaurants is a growth strategy. For many entrepreneurs opening one restaurant may be the end goal, but others will have larger aspirations. Joey Crugnale, replicating the earlier successes he had with Steve's Ice Cream and Bertucci's, now has opened seven Naked Fish restaurants. Frank Day's restaurant empire includes 89 outlets of Old Chicago, Jose Muldoons, and the Rock Bottom Brewery among others. Both Crugnale and Day are role models for creating hugely successful businesses. They "got into the game" by opening one restaurant which they used for experience and learning. Crugnale started at age 23 with a single ice cream shop and bought a competitor a few years later in 1976. That shop drew a number of customers, piquing interest in some nearby restaurant space that lay vacant. Crugnale didn't want other restaurateurs feeding off his business, so he leased the space and started a pizza parlor named Bertucci's. Frank Day, in order to differentiate his Old Chicago in Boulder, Colorado, began offering a selection of 110 beers. As he expanded the chain to new locations, Day allowed the restaurants to reflect their local communities and focused on the ambience. Day and Crugnale then replicated their highly successful business models and grew their businesses into multimillion-dollar chains.

This strategy works across industries and marketplaces. P'kolino, for example, is entering the children's furniture market with a few designs. As they start selling their products and learning what aspects customers like and don't like, its owners will continue to add designs. Further down the road, they expect to enter different segments by offering different levels of quality. This type of learning reduces your up-front costs and exposes you to new opportunities that you might not otherwise perceive because you are interacting with customers. Finally, if the worst case should occur and you fail, you will lose less than if you boldly jumped in with multiple restaurants or products all at once.

Opening that first restaurant or selling your first product is your entry into the marketplace. You'll need to have an overriding entry strategy as we discussed earlier—perhaps differentiation. You'll also need to have marketing, operating, and financial plans in place to help achieve your strategy. Much of this is covered in other courses you've taken, and we will explore business planning in-depth in Chapters 7 and 8 as well. The key for your entry strategy is to find a pathway into the industry and a way of surviving the first two to three years when most businesses are operating with a negative cash flow. Starting in year three, you need to envision how you will not only grow your firm, but how you will thrive.

Growth Strategy

The first two to three years of any new venture are about survival. The firm has to prove that its customers are interested in its offerings, refine its operations, and increase its visibility. After the first couple of years, many firms will seek growth. In Figure 4.4, we see growth as a function of adding more company-owned restaurants and then ultimately franchising the concept. Managing growth is difficult, and Chapter 14 goes into greater detail on these issues. Our goal here is to think about strategies for growth—what works, when it works, and why it works. Although experience suggests that the first few years of a new venture should focus on testing the market and refining your business model, it is never too early to start thinking about how you will grow. We will explore several common growth strategies.

Franchising. As shown in the example in Figure 4.4, franchising is a strong growth strategy if you have a replicable business model. Most often, franchising is used with retail concepts, such as McDonald's or Mail Boxes Etc. We can summarize the keys to success with franchising as follows:

- Replicability—The business model is well established and proven. As the franchisor, you have worked out the processes of opening and operating a business unit (which is captured in the Uniform Franchising Offering Circular and details the operations, quality controls, policies, procedures, and financial aspects of the business).

- Control—The brand is the life blood of your business. A poor franchisee can damage your brand, so you need to have monitoring systems in place. Control is also important to ensure that the franchisee is accurately reporting revenues, because this controls the revenue you'll receive from your franchising royalty.

Franchising leads to two types of growth. First, it speeds growth as it brings in new capital to fund growth. Specifically, the franchisees fund new unit development. SUBWAY is the classic example. In fact, many critics argue that SUBWAY takes advantage of its franchisees (see box). SUBWAY's growth was phenomenal. Starting with 3 company stores in 1965, it grew to 134 by 1979 and has exploded to more than 25,000 franchises today. SUBWAY is ubiquitous in the United States and operates in 83 other countries around the world. It has focused on long-term growth and expanding in countries with high population density, available disposable income, and political and economic stability.[22] Figure 4.5 shows the top 10 franchise operations in the world, the year started, the number of units and current revenues.

The Dark Side of Franchising: Does SUBWAY Take Advantage of Its Franchisees?

Although franchising is an excellent growth strategy for the franchisor as well as a means for individuals to start their own tried-and-true business (franchisee), franchising is not without its problems. For example, many critics and franchisees feel that SUBWAY is not a good partner. In 1998, Dean Sagar, the staff economist of the U.S. House of Representative's small business committee said, "SUBWAY is the biggest problem in franchising and emerges as one of the key examples of every abuse you can think of."[23]

Today SUBWAY has over 26,000 restaurants,[24] but that rapid growth has caused some dissension. Many franchisees believe that SUBWAY has violated their agreements by allowing new franchisees to open close to existing restaurants, thereby canalizing sales. "In many markets SUBWAY has overbuilt," says International Association of Independent SUBWAY Franchisees (IAISF) Executive Director Leslee Scott. "There are guys who were doing $8,000 a week three or four years ago who today are doing $4,500."[25]

Although most SUBWAY franchisees are happy and profitable, the franchise business model is ripe for conflict. "The franchising business is, at its core, antagonistic" says Tom Schmidt, an attorney who is suing the Houston-based Marble Slab Creamery ice cream chain on behalf of nine Marble Slab franchisees. Schmidt continues, "Franchisees must also play by strict rules, and those rules are constantly changing according to the parent company's whims."[26] Thus, franchisees and franchisors need to be aware of and prepare for likely conflict.

Franchisor	Year Started	Number of Units in 2005	Revenues for 2005
McDonald's	1955	28,000	$20 billion
SUBWAY	1965	25,140	$6.2 billion
Pizza Hut*	1958	13,000	$5.2 billion
Burger King	1954	11,220	$12 billion
Starbucks	1971	8,500	$6.4 billion
Domino's Pizza	1960	8,000	$4.8 billion
KFC*	1952	7,500	$5.0 billion
Taco Bell*	1954	6,800	$4.7 billion
Wendy's	1969	6,600	$3.8 billion
Dunkin' Donuts	1950	6,000	$3.4 billion

* Jointly owned by Yum! Brands, revenues have been separated from aggregate figures

Figure 4.5

Top 10 franchisors

Franchising also adds new revenues—the royalty fee and the franchising fee. Franchisees owe the franchisor a royalty ranging from 2% to 12.5% on every dollar earned.[27] For this royalty, the franchisor promises to support the franchisee. Often the fee will include royalties the franchisees must pay for advertising, but sometimes this charge is a separate fee. The franchisor pools together the advertising royalties and spends it on behalf of the franchisees for ads in regional and national TV, radio, newspapers, magazines, and the Internet.

The franchisees also pay a fee to secure the rights to the franchise. This ranges from $25,000 for a relatively undeveloped brand to $45,000 for a McDonald's (plus another $500,000 to $1 million in pre-opening and equipment costs; moreover, McDonald's requires the franchisee to have $200,000 in nonborrowed equity).[28] For the most part, these fees cover the overhead for managing and monitoring the system, but they are also a source of growth capital.

Some franchisors bring in additional revenue by selling supplies to their franchisees. In fact, the franchising business model can be so lucrative that William Ackman, whose Pershing Square Capital Management owns 4.9% of McDonald's stock, challenged the firm to spin off all its company-owned stores, which according to his analysis, drag down the firm's profit. However, it is necessary to have company-owned stores in the launch and early years, while the entrepreneur tests and refines the basic operations and market acceptance of the concept. Successful company-owned stores also allow the franchisor to charge larger franchise fees.

Expanding Your Product Mix. Many companies start with one product, but as they gain traction in the marketplace, they recognize new opportunities to add to their product mix. Building your product mix should increase your revenue at a rate greater than the associated costs. In other words, you should be able to spread your existing costs across a larger product base. You might use the same vendor to provide raw materials or to produce your product. That would increase your power to secure better terms when negotiating. You also might leverage your existing distribution channels. By selling more products through these channels, you increase your negotiating power.

The key is to leverage your firm's experience as you become more familiar with your core customers and your own operations. Whole Foods, for example, has included lifestyle departments at its stores in Austin and Los Angeles, selling all-natural housewares and clothing. "The development and incorporation of Whole Foods Market Lifestyle reflects the company's founding values into other aspects of life," said Marci Frumkin, a Whole Foods regional marketing director. "The new lifestyle store is another example of how Whole Foods leads by example . . . educating consumers about organic food, natural products and ethical business practices."[29] Like Whole Foods, you should search for ways to extend your product mix that leverage your existing production or customer relationships.

Adding products is a means to grow, but it is not risk-free. Eighty percent of new products are failures.[30] The risk is that the company will incur development expenses, the market may not accept the new product, and the unsuccessful product line could reflect unfavorably on the reputation of the existing products. You need a coherent strategy to minimize the risks of new products. Start with your firm's competitive advantage. What do you do better than anybody else? For P'kolino, that advantage is innovative furniture designs. Adding designs increases P'kolino's power by giving it more visibility with its distributors, such as FAO Schwartz. P'kolino also decreases its cost of direct distribution by selling a wider range of products on its Web site and having enough products in a catalog to try a direct-mail strategy. Furthermore, this strategy gives the company more leverage with its vendors. More products ideally result in a larger production volume, which suggests that P'kolino can negotiate better terms.

iRobot was a Massachusetts-based startup focused on building robots on specification for government agencies and industry, until it created the Roomba. This innovative self-propelled and self-controlled vacuum cleaner helped iRobot move into the lucrative consumer products market. Rather than partnering with another firm and selling the technology, iRobot decided it could manufacture the Roomba overseas. Although it still builds robots for military and industrial use, iRobot is focusing on branching into other consumer products.[31]

A product growth strategy identifies synergies within the firm and then leverages those synergies in conjunction with the company's customer knowledge. While sound management imagines what the firm will pursue for product growth during the launch phase, in reality many new opportunities will only appear once you have started selling your first product and gained first-hand market intelligence.

Geographic Expansion. Expanding geographically is another common growth strategy. This natural growth is based on the underlying assumption that customers should like your product or service elsewhere if they like it in the location where you founded the company. All the larger retail companies in existence today had roots in one geographic region before they grew outward. Wal-Mart started in Arkansas, while McDonald's was originally located in Bakersfield, California.

You can plan geographic expansion systematically or it can happen haphazardly. Oftentimes, potential customers will come across your product through the media or the Internet and want it. The MouseDriver,[32] a one-product company that developed a computer mouse in the shape of a Big Bertha golf driver, received unsolicited inquiries from potential distribution agents as far away as Japan. While opportunistic growth can be a smart move, entrepreneurs benefit from developing and following a coherent strategy.

When planning geographic expansion you'll want to weigh a number of factors:

- Customers—First and foremost, are the customers in the new location similar to those in areas with existing operations? Your initial strategy is predicated on delivering a product or service that satisfies the needs or wants of a core customer group. For your initial expansion, you want to leverage the knowledge you've gained from serving customers in your initial location. For example, College Coach,[33] a college-advisory service, targets well-to-do parents through two primary channels. First, the company sets up retail stores in affluent suburbs, and second, it partners with large Fortune 500 companies such as AIG to provide human resource benefits. College Coach was founded and based in Newton, Massachusetts, an affluent suburb of Boston. Its initial expansion efforts have been to the suburbs of New York City and more recently to Chicago. The rationale behind these locations is the prevalence of well-to-do parents who are focused on getting their children into Ivy League schools and other top universities across the country. Thus, College Coach needs to find affluent pockets where a high percentage of kids apply to top-tier universities.

- ◉ Vendors—Can you continue to use the same vendors? If not, what costs will you incur to establish new relationships? Remember, the greater your volume, the stronger your negotiating position. If you can continue with the same vendors, you will have greater bargaining power, but that power becomes diluted as you add vendors.

- ◉ Distribution—Can you use the same distribution channels? As with vendors, you can increase your leverage and reduce your marginal costs by moving more volume through existing distribution channels.

These factors should guide your decision making as you formulate your growth strategy. If you look at geographic expansion for retail operations, you'll note that they strive for a critical mass within a region before moving to another region. For example, Dunkin' Donuts is highly concentrated in the northeastern United States. There is approximately one Dunkin' Donuts outlet for every 3,230 residents in Boston. Customers in the Boston area know the company well, and its core customers view stopping at Dunkin' Donuts for their morning coffee as integral to their morning routine. Not only does this high concentration keep the brand at the forefront of the customer's mind, it gives Dunkin' Donuts considerable operating efficiencies. The key is balancing your company's saturation point—the point when new expansion within the region cannibalizes existing operations—against its opportunities to expand to new regions.

Today with the Internet, it is easier than ever to expand across many regions simultaneously. Potential customers find out about your product and then contact you about buying the product or representing your company in a new region. Before accepting these offers, make sure you understand the trade-offs. First, most sales and even unsolicited orders require time and effort on your part. This is time and effort that is diverted from establishing your company in its existing regions. Second, your company may not have the infrastructure in place to support the buyer after the sale. Third, consider any additional costs for transporting the product to the customer. While unsolicited orders can be attractive, make sure you understand the hidden costs (mostly in time and effort) that you incur as you fill them.

International Growth. International growth is a special case of geographic expansion. In today's global economy, new entrepreneurial firms often should consider expansion at their inception. Advances in logistics, technology, and manufacturing have allowed smaller and younger firms to compete globally. Firms that look globally from the outset often have tightly managed organizations, innovative products, and strong networks for marketing. They also have more aggressive growth strategies, use more distribution channels, and have more experienced management teams. They don't simply export, but instead choose foreign direct investment in the countries in which they seek to operate. With their global reach, they can introduce innovative products to new markets, giving

Figure 4.6

The entrepreneurial firm international expansion process

them an advantage over startups that operate only in the domestic sphere. They also may operate in industries that are globally integrated from the start.[34]

A study by Paul Reynolds[35] suggests that 20,000 of the 35,000 transnational firms in the world are small and medium-sized Enterprises (SMEs—firms with fewer than 500 employees). Reynolds predicts that by 2005 more than 80% of all SMEs will be affected by or involved in international trade. In another study, Rodney Shrader and colleagues[36] estimate that one-third of all small manufacturing firms derive at least 10% of their revenues from foreign sources. Unfortunately for a new venture, going global increases risk and costs money. Pat Dickson[37] provides a model that illustrates when and how entrepreneurial ventures go global (see Figure 4.6)

Dickson notes that there are three types of global entrepreneurial firms. The first, *gradual globals*, enter international markets in stages in order to reduce their risk. During their initial entry, gradual globals will enter countries similar to their domestic market and use processes that require lower costs and commitment, such as exporting. Over time, they will enter more, and increasingly dissimilar, countries. Gradual globals will also expand their entry modes, moving from exporting to foreign direct investment (FDI), for example. The second category of entrepreneurial firms is *born global*. These firms plan to enter international markets right from their outset. The final category, *born-again globals*, have been operating only domestically, but some event triggers them to move rapidly into new international markets, such as an unsolicited order from abroad. Although there is a lot of debate about which type of firm is more likely to succeed globally, entrepreneurs need to think about international business from day one.

Dickson suggests that entrepreneurs pursue enabling strategies, given that new ventures are resource constrained. For instance, they can use intermediaries to reduce needed resources or use low-cost methods, such as the Internet, that enable them to make contact with potential international partners. In many cases, entrepreneurs can tap their existing networks, such as employees, investors, vendors, or customers, to facilitate international entry. One of your vendors, for instance, may have distribution in another country that you can use on a variable-cost basis. You might also pursue alliances with other companies. Faxes and the Internet enable entrepreneurs to directly access international markets in a low-cost manner. You can market to firms worldwide by simply putting up a Web site. You can proactively manage relationships overseas by using the Internet and e-mail. The toy designers at Kidrobot communicate with their subcontractors from afar, electronically sending their plans and product changes to China.[38] Whatever the enablers you use, it is easier today to enter global markets than ever before.

Dickson's model moves from enablers to enacting processes. There are eight primary means to expand globally.

- Technology transfer (joint venture)—When firms choose to enter the global market, they may need to decide whether to sell their technology or produce it abroad themselves. Producing technology overseas can involve significant risk and investment. Having a partner firm in the target country or region to produce and distribute your product instead can reduce your entry costs. The costs of technology development and production often lead young firms to build alliances and joint partnerships and to focus on niche markets.[39] However, there is a risk you'll lose control of the technology, because the partner firm will gain insight into how you produce the product.

- Technology licensing—Perhaps the most common means to enter a foreign market is to secure an agent to represent the company abroad. Here the entrepreneur may decide that he or she is better off letting a foreign company produce and sell the product, perhaps rebranded under its own name, and taking a royalty as compensation. Licensing reduces risk from an operational perspective. While this is an excellent means of generating revenue and conserving resources, it also is a lost opportunity to extend your own brand into new markets.

- Outsourcing—Outsourcing allows businesses to handle key attributes of their products while handing over the responsibility for development and manufacturing to a subcontractor. The outsourced production may be sent back to the company's home country for sale. It is often the first logical step as a firm seeks to expand globally. This is basically the strategy that P'kolino is considering, and the primary reason to look at global outsourcing is cost savings.

- Exporting—The cheapest and easiest way to enter new markets is to sell from your headquarters. However, as always there are trade-offs. First, it is harder to establish a critical mass in the country if you don't have anyone on the ground, and as mentioned earlier, you may incur additional costs in after-sales support. Your customers also may have difficulty contacting you or providing information about the market and their needs. You incur the transportation costs and risks of getting your products through the target country's customs. A second alternative is to hire a sales representative in the target country. The advantages are that sales representatives have deep knowledge of the country and presumably a strong network they can leverage in selling the product. However, agency theory suggests there are risks to consider.[40] First, it is difficult for you to confirm that agents are as skilled as they might claim (which is referred to as *adverse selection*). Second, it is difficult to ensure that the agent is honoring the contract (which is referred to as *moral hazard*).

- Foreign direct investment (FDI)—Under this strategy, companies set up a physical presence in the countries of interest, whether that is a sales office, retail outlets, production facilities, or something else. The startup retains control of the assets and facilities, an issue that can prove expensive. The primary means of FDI are acquiring foreign assets and building and expanding current facilities overseas. FDI is usually beyond the means of most early-stage companies. French clothing line Chloé tested the Chinese market by exporting the product first through retail stores. Then once it learned that Chinese customers liked the product, it started to establish its own retail outlets in Beijing and then Shanghai. It plans to branch out slowly from those locations.[41] Similarly, Jeff Bernstein started Emerge Logistics by using China's bureaucratic red tape and the unwillingness of American companies to invest in Chinese facilities to his advantage. Bernstein's logistics company stocks three overseas warehouses with industrial parts for clients like DaimlerChrysler and Gates Rubber.[42]

◉ Franchising—Some see franchising as a low-risk method of entering a foreign market because it allows the firm to license an operational system. Yet there can be difficulties in monitoring the international franchisee and ensuring that it protects the company's brand (moral hazard). Until recently, the Chinese as a whole had a dim view of franchises. The media in China highlighted several news stories about franchise owners receiving payment but failing to provide services. And as a parent company, KFC had difficulties in convincing its franchisees in China to collectively bargain in order to receive lower prices from suppliers.[43]

◉ Venture financing—According to Dickson, venture capital is both an enabling and an enacting mechanism. What he means is that the available capital and expertise provided by VCs may enable a firm to go international using any of the previously mentioned means to enter a market. However, research suggests that venture capital often leads to mergers and acquisitions with foreign companies.

◉ Mergers and acquisitions (M&A)—For some businesses, buying an overseas firm may be the most efficient manner to enter a foreign market. You gain an instant presence in the country with an established infrastructure. M&As also allow an entrepreneurial company to grow and expand quickly. Some research shows that firms that use acquisitions for expansion have a higher survival rate than those that choose a startup.[44] The capital required means that the firm must secure venture capital or go public; thus, this method is beyond the means of most early-stage entrepreneurs.

As the world becomes increasingly connected, entrepreneurs need to look beyond their home borders to see whether they can expand on their initial opportunity. While it is more difficult to enter and operate in a country that you are not familiar with, technology and increasing trade are reducing the knowledge gap. As research points out, more and more entrepreneurs are becoming global early in their companies' lives. As an entrepreneur you need to be aware of your options, and the Dickson model provides a solid framework for understanding them.

☐ CONCLUSION

This chapter moves beyond opportunity recognition to implementation. Once you understand your business model, it is time to think about how you will enter the marketplace and grow your firm. During entry, you are proving that your business model is viable and profitable. Are customers buying your product at the prices you need to be profitable? As you learn more about your customer and business, you'll modify your original vision. Entry into the marketplace provides a platform to identify new opportunities and to reshape your business so that it is best positioned to grow and thrive. Thus, it's wise to think about your growth strategy from the very beginning. Today that growth is more likely than ever to mean you'll consider international expansion.

Reflection Point

1. Describe your business model. What are your primary sources of revenue? What are your revenue drivers? Your COGS? Your operating expenses?

2. What is your overall strategy? Why does this strategy help you sell to customers? What tactics can you employ to increase your revenues?

3. What is your entry strategy? How does this create a platform for your business to grow?

4. What is your growth strategy? How big do you want your firm to be? How long might it take for it to get there?

Your Thoughts...

WEB EXERCISE

Pull the income sheets from three companies in the industry that you are interested in entering. Try to find companies that are pursuing different strategies. Examine their business models and see if you can identify the drivers that they are influencing to achieve their strategy. What lessons can you learn for your own venture? What new elements can you incorporate into your business model? How do you tie these elements to your strategy?

NOTES

[1] Demery, P. The New Wal-Mart? *Internet Retailer.* 2004. www.internetretailer.com/article.asp?id=11898.

[2] Mangalindan, Mylene. "How Amazon's Retail Alliance with Toys "R" Us Soured; Online, Retail Titans Clash in U.S. Court Over Contract Terms." *The Wall Street Journal Europe.* January 24, 2006.

[3] The actual accounting definition is that COGS is the inventory at the beginning of the period, plus the costs of inventory purchased during the period, minus the inventory remaining at the end of the period.

[4] Although many software firms amortized R&D and include it in COGS.

[5] Copeland, Michael V. and Tilin Andrew. "The New Instant Companies. Cheap Design Tools, Offshore Factories, Free Buzz Marketing. How Today's Startups are Going from Idea to $30 Million Hit—Overnight." *Business 2.0.* June 2005. Vol. 6, Issue. 5, pp. 82–94.

[6] Ibid.

7 "Happy e-birthdays; Internet businesses" *The Economist.* July 23, 2005. Vol. 376, Issue 8436, p. 62.

8 Bygrave, W. Beautiful Legs by Post. Wellesley, MA: Babson College. 1996.

9 McElligot, Tim. "eBay PlacesVoIP's Biggest Bet." *Telephony.* September 19, 2005.

10 Millot, J. Amazon.com expects to generate $34 million from IPO. *Publishers Weekly New York*: March 31, 1997. Vol. 244, Issue 13, p. 11.

11 Tellis, Gerald J. and Golder, Peter N. "Will and Vision: How Latecomers Grow to Dominate Markets." New York, NY: McGraw-Hill. 2002.

12 Ibid.

13 Ibid.

14 Xie, Tian "Frank." "Enduring Market Performance: The Role of Entry Time Momentum and the Myth of the First Mover Advantage." Georgia State University. 2003.

15 Now Books.com, although it appears that Barnes & Noble has the domain name today. Gately, Gary. "Online Book Price War Worries Wall Street." *eCommerce News.* May 18, 1999.

16 Ibid.

17 Gittell, J., & O'Reilly, C. JetBlue Airways: Starting from scratch. Harvard Business School Publishing, Case 9–801–354. 2001.

18 Ibid.

19 Grescoe, Paul. "Maxims of the Mavericks: Looking for Sage Business Advice?" *Profit.* October 1, 1999. Vol. 18, Issue 6, p. 49.

20 Elizabeth Riley is a successful entrepreneur who started Mazza and Riley, Inc., an internationally recognized executive search firm, and has spent much of her career placing people in venture-backed companies.

21 Salter, C. And now the hard part. *Fast Company.* May 2004, p. 66.

22 Duecy, E. Global growth, urban sites speed Subway along track toward overtaking McDonald's. *Nation's Restaurant News.* February 7, 2005. Vol. 39, Issue 6, p. 4.

23 Behar, Richard. "Why Subway is the Biggest Problem in Franchising." *Fortune.* 1996. March 16, 1998.

24 From www.Subway.com.

25 Goff, L. "Encroachment complaints hasten litigation, unity." *Franchise Times,* 1996. 2:4(3–4).

26 McCuan, J. "Should you consider franchising?" Smartmoney.com. April 5, 2005.

27 http://money.cnn.com/2004/04/29/pf/howmuchfranchise/.

28 www.franchiseadvantage.com/handbook/mcdonalds.ihtml.

29 Desjardins, Doug. "Whole Foods Goes Hollywood with Lifestyle Store." *DSN Retailing Today.* November 7, 2005.

30 Shanahan, L. Designated shopper. *Brandweek.* January 4, 1999. Vol. 40, Issue 1, p. 38.

31 Buchanan, Leigh. "Death to Cool." *Inc.* July 2003. Vol. 25, Issue 7, pp. 82–88.

32 www.mousedriver.com.

33 www.getintocollege.com.

34 McDougall, Patricia P., Oviatt, Benjamin M., and Shrader, Rodney C. "A Comparison of International and Domestic New Ventures." *Journal of International Entrepreneurship.* 2003.

35 Reynolds, Paul D. "New and small firms in expanding markets." *Small Business Economics* 9, 1997. No. 1: 79–84.

36 Shrader, Rodney C., Oviatt, Benjamin M., and McDougall, Patricia P. "How new ventures exploit trade-offs among international risk factors: Lessons for the accelerated internationalization of the 21st Century." *Academy of*

Management Journal 43, No. 6 (2000): 1227–1247.

[37] Dickson, P. Going global. In A. Zacharakis & S. Spinelli (Eds.) *Entrepreneurship, Volume 2.* Geenwich, CT: Praeger Publishers. (Forthcoming in 2006.)

[38] Copeland, Michael V., and Tilin, Andrew. "The New Instant Companies. Cheap Design Tools, Offshore Factories, Free Buzz Marketing. How Today's Startups are Going from Idea to $30 Million Hit—Overnight." *Business 2.0.* June 2005. Vol. 6, Issue 5, pp. 82–94.

[39] Eden, L., Levitas, E., and Martinez, R. J. "The production, transfer and spillover of technology: Comparing large and small multinationals as technology producers." *Small Business Economics* 9, 1997. No. 1:53–66.

[40] Zacharakis, A. L. Entrepreneurial entry into foreign markets: A transaction cost perspective. *Entrepreneurship: Theory and Practice.* 1997. 21(3): 23–39.

[41] Movius, L. Chloe launches in China. *WWD.* December 29, 2005. Vol. 190, Issue 137.

[42] Flannery, Russell. "Red Tape." *Forbes.* March 3, 2003. Vol 171, Issue 5, pp. 97–100.

[43] Chang, Leslie. "From KFC to Beauty Spas, Chinese Are Embracing Franchises—As Maturing Retail Market Moves Past Fraudsters, Chain Stores Take Root." *The Wall Street Journal.* April 18, 2002.

[44] Vermeulen, Freek, and Barkema, Harry. "Learning through acquisitions. *Academy of Management Journal,* 44, No. 3 (2001):457–476.

Adam Aircraft

As the sleek, six-seat Adam A500 performed a graceful arc overhead, Babson College MBA John Hamilton, Vice President of Marketing for Adam Aircraft Industries (AAI), had to smile. Earlier that morning, he had read an article describing the difficulties and pitfalls associated with designing, building, and certifying new aircraft. In the last 30 years, there were countless examples of startup aircraft manufacturers that had tried and failed to deliver new products to the small and mid-sized aircraft markets. In fact, the only two startup companies that had recently succeeded had been builders of very basic, single-engine aircraft.

Like most MBAs, John had been taught to analyze companies based on all the standard metrics; the management team, product viability and appeal, market demand, capitalization, and financing potential. While Adam Aircraft appeared to be a winner on all counts—including the progress it was making in the lengthy and complex certification process—the company did not have the many millions of dollars it would need to bring its products to market and reach positive cash flow.

Talking with some of his peers in venture capital, John had come to understand that private equity investors were a fickle bunch. The vast majority preferred to invest in bio-technology, telecommunications, and other industries with historically well-defined harvest potential. Following the market correction in 2000, the flow of venture capital had significantly diminished, and investments outside of these core industries had all but ceased.

John had grown up in a family of aviators. He had been a licensed pilot for over eighteen years. Since flying machines were not only his vocation but also his passion, he had to wonder whether this love was clouding his analysis. The market was clearly desperate for products like the plane performing flawlessly overhead, but did Adam Aircraft have what it would take to succeed where so many had failed? Could they continue to advance toward certification and full-production capability, or would the challenges that lay ahead slow them down enough to increase their burn rate to a level that would discourage even the most ardent investor?

John did know that in less than five years, company founder Rick Adam had orchestrated the fabrication of two flying prototypes—the A500 twin piston and the A700 jet—at a speed of design and production that had turned heads in all sectors of the aviation industry. Certification on both models was expected in the coming year—two years ahead of a number of well-funded competitors. With their third product—the A600 twin turboprop—nearly ready to fly, Adam Aircraft had become the one to watch in 2004.

John zipped up against the cold December wind and tracked the A500 as it snapped a sharp wing-turn on its approach to their home field at Centennial Airport in Englewood, Colorado. Another successful flight test. He smiled; definitely the one to watch . . .

The Entrepreneur

George Adam Sr. had been a career Air Force officer who had flown B-17 and B-29 bombers during World War II. His son Rick, born in 1946, grew up on Air Force bases

Carl Hedberg and John Hamilton prepared this case under the supervision of Professor William Bygrave, Babson College, as a basis for class discussion rather than to illustrate either effective or ineffective handling of an administrative situation. Funding provided by the F. W. Olin Graduate School and the gift of the Class of 2003, and the Frederic C. Hamilton Chair for Free Enterprise. Copyright © by Babson College 2004.

and had always expected to follow his father into the military cockpit. When a color-vision deficiency kept him out of the Air Force Academy flight program, he joined the Army, attended West Point, and then switched his commission to the Air Force.

Rick specialized in computer science, and as an Air Force captain he ran the Real-Time Computer Centers at the Kennedy Space Center and at Vandenberg Air Force Base. During that time he earned his MBA at Golden Gate University, and later, as a civilian, he found his way to Wall Street. At Goldman Sachs he ran the IT department as a general partner. In 1993, Rick left Goldman to start his own business: New Era of Networks, an Enterprise Application Integration software developer. The wildly successful company went public and grew to a market capitalization of over $1 billion. It was later acquired by the Sybase Corporation.

All the while, Rick had never lost sight of his first love, and in the early 1990s he learned to fly. Since his business required lots of travel, he was able to log over a thousand pilot-hours in just a few years by flying himself to meetings. He started in an old Skymaster, moved into a 1978 Mitsubishi MU2, and ultimately got type-rated in a 1993 Citation jet. While Rick had had the opportunity and the personal wealth to progress quickly as a pilot, he recognized that the majority of owner-operators weren't as fortunate:

> As a pilot you have to go in steps; you can't get ahead of yourself. So, as you log more and more hours in the air, you can begin to fly increasingly more complex airplanes. The problem is, that when you are ready to make the move from a single to a twin-engine aircraft, there are very few products to choose from. Most of the aircraft are based on old designs, which makes them tough to fly and expensive to own and operate.
>
> One of the most popular production twin-engine planes on the market is the Beechcraft Baron—introduced in 1961! Because they quit building their more capable pressurized twins in the mid-80s, and stopped innovating at the same time, the old Baron is still their frontline light twin—and a new one costs over a million dollars. See, as the volume of orders has gone down, the prices have continued to climb (see Exhibit 4.1).

Rick added that the alternative to buying a new version of an old design was far worse:

> Demand for used planes is huge, because they are cheaper than new ones, and, since nothing has changed in the industry, pilots can buy something that may have been manufactured in the 70s or 80s, but it looks like a new plane. Right now the average age of a general aviation[1] aircraft is over thirty years (see Exhibit 4.2), and it's getting one year older every year.
>
> And frankly, these airplanes become unsafe. If you look at the accident rate in aircraft, it climbs dramatically with age. So even though there are strict regulations on maintaining these aircraft, it's hard to keep an old plane in good shape. Things like the wiring and systems just get to a point where they are too old to be reliable.

The more Rick thought about this aging factor, the more certain he became that the only solution would be an entirely new generation of general aviation products. It wasn't long before he had begun to evaluate the commercial viability of such a venture.

---

[1] General aviation (GA) is a term comprising all of aviation other than government and scheduled air transport (commercial airlines), and includes privately owned aircraft, charter services, business-owned aircraft, and many more types of working aircraft that are not, strictly speaking, for transportation. Although a large part of GA consists of recreational flying, an equally large part involves important, commercial activities such as flight training, shipping, surveying, agricultural application, air taxi, charter passenger service, corporate flying, emergency transport, and firefighting.

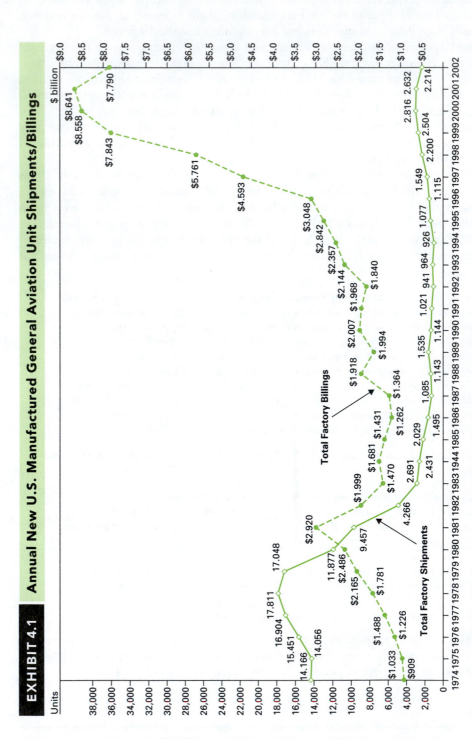

EXHIBIT 4.1   Annual New U.S. Manufactured General Aviation Unit Shipments/Billings

Source: General Aviation Manufacturers Association (GAMA) Statistical Databook 2002

EXHIBIT 4.2	Average Age of U.S. General Aviation Fleet in 2002		
Aircraft Type	**Engine Type**	**Seats**	**Average Age in Years**
Single-Engine	Piston	1–3	36
		4	33
		5–7	28
		8+	43
	Turboprop	All	12
	Jet	All	31
Multi-Engine	Piston	1–3	36
		4	33
		5–7	33
		8+	37
	Turboprop	All	26
	Jet	All	28
All Aircraft			**31**

Source: General Aviation Manufacturers Association (GAMA) Statistical Databook 2002

Spotting the Opportunity

Almost immediately upon joining the ranks of experienced aviators, Rick began to contemplate the type of effort that would be required to deliver a new plane to the marketplace:

> *Every time I went to a cocktail party or barbeque, all the pilots would go off into a corner and start talking pilot stuff. And since everybody was moaning about the lack of new products, I became convinced that there was a huge demand. So in the early 90's I started developing strategies for launching a new aircraft company.*
>
> *Now, I have launched a few entrepreneurial ventures, and when you think there is a big opportunity, you make sure to stop and evaluate why it hasn't been done before. Why isn't anyone pursuing this opportunity? What do I know, or what do I see that nobody else is seeing? Very often, entrepreneurial opportunities occur when a series of prior developments make it possible to accomplish the once unachievable. You reach a point where you finally have all the ingredients to make it happen.*

To illustrate, Rick referred to the electronic organizer on the table:

> *There were at least a dozen attempts to bring out handheld devices ahead of the Palm Pilot. The most notable was Jerry Kaplan's GO Corporation. Kaplan saw the opportunity, had the right idea, and raised $50 million in funding back in the early 90s. But since the chips weren't small enough, the displays weren't big enough, and the batteries weren't powerful enough, his product looked like a brick. He spent 50 million bucks and failed, simply because his great idea was ahead of the prevailing technology.*

In a similar way, the Beechcraft Corporation was ahead of its time when, in the late 1970s, it set out to develop a new class of business aircraft. The five-and-a-half year, $300 million development program resulted in the federally-certified Starship (see Exhibit 4.3).

| **EXHIBIT 4.3** | **The Beechcraft Starship** |

The Beechcraft Starship, a twin-turboprop pusher design, was the first all-composite pressurized airframe ever certified by the FAA. The task was larger than simply developing an all-new aircraft. Beechcraft had to master an innovative technology, work hand-in-hand with FAA regulators, build a new manufacturing facility, and train a specialized workforce. Much of this effort was concentrated on areas the industry had not addressed before. The company built 53 Starships in all before ceasing production in the early 1990s.

The futuristic craft was the world's first pressurized, all-composite[2] business turboprop. Many in the industry had high hopes that the Starship would usher in a new age of modern propeller-driven aircraft, but that was not to be.

Developed by Scaled Composites, a cutting-edge aircraft design enterprise founded by visionary Burt Rutan,[3] the Starship project brought about the development of Federal Aviation Authority (FAA) standards for the construction of composite aircraft. Unfortunately for Beechcraft, this was a very long and difficult process resulting in an aircraft that was heavier and more expensive than predicted. As a result, the Starship's performance was only marginally better than the existing fleet—and yet its price was far higher. Despite its commercial failure, this project was the first in a series of events that would begin to spark new life into the long-ailing general aviation aircraft industry in America.

---

[2] An easy-to-understand composite material would be an adobe brick: wet mud and straw mixed together and dried. The result is a material stronger than either mud or straw. Composite airframes typically consisted of a carbon, graphite, or glass fiber reinforcing material, and an epoxy resin binder. Alone, these substances had very little strength, but when combined and properly cured, they became a composite structure that was very strong. Since this construction process lent itself to fluid design, composite airframes were often sleeker and more pleasing to the eye than their aluminum counterparts.

[3] As a schoolboy, Burt Rutan had designed award-winning model aircraft, and by age 16 had learned to fly. After receiving a bachelor's degree in aeronautical engineering from California Polytechnic State University he worked for the U.S. Air Force as a flight test project engineer at Edwards Air Force Base in California. In 1972, at age 29, he founded Rutan Aircraft Factory, which sold plans and kits for Rutan-designed aircraft. His science-fiction-like aircraft designs were considered "risky" by established aircraft manufacturers, who made sure that the regulators of the Federal Aviation Administration were aware of their "concerns." While he successfully sold a number of different unique designs, he became frustrated by the litigious regulatory environment and substantial liability claims that had put many private aircraft manufacturers out of business. In 1982, Rutan chose to leave the home-built industry in favor of larger-scale designs for companies. His new firm was Scaled Composites.

A Convergence of Factors

Between 1978 and 1992, the general aviation industry had suffered a 95% unit sales decline and the loss of over 100,000 jobs. Over that same period, GA manufacturers had spent as much to defend product liability suits as they had spent to develop new aircraft in the 30 years following the Second World War.

When Congress enacted the General Aviation Revitalization Act (GARA) in 1994 to protect aircraft builders from lawsuits on planes that were older than eighteen years, it revitalized an industry nearly wiped out by two decades of what lawmakers were calling lawsuit abuse and trial lawyer profiteering.

The 1990s also brought about enormous advances in computing power and computer-aided design and modeling (CAD/CAM) software. Airframe geometry could now reside in the computer, with all of its internal structures defined electronically as three-dimensional models. By the end of that decade, expensive wind tunnels and physical scale models were being replaced by computational fluid dynamics software. Manufacturing and tooling capabilities had made great strides as well.

Rick said that after a couple of kit manufacturers[4] managed to achieve commercial certification for their composite designs, he figured that the time was right:

> In the early '90s, all the innovation was being done in composites and kits. Then Lancair and Cirrus announced that they were going to take what they had learned and build production airplanes. Everybody who loves flying was rooting for them, hoping they would make it, and sure enough, they both got certified.
>
> I'm watching this process and realizing that while there were quite a few single-engine, non-pressurized, fixed-gear startups out there, nobody had yet brought an innovative product into the middle market. It was real clear to me that pilots wanted a new twin, and once I had seen the success that the composite guys had down in single engines, I came to the conclusion it could be done in the twin-engine area.

By the latter half of the 1990s, a number of well-financed firms were competing to introduce a personal jet into this middle-market space by 2006. Rick looked at these projects and wondered: would it be possible to design a single airframe that could accommodate jet engines as well as twin-pistons? He didn't have the answer, but he knew who would.

The Project Begins

Although he was still running his software venture, in 1998, Rick decided to put up a million dollars to get into the aviation business. At the same time, he brought in a talented partner; former FAA trial attorney John Knudsen, an experienced aviator with a career in the U.S. Navy as a carrier-based attack pilot. Understanding that a commercially viable new design—whether it was a jet or a twin-piston—would have to blend superior performance capabilities with "curb appeal," Rick said that they contacted the best in the business:

---

[4] Kit planes were considered "experimental" by the Federal Aviation Administration. This designation was originally intended for aircraft designers who wanted to do research, or for amateur pilots who wanted to learn about aerodynamics as they built their own planes. Because these aircraft were barred from commercial use, the FAA felt that there was no need to impose its exhaustive and very expensive certification process on this class of aircraft.

We met with Burt Rutan and showed him some requirements, definitions, and preliminary designs for a twin piston. Since carbon fiber lends itself to much more aerodynamic shapes than you can get with aluminum construction, I told him to make it look as much like a jet as possible.

As always, he had some wild stuff and he had some stuff that was more middle of the road. We narrowed four or five design concepts down to an in-line, front and back engine configuration, with twin booms to get to the tail.

If this plane was going to be the step-up for single-engine pilots that Rick was envisioning, they understood that ease of operation would be critical. With this in mind, they chose a centerline thrust arrangement, since, compared to twins with the power plants mounted on the wings, the push-pull design significantly reduced the difficulty of flying with one engine not functioning. Having settled on what he felt was an exciting airframe, Rick noted that they had no desire to conquer more than one frontier at a time:

The Eclipse 500 project has raised $400 million so far in its effort to build a light business jet. They tried to develop a new airframe and a new engine at the same time. The engine didn't work, and now they are two years off schedule.

I'm a raging incrementalist; the way to innovate is to take one step at a time. We chose power plants, avionics, and construction methods that had previously been certified by the FAA for other planes; our only major innovation initially will be with the shape of the airframe. I figured that once we had that done, we could innovate on something else later on. It's just so tough to bring a certified new airplane to market; we had to be very careful to avoid adding layers of complexity—and lots of time and money.

The team at Scaled Composites began work on the conceptual designs for Adam Aircraft in May of 1999, and cut the first tool[5] in late August. When the M-309 (see Exhibit 4.4) lifted off on its maiden flight in March of 2000, it marked the most rapid manned-aircraft development program in the company's history.

Despite the price tag, Rick understood that this "experimental" was a one-of-a-kind, hand-built model that would serve only as a research vehicle. Conventional evidence suggested that the development of an FAA-certified version of the M-309 would take a few years, at least a couple more flying test planes, millions of engineering man-hours, and hundreds of millions of dollars. Rick was determined, however, to make sure that his aircraft company was anything but conventional.

Research and Innovation

With the M-309 outfitted with an array of data collection equipment, the AAI team proceeded to log over 300 flight hours in 2000 as they scrutinized the full range of the craft's aerodynamic characteristics and performance capabilities. Rick explained that with regard to understanding the commercial viability of the plane, their destinations were often just as important as their in-flight calculations:

We collected aerodynamic data as we flew the M-309 to air shows around the country, and that gave us the opportunity to survey the market and listen to what potential customers had to say. We completely re-engineered the original design. For example, we increased the size of the empennage,[6] and also moved the door for easier access to the cabin. By the fall of 2000, I had come to the conclusion that there was a significant market for this kind of aircraft.

---

[5] In composite engineering, a tool was the master mold that the composite material was layered into before being vacuum-compressed and then oven cured—a process known as thermosetting—at 240 degrees.

[6] The empennage, commonly called the tail assembly, is the rear section of the body of the airplane. Its main purpose is to provide stability to the aircraft.

EXHIBIT 4.4   The M-309

Named for Burt Rutan's 309th completed design, the Model 309 was built with the aim of delivering a very safe twin-engine aircraft that would give good performance and benign single-engine handling qualities. The pressurized cabin was designed to carry a pilot and five passengers.

The central goal of this program was to develop and aerodynamically refined aircraft. However, there were several features that were more representative of a full-production airplane. For example, there are several major structural components that have been produced as single-cure parts. The outboard wings, horizontal tail, elevator, rudders, and flaperons have no secondary bonds in their primary structure. This allows for a lighter, stronger, and safer structure due to the significant elimination of fasteners and secondary bonds.

Source: www.scaled.com

Rick, who was self-funding most of the startup costs, had been busy recruiting a top-tier management group. Nearly everyone on his ten-member executive staff was an accomplished pilot, and, collectively, they had many years of experience from all corners of the aviation industry, including Boeing, Beechcraft, Martin Marietta, Cirrus, Lancair, Scaled Composites, Eclipse, the U.S. military, and the FAA.

In December, Adam Aircraft established its home base at Centennial Field, just south of Denver. As they got down to the business of fitting the factory in advance of tooling design for the first production model, now called the Adam A500, Rick said that because of the direct relationship between time to market and project cost, they had no choice but to innovate:

> I had recently heard from an industry expert that the standard budget for a new airplane project is about $250 million. Since there has been so little success in this industry to date, it would be nearly impossible to raise that kind of money for a startup airplane company like ours. We knew that the only way we could make financing achievable was by cutting development costs by at least 75%.

He added that to accomplish such a feat would not only require brilliant engineering, but the development of a culture unheard of in aviation manufacturing:

Being a lifetime computer guy, speed and innovation seem very natural to me. We knew right off that time was not our friend; either we get this plane up and certified quickly, or we'd attract competitors and run out of money. One of the first things we did was to institute the kind of 24-hour scheduling that we had used to run our data centers and networks.

Our people now work twelve-hour, overlapping shifts: three-day weeks, with voluntary overtime on Sundays. So while our competitors are putting in five shifts in a calendar week, we are getting up to 21—in addition to high morale and very low attrition.

Over the past few decades, powerful aircraft builders like McDonnell Douglas, Lockheed, and Boeing had developed highly sophisticated modeling design tools that were powered by multi-million-dollar mainframe computers. The PC age had put those capabilities into the hands of small shops like Adam Aircraft. For an off-the-shelf cost of about $3,000 per system, the company was able to set up a 40-station CAD/CAM engineering center with all the capabilities of the big guys. Rick said that by tying this powerful design architecture into the tooling mill downstairs (see Exhibit 4.5), the company was able to add efficiencies by keeping the entire design process in-house:

With aluminum technology, you design the part, and then you bid it out for tooling. You award the tooling—which typically costs over a million dollars—and six to nine months later, the tool comes back. If it's wrong or you want to make a design change, you have to start all over. Because we have our own tooling mill, we can do it fast the first time, and more importantly, continue to modify the tool quickly until we get it right.

The management team understood that merely coupling rapid application development with a 24/7 working environment would not provide enough of an edge to develop the full line of airplanes they were envisioning. Rick explained that for that to happen, they would need to adopt a computer industry concept that, if successful, would change the face of general aviation manufacturing forever:

PCs are developed around a common set of rules as to how the parts interact with each other. That way, you can change the keyboard, the disc drive, the screen, whatever you want, and it won't tear up your memory or your software; that's called modular architecture.

There has been little progress in modular architecture in airplanes—until now. We are building enormous modularity into our design so we can do things like move the wing location, modify the cabin size, change the power plants—all kinds of things. What that means is that we will bring this first plane to certification status for about $50 million bucks. For another ten million, we'll adjust the modules slightly and get a jet. For another five million, we'll get a turboprop.[7]

Detractors felt that this was wishful thinking, and pointed out that the modular architecture approach could potentially compromise performance. Some noted that since each power plant system would have different weight and structural characteristics, installing all three on essentially the same airframe could cause center of gravity problems. In addition, critics felt that using a single wing and empennage design would mean that two of the planes, or maybe even the whole line of products, would fly at less than optimum performance.

The AAI team felt that they were on top of those challenges with innovations like their "smart tunnel," a device that enabled engineers to shift the wing location on the

---

[7] Turboprops were designed to carry high passenger (or cargo) loads over relatively short distances (under 300 miles or so). Short-field take-off and landing capabilities, and the ability to use kerosene instead of aviation fuel, had contributed to the popularity of turboprops, particularly in developing countries.

| EXHIBIT 4.5 | Five-Axis Tooling Mill |

Fabricating the Air-Stair door tool out dense foam material.

fuselage in order to control the range of the aircraft's center of gravity. The team felt that this technology and other specialized systems they were devising would give AAI engineers the means to modify the underlying airframe to accommodate a wide range of engine choices and configurations. In addition, they felt that this engineering strategy would enable them to leverage their research and development spending over at least three commercially viable aircraft designs. Time would tell.

Working with the FAA

Throughout 2001, all manner of government and industry groups had visited the plant to witness the A500 project as it came together very nearly on schedule, and on budget. Predictably, the one group that would not be offering praise or extra points for speed of design and assembly was the Federal Aviation Authority.

The task of the FAA was to see to it that the Type Certification (TC) approval process (see Exhibit 4.6) proceeded in a careful and thorough manner. The complex system of

EXHIBIT 4.6   **FAA Type Certification Process**

Familiarization Meeting — Meeting to establish a partnership with the applicant. It is an opportunity to develop mutual understanding of the type certification process as it applies to the applicant's design. It's highly recommended as a beginning point in the process.

Formal Application — Applicant's formal application for a Type Certification (TC) includes a cover letter, Form 8110-2, and a three-view drawing

Preliminary Type Certification Board — At this initial formal meeting, the project team collects data about the technical aspects of the project and the applicant's proposed certification basis, and identifies other information needed to start developing the Certification Program Plan. Special attention items are also identified at this time.

Certification Program Plan (CPP) – A key document, the Certification Plan addresses:

- The proposed FAA certification basis
- Noise and emission requirements
- Issue papers
- Special conditions, exemptions, and equivalent level of safety findings
- Means of compliance
- Compliance checklists and schedules
- Use of delegations/designees

Technical Meetings – Held throughout the project, technical meetings, e.g., specialist and interim TC meetings, cover a variety of subjects. Team members may:

- Approve test plans and reports
- Review engineering compliance findings
- Close out issue papers
- Review conformity inspections
- Review minutes of board meetings
- Revise the Certification Program Plan
- Issue new FAA policy guidance
- Review airworthiness limitations
- Review instructions for continued airworthiness

Pre-Flight Type Certification Board — Discussions at the pre-flight TC board center on the applicant's flight test program, including conformity inspections and engineering compliance determinations.

Type Inspection Authorization (TIA) — Prepared on FAA Form 8110-1, the TIA authorizes conformity and airworthiness inspections and flight tests to meet certification requirements. The TIA is issued when examination of technical data required for TC is completed or has reached a point where it appears that the product will meet pertinent regulations.

Conformity Inspections and Certification Flight Tests — Conformity inspections ensure that the product conforms with the design proposed for type certification. Flight tests are conducted in accordance with the requirements of the TIA.

Aircraft Evaluation Group (AEG) Determinations — The AEG works with certification engineers and FAA flight test pilots to evaluate the operational and maintenance aspects of certificated products through such activities as:

Flight Standardization Board (FSB)

- Pilot type rating
- Pilot training checking, currency requirements
- Operational acceptability

Flight Operations Evaluation Board (FOEB)

- Master Minimum Equipment List (MMEL)

Maintenance Review Board (MRB)

- Maintenance instructions for continued airworthiness

EXHIBIT 4.6 (Continued)

Final Type Certification Board — When the applicant has met all certification requirements, the ACO schedules the final formal TC board. The board wraps up any outstanding items and decides on the issuance of the TC.

Type Certificate — The certifying ACO issues the TC when the applicant completes demonstration of compliance with the certification basis. The TC data sheet is part of the TC and documents conditions and limitations to meet FAA requirements.

Post-Certification Activities — This includes the Type Inspection Report (TIR) — to be completed within 90 days of issuance of the unique technical requirements and lessons learned — the Certification Summary Report (CSR), and the Post-Certification Evaluation, which closes out the TC project and provides the foundation for continued FAA airworthiness monitoring activities such as service bulletins, revisions to type design, malfunction/defect reports, and Certificate Management for the remainder of the aircraft's life cycle.

---

inspections and testing was similar to what health-care companies faced with the Federal Drug Administration (FDA). Like the FDA, the FAA requires exhaustive proof that products are safe before they can be marketed to consumers. In the aviation industry, that regulatory oversight translates into lots of time and money. While it was true that successful new entrants like Lancair and Cirrus had helped pave the way for subsequent efforts, Rick said that getting through the regulatory process would still be one of their greatest challenges:

> Although the FAA is constantly working to improve the aircraft certification process, for good reason it is designed to be extremely arduous. Nevertheless, we do have a number of advantages over our predecessors. For example, as opposed to submitting aircraft designs on paper, we can now send designs to the FAA electronically. By doing this, we save a ton of time and, most importantly, are assured of the highest degree of accuracy in our documentation process.

By the time the A500 had been cleared for its inaugural flight in July of 2002, a second test aircraft was already under construction (see Exhibit 4.7), and fabrication of parts for a third had begun as well. Comprising the entire testing fleet, these three aircraft would each undergo a series of exhaustive flight and static tests—many requiring the construction of customized systems and fixtures (see Exhibit 4.8). If all proceeded as planned, AAI expected to achieve certification for the A500 by the first half of 2004.

The Customers

When Adam Aircraft flew its A500 to the Experimental Aircraft Association's (EAA) AirVenture Convention in Oshkosh, Wisconsin that summer, the company brought along a full-size mockup of the plane's cockpit and fully appointed interior. Vice President of Marketing John Hamilton noted that Oshkosh was an excellent show since it attracted buyers from all the major markets for its $895,000 twin piston:

> There are two basic markets for aircraft like the A500: owner-flown and professionally flown. The owner-flown market is just that—the owner of the aircraft is also the pilot in command. In the professionally flown market, non-owners fly the aircraft. It sounds like a silly distinction, but it makes a difference in how you market the aircraft.

EXHIBIT 4.7	Fuselage Construction of the A-500 SN002

a.

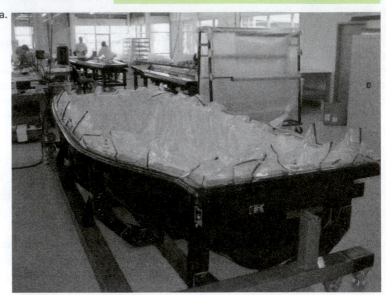

Vacuum bag on fuselage tool.

b.

Laying up the carbon material into the tail boom tool.

I would say between 70 and 80% of our A500 customers will be owner-operators. These folks are evaluating our aircraft from the pilot's seat. They will be very tuned in to things like the performance of the aircraft, its handling characteristics, and the electronic systems in the instrument panel. In addition, because they also manage the scheduled maintenance requirements, they will be very sensitive to serviceability.

Marketing to the professionally flown segment is a bit different since they are more focused on the needs of their client-passengers. They'll be interested in things like how comfortable the seating is, how much baggage area is available, and whether the plane has a toilet or an entertainment system. They'll also want a pressurized cabin so they can fly over weather, a plane that looks and feels safe and substantial—and a plane that is appealing to the eye.

EXHIBIT 4.8　Custom-Built Static Test Rig

In addition, John emphasized that aviation consumers of all types demanded top service and easily maintainable aircraft:

You have to have absolute first-rate service. Customers can't have difficulty getting parts, or finding somebody to work on their airplane.

Pilots are also hesitant to adopt something that is new. We're not Cessna, we're not Beechcraft, and we're not Piper. Those guys have been around forever, and they've built a ton of airplanes.

That's why with everything we do—from delivery, to flight training, to service and parts—we have to prove to our customers that there is a very compelling reason why they should adopt this new aircraft.

John added that the company's unique design modularity would play an important role in serviceability:

One feature of the A500 that customers will love is how easy it is to access the systems on the aircraft that need to be inspected and/or replaced. A great deal of engineering work has been performed to dramatically reduce the amount of time it takes maintenance personnel to complete the necessary service tasks. This will result in reduced down-time and lower costs of operation. Going the extra mile for owners in this area will pay substantial dividends in customer satisfaction.

Eyeing the Future

In October of 2002, the company announced its plan to introduce the next aircraft. The company also indicated that due to the modular systems, the A700, a six- to eight-seat stretched-fuselage twin jet, would share 80% part commonality with the A500. Some critics doubted Rick's assertion that since the A700 would present only an incremental development challenge for his talented engineers, AAI would be able to build a flying model within a year.

Ten months after completing preliminary design work, the A700 jet shocked and amazed the general aviation world by making a surprise appearance at the 2003 EAA AirVenture event. Industry dignitaries such as Secretary of Transportation Norman Mineta and FAA Administrator Marion Blakey welcomed the aircraft with words of support and congratulations. The aviation press was buzzing; if the company was able to hold to its schedule and achieve FAA certification for the A700 in the fourth quarter of 2004, the $1.995 million craft would be the first to market in this emerging, closely-watched segment (see Exhibit 4.9).

John explained that this keen interest in light jets was directly related to the need for more efficient transportation solutions:

> The average mission is less than a two-hour flight, with three-and-a-half people on board—meaning nearly every business jet in America is oversized for what it does.
>
> This emerging personal jet segment is based on the same concept that Japanese auto makers used to take on Detroit 30 years ago. With gas prices going up, why not build a car which was more suitably sized to the average driver's need? Reducing the size and weight of the machine dramatically improved its operating efficiency. We're building a smaller and lighter aircraft designed for the most common trip length and passenger load to deliver optimal efficiency in the twin jet category.

In addition to the benefits of an incremental improvement in the efficiency of twin-engine jets, personal jet aircraft were being viewed by some as the solution to the gridlock in the hub-and-spoke airline system. Rick Adam described one official's views on the subject:

> Dr. Bruce Holmes at NASA[8] has performed extensive studies of the transportation system and has concluded that the best way to increase capacity in the air is by directing more traffic to the 5,000 underutilized regional airports in this country. Regional travelers would fly point-to-point out of small airports and never enter the hub-and-spoke system unless they plan to fly across the country or abroad.
>
> Because this air taxi system would require a massive fleet of aircraft to achieve network coverage, the price of the aircraft and its operating cost are critical components to the success of the system. Aircraft like the A700 could get the cost-per-seat mile down to a level where the average business traveler could afford the service.
>
> We don't need the air taxi model to take off for the A700 to be a successful project, but it would certainly provide a fantastic upside to our company.

With two distinct models flying, Rick and his company now had a real story to tell. CFO Mike Smith observed that for outside investors and municipal development groups, one of the most attractive aspects of the AAI plan was that the economics seemed entirely within the range of possibility:

> We could break even right out of this facility [at Centennial Field] by adding roughly 100 production people to our current staff of 150. With the A500, the current overhead breaks even at somewhere between 35 and 40 planes a year, and the jet would be roughly a third of that. We have a component capacity for about 100 planes a year, and an assembly capacity for about 40 or 50. The great thing about this company is at just 50 airplanes a

---

[8] Dr. Bruce Holmes led the Small Aircraft Transportation System (SATS) Program unit at NASA. SATS was a driving force in the incubation of innovative technologies necessary to bring affordable, on-demand flight service by small aircraft in near-all-weather conditions to small community airports.

EXHIBIT 4.9 Very Light Jet Segment—Competitor Profiles

Manufacturer	Product	List ($000)	Seats	Cruise Speed	First Delivery	Orders to Date (11-03)	Home Base
Avocet	Pro-Jet	2,000	6–8	420	Late 2006	200	Westport, Connecticut
Cessna	Citation Mustang	2.295	6	391	Late 2006	300+	Wichita, Kansas
Safire	Safire Jet	1,395	6	437	2006	300+	Miami, Florida
Eclipse	Eclipse 500	950	3–6	432	2006	2,060	Albuquerque, New Mexico

a

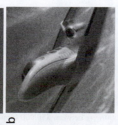
b

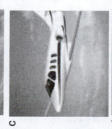
c

d

year, we're making money. So far we have taken deposits for over 50 twin pistons.[9] *Once we are certified, we anticipate a surge in orders.*

By late 2003 the planes had appeared on a host of aviation magazine covers and in a wide range of business publications including *The New York Times, The Wall Street Journal*, and *Forbes Magazine*. Nearly all seemed to be anticipating a significant American success story.

The Critical Juncture

Heading out for a meeting over in Boulder, John fired up his twin-engine Beechcraft as the A500 crossed his path on its way back to the hanger for further testing. As he taxied out in preparation for take-off, John recalled an earlier meeting with a reporter from an aviation magazine. When she had asked him whether he thought much about the possibility of failure, he prefaced his response with a story:

> *You know, we were speaking with some guys in the airborne fire-fighting business. They currently use airplanes that are roughly in the A500 class to fly lead-in for fire-fighting tankers. These spotter planes fly low and left of the tankers, and tell those pilots where to make the drop.*
>
> *They asked if we could put a window overhead on the A500 so their lead pilots could have good visibility of the tanker high and right. They told us that none of the established competitors they had spoken with would even consider that kind of modification. Our engineers told him that it would take us about a week to figure that out.*
>
> *The point is, that's why I don't spend much time thinking about the business risk of this venture. Adam Aircraft has been surprising the experts and our potential customers from the very beginning; there is no reason to assume we won't continue to do so.*

As John lifted off and banked north toward Boulder, he realized that his thrill of flying had never waned since he was a kid. Although he loved his 30-year-old Beech, he knew it wouldn't last forever—and there were a bunch of pilots just like him out there waiting for something new. He felt certain that Adam Aircraft would be the one to answer that call.

Preparation Questions

1. What is Adam Aircraft's business model?
2. Do you believe that Rick Adam can bring a new aircraft to market for so much less than conventional wisdom says it should cost?
    a. What are the factors that are critical to the success of Adam Aircraft?
    b. Which of those factors are the biggest risks?
    c. What can he do to control those risks?
3. If you were a potential investor, how would you compare the potential risks and rewards from an investment in Adam Aircraft with an investment in Jim Poss's company (Seahorse Power Corporation)?

---

[9] Initial deposits to secure a delivery position for an A-500 were between $50,000 (non-escrowed) and $100,000 (escrowed). An additional $50,000 progress payment would be due at aircraft type certification, with an additional $100,000 progress payment due six months prior to the scheduled delivery date of the aircraft. The balance would be due upon delivery.

(*Source*: Porter Gifford/Getty Images/News and Sports Services)

ENTREPRENEURIAL MARKETING

Marketing is at the heart of an organization because its task is to identify and serve customers' needs. In essence, marketing spans the boundaries between a company and its customers. It is marketing that delivers a company's products and services to customers, and marketing that takes information about those products and services, as well as about the company itself, to the market. In addition, it is marketing's role to bring information about the customers back to the company. Although many people relate the term "marketing" to advertising and promotion, the scope of marketing is much broader. The American Marketing Association defines marketing as:

> *An organizational function and a set of processes for creating, communicating, and delivering value to customers and for managing customer relationships in ways that benefit the organization and its stake holders.*[1]

Successful entrepreneurs select and optimize the marketing tools that best fit their unique challenges. Marketing practices vary depending on the type of company and the products and services it sells. Marketers of consumer products, such as carbonated soft drinks, use different tools than marketers of business-to-business products, such as network software. Companies in the services sector, such as banks, market differently from companies that sell durable goods, such as automobile manufacturers.

This chapter written by Abdul Ali and Kathleen Seiders.

Why Marketing Is Critical for Entrepreneurs

Marketing is a vital process for entrepreneurs because no venture can become established and grow without a customer market. The process of acquiring and retaining customers is at the core of marketing. Entrepreneurs must create the offer (design the product and set the price), take the offer to the market (through distribution), and, at the same time, tell the market about the offer (communications). These activities define the famous **Four Ps** of marketing: product, price, place (distribution), and promotion (communication).

Entrepreneurs often are faced with designing the entire "marketing system"—from the product and price to distribution and communication. Because it is difficult and expensive to bring new products and services to market—especially difficult for new companies—they need to be more resourceful in their marketing. Many entrepreneurs rely on creativity rather than cash to achieve a compelling image in a noisy marketplace.

An important part of gaining the market's acceptance is building brand awareness, which, depending on the stage of the venture, may be weak or even nonexistent. Entrepreneurs must differentiate their company's product or service so its distinctiveness and value are clear to the customer. This is the job of marketing.

Marketing also plays a central role in a venture's early growth stages when changes to the original business model may be necessary. Companies focused on growth must be able to switch marketing gears quickly and attract new and different customer segments.

Entrepreneurs Face Unique Marketing Challenges

Entrepreneurial marketing is different from marketing done by established companies for a number of reasons. First, entrepreneurial companies typically have limited resources—financial as well as managerial. Just as they rarely have enough money to support marketing activities, they also rarely have proven marketing expertise within the company. Most entrepreneurs do not have the option of hiring experienced marketing managers. Time—as well as money and marketing talent—is also often in short supply. Whereas larger corporations can spend hundreds of thousands or even millions on extensive marketing research, testing their strategies, and carefully designing marketing campaigns, new ventures find creative and less costly means to validate their ideas and reach customers.

Most entrepreneurs face daunting challenges. Their companies have little or no market share and a confined geographic market presence. As a result, they enjoy few economies of scale; for example, it is difficult for small companies to save money on "media buys" because their range of advertising is so limited. Entrepreneurs usually are restricted in their access to distributors—both wholesalers and retailers. On the customer side, entrepreneurs struggle with low brand awareness and customer loyalty, both of which must be carefully cultivated.

Not only is market information limited, but decision making can be muddled by strong, personal biases and beliefs. Early-stage companies often stumble in their marketing because of a product focus that is excessively narrow. Companies frequently assume that their products will be embraced by enthusiastic consumers when, in reality, consumer inertia prevents most new products from being accepted at all. Research has shown that common marketing-related dangers for entrepreneurs include overestimating demand, underestimating competitor response, and making uninformed distribution decisions.

Entrepreneurs market to multiple audiences: investors, customers, employees, and business partners. Because none of these bonds is well established for early-stage companies, entrepreneurs must be both customer-oriented and relationship-oriented. A customer orientation requires understanding the market and where it is going. A relationship orientation is needed to create structural and emotional ties with all stakeholders. *Thus, marketing helps entrepreneurs acquire resources by selling their ideas to potential investors and partners. It also allows entrepreneurs to leverage scarce resources through innovative business approaches.*

In this chapter, we consider entrepreneurial marketing in depth. Building upon the opportunity defining and refining discussion in Chapter 3, we provide direction on market research, that is, collecting information useful to making marketing and strategy decisions. Next, we focus on implementing marketing strategies that make the most of these opportunities. We also look at how certain marketing skills serve to support a new company's growth.

Acquiring Market Information

An entrepreneur needs to do research to identify and assess an opportunity. Intuition, personal expertise, and passion can take you only so far. Some studies show that good pre-venture market analysis could reduce venture failure rates by as much as 60%.[2] But many entrepreneurs tend to ignore negative market information because of a strong commitment to their idea. Whereas Chapter 2 defined what an opportunity is, and Chapter 3 presented a checklist on assessing how attractive your opportunity might be, this chapter provides a drill-down on how you collect data to validate your initial impressions of the opportunity.

We define **marketing research** as the collection and analysis of any reliable information that improves managerial decisions. Questions that marketing research can answer include: What product attributes are important to customers? How is customers' willingness to buy influenced by product design, pricing, and communications? Where do customers buy this kind of product? How is the market likely to change in the future?

There are two basic types of market data: **secondary data**, which marketers gather from already published sources, like an industry association study or census reports, and **primary data**, which marketers collect specifically for a particular purpose through focus groups, surveys, or experiments. You can find a great deal of market information in secondary resources. Secondary research requires less time and money than primary research, and it should be your first avenue. Entrepreneurs sometimes use databases at college libraries to collect baseline information about product and geographic markets (Figure 7.5 in Chapter 7 lists some common databases).

Some types of primary data are easy to collect, for instance, with personal interviews or focus groups, but keep in mind the limitations of such data, such as lack of statistical significance (because the samples are small). To ensure that they obtain high-quality data, some entrepreneurs hire marketing research firms to perform research studies. Lower-cost alternatives do exist: for example, business school professors might assign the company's project to a student research team. In choosing a research approach, balance your quality and time constraints with the possible cost savings.

The appendix at the end of this chapter provides a checklist of possible questions to address in a customer research interview. You can structure such an interview as one-on-one or as a focus group. In focus groups, a discussion leader encourages five to ten people

Stage		Examples of Effective Questions
Introduction	◉	Think of the last time you purchased Product X. What prompted or triggered this activity?
	◉	How often do you use X?
Rapport Building	◉	What are some of the reasons for so many products in this industry?
In-depth Investigation	◉	Here is a new idea about this market. In what ways is this idea different from what you see in the marketplace?
	◉	What features are missing from this new product?
	◉	What would you need to know about this idea in order to accept it?
Closure	◉	Is this focus group discussion what you expected?

■ Figure 5.1

Focus group overview

to express their views about the company's products or services. The focus group has distinct stages, and you will need to ask specific questions to get good-quality information from the group participants. Figure 5.1 displays these stages and the techniques for asking effective questions in each.

Customer acceptance of an entrepreneur's idea is proof that the opportunity is worth pursuing. Entrepreneurs must understand the customer decision-making process and how to influence the customer's choice. Such customer understanding enables entrepreneurs to develop the right products at the right prices (create and capture value) and then market these products to the right customers in the right place (communicate and deliver value). Further, such knowledge of customers' behavior at each stage of the decision-making process helps entrepreneurs to be effective and efficient with their communication strategy to reach the target customers. Figure 5.2 provides an illustration of the role marketing tools play in the customer choice process.

Provider

- Create and Capture Value
  - Product/service features
  - Price
- Deliver and Communicate Value
  - Availability
  - Advertising
  - Sales force
  - Public relations
  - Guerrilla marketing

Customer

➤ Awareness
  ↓
➤ Perceptions
  ↓
➤ Preferences
  ↓
➤ Choice
  ↓
➤ Satisfaction/loyalty

■ Figure 5.2

Understanding the customer choice process

Marketing Strategy for Entrepreneurs

A company's marketing strategy must closely align with its resources and capabilities. Entrepreneurial companies with limited resources have little room for strategic mistakes. Segmentation, targeting, and positioning are key marketing dimensions that set the strategic framework. We begin this section by discussing these three activities and their role in marketing strategy. Then we examine the widely studied marketing elements known as the marketing mix: product, price, distribution (place), and communications (promotion).

Segmentation, Targeting, and Positioning

Segmentation and *targeting* are the processes marketers use to identify the "right" customers for their company's products and services. In Chapter 3, we talked about the segment your opportunity would initially target, what we call the Primary Target Audience or PTA. As we move beyond opportunity recognition into implementation of a marketing strategy, we need to revisit our initial conceptions and refine what that PTA segment really means. A **segment** is a group of customers defined by certain common bases or characteristics that may be demographic, psychographic (commonly called *lifestyle characteristics*), or behavioral. Demographic characteristics include age, education, gender, and income; lifestyle characteristics include descriptors like active, individualistic, risk-taking, and time-pressured. Behavioral characteristics include consumer traits such as brand loyalty and willingness to adopt new products.

Marketers identify the most relevant bases for segmentation and then develop segment profiles. It's common to define a segment using a combination of demographic and lifestyle characteristics, for example high-income, sophisticated, baby boomers. Marketers also segment customers based on where they live (geography), how often they use a product (usage rates), and what they value in a product (product attribute preferences).

Targeting compares the defined segments and then selects the most attractive one, which becomes the PTA. Target market definition is essential because it guides your company's *customer selection* strategy. The attractiveness of a segment is related to its size, growth rate, and profit potential. Your targeting decisions should also reflect your company's specific capabilities and longer-term goals. Accurate targeting is important for entrepreneurs: it is not always clear which customer segment(s) represents the best target market, and finding out may require some research and some trial and error. As we noted in Chapter 3, it is wise to identify Secondary Target Audiences (STAs) in case the PTA doesn't prove out as expected. Nevertheless, identifying the appropriate target market early on is critical because pursuing multiple targets or waiting for one to emerge is an expensive strategy.

To illustrate segmentation and targeting, let's look at the example of Nantucket Nectars, the beverage company founded by marketing-savvy entrepreneurs Tom Scott and Tom First. Relevant segment characteristics for this company are age, individualism, and health-consciousness. In Nantucket Nectar's early days, its primary target market was young, active, health-oriented consumers who enjoyed breaking with conformity by choosing a noncarbonated soft drink alternative. As Nantucket Nectars gained public awareness, it gave the company power to move beyond its PTA to STAs and ultimately the broader, nationwide drink market. Scott and First started the company with an initial investment of $9,000 and a production run of 1,400 cases. In 1997 they sold a majority stake in the business to Ocean Spray for $70 million. Cadbury bought the firm from Ocean Spray in 2002. At the time, Nantucket Nectars had estimated revenues of $80 million.[3]

While segmentation and targeting profile a company's customers, **positioning** relates to competitors and to customers' *perceptions* of your product. Positioning usually describes a company's offering relative to certain product attributes—the ones customers care about most. Such attributes often include price, quality, and convenience, all of which can be scaled from high to low. For example, if brands of single-serve beverages were shown on a positioning map (see Figure 5.3) with the two dimensions of *price* and *quality*, Nantucket Nectars would be positioned in the high-price, high-quality (upper-right) quadrant, whereas a store-brand juice would likely be positioned in a lower-price, lower-quality (lower-left) quadrant.

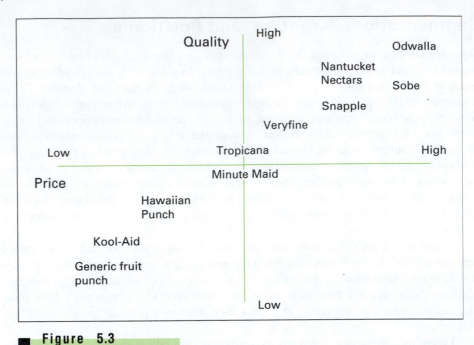

Figure 5.3

Nantucket Nectars position map

The Marketing Mix

The marketing mix—the Four Ps of product, price, place, and promotion—is a set of tools your company can use to achieve its marketing goals. In fact, the marketing mix is so basic to a company's business model that *marketing* strategy often defines company or corporate strategy. In this section, we discuss the individual elements of the marketing mix, shown in Figure 5.4. Our focus is on the particular challenges entrepreneurial marketers face.

Figure 5.4

Marketing mix strategy for an entrepreneur

Product Strategy. We can divide product strategy into the **core product** and the **augmented product**. The core product is the essential good or service, while the augmented product is the set of attributes peripherally related to it. For example, Apple manufactures and markets its iPod, the core product, but it also provides iTunes for downloading music and product troubleshooting as augmented services.

Another way to look at the product variable part of the marketing mix is in terms of goods and services (the word *product* here can refer to either a service or a good). Whereas beverages and computers are obviously tangible goods, supermarkets, Internet service providers, and banks are services *and* offer service products, such as food shopping, Internet access, and debit accounts. The line between products and services has been eroding for some time. Furthermore, we live in a service economy, and a large part of the gross national product and new job creation are tied to services.

In your product strategy, you'll pay attention to the strength of the *value proposition* you are offering customers, and make sure your products are clearly *differentiated*. You'll also be guided by the *product life cycle* in crafting your strategy, and by *product diffusion theory* in assessing how fast consumers will adopt your products. Finally, from the beginning, you should be obsessively focused on *quality*.

Many entrepreneurs establish companies based on a new product or product line. When developing any new product, your company must ensure that it is truly addressing an "unmet consumer need"—that there is a real **customer value proposition (CVP)**. **Customer value** is the difference between total customer benefits and total customer costs, which are both monetary and nonmonetary. A product attribute is not a benefit until consumers buy into the advantage.

Identifying a customer value proposition, also known as a *positioning statement*, is an essential step in the marketing of a product or service, regardless of your industry. Any positioning statement has four elements: (1) target group and need, (2) brand, (3) concept, and (4) point of difference. The formula is straightforward. Entrepreneurs need to know which attributes customers consider important and how customers rate the company's products—and competing products—on each attribute. Figure 5.5 shows how you can identify the product/service attributes you'll consider when designing your offerings.

Product differentiation is important for initial product success as well as for longer-term brand building. In its early days, Maker's Mark, a sixth-generation, family-run Kentucky bourbon producer, leveraged the product-related attributes that make its bourbon unique (for example, wheat instead of rye, six-year fermentation, and small batch production) to build a distinctive image for the brand. For decades, the company has been able to rely on these product differences to reinforce its quality position.

A venerable framework for understanding product strategy is the **product life cycle**. The stages of the product life cycle are **introduction, growth, maturity, and decline**. Product life-cycle analysis can help you recognize how marketing requirements differ at each stage of a company's growth. During the introduction stage, marketers must educate the customer and secure distribution. During the growth stage, they cultivate customer loyalty and build the brand. Differentiation is important during maturity, and marketing efficiency is critical during the decline stage.

In a business environment with intense global competition and fast-paced technology, entrepreneurs must continue to develop new products in order to maintain a profitable market position, even after creating a winning new venture. New product development is

| | | Perceived Performance | |
		"Poor"	"Good"
Attribute	High	Improve	Maintain
Importance	Low	Monitor	De-emphasize

Source: Adapted from John A. Martilla and John C. James[4]

Figure 5.5

Importance-performance analysis

Courtesy Maker's Mark

critical for market longevity. Entrepreneurship combined with innovation equals success. Naturally, entrepreneurs need to understand new product opportunities and the new product development process if they are to ensure their venture's survival.

Because new products have varying levels of *newness* to both the company and the marketplace, entrepreneurs must make different kinds of *risk-return* trade-offs. At one extreme, pioneering or radical innovation represents a technological breakthrough or "new-to-the-world" product. Although pioneering products may be risky investments, they can produce handsome returns. At the other extreme, entrepreneurs may develop *incremental* products, which are modifications of existing products, or *product line extensions*. Incremental products are less risky to develop but typically produce a more modest return. Regardless of the type of new products you develop, bringing products to market quickly—by mastering the new product development process—is critical for gaining a competitive advantage.

If you introduce highly innovative products, be particularly attentive to consumer adoption behavior. Consumer willingness to adopt a new product is a major factor in the realm of technology products. The **product diffusion curve** (see Figure 5.6) captures adoption behavior graphically, showing customer segments called innovators, early adopters, early majority, late majority, and laggards. A number of factors affect the *rate of diffusion*, or how fast customers adopt a new product. If a product represents risk or is complex, or is not completely compatible with existing products, then the market usually will adopt it at a fairly slow rate.

Entrepreneurs sometimes err in being overly product focused, concentrating on the product as they conceive it rather than as customers may want it. One way to offset the danger of this mindset is to involve the customer in the design process. Custom Research, a Baldrige National Quality Award-winning marketing research firm, performs a comprehensive survey of each of its clients prior to beginning a project. This allows the company to learn exactly what the client expects and hopes to gain from its investment. The practice of studying the customer upfront not only results in better service quality, but also enables you to deliver a highly customized product.

Finally, perhaps the most important product attribute for entrepreneurs is quality, which serves as a powerful differentiator and is needed to gain the recommendation of customers. Positive word-of-mouth recommendations are essential because most customers are not yet familiar with the

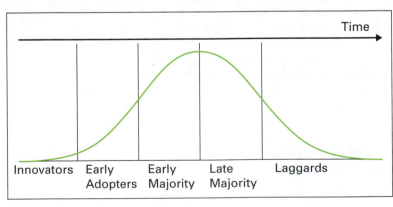

Figure 5.6

Product diffusion curve

company. Entrepreneurial companies with a quality orientation also find it easier to engage in internal marketing: employees are more enthusiastic about and proud to be selling high-quality products than products of mediocre quality.

Pricing Strategy. Developing an optimal pricing strategy is a daunting challenge for even the most sophisticated entrepreneurial company. Figure 5.7 shows various price-setting options.

Entrepreneurs incur many costs in starting a venture. Some are *fixed costs*, which do not change with the volume of production (such as facility, equipment, and salaries), and some are *variable costs*, which do change with the volume of production (such as raw materials, hourly labor, and sales commissions). The price of a product/service must be higher than its variable cost (point A in Figure 5.7) or you will sustain losses with the sale of each additional unit. To operate successfully, an entrepreneurial venture must not only recover both fixed (point B) and variable costs but also must make a reasonable profit (point C). The crash of many early dot-com businesses illustrates this simple financial logic, as a number of these companies followed a "get-big-fast" strategy by aggressively selling their products below cost. Online grocery businesses such as Webvan fell into this trap: the expense of filling and delivering each order exceeded the profitability of the sale.

Many entrepreneurs, in setting prices, use a *cost-based method*, marking up a product based on its cost plus a desired profit margin (point C in Figure 5.7). Another method, often used in conjunction with a mark-up, is matching competitors' prices. A common problem with these methods is that they allow entrepreneurs to price too low, thereby "leaving money on the table." Pricing too low can hurt the long-term profitability of the venture. Of course, pricing too high also has a serious downside, as it can create a purchase barrier and limit sales.

So what choices does an entrepreneur have in identifying the most appropriate price? An alternative to cost-based and competitive pricing is *perceived value pricing* (point D), which is especially viable for pricing a new or innovative product or service. Entrepreneurs also can pursue strategies that trade off high profit margins for high sales, or vice versa. Determining the full value of a product/service and then using effective communications to convince target customers to pay for that value are challenging tasks even for an established company.

If possible, approach perceived value pricing with pre-market price testing, estimating the number of units customers will purchase at different price points. Two well-known pricing strategies, which represent opposite ends of the pricing spectrum, are price skimming and penetration pricing. **Price skimming** sets high margins; you can expect to gain limited market share because your prices will be relatively high. **Penetration**

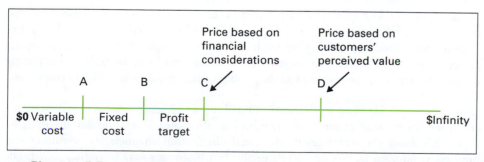

Figure 5.7

Pricing decision for an entrepreneur

pricing aims to gain high market share with lower margins and relatively lower prices. For entrepreneurs with a product that brings something new to the marketplace, a skimming strategy is usually best. Unless your channels of distribution are very well established, a penetration strategy, generally reserved for mature products, is hard to implement.

We can represent price in a variety of ways. There are basic **price points** (also called *price levels*) for products, which are standardized or fixed, and there are **price promotions**—a tool by which marketers can achieve specific goals, such as introducing a product to a new customer market. Price promotions are short term and use regular price levels as a base to discount from; they provide a way to offer customers good deals. Price promotions let you increase sales, reward distributors, gain awareness for a new product, and clear excess inventory. Periodically, Nantucket Nectars coordinates a price promotion with its retailers, who offer its 16-ounce juices (such as Peach Nectar) with an advertised, 25%-off price. This type of promotion typically doubles sales on the products, benefiting both the manufacturer and the retailers.

Price promotions often are necessary to maintain good relationships with distributors: both wholesalers and retailers must offer price promotions in order to stay competitive. In business-to-business markets, companies often reward their business customers with volume discounts applied to the ongoing purchase of particular goods and services. Promotions are an important tool for entrepreneurs, too, who often use them to gain an initial position in the marketplace. At its earliest stage, Nantucket Nectars used *trade promotions* to motivate retailers to make the initial "buys" of their products and *customer promotions* to motivate the retailers' customers to try the products.

A common pricing strategy is **price discrimination,** which charges different prices to different customer segments. Examples of this practice are highly varied and include the lower prices received by shoppers using store loyalty cards and the differing price structures used to charge airline passengers. *Couponing* is a widely used form of price discrimination that rewards customers who care about receiving a discount, but does not reward those who don't care enough to put forth the extra effort to redeem the coupon.

Pricing is important to entrepreneurs, not just because it affects revenue and profit, but also because price plays a role in how consumers perceive a product's position in the market. Price serves as a quality cue to consumers, especially when they have had limited experience with the product. The *economic perspective* views consumers as rational actors who buy when the perceived benefits of a product exceeds its price. Those who study consumer behavior, however, understand that consumers' *willingness to pay* is not totally rational but is affected by a variety of psychological factors.

Entrepreneurs can use some marketplace wisdom relative to pricing. First, the selling effort for a product must match its price. Price skimming, for example, must be accompanied by a sophisticated, effective selling process. It is easier to lower than raise prices because customers are resistant to price increases. The more established the differentiation and/or quality of a product or service, the more price-insensitive the consumer—if he or she values the perceived benefits. Customers also are less price-sensitive when products and services are bundled into a single offer, because this makes prices more difficult to compare. A good entrepreneur will be aware of both the pricing practices of competing companies and the pricing-related purchase behavior of consumers.

Distribution Strategy (Place). Distribution presents special challenges for entrepreneurs because channels of distribution often are difficult to set up initially. Figure 5.8 shows the structure of traditional distribution channels for consumer and business-to-business marketing. While established businesses may introduce new products, price points, and communications strategies, they usually rely on existing channels of distribution. For example, Crest, a Procter & Gamble brand, may introduce a new type of electric toothbrush with a distinctive price position and an innovative advertising

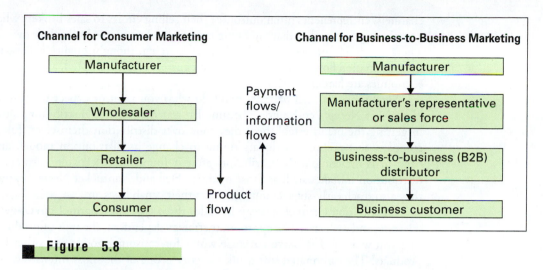

Figure 5.8

Traditional distribution channels

campaign, but it will use its existing network of wholesalers and retailers to actually distribute the product. Entrepreneurs usually don't have this luxury.

Finding the right channel can be far less difficult than breaking into the right channel. Entrepreneurs who want to market food products, for instance, face enormous barriers when they try to get their products on supermarket shelves, as the Gourmet Chili case in Chapter 3 illustrated. Most supermarkets are national chains that charge large slotting fees. Even when brokers and distributors accept new products into their lines, they may be unwilling to dedicate much effort to selling them when the products are unknown.

Distribution can be problematic for entrepreneurial service companies as well as for those that manufacture goods. Distribution decisions for a service company often are location decisions, because many services require that service providers interact directly with customers. Effective distribution is the availability and accessibility of a service to its target customers. As early-stage service companies grow, new locations often are the most important means of attracting new customers and increasing sales.

Starbucks is an international services-sector company with thousands of stores; nevertheless, the service is sold locally, and one location may be more or less successful than another. If a Starbucks location is unsuccessful, the company can cancel its lease and open an alternative location in that neighborhood, or focus on locations in other neighborhoods. But if entrepreneurs make a bad location decision for their first or second or even third location, the financial loss can paralyze the company.

Poor distribution decisions have haunted many entrepreneurial companies. Dell Computer, in its early years, became worried about the limitations of its direct-to-consumer model and decided to go into the retail marketplace with its personal computers. The low product margins and high promotional costs of the new channel took Dell by surprise, and the company lost millions of dollars before it quickly pulled out of the retail channel. Were it not for Michael Dell's brave decision to admit his mistake and execute a fast about-face, Dell might have stumbled fatally trying to make the strategy succeed.

There is a great deal of *interdependency* in a distribution channel: each channel member has a particular function to perform, and each relies on the others. Entrepreneurs especially are inclined to rely on other companies to fulfill certain distribution tasks. Many companies were able to enter the Internet retailing sector quickly because they could outsource *fulfillment*—warehousing, packing, and delivering the order—to another company, allowing them to maintain *virtual* companies with low fixed costs. In business-to-business channels, entrepreneurs often outsource their selling efforts to sales brokers who work for a marketing firm, rather than investing the time and money to build their own sales force. There are disadvantages to this kind of outsourcing, though: quality is hard to control, the information flow between you and your customer is interrupted, and longer-term cost economies are harder to achieve.

Sometimes channel partners don't do what you want or expect them to do. When Nantucket Nectar's co-founders became frustrated with their distributor's slow progress in getting the brand established, they took over distribution themselves. Like Dell, the company lost millions of dollars trying to change its distribution model, and it went back to contracting with distributors after it found more capable partners. Although distribution mistakes such as those made by Dell and Nantucket Nectars extract a price, they also teach early-stage companies what their capabilities are.

Distribution channel strategy includes three types of **channel coverage**: intensive, selective, and exclusive. The appropriate strategy depends on the type of product or service that you will sell. **Intensive** coverage works for consumer goods and other fast-moving products. The carbonated soft drink category is one of the most intensively distributed: products are sold in supermarkets, drug stores, convenience stores, restaurants, vending machines, sporting event concessions, and fast-food outlets. **Selective** distribution brings the product to specific distributors, often limiting selection geographically by establishing a dealer network. Kate Spade sells her handbags and other fashion accessories to high-end department stores but not to mainstream retailers or mass merchandisers. Selective distribution can protect dealers and retailers from competition, while helping manufacturers maintain prices by thwarting price competition. The third coverage strategy, **exclusive** distribution, is often used for luxury products. For some time, Neiman Marcus had exclusive rights to distribute the Hermès line of very high-end leather goods and fashion accessories.

Channel partnerships (or *relationships*) have important implications for entrepreneurs. Often the channel member with the most power will prevail; for this reason, **channel power** is an important concept in distribution strategy. While channel partnerships can speed a young company's growth, preserve resources, and transfer risk, entrepreneurs must be careful not to sacrifice their direct relationship with customers. Most important, entrepreneurs must carefully manage their relationships with channel partners and monitor them over time.

Another widely applied concept, **channel conflict,** refers to situations where differing objectives and turf overlap lead to true disharmony in the channel. Channel conflict was a high-profile phenomenon in the early days of the Internet, when many startup companies were using the strategy of **disintermediation**—cutting intermediaries out of traditional distribution channels by selling directly to customers. Amazon.com, the online bookseller, created conflict between book publishers and distributors and traditional book retailers. Because Amazon could buy in volume and avoid the high occupancy costs retailers pay, it could offer an enormous assortment at deeply discounted prices. Amazon's volume allowed it to negotiate low prices from publishers and wholesalers, who in turn alienated their other customers, the traditional book retailers in the channel.

Entrepreneurs succeed with their distribution strategies when they have a strong understanding of channel economics. Giro, the bicycle helmet company that outfitted both Greg LeMonde and Lance Armstrong—famous American winners of the Tour de France—gained initial access to the retail channel by offering high margins and selective distribution to preferred bike shops. This allowed the company to maintain its premium prices and establish loyalty among experts and cycling enthusiasts.

Current practice reflects a focus on multi-channel distribution, which gives a company the ability to reach multiple segments, gain marketing synergies, provide flexibility for customers, save on customer acquisition costs, and build a robust database of purchase information. J.Crew, for instance, has been successful diversifying its store-based business to include strong catalog and online channels. But a multi-channel strategy adds operating complexity and demands more resources, so entrepreneurs are best to approach these opportunities cautiously and be careful that their timing is in line with their capabilities and resources. For example, TiVo's strategy to push its innovative product through both specialty stores like Tweeter and consumer-electronics superstores like Best Buy created problems for the successful launch of its product. TiVo should have used the specialty store channel exclusively in the beginning rather than both channels. Specialty stores are not willing to provide time and service to develop the market for an innovative product when they have to compete on price with consumer-electronics superstores.

Research shows that many of the most serious obstacles to entrepreneurial success are related to distribution. Specifically, entrepreneurs tend to be overdependent on channel partners and short on understanding channel behavior in their industry. It is critical that entrepreneurs take the time to learn about distribution and make fact-based decisions about channel design and channel partnerships to overcome these threats to good distribution strategy.

Marketing Communications Strategy (Promotion). Marketing communications convey messages to the market—messages about the company's products and services as well as about the company itself. The marketing communications element of the marketing mix is a mix within a mix: the **communications mix** is defined as *advertising, sales promotion, public relations, personal selling,* and *direct marketing* (sometimes included with advertising). The marketing communications mix and some of its key elements are shown in Figure 5.9.

The components of the communications mix, like the marketing mix, are often referred to as *tools,* and the use of these tools by marketers differs substantially across business and industry contexts. To illustrate, consumer product companies' communications are often aimed at mass markets and include advertising and sales promotions, whereas

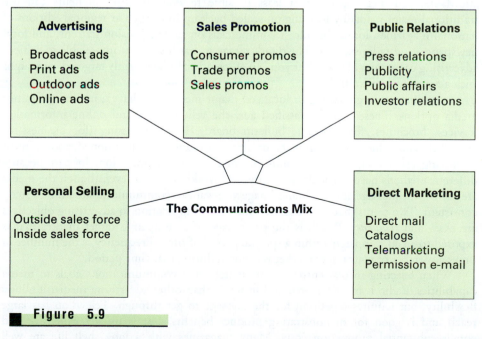

Advertising

Broadcast ads
Print ads
Outdoor ads
Online ads

Sales Promotion

Consumer promos
Trade promos
Sales promos

Public Relations

Press relations
Publicity
Public affairs
Investor relations

Personal Selling

Outside sales force
Inside sales force

The Communications Mix

Direct Marketing

Direct mail
Catalogs
Telemarketing
Permission e-mail

■ **Figure 5.9**

Marketing communications

business-to-business companies use more customized, interactive tools, such as personal selling by a sales force. Of course, the communications a marketer uses are closely aligned with the specific type of product the company is attempting to sell, as well as with the company's marketing objectives.

It is common marketing wisdom to use a variety of tools in marketing any product or service. Because of this focus on multiple methods, and the need to integrate and coordinate these methods, we often call the process **integrated marketing communications.** A range of factors—including cost, timing, and target market—determines the selection of a company's key communications tools. The question you must answer is: "What is the most effective way to communicate with my customers and influence their actions?" And the sooner you can answer this, the better.

Two communications strategies are *push* and *pull*. A **push** strategy aims to push a product through the channel using tools such as trade promotions, trade shows, and personal selling to distributors or other channel members. A **pull** strategy's goal, on the other hand, is to create end-user demand and rely on that demand to pull the product through the channel. Pull strategies, which are directly targeted to end users, include advertising and consumer sales promotions, such as in-store specials. These strategies also are relevant for service companies. Fidelity Investments, for example, can push its mutual funds through brokers or advertise them directly to investors, who, the company hopes, will then request them.

Marketing communications is a broad and sophisticated field. Many of the most visible tools are primarily accessible to large companies with deep marketing budgets and in-house marketing talent. This is usually the case for large, national television and print advertising and high-penetration direct mail campaigns. Probably the greatest breadth of tools exists within the domain of advertising, which includes everything from billboards to Web sites to local newspapers to Super Bowl commercials. There also are various direct marketing tools, including catalogs, direct mail and e-mail, telemarketing, and infomercials (vehicles for direct selling).

What *advertising* choices are available to an entrepreneur? Anything that is appropriate, affordable, and measurable, or at least possible to evaluate. Entrepreneurs can use traditional major media by focusing on scaled-back options, such as regional editions of national magazines, locally broadcast commercials on cable television stations, and local newspapers and radio stations. The disadvantage is that it's almost impossible to achieve advertising economies of scale. But you can efficiently conduct tightly targeted campaigns with a focus on cost control.

In addition to regionalized or localized major media, you have a number of minor media options. These include classified ads, the yellow pages and online information services, brochures, flyers, online bulletin boards, local canvassing (for business-to-business), and educational seminars or demonstrations. As mentioned above, most marketing experts support using multiple methods in combination, in part because different methods have particular strengths and weaknesses. But even though the media are varied, the message and the brand image you want to communicate should be strictly consistent. Two terms that are frequently mentioned in relation to advertising objectives are *reach* and *frequency*. **Reach** is the percentage of a company's target market that is exposed to an ad campaign within a specific period of time. **Frequency** is the number of times a member of your target market is exposed during that time period.

When selecting media, entrepreneurs match their communications goals to media capabilities. Radio is more targeted and intimate than other advertising media; it allows flexibility, but requires repetition for the message to get through. Television has large reach and is good for demonstrating product benefits, but is usually expensive and entails substantial production costs. Many magazines with a long shelf life are well targeted (consider how many times a magazine may be read in a doctor's waiting room).

Newspapers are good for geographical targeting and promotional advertising, but have a very short shelf life. Infomercials, which we may also consider a direct marketing tool, have production costs and a short life span, but are persuasive and good for telling the product story. Online advertising, which continues to grow in importance, allows companies to reach a specific and often desirable customer market. Figure 5.10 presents brief guidelines for the strategic use of advertising media.

Advertising Medium	Key Factors for Entrepreneurs to Consider
Brochures and flyers	◉ Allows creative flexibility and focused message
	◉ Production quantity and distribution must be well planned
Direct mail and e-mail	◉ Permits precise targeting and encourages direct response
	◉ Results are measurable and can guide future campaigns
Infomercials	◉ Effective for telling a story and communicating or endorsing product benefits
	◉ Costly to produce but measurable and good for collecting data
Internet communications	◉ A variety of options, such as banner ads and permission e-mail marketing
	◉ Superior for collecting data and measuring responses
Magazines	◉ Can easily be targeted, are involving for readers, and have a long shelf life
	◉ Offer budget flexibility but involve a long lead time
Newsletters	◉ Good creative opportunities and maximum control
	◉ Cost factors (time and money) should be carefully considered
Newspapers	◉ Best medium for advertising promotions and reaching a geographically based or local market
	◉ Shelf life is fairly short and ads are usually not carefully read
Outdoor	◉ Can have strong visual impact and repeat exposure; this medium is believed to offer a high return on investment
	◉ Targeting is difficult because ads are location-bound
Radio	◉ Good potential for creativity and connecting with the audience; message can be easily varied
	◉ Excellent for targeting but ads must be repeated to be effective
Telemarketing	◉ Interactive communication with one-on-one selling capabilities
	◉ A direct response method that has faced increased regulation because it is seen by many to be intrusive
Television	◉ High media and production costs but superior reach; most effective way to present and demonstrate a product
	◉ Commonly used for brand building
Yellow pages	◉ An important local medium used as a basic reference by consumers; necessary for credibility
	◉ Low cost, but standardized format limits creativity

Figure 5.10

Strategic use of advertising media

Even entrepreneurs often go to marketing experts for advice about how to execute campaigns and how to frame an effective message. While some early-stage companies use established advertising agencies, others contract with freelance marketing professionals, many of whom have experience in the entrepreneurial domain. You'll want to learn the basics of advertising, public relations, and marketing research in order to be able to select and evaluate agencies or individuals you bring in to assist your company with its early-stage marketing.

The three primary types of **sales promotion** are consumer promotions, trade promotions, and sales force promotions. **Consumer promotions** are deals offered directly to consumers to support a pull strategy. **Trade promotions** are deals offered to a company's trade or channel partners—such as distributors or retailers—to support a traditional push strategy. **Sales force promotions** motivate and reward the company's own sales force or its distributors' sales forces.

There are two basic types of sales promotions: price and nonprice. We discussed price promotions earlier in the section on pricing strategy. *Consumer* price promotions include coupons, rebates, and loyalty rewards; *trade* price promotions include discounts, allowances, buy-back guarantees, and slotting fees. Types of *consumer* nonprice promotions include product sampling, advertising specialties (such as t-shirts with a brand logo), contests, and sweepstakes. *Trade* nonprice promotions include trade shows and sales contests.

The effects of sales promotions differ from the effects of advertising. In general, sales promotions produce more immediate, sales-driven results whereas advertising produces a more long-term, brand-building result. Sales promotions have become increasingly popular with companies in the last couple of decades.

Many entrepreneurs derive great value from using **public relations (PR)** as a strategic communications tool. PR has two major dimensions: *publicity* and *corporate communications*. When Merrill Lynch published a full-page tribute to the victims of the September 11th World Trade Center attack, that was a corporate communication designed to convey sympathy. When Merrill Lynch presents itself as the sponsor of a public television fundraiser or a golf tournament, or issues a press release announcing the promotion of an executive, it does so to gain positive publicity. Bill Samuels Jr., the CEO of Maker's Mark Bourbon, used a personal connection and an elaborate plan to gain major-league publicity:

> Dave Garino covered the Kentucky area for The Wall Street Journal. *Bill Jr. discovered that he and Dave had a mutual friend, Sam Walker, with whom Dave had gone to journalism school. Bill Jr. knew Dave was going to be in town covering an unrelated story and decided to try a unique approach to persuade him to do a story on Maker's Mark. Bill Jr. staged an event at the distillery and awarded exclusive rights to cover the show to a local news station. He found out which hotel Dave Garino was staying in and had Sam Walker arrange to meet Dave for cocktails in the hotel's bar. Next, Bill Jr. convinced the bartender to turn all the televisions above the bar to the local station that was covering the distillery show. When Dave saw the news footage he asked Sam what Maker's Mark was and why, if there was so much interest in this distillery, had he never heard of it. When Sam replied that it was the local favorite and offered to introduce him to Bill Jr., he accepted. Subsequently, Dave and Bill Jr. spent three days developing a story that was published on the front page of* The Wall Street Journal *in August of 1980.*
>
> *Bill Jr. recalled: "From that one story we received about 50,000 letters inquiring about our product. The phone lines didn't stop ringing for weeks. We had one salesman at the time and we were trying to figure how to best capitalize from all this publicity."*

And the rest, as they say, is history.[5]

It is often argued that publicity is an entrepreneur's best friend, more valuable than millions of dollars of advertising. The reason is that PR is perceived as more credible and more objective; a reporter's words are more believable than those of an advertising agency. Also, the argument goes, PR is free! This, of course, is not true—it takes a significant amount of time and effort, sometimes money, and always the ability to leverage connections to generate good PR. If this were not the case, there would not be so many public relations firms charging high fees and battling for the media's attention.

For companies operating in a business-to-business environment, or those that need to sell into an established distribution channel, *personal selling* is a core component of the communications mix. Although some companies separate sales and marketing, a company's sales force is often its primary marketing tool. Establishing and managing a sales force requires decisions related to sales force size, training, organization, compensation, and selling approaches.

A sales force is often considered to be a company's most valuable asset. Maintaining a strong sales force is an expensive proposition, though, and startup companies often face a difficult decision: whether to absorb the expense and sell directly or hire manufacturers' representatives (*reps*, sometimes called *brokers*) to sell the company's products (along with those of other companies) on commission. Reps are advantageous in that they have existing relationships with customers, but a company has more control—and a closer relationship with its customers—if it invests in its own sales force. A sales force may be organized geographically, by product line, by customer size, or by customer segment or industry. Compensation is usually some mix of base salary and commission, and incentives may be linked to gaining new customers, exceeding sales quotas, or increasing profitability. Current marketing practice places a high value on selecting and retaining customers based on their profit potential to the company. The sales force typically should have access to effective selling materials, credible technical data, and sales automation software that will ensure an effective and efficient selling process.

Personal selling is an important activity for entrepreneurs on an informal, personal level—through professional networking. Leveraging personal and industry connections is a key success factor, especially in the startup or early growth stage of the venture. But this is a time-consuming and often laborious process, which is often neglected and rarely fully optimized. Giro's founder personally attended top triathlons and other high-profile races across the country, demonstrating his helmets and giving them to the best cyclists. He was ahead of his time in understanding the value of endorsements from world-class athletes.

Entrepreneurs can implement *direct marketing* campaigns to be broad-based or to be local or limited in scope. Direct marketing methods include direct mail, catalogs, telemarketing, infomercials, and permission e-mail (where consumers "opt-in" to receive messages). The effectiveness of direct media is easy to measure, and these media are ideal for building a database that can be used for future marketing and analysis. Direct marketing is an important tool for communicating with new or existing customers, whom you can target for mailings that range from thank-you notes to announcements of future promotions.

With the increased use of technology and databases in marketing, and the growth of the Internet channel, the practice of "one-to-one" marketing has become pervasive. This type of marketing is interactive and has qualities similar to personal selling: your company can address a customer on an individual level, factoring in that customer's previous purchasing behavior and other kinds of information, and then respond accordingly. It is the use of databases that allow marketers to personalize communications and design customer-specific messages.

Customer Relationship Management (CRM) systems are designed to help companies compile and manage data about their customers. While CRM systems are usually large-scale and expensive, an astute entrepreneur can set up a more fundamental system to capture and use customer data to facilitate relationship building. Part of this process is capturing the right metrics—for example, the *cost of customer acquisition* or the *average lifetime value of a customer*—and knowing how to act on them.

Guerrilla Marketing

Guerrilla marketing is marketing activities that are nontraditional, grassroots, and captivating—that gain consumers' attention and build awareness of the company. Guerrilla marketing is often linked to "creating a buzz" or generating a lot of word-of-mouth in the marketplace. The terms *buzz*, *viral*, and *word-of-mouth* marketing aren't interchangeable. According to the Word of Mouth Marketing Association (WOMMA), the three concepts are defined as in the following box.[6]

Entrepreneurs may use all of these nontraditional promotion campaigns to get people's attention, especially younger generations who may not pay attention to TV campaigns and print media. Guerrilla marketing is also attractive to entrepreneurs because often they have to work with a limited or nonexistent promotion budget, and traditional media are very expensive. Unfortunately for entrepreneurs, such nontraditional promotional methods are getting the attention of big marketers, who want to break through the clutter of existing media. BzzAgent, a Boston-based word-of-mouth marketing agency, has more than 130,000 agents who will try clients' products and then talk about them with their friends, relatives, and acquaintances over the duration of the campaign. It has worked with companies like Anheuser-Busch, General Mills, and Volkswagen. Procter & Gamble's 4-year-old Tremor division has a panel of 250,000 teenagers who are asked to talk with friends about new products or concepts that P&G sends them. Some experts suggest that traditional marketers underused public relations or used it only as an afterthought, thus opening the door for creative guerrilla marketers.

It is easier to define what guerrilla marketing *does* than what it *is*. Guerrilla marketing is heard above the noise in the marketplace and makes a unique impact: it makes people talk about the product and the company, effectively making them "missionaries" for the brand. It creates drama and interest and positive *affect*, or emotion—all pretty amazing results. But in fact, truly good guerrilla marketing is as difficult—and maybe more so—than good traditional marketing. Because lots of companies are trying to do it, it's harder to break free of the pack.

Think of guerrilla marketing as guerrilla *tactics* that you can apply to various media or elements of the communications mix, rather than as entirely different communications tools. You can use guerrilla tactics in advertising (riveting posters in subways) and in personal selling (creative canvassing at a trade show), but you'll most likely use them as a form of PR—as tactics that garner visibility and positive publicity. The president of Maker's Mark practiced guerrilla marketing when he inspired *The Wall Street Journal's* reporter to learn about and write the story of his bourbon. Nantucket Nectars' Tom and Tom were relentless guerrilla marketers, dressing up like grapes and making a stir on

TYPES OF GUERRILLA MARKETING

- ◉ Word-of-mouth marketing: "Giving people a reason to talk about your products and services, and making it easier for that conversation to take place."

- ◉ Buzz marketing: "Using high-profile entertainment or news to get people to talk about your brand."

- ◉ Viral marketing: "Creating entertaining or informative messages that are designed to be passed along in an exponential fashion, often electronically or by e-mail."

ISSUES IN GUERRILLA MARKETING

- ◉ Identify challenges and develop creative solutions

- ◉ Find the "inherent drama" in your offerings and translate that into a meaningful benefit

- ◉ Get people's attention and get a "foot in the door" (generating the first sale)

- ◉ Create "buzz" once you get in the door (word-of-mouth marketing)

the Cape Cod highway on Memorial Day weekend as thousands of motorists were stuck in traffic, and sending purple vans to outdoor concerts to distribute free juice before it became a common practice.

Much of what we now call *event marketing* is in the realm of guerrilla marketing, because it is experiential, interactive, and light-hearted. But as we noted earlier, guerrilla tactics are becoming more and more difficult for entrepreneurs to execute, because every corporate marketing executive is trying to succeed at guerrilla marketing too and has a much larger budget to employ. Sony Ericsson Mobile executed a guerrilla marketing campaign in New York City in which trained actors and actresses pretended to be tourists and asked passersby to snap a picture with the company's new mobile phone/digital camera product. Deceptive? Yes, but too commonplace a tactic to truly be controversial. Not every guerilla campaign escapes controversy. In the fall of 2005, Sony's guerrilla marketing campaign for its PlayStation Portable used graffiti-style paintings of wide-eyed kids with a hand-size gadget painted on walls in urban areas of California, New York, and Florida. Though the buildings were on private property, the stunt raised complaints of vandalism.

An elaborate guerrilla marketing campaign in Toronto, designed to promote an HBO comedy series, featured street teams with TV-equipped backpacks to show pedestrians 30-second promotional clips, chalk drawings promoting the series at major intersections, and ads in the bathrooms of major media agencies that showcased giant quotes from reviews of the show. The attempt by large corporations and advertising agencies to set the standard for guerrilla marketing makes these tactics less accessible to small companies. Still, as long as entrepreneurs are sparked by creativity, guerrilla successes can still be possible, even though they require a continuous stream of ideas and energy.

In conclusion, entrepreneurs who create successful marketing strategies must have a clear vision of their goal. They also must understand how one strategic element affects another, because if the marketing mix elements of product, price, distribution, and communications are not perfectly compatible—if the mix is not internally logical—the strategy will not work. Even a good beginning strategy is not enough, however, because the marketplace is dynamic. Entrepreneurial companies, more so than mature businesses, must constantly reevaluate their strategy and how it is affecting growth.

Marketing Skills for Managing Growth

It is beyond the scope of this chapter to offer a comprehensive discussion of the next step: the marketing processes and capabilities a young company needs in order to pursue strong growth. However, two key areas for you to focus on are *understanding and listening to customers* and *building a visible and enduring brand*.

Understanding and Listening to the Customer

Although intuition-based decision making can work well initially for some entrepreneurs, intuition has its limitations. Entrepreneurs must be in constant touch with their customers as they grow their companies. When a company decides to introduce its second product or open a new location, for example, it needs to be able to determine whether that product or location will be welcomed in the marketplace. Entrepreneurs with a successful first product or location often overestimate demand for the second, sometimes because their confidence encourages them to overrely on their own intuition.

Entrepreneurs must obtain information that will allow them to understand consumer buying behavior and customer expectations related to product design, pricing, and distribution. They also need information about the best way to communicate with customers and influence their actions. Finally, they need information about the *effectiveness* of their own marketing activities, so they can continue to refine them. Marketers build relationships, in part, by using information to customize the marketing mix. Good entrepreneurial marketers do whatever it takes to build relationships with customers.

Entrepreneurs following a high-growth strategy need to continuously find new customer segments to support that growth. Bill Samuels Jr. recognized that for Maker's Mark to grow significantly, the company would have to reach a new segment—drinkers of other types of alcohol—because the bourbon connoisseur market was near saturation. Rather than relying on his own intuition, Samuels studied the consumer market to understand where he would find his new customers and how he would attract them.

There are a number of ways to listen to customers; some require formal research, and others use informal systems for soliciting information and scanning the market environment. Leonard Berry cites a portfolio of methods that entrepreneurs can use to build a *listening system.*[7] These include:

- *Transactional surveys* to measure customer satisfaction with the company
- *New and lost customer surveys* to see why customers choose or leave the firm
- *Focus group interviews* to gain information on specific topics
- *Customer advisory panels* to get periodic feedback and advice from customers
- *Customer service reviews* to have periodic, one-on-one assessments
- *Customer complaint/comment capture* to track and address customer complaints
- *Total market surveys* to assess the total market—customers and noncustomers

Building the Brand

All entrepreneurs face the need for **brand building**, which is the dual task of building brand awareness and building brand equity. **Brand awareness** is the customer's ability to recognize and recall the brand when provided a cue. Marketing practices that create brand awareness also help shape **brand image**, which is the way customers perceive the brand. **Brand equity** is the effect of brand awareness and brand image on customer response to the brand. It is brand equity, for example, that spurs consumers to pay a premium price for a brand—a price that exceeds the value of the product's tangible attributes.

Brand equity can be positive or negative. Positive brand equity is the degree of marketing advantage a brand would hold over an unnamed competitor. Negative brand equity is the disadvantage linked to a specific brand. Brand building is closely linked to a company's communications strategy. While brand awareness is created through sheer exposure to a brand—through advertising or publicity—brand image is shaped by how a company projects its identity, through its products, communications, and employees. The customer's actual experience with the brand also has a strong effect on brand image.

Maker's Mark used its communications strategy, implemented through humorous, distinctive print advertising in sophisticated national magazines like *Forbes* and *Business Week* to create a brand image that would help establish a high-end market for bourbon where none had existed in the past. The company created a likeable, genuine brand personality for its bourbon. Because many of the advertisements were in the form of an open letter from Bill Samuels Jr. to his customers, Samuels was able to represent and personalize the brand.

CONCLUSION

Marketing is often described as a delicate balance of art and science. Certainly developing the expertise to be a master marketer is difficult, especially for entrepreneurs who are constantly pulled in a thousand directions. Nevertheless, the task remains: to have customer knowledge and PR mastery, and to recognize effective advertising as well as effective experiential promotion. Entrepreneurial marketers must, first and foremost, be able to sell: sell their ideas, their products, their passion, their company's long-term potential. And they must learn the skill of knowing where the market is going, now and into the future.

Early-stage companies often find it necessary to scale up or change focus. In these scenarios, competition can be a potent driver of marketing decisions, whether you are staying under the radar screen of giant companies or buying time against a clone invasion. But successful entrepreneurs will have a strong, focused marketing strategy—a consistent strategy—and therefore will not easily be thrown off course.

YOUR OPPORTUNITY JOURNAL

Reflection Point	Your Thoughts...
How do you learn about your customer?	
What secondary sources can you use?	
What primary data will you collect?	
How do you segment your market? Who's your PTA? Who are your STAs?	
How will you price your product?	
How will you distribute your product?	
What channels are available? Which channels are best? When will you add new channels?	
What is your marketing communications strategy? What mix of advertising, PR, personal selling, and direct marketing are most effective?	
What "guerilla tactics" can you use to create a buzz? How will you get your product to be heard above the noise?	
Articulate what you would like your brand to be. How will you build it during launch? During growth?	

WEB EXERCISE

Scan the Web and identify the Internet marketing techniques of two to three companies. Start with the company's home page. What functionality does the page contain (just information, online selling interface, etc.)? Evaluate the homepage's communications effectiveness. Next, go to a search engine such as Google. What key search terms bring this company up on the first two or three pages? Does the company use paid Internet advertising? Affiliate programs? Are there any other unique aspects about the company's Internet strategy? How does what you've learned inform your Web strategy?

Appendix: Customer Interview

To whom should we ask the questions?
What possible information would be asked?
Should the questions be open-ended or structured?
How should the questions be sequenced?

General Outline: It Needs to be Tailored to Meet your Research Needs.

1. Opening discussion (introduction and warm up):

   Briefly, describe research purpose, introduce self, ensure confidentiality of response, and state expected duration of the interview session.

   Opening statement: Think of the last time you purchased or used such a product. What prompted or triggered this activity? What specific activities did you perform to get the product or service? What was the outcome of your shopping experience?

2. Current practice:

   How do you currently purchase or use a product/service of interest? How did you go about deciding on what to buy? How frequently do you buy/use this product/service? How much do you buy/use each time? Where do you buy?

3. Familiarity/awareness about product/service:

   What other products/services/stores have you considered before deciding on the final product/service you bought?

4. Important attributes:

   If you were shopping for such a product, what would you look for? What is important? What characteristic(s) are important to you?

5. Perception of respondents:

   How would you compare different products/services? How well do you think of the product/service you bought compared with those of its competitors with respect to these attributes?

6. Overall satisfaction with or liking of the product/service:

   Ask satisfaction level and preference ranking among competitive products.

7. Product demo/introduction/description:

   Purpose: Get reactions to the product concept and elicit a response that may identify additional decision drivers.

   What do you like about this idea? What do you dislike? Does listening to this idea suggest some factors that you would consider important and which we have not discussed so far? Does it change the importance you attach to different factors before choosing a product or service?

   Purchase intent of new product or service: What will be the level of interest or willingness of respondents to buy or use this new product/service? At what price?

   We would like to know how likely it is that you would buy such a product or service.

   - ☐ Would definitely buy
   - ☐ Would probably buy
   - ☐ Might or might not buy
   - ☐ Would probably not buy
   - ☐ Would definitely not buy

   We would like to know now how much you would be willing to pay for such a product or service:

   - ☐ Would definitely pay $_____ .

   Please note that comparable products are priced at $_____ . Now how much will you be willing to pay for such a product or service?

   - ☐ Would definitely pay $_____ .

8. Media habit:

   How do you find out about a product or service?

   What (*media*) do you read, listen, or watch?

9. Demographic information:

   Personal information should be asked at the end of the interview.

   Age, income, occupation, gender, education, etc.

   Size of the firm (revenue, total full-time staff, R&D staff), resources, experience, skills, etc.

10. Wrap-up:

    Any final comments or ideas?

    Thank you for your time.

NOTES

[1] American Marketing Association, 2004. www.marketingpower.com/content21257.php.

[2] Lodish, Leonard M., Morgan, Howard Lee, and Amy Kallianpur. *Entrepreneurial Marketing*, Hoboken, NJ: John Wiley & Sons, Inc. 2001. P. xi.

[3] "Cadbury Does Yet Another Deal," *Beverage Digest*, May 2002.

[4] Adapted from John A. Martilla and John C. James, "Importance-Performance Analysis," *Journal of Marketing*, January, 1977, pp. 77–79.

[5] From an interview with Bill Samuels Jr., Louisville, Kentucky.

[6] Taylor, Catherine P., "Psst! How do you measure Buzz?" *AdWeek*, October 24, 2005.

[7] Berry, Leonard L. *Discovering the Soul of Service*. New York, NY: The Free Press, 1999, pp. 100–01.

ClearVue

Brooks O'Kane sat in his chair on the front porch staring at a bottle of ClearVue glass cleaner. He was wondering in what direction he should go with this product. He had taken it from being mixed once a week in a vat in his father-in-law's warehouse to a $4 million business that was now in direct competition with the nation's top glass cleaners.

As the success of ClearVue grew, Brooks' choices narrowed. In a short time, Brooks had done wonders marketing the product in two different categories. Distribution was spilt 50/50 between regional grocery accounts and national automotive accounts. However, with each marketing success he achieved, he learned there were many other variables that must be considered if success were to continue, and the product were to compete nationwide in either distribution channel.

ClearVue's prosperity was remarkable given the company's human-resource overhead. Due to a large order from Wal-Mart, the company had been forced to outsource production and transportation, making ClearVue, in effect, a virtual corporation with sales of $2 million per employee.

As he sat on his front porch, Brooks thought about the challenges of marketing ClearVue. The grocery market had needs quite unlike the automotive market. Both markets demanded his full attention across the board: public relations, advertising, packaging, product development, direct sales, and marketing. Something had to give, and Brooks knew his choices weren't as clear as the bottle of glass cleaner before him.

Brooks O'Kane

Brooks had graduated from a New Hampshire state college in 1983 with a degree in marketing. He then worked as an account executive in one of the area's larger advertising agencies before moving to a smaller agency where he felt he would have more creative input, but that agency went out of business in the late 1980s. Brooks then focused his energy on renovating investment properties until a subsequent industry downturn. According to Brooks, "The real estate market died. I didn't make a dime. I didn't lose a dime, but I probably wasted two years of my life."

At about this time, Brooks' father-in-law and president of Lawrence Plate Glass, Walter Demers, Jr., approached him about becoming the marketing director of his small family-run glass business in Lawrence, Massachusetts (see Exhibit 5.1). Brooks became the Lawrence Plate Glass Company's director of marketing in 1989. His first priority had been developing a consistent image for the company, which had six locations, all with different letterheads, logos, and signage. Then one day, several months after Brooks had taken the position with Lawrence Plate Glass, Demers appeared in the doorway of Brooks' office and asked him to "take care of ClearVue," the company's $60,000-a-year glass-cleaning product. Brooks got the distinct impression that this was not considered an important assignment.

This case was prepared by Carole Guarante, Dan D'Heilly, and Andrea Alyse under the direction of Professor William Bygrave. Funding provided by the Ewing Marion Kauffman Foundation.

| **EXHIBIT 5.1** | **Lawrence Plate Glass Co.—1989 Profile** |

Total Sales: $18 million
Employees: 150
Branch Locations:

Lawrence, MA (3 locations)	Beverly, MA
Haverhill, MA	Manchester, NH
Lowell, MA	Lewiston, ME

Business Segment Breakdown:

Residential Glass & Repair	$5,000,000
Wholesale Glass Division	$3,000,000
Contract Glazing Division	$8,000,000
Garage Door Division	$2,000,000
ClearVue Glass Cleaner	$60,000

Glass Cleaner Industry

The $160 million glass-cleaner segment of the cleaning-products market was dominated by three major players in the early 1990s: Windex, Glass Plus, and SOS Glass Works. Windex, the industry leader with a market share of almost 45%, was wholly-owned by Bristol-Myers Squibb. Glass Plus, owned by Dow Chemical, and SOS Glass Works, owned by Miles Inc., a subsidiary of Germany's Bayer conglomerate, each had approximately a 15% market share. The remaining market was mostly made up of private-label and regional brands.

Because total industry sales in this market were flat, allotted grocery shelf space in this category remained constant, and competition had intensified in the industry. Brooks recalled the competitive response when ClearVue gained a regional market share of only 4.5%.

> *The deals and promotions were incredible. The Cinch product came out and Proctor & Gamble spent a fortune on it. Then they came out with another product that was the same exact product and called it Mr. Clean ... exact same bottle, different color. This made me mad because they were trying to dominate the shelves, and keep people like me off—and they had the money to do it.*

However, increased competition also resulted in the creation of niche segments. Industrial-strength, private-label, and regional cleaning products such as ClearVue were a growing segment in this otherwise mature industry. In addition, throughout the 1990s, consumers became increasingly price-sensitive to the cost of cleaning products and more willing to substitute a regional or private-label brand, sometimes saving as much as 50%.

Although the automotive cleaning-products segment was dominated by players such as Armor All and Turtle Wax, the automotive glass-cleaning segment remained fragmented through 1995. Total after-market retail sales in the automotive cleaning-products segment grew almost 19% from 1994 to 1995, from $270 million to $322.4 million. Retailers averaged a 47.4% gross margin on sales of these products in 1995, slightly lower than the 1994 average gross margin of 51.5%, and projected a 6.3% growth in this category for 1996. Automotive chains and discount stores were the best channels for glass cleaner in 1995, but nonauto retailers and department stores also achieved success in selling automotive glass-cleaning agents.

Opportunity Knocks: ClearVue

Walter Demers Sr. founded Lawrence Plate Glass in 1918. In about 1950, he developed ClearVue because he needed a product that cleaned glass better and more cheaply than those already available on the market. A low-tech operation, the cleaner was mixed in a 300-gallon tub in a corner of the plant by an employee on Saturday mornings. Originally, Demers had no intention of selling it, but people frequently asked what he used at the shop, so Demers packaged ClearVue for sale. Brooks said:

> It became popular by word of mouth. People loved it. When people vacationed in Boston, or moved from Boston, they took ClearVue with them across the country. ClearVue never advertised, but it developed a loyal, cult-like following.

When Brooks became director of marketing, ClearVue was still being made in a tub in the back of the company's warehouse by a guy named Bert. Brooks' father-in-law gave him an old accounts-receivable ledger and a file of ClearVue fan letters from around the world. Brooks became convinced that there was additional market-potential for this product.

> I knew right then and there—I had to do something with this. It amazed me that people would write fan mail about a glass cleaner. I knew I had a terrific product and a great story. Then I thought about this guy Bert, out back with an oak paddle. I thought, "I've got Bartles & James, the Keebler Elves, and Ben & Jerry all rolled into one. I can do something with this."

But before Brooks told the story, he wanted to refine his presentation.

Clearly Superior Packaging

One of Brooks' first moves was to improve the old ClearVue package, because he knew that sometimes people sampled new products simply because they liked the way they looked. After meeting with a package designer who wanted a hefty $25,000 to redesign ClearVue, Brooks knew he had to find a creative solution. He decided instead to work on the design project with the graphic artist who had done his newspaper advertisements:

> My whole objective was to have a label that looked as good as the product worked. I wanted clean, crisp, different—top-shelf all the way, but I couldn't pay top-shelf prices. I paid $2,500 and we won three national packaging awards. All of it was decided by gut feelings and talking with people—no focus groups or any market research. It was bootstrap marketing at its finest.

The "quality first" strategy also applied to the bottle Brooks chose for ClearVue, which had previously been sold in a drab, white plastic bottle. The glass-cleaning industry was already using PVC (a clear plastic material), but Brooks decided to use PET (a higher grade of clear plastic than PVC). Although $.01 more per bottle, PET is both easier to recycle and clearer in appearance—setting ClearVue's packaging apart from the rest. Also, his competitors were dyeing their liquids blue, while ClearVue remained true to its name—clear. Since then, competitors have adopted many of ClearVue's strategies. According to Brooks, "Now everyone is using the best PET plastic and clear liquid. We caught the front end of a trend."

To further emphasize the high-quality appearance, Brooks decided to use special labels that allowed him to print on both sides, so that consumers could read the story of Bert on the back of the label—right through the liquid in the bottle.

PPG Industries

Demers didn't initially share his son-in-law's enthusiasm. He did not want Brooks to grow ClearVue; he simply wanted to free up the person who was managing it, so that person would have more time for other things. As a result, Brooks wore two hats for a couple of years: in addition to being the marketing director of Lawrence Plate Glass, he was the sole person marketing ClearVue.

> For a long time, it was kind of like I was making phone calls when he (Demers) wasn't looking. I gradually wore him down. I had some early successes that opened his eyes. The key one was PPG (Pittsburgh Plate Glass) Industries, the world's largest glass company. When I told my father-in-law I was going after it, he literally laughed in my face—but I got their business.

In 1989 Brooks called the local PPG branch that Lawrence Plate Glass dealt with and asked for the corporate number. He was lucky. Within ten minutes of picking up the phone, he was talking to the PPG sundries and accessories buyer in their corporate office, who told him, "Brooks, your timing is perfect. We need a better glass cleaner." At the buyer's request, Brooks sent samples to 100 PPG warehouses along with a questionnaire about ClearVue. Within four months, they had a contract with PPG. PPG became ClearVue's exclusive glass-industry distributor in North America.

> PPG is a $7 billion glass company. If I knew at the beginning what I know now, I would never have done it. I would have been too smart. I would never have picked up the phone and asked. It's like the pretty woman not getting any dates because everyone is too intimidated to ask. I learned you can pick up the phone and call anyone. Don't assume anything—just do it. The PPG sale is what opened my father-in-law's eyes to the potential of ClearVue.

ClearVue became a separate company at the end of 1989.

Distribution

While looking at old sales records, Brooks noticed that ClearVue had one grocery-store client—so why not go after others? He successfully landed a couple of small accounts, but was advised to get a food broker if he wanted to pursue larger ones.

Brooks was referred to Chase, Kolbin, and Allen, one of the largest food brokers in New England, which managed national accounts like Coca-Cola and Clorox. Brooks called and asked to speak directly to senior partner Freeman Chase, who was impressed with Brooks' enthusiasm and passed his name along to an account manager. However, Brooks was not satisfied with being assigned to an account manager, so he asked Chase to attend his presentation to the account-management team. Everyone except Brooks was surprised when Chase showed up at the ClearVue account meeting.

> *Freeman became my mentor and personally managed the ClearVue account. You go in with a regular account manager and you talk to associate buyers. With Freeman, we went in three levels up—he knows people who make the real decisions. This was a huge advantage. I came in with a lot of credibility.*

Freeman advised Brooks, "Don't make price a barrier for people sampling the product—there's always time to raise the price down the road." As a result, Brooks set the price 30 cents cheaper than national brands, such as Windex, in the grocery stores.

Prohibitive slotting fees were an obstacle to ClearVue's grocery distribution. Stop & Shop's fee at that time, for instance, was $25,000 per item. Brooks creatively negotiated around slotting fees, mostly with agreements that included payment-in-kind. Sometimes he would offer a pallet of product at wholesale in lieu of cash for most of the slotting fee, then about 10% of the fee in cash. He also negotiated deals that induced grocers to actively promote ClearVue. For example, he negotiated one slotting fee that consisted of a 5% discount per case for the first six months, with a cash guarantee at the end of six months if the additional profit fell short of the slotting fee. However, if the store sold more than the fee would have generated, it was theirs to keep, thereby motivating them to give ClearVue good placement and promotion.

Initially, Brooks estimated it would take at least three years to get grocery distribution in New England. However, he made presentations to Stop & Shop, Star Market, and Purity Supreme, and they all signed deals the same day. In three months, ClearVue had achieved an 80% New England market penetration.

Encouraged by his success with PPG and the New England grocers, Brooks went after Wal-Mart. He tried letters and phone calls to Wal-Mart buyers, all without success, so he sent a handwritten note to the top decision maker, Sam Walton: "Sam, I need your help . . . I'm a young guy just starting out and I've got the best glass cleaner in the world . . ." Soon after, a household buyer from Wal-Mart called Brooks to order 15,000 cases of ClearVue as a test. Although ClearVue held its own against the other glass-cleaner giants, it did not earn a permanent place in the household section. Next, Brooks called Wal-Mart's automotive buyer and convinced him that ClearVue would attract women shoppers to the automotive department. Brooks had created a new market niche, complete with national distribution.

When Wal-Mart ordered those 15,000 cases, they didn't know that ClearVue had produced only 72 cases at any one time. Not only had ClearVue grown beyond grocery store aisles and into automotive, it had also outgrown Bert's paddling in the back room. Unable to fulfill the order, Brooks stopped producing ClearVue in the back room of the glass company and hired a New Hampshire contract bottler.

Getting the ClearVue Word Out

Brooks knew how to get free publicity from his days in advertising. He collected magazine and newspaper editorial schedules, then contacted editors to fit the ClearVue story into their publications. Every time a story ran, people would call him with ideas about everything from chemical suppliers to food brokers to package designers. Consultants began coming to Brooks instead of his having to track them down. He also made use of other innovative marketing to get the ClearVue word out. He told the folksy, fun ClearVue story wherever and whenever he could, gave out samples everywhere he went, and personally answered every fan letter with a handwritten reply:

> *If someone's wacko enough about my product to write me a letter, I not only want to keep that person as a customer, I want to turn them into a salesperson. That's why I take the time to write them a handwritten note and send them coupons. It's something the big guys can't duplicate.*

Brooks also penned an annual newsletter, which he sent to anyone who had a connection with his product (see Exhibit 5.2). The newsletter was sent to 7,500 people in 1995.

In addition to having many articles written about ClearVue, Brooks has also appeared on the television show *Chronicle* with the ClearVue story. It took him a couple of years of lobbying the show's producers to get his chance in the spotlight. At one point he sent the show's producers a plaque he had had made, inscribed, "I do hereby declare on April 1, that I will appear on *Chronicle* before Dec. 31." Then, through his newsletter, he organized a write-in campaign for supporters to help him get on the show.

Initially, Brooks didn't have enough money to pay for advertising. However, as revenues increased, he decided to buy time on talk-radio because "people don't push those buttons" and ClearVue appealed to the talk-radio audience—women over 35 years old.

New Roads: New Challenges

Brooks' problems with automotive and grocery vendors were not the same:

> *What's becoming an issue, and I'm surprised it's not more of an issue on the grocery side, is being a one-SKU vendor. Automotive departments are constantly wanting to reduce the number of vendors and items they carry. I had an advantage initially because there weren't any auto-glass cleaners out there—now they are coming out of the woodwork. Why would they want to buy an auto-glass cleaner from me when they can buy it from Armor All or Turtle Wax or someone like that, when they are already buying 50 other items from them? Why have to cut another purchase order and have to set me up as another vendor?*
>
> *The grocery stores were more concerned with promotional support and slotting fees. First you pay your way in, then they want you to produce coupons and FSIs, so you have to pay to keep your spot.*

The biggest decision Brooks pondered was: Should he align himself with automotive or grocery? He needed to find someone who could provide an automotive product line, or a food distributor who could help finance his national expansion. He felt compelled to find a distributor for one line or the other:

> *I need to be focused. I don't have the resources, personnel, or money to be good at the automotive, the hardware, the club stores, the grocery stores . . . I can't do it all—it's too sophisticated. The one-SKU thing is a problem, and I don't have the resources to have a broad product line on both the grocery and automotive sides.*

EXHIBIT 5.2 **ClearVue's Newsletter**

The World's Finest Glass Cleaner !

The ClearVue Sun

FREE Pull-Out Poster!

A Publication of ClearVue Products, Inc.

Issue # 4

Fall / Winter 1994

Update:

Recently a thought occured to me as I was planning next year's advertising budget. Since you folks are doing such a great job with your "word of mouth" advertising, why not just expand upon that idea? Here's my plan: If each one of you were to tell 10 of your friends about ClearVue, and then they in turn told 10 of their friends . . . and so on . . . well, within 8 "rotations" we will have spread the gospel of ClearVue to one billion consumers! Then if just 10% of these people bought one bottle of ClearVue per year, we'd sell 100 million units. And the most beautiful part of the whole thing is that **100% of the profits go to needy children.** (mine)

Now, granted this might take a few weeks to put together, but can you think of a more worthwhile cause? We're just a tiny little company that's trying to compete against those big evil, devil - worshipping, seal clubbing, bunny stomping, greedy conglomerates - we need your help! Please make certain you send us your contact names soon - as we'd like to add these billion new names to our mailing list in time for Christmas.

Thanks again - and please remember to keep "facing" those shelves and put to CV in other people's shopping carts when they're not looking.

Brooks O'Kane

Growth Continues!

Company Doubles Workforce

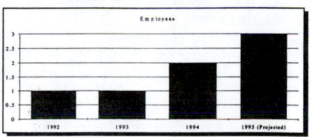

LAWRENCE, MA - In a move that stunned industry analysts, ClearVue Products , Inc recently doubled the size of it's workforce - literally overnight.

The company, which markets a super- premium, fat free, low cholesterol, high fiber, cruelty free, dolphin safe, ozone friendly glass cleaner, accomplished the feat when a new secretary was hired recently. The company now has 2 full-time employees.

Another 75 sq. ft. addition was added on to the sprawling ClearVue Products headquarters to accomodate the dramatic increase in size.

Mail:

"Today I was fortunate enough to find your glass cleaner at the grocery store. This is the best thing since chocolate ice cream. ... you give new meaning to the phrase""Made in America"". "
York, PA

"My husband will not use anything else for his truck windows ... it is absolutely the BEST!"
Westminster, MD

" I like the product but wish I could find a willing young man to use it more often ... I am 86 - so you can see I am only interested in my windows shining."
Lake George, NY

"I've been using ClearVue for about a year now and feel so strongly about it that I took it with me last year to clean my elderly Mom's black stove while visiting Long Island. It worked like a charm. I am so proud to be using your product and to be able to recommend it to friends."
Marblehead, MA

EXHIBIT 5.2 **(Continued)**

The ClearVue Sun

Current Accounts

We get a tremendous amount of calls and letters from consumers looking for a supply of ClearVue. Even though we still have a long, long way to go in having truly national distribution, most consumers can get their hands on a bottle. Much of the reason for this is the fact that we landed the Wal-Mart account **(in the automotive section)** several years ago. They pretty much cover 48 of the 50 states.

Below is a listing of some of our major accounts around the country.

Note: Any account with an "A" next to it signifies an automotive store or that it would appear in the automotive section of that particular chain. If you can't find it, please call us (508) 794-3100.

New England:
Stop & Shop
Shaws
Star Mkt.
BJ's Wholesale Club
DeMoulas/Mkt. Basket
A&P / Foodmart
Finast/Edwards
Shop & Save
Purity Supreme
Almacs
Bradlees (A)
Auto Palace (A)
VIP Discount Auto (A)
Spags
Aubuchon Hardware
Ames (A)
Hills (A)
Caldor (A)
The Fair
Ann & Hope
Christy's Mkt.

New England (cont.)
Big Y
Victory Markets
Big D
Benny's
Ann & Hope

PA/NJ:
Weis Mkts.
Acme Markets
Genuardi Mkts.
Clemens
Giant Food
Fox's Markets
Jamesway (A)
Pep Boy's (A)
Clover (A)
Scott Grocery
R&S (A)

Florida:
Pep Boy's (A)
Wal-Mart (A)
Discount Auto (A)
BJ's Wholesale Club
Rose Auto (A)

IL:
Pep Boys (A)
Wal-Mart (A)
Straus Auto (A)

MI:
Murray's Automotive

Texas / AZ:
Pep Boys (A)
Wal-Mart (A)

California:
Pep Boys (A)
Wal-Mart (A)
FEDCO (A)

New York:
Price Chopper
Tops Markets
Shop n' Save
Wheels (A)
Great American/Victory
Aid Auto

Who Uses What?
Recent Poll Very Revealing

Windex   ClearVue

EXHIBIT 5.2 (Continued)

The ClearVue Sun

ClearVue Organizational Chart
Duties Re-defined in Restructuring

Brooks O'Kane
President

Michelle Ordway
Secretary

O'Kane   Ordway

Job Duties /Descriptions:

O'Kane - Customer golf and ski outings, writes company newsletter, schmoozes with other high-powered CEO types, selects "Employee of the Month", waters plants and a whole lot of other **really important** stuff.

Ordway - New business development, vendor relations, finance, marketing/advertising, logistics, market research, inventory control, production, office management , chemical engineering and customer service.

Strange Uses for ClearVue

Over the years we've received letters from some of our customers touting CV's effectiveness at cleaning surfaces other than glass, mirrors, windshields etc.

Among the more unusual submissions:

- Cleans golf balls, clubs and shoes
- Shines military boots
- "Spray my chandelier with it."
- " gets the St. Bernard slobber off my car windows".
- Cleans Poodle pee off the floor.
- Removes tree frog guts from sliding doors.
- Eliminates puppy "nose art"
- Uses as a nail polish remover
- Bug killer
- Mace Substitute
- Cleans Iguana spit
- Carpet Cleaner
- Cleans Marine Corp Sword
- Jewelry Cleaner
- Automotive wheel cleaner
- Chalkboards
- "Great for cleaning computers !"
- "clean my best crystal with it"
- Bowling Balls

NOTE: We do not recommend using CV on carpets, shoes, wood, painted surfaces or plastics.

... fan mail

"I was at the hardware store and the lady working there strongly recommended ClearVue ... have never been so pleased ... telling everyone I know about it".

Roanoke, VA

"I can't believe how good your glass cleaner works ... everything sparkles with very little effort."

Indianapolis, IN

"As soon as our monsoons subsided, I went to our Wal-Mart and cleaned out their stock of ClearVue."

Park Ridge, IL

"I'm hooked on ClearVue...it is the product of my dreams!"

Tenants Harbor, ME

"in my 62 years of washing windows, this is by far the very best cleaner I've ever used."

Chittenango, NY

"I LOVE IT!!!"

Woodbury, MN

"Help - I need ClearVue... I'll travel anywhere within 40 miles of Detroit to get some."

Detroit, MI

EXHIBIT 5.2 (Continued)

Misc. Tidbits

• Visiting Lawrence, MA? Well why not take a tour of ClearVue Products World Headquarters? FREE tours are offered Mon. - Fri. 8:00 AM - 5:00 PM. Due to space constraints tours are limited to one person each.

• The geniuses at Windex recently added a "Potpouri" scented glass cleaner to their product mix. *(Now, that deserves a Nobel prize.)*

• We will sell approximately 350,000 gallons of ClearVue this year - or to put it another way, enough glass cleaner to fill 350,000 one gallon containers. *(I think)*

• If you are dead or have recently relocated, please let us know so that we can update our mailing list.

CV Makes Mag Cover
Spring Edition of "Your Company"

Note: Thanks to my Mom this issue of "Your Company" was a complete sellout. She still has several thousand copies if anyone needs one.

... fan mail

"ClearVue is absolutely terrific ... really is great ... I saw you on TV the other night - hurrah for the little guy."
Yonkers, NY

"... it really does a superior job ... God bless you!"
Hauppauge, NY

"I used to buy Windex, but was never satisfied ... ClearVue is GREAT! ... it's the only one that doesn't leave streaks."
Crown Point, IN

"Nothing like doing the windows once and not having to worry about streaks."
Vernon, CT

"I am a day care Mom ... ClearVue is the best!"
Pasadena, MD

ClearVue Products, Inc.
P.O. Box 567
Lawrence, MA 01842

 TO:

The World's Finest Glass Cleaner

EXHIBIT 5.3	ClearVue Operations, 1995
Sales	$4,000,000
Cash	85,000
Accounts Receivable	535,000
Inventory	329,000
Total Current Assets	$975,000
Accounts Payable	412,000
Total Current Liabilities	$418,000
Gross Profit	39%
Net Profit	6%

While Brooks and his secretary had run the ClearVue show so far, he was now considering hiring a marketing professional to help him expand. Brooks thought that ClearVue was generating enough cash to grow (see Exhibit 5.3).

Opportunity Knocks (Again): Red Cross Nurse

Brooks was leaning toward grocery because another product opportunity had just about fallen in his lap: The 68-year-old owner of Red Cross Nurse (RCN), a household cleaning product, was looking to retire and had approached Brooks about the possibility of selling the company to him:

> He sees my distribution and sales expertise. I have access to the Wal-Marts and Kmarts; a royalty on my sales is more than he's making now.
>
> Basically, its like a no-money-down real estate deal: I pay a token payment up front of $2,500, guarantee of a couple of thousand a month as a base, and 5% of sales for 10 years. Then I own the brand outright—I would own the name, "Red Cross Nurse!" I can't even guess at how much the name "Red Cross" is worth.

A few days after the owner of RCN approached him, Brooks was visiting one of his major supermarket accounts when the ClearVue buyer told him that RCN was a very good product. RCN had been around since 1869. Previously a well-established brand, its sales peaked at $500,000 in 1990, but had declined precipitously (see Exhibit 5.4).

Brooks had heard from a friend that disinfectants were a good market. He felt that if he bought RCN, not only could he turn the company around, but, in addition to

EXHIBIT 5.4	Red Cross Nurse Income Statement 03/31/94				
	3/94	**4/93–3/94**		**3/94**	**4/93–3/94**
INCOME			**EXPENSES**		
Sales	$16,959	$227,100	Salaries	$3,950	$53,578
Sales Discount	(196)	(3,477)	Payroll Taxes	313	4,268
Net Sales	$16,762	$223,623	Advertising	31	1,815
COGS			Auto Expense	674	6,852
Beginning Inventory	$0	$(2,892)	Bank Service Charges	12	263
Purchases Alcohol	5,132	20,333	Commissions	970	6,240
Purchases Oils	3,974	11,981	Coupons	185	3,099
Purchases Boxes	0	2,643	Dues & Subscriptions	40	1,018
Purchases Bottles	671	22,345	Pesticide Registration	0	1,133
Purchases Sprayers	4,160	12,325	Delivery Expense	270	2,269
Purchases Chemicals	117	1,981	Insurance	2,573	30,258
Ending Inventory	(8,812)	(346)	Misc. Expense	0	83
Total COGS	$5,243	$68,369	Office Expense	390	6,968
			Professional Fees	0	1,060
Gross Profit	$11,519	$155,254	Rent	1,000	12,000
			Repairs & Maintenance	(33)	1,328
			Subcontractor	249	2,227
			Taxes	0	4,425
			Entertainment	36	1,344
			Travel	0	143
			Utilities	390	5,617
			Total Expenses	$11,052	$145,987
			EBIT	468	9,267
			Interest Expense	764	8,256
			NET INCOME	$(296)	$1,011

having two grocery items, he could basically put any product under his brands—as long as it cleaned or killed germs—to build a grocery-product line.

Brooks thought about the future possibilities for ClearVue and Red Cross Nurse: "The owner of RCN has a lousy package, and he doesn't do any promotion or advertising. I think RCN has great potential—this could be even bigger than ClearVue."

Preparation Questions

1. Evaluate Brooks O'Kane's marketing and selling strategies and tactics?
   a. Why have those strategies been successful?
   b. What other kind of products might be suitable for selling and marketing with O'Kane's strategies and tactics?
2. What is ClearVue's business model? What are its advantages and disadvantages?
3. Do you think that Brooks should acquire Red Cross Nurse? What factors should O'Kane consider before he makes that decision?

The Italian Football (Soccer) team celebrates its 2006 World Cup Championship. (*Source*: Jochen Luebke/AFP/Getty Images/News and Sports Services)

BUILDING THE FOUNDING TEAM

Despite the glowing tributes to superstar entrepreneurs that we all read about in the popular press, entrepreneurship is a team sport. Even the richest man in the world, Bill Gates, did not start Microsoft by himself. Instead, he and Paul Allen led a hardy team of bright young engineers to the dry semi-desert of Albuquerque in 1975 to develop the original microcomputer software, BASIC. The group included four programmers, a project manager, a production manager, a lead mathematician, a technical writer, and a bookkeeper. Despite their incredible intelligence and drive, Gates and Allen recognized that the company would never reach its potential with just the two of them.

Today, from its humble beginnings, Microsoft has become the leading software company in the world with sales of almost $40 billion and 61,000 employees worldwide as of 2005. Indeed, we could look at all the top companies in the world today and identify the team behind the lead entrepreneur, but the point is the same: Successfully launching a business requires support. Even if you are launching a small business, you'll

This chapter written by Andrew Zacharakis

quickly find that your potential to grow beyond a self-employment business requires a team, whether it's your spouse for moral support, or a trusted advisor who mentors you through the growing pains you'll inevitably encounter. This chapter will look at the issues entrepreneurs face as they build their initial team and lead this group through the challenging launch process.

Power of the Team

Teams provide multiple benefits. First and foremost, a team enables the entrepreneur to do more than he or she could accomplish alone. No matter how strong the entrepreneur, how many hours she puts into the business, or how many days a week she is willing to work, at some point a team becomes necessary to increase the capacity of the business. Babson College and the London Business School have been studying the impact of entrepreneurship on economies around the globe since 1999. One consistent finding is that businesses with growth aspirations plan on employing more than twenty people within the next five years.[1]

The size of your organization is also directly correlated to the amount of revenue your business can derive. For example, if you are launching a retailing business, your average sales per person will range from $55,000 per employee for a confectionary store to $500,000 per employee for a new car dealer.[2] The figures are lower for restaurants, averaging around $30,000 per employee.[3] So if you hope to grow a million-dollar business, you'll need to build up an organization capable of generating that kind of revenue. For a restaurant, that means you'll need 30-plus employees. Keep in mind that these figures are revenue and not profits. Thus, if you want $100,000 or more in profits each year, you'll likely need a much larger business. For a restaurant, which according to Robert Morris Associates generates an average of 4.5% net income margin before taxes, you'd need sales of $2.25 million per year to pull out $100,000 in profits. Understanding these relationships going into your business will help you set goals and objectives for growing your company.

For growth, it's important to add employees who generate revenue. Too often, firms add support staff. While such employees can improve the effectiveness of the people they work for, their impact on revenue is often not large enough to pay for their salary, especially for the early-stage entrepreneurial company. Instead, hire a salesperson who will directly lead to new revenue. In the early years, it is critical to be focused on revenue-generating employees.

The power of the team extends beyond adding sales. Solo entrepreneurs suffer from a number of shortcomings, including a limited perspective, little moral support, and a small network. Research finds that teams have a higher chance of success due to increased skill set,[4] improved capacity for innovation,[5] and higher social level of support,[6] among other factors.

Entrepreneurs benefit by hearing and evaluating suggestions from others about how to better define and shape their business concept. No matter how brilliant your idea is, it can be better. Solo entrepreneurs often fail to get feedback on their idea that could help them better match customer needs and thereby increase product demand. Remember, initially your concept is based upon your own perception of a customer need. Just because you are enthralled with the idea doesn't mean that it will generate wide-spread demand. Your team provides a good initial soundingboard for ways to improve your idea. Granted, you can solicit this feedback from people outside your founding team (and you should), but you're likely to find that team members will provide more detailed suggestions because your success directly affects their own well-being. Moreover, your team members can help you evaluate the feedback you receive from outsiders. As we discussed in Chapter 3, your idea will continue to evolve during the entire entrepreneurial process, from pre-launch all the way through rapid growth. Getting different perspectives on the opportunity will help you come up with a more robust product or service.

Starting a business is hard work. You'll face a rollercoaster of emotion as you achieve important milestones (your first sale) and hit unexpected pitfalls (your first unhappy customer). Unfortunately, most new ventures encounter far more pitfalls than milestones in the launch phase. It is all too easy to fold up and find regular employment when you hit a particularly tough problem. Having a team around you provides moral support. You're all in this together. You have a shared responsibility to work hard on each other's behalf, because if the business fails, it is not only you who needs to find alternative employment or opportunities, but the rest of the team as well. Furthermore, a team means there are people you can confide in and share your frustrations with because they are facing them as well. The sympathetic ear enables you to let off steam and then refocus your attention on the problem at hand. Finally, it is more fun and rewarding to share the successes with a group of people who have been working toward the same goals. The power of a team is its shared vision of success.

Business is all about relationships. You need to establish relationships with suppliers, distribution channels, customers, investors, bankers, lawyers, accountants, and countless others. While well-networked individuals make better entrepreneurs, a team dramatically multiplies the size of even a good network. If you build your team wisely, you will gain access to a broader range of contacts that can help your business. This is often most evident in the fund-raising phase. Early on, you will likely need to raise equity capital, and the bigger your team, the more contacts you have as you embark on finding that investment. At the very least, your team is a great source for co-investment. In the 2003 edition of the *Inc. Magazine* list of the 500 fastest growing firms, 17% of the entrepreneurs reported that co-founders were a source of seed financing. Even if the co-founders don't invest directly, they can tap their own friends and family for startup capital, as was the case at 10% of the 2003 *Inc.* listing of fastest growing companies.[7] Thus, the power of the team greatly enhances your network, which is the lifeblood of any business.

A team also rounds out the skill set needed to launch a business. Most lead entrepreneurs have a vision of the initial product, and many even have the skills necessary to build a prototype—such as a software engineer who identifies a new video game opportunity. But it is almost impossible for one individual to possess all the skills necessary in the launch phase. For instance, a person with strong technical skills may lack the business know-how required to successfully introduce a new product to market, or a business guru may see a product need but lack the technical skill to build it. Even a business superstar is unlikely to possess all the business skills needed for long-term success. For example, a financial expert likely will need team members with marketing, sales, operations, and production experience, among others. The key is to understand your own strengths and weaknesses. Know what you know, and more importantly, know what you *don't* know. Once you have a strong sense of who you are, you can create a strategy to construct a powerful team. As you start to build up your team, identify the critical skills for success. Create job descriptions and a timeline of when you need these people. Then work through your network to find the right candidates.

Where Do You Fit?

Just because the business is your idea doesn't mean you must be the CEO. Every entrepreneur needs to take a hard look at himself or herself and decide how to best contribute to the venture's success. Jed Smith, founder of Drugstore.com (the online pharmacy), is a case in point. He took his concept to Kleiner Perkins, a pre-eminent venture capital firm, and with some seed funding further developed the business plan. John Doerr and Brook Byers, the senior partners at Kleiner Perkins overseeing Drugstore.com, solicited Jeff Bezos, CEO of Amazon.com, to serve on the board. With a strong board of highly networked individuals, Drugstore.com was positioned to attract quality team members. Once the plan was complete, Smith, with the help of Doerr, recruited a former Microsoft executive, Peter Neupert, to be CEO. Smith himself became VP of Strategic Partnerships.[8] Why did he relinquish the role of CEO? It's likely that Smith and the venture capitalists felt this rapid growth opportunity required someone with senior executive experience in the technology industry. Although Smith had previously co-founded a retailing concept with his father (Cyber-Smith), his skills weren't easily transferable to Drugstore.com.

Granted, creating a new venture requires most people to develop new skills on the job, but you'll be encountering a plethora of new challenges in the launch process and you need to understand your personal limits. Stubbornly keeping the CEO job could limit the potential of your venture and may even lead to its premature demise. So the question is, how do you gauge what you already know and what you can comfortably grow into as your business evolves?

The first thing to do is to update your resume. This document best captures your skill set to date. The key to revising and reviewing your resume is to do an *honest* and complete assessment of your demonstrated skills. This is not the time to exaggerate your accomplishments, because the only person you're fooling is yourself. You need to understand how your skill set will help you achieve success.

A second thing to keep in mind as you update your resume is, what do you really like to do and what do you dislike? Too many product people fail as CEO because they don't like to sell. These entrepreneurs want to design a product, and then redesign it over and over until it is perfect. While there is definitely a place for this type of founder within a new venture, it's not in the CEO role, which is about selling your company to customers, investors, and vendors.

Even if you're still a student and have limited work experience, building your resume will help you examine what you have achieved. Do you see patterns in your resume that suggest some underlying strengths? Can you leverage these strengths as you try to launch a startup? Even if you are relatively young, recognize that many young entrepreneurs built companies large and small starting from their strengths. Michael Dell, for example, started Dell Computer as a college student at the University of Texas. He launched the company on his strengths: incredible technical skills during a time when most people didn't really understand how PCs worked. He originally started by purchasing computers from local retailers and upgrading them so that they better met his business customers' needs. His strengths lay in his ability to understand customer needs and how to best deliver PCs in a cost-effective, mass-customized manner, because he understood that the market was looking for lower-cost computing with superior customer service.

Likewise, Jeremy Weiner took his business plan for Cover-It, which had won an undergraduate business-school competition, and grew the business to the point where his largest competitor bought him out, making him a millionaire by the age of 26. Weiner's strengths lay in his tenacious ability to bootstrap the business, the strong connections he forged with his customers (high schools and national brand advertisers), and his ability to offer the service at a lower cost than his competitor. In addition, he worked hard to get an audience with a potential client and didn't give up until he closed the sale.

Dell and Weiner both started modestly and grew their businesses incrementally (at least in the beginning), which allowed them to develop their own skills in line with the growth of the business. Yet, both of them had a key strength they could leverage in the early days, a platform from which they could launch their business. As you examine your resume, what key strength pops out at you? Is that strength a strong platform from which you can develop the skills necessary to be the company's CEO, or might you be better off taking another role, such as Jed Smith did, and bringing in a more seasoned leader? Can you sell, or are you better suited to another role? You can't build a successful team until you understand your strengths and the best place for you in the company today at its launch and in the future as it progresses through various stages of growth.

While most people are pretty good at identifying their own strengths, they often have trouble understanding their weaknesses. Peter Drucker, the management guru who published over 30 books and received the 2002 Presidential Medal of Freedom, suggests that we can all improve our own self-awareness by conducting feedback analysis.[9] His methodology is simple: Every time you make a major decision or take a significant action, record what you expect to happen. For instance, as you decide to take an entrepreneurship class, write down what you expect to learn and what grade you believe you will earn. Several months later, after an outcome has occurred, compare it to what you originally recorded. Are your expectations and your actual results similar? What's different, and why is it different? Drucker asserts that this exercise focuses you on performance and results so you can identify your strengths and work to improve them. Although this exercise and others can help you understand your own strengths, many times people who know you are better judges of you than you are.

Talk to those people in your sphere of influence, people who know you well and whom you respect. Talk to your parents, friends, bosses, employers, coaches, professors, and others who can gauge your capabilities. Ask them, "What do you see me doing? What are my strengths and how can these attributes translate into launching a successful venture? What areas do you think I need to work on, and how should I go about it?" It is also important to ask them about your weaknesses. "What characteristics might impede my success? How can I work to rectify them?" Understanding your weaknesses will help you devise a plan to overcome them, whether that be through self-improvement or by hiring the right people to compensate for your weaknesses.

When it comes to self-awareness, there are two types of people. First, there are those who are overly conscious of their own weaknesses; they are their own worst critics. This group may be reluctant to pursue a venture because they fear their own shortcomings will lead to failure. In contrast, the second group seems oblivious to their own weaknesses. While this group may be more likely to launch a business, they are also more likely to fail once they do so because they won't seek help or even recognize that they need help. It is important to strike the right balance between these two extremes. The key to doing so is to develop deep self-awareness.

In addition to self-reflection and feedback from friends and family, there are also a wide array of psychological and personality tests available. Some classic examples are the Myers-Briggs personality type indicator, the California Personality Inventory, and the PIAV (Personal Interests, Attitudes and Values profile). These tests, which vary widely in cost, are designed to help individuals understand things like their underlying interests, motivations, and communication styles. They can provide valuable insights, but there are several important caveats to keep in mind when using them. First, always remember that no test, no matter how carefully designed and applied, can accurately predict an individual's likelihood for success in an entrepreneurial endeavor. Few things in life are as dynamic and unpredictable as an entrepreneurial environment, and for this reason, expect these tests only to give you a deeper understanding of your own strengths and weaknesses. Second, should you decide to take advantage of these resources, industry newsletter *HRfocus* strongly recommends that you have a trained professional administer and interpret the test for you, and that you insist upon a test that has been statistically validated. This is a field with little regulation, and as a result it is essential that you use assessments that have a proven track record.[10]

Finally, keep in mind that no single personality or demeanor is best suited for entrepreneurship. In fact, a study by *Inc. Magazine* found that many of the most common assumptions about entrepreneurs were misleading or wholly inaccurate. For instance, a classic label applied to entrepreneurs is that they are risk takers. In reality, the study found that CEOs of the *Inc. 500* companies varied widely in their levels of risk tolerance. What many had in common, however, was an ability to work well under highly stressful conditions.[11] The lesson here is that entrepreneurs come in all shapes and sizes, and you need to be careful about letting common myths about entrepreneurs dissuade you from starting a business. Tests can't tell you whether you will be successful, but they can provide you with insights that you can use to help ensure your success.

The key thing to remember is that entrepreneurship is hard work. You will not become a millionaire overnight, or in five years. As Walter Kuemmerle, a Harvard Business School professor, notes, entrepreneurship requires patience.[12] As the Internet boom and bust taught us, it can be a mistake to grow too big too fast. It is cheaper to test the business model when a company is small and then shift strategies quickly to better adapt the model to the market reality.[13] This will take years, not months. So you need to ask yourself whether you have the patience to be an entrepreneur—this can be harder for the young and brash.

Once you understand who you are and what skill set you bring to the venture, the next step is to identify what other skills are necessary to successfully launch the business. Create a staffing plan that not only identifies key roles, but also tells you when you need to fill those roles. Figure 6.1 provides an example, but staffing plans vary based on the type of company, stage of development, type of industry, and so on. Early on, you likely need only one or two other team members. At this stage, each team member needs to understand that early-stage companies are flat and nonhierarchal. It is more important to know what needs to be done than worry about who should do it. Nonetheless, the roles for these members should be complementary, and each co-founder should also participate extensively in shaping the vision of the business. An ideal combination might have team members coming from different disciplines such as science and business. Or if they are in the same major field of study, they might have different functional specialties, such as finance and marketing or biology and microbiology. The co-founders will work together on the overall direction of the business, but it is also wise for them to identify and divide primary responsibilities. Many co-founders make the mistake of working on every task and decision together, which often leads to frustration and inefficiency. While everyone's input is valuable, consensus is often a deterrent to success. Someone needs to be in charge.

The sample staffing plan in Figure 6.1 is a working document that grows and evolves as the founding team achieves milestones and moves on to new tasks. The value in creating the staffing plan is that it helps you anticipate where the company is going and to plan

Role	Primary Duties	Person Filling Role	When Needed
Product Development	Develop prototype	Lead entrepreneur	Now
Market Development	Customer research Channel development	Founder	Now
Finance	Raise outside capital	To be determined	Next month
Production	Identify manufacturing partners	To be determined	3 months from now

Figure 6.1

Staffing plan

for those needs. Note that not all the positions are currently filled. It is wise in the launch stage to conserve resources, especially cash. Thus, the founders may take on some of the future roles as their skills permit. If, for example, the team needs a strong finance person with previous experience raising equity capital, it makes sense to start identifying that person early on, but to delay bringing him onto the team until needed (which might be when the company raises a significant round of financing from angels or through a private placement). While we have found the staffing plan highlighted in Figure 6.1 to be useful, the Management Function Analysis worksheet[14] is another useful staffing planning device.

How to Build a Powerful Team

Your staffing plan is the first step in building a powerful team. Your next challenge is to identify the individuals to fill the gaps. How do you identify the best candidates? The simple answer is to tap your personal network and the network of your advisors, but you'll want to go outside that network to broaden the pool of quality candidates. Work with your professors to make contacts with alumni. Search your college's alumni database to find people in the right industry and the right kind of position. More often than not, alumni are willing to speak with current students. Even if the alumni isn't willing or able to join your team, she may be able to recommend someone from her network. You should also check with your investors, accountant, lawyer, or other people affiliated with your efforts (if you have these people lined up already). Oftentimes, entrepreneurs will hire a lawyer or accountant earlier than they might need that individual, just to tap into his network. Moreover, many law firms are willing to work for promising new ventures pro bono, at reduced rates, or for deferred compensation. Thus, it may make sense to hire your lawyer early in your launch process. The key to your success is continually building your network. This will help you meet challenges beyond filling out your team.

A natural place to find co-founders and other team members is your family and friends. A look at the *Inc. 500* shows that 58% of entrepreneurs teamed up with a business associate, 22% with a personal friend, and 20% with their spouse or other family members.[15] Just remember that working with a close friend or family member can be a double-edged sword. On the plus side is that you know these people well, so you have a strong sense of their work ethic and personal chemistry. This was definitely the case for Sarah Eck and Brook Jay, of the Chicago-based events marketing firm All Terrain Productions. Close friends before going into business together, they found that their skills complemented each other's very well. Perhaps more importantly, their relationship added a level of trust that can only be found between friends.[16]

It can be difficult, however, to order your parent or spouse to do some tasks. Jeremy Weiner, the young millionaire entrepreneur we spoke of earlier, relates a story of hiring his mom, reversing their customary roles. Whereas Weiner's mother had been used to directing and advising him as he grew up, now he was in a position to direct and advise his mother. Finally one day, his stepfather scolded him for not "being nicer to his mother at work." Similar dynamics occur when you hire friends. You need to relate to your friends in a different manner—a more professional manner—and this can stress the friendship. Recognizing the consequences of this new dynamic is the first step toward managing it, but there is more that you can do.

Before entering into a team relationship with family or friends (or anyone for that matter), lay out as much as possible the previous accomplishments, industry profile, and years of experience that the person has, and what roles and responsibilities the person will fill in your organization going forward. Define decision and reporting responsibility.

Courtesy Jeremy Weiner

Jeremy Weiner, founder of Cover It and Zim Squared, directs his mother on an important task.

We are not saying you need to have a highly formalized structure at an early stage of your venture's development, but you do need to clearly state expectations, tasks, and objectives. We have seen more teams self-destruct because of personal conflicts than for lack of funding.

During the Internet boom, a three-student team was offered $100,000 seed investment by Idealab (a venture-capital-oriented incubator) for nothing more than a 20-page business plan and an interesting idea. However, two of the team members could barely sit in the same room together, and the third felt that his primary role was to mediate between the other two. Clearly, this dysfunctional team dynamic wasn't going to be able to develop the concept further. Unfortunately, the trio also couldn't decide to whom the intellectual capital belonged, so they disbanded the nascent venture before it ever got off the ground. Although that experience was painful, it would have been far worse to come to this realization after they had investors and other employees.

It is not at all uncommon for friends to dive into starting a business before they have really considered how it could affect their relationship. An excellent example unfolds in the movie *Startup.com*. This outstanding documentary follows two close friends through the rise and fall of their company during the Internet boom, and provides a dramatic example of how working together can affect the relationship of two lifelong friends. Although Kaleil Tuzman had to make the difficult and painful decision to fire his friend and co-founder, Tom Herman, the two were ultimately able to piece their friendship back together. This is just one example of the difficulties you may face. Again, the key is to have clear expectations of each other and understand that pitfalls will test your friendship.

Once you have identified the right co-founders or team members, there is still the hurdle of opportunity costs. The best candidates often are already employed in good jobs, often in the industry where you will be competing. That means at some point they will need to leave a well-paying job to join your venture, and most new businesses can't afford to pay market rates during the cash-strapped startup phase. In addition, there is much greater risk that a new business will fail, which compounds the personal opportunity costs that co-founders and early team members face. As the lead entrepreneur you need to convince potential candidates that the job itself is intrinsically rewarding and growth oriented (team members get to do something they like and be part of creating something new and exciting), and that in the long run the financial payoff will be much greater. A young company offers potential team members opportunities to grow into higher management positions (and therefore higher deferred tax-advantaged pay) than might be possible at their current company, and also the opportunity to have some ownership in the new venture (either through options or founders stock). These are both powerful tools for convincing talented candidates to take a risk with your company. The more successful the targeted candidate, the harder it will be for you to successfully make these arguments, yet our research indicates that many people are willing and eager to jump into the entrepreneurial fray for the right opportunity. Make sure to present your best case. Sell candidates on the vision and back that up by showing them what you've accomplished to date, such as building and testing a prototype or securing outside financing.

Bootstrapping: Building the Team Based on Stage-of-Venture Life

Building your team requires resources, something that's scarce in most nascent ventures. Co-founders must often live off their savings or their spouse's income during the early days, as it may be impossible to draw a salary. Recognizing that difficulty, you are likely to find that it is better to bootstrap your team build-out, rather than putting everyone in place from day one. It's common for founders of smaller companies to continue working at their current jobs and work on the business part-time at night and on weekends. Many companies are able to successfully develop prototypes or raise the first round of outside investment while the founders are still at their current job (although you should not continue working for a firm that you'll directly compete with).

Be careful, though, not to commingle activities. When you're at your current job, your attention should be focused on those duties that help your employer succeed. You should *not* use your employer's resources, like computers and copiers, without explicit permission. You should *not* expropriate intellectual property from your current employer to use in your new venture. And, you should most certainly *not* solicit your employer's customers while you are still taking a paycheck from that employer. If you handle your startup well, you will often find that your current employer is supportive, especially if the business isn't directly competing with your proposed venture. Thus you should notify your employer of your intentions as soon as possible.

Another means of earning a salary during the early days is to take a part-time job. While this may mean working as a waiter or for a temp agency, entrepreneurs will often consult in a related field until their main product or service is ready to go to market. For example, Rezwan Sharif, founder of Ferrate Solutions, a producer of water treatment compounds that are more effective and environmentally friendly than chlorine, is consulting with a South American water treatment plant while his technology goes through field tests. He has also applied for and received a number of grants, and won several cash and services-in-kind prizes for competing in business plan competitions nationwide. All these efforts bring the cash and resources needed to build the business to the point where it will be more attractive to outside equity investors.

As a lead entrepreneur, you need to prepare for a diminished personal cash flow during the early years of your business, as you will often have to defer drawing a salary. Continuing to work for your current employer, building up a savings war chest, and delaying purchases of new cars or a house all contribute to sustaining you during the beginning. While painful, this frugality is often a small tradeoff to pursue your dream, and if you are successful, you will likely receive a future payoff that will be well worth the initial risk and sacrifice.

Perhaps the most common means to protect your personal cash flow is to continue working in a full-time job during the early phases. The weekend and nighttime entrepreneur is common, but at some point you have to quit and work on your dream full time. Alan Knitowski started Vovida Networks while still working 50 to 60 hours a week with an operations consulting firm.[17] The tradeoffs of this approach are clear. While you do maintain your personal income, every waking hour is devoted to either your regular job or your new venture. This dual-job strategy usually only works during the planning stages of your new venture—you can write a business plan, build a prototype, and start to make some key vendor and customer contacts, but you likely can't launch the business while working full time elsewhere.

In addition to the time constraints, there are other issues to consider. If you are being paid, that means your time and effort should go toward your current job. Make sure to work on the startup on your own time. There is also the potential for a lawsuit if your new business uses intellectual property developed on the company's time. Once you leave your full-time job, your previous company may feel like a jilted lover. Working to maintain a relationship with your former company is difficult, but not impossible. Alan Knitowski, for example, informed his boss that he was thinking of leaving to launch his business, and both sides agreed to give the other six months notice as to when that would happen.[18] The risk, of course, is that your current company might terminate you immediately after you inform them, but for the long term it is better to be straight with those affected by your decision.

When you're bringing on team members, many of the same principles apply. Examine your staffing plan to assess when you need that individual on a part-time basis and when you need her on a full-time basis. If the person is critical to building your product, you'll need her sooner. If she will be your primary salesperson, you won't need her until you go to market. Accurately timing when different people join the team conserves company cash and helps the new-hire manage her own personal finances. There are tradeoffs, however. First, you need to plan ahead. It often takes four months or more to identify and hire key employees. Second, it is easy for a part-time worker to become disengaged from the startup. If your team member is still at his current job, that will likely take priority over your venture, especially if some special projects come up. Third, people who are already working on the startup full time may resent that the other person isn't as heavily involved in the sweat and tears that characterize the venture. They may feel this person is getting a free ride. As the lead entrepreneur, you need to manage these perceptions and work to keep the part-time and future team members fully apprised of what is happening. Finally, until a person signs up, she is at greater risk of either changing her mind about joining the venture or walking away for another new opportunity. Understanding these risks will help you manage them and still preserve your cash flow. One way to handle these situations is to develop a compensation plan that excites your current and future team members.

Compensation

As resource-constrained as new ventures are, you are likely hard pressed to think about compensation for you and your team. At some point, however, you'll need to pay yourself and others in your organization. The more powerful your team, the more compensation they will expect, whether that is in salary or equity (but usually a combination). So how does a startup company determine what to pay its employees? How does it choose between wages, salary, bonuses, equity, or some combination of these options? The answers to these questions depend not only on the nature of your company, but also on the nature of your team and employees.

Equity

There are several good reasons why most new ventures distribute equity to at least some of their employees. First, new companies often can't pay market rates for salary and wages. Equity can induce people to work for below-market rates with the expectation that at some point in the future they will be handsomely rewarded. As Lalitha Swart of Silicon Valley

Bank put it, "People don't leave large corporations and take on risk without knowing there is an upside in stock."[19] Second, including some equity in the compensation package aligns the employee's interests with those of the company. Basically, the employees become owners and their stock or options increase in value as the company prospers. Finally, the sense of ownership boosts morale as employees perceive that everybody is in this together. This added camaraderie helps the team to stick together during the inevitable rough times in the early-launch phase. Of course, distributing equity throughout an organization isn't costless. It dilutes the founders' and investors' equity. You need to understand the tradeoff between motivating employees, conserving cash flow, and preserving your own equity. Understanding the tradeoffs helps you develop a compensation plan.

There are two basic ways of distributing equity: founder shares and an option pool. As the name implies, **founder shares** are equity earned by founders of the company at the time it is officially established, or when the first outside equity capital is invested (usually when it is first incorporated, although the shares may vest over time). Founder shares are most often given with no or minimal investment (maybe one cent per share) and are an acknowledgment of the "sweat equity" that each of the founders has invested in turning their idea into a company, or as acknowledgment of the track record and value of the founders. There are several considerations to keep in mind when granting founder shares. First, remember that granting shares to new parties dilutes your personal ownership, but this dilution is more than offset if you are granting shares to valuable co-founders who can help the company grow. For example, if you are opening a French restaurant and you have front-room experience as a maître d', it makes sense to co-found the restaurant with an accomplished French chef who can design and run the kitchen. It makes less sense to award founder shares to waiters, dishwashers, busboys, and other staff who are more transient and less central to the restaurant's competitive advantage. Founder shares should be reserved for those team members who are essential to turning the idea into reality.

How many people should get founder shares? It's a serious question. We advise entrepreneurs to keep this group small, usually no more than three people. Again, keep in mind the principle of preserving your equity by avoiding dilution. Once the founding team gets to be five or more, dilution can dramatically affect the capital appreciation that each founder receives, especially if the company needs to raise outside equity. Investors like to see founders with a significant stake in the company because "having skin in the game" focuses entrepreneurs on growing the company's future value rather than on maximizing current salaries. If, after a few rounds of outside investment, the founders have only 1% to 5% percent of the equity each, they may start to recognize that no matter how big the company becomes, the long-term gain won't be sufficient to compensate them for all the hard work of getting the company to that point. Therefore, the founders might be more inclined to leave the new venture for greener pastures, and disruption in the leadership team is very difficult for emerging ventures to survive. The smaller the group of people who receive founder shares, the smaller this dilution problem becomes. This is not to say that other team members should be precluded from equity participation, just that founder shares are not the best way to distribute equity to employees. Options are a better choice, and we'll touch on that topic shortly.

A third consideration regarding founder shares is how to divide them between the founders. Many first-time entrepreneurs fall into the trap of evenly dividing the shares among the founders. So if you have four founders, you might give each person 25% of the founder shares. A number of problems can arise from equal distribution. First and foremost, if each founder has an equal share, it can be hard to make important decisions because the group will want to have consensus. Even if one founder has been designated CEO, the others may perceive that their input needs to be given full consideration. At a minimum this situation slows the decision-making process, but it can sometimes lead to disaster as the team stalls and becomes incapable of taking action. Another factor is that ambitious people tend to benchmark themselves against their peers. This means that a CEO will benchmark her compensation against that of other CEOs. If the founder shares are equally distributed, it is only a matter of time before the CEO recognizes that she is doing as much work as her peers but has less potential upside. This discrepancy acts as a disincentive to maintaining the level of commitment required by startups.

While there are no hard-and-fast rules for splitting founder stock, keep in mind these guiding principles centering on past contribution and expected future contribution. First, acknowledge the time and value of past contributions.[20] The entrepreneur who initiated the idea, started doing the leg work, and enticed co-founders to join deserves consideration for all of these efforts, and also for her expected contribution going forward; maybe as much as 50% if the founder also continues in a major role as CEO or some other high-level manager. Second, the founder who is CEO should have most of the equity, often as much as 50% of the founder shares. Next, the founder who brings in the intellectual capital, say a patent or invention, should have 20% to 30% of the founder shares. As you can see, it is difficult to put hard-and-fast rules on founder shares as founders may assume multiple roles.

While these principles can guide the distribution, the final split comes down to a negotiation. Detail each founder's past and expected future contribution and the role he will assume in the organization, and then divide the founder's stock accordingly. It can be useful to engage a lawyer with experience in this area. The lawyer can help you benchmark against other companies and offer outside validation that each founder is getting her due share.

Since you will want to minimize the distribution of founder shares, another way to reward other employees and future hires is through an option pool. An **option pool** is equity set aside for future distribution. Options basically give the holder the right to buy a share in the company at a below-market rate. The option price is often determined by the market price of the stock on the day the employee is hired (or in the case of a private company, the price at the last round of financing).

The principles we discussed about founder shares apply to options as well. An option pool will dilute the founders' equity, but to a much lower degree than broadening the number of people who receive founder shares. Granting options also helps align the employee interests with those of the founders by making the employees partial owners of the company. Additionally, to exercise their options recipients must pay for the shares, which brings money into the company (although the amount is usually too small to be considered as a source of growth capital). During the Internet boom, companies liberally granted options. Unfortunately, as the boom turned to bust, many employees found their options "under water," meaning that the exercise price was greater than the current market price for the share. If options lose their value, they cease to be an incentive and retention tool. When this happens, employees are more likely to leave to seek new opportunities. However, if a company is growing, the value of the options should continue to grow, which increases the incentive and value for the employees.

Since granting options can mean giving up a significant piece of the organization, it is essential that owners know how to use these motivational tools effectively. The worst-case scenario is one in which the entrepreneur gives up equity in the company and receives little or none of the value that equity is supposed to create. Many rank-and-file employees have difficulty understanding exactly how they contribute to the value of the organization. Communicating with employees about the importance of their roles, and training everyone about how they can increase shareholder value, is essential.

According to the Beyster Institute, a nonprofit organization dedicated to improving the use of employee ownership, entrepreneurs can take several key steps to ensure that options improve organizational performance. First, employees need to fully understand the stock ownership program and how they will participate in it. Related to this point, employees should have a solid understanding of how the company is performing. Second, the staff must know how to measure company success, and receive training on how to achieve it through their individual roles. Third, as we have mentioned, one of the great benefits of offering options is that it makes employees owners of the company, and therefore encourages them to think like owners. However, the key here is that owners are typically more motivated to find solutions to problems or to develop innovations. An entrepreneur who offers options and doesn't harness or listen to this highly motivated workforce is failing to capitalize on the greatest benefit of offering ownership. Fourth, a stock-ownership plan should offer employees a true opportunity to earn a financial reward. This potential for financial windfall is the key to stock-ownership plans.[21]

Once the company decides it wants to use options to motivate and reward employees, the question is how many options to issue and to whom. Research suggests that issuing options generates increased overall company value through gains in employee productivity, and that this increased value offsets the dilution effect.[22] It is common for many technology firms to put aside 15% to 20% of their equity for employee options after a major investment round. From that pool, the company can decide to distribute options to all or just key employees. Don't make the mistake of distributing all the options to existing employees, but anticipate how many new hires you'll make over the coming years. Then you can come up with a distribution plan based on employee level. Higher-level employees, say vice presidents and other upper-management employees, will get more options than lower-level employees. Keep in mind that you'll vest shares over an employee's tenure.

Although options are the most commonly used form of equity compensation, new Financial Accounting Standards Board (FASB) regulations put into place in 2005 make them more expensive for both private and public companies. Specifically, companies must list options as an expense on their income sheet rather than just as a footnote to their financials.[23] While it appears that the FASB rule hasn't dampened the use of options, there are other similar means to reward employees including restricted stock, stock appreciation rights, and phantom stock.[24] **Restricted stock** are actual shares, rather than the option to buy shares, that are vested over time. The upside is that the expense is the current share price, rather than the expected exercise price of an option. The downside is that the recipient gets the stock regardless of company performance, whereas employees exercise options only when the company's stock price increases. **Stock appreciation rights** accrue to employees only if the stock price increases (similar to options). Their advantage over options is that they tend to be lower cost to the company. Finally, **phantom stock** isn't really issued equity, but a cash bonus paid to employees if the stock price appreciates over a set period of time. Phantom stocks are expensed over the vesting period, but they have the benefit of lowering dilution. The downside is that you'll need cash once the phantom stocks are exercised, and for a resource-constrained startup, cash is at a premium.

One of the main reasons to award options, founder stock, or one the hybrids just mentioned is to keep key employees with the firm. However, what happens if you decide that someone needs to be fired due to poor performance, nonperformance, or any variety of other reasons? If it is a co-founder, that person likely has a sizable chunk of equity and any voting rights associated with it. That may mean the person can interfere with the operations of the business. An important means to protect you from an employee or co-founder who doesn't pan out as expected is to create a vesting schedule. **Vesting** basically means that people earn their shares or options over time, usually over four or more years. For example, if a co-founder is entitled to 25% of the company's shares, you may vest those shares in equal chunks over four years. That way if the person leaves or is fired in the first year, he walks away with only a quarter of the shares he would have been entitled to if he stayed. This maintains the unvested shares for distribution to future hires.

You can also structure an employment contract to permit the company to repurchase the employee's shares at cost, or some other predetermined rate, when she leaves or is dismissed from the company. You may negotiate a right-of-first-refusal that gives the company or other existing shareholders the right to buy the equity of an ex-employee at the prevailing market rate. If you are firing the individual, it will be important for your employment agreement to state that the employee is an at-will employee regardless of her ownership position in the company. Failure to take this step can open your company up to the possibility of a minority shareholder lawsuit. To avoid lawsuits, you should define fired for cause, touching on what the company considers to be fraud, negligence, nonperformance, and so forth. Lawsuits aside, having a right-of-first-refusal or the option to repurchase shares when the employee leaves preserves all the shares for redistribution among the remaining founders and employees. To avoid the time and energy of litigation, companies usually buy out fired co-founders after they reach a settlement.

The Dilution Effect: An Example

This hypothetical example shows what happens to an entrepreneur as her firm achieves various milestones/benchmarks of a successful launch and on to a harvest/liquidity event. To demonstrate dilution, assume valuations at different rounds (valuation is covered in detail in Chapter 10). The following are some typical milestones that a successful venture might reach.

Milestone Events

1. Entrepreneur entices technology partner to join her firm, gives him **40%** of the equity.

2. Raises **$200,000** in equity from family and friends. The idea is valued post-money at **$1.0 million**.

3. Idea is technically feasible. Needs to hire **software engineers** to build a working prototype. Raises **$1 million** from angels on a **$2.5 million** post-money valuation. Establishes a **15%** option pool to provide equity to current engineers as well as future hires.

4. Prototype looks promising and company successfully raises **$3 million** of venture capital on a **$7 million** post-money valuation to start sales. The VC imposes the following terms: Company needs to hire an experienced CEO, CFO, and VP of Sales, giving the three options worth **10%**, **3%**, and **7%**.

5. Sales growth is on plan and the firm needs to ramp up to meet increasing demand. Raises **$10 million** of additional venture capital on a **$30 million** post-money valuation.

6. Firm receives acquisition offer from a large company (e.g., Microsoft, Cisco, etc.) for **$100 million in the large company's stock.**

Note that while our entrepreneur is being diluted, the increasing value of her firm offsets this dilution.

Event	Entr. Share	Co-Founder	Family/ Friends	Angels	Option Pool	CEO	CFO	VP Sales	VC Rnd1	VC Rnd2	Total	Valuation (000)	Ent's. Value
1	60%	40%									100%		
2	48%	32%	20%								100%	$1,000	$480
3	22%	14%	9%	40%	15%						100%	$2,500	$540
4	8%	5%	3%	15%	6%	10%	3%	7%	43%		100%	$7,000	$562
5	5%	4%	2%	10%	4%	7%	2%	5%	29%	33%	100%	$30,000	$1,605
6	5%	4%	2%	10%	4%	7%	2%	5%	29%	33%	100%	$100,000	$5,349
Harvest Value for All Stakeholders	$5,349	$3,566	$2,229	$9,905	$3,714	$6,667	$2,000	$4,667	$28,571	$33,333			

This example highlights a successful venture. Founders who distribute equity wisely grow the value of their firm, which leads to a higher return for all involved, even as dilution occurs. However, student entrepreneurs often make the mistake of giving too much founder's stock to too many different people. If, for example, the firm started with five student founders with equal ownership and still progressed through each step, the final harvest value for each founder would be $1 million. While this sum is attractive, keep in mind that this growth projection likely takes five or more years, and in the early years the founders will be paid below-market salaries (and probably no salaries until the angel round).

Also, if there is any kind of problem that leads to a lower valuation than projected here, the final payoff for the founders is greatly impacted. If, for example, the valuation that the firm receives when the first VC comes in is only $5 million versus $7 million, the entrepreneur (as sole initial founder) earns a harvest value of $2.8 million. If there were five initial co-founders who get equal shares, each would earn a bit less than $600,000 each for many years of hard work and below-market pay. The lesson is to distribute equity wisely. Make sure that all co-founders will contribute throughout the entire time it takes to build and harvest the company, and that each can increase the value of the company.

Salary

Although equity can compensate for a below-market salary, most of your team will need at least a subsistence salary during the launch phase. The difficulty is trying to set that initial salary. You can start by researching the current market rate for the position you are trying to fill at online resources such as www.salary.com. The Web site provides general parameters for the position and then allows you to personalize your search by company size, industry, and other factors. For instance, an information technology director might earn anywhere from $130,000 to $180,000 in the Boston metropolitan area. The person's salary would be adjusted by her previous work experience, the industry focus of your company, and other mitigating factors specific to the individual or your company. You can also double-check your market figure by looking at some of the Internet job sites like www.monster.com. A scan of that site found that a CTO position was being offered around $150,000 in an early-stage software firm. The market rate is a reference parameter, and you'll adjust it by considering the person's expertise and perceived contribution to the company. A younger, less experienced co-founder will earn well below the market rate. A more senior, experienced co-founder with a long record of success might earn close to or above the market rate, but paying the market rate is probably impossible for a startup.

Once you know the market rate, you can negotiate a current salary and expected increases based on your company's improving cash flow. For instance, you might tie an increase to closing the next round of funding. Other increases might be linked to increasing cash flow due to improved sales. Instead of making firm commitments to future salary increases, consider using performance-based bonuses in the early years. This further aligns the team's efforts with the venture's overall goals and preserves cash flow. If team members successfully execute, the venture should have increasing sales, which in turn can lead to rapid growth in bonuses and other profit sharing. The key is to be creative and motivate your team to work toward common goals. That means deferred current income (lower salaries) with the promise of larger returns in the future (bonuses, appreciation of equity, and options).

Although startups should negotiate below-market salaries, it can be helpful to understand the implications of a fully loaded business model. When constructing your pro forma financials, see what happens to your expected profitability if you paid everyone their market rates. All too often, entrepreneurs launch into a business expecting attractive profit margins only to realize that these margins are a mirage; once people are paid according to the market rate (say in the fifth year), the profits disappear. Some entrepreneurs choose to promise market rates but defer payment until cash flow improves. In this case, they are creating a deferred liability that obligates the company to pay back some portion of the lower-market salary in the future. This means the market salary is reflected in the income statement, the actual pay is shown on the cash flow, and the remainder appears on the balance sheet as a deferred liability. However you decide to compensate your team, be cognizant of the full range of possibilities and keep in mind that you need to preserve cash flow in the early years to fund growth.

Other Compensation Considerations

In addition to equity and salary, as the owner of a company you will need to think through a number of other issues in overall compensation. You will be competing with companies of all shapes and sizes for the most skilled people in the workforce. Putting together a competitive compensation package means thinking beyond just the monetary side of compensation. For instance, while they may not be feasible in the earliest parts of the startup phase, as quickly as possible you will want to consider things like health and dental plans, and retirement savings programs like 401(k)s. Even from the start, you will need to figure out a holiday and vacation package that makes sense for your company.

Every organization is different, and it's important to align your benefits package with the types of people you intend to hire. If your business will rely on recent college graduates, something like company-sponsored life insurance will probably be unnecessary. However, if your staff will be older, married people who have families, life insurance and a solid family health-care plan will be essential. The key is that all of these benefits are strategic in nature. Your goal in developing a compensation package is to attract and motivate the best talent in the most cost-effective way possible. You should never underestimate the effect that a thoughtful benefits plan can have on employee satisfaction and loyalty. There are few things as powerful as having a workforce that feels they work for a great company.

External Team Members

Although your core team is critical to your venture's success, you will leverage their efforts by building a strong **virtual team**—that is, all those who have a vested interest in your success, including professionals you contract for special needs, such as lawyers, accountants, and consultants. It also includes those who have invested in your business, especially if they have valuable expertise. For instance, you'll be well served if you secure angel investors who are successful entrepreneurs in your industry. You may also be able to gain help from those who haven't financially invested in your firm but are interested in helping new businesses succeed, perhaps by serving on advisory boards for new companies. Finally, at some point you'll likely pull together a board of directors, which is required by law if you are incorporated. Let's examine each of these outside team members in more detail.

Outside Investors

When you are considering bringing on outside investors, whether in the form of angel investors or venture capitalists, never underestimate the value these team members can bring with their experience and wisdom. For many angel investors in particular, the experience of working with a startup is as much about the satisfaction of mentoring a young entrepreneur as it is about financial gain. Take, for example, the story of Norm Brodsky, the long-time entrepreneur and contributor to *Inc. Magazine*. In describing his decision to invest in David Schneider's New York City restaurant, he said that, "Yes, making money is important. I wouldn't go into a deal unless I thought I could get my capital back and earn a good return. But I don't really do this type of investing for the money anymore. I'm more interested in helping people get started in business. Whatever I make is a bonus on top of the fun I have being a part of it and the satisfaction I get from helping people like David succeed."

For an aspiring entrepreneur, finding an investor with that kind of an attitude is invaluable. As Schneider put it, "I really liked the idea of having somebody I could go to who cared about this place as a business... It's like he's always pushing people to better themselves. He wants you to move on, to expand, to grow."[25] In business, experience is the greatest competitive advantage, and an investor can bring that asset to a fledgling company. But Schneider's comments also point to another key benefit of having a strong investor on your side: You'll have someone to hold you accountable and keep you focused. Many entrepreneurs underestimate the challenge being your own boss can pose. When the going gets tough or decisions get complicated, it can be incredibly helpful to have someone prodding you forward. For all these reasons, choose carefully if you decide to raise capital through angel investors.

Lawyers

Every new venture will require legal advice. Although you may be able to incorporate on your own, other aspects of your venture will benefit from your attorney's guidance. As discussed earlier, your lawyer can draft an appropriate template for employee contracts. If your business is developing some intellectual property, you may wish to file a patent. The right attorney can help you search existing patents and decide which elements of your intellectual property are patentable. She will devise a suite of patents and then, if you deem it appropriate, help you patent your product in several important countries. Lawyers can also consult on the myriad unforeseen issues that are likely to arise, which is why it is so essential to choose your attorney carefully.

When making a decision to hire a lawyer, consider several factors. For instance, a smaller firm is likely to offer lower billing rates, a factor that can be very important to a startup. However, small firms are often heavily dependent on a small handful of clients who make up the bulk of their business. For this reason, you may find that your company is a low priority for a small firm with several key accounts. In contrast, while a large firm may bill out at a higher rate, it will almost always have someone available to answer your questions, and it will also offer the benefit of a large pool of lawyers with diverse areas of expertise to draw from. Since your legal issue may cover everything from employment law to intellectual property, a large firm isn't necessarily a bad choice. While you may pay more, you may also find that a larger firm is more willing or able to set up a flexible payment plan.

In addition, when choosing your lawyer it is essential that you find someone you like, who shows an appreciation for and interest in your company, and most importantly, who has deep knowledge

When Ajay Bam started his company, Vaysu/Mobilelime.com, he was determined to get the best legal advice possible, but he had no money to pay for the service. He heard John Hession speak at an MIT Enterprise Forum and decided he was the right lawyer for Vaysu. Bam pursued Hession with phone calls and e-mails. He arranged a personal meeting and they clicked. Hession knew that a startup like Bam's couldn't afford his fees so he told Bam, "You educate yourself on a lot of the legal stuff so I don't have to spend time telling you what it means, and you will save some money. You will prepare all the drafts." Hession sent Bam typical legal document templates such as stock agreements and told Bam to cut and paste his own documents and then bring them to him for a final review. In that way, Bam saved thousands of dollars and got an education.

of your industry. The last thing you want is to be paying several hundred dollars an hour to talk with someone who is distant or aloof. And as for hourly rates, yes, you should expect to pay a minimum of $150/hour, and likely much more than that. For this reason it is critical that you do as much preparation and research as possible before you sit down with your attorney. Most firms bill in increments of as little as 10 minutes, so you need to use your time with an attorney as effectively and efficiently as possible. Also keep in mind that while it is important to have a lawyer from the beginning to ensure that you avoid many of the classic mistakes, there are also a wide variety of free resources available to small businesses. These include everything from online templates for standard agreements and forms, to nonprofits and government-sponsored law centers that can provide low-cost or pro bono advice. While you should always turn to your lawyer for the final word, you can save your company a lot of money by using the available resources to get some of the legwork out of the way. Just remember that as your company grows, your time will become more valuable, and at some point spending hours doing your own research becomes counterproductive.

Accountants

It's often wise to hire an accountant to handle tax filings in the early years, because you're likely to be too busy to do it yourself and too small to have an in-house person, such as a controller or CFO, to manage the process for you. Many of the same caveats about working with lawyers apply to accountants, though you may be well served by an accountant who is a sole proprietor. The nature of accountants' work is somewhat different from that of lawyers, and for this reason you needn't work with a larger firm in your early years. Beyond filing tax returns and keeping your filings up to date, don't forget that an accountant is a trained business professional who can help you analyze the strengths and weaknesses of your company's financial performance. He or she may be able to help you find ways to improve cash flow, strengthen margins, and identify tax benefits that can save you money down the road. Furthermore, both lawyers and accountants represent another spoke in your network, as both groups frequently have a long list of business and professional contacts. This can include everything from potential partners and customers to angel investor networks and venture capital firms.

Board of Advisors

A board of advisors can be extremely powerful to the early-stage company. Unlike a board of directors, a board of advisors has no fiduciary duty to shareholders. Instead, the goal is to offer a source of expert guidance and feedback to the lead entrepreneur. In choosing a board you should look to enlist people with expertise in your field and a sincere interest in mentoring an emerging business. Good sources are your professors, current and former entrepreneurs, professional investors such as venture capitalists and angels, suppliers for your firm, and individuals who may have insight into your target customers. Beyond advice, this group can expand your personal network and provide leads to new customers or investors. In fact, board of advisor members will often become investors if your firm goes through a private placement.

One final note on boards of advisors relates to communication. Many first-time entrepreneurs struggle to strike the right balance between too much and too little communication. Keep in mind that if you have developed a powerful board of advisors, they are busy individuals. Don't e-mail or phone them every time you have a question. Instead, accumulate questions and think about which ones are most critical to your firm and where the advisor can add the most value. Do some preliminary legwork to find alternative answers to these questions and options you might be inclined to pursue. If you are prepared, you will have a more productive conversation with your advisors and they will be even more supportive of your future efforts.

The flip side to overcommunicating with advisors is touching base with them rarely, or only when you want help raising money. This type of communication suggests the entrepreneur is only interested in the advisor's network, but the advisor is less inclined to open up that network unless he has a strong understanding of the company's progress. Produce a monthly or bi-monthly e-mail newsletter that keeps all your important stakeholders, including your board of advisors, informed about the company's progress. This newsletter should be short and concise so that it will get read. More often than not, the newsletter will prompt an advisor to contact you with some useful input or connection to someone in her network. Properly managing your board of advisors will pay dividends, so don't neglect it.

Board of Directors

When incorporating a company, entrepreneurs must establish a board of directors whose purpose is to represent the interests of the equity holders. Thus, when you initially incorporate, the only shareholders might be you and your co-founders. Once you seek outside financing, it becomes important to fill out the board beyond the co-founders. Venture capitalists and more sophisticated angels often require representation on the board. A common board structure for the early-stage firm is five board members; these might include two insiders like the CEO and CFO, two members from the lead investors, and one outsider, who most often is selected with strong input from the investors. The outsider is often a person who has significant vertical market expertise and who can add value to the strategic operating decisions.

The board is in charge of governance and represents the shareholders. It meets quarterly to review the company's progress and its strategy going forward. The board will determine compensation for the company's officers and also oversee financial reporting. With the passage of the Sarbanes-Oxley Act, the responsibilities and potential liability of the board has greatly increased. While the legislation applies only to public companies, more and more small businesses are finding it necessary to align with the act if they hope one day to sell to a public company or go public themselves. It's a voluntary choice to do so, but the act's standards are rapidly becoming the "best practices" for accounting and financial control at well-managed companies. This means that developing a clear set of expectations, ethical standards, and procedures for board members is essential. Furthermore, you'll want to ensure that your board has at least one or two members who can be considered independent, which means they are not susceptible to potential conflicts of interest. Board members should be encouraged to act in the best interest of all the shareholders, not just the principal owner.

We believe the entrepreneurial team should extend beyond the co-founders and early employees to include external individuals who can provide invaluable wisdom and input. Entrepreneurship is truly a team sport—the stronger your team, the stronger your bench, the more likely you'll not only survive but thrive. The next section looks at some difficulties you might incur once the team is in place.

Keeping the Team Together

We've looked at the value of a well-functioning team. But not every team functions well, even if it's filled with superstars. Consider the New York Rangers of the National Hockey League. Since winning the Stanley Cup in 1994, the team consistently failed to make the playoffs despite having signed some of the biggest names in the sport, including Wayne Gretzky, Jaromir Jagr, and Eric Lindros, to name but a few. Why has this happened? Common sense dictates that the team with the best talent should win, but a dysfunctional team often fails. The key here is chemistry: sometimes the whole really is greater than the sum of the parts. Consider the Oakland A's of Major League Baseball. Although as of the writing of this book they have not won the World Series since 1989, they have consistently achieved a winning record despite having one of the lowest payrolls in the major leagues. Their general manager, Billy Beane, argues that a manager can put together a winning combination as long as he understands the gaps in his team, works to fill those gaps, and focuses on finding players who match the team's culture and work ethic. While we're not advocating the statistical construction of teams, we do believe that understanding and effectively directing your team toward its ultimate goal can make all the difference in the world.

You can hardly overestimate the importance of culture and fit. The key to building and growing a successful team is establishing a company culture and working to bring in team members who subscribe to that culture. Culture starts at day one in any new venture and evolves from the way the founders interact among themselves and with other early employees. Picture culture as analogous to duck imprinting. When a duckling is born, she follows the first thing she sees, which is usually her mother. Likewise, when a person joins a company she quickly acculturates to the environment she is in—or leaves shortly thereafter.

Once established, a company culture is incredibly difficult to change. So decide what type of culture you want, and then work to create it. Company culture is an enigmatic and amorphous thing, and the ways in which it affects organizational performance are not completely understood. It often filters down from the very top of the company, and thus it reflects the values and skills of the CEO and other leaders. If you want a company with an open, trusting environment, then you need to foster an open and trusting relationship with your direct reports. If you lead with fear and intimidation, this approach will filter its way down to all levels of your organization. The bottom line is that you need to think through the culture you want to create, decide on one you are comfortable with, and work daily to communicate the values behind that culture. The most successful cultures are those rooted in core values and beliefs that are a part of the company's mission, vision, and mantra.

Keep in mind that not everyone will fit the culture of your company. For many first-time entrepreneurs this represents a source of frustration and internal conflict, but it shouldn't. There are people who like buttoned up, conservative work environments, and people who like laid-back, laissez-faire workplaces. One person's "unprofessional" atmosphere makes another person's ideal company. Don't fight this, but do recognize the culture you are trying to create, and seek to hire people who will feel comfortable in it.

As a company grows, it's common for the culture to evolve. The classic example is the loosely organized startup culture where the pace of work is relentless, and as a result a lot of misgivings are overlooked. Nine times out of ten this culture will evolve toward a more structured "corporate" culture as the company gets bigger, and the chaos that was so critical to the early stage begins to erode the company's success. Every startup will see certain elements of its culture evolve, and certain elements stay the same year after year. The most important point is to make the change deliberate, and recognize the long-term commitment needed to instill it.

Even if a venture has a strong culture, problems with the team are inevitable. Just as the best cure is prevention, the best way to keep your team functioning well is to avoid some of the common pitfalls. We will take a look at some of the problems that most new venture teams face and then examine ways to avoid them.

Burnout

We've all heard the stories of Internet startups during which the team ate and slept in the office for weeks at a time. A diet of pizza and Red Bull are synonymous with the crazed hours of the classic launch phase. The atmosphere is relaxed but energized, and the people are highly motivated by the fast-paced environment and the thrill of being on the cutting edge of an emerging technology.

While this approach works for many early-stage ventures, it's not for everyone, and it has its drawbacks. On top of the long hours, there's the uncertainty that your product will work as intended or that the market will respond to the product or service as you hoped. Every minor misstep seems to take on epic importance and increases the stress levels of your team. Moreover, your team will notice that the balance between personal and professional life is out of whack, and they may start questioning whether this sustained effort is worth it. As these pressures increase, the risk of losing a critical team member mounts. It's important to manage and relieve these stresses as much as possible.

As the lead entrepreneur, you need to act as the coach of the team and keep them focused on the end goal. This means that communication is critically important. Although e-mail is the standard business communication form these days, in the startup phase, you should make a point of having daily face-to-face communication with every team member. Listen to each, not only about the progress of their assignments, but also about the stresses they may be feeling. Present them with regular updates on the overall progress of the venture, and give them realistic progress reports on how things are going. It is far more damaging to withhold negative information they will ultimately discover for themselves. If they understand that the venture is falling behind schedule or that the product isn't functioning quite as planned, they can be energized to correct these problems.

New ventures also have planned stress-relieving activities, or bonding experiences, such as the Friday happy hour, or the lunchtime basketball game. Get away from your workspace and share some downtime with each other. The upside of these extracurricular activities is the strong bonds it helps the team build. A startup can be like your college days, where you'll make some of your life-long friends. Many new ventures also have stress relievers right in the workplace, such as foosball tables, dartboards, and other distractions so that individuals can break from their work for a few minutes and clear their minds. It's often a good idea to provide free soda, coffee, and snacks as well. These little perks are cost-effective and build goodwill and camaraderie. Relieving stress will help keep your team strong and cohesive.

Family Pressure

If working long hours stresses your team members, it also stresses their families. Spouses and significant others complain to their partners about their never being home or being too tired to pay attention to their families. Missing a child's ball games and school performances can create resentment. Stress at home can negatively affect performance and increase the risk of turnover. If spouses continually ask why their partner has left a good-paying job for lower pay and the promise of a future payoff, your team members will question their own motives. So it's imperative that open communication occur on the home front as well.

Counsel your team members to set the expectations of their families even before they join your team. If a spouse is forewarned of the long hours, it minimizes the angst. It's also a good idea to include families in stress-relieving events on a regular basis. Company picnics are a nice way for spouses to connect with other spouses. In this way they can develop an informal support group with people who are facing the same difficulties. In fact, some new ventures formalize these family support groups by organizing a few events that are spouse-specific. It is important to remember and remind all involved that the long hours will subside, and that if the venture is successful, everyone will benefit.

Interpersonal Conflicts

In such a charged environment, interpersonal conflicts among team members are common. Resolve these disputes as quickly as possible or they may escalate to the point where they become destructive. Lead entrepreneurs typically find that they spend as much time coaching and managing team issues as they do directly working on the business. If you find yourself in this situation, don't worry—this is a valuable and effective use of your time. If you can keep your team working together, you'll have more success than if you try to carry the burden all alone.

As the coach, you may be able to resolve some conflicts only by firing one of the team members. While firing is a necessary part of running a company, you need to be prepared for the inevitable disruption it will cause (although it can be therapeutic to those who remain if it removes some of the stress that the fired individual brought to the company). Depending on the person's agreement with the company, his departure may require a buyout of equity and a lump-sum settlement. That's why firing is usually undertaken only if the person is not only prone to interpersonal conflicts, but also underperforming in some way (either not skilled enough to do the jobs required or shirking his responsibilities). First try to resolve the conflict by mediating between the parties, and be sure not to appear to be favoring either one. It may be prudent to hire an outside expert who is perceived as a neutral party. Whatever resolution you agree upon, make sure that it is implemented as planned.

☐ CONCLUSION

Entrepreneurship is a team sport. The most critical task any lead entrepreneur undertakes is defining who should be on the team and then creating an environment in which that team can flourish. This chapter has identified the type of team members ventures might need, how to entice and compensate them, and how to build a strong, supportive culture. Maintaining a team requires ongoing effort, and many organizations find that team dynamics suffer when the firm experiences rapid growth. Chapter 14 revisits these issues and suggests ways that organizations can keep their entrepreneurial orientation.

Reflection Point	**Your Thoughts...**	

1. What are your three strongest attributes?

2. Talk to a close mentor and ask what he or she sees as your strengths. Do these match the attributes you identified above?

3. What skills do you need to develop prior to launch? What skills can you develop during the launch and early stages of your company? Create a plan to develop those skills.

4. Create an organization chart for your venture. Show positions to be filled immediately and those to be filled later (along with the dates of filling those positions). Create a staffing plan based on your organization chart.

5. Think about the types of employees you'd like to hire. What kind of values are you looking for? Remember, this is the point that you create your company's culture.

WEB EXERCISE ☐

Scan Monster.com, Salary.com and other job sites. Look at the postings for CEO and other key employees of early-stage companies in the industry that you are interested in pursuing. What skills are being sought? What level of previous experience is desired? How much are they offering for these key employees? Use this information to start creating your own staffing plan.

NOTES ☐

[1] Minniti, M., Bygrave, W., and Autio, E. *Global Entrepreneurship Monitor: 2005 Executive Report.* Babson College and London Business School. 2006.

[2] http://bizstats.com/emprodretail.htm.

[3] http://bizstats.com/emprodaccom.htm. For other industries, check http://bizstats.com/.

[4] Lechler, T. Social interaction: A determinant of entrepreneurial team success. *Small Business Economics,* 16: 263–278. 2001.

[5] Ruef, M. Strong ties, week ties and islands: Structural and cultural predictions of entrepreneurial team success.

Industrial and Corporate Changes, 11: 427–449. 2002.

6   Bird, B. *Entrepreneurial Behavior.* Glenview, IL: Scott Foresman. 1989.

7   Hofman, M. The Big Picture. *Inc. Magazine*, October 15, 2003: 87–94.

8   Nolan, R. Drugstore.com. Harvard Business School Publishing, case 9-300-036. 2000.

9   Drucker, P. Managing Oneself. *Harvard Business Review*, 83(1): 100–105. 2005.

10   *HRfocus*, September 2005, Vol. 82, Issue 9, pp. 8–9.

11   McFarland, K. The Psychology of Success. *Inc. Magazine*, November 15, 2005: 158–159.

12   Kuemmerle, W. A test for the fainthearted. *Harvard Business Review*, 80(5): 122–126. 2002.

13   Ibid.

14   www.eventuring.org/eShip/ appmanager/eVenturing/ShowDoc/ eShipWebCacheRepository/ Documents/FTNV-pp276-279.pdf.

15   Brief profile of 2003 Inc. 500 companies. *Inc. Magazine*, October 2003.

16   Sherman, A. P. You can count on me. *Entrepreneur Magazine*, November 2004, p. 36.

17   Howard, B. (2000) Not ready for the burden of a full-time business? How do your evenings and weekends look? *Entrepreneur Magazine*, June 2000.

18   Ibid.

19   Spirrison, J. B. Startups Ponder Equity Compensation Conundrum. *Private Equity Week*, October 4, 1999, pp. 1–2.

20   Robbins, S. Dividing equity between founders and investors: How to figure out who gets what percentage of the business when investors come on board. *Entrepreneur Magazine*, October 13, 2003.

21   Beyster Institute. Employee Ownership Plans—"Keys to Success." www.beysterinstitute.org/about_ employee_ownership/keys_to_success .cfm.

22   Burlingham, B. The boom in employee stock ownership. *Inc. Magazine*, 22(11): 106–110. August 2000.

23   Sisk, M. Taking stock. *Inc. Magazine*, 27(4): 34. April 2005.

24   Ibid.

25   Burlingham, B. Touched by an Angel. *Inc. Magazine.* 19(10): 46–47. July 1997.

Ajay Bam

With the quiet click of the meeting room door, Ajay Bam was left with one fewer person on his team. It was the spring of 2002, and Walter Stock—Ajay's friend and partner—had finally succumbed to the pressures of time and money. Troy Chen, the other founding partner, had exited two months earlier.

Ajay dialed new-venture attorney John Hession to vent his frustrations. Maybe at 27 he was just too young and inexperienced, right? Of course he had understood that it was not going to be easy to start up a wireless payment and loyalty solution in the U.S., but did it have to be this draining, this fraught with rejection and nay sayers? Sure, he had assembled a top-flight board of seasoned advisors, but what good was that if he was unable to keep his team together or get any traction with investors? Broke and exhausted, Ajay confessed that even though he had worked for two years to earn an MBA degree in Entrepreneurship, he was giving a lot of thought to a six-figure job that was still waiting for him with Lehman Brothers in New York.

As Ajay clicked off his cell phone, he was suddenly struck by the fact that the attorney had said almost nothing. He swallowed hard as he realized why; he had been talking like a quitter—maybe not worth the free advice and networking support that the skilled lawyer had been providing for months. And what about all the other professionals who had given Ajay so much of their time and encouragement over the past two years—including a major venture-capital investor that he now considered his mentor? Was he willing to make a similar call to them as well? This is just too hard, too lean.

Ajay rubbed his tired eyes and looked out at the cold April rain. What had he missed? What else could he try? Should he keep at it, or cut his losses now and attempt something else at a later time after he had rebuilt his personal savings a bit?

In addition to his precarious financial situation and his state of exhaustion, Ajay was certain of at least one other thing: if he didn't start up a mobile payments and loyalty enterprise soon, someone else would.

Ajay Bam

Ajay Bam grew up in Pune, India, just north of Bombay. His father, a textile manufacturer, and his mother, a greenhouse business proprietor, had raised their children to be independent, critical thinkers. Looking back, Ajay said that although he wasn't always in agreement with their choices, he could see they had been pushing him in the right direction:

> I am so grateful to my parents. I remember when I went to prep school, I hated it . . . I didn't realize at the time what my parents were doing, but they did the best thing. I have seen a lot of amazing things, and I am cosmopolitan because I am very world traveled. It puts a lot of things in perspective. . . You know who you are, where you have come from, and what you have.

By his early twenties, Ajay had earned an undergraduate degree in computer engineering and a master's degree in software engineering. He then landed a job as a

This case was prepared by Carl Hedberg under the direction of Professor William Bygrave. © Copyright Babson College, 2002. Funding provided by the Ewing Marion Kauffman Foundation. All rights reserved.

technology analyst for Lehman Brothers in the World Trade Center complex in New York City. He was young, single, successful, and growing restless:

> *The pay was great. Everything was fantastic, but it gets to a point where the money doesn't matter anymore. You know you are good and you know you are going to make a good living . . . In the back of my mind I always knew I wanted to go for my MBA . . . so after getting two years of full-time experience I decided to apply to a number of schools . . . Babson, being number one in Entrepreneurship, was my first choice.*

Babson College

Ajay left Wall Street, and in the fall of 1999 began a two-year program at Babson College. He immediately applied for and was accepted into a new offering at the school: the Entrepreneurship Intensity Track (EIT) program. EIT was "a compressed and highly focused entrepreneurial curriculum designed to provide students with the necessary skills to take a business idea through the critical stages of exploration, investigation, and refinement." Ajay was thrilled with the opportunity to meet the many successful entrepreneurs who were participating in the program, as well as to work with a diverse, talented group of instructors and students. He recalled that the learning experience was quite different from his more bookish engineering studies:

> *To me getting an MBA was 50% networking, 20% classes, and 30% doing what I wanted to do. It was not about what your professors did for you; it was about your level of participation.*

Following his second semester, Ajay signed up for a four-month international management internship. Eager to travel again and test his proficiency with at least one of several languages he had learned academically, Ajay chose a startup in Munich, Germany. Ajay enjoyed working for the COO, who agreed to let him sit in on board meetings:

> *The great challenge for me was that the meetings were in technical German. It was hard to understand every word. So I would come out of these meetings and ask, "What just happened? I got bits and pieces but could you put the story together for me?" I think they liked it because they thought it was very challenging of me to be sitting in and trying to understand what was going on.*

The COO encouraged his soft-spoken, hard-working intern to take three-day travel weekends. Ajay grew particularly fond of Western Europe, and it was there that he began to see cell phones in a new light:

> *As I traveled around, I noticed that people had very fancy phones—sometimes several; like one for a party, one for the office, one for home . . . I still had my phone from the States and it was just a clunky old black box . . . I just hated it . . . I decided that mobile applications were going to be the next big thing in the U.S. When I came back from Germany I decided that this was the space I wanted to work in.*

Vayusa

In the fall of 2000, Ajay and fellow MBA Walter Stock were meeting at Starbucks to brainstorm consumer applications for mobile technology. When the discussion gravitated toward the hassle of coffee cards, the pair spied their opportunity. Ajay explained:

I carry a lot of loyalty cards. I have four coffee cards in my wallet. To be honest, it is a pain carrying all these cards; I don't have them when I need them, I lose my rewards, it's a pain to sign up, and it's a pain if you lose them. And for merchants, the struggle is getting their card into your wallet.

Walter and I started thinking about building a mobile coffee card which would allow you to track your coffees on your cell phone and let you know that you have, say, eleven coffees on your card. Then you wouldn't need to carry all these loyalty cards.

Over the next few weeks, Ajay's EIT sessions helped to shape the business model and they began to gain an understanding of the challenges that merchants were facing. The new venture would develop a technology platform that would enable customers to carry out payments and participate in loyalty programs using any type of cell phone. The partners viewed the loyalty component as key, since vendors large and small were discovering that loyalty-marketing programs developed from actual customer behavior—a discipline known as Customer Relationship Management, or CRM—could produce stunning returns on investment. Ajay explained how the transaction would work:

As a first-time [user] you have to sign up your mobile phone and credit card into the Vayusa portal. Once you do the sign up process, you walk into a participating store, say, Blockbuster, and they ask you how you would like to pay: Visa card, Visa phone, or cash. Our vision is to be the Visa phone.

There is a pre-programmed [toll free] number on your phone that will ask you for the . . . unique tonal [point of sale ID displayed by that merchant]. Say it's 100. Press 100. Simultaneously, the Blockbuster guy enters $4.99, and on his tonal he says, "Visa mobile."

When you authorize the payment, [the system] automatically reads your [online] coupons and lets you know whatever the best one is. Then you enter your pin number to complete the transaction.

Afterwards you get a text receipt on your cell phone and an e-mail receipt sent to your e-mail address. Then we automatically update your loyalty rewards with Blockbuster. Again, you don't need to carry [a vendor] card in your wallet. You don't even need to carry credit cards.

The company name, Vayusa—Sanskrit for "rhythm in the air"—was chosen to evoke the effortless mobile transactions they were hoping to foster (see Exhibit 6.1).

Ajay and Walter had no illusions about the odds against two young MBAs (with no industry experience) developing a complex technology enterprise that would likely require a significant infusion of venture capital, in addition to corporate alliances and partnerships. Ajay set out immediately to understand the payments industry, and, at the same time, build a top-tier board of advisors.

A Legal Education

Although he had no money to pay for such services, Ajay was determined to secure the best new-venture legal advice in the Boston area. After hearing attorney John Hession, an attorney with Testa Hurwitz, one of leading U.S. law firms specializing in technology new ventures and venture capital, speak at an MIT venture forum, Ajay decided that he fit the bill. Ajay recalled that, predictably, the busy attorney was not an easy sell:

I pursued him. I sent him e-mails, I called him up. I told him that I have to work with you; you have to hear my story. So John and I met one day for breakfast and we just clicked. He said okay; let's see where we can go. One reason why John and I clicked was that he wasn't about making money with startups. He knew that startups don't have money.

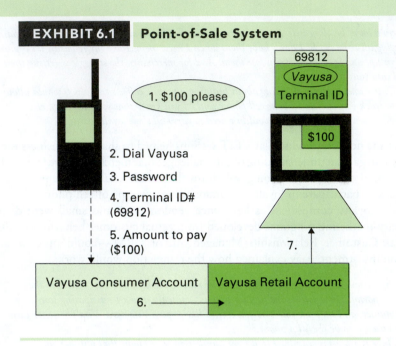

EXHIBIT 6.1 **Point-of-Sale System**

69812

Vayusa

Terminal ID

1. $100 please

$100

2. Dial Vayusa

3. Password

4. Terminal ID# (69812)

5. Amount to pay ($100)

7.

Vayusa Consumer Account

Vayusa Retail Account

6. ⟶

He said, this is how I work: You educate yourself on a lot of legal stuff so I don't have to spend a lot of time telling you what it means, and you will save some money there. You [Ajay] will prepare all the drafts. He sent me stock agreements, things like that. He said you are going to cut and paste to put documents together and then you are going to come back to me for a final review. He said that he would rather spend his time on people who are paying him, and it made sense. It is a great philosophy. So I saved myself thousands of dollars, and I got an education.

When John saw that the young man had an insatiable thirst for learning and for meeting people who might be of assistance, he opened his Rolodex. In addition to referring Ajay to a number of business leaders, John provided him with free passes to the many entrepreneurship and technology events that were being sponsored by his firm. Ajay attended every one of them.

SeaPoint Ventures

Babson Professor Jeffrey Timmons put Ajay in touch with his close friend, Tom Huseby, the managing partner at SeaPoint Ventures—a Seattle-based venture capital firm specializing in telecommunications. Ajay said that after a couple of phone conversations, the venture capitalist invited him over for dinner and a sail:

I spent my Thanksgiving with Tom's family in Seattle. I flew to Seattle and had one of the most wonderful times with Tom. He was a great guy. He's a Stanford MBA. He has started four different telecom companies, was very successful, made money, and decided to start a venture fund. It was my first visit to a VC office and it kind of blew me away. It was grand, something totally unexpected.

Tom took me out for four hours on his million-dollar sailboat, and in that four hours he explained to me the entire process of how a startup works, how to reduce risk, and what it was going to take for him to invest in my company. So that was fascinating, and it motivated me. Wow, this is how I want to be. I want to have money, I want to do a lot of philanthropy, and I want to be in a position where I can control and do more. I came back and decided that Tom was going to be my mentor for life.

Cracking the Chicken and Egg Cycle

By late 2000, Ajay and Walter found themselves running in circles. Potential merchant-clients were interested in their idea, but would not commit to anything until Vayusa could demonstrate the application. Developing a prototype would require funds they didn't have, and funding sources explained that before they would be willing to invest, Vayusa would have to sign up some merchants.

The pair decided to concentrate on the technology piece of the puzzle, since that was the element over which they had the most control. In January, Ajay began looking into product development grant programs, and came across the National Collegiate Inventors and Innovators Alliance at Hampshire College in western Massachusetts. Launched in 1995, the NCIIA was created "to support educational initiatives in creativity, technological innovation, and entrepreneurship." Ajay sensed a fit, but he immediately encountered his first obstacle in the grant process:

When I started looking at NCIIA I found out Babson needed to be a member of NCIIA. That would cost $500 ... While I was at Babson I was significantly involved in a lot of different activities on campus, and that helped my credibility with my professors. Everyone knew me, and I was talking to the Associate Dean, Wendy Baker, every day. I told Wendy that Babson needed to be a member in order for me to apply for this grant. Nobody had done this before, so I said that it is likely that if we do this now, more Babson students will end up getting grant money in the future.

In February, Ajay and Walter had brought in a third partner: Babson MBA student Troy Chen. In March, after Ajay had successfully enrolled the college as an NCIIA member, he was faced with new hurdles:

My partners refused to apply for the [NCIIA] grant. They said this is all crap; just a lot of paper work. I just said that I was going to work at it and get the grant. I remember that I applied for a [$20,000] grant a day after the deadline and I called them and I said my partners are not listening to me, I want to do this, will you still accept my app? They said we'll do it as long as you FedEx it within a day ... They got it the next evening and they agreed to take it.

While Ajay was busy investigating grant opportunities, he was also helping his partners search for an engineer who might be willing to develop their prototype software for an equity stake in Vayusa. In March they signed up Tim Patel, a recent computer engineering graduate from Tufts University.

It was early spring of 2001 when Ajay started to run short on cash. To cover his rent, he began to cast around for some sort of employment that would not seriously undermine his final semester of MBA studies, or his work with Vayusa. He discovered the answer in his own academic backyard:

The Olin Engineering School had opened and they were looking for a student housing director. So I applied, and guess what? I was accepted because [at the time] I was a student housing director with Babson. With Olin it was exciting to be part of something new, exciting, and something very entrepreneurial. I just moved from one side of the campus to the other.

With all his commitments, Ajay found himself screaming along at a breakneck pace of 18-hour days. One of his favorite posts was serving as the director of the Babson Technology Venture Group. In that capacity, he traveled to technology conferences around the country, led Babson College to the Harvard Cyberposium—the largest gathering of MBAs in the high-tech industry—and spoke with a wide range of entrepreneurial and technology experts about the mobile payment and loyalty space.

Even with solid work experience, two engineering degrees, an interesting business model, and boundless energy to promote and network, Ajay was still hard-pressed to gain any traction for Vayusa. As they neared graduation, his partners appeared to be losing interest. Just then, they received word that the NCIIA would be awarding Vayusa a grant of $12,500, and that Babson College would kick in an additional $8,500 from its seed fund.

VeriFone

In June, flush with renewed spirit, resolve, and a bit of cash, the team moved into Idealab in downtown Boston. They were building the product, talking to a wide range of funding sources, attempting to bring merchants on board, and researching potential competitors (see Exhibit 6.2). As their vision for a mobile payment and loyalty solution took shape, they began to realize that the only feasible way to capture significant market share quickly would be to design technology that would work with an existing point-of-sale (POS) device (see Exhibit 6.3).

The team reasoned that since the value of a POS systems manufacturer alliance would be directly proportional to the market strength of that partner, they needed to aim high. They learned that the number one POS payment company, with over four million units worldwide, was VeriFone. Ajay recalled with a grim smile that the company, which was restructuring following a spin-off from parent Hewlett-Packard, gave him less than a warm reception when he described what his team had in mind:

> *VeriFone wouldn't talk to us because they were like, who are you guys in Boston, out of nowhere, wanting to use a VeriFone box for mobile payments? Stay away! They wouldn't even give us a contact name or number for anyone at VeriFone who would want to talk to us. So I said, somehow I have to crack this. I called them every day. Finally after three months they gave in. Okay, okay, here is the guy you should talk to.*

The VeriFone contact took a liking to the enthusiastic MBA, and ultimately provided Ajay with a list of VeriFone vendors and contacts. He suggested that Ajay work through the list. Ajay did. One of the people he met over the phone was Nick Epperson, a former chief marketing officer at VeriFone and the chief technical architect who had designed the VeriFone box.

As the summer of 2001 drew to a close, Ajay felt that he was beginning to build a good relationship with Mr. Epperson and a number of other potential investors and advisors. Although the prototype was still in the design stage, and investors appeared to be waiting for merchants to sign on, the overall momentum seemed to be in their favor.

Then came 9–11.

EXHIBIT 6.2 **Competitor Matrix**

	Vayusa	WIRCA	Mint	Speedpass	Prepaid cards
Utilizes current infrastructure	✓	✓	✓		✓
Loyalty program integration	✓		✓	✓	
Safe and secure	✓	✓	✓		
Transaction speed	✓		✓	✓	✓
Wireless	✓	✓	✓		✓
CRM	✓			✓	✓

The Aftermath

The terrorist attacks in September exacerbated a downturn in the capital markets that had been showing signs of weakness for some time. The drying up of the investor pool was a tough reality, but for Ajay, the horror of 9–11 had hit far closer to home:

> I lost six of my friends in the September eleventh tragedy . . . The next three months after that were very depressing . . . Troy was supposed to have gotten married on September fifteenth in New York . . . His grandmother was now stuck on a flight from Japan in Seattle for three days . . . Everyone was depressed . . . The wedding was postponed . . . October was Walter's wedding, and that wedding happened. With the weddings we had a precondition that you could not take a long vacation, so they came back after two weeks. So he was married now and it just was worse. He had more responsibilities . . . For me, I am still single so it makes it easier to do things, to make decisions . . . It was a terribly emotional ride.

In early November, despite clear indications that the gathering would be dismal at best, Ajay decided to attend the West Wireless Conference in California. He explained that even though he had been correct about the conference, his decision to attend yielded a golden connection:

EXHIBIT 6.3	The Concept

Executive Summary Highlights

The Vision

With mobile phones becoming the most ubiquitous communication device of the times, Vayusa offers innovative mobile payment and loyalty program solutions to enterprises in the telecom, retail, and hospitality industry. The solutions extend the use of mobile phones beyond voice to data, messaging, transaction, and multimedia.

The Problem

Carriers are starved for new sources of revenue as they reach saturation with voice services and are looking for compelling applications to drive next-generation phones, messaging, and services. Currently merchants spend significant dollar amounts on payment fees and millions of dollars to manage loyalty programs, none of which are affordable to small and mid-size businesses. Merchants are thus looking to a new, convenient, and cost-effective customer relationship offerings and services via the mobile channel.

The Product

Vayusa's product is a mobile payment and loyalty program technology platform that is device and point-of-sale (POS) neutral. The software platform transforms the existing POS into a very powerful mobile transaction and marketing device by enabling it to accept mobile payments and trigger loyalty programs with only a change in software.

The platform has two offerings:

- Mobile payments — Enabling merchants to accept a mobile phone as an acceptable means of payment instrument either at the point-of-sale or remotely. Vayusa offers merchants a low-cost prepaid service (stored value) in addition to access to existing debit and credit models. The payment solutions are secure and as fast as existing payment technologies. With e-mail and SMS being the key messaging drivers, Vayusa enables consumers to receive digital receipts and transactional information on their mobile phones.

- High-impact loyalty offerings and services — A wide array of tools and one-to-one marketing programs now provide instant marketing promotions, interactive rewards, and better ROI. Loyalty offerings include SMS-based coupons, promotions, notifications, and digital tags to drive customers to the stores and offer better customer service and product/service information. The offerings make it very easy and convenient for consumers to manage their payments/receipts and loyalty programs, providing access to all the information from anywhere at anytime.

Differentiation

Vayusa's technology platform works on existing infrastructure, thereby providing immediate accessibility to markets and consumers. Vayusa is also the first to provide an

EXHIBIT 6.3 (Continued)

end-to-end electronic transaction processing system leveraging e-mail, SMS, and voice channels. By connecting the point-of-sale to the Web, Vayusa will be one of the first companies to offer new applications that leverage the Internet to provide faster and better services.

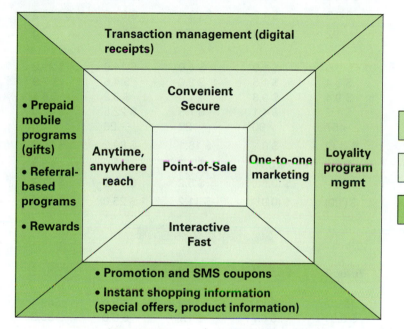

Vayusa Products
Payment and receipt engine
Alert and couponing engine
Referral service

My timing was so lucky. It turns out Nick Epperson had just left VeriFone and was looking for his next gig. VeriFone had kept him as a consultant ... The conference was so bad. There was no one there. I don't even know why I showed up. But I met Nick in person. He and I clicked and he said, "I'm on board; let's do this."

I went back to VeriFone and I said, "Guess what? I just got Nick as my advisor. Do you want to work with us?" VeriFone replied, "Absolutely"—because now we had credibility. It is all about having the right people.

After the conference, Ajay flew north to spend his second Thanksgiving with the Huseby family in Seattle. Ajay presented his Vayusa plan to Tom's three general partners at SeaPoint Ventures. In summary, Ajay explained that Vayusa needed to raise two million dollars in the first year to support the beta development and implementation, and to hire senior management. Vayusa would then need another five million in funding to reach a

EXHIBIT 6.4 Financial Projections

Years 1 to 5
(000,000)

Income Statement

	Year 1	Year 2	Year 3	Year 4	Year 5
NET REVENUES	$ 0.3	$ 4.6	$ 34.6	$ 85.6	$ 169.8
COST OF REVENUES	$ 0.02	$ 0.4	$ 9.0	$ 24.0	$ 51.0
GROSS	$ 0.3	$ 4.2	$ 25.6	$ 61.6	$ 118.9
% of	92	92	74	72	70
OPERATING EXPENSES					
Sales & Marketing	$ 0.5	$ 1.9	$ 4.0	$ 14.6	$ 29.2
Research & Development	$ 0.4	$ 1.5	$ 2.0	$ 4.6	$ 7.9
General & Administration	$ 0.4	$ 0.8	$ 1.4	$ 3.2	$ 5.5
Total Operating Expenses	$ 1.3	$ 4.1	$ 7.5	$ 22.5	$ 42.6
% of	457	90	22	26	25
EARNINGS BEFORE INTEREST & TAXES	$ (1.0)	$ 0.1	$ 18.1	$ 39.2	$ 76.3
DEPRECIATION	$ 0.0	$ 0.70	$ 1.7	$ 3.0	$ 5.3
TAXES	$—	$ (0.55)	$ 5.2	$ 11.2	$ 21.7
NET EARNINGS (LOSS)	$ (1.0)	$ (0.07)	$ 11.2	$ 25.0	$ 49.4

Years 1 to 5
(000,000)

Statement of Cash Flows

	Year 1	Year 2	Year 3	Year 4	Year 5
OPERATING ACTIVITIES					
Net Earnings	($1.0)	($0.1)	$11.2	$25.0	$49.4
Depreciation	$ 0.01	$ 0.7	$ 1.7	$ 3.0	$5.3
Working Capital Changes					
(Increase)/Decrease Accounts Receivable	($0.0)	($0.1)	($1.8)	($2.8)	($4.6)
(Increase)/Decrease Other Current Assets	$0.0	$0.0	$0.0	$0.0	$0.0
Increase/(Decrease) Accounts Payable	$0.0	$0.0	$0.5	$0.8	$1.5
Increase/(Decrease) Other Current Liab	$0.0	$0.0	$0.0	$0.0	$0.0
Net Cash Provided by Operating Activities	($1.0)	$0.5	$11.6	$26.0	$51.5
INVESTING ACTIVITIES					
Technology & Equipment	($0.20)	($1.9)	$(2.9)	$(4.0)	$(9.0)
Other	$0.0	$0.0	$0.0	$0.0	$0.0
Net Cash Used in Investing Activities	($0.20)	($1.9)	($2.9)	($4.0)	($9.0)
FINANCING ACTIVITIES					
Increase/(Decrease) Short-term Debt	$0.0	$0.0	$0.0	$0.0	$0.0
Increase/(Decrease) Long-term Debt	$0.0	$0.0	$0.0	$0.0	$0.0
Increase/(Decrease) Common Stock	$0.01	$0.0	$0.0	$0.0	$0.0
Increase/(Decrease) Preferred Stock	$2.0	$0.0	$5.0	$0.0	$0.0
Net Cash Provided/(Used) by Financing	$2.0	$0.0	$5.0	$0.0	$0.0
INCREASE/(DECREASE) IN CASH	$0.8	($1.4)	$13.7	$22.0	$42.5
CASH AT BEGINNING OF YEAR	$0.0	$0.8	($0.6)	$13.1	$35.2
CASH AT END OF YEAR	$0.8	($0.6)	$13.1	$35.2	$77.7

EXHIBIT 6.4 (Continued)

Years 1 to 5
(000,000)

Balance Sheet

	Year 1	Year 2	Year 3	Year 4	Year 5
ASSETS					
CURRENT ASSETS					
Cash	0.8	0.6	13.1	35.2	77.7
Accounts Receivable	0.0027	0.1	1.9	4.7	9.3
Other Current	0	0	0	0.0	0.0
Total Current	0.8	(0.5)	15.0	39.9	87.0
FIXED ASSETS					
Technology & Equipment Cost	0.2	2.1	5.0	9.0	18.0
Less Accum. Depreciation	0.0	0.7	2.4	5.4	10.7
Net Book Value	0.2	1.4	2.6	3.6	7.3
TOTAL ASSETS	1.0	0.9	17.6	43.5	94.3
LIABILITIES & SHAREHOLDERS' EQUITY					
CURRENT LIABILITIES					
Short-Term Debt	0	0	0	0	0
Accounts Payable	0.0002	0.0	0.5	1.3	2.8
Accrued Expenses	0	0	0	0	0
Other Current Liab	0	0	0	0	0
Total Current Liabilities	0.0002	0.0	0.5	1.3	2.8
LONG-TERM DEBT	0	0	0	0	0
STOCKHOLDERS' EQUITY					
Common Stock	0.01	0.01	0.01	0.01	.01
Preferred Stock	2.0	2.0	7.0	7.0	7.0
Retained Earnings	(1.0)	(1.1)	10.1	35.1	84.5
Total	1.0	0.9	17.1	42.1	91.5
TOTAL LIABILITIES & EQUITY	1.0	0.9	17.6	43.4	94.3

positive cash flow position in year three (see Exhibit 6.4). The presentation went well, and all but one of the partners seemed to be on board. Unfortunately, that was one fewer than Vayusa needed to garner a SeaPoint term sheet.

Spring Exodus

By January of 2002, Vayusa had a working prototype to support a detailed business plan, and a board of advisors that included—in addition to Tom from SeaPoint Ventures and Nick from VeriFone—a former CEO of NYNEX, a former CEO of Citibank, and Bob Anderson, director of the MIT Enterprise Forum and former CEO of GenRad. Nevertheless, the founding team had been unable to make much progress with the Boston merchants or secure commitments for a first round of venture funding.

Each month, Ajay was painfully reminded of their need for a capital infusion by a persistent Indian national whom he had met through an organization of Southeast Asian Entrepreneurs:

Rahul used to call me every month to see if I was interested in working with him. He was based in Boston and had an outsourcing company in India to write software code. Every month he used to call me and say like, "Hey I like your idea, would you be interested in working with me? I want to work with you."

Due diligence by contacts Ajay had back in India verified that Rahul would be an excellent choice to build the software platform, so Ajay continued to string him along until he could raise enough capital to take that next step. Ajay had applied for a follow-on NCIIA grant, but that money would likely be less than the first award, and far less than they would need to move ahead in a substantial way.

Troy, whose wedding had been rescheduled for April, announced in late January that he was leaving the team and moving back to New Jersey. The following month, Ajay kept a meeting that Troy had scheduled long before with a gentleman recommended by a venture firm that had liked their concept but did not participate in early-stage funding. Ajay described the meeting with Jack Weston, a twenty-year credit card industry veteran who had recently joined a startup that was building applications to store coupons on charge cards:

When I showed Jack what we were doing, it struck him that we were one step ahead [of his company] because we had the chip and our solution was with every cell phone . . . He loved the demo and we ended up having a two-hour conversation. When he started asking me about the team, I realized that he might be looking for his next gig. I hinted to him in the meeting that we were looking for senior people or someone from the industry who knows the space. I asked if he would be interested. He said, "Let me think about it." We started meeting once a week after that.

Two months later Mr. Weston joined Vayusa as an advisor, but at the same time, their software designer Tim Patel decided to leave the team. Soon after, Walter brought in Phuc Truong, a Babson MBA with whom Ajay had never worked. Ajay commented that his initial skepticism was soon allayed;

Phuc was running Club Nicole in Boston. Phuc and Walter had worked together in some of their classes. I didn't know Phuc at all then. Walter said that Phuc wants to join the team and that he had a lot of merchant contacts . . . he knew a lot of wealthy people in town as well . . . I'm like, I don't know Phuc, and he runs a club; what is he going to bring to the table?

It turns out that all the merchants in Boston knew Phuc because he had worked before for a startup that was a retail business and he knew every damn merchant in the city . . . It made a lot of sense because I didn't have time to go out and talk to a lot of merchants. I needed someone who knew the merchants on a very personal level, [because] with a lot of shops—like small mom and pop shops—it is very much about personal relationships.

While it had seemed that Walter had suggested Phuc as a substitute for Troy, when Walter called it quits less than a month later, it was clear that he had not wanted to leave his good friend Ajay standing alone at the helm.

Go or No Go?

With all of his original partners gone and Phuc barely up to speed, Ajay was once again standing on the edge of a decision to try to keep moving forward, or cut his losses and head back to Wall Street. It was maddening. Without a substantial startup investment soon, Vayusa would most certainly fail. Ajay leaned back, glanced at his cell phone for the time, and considered his next move.

Preparation Questions

1. What traits does Ajay exhibit that have helped him get this far?

2. Imagine you are a potential investor. Ajay has just given you his rocket pitch. What are your concerns? Would you invest?

3. If Ajay decides to move forward, what more can he do to build credibility and improve his chances of securing venture capital?

J.B. Schneider and Antonio Turco-Rivas, founders of P'kolino. (*Source*: Courtesy Antonio Turco/Rivas and J.B. Schneider)

THE BUSINESS PLANNING PROCESS

The most important aspect of writing the business plan is not the plan itself, but all the learning that goes on as you identify your concept and then research the concept, the industry, the competitors, and, most importantly, your customers. The written plan has its place (as an articulation of all the learning you have achieved), but even a technically well-written plan does not necessarily ensure a successful new venture. *Inc. Magazine* finds that few if any of the fastest growing companies in the country have a business model exactly the same as the one in their original written business plan: of those that wrote a formal business plan, 65% admitted that the existing business was significantly different from their original concept.[1]

This chapter takes the view that the *process* undertaken in developing a tight, well-written story is the most important thing. Furthermore, our research indicates that students who write a business plan, even if it is for an entrepreneurship class, are far more likely to become entrepreneurs than students who haven't written a business plan.[2] Business planning isn't just writing; it's research, it's talking to others, it's iterative, it's a *learning* process . . . and given that, a three-ring binder that catalogs all your learning is the best place to start.

The purpose of business planning is to tell a story: the story of your business. The plan must establish that there is an opportunity worth exploiting and must detail how

This chapter written by Andrew Zacharakis.

you will accomplish it. During the dot-com boom of the late 1990s, many entrepreneurs and venture capitalists questioned the importance of business planning. Typical of this hyper-startup phase are stories like that of James Walker, who generated financing for a 10-day-old company based on "a bunch of bullet points on a piece of paper." He stated, "It has to happen quick in the hyper-competitive wireless-Internet-technology world. There's a revolution every year and a half now."[3] The implication was simple. Business planning took time—time that entrepreneurs didn't have.

Media stories abounded of the whiz-kid college dropout who received venture capital, zoomed to IPO, and cashed out a multimillionaire in 18 months or less. The mythology of the dot-com entrepreneur was that she didn't have a business plan, only a couple of PowerPoint slides. That was all it took to identify the opportunity, secure venture backing, and go public—why spend the weeks of effort that solid business planning often takes? The NASDAQ crash of April 2000 and the subsequent demise of many high-flying dot-coms revealed that the majority of these businesses never had the potential to generate profits—not then, not now, and not any time in the future. The easy money and quick returns of the late 90s have disappeared. Today, entrepreneurial gold is found by executing on solid business plans targeted at significant, well-researched market opportunities.

It's a common misperception that a business plan is primarily used for raising capital. Although a good business plan assists in raising capital, the primary goal of the process is to help entrepreneurs gain a deeper understanding of the opportunity they see. Because they lack a deep understanding of the business model, many would-be entrepreneurs doggedly pursue ideas that will never be profitable. Given the enormous financial and emotional toll a failed startup can have, the weeks or months it will take to complete a thorough business plan are a relatively small investment. For example, if you make $100,000 per year, spending 200 hours on a business plan equates to making a $10,000 investment in time spent ($50/hour times 200 hours). In comparison, the cost of launching a flawed business concept can quickly accelerate into millions in lost capital for the founders and investors. So do yourself a favor and spend the time and money up front.

The business planning *process* raises critical questions about the feasibility of the venture. Researching and then answering those questions helps the entrepreneur shape his original vision into a better opportunity. For example, one question that every entrepreneur needs to answer is, "What is the customer's pain?" Conversations with customers and other trusted advisors assist in better targeting product offerings to what customers need and want. This pre-startup work saves untold effort and money that an entrepreneur might spend trying to reshape the product after the business has been launched. While all businesses adjust their offerings based on customer feedback, the business planning process helps the entrepreneur anticipate some of these adjustments in advance of the initial launch.

The most valuable outcome of business planning for us was that it gave us a direction to start in. We took a snapshot of the world as we understood it at that time, and it told us in which direction to take our next step. The important thing was not to take the second step according to that original business plan but to continually re-evaluate at every step along the way. Because of this, a formal written business plan is not very useful operationally. You need to do all the strategic planning, competitive analysis and financial analysis but it is impossible to have a written business plan that you stick to as you build the company because when you wake up on Wednesday, the world is completely different than it was when you went to bed on Tuesday.

Ed O'Malley, Vice President
Black Rock Systems
www.blackrockapu.com

The most valuable outcome of business planning is that it gave me a framework with which to ask the right questions and research the most critical aspects of my business and industry. Therefore,

Courtesy Gina Maschek

Gina Maschek, Co-founder of Beyond Blossoms, shows off some of her flowers.

the process helped me to gain a thorough understanding of the industry and the challenges and opportunities within that industry. In the end, I would say the most positive outcome of the process has been that it has given me confidence in talking with potential investors, partners and other stakeholders. Although these stakeholders didn't often look at my business plan, they did ask questions to which I wouldn't have known the answers had I not gone through the business planning process.

Ryan Bettencourt, Founder and President
LifePrints

Business planning really helps you understand your business, especially the drivers of the business. For example, what happens if I tweak my customer retention rate? How does that change my customer acquisition cost, etc.? How does that prolong or shorten the time to break even . . . ? It gives you a basis to make important decisions.

Gina Maschek, Co-founder
Beyond Blossoms
www.beyondblossoms.com

Perhaps the greatest benefit of the business planning process is that it allows the entrepreneur to articulate the business opportunity to various stakeholders in the most effective manner. First, the plan provides background information that enables the entrepreneur to communicate the upside potential to investors. Second, it provides the validation needed to convince potential employees to leave their current jobs for the uncertain future of a new venture. Finally, it can also help secure a strategic partner, key customer, or supplier. In short, the business plan provides the entrepreneur with the deep understanding she needs to answer the critical questions these various stakeholders will ask. Completing a well-founded business plan gives the entrepreneur credibility in the eyes of each group.

Think of the business plan as a compilation of learning (both literally and figuratively). Start with a three-ring binder divided into categories, and then start collecting information in each section. Write a synopsis for each of these sections that includes your interpretation of what the information means and how that implies that you should shape and reshape your concept. You can also compile all this information on your computer, but whatever method you choose to catalog it, the point is the same—you need a mechanism to start organizing your learning.

The Planning Process

Business planning literally begins when you start thinking about your new venture. In Chapter 3, we highlighted the opportunity recognition process. That is the genesis of planning. It progresses from there when you start sharing your thoughts with potential co-founders over a cup of coffee or lunch. It moves on from that point when you share the idea with your significant other, friends, family, colleagues, and professors, among others. At each interaction, you are learning about aspects of your business opportunity. Do your friends think they would buy this product or service (potential customers)? Have they said things along the lines of, "This is just like XYZ Company..." (potential competitors)? Have they informed you of potential suppliers or other people you might want to hire or at least talk to or learn from? All these bits and pieces of information are valuable learning that you should document and catalog in your three-ring binder.

Once you acquire a critical mass of learning, it's time to start organizing your information in a meaningful way. First, write a short summary (less than five pages) of your current vision. This provides a roadmap for you and others to follow as you embark on a more thorough planning process. Share this document with co-founders, family members, and trusted advisors. Ask for feedback on what else you should be thinking about. What gaps do the people who read this summary see? What questions do they ask and how can you gain the learning necessary to answer those questions in a convincing and accurate manner? This feedback will provide a platform for you to attack each of the major areas important to launching and running a new venture.

Your planning process will focus on critical aspects of your business model; not coincidentally, these critical aspects map well to the typical format of a business plan (see Figure 7.1). Now that you have some feedback from your trusted advisors, you can begin attacking major sections of the plan. It really doesn't matter where you start, although it is often easiest to write the product/service description first. This is usually the most concrete component of the entrepreneur's vision. Wherever you begin, don't let the order of sections outlined in Figure 7.1 constrain you. If you want to start somewhere else besides product description, do so. As you work through the plan, you'll inevitably find that this is an iterative process. Every section of the plan interacts with the other sections, and as a result, you'll often be working on multiple sections simultaneously. Most important, keep in mind that this is *your* business planning process; this is your learning. You should follow whatever method feels most comfortable and effective.

Wisdom is realizing that the business plan is a "living document." Although your first draft will be polished, most business plans are obsolete the day they come off the presses. The best entrepreneurs are continually updating and revising their business plan—they recognize it is a learning process, not a finished product. You'll continue learning new things that can improve your business for as long as you're involved with the business, and the day you stop learning how to improve it is the day that it will start its decline towards bankruptcy. So keep and file each major revision of your plan, and occasionally

I.	Cover
II.	Table of Contents
III.	Executive Summary
IV.	Industry, Customer, and Competitor Analysis
V.	Company and Product Description
VI.	Marketing Plan
VII.	Operations Plan
VIII.	Development Plan
IX.	Team
X.	Critical Risks
XI.	Offering
XII.	Financial Plan
XIII.	Appendices

Figure 7.1

Business plan outline

look back at earlier versions for the lessons you've learned. Remember, the importance of the business plan for you isn't the final product, but the learning you gain from writing it. The plan articulates your vision for the company, and it crystallizes that vision for you and your team. It can also provide a history of the birth, growth, and maturity of your business. Although it's daunting, writing a business plan is exciting and creative, especially if you are working on it with a founding team. So now let us dig in and examine how to go through an effective business planning process.

The Story Model

One of the major goals of business planning is to attract various stakeholders and convince them of the potential of your business. Therefore, you have to keep in mind how these stakeholders will interpret your plan. The guiding principal is that you are writing a story, and all good stories have a theme—a unifying thread that ties the setting, characters, and plot together. If you think about the most successful businesses in America, they all have well-publicized themes. When you hear their taglines, you instantly gain insight into the businesses. For example, when you hear "absolutely, positively has to be there overnight," most people think of Federal Express and package delivery. On top of that, they think of reliability, which is the quality FedEx wants to embody in the minds of its customers. Similarly, "Just do it" is intricately linked to Nike and the image of athletic excellence (see Figure 7.2).

A tagline is a sentence, or even a fragment of a sentence, that summarizes the pure essence of your business. It's the theme that every sentence, paragraph, page, and diagram in your business plan should adhere to—the unifying idea of your story. One useful tip is to put your tagline in a footer that runs on the bottom of every page. Most word-processing packages, such as Microsoft Word, enable you to insert a footer that you can see as you type. As you are writing, if the section doesn't build on, explain, or otherwise directly relate to the tagline, it most likely isn't a necessary component to the business plan. Rigorous adherence to the tagline helps you write a concise and coherent business plan. You might also want to put your tagline on your business card, company letterhead, and other collateral material you develop for the business. It's a reminder to you and your team about what you are trying to accomplish, as well as an effective marketing tactic that helps build your brand.

Now, let's take another look at the major sections of the plan (refer back to Figure 7.1). Remember that although there are variations, most planning processes will include these components. Keep your plan as close to this format as possible, because many stakeholders are accustomed to it and it facilitates spot reading. If you are seeking venture capital, for instance, you want to make quick reading possible because venture capitalists often spend

Nike	*Just Do It!*
Fed Ex	*Absolutely, Positively Has to Be There Overnight*
McDonald's	*I'm lovin' it.*
Cisco Systems	*Discover All That's Possible on the Internet*
Microsoft	*Where do you want to go today*
Wal-Mart	*Always low prices. Always!*

Figure 7.2

Taglines

as little as five minutes on a plan before rejecting it or putting it aside for further attention. If a venture capitalist becomes frustrated with an unfamiliar format, it is more likely that she will reject it rather than try to pull out the pertinent information. Even if you aren't seeking venture capital, the common structure is easy for other investors and stakeholders to follow and understand.

The Business Plan

Although it's the business planning *process* that's important, it is easier to discuss that process by laying out what the final output, the business plan, might look like. We will progress through the sections in the order that they typically appear, but keep in mind that you can work on the sections in any order that you wish. Business planning is an iterative process. Also, you may find it useful to refer to the P'kolino business plan at the end of this chapter as you read each of the following sections. You'll notice areas where the P'kolino plan follows our suggestions and areas where it doesn't. The most important point is that you evaluate the P'kolino plan's strengths and weaknesses on the basis of how well it articulates the P'kolino story.

The Cover

The cover of the plan should include the following information: company name, tagline, contact person, address, phone, fax, e-mail, date, disclaimer, and copy number. Most of the information is self-explanatory, but here are a few things to keep in mind. First, the contact person for a new venture should be the president or some other founding team member. Imagine the frustration of an excited potential investor who can't find out how to contact the entrepreneur to gain more information. More often than not, that plan will end up in the reject pile.

Second, business plans should have a disclaimer along these lines:

> *This business plan has been submitted on a confidential basis solely to selected, highly qualified investors. The recipient should not reproduce this plan or distribute it to others without permission. Please return this copy if you do not wish to invest in the company.*

Controlling distribution is particularly important when seeking investment, especially if you do not want to violate Regulation A of the Securities Exchange Commission, which specifies that you may solicit only qualified investors (high-net-worth and high-income individuals). Although you cannot physically control what someone else might do with your plan, the statement at least reminds them to respect your wishes and that is usually good enough.

The cover should also have a line stating which number copy it is. So, for example, you will often see on the bottom right portion of the cover a line that says "Copy 1 of 5 copies." Keep a log of who has copies so you can control for unexpected distribution.

Finally, the cover should be eye-catching. If you have a product or prototype, a picture of it can draw the reader in. Likewise, a catchy tagline draws attention and encourages the reader to look further.

Table of Contents

Continuing the theme of making the document easy to read, a detailed table of contents is critical. It should include major sections, subsections, exhibits, and appendices. The table of contents provides the reader a roadmap to your plan (see Figure 7.3). Note that the table of contents is customized to the specific business, so it doesn't perfectly match the business plan outline presented earlier in Figure 7.1. Nonetheless, a look at Figure 7.3 shows that the company's business plan includes most of the elements highlighted in the business outline, and that the order of information is basically the same as well.

Executive Summary

This section is the most important part of the business plan. If you don't capture readers' attention in the executive summary, it is unlikely that they will read any other parts of

Figure 7.3

Table of Contents

the plan. A good analogy is the jacket copy on a book. The reader is likely to buy the book only if she is impressed with the notes on the cover. In the same way, you want to hit your readers with the most compelling aspects of your business opportunity right up front. *Hook the reader.* That means having the first sentence or paragraph highlight the potential of the opportunity.

> *"The current market for widgets is $50 million, growing at an annual rate of 20%. Moreover, the emergence of the Internet is likely to accelerate this market's growth. Company XYZ is positioned to capture this wave with its proprietary technology; the secret formula VOOM."*

This creates the right tone. The first sentence tells the reader that the potential opportunity is huge and, the last sentence that Company XYZ has a competitive advantage that will enable it to become a big player in this market. Too many plans start with "Company XYZ, incorporated in the state of Delaware, will develop and sell widgets." Ho-hum. This kind of opening is dull and uninspiring—at this point who cares that the business is incorporated in Delaware? Capture the reader's attention immediately or risk losing her altogether.

Once you have hooked the reader, you need to provide compelling information about each of the following subsections:

- Description of Opportunity
- Business Concept
- Industry Overview
- Target Market
- Competitive Advantage
- Business Model and Economics
- Team and Offering

Remember that you'll cover all these components in detail in the body of the plan. Given that, your goal in the executive summary is to touch on the most important or exciting points of each section. Keep it brief and make it compelling.

Since the executive summary is the most important part of the finished plan, write it *after* you have gained a deep understanding of the business by working through all the other sections. Don't confuse the executive summary included in the plan with the short summary that we suggested you write as the very first step of the business plan process. As a result of your research, the two are likely to be significantly different. So don't recycle your initial summary. Rewrite it entirely based on the hard work you have done by going through the business planning process.

Industry, Customer, and Competitor Analysis

Industry. The goal of this section is to illustrate the opportunity and how you intend to capture it. However, before you can develop your plot and illustrate a theme, you need to provide a setting or context for your story. Refer back to Chapters 2 and 3 where we described characteristics that create an attractive opportunity. In your plan you'll need to delineate both the current market size and how much you expect it to grow in the future.

In addition, you need to indicate what kind of market you're facing. History tells us that often the best opportunities are found in emerging markets—those that appear poised for rapid growth and that have the potential to change the way we live and work. For example, in the 1980s the PC, disk drive, and computer hardware markets revolutionized our way of life. Many new companies were born and rode the wave of the emerging technology, including Apple, Microsoft, and Intel. In the 1990s, the Internet drove the pace of social and economic change, and as we enter the twenty-first century, biotechnology may be the next major shift. Another market structure that tends to hold promise is a fragmented market where small, dispersed competitors compete on a regional basis. Many of the big names in retail revolutionized fragmented markets. For instance, category killers such as Wal-Mart, Staples, and Home Depot consolidated fragmented markets by providing quality products at lower prices. These firms replaced the dispersed regional and local discount, office supply, and hardware stores.

Another key attribute to explore is industry economics. For example, do companies within the industry enjoy strong gross and net income margins? Higher margins allow for higher returns, which again leads to greater growth potential. This typically happens when the market is emerging and demand exceeds supply. So again, you'll want to explore where the margins are today, but also where you expect them to go in the future.

You'll note that we keep referring to the future. A good market analysis will look at trends that are shaping the future. For instance, as the world continues to adopt wireless communication, more and more people are connected 24/7. What might this mean for your business? Another trend that has had tremendous ramifications on U.S. society is the life cycle of the baby boom generation. Over the last fifty years business has responded to this generation's needs and wants. In the 50s and 60s that meant building schools. In the 70s and 80s it meant building houses and introducing family cars like the minivan. In the 90s, it led to Internet concepts as this group was more affluent and computer savvy than any generation before it. Today, the baby boomers are approaching retirement. What opportunities does this trend portend? Identify the trends, both positive and negative, that will interact with your business.

You need to describe your overall market in terms of revenues, growth, and future trends that are pertinent. In this section, avoid discussing your concept, the proposed product, or service you will offer. Instead, use dispassionate, arm's-length analysis of the market with the goal of highlighting a space or gap that is underserved. Thus, focus on how the market is segmented now, and how it will be segmented into the future. After identifying the relevant market segments, identify the segment your product will target. Again, what are the important trends that will shape this segment in the future?

Customer. Once you've defined the market space you plan to enter, you'll examine the target customer in detail. As we discussed in Chapters 4 and 5, an accurate customer profile is essential to developing a product that customers truly want and marketing campaigns they will actually respond to. Define who the customer is by using demographic and psychographic information. Although you may argue that everyone who is hungry is a restaurant's customer, such a vague definition makes it hard to market to the core customer. For instance, since I'm a middle-aged man, my eating habits will be different from what they were when I was twenty-something. I will frequent different types of establishments and expect certain kinds of foods within a certain price range. I'm beyond fast food, for example. Thus, you'd have very different strategies to serve and reach me than you would to reach younger people. Unless you develop this deep an understanding of your customer, your business is unlikely to succeed.

A venture capitalist recently said that the most impressive entrepreneur is the one who comes into his office and not only identifies who the customer is in terms of demographics and psychographics, but also identifies that customer by address, phone number, and e-mail. You can even go one step further by including letters of interest or intent from key customers who express a willingness to buy once your product or service is ready. When you understand who your customers are, you can assess what compels them to buy, how your company can sell to them (direct sales, retail, Internet, direct mail), and how much it is going to cost to acquire and retain them as customers. An exhibit describing customers on the basic parameters and inserted into the text of your plan can be very powerful, as it communicates a lot of data quickly.

Too often entrepreneurs figure that if they love their product concept, so should everybody else. Although your needs and wants are the best place to start, you must recognize that they may not be the same as everyone else's. So to truly understand your customers, you need talk to them. Early in your conceptualization of your product or service, go out and interview potential customers (the appendix at the end of Chapter 5 provides some questions that might be useful). Keep your questions open ended and try not to direct the customer's answers. It is critical to *listen* at this stage, rather than talk or tell about your concept. After each customer interaction, go back and reevaluate your concept. Can you cost-effectively incorporate features that will make this product better fit the customer's need? After several individual conversations, run a focus group, then maybe a broader customer survey. At each step along the way, refine your concept and start to define the demographic and psychographic characteristics of your primary target audience. This process helps you create a better product that is more likely to gain customer acceptance than if you boldly (and blindly) charge ahead with your initial concept. As you get closer to launching, you'll likely have a beta customer use your product or service to further refine the concept. The key once again is that business planning is the *process*, not the output (written plan).

Competition. The competition analysis falls directly out of the customer analysis, and you should complete it using a competitive profile matrix. You have already identified your market segment, profiled your customer, and described what he wants. Armed with this information, you can begin to research how your direct and indirect competitors are meeting those needs. The basis of comparison will be the different product features and attributes that each competitor uses to differentiate itself from the pack. A competitive profile matrix not only creates a powerful visual catch-point, it conveys information about your competitive advantage and is the basis for your company's strategy (see Figure 7.4).

The competitive profile matrix should be at the beginning of the section and be followed by text describing the analysis and its implications. Figure 7.4 shows a sample competitive profile matrix for a new retail concept—a specialty store targeting the history enthusiast. The entrepreneur rates each competitor (or competitor type) on various key

	My Concept	Big Box	Amazon	The History Channel Web site	Museum Stores	Specialty Web sites
History book selection	2	3	1	3	4	3
Display of artifacts	1	5	5	5	3	5
History-related gift items	1	5	4	2	1	2
Videos/DVDs	1	4	3	3	5	2
Price	3	2	1	2	3	3
Atmosphere	1	2	5	5	4	5
Employee knowledge	1	4	5	5	2	5
Ease to shop specific item	2	2	1	1	3	4
Location	4	1	1	1	5	3
Ease to browse	1	2	3	3	2	4

Figure 7.4

Competitive profile matrix

Infotrac — Index/abstracts of journals, general business and finance magazines, market overviews, and profiles of public and private firms.

Factiva — Searchable index of articles from over 9,000 U.S. and international newspapers, trade journals, and more.

LexisNexis — Searchable index of articles.

Dun's Principal International Businesses — International business directory.

Dun's One Million Dollar Premium — Database of public and private firms with revenues greater than $1M or more than 8 employees.

Hoover's Online — Profiles of private and public firms with links to Web sites, etc.

CorpTech — Profiles of high technology firms.

RDS Business Reference Suite — Linked databases providing data and full-text searching on firms.

Bloomberg — Detailed financial data and analyst reports.

■ **Figure 7.5**

Sample sources for information on public/private companies

success factors using a five-point scale (with one being strong on the attribute and five being weak). Often entrepreneurs include product attributes such as the product color, dimensions, specifications, and so forth, but you should omit this unless you believe it is the main criterion customers will use to decide to buy your product over competitors. Instead, focus on the key success factors that often lead a customer to buy one product over another, such as price, quality, speed, and so on. It is also a good idea to list your own concept in the matrix. Up until this point your plan has been painting a picture of the industry and market. By including your concept in the matrix, you begin to shift the focus toward your company and the opportunity you believe it can capture.

Finding information about your competition can be easy if the company is public, harder if it is private, and very difficult if the company is operating in "stealth" mode (it hasn't yet announced itself to the world). Most libraries have access to databases that contain a wealth of information about publicly traded companies (see Figure 7.5 for some sample sources), but privately held companies or "stealth ventures" represent a greater challenge.

The best way for savvy entrepreneurs to gather competitive information is through their network and trade shows. Where in your network should you look? First and foremost are your potential customers. Your existing competition is interacting with this group every day, and as a result your customers are the best source of information about the "stealth" competition on the horizon. Although many entrepreneurs are reluctant to discuss their business opportunity for fear that valuable information will fall into the wrong hands, the reality is that entrepreneurs who openly talk about their ideas with as many people as possible are far more likely to succeed. Take the risk. Talking allows entrepreneurs to get the kind of valuable feedback that can make the difference between success and failure in a venture.

Company and Product Description

The dispassionate analysis described in the previous section lays the foundation for describing your company and concept. In this section you'll introduce the basic details of your company before moving on to a more detailed analysis of your marketing and operations plans.

You can begin by identifying the company name and where the business is incorporated. After that you should provide a brief overview of the concept for the company, and then highlight what the company has achieved to date. If you have reached any major milestones, be sure to list them, but don't worry if the business plan is your first step. Subsequent drafts will provide you with opportunities to showcase what you have achieved.

Once you have provided an introduction, take some time to communicate the product and its differentiating features. You can do this in writing, but keep in mind that graphic representations are visually powerful. You'll note in the P'kolino case at the end of this chapter that the photos create a powerful message communicating much about how this market is different from the existing alternatives. Highlight how your product fits into the customer value proposition. What is incorporated into your product and what value-add do you deliver to the customer? Which of the customer's unmet wants and needs are fulfilled by your offering? In essence, you need to tell us why your product is better, cheaper, or faster, and how that creates value for the customer. Your advantage may be a function of proprietary technology, patents, distribution, and/or design. In fact, the most powerful competitive advantages are derived from a bundle of factors, because this makes them more difficult to copy.

Entrepreneurs also need to identify their market entry and growth strategies. Since most new ventures are resource-constrained, especially for available capital, it is crucial that the lead entrepreneur establish the most effective way to enter the market. We discussed in Chapters 3 and 5 how to identify your Primary Target Audience (PTA) based on analysis in the market and customer sections. Focusing on a particular niche or subset of the overall market allows new ventures to effectively utilize scarce resources to reach those customers and prove the viability of their concept.

The business plan should also sell the entrepreneur's vision for the company's long-term growth potential. If the venture achieves success in its entry strategy, it will either generate internal cash flow that can be used to fuel continued growth, or it will be attractive enough to get further equity financing at improved valuations. The growth strategy should talk about the Secondary and Tertiary Target Audiences that the firm will pursue once it meets success with the PTA. For instance, technology companies might go from selling to users who want the best performance (early adopters) to users who want ease of use (mainstream market). Whatever the case, you should devote at least a paragraph or two to the firm's long-term growth strategy.

Marketing Plan

Up to this point, you've described your company's potential to successfully enter and grow in a marketplace. Now you need to devise the strategy that will allow it to reach its potential. The primary components of this section are a description of the target market strategy, the product/service strategy, pricing strategy, distribution strategy, marketing communications strategy, sales strategy, and sales and marketing forecasts. Let's take a look at each of these subsections in turn.

Target Market Strategy. Every marketing plan needs some guiding principles. In targeting and positioning your product, you should lean heavily on the knowledge you gleaned from the customer analysis. For instance, product strategies often fall along a continuum whose endpoints are rational purchase and emotional purchase. For example, when a person buys a new car, the rational purchase might be a low-cost reliable option such as the Ford Focus. In contrast, some people see a car as an extension of their personality, and therefore might buy a BMW or Audi because of the emotional benefits it delivers. Within every product space there is room for products measured at different points along this continuum. You can also use this idea of a continuum to find other dimensions that help you classify your marketplace. These tools help entrepreneurs decide where their product fits or where they would like to position it, and once you have solidified your target market strategy you can begin working on the other aspects of the Marketing Plan.

Product/Service Strategy. Building from the target market strategy, this section of the plan describes how you will differentiate your product from the competition. Discuss why the customer will switch to your product and how you will retain customers so that they don't switch to your competition in the future. You can create a powerful visual by using the attributes defined in your customer profile matrix to produce a product attribute map. This tool is a great way to illustrate how your firm compares to the competition. In creating it you should focus on the two most important attributes, putting one on the x-axis and the other on the y-axis. The map should show that you are clearly distinguishable from your competition on desirable attributes.

Figure 7.6 shows the competitive map for the retail concept that focuses on the history enthusiast. The two attributes on which it evaluates competitors are atmosphere (Is this a place where people will linger?) and focus (Does it have a broad topic focus or is it specialized?). As you can see from Figure 7.6, our retail concept plans to have a high level of history specialization and atmosphere, which places it in the upper right quadrant. From the product attribute map it is easy to see how our retail concept will distinguish itself from the competition. The map implies that history specialization and atmosphere will attract history buffs and entice them to return time and again.

This section should also address what services you will provide the customer. What type of technical support will you provide? Will you offer warranties? What kind of product upgrades will be available and when? It is important to detail all these efforts, because they will affect the pricing of the product. Many times entrepreneurs underestimate the costs of these services, which leads to a drain on cash and ultimately to bankruptcy.

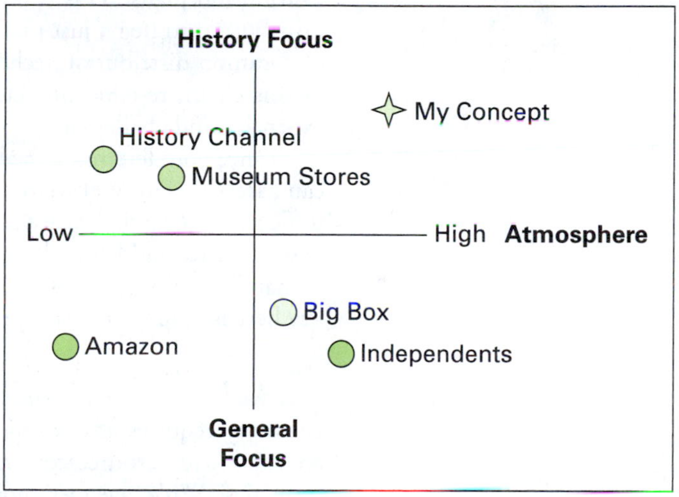

Pricing Strategy. Pricing your product is challenging. Canvassing prevailing prices in the marketplace helps you determine what the perceived value for your product might be. If your product is of better quality and has lots of features, price it above market rates. We saw in Chapter 5 that a price skimming strategy is best in the beginning, to gain a sense of what customers are willing to pay—that means pricing a bit higher than you believe the perceived value to be. It is always easier to reduce prices later than to raise them. Most importantly, if during the course of researching possible prices you find that you can't price your product well above what it will cost you to produce it, the business planning process will have saved you untold time and pain. You have two choices: redesign your concept or abandon it.

Figure 7.6

Product attribute map

Remember to avoid "cost plus" pricing (also discussed in Chapter 5). First, it is difficult to accurately determine your actual cost, especially if this is a new venture with a limited history. New ventures consistently underestimate the true cost of developing their products. For example, how much did it really cost to write that software? The cost includes salaries and payroll taxes, computers and other assets, overhead contribution, and more. Since most entrepreneurs underestimate these costs, they underprice their products. Second, we often hear entrepreneurs claim that they are offering a low price in order to penetrate and gain market share rapidly. One major problem with launching at a low price is that it may be difficult to raise the price later. In addition, demand at that price may overwhelm your ability to produce the product in sufficient volume, and it may unnecessarily strain cash flow.

Distribution Strategy. This section of your written plan identifies how your product will reach the customer. Since much of the cost of delivering a product is tied up in its distribution, your distribution strategy can define your company's fortune as much as or more than the product itself. Distribution strategy is thus more than an operational detail. For example, the e-commerce boom of the late 1990s assumed that the growth in Internet usage and purchases would create new demand for pure Internet companies. Yet, the distribution strategy for many of these firms did not make sense. Pets.com and other online pet supply firms had a strategy calling for the pet owner to log on, order the product from the site, and then receive delivery via UPS or the U.S. Postal Service. The strategy was fantastic in theory, but in reality the price the market would bear for this product didn't cover the exorbitant costs of shipping a forty-pound bag of dog food.

It's wise to examine how the customer currently acquires the product. If you're developing a new brand of dog food and your primary target customer buys dog food at Wal-Mart, then you will probably need to include traditional retail outlets in your distribution plans. This is not to say that entrepreneurs are limited to a single channel distribution strategy, just that to achieve maximum growth will probably require the use of common distribution techniques. While it may be appealing to take retail outlets out of this chain, re-educating customers about a new buying process can be prohibitively expensive and challenging.

Once you determine the best distribution channel, the next question is whether you can access it. The Wal-Mart example is a good one. A new startup in dog food may have difficulty getting shelf space at Wal-Mart. A better entry strategy might focus on boutique pet stores to build brand recognition. Once your product is well known and in high demand, retail stores like Wal-Mart will be much more likely to carry your brand. The key here is to identify appropriate channels and then assess how costly it is to access them.

Marketing Communications Strategy. Communicating effectively to your customer requires advertising and promotion, among other methods. Since these tools are expensive, resource-constrained entrepreneurs need to carefully select the appropriate strategies. What avenues most effectively reach your Primary Target Audience? Your options include mass advertising, direct mail, and public relations. While mass advertising is often the most expensive approach, it is also one of the most effective tools for building a brand. In contrast, if you can identify your PTA by name, then direct mail may be more effective than mass media blitzes. Similarly, grassroots techniques such as public relations efforts geared toward mainstream media can be more cost-effective. Sheri Poe, founder of Ryka shoes, appeared on the Oprah Winfrey show touting shoes designed by women made for women. The response was so overwhelming that she couldn't supply enough shoes to meet the demand. This is a classic example of a public relations success. In contrast, the dot-com boom of the late 1990s offers striking examples of advertising failures, such as Computer.com's exorbitant media buy during the 2000 Super Bowl. The firm spent $3 million of the $5.8 million it had raised on three ads.[4] Needless to say, the gamble failed, and now it represents a textbook example of the importance of using advertising carefully.

As you develop a multipronged advertising and promotion strategy, create detailed schedules that show which avenues you will pursue and the associated costs (see Figures 7.7a and 7.7b). These types of schedules serve many purposes, including providing accurate costs estimates, which will help in assessing how much capital you need to raise.

Promotional Tools	Budget Over 1 Year
Print advertising	$ 5,000
Direct mail	3,000
In-store promotions	2,000
Tour group outreach	1,000
Public relations	1,000
Total	$12,000

Figure 7.7a

Advertising schedule

Publication	Circulation	Ad Price for Quarter Page	Total Budget for Year 1
Lexington Minuteman Newspaper	7,886	$ 500	$4,000
Boston Magazine	1,400,000	$1,000	$1,000

Figure 7.7b

Magazine advertisements

They also build credibility in the eyes of potential investors by demonstrating that you understand the nuances of your market.

Sales Strategy. The section on sales strategy provides the backbone that supports all of the subsections described so far. Specifically, it illustrates what kind and level of human capital you will devote to the effort. You should complete a careful analysis of how many salespeople and customer support reps you will need. Will these people be internal to the organization or outsourced? If they are internal, will there be a designated sales force or will different members of the company serve in a sales capacity at different times? Again, a thoughtful presentation of the company's sales force builds credibility by demonstrating an understanding of how the business should operate.

Sales and Marketing Forecasts. Gauging the impact of sales efforts is difficult. Nonetheless, to build a compelling story, entrepreneurs need to show projections of revenues well into the future. How do you derive these numbers? There are two methods: the comparable method and the build-up method. After detailed investigation of the industry and market, entrepreneurs know the competitive players and have a good understanding of their history. The **comparable method** models the sales forecast after what other companies have achieved, and then adjusts these numbers for differences in things like the age of the company and the variances in product attributes. In essence, the entrepreneur monitors a number of comparable competitors and then explains why her business varies from those models.

In the **build-up method**, the entrepreneur identifies all the possible revenue sources of the business and then estimates how much of each type of revenue they can generate during a given period of time. For example, a bookstore generates revenues from books and artifacts. Thus, a bookstore owner would estimate the average sales price for each product category. Then he might estimate the number of people to come through the store on a daily basis, and what percentage would purchase each revenue source. From these numbers he could create a sales forecast for a typical day, which could then be aggregated into larger blocks of time (months, quarters, or years). These rough estimates might then be further adjusted based on seasonality in the bookstore industry. In the end, the bookstore owner would have a workable model for sales forecasts.

The build-up technique is an imprecise method for the new startup with limited operating history, but it is critically important to assess the viability of the opportunity. It's so important, in fact, that you might want to use both the comparable and build-up techniques to assess how well they converge. If the two methods are widely divergent, go back through and try to determine why. The knowledge you gain of your business model will help you better articulate the opportunity to stakeholders, and it will provide you with invaluable insights as you begin managing the business after its launch. Chapter 8 provides more detail on how to derive these estimates.

While we know for certain that these forecasts will never be 100% accurate, it is essential to minimize the degree of error. Detailed investigation of comparable companies can help you accomplish this goal, as can triangulating the comparable method results with your build-up method results. However you go about building your forecast, always keep in mind that the smaller the error, the less likely your company will run out of cash. Beyond building credibility with your investors, rigorous estimates are also the single best tool for keeping your company out of financial trouble.

Operations Plan

The key in the Operations Plan section is to address how operations will add value for your customers. Here you'll detail the production cycle and gauge its impact on working capital. For instance, when does your company pay for inputs? How long does it take to produce the product? When does the customer buy the product and, more importantly, when does the customer pay for the product? From the time you pay for your raw materials until you receive payment from your customers, you will be operating in a negative cash flow. The shorter that cycle, the more cash you have on hand and the less likely you are to need bank financing. It sounds counter-intuitive, but many rapidly growing new companies run out of cash even though they have increasing sales and substantial operating profit. The reason is that they fail to properly finance the time their cash is tied up in the procurement, production, sales, and receivables cycle.

Operations Strategy. The first subsection of your Operations Strategy section provides a strategy overview. How does your business compare on the dimensions of cost, quality, timeliness, and flexibility? Emphasize those aspects that provide your venture with a comparative advantage. It is also appropriate to discuss the geographic location of production facilities and how this enhances your firm's competitive advantage. Your notes should cover such issues as available labor, local regulations, transportation, infrastructure, and proximity to suppliers. In addition, the section should also provide a description of the facilities, discuss whether you will buy or lease them, and explain how you'll handle future growth (by renting an adjoining building, perhaps). As in all sections detailing strategy, support your plans with actual data.

Scope of Operations. What is the production process for your product or service? Creating a diagram makes it easier for you to see which production aspects to keep in-house and which to outsource (see Figure 7.8a). Considering that cash flow is king and that resource-constrained new ventures typically should minimize fixed expenses on production facilities, the general rule is to outsource as much production as possible. However, there is a major caveat to that rule: Your venture should control aspects of production that are central to your competitive advantage. Thus, if you are producing a new component with hard-wired proprietary technology—let's say a voice recognition security door entry—it is wise to internally produce that hard-wired component. The locking mechanism, on the

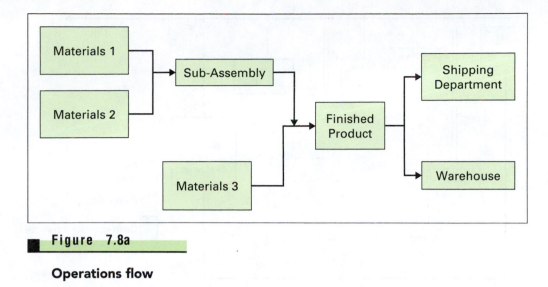

Figure 7.8a

Operations flow

other hand, can be outsourced to your specifications. Outsourcing the aspects that aren't proprietary reduces fixed costs for production equipment and facility expenditures, which means you have to raise less money and give up less equity.

The Scope of Operations Section should also discuss partnerships with vendors, suppliers, and partners. Again, the diagram should illustrate the supplier and vendor relationships by category, or by name if the list isn't too long and you have already identified your suppliers. The diagram helps you visualize the various relationships and ways to better manage or eliminate them. The operations diagram also helps identify staffing needs; for example, how many production workers you might need depending on the hours of operations and number of shifts.

Ongoing Operations. This section builds upon the Scope of Operations section by providing details on day-to-day activities. For example, how many units will you produce in a day and what kinds of inputs will you need? An operating cycle overview diagram graphically illustrates the impact of production on cash flow (see Figure 7.8b). As you complete this detail, you can start to establish performance parameters, which will help you monitor and modify the production process into the future. If this plan is for your use only, you may choose to include such details as the specific job descriptions. However, for a business plan that will be shared with investors, you can get by with a much lower level of detail.

Development Plan

The Development Plan highlights the development strategy and also provides a detailed development timeline. Many new ventures will require a significant level of effort and time to launch the product or service. This is the prologue of your story. For example, new software or hardware products often require months of development. Discuss what types of features you will develop and tie them to the firm's competitive advantage. This section should also discuss any patent, trademark or copyright efforts you will undertake.

Development Strategy. What work remains to be completed? What factors need to come together for development to be successful? What risks to development does the firm face? For example, software development is notorious for taking longer and costing more

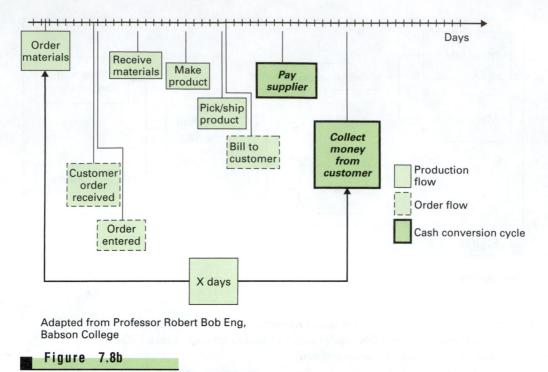

Adapted from Professor Robert Bob Eng,
Babson College

Figure 7.8b

Operating cycle

than most companies originally imagined. Detailing the necessary work and what needs to happen for you to consider the work successful helps you understand and manage the risks involved. After you have laid out these details, you can assemble a development timeline.

Development Timeline. A development timeline is a schedule that highlights major milestones and that you can use to monitor progress and make changes. It's often useful to illustrate timelines as Gantt charts. Figure 7.9 illustrates a typical Gantt chart for the History Shoppe we discussed earlier.

The timeline helps you track major events, delegate responsibilities for project tasks, and schedule activities to best execute on those events. In addition to plotting future milestones, it is also a good idea to illustrate which development milestones you have already achieved as of the writing of the business plan. Finally, keep in mind that, as the old adage says, "time is money." Every day your product is in development and not on the market, you lose a day's worth of sales. You will have to work hard to meet deadlines, especially in those industries where speed to market is critical.

Team

We mentioned in Chapter 2 that Georges Doriot would rather back a "grade-A man with a grade-B idea than a grade-B entrepreneur with a grade-A idea". For this reason, the Team section of the business plan is often the section that professional investors read right after the executive summary. This section is also critically important to the lead entrepreneur. It identifies the members responsible for key activities and conveys why they are exceptionally qualified to execute on those responsibilities. The section also helps you consider how well this group of individuals will work together. It is well established that ventures started by strong teams are much more likely to succeed than those led by weak teams.

Gantt chart for History Shoppe

Activity	12	11	10	9	8	7	6	5	4	3	2	1	Opening Month
10–12 Months Prior to Opening	■	■	■										
1) Finalize business plan and financials													
2) Review plans with local book-stores/ specialty shop owners													
3) Fill in skill gaps with advisory board													
4) Determine exact location possibilities													
7–9 Months Prior to Opening				■	■	■							
5) Register rights to business name													
6) Seek funding from appropriate sources													
7) Update business plan per feedback from potential financiers													
8) Initial contact with product vendors													
9) Contact for POS/inventory vendors and store designers													
4–6 Months Prior to Opening							■	■	■				
10) Determine exact store design													
11) Finalize product vendors													
12) Confirm funding													
3 Months Prior to Opening										■			
13) Finalize store design plans													
14) Open vendor/bank accounts													
15) Place fixture orders													
16) Finalize marketing plan and implement to announce store opening events													
17) Submit merchandise orders with all vendors													
One Month Prior to Opening											■	■	
18) Contact local media re: placement in local newspapers and magazines													
19) Code merchandise category data in inventory management system													
20) Recruit and train staff													
21) Receive merchandise, fixtures, and complete setup of store													
Opening Month												■	■
22) "Soft opening" of store to assess customer response, training, and system functioning													
Grand Opening of Store													

Figure 7.9

Gantt chart for History Shoppe

Team Bios and Roles. Every story needs a cast of characters, and the best place to start is by identifying the key team members and their titles. Often, the lead entrepreneur assumes a CEO role. However, if you are young and have limited business experience, it is usually more productive to state that the company will seek a qualified CEO as it grows. In these cases, the lead entrepreneur may assume a Chief Technology Officer role (if she develops the technology) or Vice President of Business Development. However, don't let these options confine you. The key is to convince your investors that you have assembled the best team possible and that your team can execute on the brilliant concept you are proposing.

A simple, relatively flat organization chart is often useful to visualize what roles you have filled and what gaps remain. It also provides a roadmap for reading the bios that follow. The bios should demonstrate records of success. If you have previously started a business (even if it failed), highlight the company's *accomplishments*. If you have no previous entrepreneurial experience, discuss your achievements in your last job. For example, bios often contain a description of the number of people the entrepreneur previously managed, and, more importantly, a measure of economic success, such as "grew division sales by 20-plus percent." The bio should demonstrate your leadership capabilities. Include the team's resumes as an appendix.

Advisory Boards, Board of Directors, Strategic Partners, External Members. Many entrepreneurs find that they are more attractive to investors if they have strong advisory boards. In building an advisory board, you want to create a team with diverse skills and experience. Industry experts provide legitimacy to your new business as well as strong technical advice. Other advisors should bring financial, legal, or management expertise. Thus, it is common to see lawyers, professors, accountants, and others who can assist the venture's growth on advisory boards. Moreover, if your firm has a strategic supplier or key customer, it may make sense to invite him onto your advisory board. Typically, these individuals are remunerated with a small equity stake and compensation for any organized meetings.

By law, most organization types require a board of directors. While these members can also provide needed expertise, a board of directors is different from an advisory board. The directors' primary role is to oversee the company on behalf of the investors, and to that end the board has the power to replace top executives if it feels doing so would be in the best interests of the company. Therefore, the business plan needs to briefly describe the size of the board, its role within the organization, and any current board members. Most major investors, such as venture capitalists, will require one or more board seats. Usually, the lead entrepreneur and one or more inside company members such as chief financial officers or vice presidents will also have board seats.

Strategic partners may not necessarily be on your advisory board or your board of directors, but they still provide credibility to your venture. For this reason, it makes sense to highlight their involvement in your company's success. It is also common to list external team members, such as the law firm and accounting firm that your venture uses. The key in this section is to demonstrate that your firm can successfully execute the concept. A strong team provides the foundation that can ensure your venture will implement the opportunity successfully.

Compensation and Ownership. A capstone to the team section should be a table listing key team members by role, compensation, and ownership equity. A brief description in the text should explain why the compensation is appropriate. Many entrepreneurs choose not to pay themselves in the early months. Although this strategy conserves cash flow, it would misrepresent the individual's worth to the organization. Therefore, the table should contain what salary the employee is due. If necessary, that salary can be deferred until a time when cash flow is strong. Another column that can be powerful shows what the person's current or most recent compensation was and what she will be paid in the new company. Highly qualified entrepreneurs taking a smaller salary than at their previous job make an impressive point. While everyone understands that the entrepreneur's salary will increase as the company begins to grow, starting at a reduced salary sends the message that you and your team believe in the upside of your idea. Just be sure the description of the schedule underscores the plan to increase salaries in the future. In addition, it is also a good idea to hold stock aside for future key hires and to establish a stock option pool for critical lower-level employees, such as software engineers. The plan should discuss such provisions.

Critical Risks

Every new venture faces a number of risks that may threaten its survival. Although the business plan, to this point, is creating a story of success, readers will identify and recognize a number of threats. The plan needs to acknowledge these potential risks; otherwise, investors will believe that the entrepreneur is naïve or untrustworthy and may possibly withhold investment. How should you present these critical risks without scaring your investor or other stakeholders? Identify the risk and then state your contingency plan. Critical risks are critical assumptions—factors that need to happen if your venture is to succeed as currently planned. The critical assumptions vary from one company to another, but some common categories are Market Interest and Growth Potential, Competitor Actions and Retaliation, Time and Cost of Development, Operating Expenses, and Availability and Timing of Financing.

Market Interest and Growth Potential. The biggest risk any new venture faces is that once the product has been developed, no one will buy it. Although you can do a number of things to minimize this risk, such as market research, focus groups, and beta sites, it is difficult to gauge overall demand, and the growth of that demand, until your product hits the market. State this risk, but counter it with the tactics and contingencies the company will undertake. For example, sales risk can be reduced by mounting an effective advertising and marketing plan or by identifying not only a Primary Target Audience but also Secondary and Tertiary Target Audiences that the company will seek if the PTA proves less interested.

Competitor Actions and Retaliation. Too many entrepreneurs believe either that direct competition doesn't exist or that it is sleepy and slow to react. Don't rely on this belief as a key assumption of your venture's success. Most entrepreneurs passionately believe that they are offering something new and wonderful that is clearly different from what is currently on the market. They go on to state that existing competition won't attack their niche in the near future. Acknowledge the risk that this assessment may be wrong. One counter to this threat is that the venture has room in its gross margins to operate at lower than anticipated price levels, and the cash available to withstand and fight back against such attacks. You should also identify the strategies you will use to protect and reposition yourself should an attack occur.

Time and Cost of Development. As mentioned in the Development Plan section, many factors can delay and add to the expense of developing your product. The business plan should identify the factors that may hinder development. For instance, during the extended high-tech boom of the late 1990s and into the new century, there has been an acute shortage of skilled software engineers. You need to address how you will overcome the challenge of hiring and retaining the most qualified professionals, perhaps by outsourcing some development to the underemployed engineers in India. Compensation, equity participation, flexible hours, and other benefits that the firm could offer might also minimize the risk. Whatever your strategy, you need to demonstrate an understanding of the difficult task at hand, and assure potential investors that you will be able to develop the product on time and on budget.

Operating Expenses. Operating expenses have a way of growing beyond expectations. Sales, administration, marketing, and interest expenses are some of the areas you need to monitor and manage. The business plan should highlight how you forecast your expenses (comparable companies and detailed analysis), and also lay out your contingency plans for unexpected developments. For instance, you may want to slow the hiring of support staff if development or other key tasks take longer than expected. Remember, cash is king, and your plan should illustrate how you will conserve cash when things don't go according to plan.

Availability and Timing of Financing. We can't stress enough how important cash flow is to the survival and flourishing of a new venture. One major risk that most new ventures face is that they will have difficulty obtaining needed financing, both equity and debt. If the current business plan is successful in attracting investors, cash flow will not be a problem in the short term. However, most ventures will need multiple rounds of financing. If the firm fails to make progress or meet key milestones, it may not be able to secure additional rounds of financing. This can put the entrepreneur in the uncomfortable position of having to accept unfavorable financing terms or, in the worst-case scenario, force the company into bankruptcy. Your contingency plans should identify viable alternative sources of capital and strategies to slow the "burn rate."[5]

A number of other risks might apply to your business. Acknowledge them and discuss how you can overcome them. Doing so generates confidence among your investors and helps you anticipate corrective actions that you may need to take.

Offering

Using your vision for the business and your estimates of the capital required to get there, you can develop a "sources and uses" schedule for the Offering section of your business plan. The Sources section details how much capital you need, and the types of financing such as equity investment and debt infusions. The Uses section details how you'll spend the money. Typically, you should secure enough financing to last 12 to 18 months. If you take more capital than you need, you have to give up more equity. If you take less, you may run out of cash before reaching milestones that equate to higher valuations.

Financial Plan

Chapter 8 illustrates how to construct your pro-forma financials, but you will also need a verbal description of these financials. We will defer discussion of this section until the next chapter.

Appendices

The appendices can include anything and everything that you think adds further validation to your concept, but that doesn't fit or is too large to insert in the main parts of the plan. Common inclusions would be one-page resumes of key team members, articles that feature your venture, and technical specifications. If you already have customers, include a few excerpts of testimonials from them. Likewise, if you have favorable press coverage, include that as well. As a general rule, try to put all exhibits discussed in the written part of the plan on the same page that you discuss them so the reader doesn't have to keep flipping back to the end of the plan to look at an exhibit. However, it is acceptable to put very large exhibits into an appendix.

Types of Plans

So far in this chapter we have laid out the basic sections or areas you want to address in your business planning process. The earliest drafts should be housed in a three-ring binder so you can add and subtract as you gain a deeper understanding, but at some point you may want to print a more formal-looking plan.

Business plans can take a number of forms depending on their purpose. Each form requires the same level of effort and leads to the same conclusions, but the final document is crafted differently depending on who uses it and when they use it. For instance, when you are introducing your concept to a potential investor, you might send a short, concise summary plan. As the investor's interest grows and she wants to more fully investigate the concept, she may ask for a more detailed plan. Even though the equity boom of the late 1990s essentially equated entrepreneurship with venture capital, a business plan serves so much more than the needs of potential investors. Employees, strategic partners, financiers, and board members all may find use for a well-developed business plan. Most importantly, the entrepreneur herself gains immeasurably from the business planning process because it allows her not only to run the company better, but also to clearly articulate her story to stakeholders who may never read the plan. In sum, different consumers of the business plan require different presentation of the work.

Your three-ring binder is basically what we would call an *operational plan*. It is primarily for you and your team to guide the development, launch, and initial growth of the venture. There really is no length specification for this type of plan, but it's not unusual to exceed 80 pages. The biggest difference between an operational plan and the one you might present to a potential investor is the level of detail, which tends to be much greater in an operational plan. Remember, the creation of this document is where you really gain the deep understanding so important in discerning how to build and run the business.

If you need outside capital, a business plan geared toward equity investors or debt providers should be about 25 to 40 pages long. Recognize that professional equity investors, such as venture capitalists, and professional debt providers, such as bankers, will not read the entire plan from front to back. That being the case, produce the plan in a format that facilitates spot reading. The previous discussion highlighted sections that these readers might find useful. The key is to present a concise version of all the material you have produced in your planning process. Focus on what the investor values the most. Thus, operational details are often less important unless your competitive advantage derives from your operations. Our general rule of thumb is that "less is more." For instance, we've found that 25-page business plans receive venture funding more often than 40-page plans (other things being equal).

You may also want to produce an expanded executive summary. These plans are considerably shorter than an operational plan or the 25–40 page plan discussed above; typically no more than 10 pages. The purpose of this plan is to provide an initial conception of the business in order to test initial reaction to the idea. It allows you to share your idea with confidantes and receive feedback before investing significant time and effort on a longer business plan.

After you've completed the business planning process, rewrite the expanded executive summary. You can use this expanded summary to attract attention. For instance, send it to investors you have recently met to spur interest and a meeting. It is usually better to send an expanded executive summary than a full business plan, because the investor will be more apt to read it. If the investor is interested, he will call you in for a meeting. If the meeting goes well, the investor often then asks for the full business plan.

Style Pointers for the Written Plan and Oral Presentation

Once you start writing plans for external consumption, the way you present the information becomes important. Not only do you need to capture the reader's attention with a well-researched opportunity, you need to present your case in a way that makes it easy and interesting to read. Too many business plans are text-laden, dense manifestos. Only the most diligent reader will wade through all that text. The key is to create visual catch-points.

Use a table of contents with numbered sections, as we described earlier in this chapter. Then use clearly marked headers and subheaders throughout the document. This allows the reader to jump to sections she is most interested in. Another way to draw the reader to important points is to use bulleted lists, diagrams, charts, and sidebars.[6] Your reader should be able to understand the venture opportunity by just looking at the visual catch-points of a plan. Work with your team and trusted advisors on ways to bring out the exciting elements of your story. The point is to make the document not only content rich, but visually attractive.

Some investors have no interest in a plan at all. Instead, they prefer to see an executive summary and PowerPoint slides, and they often read the PowerPoint slides instead of asking the entrepreneur to personally present those slides. We have already discussed executive summaries, so let's spend a few moments on PowerPoint slides. You should be able to communicate your business opportunity in 10 to 12 slides, possibly along the following lines:

1. Cover page showing product picture, company name, and contact information
2. Opportunity description emphasizing customer problem or need that you hope to solve
3. Illustration of how your product or service solves the customer's problem
4. Some details (as needed) to better describe your product
5. Competition overview
6. Entry and growth strategy showing how you get into the market and then grow
7. Overview of your business model—how you will make money and how much it will cost to support those sales
8. Team description
9. Current status with timeline
10. Summary including how much you need and how that money will be used

The key to creating a successful presentation is to maximize the use of your slides. For example, graphs, pictures, and other visuals are more powerful and compelling than texts and bulleted lists. Entrepreneurs who create bulleted lists often use them as cue cards during an oral presentation, and either stare at the screen behind them as they talk or continually look back and forth between the screen and their audience. In either case, this behavior might prevent you from creating a personal connection with your audience.

This connection is important because it conveys that you have confidence in your plan and that you have a strong command of the concept. A second problem with bulleted lists is that your audience will tend to read them, and their attention will be focused on the slide and not on what you are saying. Again, you want to create a strong personal connection with your audience. You should be able to use graphics to communicate the key points. Doing so will better engage your audience and make them more inclined to view your opportunity favorably.

CONCLUSION ☐

The business plan is more than just a document; it is a process, a story. Although the finished product is often a written plan, the deep thinking and fact-based analysis that goes into that document provides the entrepreneur the keen insights needed to marshal resources and direct growth. The whole process can be painful, but it almost always maximizes revenue and minimizes costs. The reason is that the process allows the entrepreneur to better anticipate instead of react.

Business planning also provides talking points so that entrepreneurs can get feedback from a number of experts, including investors, vendors, and customers. Think of business planning as one of your first steps on the journey to entrepreneurial success. Also remember that business planning is a process and not a product. It is iterative, and in some sense it never ends. As your venture grows you will want to come back and revisit earlier drafts, create new drafts, and so on for the entire life of your business. Keep your three-ring binder close by and continue to add to and revise it often. It is the depository of all the learning that you have achieved as well as your plans for the future. While the first draft of any plan is tough, the rewards are many. Enjoy the journey.

YOUR OPPORTUNITY JOURNAL ☐

Reflection Point	Your Thoughts...

1. What data have you gathered about your opportunity?
   a. What does this data suggest as far as reshaping your opportunity?
   b. What new questions does it raise, and who should you talk to in order to answer these questions?

2. Who have you shared your vision with?
   a. Who have they referred you to?
   b. What new learning have you gained from these conversations?

3. What is your "tagline?"

4. Does your executive summary have a compelling "hook?"

5. Does your business planning process tie together well? Do you have a compelling, articulate story?

WEB EXERCISE

Scan the Internet for business plan preparation sites. What kinds of templates are available? Do these make it easier to write a plan? What is the downside, if any, of using these templates? What are the benefits? Find some sample plans online. These plans are often advertised as superior to "typical" plans. Are they better? What makes them better?

NOTES

[1] Bartlett, S. Seat of your pants. *Inc. Magazine*, October 2002.

[2] Lange, J., Bygrave, W., and Evans, T. Do Business Plan Competitions Produce Winning Businesses? Paper presented at 2004 Babson Kauffman Entrepreneurship Research Conference, Glasgow, Scotland.

[3] Thomas, P. Rewriting the rules: A new generation of entrepreneurs find themselves in the perfect time and place to chart their own course. *Wall Street Journal,* May 22, 2000, R4.

[4] Sacirbey, O. Private Companies Temper IPO Talk. *The IPO Reporter*, December 18, 2000.

[5] *Burn rate* is how much more cash the company is expending each month than earning in revenue.

[6] A running sidebar, a visual device positioned on the right side of the page, periodically highlights some of the key points in the plan. Don't overload the sidebar, but one or two items per page can draw attention to highlights that maintain reader interest.

P'kolino

Executive Summary

Pίkolino, LLC

(pee-ko-lee-no)

P'kolino

QUICK FACTS:

Management:
J.B SCHNEIDER: President, Marketing
ANTONIO TURCO-RIVAS: Operations
Sales, Finance
RISD: Design and Development

Industry: Play at Home – Play Furniture

Business: Improving play at home with products like this:

Patents: Currently filing provisional patents

Law Firm: Brown Rudnick, and Berlack Israels LLP

Auditors: N/A

Current Investors: Founders

Financing Sought: $400K

Use of Funds: Manufacturing, Marketing and Product Development

Employees: Founders (2)

Clients: Conversations with specialty retailers (e.g. Museum of Modern Arts)

Exit Strategy: Acquisition by toy manufacturer, furniture retailer or furniture manufacturer

CONTACT INFORMATION:
600 West Cummings Park, Suite 5350
Woburn, MA 01801
Phone: (781) 497-0913
Email: jb@pkolino.com or
atrn@pkolino.com
Website: www.pkolino.com

Summary:
P'kolino is committed to improving play at home by developing and marketing innovative play products and accessories. P'kolino believes that play should be fun and that play is critical to a child's physical, mental and social development. We hear from parents that they believe this too. Our products,
- are designed for optimal usage by the child,
- grow and adapt to the child's stage of development, and
- integrate with toys and activities to encourage and enhance play.

P'kolino not only improves play at home but its business of "growing" products, toy integration and complementary accessories serves as the foundation for a solid business with recurring, high margin sales.

Strategy:
Our goal is for P'kolino to become synonymous with play at home, and to accomplish this we have designed a progressive growth strategy. Through research we determined that the basis for play, the play space and its furniture, are in need of improvement. We've identified four key areas for improvement:
- Existing play furniture hinders play because it is designed for miniature adults.
- Play furniture rapidly loses its value because children outgrow it.
- The child loses interest in the play furniture quickly because it has few applications.
- Play spaces are cluttered and unorganized

P'kolino addresses these needs by:
- Making play more productive by designing furniture for the ones who use it: children.
- Increasing the useful life of the furniture by designing it to grow with the child
- Maintaining interest in the furniture by increasing its uses. Add-on toy kits integrate with the table for unlimited uses.
- Organizing the play spaces by designing these toys kit to simply fold-up and store away in a child friendly storage unit.

We will build distinctive, high quality products and focus on developing a strong brand. P'kolino will first target the high-end market because it values the brand, its consumers are influencers, and it has the highest margins. We will grow by introducing additional products to the high-end markets and expanding with a different product line into the higher volume mid-market.

Distribution will primarily be direct, however we will partner with key retail showrooms to create familiarity with our products. A strong direct channel will enable us to develop extended relationships with our customers for repeat sales of upgrades, accessories and toy kits.

Market:
Play furniture is a $1.2 billion market. The High-end segment is $51million, growing at 9% and strong margins of 55% gross/20% net. The Mid segment is estimated at $300 million, growing at 8% per year and margins of 48% gross/14% net. The mass segment is estimated at $800 million, growing at 7% and margins of 37% gross and 5% net.

Operations:
Outsourcing Manufacturing, and using a collaboration model for product development.

Management Background:
- Antonio Turco-Rivas: co-founder and Sales & Operations Manager is a Babson MBA 2005. Antonio is a proven entrepreneur who successfully launched two ventures. He has managerial and sales experience.
- J.B. Schneider: co-founder and Marketing & Product Development Manager is a Babson MBA 2005 with over 10 years of marketing strategy and communications experience for several Fortune 500 companies.

	Year 1	Year 2	Year 3	Year 4	Year 5
Revenues	612K	1 783K	2 922K	4 168K	5 793K
Expenses	643K	1 761K	2 806K	3 786K	5 093K
Net Profit	-31K	22K	115K	382K	700K
Head Count	4	7	13	14	14

Pkolino™

Business Plan
May-2005

Prepared by:
J.B. Schneider &
Antonio Turco-Rivas N.

Contact Information:
Phone: (781) 497-0913
Email: jb@pkolino.com
          atrn@pkolino.com
Address:
600 West Cummings Park
Suite 5350
Woburn, MA 01801

Confidential Information
Business Plan - Dated May-2005
Woburn, Massachusetts – USA

1	**Mission Statement**

"P'kolino will develop innovative playroom furniture designed for the child to improve play"

"P'kolino is a product development and marketing company. Our goal is to improve play at home by developing and marketing innovative playroom furniture <u>designed for the child</u>. Our products will grow and adapt to the child's stage of development and integrate with toys and activities to encourage and enhance play".

2	**Industry Overview**

2.1 <u>Understanding the Playroom Market</u>

Four million children are born in the United States each year[1]. Thus, at any given time, there are 30 million children ages 8 or younger. This large base fuels the $38 billion children's toy and furniture market, currently growing at 13% per year (according to the industry trade publication "Playthings"). The playroom market (meaning the area of the house set aside for children's recreation and play) is part of this pie, and includes elements of both the furniture and the toy industry.

"Children's playroom furniture market is estimated at $1.2 billion, growing at 7% annually for the next five years"

P'kolino will compete in the children's playroom furniture space, estimated to be a $1.2 billion market, growing at 7% annually for the next five years (according to marketresearch.com). However, a playroom is not a playroom without toys. For this reason, P'kolino will develop furniture products and accessories designed to integrate with toys and activities to complete the playroom offering and enhance their play value.

Exhibit 2-A
The Playroom Market
(US$ Billions)

■ Toy + Furniture Market
□ Playroom Furniture

The dynamics of the playroom market are influenced by both the furniture and toy industry. An overview of each of these industries follows.

2.2 <u>Furniture Industry Highlights</u>

Households in the US spend over $24 billion a year on furniture and this figure is expected to grow at 2% per year according to the American Furniture Manufacturer Association (AFMA). The industry has traditionally been highly segmented, but because of lower margins fueled by intense competition from imports, it has started to consolidate. Last year, for example, products manufactured and imported from other countries (especially China) represented 45%[2] of total purchases.

---

[1] Source: U.S. Census Bureau – www.census.gov
[2] Source: US Department of Commerce – www.commerce.gov

Confidential Information
Business Plan - Dated May-2005
Woburn, Massachusetts – USA

Companies competing in this market are:
- Furniture Brands International, the largest maker of residential furniture and owner of brands like Henredon, Drexel, and Maitland-Smith (the company has over $2.3 billion in revenues[3]).
- Lay Z Boy ($1.9 billion in revenues).
- Ashley Furniture ($1.7 billion in revenues)
- and others; like Ethan Allen and local players.

These companies distribute products through a network of furniture centers, independent dealers (specialty retailers), national and local chains, and department stores.

According to the AFMA, children's furniture generated $4 billion in 2003, 90% related to children's bedroom furniture sales (cribs, changing tables, etc.) and the remaining 10% or <u>$400 million</u> to children's tables, chairs, storage and toys. Niche players have dominated this segment of the industry, and according to the American Home Furnishings Alliance (annual publication) it is the fastest growing segment (8% in 2003).

"Children's furniture is the fastest growing segment in the Furniture Industry with 8% growth in 2003"
American Home Furnishing Alliance

We believe the Furniture Industry will continue to face strong competition from foreign manufacturers (selling at lower prices). Local manufacturers will have to invest in technology and compete on quality and speed. In the children's furniture market, the large companies have been traditionally focused on bedroom furniture. Niche players have been taking over the more specialized products - those requiring expertise in other areas - like child development (i.e. the playroom furniture).

Exhibit 2-B
Furniture Industry
(US$ Billions)

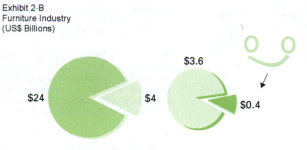

$3.6
$24
$4
$0.4

■ Furniture Industry □ Children's Bedroom ■ Children's Playroom

---

[3] Source: Hoovers Online – www.hoovers.com

2.3 Toy Industry Highlights

The Toy Industry accounted for $34 billion in 2003[4]. On both the manufacturing and retailing side it is a highly concentrated industry. For the past few years it has been growing at 5-9% per year, with almost 60% of the products being imported from other countries[5].

According to "Playthings annual report" the Toy industry is highly seasonal with almost 70% of all toy purchases occurring during the Holiday season (Christmas).

The "Playthings annual report" for 2003 also stated the main forces driving the industry as follows:

Exhibit 2-C
The Toy Industry
(US$ Billions)

- "Educational toys": after many ups and downs, it seems like American parents have become more aware of the importance of play and education in the early years. This has resulted in sales growth of 9% per year.
- "Word of mouth and Brand": proven ways to build sales in this industry.
- "Technology is king": almost 39% all of toys sales (in terms of US$) are video games or what they like to call "technology related products".
- "Merchant power": Mass merchandisers; in particular Wal-Mart (sells 25% of the toys sold every year in America), have taken the industry by storm, lowering prices to consumer but also lowering margins to manufacturer.
- "China": manufacturing has gone overseas

"Parents have become more aware of the importance of play and education in the early years... educational toys sales are up 9% per year"
"Playthings"

Retail sales of toys and games are expected to grow 4.3 percent per year to total $37.8 billion in 2007[6]. New video game technologies and the introduction of next generation systems are expected to be the main driver of growth. With respect to toys the leaders in the industry are Mattel [7] ($4.9 billion in sales), Hasbro ($3.1 billion), Lego ($1.6 billion), and Leap Frog ($600 million). Sony takes the lead in video games.

Regarding the playroom furniture market, some companies like Rubbermaid (using the Little Tykes brand) have developed; role-play toys, ride-on toys, sandboxes, activity gyms and climbers, and plastic juvenile furniture. These products are sold in toy stores (not furniture stores) and have been targeting the price sensitive consumer. Our research indicates that these types of

---

[4] Source: Industry trade publication "Playthings"
[5] Source: Industry trade publication "Playthings"
[6] Source: Marketreseach.com
[7] Source: revenues for Toy industry leaders from Hoovers Online

Confidential Information
Business Plan - Dated May-2005
Woburn, Massachusetts – USA

"$800 million in playroom furniture products are sold each year by Toy Industry related companies

products carry very low margins (average 5% profit margins[8]). To compete, companies like Brio, another strong player in this niche, sells low price train tables to encourage parents to buy their higher margins trains (they lose money on the furniture to sell the toy).

According to the Marketresearch.com industry report, of the $34 billion, $6 billion accounts for furniture products. However, this number includes car seats, play pens, strollers, etc. For playroom furniture, our research[9] indicates that approximately $800 million is sold each year.

Exhibit 2-D
Toy Industry
(US$ Billions)

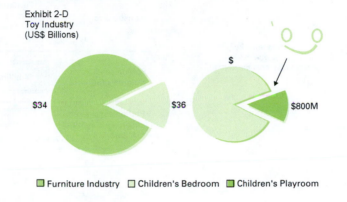

☐ Furniture Industry   ☐ Children's Bedroom   ☐ Children's Playroom

Our research concluded that large toy companies dominate the price-sensitive segment of the playroom furniture market. However for mid and high-end play furniture products, niche manufacturers and retailers like Pottery Barn Kids and Land of Nod have taken the lead.

---

[8] Sources: According to 10K fillings for the SEC and/or public financial statements from: Graco, Rubbermaid, Brio and others.
[9] Based on Marketresearch.com Industry Report and Sales of top ten manufactures of playroom furniture products

Confidential Information
Business Plan - Dated May-2005
Woburn, Massachusetts – USA

2.4 How it all Comes Together (Furniture & Toy Industry)

Furniture meets toys in the playroom; both Industries converge and influence the $1.2 billion market.

Exhibit 2-E
The Playroom Furniture Market
(US$ Billions)

"The Furniture and Toy industry converge in the furniture playroom market"

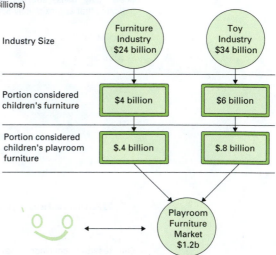

The Playroom furniture market (where P'kolino will compete) has inherited many of the competitive dynamics of its parent industries:

- Is growing at an average of 7% annually[10]
- Is highly seasonal (almost 70% of sales during the Holiday season)
- Almost 60% of the products are manufactured abroad[11]
- For highly price sensitive consumers the market is highly concentrated, but at mid and high-end income levels niche players dominate
- Word of mouth and brand are the main drivers of sales

---

[10] Source: Marketresearch.com Industry Report
[11] Based on the Management calculations, supported by AFMA information on Furniture Imports

Confidential Information
Business Plan - Dated May-2005
Woburn, Massachusetts – USA

2.5 Trends Influencing the Playroom Market

More children are being born: According to the latest statistics from the National Center for Health Statistics, women in the United States are having more children now than at any time in almost 30 years. During most of the 1970s and 1980s, the average birthrate was fewer than two children per woman, today that average has increased to 2.1 children. As a result of this trend, the population of children age 5 and under is expected to grow in 2004, and to experience gradually increasing annual percentage gains through 2010.

"...More babies, more disposable income and more spending in children's furniture are also driving the playroom market"

Mom's with more income and spending more: More women are having babies later in life, when their income tends to be higher and more stable. The birth rates for women in their 30s and older are at their highest level in three decades, up 2%-3% since 1990 for women in their 30s, and up more than 7% for women in their 40s.[12] As a result many of them are coming into the toy and furniture markets with higher disposable income than was previously the case.

Grandparents are spending more: According to the U.S. Census Bureau, greater longevity and higher disposable income of a growing U.S. population of grandparents is also boosting average per capita spending on home furnishings and toys for young children. There are about 70 million grandparents in the United States today. As a result of divorces and remarriages, many American children have six to eight adults in the "grandparent" role. According to the Research Firm Interep, (supported by Simmons database) grandparents are spending over $60 billion on grandchildren each year.

More aware/educated parents: Parents these days are being bombarded by advice from experts about developing children's mental, physical, and social skills. Parents understand the value play has on this development and look for products to encourage it. In an interview with the trade publication Playthings (May 2002), Susan Oliver, executive director of the non-profit organization Playing for Keeps, explains:

"Parents with dollars to spend, typically those who have greater amounts of education, are increasingly aware of the connection between play and healthy development. There has been a lot of media coverage about brain development, with an emphasis on the critical role of a stimulating environment during the first three years of a child's life." As long as the market approach is toward kids learning more at a younger age, consumers will pay to get on the higher rung of the educational ladder"

---

[12] Source: U.S. Census Bureau – www.census.gov

Confidential Information
Business Plan - Dated May-2005
Woburn, Massachusetts – USA

New laws: New safety legislation has propelled safer product designs as the industry and the media warn consumers not to use older products that do not meet current safety standards[13].

Home remodeling: With new TV shows encouraging makeovers of home spaces, Americans are likely to spend more on home furnishing in 2005.

"...The Power of Play program, continues to reach literally millions of people...play has a positive effect on children's overall well-being is instrumental in the child's development"

The Power of Play Campaign: Children appear to be growing up much faster; they look more mature and they know more about the world at younger and younger ages. Child development experts stress that despite appearances, a child is still a child. This message is a major focus of "The Power of Play" program, which continues to reach literally millions of people throughout our nation as a result of the second phase of broadcast and print public service announcements sponsored by the Toy Manufacturer Association.

The importance of this message was discovered as a result of a national survey conducted in 1999 on behalf of the American Toy Institute, the industry's charitable and educational foundation, recently renamed the Toy Industry Foundation. Ninety-one percent of the survey participants, made up of parents, teachers and child experts, stated that play has a positive effect on children's overall well-being and was instrumental in the development of a child's imagination, self-confidence, self-esteem, creativity, problem-solving and cooperation.

Toys March Up-market: A recent article in the <u>Wall Street Journal</u> (please refer to Appendix 11.1) explained the profit killing price war landscape for toy-making and retailing in the mass market, and highlighted how premium priced toys appear to be outgrowing the simpler less expensive versions.

David Shaw, the new owner of the FAO Schwarz retail stores stated "the admittedly small niche is a vibrant marketplace full of customers looking for something different from what's available at mass retail stores... is a niche that small retailers and catalogs dominate".

A customer commented as she visited one small specialty retailer in New York City "these toys aren't cheap... but they are really good-quality...I know my kids will love them".

---

[13] Source: The U.S. Public Interest Research Group

2.6 Playroom Furniture Market Structure and Competition

The Playroom Furniture Market has three main segments: mass ($800 million), mid ($300 million) and high-end ($51 million). These segments are derived from a market segmentation based on product quality, price, distribution channel and type of customer.

High-end segment: P'kolino will enter the playroom furniture market in this segment. This segment refers to exclusive products sold primarily through catalogs, interior-designer depots, trade events, specialty small retailers and direct from the designer/manufacturer. These products are expensive and branded with the designer's name. Most of these products are usually designed in Italy, Germany, Spain, Netherlands, among others European countries. Buyers are looking for something unique and beautiful. Interior designers are the main promoters in this segment; however, some specialty furniture boutiques have also begun to carry premium furniture for play. Furniture usually takes 6 to 8 weeks for delivery.

"P'kolino market entry strategy will be to target the High-end segment, a small but profitable spot"

Exhibit 2-F
Playroom Furniture Market (US$ MM)

$51

$300

$800

☐ Mass   ☐ Mid   ☐ High

Customers in this segment are resorting to custom designed playroom solutions using interior designers; some of them even specialized on child-spaces. Customers are also buying from product boutiques that sell furniture as well as other children products (e.g. clothing, toys, and accessories). Small independents design firms (e.g. Truck Architecture) generally design the products sold in these stores. These design shops are usually niche players, who specialize in products such as hand painted furniture, or replications of classic styles. Their value to the boutique is the uniqueness of the product; you cannot find them at the mid or mass market stores.

To summarize, our main competitors in this market are the interior designers (custom made) and the niche product designers. They are often

small in size with limited reach and resources. According to our research this segment is growing at 9% per year with strong margins of 55% gross/20% net[14] .

Due to the distinctive characteristics of the High-end segment it is difficult to pinpoint a single market or list of the most prominent competitors. However, we will provide examples of the type of competition P'kolino will face as it enters the high-end segment:

- **Truck Architecture:** is a good example of a design firm. With offices in New York City and a team of 3 designers the company has developed high-end playroom furniture products with a very contemporary style. Truck has been in business since 2000, and sells its products through specialty retail stores, online retailers and in an affiliate web-based store (Offi). Truck founders Jennifer Carpenter, Jonathan Marvel and Rob Rogers have been successful with PR, and have managed to showcase its products in high visibility places like the Museum of Modern Arts (MoMA) Stores in San Francisco and New York.

- **Casakids – Roberto Gil:** Born in Buenos Aires, Argentina and educated at Harvard University, Roberto Gil trained as an architect before delving into furniture design. Gil's lines of children's furniture are very simple in terms of design and configuration. His products have been sold most recently at the Guggenheim Museum Store, Barney's New York; the Whitney Museum's Store Next Door, FAO Schwarz, SF MoMA, and The Land of Nod.

- **KidKraft, Inc:** Originally formed in 1968 as a manufacturer and supplier to the early-childhood sector, KidKraft began competing in the juvenile retail market in 1996. Today, KidKraft creates a wide array of room furnishings, gifts and toys, including licensed juvenile products. KidKraft (headquarter in Dallas, Texas) competes in other segments of the market as well. Its most recent line of products, hand-painted furniture pieces, is positioned at high-end price points. KidKraft has a strong distribution channel infrastructure for mid and mass market products, and is trying to leverage those channels to enter the high-end segment.

---

[14] Based on primary and secondary research – Interviews with industry experts.

Confidential Information
Business Plan - Dated May-2005
Woburn, Massachusetts – USA

"The mid segment is the sweet spot for P'kolino, with reasonable volume, high margins and less price sensitive customers…is driven by quality and looks, not price."

Mid-Segment: Retailers like Pottery Barn Kids, Bellini, Bombay Kids, Land of Nod and specialty catalogs have become the leaders in this segment. These companies are mainly furniture retail chains with products designed with a more conservative classic look and with better materials. The majority of the pieces are made from wood, normally targeting the family room and the child's bedroom. Some of the products are multipurpose (e.g. coffee table that is also a train table). Competition in this segment is considered "high" because of the limited number of players. Pottery-Barn, the market leader, is also the style setter for this segment. In contrast to the take-home approach of mass merchandisers, delivery of the product to the end customer usually takes up to 4 weeks.

Most of the products are sold by catalog, although Pottery-barn, Bellini and Bombay have all opened physical stores to showcase their children's product line.

Customers in this segment are looking for more exclusive designs and will trust companies like Pottery-Barn Kids, The Land of Nod, and Bellini because of their established reputations for high quality and visually appealing products. The largest threats for these companies are the copy-cats (e.g., Ikea and Target) as they manufacture very similar products priced 30-40% less. Copy cats successful because the brand defining product attribute - beauty - is easily replicated.

According to our research, succeeding in this segment requires a strong brand. Our strategic differentiation in this market will be to offer compelling, customer driven attributes, leveraging the functionality of our products, a grow-with-your-child proposition and furniture integration with toys/activities. For P'kolino the mid-segment is the sweet spot (good margins and healthy volume).

According to AFMA the mid-segment is growing at 8% per year and has been enjoying healthy margins of 48% gross and14% net.

Key competitors in the Mid-Segment:

- **Pottery Barn Kids (PBK):** A subsidiary of Williams-Sonoma, Inc. is the largest player in this segment with over 87 stores, an online store-front and 4 to 5 catalog issues per year. According to 10k reports revenues are split 50/50 between physical stores and direct channels. PBK competes with quality, design and brand and had revenues over $300 million last year. They entered the playroom furniture market with a number of products targeting the bedroom and family room spaces, as well as some toy like furniture pieces (e.g., kitchen play sets).

Confidential Information
Business Plan - Dated May-2005
Woburn, Massachusetts – USA

In a recent article in the <u>Wall Street Journal</u>[15] - "Williams-Sonoma: Seeing a Strong High-End Consumer," it was reported that:

"Furniture sales have increased to about 25% of total company sales from about 17% a year earlier, said Laura Alber, head of the Pottery Barn brand. "It's really a key strategic focus," Alber said. "Furniture seems to be a strong area of growth and one where we're very focused on driving profitability."

- **Bellini:** A manufacturer and specialty retail boutique chain that has been around for more than 15 years. They sell high-end European designed children's furniture and accessories. Bellini targets the big spenders with solid-wood juvenile furniture. The company franchises its retail concept and has stores nationwide. Some of its products could be considered high-end, but depending on the franchisee target, the store would more likely than not carry products at prices closer to the mid-segment. They have embraced the grow-with-your-child concept for bedroom furniture, but they are still very classic and basic in terms of their playroom offering.

- **Land of Nod:** The runner-up in terms of playroom furniture in this segment. The online-catalog based juvenile furniture store was recently acquired by Crate and Barrel. They are now in the process of opening stores following the PBK success; however, their business model is different. They sell products designed and manufactured by others. They are competing head to head with PBK in terms of design attributes, style and prices.

Mass-Segment: In this segment, furniture market characteristics more resemble those of toys than in the other segments. Together Brio, Imaginarium, Little Tykes and Fisher Price hold up to 58%[16] of the market share. Small independents that manufacture furniture products under licensed brands such as Dora the Explorer, Barnie, Barbie, Disney, etc, also hold a solid 20% market share[17].

"The mass segment is highly concentrated, suffers low margins and uses mainstream toy distribution channels"

This segment can be considered highly concentrated (few players) and price sensitive. Customers in this segment are buying playroom furniture the way they buy toys: at large discount stores (75%) like Wal-Mart, Target, Kmart or large specialized retailers like Toys R Us.

Products like play tables and chairs are sold for less than $200. They are made of plastic or composite materials and in many cases branded with cartoon characters. The majority of the products are not designed to

[15] Wednesday August 25-2004, WSJ
[16] Source: Derived from individual sales from companies financial statements
[17] Source: "Playthings" Annual Report

Confidential Information
Business Plan - Dated May-2005
Woburn, Massachusetts – USA

integrate with the toy or activity (toy/furniture integration) and competition seems to be based on price and brand, not on quality or looks. The noticeable exceptions are the train tables and some Lego tables. Brio for example, sells its train table almost at cost, but then makes a profit selling the trains.

Distribution and competitive dynamics in this segment mimic those of the toy industry in terms of levels of concentration (few players with large market shares), business cycle (70% of sales occurs during the holidays)[18] and barriers of entry (very low margins – competition based on volume). Most of the participants in this market have been losing money lately. On average, the mass segment margins have been 37% gross, and 5% profit.[19]

Some Key Competitors in the Mass-Segment:

- **Brio**: Based in Sweden, but with operations in Europe, Asia and the US. With $1.6B in sales[20] the company has complemented its toy offering with some playroom furniture pieces (especially train tables) now representing about 1/3 of total sales. The company has a strong presence in the Nordic countries and has made an effort to penetrate the US market with products priced a little above the market average. Specialty stores and mass merchandisers have been carrying Brio products in small quantities because of its price point. Brio represents the "traditional wood based" products in this segment. High quality products and a reputation for delivering on educational play support its strong brand.

- **Little Tykes**: Subsidiary of Newell Rubbermaid, Little Tykes is the largest manufacturer of plastic based tables and chairs for this segment. With operations all over the world, Little Tykes has positioned its products as safe, durable and low price playroom furniture. Its products are sold in mass merchandise stores and according to the parent company's financial statements the division has been struggling to maintain profitability because of higher raw material prices (oil based). In July 2004, the company sold its Little Tykes Commercial Play Systems (LTCPS) unit to PlayPower. Little Tykes had 28% gross and -2% profit margins in 2003.[21]

- **Imaginarium:** This Spain based company and Toys R Us affiliate since 2001 is the second largest manufacturer of play tables for this market segment. The relationship with Toys R Us guarantees shelf space in the stores to display its products and has even created barriers of entry to other manufacturers in that channel. The

"P'kolino will enter the mass-segment once it has penetrated the high and mid segments of the market and developed a strong brand"

---

[18] Source: Toy Industry Association Annual Report
[19] Source: Hoovers Online, SEC filings and Annual Reports from Mattel, Hasbro, Lego and LeapFrog
[20] Source: Brio Annual Financial Statements
[21] Source: Newell Rubbermaid Annual Report, SEC Filling, Hoovers Online

company has positioned its products similar to Brio but with a lower price tag and quality. The company has had a disappointing year in the U.S. according to the <u>Wall Street Journal</u>, but remains a competitor with a strong distribution channel and world-class product development capabilities.

The following summarizes the size and structure of the Playroom Furniture Market:

Exhibit 2-G The Playroom Furniture Market
Summary of Market Segments and Competitive Dynamics

The Furniture Playroom Market

	Market Characteristics	Market Dynamics	What's driving the customer
High-end segment (entry)	Size:$51MM / Growing: 9% Main Distribution Channels: FAO Schwarz, Toy/Furniture Boutique s Interior Designers (custom made) Direct (Internet)	Unknown number of competitors (many) Very diverse distribution channels (there is no predominant channel in this segment) No identifiable market leader High margins, low volumes Competition is based on access to customers and looks	Brand/Benefits Word of Mouth Interior Designer
Mid-market segment (sweet spot)	Size:$300MM / Growing: 8% Main Distribution Channels: Pottery Barn Kids Land of Nods Specialty stores and catalogs Direct (Internet)	Limited number of competitors Dominated by few Companies (catalogs and brand stores) Pottery Barn is the market leader Good margins, good volumes Competition is based on brand and looks	Brand/Benefits Word of Mouth Store Display/ Catalog
Mass-market segment (expansion)	Size:$800MM / Growing: 7% Main Distribution Channels: Mass Retailers (Wal-Mart "Target" Toys "R" Us Specialty stores and catalogs Direct (Internet)	Limited number of competitors Dominated by few companies (Wal-Mart, Target, and Toys "R" Us) Brio, Imaginarium, and Little Tykes are among the market leaders Low margins, high volumes Competition is based on price	Brand/Licensing Characters Advertising Discount prices

---

3	The Opportunity

Play is a child's work and education; it is how they learn and grow. Parents are more willing to pay for products that encourage or facilitate play as they become more educated about child development and the importance of play. Evidence of this trend is the growing spending on educational toys (growing at 9% for the last three years)[22], and playroom furnishings (growing at 7% per year[23]). P'kolino has identified a powerful opportunity that leverages this trend.

"Willingness to pay for products that encourage child development is on the rise."

Through our research we discovered that the basis for play - the play space and its furniture - is in need of improvement. We identified four key areas for improvement:

"The basis for play - the play space and its furniture – is in need of improvement"

- Existing playroom furniture compromises play because it is designed for miniature adults and not children.
- Playroom furniture loses its value fast because children quickly outgrow it. One size fits all in playroom furniture simply doesn't work.
- The child loses interest in the playroom furniture quickly because it has few applications.
- Lastly, and probably most obviously, play spaces are cluttered and unorganized.

"Parents want to know the right toy to buy"

We also discovered that parents are feeling the pressure of wanting to know the right toy to buy, at the right time to effectively support the development of their children.

4	Company and Product Description

4.1 Company and Description:

P'kolino, LLC is based in Woburn, MA and is a product design and marketing company. We believe play is an integral part of a child's healthy development and that current play furniture compromises play. It is our goal to improve the play experience at home. P'kolino currently has 4 product concepts under development through a partnership with the Rhode Island School of Design (RISD).

"P'kolino, improving play at home."

---

[22] According to Parents Magazine and LeapFrog SEC fillings
[23] *According to marketresearch.com*

Confidential Information
Business Plan - Dated May-2005
Woburn, Massachusetts – USA

4.2 The P'kolino Concept

P'kolino will address the opportunity in the play space by designing truly innovative play furniture and child development stage specific toy kits.

These solutions will have the following characteristics:

1. We are making play more productive by designing playroom furniture for the ones who use it, the children. **Functional.**
2. We are increasing the useful life of the furniture by designing it to grow with the child through key stages of development. **Multi-purpose.**
3. We are maintaining interest in the furniture by increasing its uses. The furniture is designed to be a toy and to transform to different activities. This transformation is made possible by add-on toy kits that change the P'kolino table from activity to activity (for example: from a Lego table to a painting table to a train table and so on). **Multi-purpose.**
4. We are organizing the play space by designing the toy kits to simply fold-up and store away in a child friendly storage unit. **Functional.**

In addition to these key differentiators P'kolino's products will be safe, beautiful and fun, as these are necessary attributes to succeed.

These solutions also address the challenges parents have of selecting the right toys for the right stage because our toy kits will be packaged for specific stages of child development.

The "grow with the child" capabilities of our products will reduce our customers' total costs of ownership and provide us with opportunities for follow-on sales. Follow-on products will be in the form of developmentally appropriate toy kits, upgrade packages and accessories.

"P'kolino's playroom furniture is designed for the child and functional for the parent. It grows and adapt to the child's stage of development and integrate with toys/activities to encourage and enhance play"

Confidential Information
Business Plan - Dated May-2005
Woburn, Massachusetts – USA

4.3 Product Description

P'kolino's first product line will include two different table designs, a storage unit, and toy kits. Constant product innovation is part of our strategy, and it will be supported with a product development effort in order to expand our current offering and include accessories and new products every year.

Initial Product line

Table A shows a very contemporary, style driven concept, with plenty of multifunctional (i.e., grow with the child) capabilities resulting from its unique modular design. It is comprised of 7 separate pieces and designed to accommodate at least four stages of the child's development. This product will be the hub for the toy kits and the foundation of our playroom offering. The product is made of wood, high-density foam and fabric.

Note: *the following are pictures of prototypes of the Table A; the actual product may be different. They are presented here for the purpose of illustrating the concept*

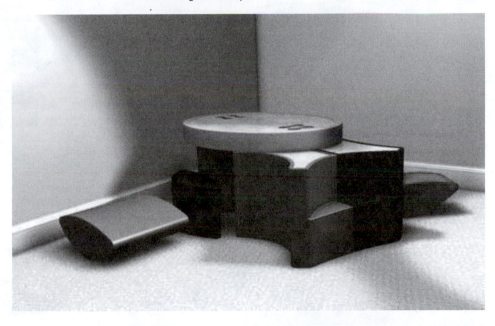

Confidential Information
Business Plan - Dated May-2005
Woburn, Massachusetts – USA

Prototypes designed at risd for P'kolino

Packaging Mode

Toddler Mode

Infant Mode

Two table Mode

Toddler Mode

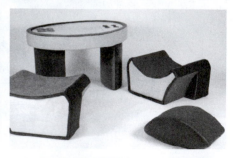

Toddler 1 Mode

Confidential Information
Business Plan - Dated May-2005
Woburn, Massachusetts – USA

Children Interacting with Table "A"

Table B shows a more playful design, with an almost endless array of configurations. This six-piece concept is designed around the belief that children can also play with the furniture itself. Most of the pieces are very light to facilitate child interaction and unit reconfiguration. This unit is intended for the more sophisticated parent, one that is willing to pay more for an exceptional product. This table is made of wood, high-density foam and fabric.

Note: *the following are pictures of prototypes of Table B; the actual product may be different. They are presented here for the purpose of illustrating the concept*

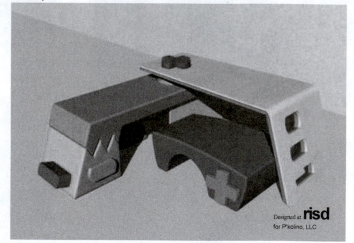

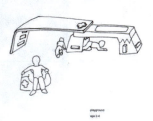

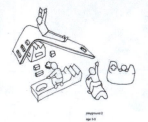

Confidential Information
Business Plan - Dated May-2005
Woburn, Massachusetts – USA

Prototypes designed at risd for P'kolino

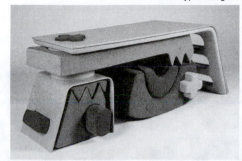

Packaging Mode

Table Mode

Table Mode

Playground Mode

Playground Mode

Table Mode

Children Interacting with Table "B"

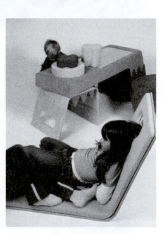

Confidential Information
Business Plan - Dated May-2005
Woburn, Massachusetts – USA

The Toy kits: These pieces are the link between the furniture and the toy. They are storage compartments that unfold on top of Table A to change the table top into an activity or toy /play enhancer. The inside of the toy kit will be designed to accommodate the requirements of a specific activity and child stage of development.

For example: if we wanted to convert the table into a toddler "Lego" table, the interior of the toy kit will have stage appropriate Lego plates attached; the unit itself will also hold the Lego blocks. When unfolded, it locks on top of Table A, transforming it into a toddler Lego table. When done, simply fold it up and store it in our storage unit.

***Note**: the following are pictures of prototypes of the Toy kits; the actual product may be different. They are presented here for the purpose of illustrating the concept*

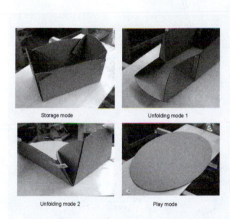

Confidential Information
Business Plan - Dated May-2005
Woburn, Massachusetts – USA

The Storage Unit: this unit will hold up to 10 toy kits and is designed to fit the design style of Table A. It allows for ease of use and accommodates a child's height and strength. The unit is made out of wood, but the drawers will be light enough so that children can open them.

Note: *the following are pictures of prototypes of the storage unit; the actual product may be different. They are presented here for the purpose of illustrating the concept*

With capabilities of holding toy kits on top of the piece or in the drawers

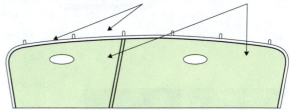

Storage Unit

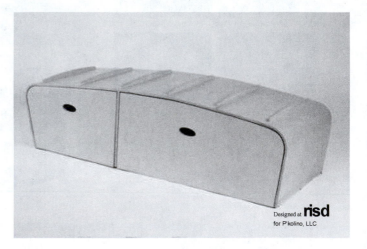

Designed at **risd**
for P'kolino, LLC

Prototypes designed at risd for P'kolino

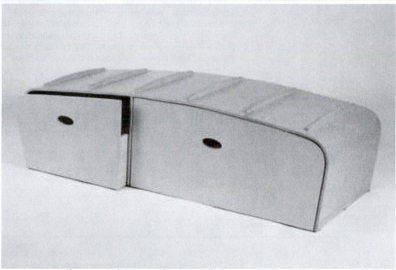

(See more pictures at the Appendix.)

Confidential Information
Business Plan - Dated May-2005
Woburn, Massachusetts – USA

4.4 Competitive Advantage

P'kolino product attributes can be summed up as follows:

"Our key differentiating benefits will be the increased functionality, the improved educational value and the multi-purpose nature of our products"

- **Multi-purpose:** modifies for changes in activity and grows with children through their stages of development,
- **Functional:** designed to better fit how children use the product (i.e. not miniature adult furniture),
- **Educational**,
- **Fun**,
- **Safe** and
- **Beautiful:** visually appealing.

(Please refer to Appendix 12.2 for details on the product attributes).

Exhibit 4-A
Key Product Attributes

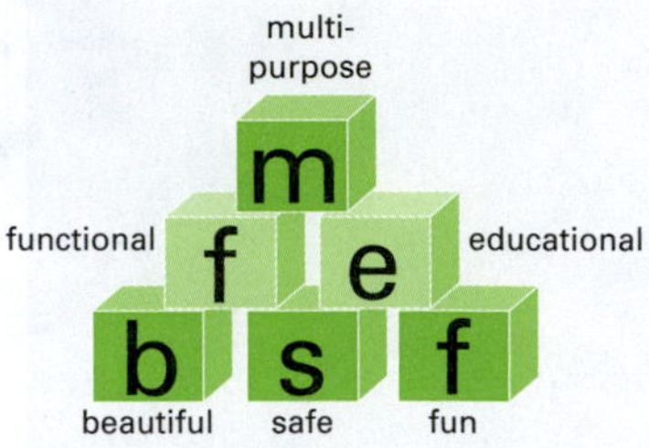

Safety, beauty and fun are absolute necessities in this market. They are the attributes that most competitors have and ones that we will build our differentiating attributes on. Our key differentiating benefits will be the increased functionality, the improved educational value and the multi-purpose nature of our products. By focusing our product development on these key attributes we will have a clear competitive advantage.

Exhibit 4-B
Attribute Comparison Chart – P'kolino's Assessment (rankings: 1 is best in the category, 10 is the worst)

Competitors	Mkt. Segment	Educational	Safe	Multipurpose	Fun	Functional	Beautiful
Pkolino	High / Mid	2	3	1	2	1	3
Brio	Mass	3	5	2	3	7	7
Fischer Price	Mass	1	2	3	1	6	8
Imaginarium	Mass	4	4	4	4	4	9
Little Tykes	Mass	5	1	6	5	2	10
Pottery Barn Kids	Mid	8	8	5	6	5	1
Land of Nod	Mid	7	7	7	7	3	2
Truck	High	9	10	8	10	8	5
Casa Kids	High	10	9	9	9	9	6
Videl	High	6	6	10	8	10	4

Confidential Information
Business Plan - Dated May-2005
Woburn, Massachusetts – USA

4.5 Our Strategy

Our strategy is designed to accomplish four key objectives:
1. Develop a strong brand → "owning the play-space at home"
2. Develop a solid customer base → " loyalty and recurring revenue"
3. Achieve predictable and sustainable growth → "good margins and repeat purchases"
4. Develop a culture of innovation → "capability of generating champion products"

Overview:
To penetrate the children's play market we will need to target influential customers and develop a strong brand. From this position we will expand our product line and extend into new markets expanding our customer base. We will maintain long relationships with our customers by offering them development stage appropriate upgrades, toy kits and accessories. This will provide us with recurring and predictable revenue.

Market Entry:
P'kolino will first target the high-end playroom market because of its favorable characteristics:
• it values innovation and brand over price,
• its consumers are market influencers, and
• it offers the highest margins.

We will focus on establishing and building a reputation for high quality products and target consumers that want the best for their children. Through a mix of public relations and grassroots marketing we will establish our products in the high-end market. Concurrently, we will develop toy-kits and accessories that integrate and complement the furniture to deliver a complete play experience.

Growth Strategy:
Growth in the high-end market is limited due to its size. In order to increase our customer base for sales of additional P'kolino products we will need to expand into the larger mid-market segment. To do this we will leverage our high-end brand reputation and introduce lower cost tables and storage with similar attributes into the larger mid-market. We expect to execute this expansion in our third year of operation.

"P'kolino targets the high-end segment because customers are market influencers, they value brand over price and offers better margins. P'kolino will later expand to the mid segment"

Confidential Information
Business Plan - Dated May-2005
Woburn, Massachusetts – USA

Exhibit 4-C
Market Penetration Strategy

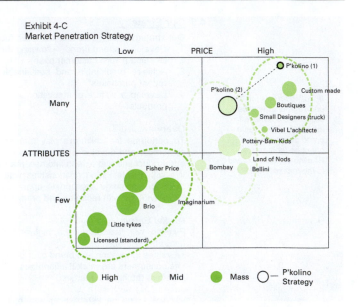

Growth will also be achieved by maintaining long term relationships with our customers to promote repeat purchases of upgrades, accessories and toy kits. Given the targeted age range (0-5 years) of our products and the average of over 2 children per household, a single customer relationship could last over 8 years with multiple sales per year. This will give us a recurring and predictable revenue stream. As we increase our customer base and product line the revenue from these repeat sales will increase dramatically.

Exhibit 4-D
Number of units sold per type of product

	Year 1	Year 2	Year 3	Year 4	Year 5
Kits	1313	3851	4818	7618	11027
Storage Units	228	477	824	1169	1533
Tables	690	1445	2551	3634	4755

Confidential Information
Business Plan - Dated May-2005
Woburn, Massachusetts – USA

Given the difficulties of the mass market, which include troubled distribution channels, intense price competition, and price sensitive customers, it is not currently part of our market extension plan. However, we will continue to evaluate it. Should conditions become more favorable, we may consider moving to this segment.

Continued product innovation is a key to this market penetration and expansion strategy. To achieve this we will focus internally on creating a culture of innovation through

• Proven product research and development methodologies,
• Creative work environments and employment arrangements, and
• Hiring proven talent that fits our dynamic, innovating culture.

5	Marketing Plan

Overview: We will bring this product to the market by targeting customers in the high-end market segment that want the best for their child. We will reach this audience through public relations, grassroots marketing, direct marketing and strategic distribution channels.

5.1 Understanding the Customer

Our primary customers will be parents who want the best for their children, and are willing and able to pay a premium for a better product.

"Our primary customers will be parents who want the best for their children, and are willing and able to pay a premium for a better product"

According to our research, our initial customers will be educated consumers who possess a strong desire to provide the best environment possible for their children to play at home. They are likely to spend a considerable amount of time researching the web for options, and have a strong bias toward friend and family recommendations (word-of-mouth).

We also see several key influencers in this purchasing decision, they are:
• "Authorities" – Experts in the field of child rearing/development. (e.g., Teachers, Care-givers, Publications).
• Children
• Grandparents
• Peers – Other parents

In addition to being influencers Grandparents are also secondary customers. Grandparents are often richer than parents, more involved and

Confidential Information
Business Plan - Dated May-2005
Woburn, Massachusetts – USA

buy large gifts for their grandchildren. The percentage of buyers of relevant children's products that are grandparents[24]:
• Games and toys 26%
• Infants' furniture 21%
• Children's furniture 16%

There are nearly 60 million grandparents in the U.S. at present and they spend an estimated $30 billion per year on their grandchildren[25]. Although grandparents exercise significant purchasing power, they are likely to ask for parent consent before they buy our products; making the parent our core customer.

5.2 Target Customer Profile

The demographics of our primary target customer are:
• House Hold Income $150K+ *
• At least one child 0-5 years old.
• Female *
• College educated* (or higher)
• Live in the Northeast*
  *These demographics have the highest indexes for infant, toddler and pre-school purchases.[26]

Additionally these consumers are:
• Not price sensitive.
• More influenced by the product benefits.
• The "concerned" parent, those who genuinely want the best for their child.
• Visionaries; they see the benefits and are going to set the trend for others in this segment to follow

These parents are in parenting groups such as Mothers Forums and Play Groups, and enroll children in early developmental classes (e.g., Creative Movements). They subscribe to parenting magazines, read parenting books or consult with Child Development/Parenting Experts. As a result, they are influenced by "Authorities" either through reading they have done themselves or by first hand interaction with teachers and care-givers.

Other customers segments in this market are the "competitive" and "compensating" parents. They have the same demographic profile but have different interests. They are the followers. The "concerned" educated parent sets the bar and these others follow.

---

[24] Source: Simmons data cited by Interep
[25] Source: Simmons data cited by Interep
[26] Source: Simmons Market Research Bureau, Fall 2002 Study of Media and Markets; Packaged Facts

Confidential Information
Business Plan - Dated May-2005
Woburn, Massachusetts – USA

As we move down market to the mid-market, the primary customer demographics and behaviors are the same except for the following.
• House Hold Income drops to $100K+
• They are influenced by the premium market
• Due to increased price sensitivity they are more pragmatic in their purchasing decisions.
• They are more likely to do their own research (more shopping around, talking to their friends). Word-of-mouth is very influential in this market.

5.3 Pricing Strategy

Market Entry – High-end pricing strategy will be market-demand pricing to maximize per sale profit. We anticipate the following price ranges per product:

"Market Entry – High-end pricing strategy will be market-demand pricing"

• Table A = $650
• Table B = $1200
• Storage Unit = $450
• Toy Kit = $50 (average)
• Providing contribution margins between 50-60%

Expansion to the mid market will require a different pricing strategy. Lower table prices (around $350) for better market penetration will increase the user/installed base and provide a larger marketing base for the toy kits and accessories.

5.4 Distribution Strategy

P'kolino's distribution goal is to have over 85%[27] of sales come from direct to the customer channels within five years. We expect that we will have to start with a distribution mix of approximately 65% of our sales through retail. Retail channels will enable customer exposure to, and interaction with, the products. As the understanding of our products grows and the brand develops we will shift the distribution mix to direct channels.

"P'kolino's distribution goal is to have over 85% of sales revenue come from channels direct to the customer"

Retail Stores: Retailers will be chosen based on their clientele. We will target non-traditional retailers that give P'kolino a "showroom" for its designs. For example, we will target The Museum of Modern Arts (MoMA) store which features uniquely designed and educationally beneficial products as one of our first outlets. This strategy will help us reach the right

---

[27] Other furniture merchants have proven success in direct channels. Land of Nod estimated at nearly 100% sales are direct; through catalog and web. Pottery Barn Kids – direct sales = 72% of its $392 million in revenue. As stated in the 11/18/04 Wall Street Journal "William Sonoma's, inc Third Quarter 2004 results."

Confidential Information
Business Plan - Dated May-2005
Woburn, Massachusetts – USA

customer and generate some exposure for our products. To encourage customer interaction with us we will offer a free Toy Kit to those who have purchased a table or storage unit through a retail channel. The customer will redeem the free kit through a direct channel (web or mail) so that we may capture relevant customer data. This customer data is critical to our direct marketing to support our migration of customers to the direct sales channels as well as to encourage future purchases.

Direct to the Customer: The goal is to have 85% of our revenue come through direct channels (web, mail and phone). Based on the proven success of other furniture merchants in direct channels (Land of Nod estimated at nearly 100% sales from direct channels like catalogs and the web[28], and Pottery Barn Kids direct sales equal 72% of its $392MM in revenue[29]) we believe this is achievable.

The primary direct channel will be through the internet as 70% of our target customers have high-speed internet access. We will also offer mail and phone orders.

We will build a website that provides consumers with an easy product review, selection and purchasing experience. Proliferation of high-speed internet access enables us to show the many benefits of our products through the latest multi-media tools (streaming video demonstrations of our products in the form of infomercials through the web).

5.5 Communication Strategy – Year 1

Overview: In the first year our communications strategy will focus on targeted marketing that can be directly attributed to sales. We will try many different tactics to determine what generates the best dollar spent to sales ratio. Additionally, we will build the brand through low cost, guerilla marketing efforts such as pubic relations and grassroots marketing.

---

[28] Our estimate based on Land of Nods business model of direct sales and no retail store to date.
[29] As stated in the 11/18/04 WSJ's "William Sonoma's, inc Third Quarter 2004 results.

Confidential Information
Business Plan - Dated May-2005
Woburn, Massachusetts – USA

Exhibit 5-A   Marketing Communications Strategy

Marketing Initiative	Estimated Cost	Estimated Table Sales	Estimated Storage Sales	Estimated Toy Kit Sales	Total Units Sold	Marketing Cost/Sale
Public Relations	$5,000	30	10	57	96	$52
GrassRoots	$5,000	80	26	151	257	$19
Word-of-Mouth	$5,000	50	17	94	161	$31
Online	$25,000	80	26	151	257	$97
Advertising	$15,000	50	17	94	161	$93
Direct Marketing	$20,000	70	23	132	225	$89
Retail Marketing Exp.	$6,000	330	109	622	1061	$6
Total $	81,000	690	228	1300	2218	$37

Public Relations

Public Relations (PR) will be at the center of our communications plan. The first phase of this plan is to utilize the PR potential of cooperation with Babson, the #1 entrepreneurship program in the country, and RISD, the #1 school of design. We have brought together these school's PR departments and have agreements to promote the story at no cost to us. To that end, we are developing a video documentary of the product design process to be used as a PR asset for the schools and P'kolino. From this PR exposure we intend to interest target market publications (e.g. Parenting Magazine) in P'kolino's story.

The PR effort will be a company priority. Management will make constant and persistent efforts to get new and compelling stories to the media. We will become a source of information for key media authorities and eventually seek product placement opportunities. Management will also seek active relationships with key media personalities to support our brand and products.

Grassroots Marketing

Grassroots Marketing will be how we get the customers interacting with the product and start the word-of-mouth engine running. We will start this grassroots effort in Boston targeting Mother's Forums, Play Groups and Day Care Centers (e.g., Bright Horizons). We will expand this effort strategically through major cities in the Northeast. These customers will be driven to the direct channels for purchase.

Word-of-Mouth

"Word-of-mouth is a powerful medium in this market."

As noted, word-of-mouth is a powerful tool is this market. We will encourage word-of-mouth by identifying key influencers in target markets and seeking to make them advocates of P'kolino products. Additionally, we will seek a child development expert endorsement to add additional

credibility. Word-of-mouth (viral marketing) tools such as referral benefits and e-mail forwarding will also be used.

Email and Web

The Web (www.pkolino.com) will be a powerful online catalog and direct purchase channel. At pkolino.com we will have product pictures, descriptions and video demonstrations to give customers as near to a physical world shopping experience as possible. The web will also be a means for us to generate awareness through targeted e-mail, keyword search, banner advertising and enhanced web advertising tools (such as rich media and dynamic banners).

Retail Sales Marketing Materials

Collateral materials such as brochures and point of purchase displays will be necessary to support our sales through retailers. Initially we will have a brochure from the RISD product development process that we can use for early discussions. We will also develop a high quality flyer for the two tables and the storage system (Storage unit and Kit). High-quality brochures and catalogs will be developed for use by retailers and distributed through mail and grassroots marketing campaigns.

Advertising

Our advertising goal will be to increase awareness of P'kolino in the high-end market. Our advertising efforts will focus on media that reach a high concentration of our target customer. The advertising will be primarily in print media because of its ability to show our product for a relatively low cost. These ads will drive customers back to pkolino.com for more information or purchase.

Direct Mail

In the first year of operation and in preparation for the 2005 Christmas season we will run a direct mail test. This mailing will target high-end customers in the Northeast to keep resources and expenses to a minimum. A successful test would result in about 1+% purchase rate of from mailed brochures. Should this test prove successful we will look to roll-out a larger direct campaign prior to the Christmas season.

5.6 Sales Strategy

The founders will serve as the sales force making direct calls to strategically identified retailers. It will be our strategy to focus on a select number of local retailers so the founders can manage these relationship and still focus on other priorities. When we expand into the mid-market (in year 3) we will hire a dedicated sales manager.

Confidential Information
Business Plan - Dated May-2005
Woburn, Massachusetts — USA

5.7 Sales and Marketing Forecast

We expect that sales will start slowly as our grassroots efforts and word-of-mouth campaign gain momentum. In the first year we expect to generate revenues of $600K based on table unit sales of 690 units. Most of these sales will be achieved through grassroots marketing efforts, web direct sales and two or three retailers in the Northeast. On average the company will spend $220 marketing dollars per each new customer, and each customer is expected to generate an average of $887 in revenues during the first year. Our expectation is that this number will drop to $451 in average revenue per customer per year as time passes.

Exhibit 5-B   Marketing Dollars per Customer

Customer Base	Year 1	Year 2	Year 3	Year 4	Year 5
New Customers	690	1,445	2,551	3,634	4,755
Customer Base	690	2,135	4,686	8,221	12,856
Customer Base Growth		409%	319%	275%	256%
Average Sales p/Customer	$887	$836	$624	$507	$451
Marketing $ p/ New Customer	$176	$246	$219	$237	$248
Marketing $ p/Customer	$176	$166	$119	$105	$92

5.8 Communications Strategy Years 2-5

In Year 2 P'kolino's communications strategy will be similar to Year 1 but with a greater focus on marketing tactics that will give us a broader reach to expand our customer base. It will also differ in that it will introduce tactics to reach existing customers for repeat purchases. We will:

- Continue our Public Relations efforts but target more national publications.
- Continue our grassroots events and word-of-mouth efforts but expand their scale.
- Look more to direct marketing, advertising and the web to increase brand awareness and drive sales.
- Begin relationship marketing and efforts to gain repeat sales from existing customers.

Year 2 will serve as preparation and learning for expansion into the mid-market where some of the guerilla tactics may still apply but our marketing efforts will have to grow to a new scale.

In Years 3-5 we will continue to shift our marketing mix to media that enable us to reach more customers. However, it will be critical to do so in an increasingly targeted manner. Direct marketing (mail and web) will be our primary medium because of its ability to target precise customer segments,

Confidential Information
Business Plan - Dated May-2005
Woburn, Massachusetts – USA

gather marketing and purchase behavior data and enable us to maintain one-to-one communications for an extended customer relationship. With this data we can become increasingly efficient at acquiring and retaining customers and thus reducing our marketing expense per sale.

It will also be important for us to maintain some advertising presence to keep brand awareness high in the general market. This awareness is necessary to help the targeted marketing break through the clutter.

6   The Team

Antonio Turco-Rivas: co-founder and Sales & Operations Manager is a Babson MBA 2005 and father of one. He has successfully launched two technology ventures in Latin America. Antonio's background also includes two years as a Corporate Finance consultant for Venezuela's most important Investment Bank and two years as a special assets Manager at the fifth largest Latin American Bank in the U.S. Antonio is a proven entrepreneur, manager and sales professional.

J.B. (Joseph B.) Schneider: co-founder and Marketing & Product Development Manager is a Babson MBA 2005 and father of three, with over 10 years of marketing strategy and communications experience. J.B. has been a project manager and led key customer acquisition and retention programs for several Fortune 500 companies. He has also been an integral part of entrepreneurial ventures and their products and marketing development.

Rhode Island School of Design (RISD): RISD's Furniture Department is ranked #1 by the US News & World Report as the best graduate industrial design program in the world, and is recognized for the creativity and quality of its students. Currently 15 designers and one Faculty member are actively designing the first versions of the P'kolino products.

Advisors: Individuals for these roles are currently being evaluated and will be filled at a later date.
- Child Development Expert
- Manufacturing Expert
- Juvenile Product Market Expert

7	Operations

7.1 <u>Operations Strategy</u>

P'kolino's core functions (design and marketing strategy) will be the main operational activities performed in-house. All other operational activities like manufacturing, packaging, shipping and some office/administrative and customer service functions will be outsourced.[30]

For manufacturing, the company has identified several manufacturers in the Bento Goncalves region in Brazil that are currently operating with underutilized (excess) capacity and have the technology and expertise to manufacture our products. We have partnered with one of these companies to manufacture our first line of products. AFECOM, our first manufacturing partner, produces over 140,000 furniture pieces per year and is well known in Europe and Latin America. Late in the 2nd year of operations, P'kolino will reexamine this strategy (when volumes increase) and evaluate alternative manufacturing options in Asia. P'kolino products are built with wood, high-density foam and fabrics. AFECOM's high density foam manufacturing technology, finishing quality, speed, volume requirements and logistic costs are better and more accommodating to P'kolino during this first stage.

The economics of the manufacturing process will be determined by our ability to negotiate with potential manufacturers. For the purpose of this document we will use industry averages[31]. For minimum orders of 150 units, the payment terms are 50% up front and 50% on shipment. For the first year of operations we plan to complete two 150 table orders. Production time is 4 weeks for prototypes and 10 weeks to manufacture and order shipment of the approved prototypes.[32]

Exhibit 7-A
Operations Cycle

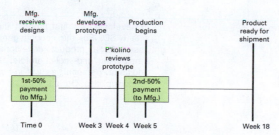

Confidential Information
Business Plan - Dated May-2005
Woburn, Massachusetts – USA

Regarding the product development process for P'kolino, it takes 9 to 12 months to develop a new product (from concept to customer[33]).

Exhibit 7-B
P'kolino Product Development Process

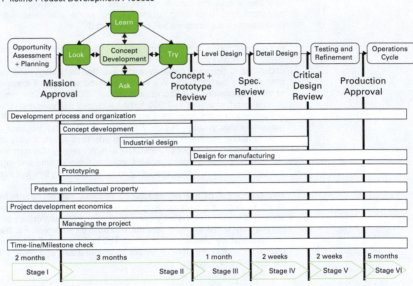

In developing the first product line, the company leveraged its relationship with RISD. For the second generation of products P'kolino will have to assemble a product development team comprised of both full-time employees and collaborators. Marketing and sales will also require additional personal, as will in-house administrative and customer service responsibilities. Our staffing plan follows:[34]

---

[33] Based on the current P'kolino product development process.
[34] Salaries are based on Boston average salaries for the respective positions according to the Career Journal (Wall Street Journal online edition) salary search (Salaryexpert.com)

Confidential Information
Business Plan - Dated May-2005
Woburn, Massachusetts – USA

Exhibit 7-C
P'kolino Staffing Plan

Staffing Plan	Year 1	Year 2	Year 3	Year 4	Year 5
CEO	1	1	1	1	1
	$40,000	$70,000	$120,000	$150,000	$220,000
COO	1	1	1	1	1
	$40,000	$70,000	$120,000	$130,000	$130,000
Product Development Manager		1	1	1	1
		$69,680	$72,467	$75,366	$78,381
Product Development Staff		1	1	1	1
		$54,080	$56,243	$58,493	$60,833
Operations and Logistics Mana			1	1	1
			$64,896	$67,492	$70,192
Marketing Manager			1	1	1
			$80,038	$83,240	$86,570
Sales Manager	1	1	1	1	1
	$35,000	$70,000	$72,800	$75,712	$78,740
Sales and Marketing Staff			1	2	2
			$58,406	$60,743	$63,172
Direct Channel Support			1	1	1
			$64,896	$67,492	$70,192
Customer Service Staff			1	1	1
			$48,672	$50,619	$52,644
Office Administration		1	1	1	1
		$33,280	$34,611	$35,996	$37,435
Accounting				1	1
				$39,370	$40,945
Advisors	1	1	1	1	1
	$20,000	$31,200	$32,448	$33,746	$35,096
Total Headcount	**4**	**7**	**13**	**14**	**14**
Total Salaries	**$135,000**	**$398,240**	**$863,334**	**$989,010**	**$1,087,371**
Benefits	$20,250	$59,736	$129,500	$148,352	$163,106
Total Compensation	**$155,250**	**$457,976**	**$992,835**	**$1,137,362**	**$1,250,476**

Benefits are estimated as a percentage of salaries (15%). Eventual hires are considered in the financial statements for the product development, sales, and marketing efforts.

7.2 <u>Development Timeline</u>

Exhibit 7-D
P'kolino Timeline

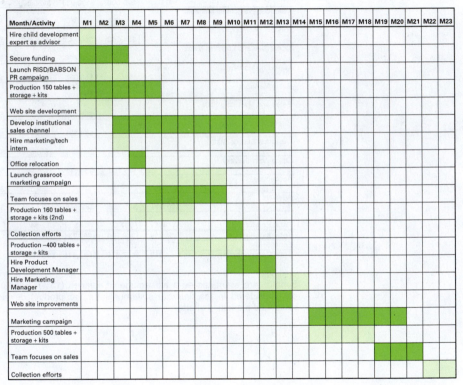

Month/Activity	M1	M2	M3	M4	M5	M6	M7	M8	M9	M10	M11	M12	M13	M14	M15	M16	M17	M18	M19	M20	M21	M22	M23
Hire child development expert as advisor	█																						
Secure funding	█	█	█																				
Launch RISD/BABSON PR campaign	█																						
Production 150 tables + storage + kits	█	█	█	█	█																		
Web site development	█																						
Develop institutional sales channel			█	█	█	█	█	█	█	█	█	█											
Hire marketing/tech intern			█																				
Office relocation				█	█																		
Launch grassroot marketing campaign					█																		
Team focuses on sales						█	█	█															
Production 160 tables + storage + kits (2nd)					█																		
Collection efforts										█													
Production ~400 tables + storage + kits							█																
Hire Product Development Manager										█	█												
Hire Marketing Manager												█											
Web site improvements												█	█										
Marketing campaign															█	█	█	█	█	█			
Production 500 tables + storage + kits																	█						
Team focuses on sales																			█	█	█		
Collection efforts																						█	

Confidential Information
Business Plan - Dated May-2005
Woburn, Massachusetts – USA

8   Critical Risks

- <u>Highly competitive market</u> – All segments of this market are highly competitive, and this is particularly true in the mid and mass segments. P'kolino will compete with a distinctive product and a different value proposition as a niche player. We will establish our brand in the high-end segment and then moving down to more competitive markets. However, the potential remains that competitor will identify our niche, before our brand has a foothold. We will rely on innovation and speed to compete if competitors attack our niche.

- <u>Copycats</u> – Intellectual property protection can be circumvented to produce competing and possibly cheaper version of our products. P'kolino will base its designs not only on beauty, but on improved usability to the end user (the child). Designing products that are better suited for children to play with, while creating identifiable differences and defining brand attributes that are more difficult to replicate.

- <u>Lawsuits</u> – Although we will take precautions to make our product safe for children it is possible that a child may injure themselves while using one of our products. We will carry product liability insurance to protect us financially from such an event but the potential brand damage must be recognized.

- <u>Product defects and/or recall</u> – P'kolino will take precautions to develop durable, reliable and safe products using materials that have proven to stand the test of time. However, it is possible given the expected useful life of these products and the use of children that these products could break creating hazards for children. Should this occur and depending on the situation P'kolino may be obligated or feel it necessary to issue a recall of the defective product. Some manufacturers carry insurance in case the defect is caused by some error during the manufacturing process. We will further explore this possibility.

- <u>Sales lower than expected</u> – In case this happens P'kolino will have the capability of adjusting production volume and shifting strategy fairly quickly because of our size and structure. We will also retain sufficient cash to support an increase in the number of inventory days.

Preparation Questions

P'kolino is a children's furniture company that was launched in 2005. As you read the business plan, keep the following questions in mind:

1. Does the business plan tell a coherent and compelling story?
2. Does the plan capture all of the learning that Antonio and JB have accumulated?
3. What three questions do you think Antonio and JB need to answer through further planning before they launch the venture?
4. What are the three strongest aspects of the plan?
5. What areas need improvement?

This business plan was prepared by Antonio Turco-Rivas and J.B. Schneider in support of their business. The original drafts were prepared in the Entrepreneur Intensity Track taught by Professor Andrew Zacharakis. © Copyright P'kolino and Babson College, 2005.

(*Source*: Jed Share/Photonical/Getty Images Inc.)

BUILDING YOUR PRO-FORMA FINANCIAL STATEMENTS

Many entrepreneurs are intimidated by numbers, even after they've gone through the business planning process. They understand their concept, they even have a good sense of the business model, but ask them to put together pro-forma financials or read an income statement and they have a panic attack.

You might feel that building your financials or understanding them isn't that important because you can always hire an accountant. Although an accountant is a useful advisor, in the pre-launch stage, the lead entrepreneur needs to understand the numbers inside and out. After all, the lead entrepreneur is the person who will be articulating her vision to potential employees, vendors, customers, and investors. If she is easily stumped by simple questions of profitability or costs, potential employees, customers, and other parties important to the new venture's success will lose confidence in her ability to execute on the concept. Financial statements serve to bridge the entrepreneur's great idea and what that idea really means in terms of dollars and cents. So, although it can be painful, learn the numbers behind your business. The rewards of gaining this deep insight are often the difference between success and failure.

This chapter written by Andrew Zacharakis.

If for no other reason, you'll need to understand the numbers so you can decide whether this business has the potential to provide you with a good living. It's too easy to get caught in a trap where a new venture is slowly draining away your investment, or where you are working, in real terms, for less than the minimum wage.[1] The goal of this chapter is to give you an introduction to entrepreneurial financial planning. Unlike existing businesses, which have an operating history, entrepreneurial ventures must develop their financials from scratch. There are no previous trends in revenue and costs that you can use as a basis to project future revenues and costs. Yet, failing to come up with solid projections may cost you your initial investment, as well as that of your investors. This chapter will help you generate sound projections.

Common Mistakes

In preparing this chapter, we sent an e-mail to several acquaintances who are professional equity investors (either angels or venture capitalists). We asked them, "What are the most common mistakes you see when you review an entrepreneur's business proposal?" We wanted to know what "red flags" made them hesitant to believe that the business could survive and succeed. Here are the six mistakes they consistently cited.

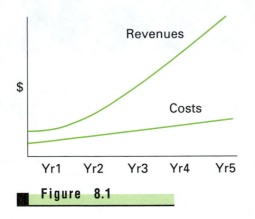

Figure 8.1

Hockey stick sales growth

1. **Not understanding the revenue drivers.** Entrepreneurs need to know what the leverage points are that drive revenues. They need to understand how many customers are likely to see the product, how many of those who see will buy, and how much, on average, they will buy each time. Although every entrepreneur claims his estimates are "conservative," 99% of the time entrepreneurs are overly optimistic in their projections. So avoid the "conservative" adjective, as it strikes most sophisticated investors as naïve.

2. **Underestimating costs.** If you were to graph the revenue and costs projections of entrepreneurs over time, you would often see revenues growing in a "hockey stick" fashion while costs slowly progress upward (see Figure 8.1). We often see revenue projections of $15 million after five years on costs of only $5 million. That is unbelievable. When we dig into those numbers, we often see that the firm has only five employees in year five. That assumes revenues per employee of $3 million, which is nearly impossible. Often, entrepreneurs underestimate how much infrastructure they need in the way of employees and physical assets to achieve that level of sales. Entrepreneurs also underestimate the cost of marketing expenditures to acquire and retain customers. Poor projections lead to cash crunches and ultimately to failure.

3. **Underestimating time to generate revenues.** Pro-forma financials often show sales occurring immediately. Typically, a business will incur costs for many months before it can generate revenue. For instance, if you are opening a restaurant, you will incur rent, inventory, and labor costs, among others, before you generate a dime in revenue. Another "red flag" is how quickly revenues will ramp up. Often, projections show the business at full capacity within the first year. That is rarely realistic.

4. **Lack of comparables.** Investors typically think about the entrepreneur's concept from their knowledge of similar businesses. They will compare your gross margins, net income margins, and other metrics to industry standards and selected benchmark companies. Yet, many entrepreneurs' projections have ratios that far exceed industry

standards, and when questioned about this above-average performance, they can't explain it. You need to understand your business model in relation to the industry and be able to explain any differences.

5. **Top-down versus bottom-up forecasting.** Investors often hear entrepreneurs claim that their revenues represent 3% of the market after year three. The implication is that it is easy to get that 3%. Investors know that, although it doesn't sound like much, the trick is how you get to that 3%. They want to see the process—the cost of acquiring, serving, and retaining the customer. Investors won't believe that you can get 3% without causing competitors to take notice and action.

6. **Underestimating time to secure financing.** The last pet peeve of investors is that entrepreneurs assume financing will close quickly. Whether entrepreneurs want to raise $25,000 or $1 million, they project it will happen in the next month. In reality, it often takes as long as six months to close a round of financing. Fred Adler, famed venture capitalist who invested in Data General, used to hand out t-shirts that said, "Happiness is a positive cash flow." Yet, if entrepreneurs are too optimistic about how quickly they can close a round of financing, they will quickly have negative cash flow, which often means they are out of business.

Understanding these pitfalls will help you generate realistic financials, and more importantly, enable you to convincingly articulate your business model so that you can sell your vision to employees, customers, vendors, and investors. Before we move on, let's take a quick overview of financial statements.

Financial Statement Overview

You'll need to include three standard financial statements in your business plan: the income statement, the statement of cash flows, and the balance sheet. Most people first want to know why there are three statements. The reason is simple. Each one provides a slightly different view of the company. Any one alone is only part of the picture. Together they provide a detailed description of the economics of your company.

The first of these statements, the **income statement**, describes how well a company conducted its business over a recent period of time, typically a quarter (three months) or a year. This indicator of overall performance begins with the company's revenues on the top line. From that accounting of sales, subtract the company's expenses. These include:

- Cost of the products that the company actually sold
- Selling, marketing, and administrative costs
- Depreciation, the estimated cost of using your property, plant, and equipment
- Interest on debts
- Taxes on profits

The bottom line of the statement (literally) is the company's profits—called *net income*. It is important to realize that the income statement represents a measurement of business performance. It is *not* a description of actual flows of money.

A company needs cash to conduct business. Without it, there is no business. The second financial statement, the **statement of cash flows**, monitors this crucial account. As the name implies, the statement of cash flows concerns itself exclusively with transactions that involve cash. It is not uncommon to have strong positive earnings on the income statement and a negative statement of cash flows—less cash at the end of the period than at the beginning. Just because you shipped a product does not necessarily mean you received the cash for it yet. Likewise, you might have purchased something like inventory or a piece of equipment that will not show up on your income statement until it is consumed or depreciated. Many noncash transactions are represented in the income statement.

What is curious (and sometimes confusing to those who have never worked with financial statements before) is the way the statement of cash flows is constructed. It starts with the bottom line (profits) of the income statement and works backward, removing all the noncash transactions. For example, since the income statement subtracted depreciation (the value of using your plant and equipment), the statement of cash flows adds it back in because you don't actually pay any depreciation expense to anybody. Similarly, the cash flow statement needs to include things that you paid for but did not use that period. For example, you might have paid for inventory that has not yet sold, or you might have bought a piece of equipment that you will depreciate over time, so you would need to put those items on the cash flow statement. After all these adjustments, you are left with a representation of transactions that are exclusively cash.

The **balance sheet** enumerates all the company's assets, liabilities, and shareholder equity. **Assets** are all the things the company has that are expected to generate value over time—things like inventory, buildings, and equipment, accounts receivable (money that your customers still owe you), and cash. **Liabilities** represent all the money the company expects to pay eventually. These include accounts payable (money the company owes its suppliers), debt, and unpaid taxes. **Shareholder equity** is the money that shareholders have paid into the company as well as the company's earnings so far. Where the income statement describes a process or flow, the balance sheet is a snapshot of accounts at a specific point in time.

All your assets come from a liability or shareholder equity. Therefore, the sum of the asset accounts must equal the sum of the liabilities and shareholder equity account.

$$\text{Assets} = \text{Liabilities} + \text{Shareholder Equity}$$

The assets are shown on the left side of the sheet with the liabilities and shareholder equity on the right. The balance sheet *always* balances. If your balance sheet does not balance, you have made a mistake.

This is of course only a partial treatment of financial statements, but it should be enough for you to understand this chapter. We strongly recommend reading John Tracy's excellent book, *How to Read a Financial Report.*[2] It is a simple, short, and easy way for novices to quickly learn the basics. The remainder of this chapter will step you through a process to generate your financials.

Building Your Pro-Forma Financial Statements

Figure 8.2 previews the points we will cover. Think of this as a checklist in developing your financials. Rigorously completing each step will lead to better financial projections and decisions. Underlying these steps are two methods: the **build-up method** and the **comparable method.** Our advice is to go through all the steps in an iterative fashion so that you not only know the numbers, but you "own the numbers."

Build-Up Method

Scientific findings suggest that people make better decisions by decomposing problems into smaller decisions. If you think about the business planning process, you are going

Build-Up Method

1. Identify all your sources of revenues
2. Determine your revenues for a "typical day"
3. Understand your revenue drivers
   a. How many customers you will serve
   b. How much product they will buy
   c. How much they will pay for each product
   d. How often they will buy
4. Validate driver assumptions
   a. Primary research (talk to customers, attend trade shows, etc.)
   b. Secondary research (industry reports, company reports, etc.)
5. Recombine. Multiply the typical day by the number of days in a year
6. Determine Cost of Goods Sold (COGS) for a typical day
7. Recombine. Multiply COGS by number of days in a year
8. Determine operating expenses by most appropriate time frame
9. Refine operating costs
10. Create preliminary income statement

Comparable Method

11. Compare revenue projections to industry metrics
12. Run scenario analysis
13. Compare common-sized cost percentages to industry averages

Building Integrated Financial Statements

13. Derive monthly income statements for first two years
14. Create balance sheet
15. Create cash flow statement

Final Steps

17. Write a two-to three-page description of financial statements

Figure 8.2

Financial construction checklist

through a series of questions that help you answer the big question: Is this an attractive opportunity? Thus, you evaluate the industry, the competition, the customer, and so forth. Based upon that analysis, you decide whether to launch the business or not. Constructing pro-forma financials is part of this process. In the build-up method, you look at the revenue you might generate in a typical day. You then multiple that day times the number of days you're open in a year to come up with your yearly revenue. You'd do a similar exercise for costs. Doing your revenues and costs on a daily basis helps you come up with more realistic annual projections.

The place to start is the income statement; the other two statements are, in part, derived from the income statement. First, identify all your revenue sources (usually, the various product offerings). Second, identify all your costs. Once you have the business broken down into its component parts, the next step is to think about how much revenue you can generate in a year, but we can decompose this estimate as well.

Revenue Projections

Instead of visualizing what you will sell in a month or a year, break it down into a typical day. For example, if you were starting the retail bookstore mentioned in the last chapter, you would estimate how many customers you might serve in a particular day and how much they would spend per visit based on the types of books and ancillary items they would buy. Figure 8.3 illustrates the process. First, it details the product mix and the average price for each item—books, maps, and other ancillary products. Second, it estimates the traffic that the store might draw on a typical day. It lists the assumptions at the bottom of the schedule. Then, it estimates how many people come into the store to buy an item and how many items they might buy. The last column gives total revenue per day by product category.

Figure 8.3 highlights critical revenue assumptions, or what we might call *revenue drivers*. Simply put, going through this exercise tells you how you will make money. It also helps you understand how you might be able to make more money. In other words, what revenue drivers can you influence? A retail shop might be able to increase its daily sales by increasing the traffic coming into the store through advertising, or increasing the number of people who buy and how much they buy through up-selling—"Can I get you anything else today?" Although this thought exercise is invaluable, your estimates are only as good as your assumptions.

How do you strengthen your assumptions? How do you validate the traffic level, the percentage of customers who buy, and so forth? The answer is through research. The first place to start is by talking to people who know the business. Talk to bookstore owners, book vendors, mall leasing agents, and others in the industry. A good way to interact with

Product/Service Description	Price	Units Sold/Day	Total Revenue
1. Books	$20	75 visitors*75%*1.5 books	$1,687.50
2. Videos	$30	75 visitors*15%*1 video	337.50
3. Maps	$50	75 visitors*10%*1 map	375.00
4. Ancillary Items	$100	75 visitors*5%*1 globe	375.00
5. Other (Postcards, Magazines, etc.)	$5	75 visitors*20%*2 items	150.00
Totals			$2,925.00

Assumptions:
Traffic — 75 visitors a day

- Books — 75% of visitors will buy 1.5 books each
- Videos — 15% of visitors will buy 1 video each
- Maps — 10% of visitors will buy 1 map each
- Globes — 5% of visitors will buy 1 ancillary item each
- Other — 20% of visitors will buy 2 misc. items

50% of sales will happen during the holiday season
30% of sales will happen during summer tourist season (May through September)

Figure 8.3

Revenue worksheet

these participants is at industry trade shows. The next thing to do is to visit a number of bookstores and count how many people come in, what portion buy, and how much they spend. Although you might feel conspicuous, there are ways to do this field research without drawing attention to yourself or interfering in the store's business. For example, you might go sit outside a bookstore and watch how many people who walk by enter the store, and how many people come out of the store with a package. Finally, talk to your expected customers, avid readers in this example. Find out how often they buy history books. Ask them how much they spend on these items a month and where they currently buy them. By going through several iterations of primary research, you will sharpen your estimates.

In addition to conducting the research yourself, you can seek out secondary sources such as industry reports and Web sites. For example, there are lots of excellent resources on retail bookstore operations such as the *Manual on Bookselling* edited by Kate Whouley and published by the American Booksellers Association (ABA) in 1996. The ABA also publishes the *ABACUS Financial Study*, which provides detailed information on all sorts of financial metrics in the industry.

Once you are comfortable that your assumptions are sound, you can then multiply the typical day by the number of days of operation in the year to arrive at yearly revenue estimates. This is a first cut. Clearly, a typical day varies by the time of the year. People do much of their shopping around the December holiday season. Therefore, most pro-forma projections for new companies typically show monthly income figures for the first two years. This allows the entrepreneur to manage seasonality and other factors that might make sales uneven for the business.

Cost of Goods Sold

Once you have your revenue projections, you next consider costs. An income statement has two categories of costs—cost of goods sold and operating expenses. **Cost of goods sold (COGS)** is the direct costs of the items sold. For a bookstore, COGS is the cost of inventory that is sold in that period. As a first cut, you might assume that COGS for a retail outlet would be around 50% (assumes a 100% markup). Since sales from Figure 8.3 were approximately $3,000 per day, COGS would be around $1,500.

As with revenue assumptions, you need to sharpen your COGS assumptions. Use a similar schedule as in Figure 8.3 to refine COGS by product (see Figure 8.4). After some investigation at Hoovers.com, you find that the gross margin on books is only 27% for the likes of Amazon.com, Borders, Barnes & Noble, and Books-A-Million. On other items you might sell, other companies' gross margins (for MTS and TransWorld Entertainment) are around 31%. Although these margins are lower than first estimated, these companies have a different business model—high volume, lower margins. Where will your bookstore operate? If it is high volume, your margins should be similar to these companies' margins. If you choose to offer a premium shopping experience, meaning highly knowledgeable sales staff and unique historical artifacts, you would likely achieve higher margins. Remember that your financials need to mirror the story you related in your business plan—be consistent. Figure 8.4 shows the price per item, the gross margin (revenue minus COGS) per item, the revenues per item (from Figure 8.3), and then calculates COGS in dollar terms [revenue times (1-COGS)]. Since the gross margins per items differ, the overall gross margin is 44%.

Operating Expenses

In addition to direct expenses, businesses also incur operating expenses, such as marketing, salaries and general administration (SG&A), rent, interest expenses, and so forth.

Product/Service Description	Price	Gross Margin	Revenue	COGS
1. Books	$20	40%	$1,687.50	$1,012.50
2. Videos	$30	50%	337.50	168.75
3. Maps	$50	50%	375.00	187.50
4. Ancillary Items	$100	50%	375.00	187.50
5. Other (Postcards, Magazines, etc.)	$5	50%	150.00	75.00
Totals			$2,925.00	$1,631.25

Total Revenue	$2,925.00
COGS	1,631.25
Gross Profit	$1,293.75
Gross Profit Margin	44%

Figure 8.4

Cost of goods worksheet

The build-up method forecasts those expenses on a daily, monthly, or yearly basis as appropriate (see Figure 8.5). For example, you might get rental space for your store at $30 per/square foot per year depending on location. You might need about 3,000 square feet, so your yearly rent would be $90,000 (put in the yearly expense column). You'll pay your rent on a monthly basis, so you would show a rent expense of $7,500 in the month-to-month income statement. At this point, however, you are just trying to get a sense of the overall business model and gauge whether this business can be profitable; showing it on a yearly basis is sufficient.

Based on the first cut, your bookstore is projecting operating expenses of approximately $315,000 per year. However, the "devil is in the details," as they say, and one problem area is accurately projecting operating costs, especially labor costs. Constructing a headcount schedule is an important step in refining your labor projections (see Figure 8.6). Although the store is open on average 10 hours per day, you can see from the headcount table that Sunday is a shorter day and the store is open 11 hours on the other days. The store operates with a minimum of two employees at all times (including either the assistant manager or the store manager). During busier shifts, the number of employees reaches a peak of six people (afternoon shift on Saturday, including both managers). Looking at the calculation below the table, you see that the new wage expense is about $66,000, a bit higher than the first estimate. This process of examining and reexamining your assumptions over and over is what leads to compelling financials.

Just as you refine the hourly wage expense, you need to also refine other expenses. For example, marketing expenses are projected to be $12,000. Create a detailed schedule of how you plan on spending those advertising dollars. If you refer back to the last chapter, Figure 7.7a has a schedule of detailed expenses. This illustrates another point: *financial analysis is really just the mathematical expression of your overall business strategy.* Everything you write about in your business plan has revenue or cost implications. As investors read business plans, they build a mental picture of the financial statements, especially the income statement. If the written plan and the financials are tightly correlated, they have much greater confidence that the entrepreneur knows what she is doing.

The Preliminary Income Statement

Once you have forecasted revenues and expenses, you put them together in an income statement on p. 319. Figure 8.3 forecasts average daily sales of almost $3,000. You need

Expense	Daily	Monthly	Yearly	Total
Store Rent			90,000	$90,000
Manager Salary			60,000	$60,000
Assistant Manager			40,000	$40,000
Hourly Employees	176			$63,360
Benefits	21		12,000	$19,603
Bank Charges			10,530	$10,530
Marketing/Advertising		1,000		$12,000
Utilities		333		$4,000
Travel			1,000	$1,000
Dues			1,000	$1,000
Depreciation		833		$10,000
Misc.			4,000	$4,000
				$0
Totals				$315,493

Assumptions:

Rent — 3,000 sq. ft. at $30/year = $90,000
Hire 1 manager at $60,000/ year
Hire 1 assistant manager at $40,000
Store is open from 9 a.m. to 7 p.m. daily, so 10 hours per day
Need 2 clerks when open and 1 clerk an hour before and after open
2 clerks × 10 hours × $8/ hour + 1 clerk × 2 hours × $8/ hour
Benefits are 12% of wages and salaries
Bank charges about 1% of sales
Advertising — $1,000/ month
Travel — $1,000/ year to attend trade shows
Dues — $1,000/ year for trade association
Depreciation — $100,000 of leasehold improvements and equipment, depreciated straight line over 10 years

Figure 8.5

Operating expenses worksheet

to annualize that figure. You can expect the store to be open on average 360 days per year (assuming that the store might be closed for a few days such as Christmas and Thanksgiving). Note that the first line is called Total Revenues and then shows the detail that creates that total revenues line by itemizing the different revenue categories. COGS are handled in the same manner as revenues; you multiply the typical day by 360 days to get the annual total.

After adjusting the hourly wages per the headcount table (which also means adjusting employee benefits), take the operating expenses worksheet (see Figure 8.5) and put it into the income statement. If you believe that you can secure debt financing, put in an interest expense. For the initial forecast, leave out interest expense because you are still not certain what amount of financing you will need to launch the business. Next, compute taxes. Make sure to account for federal, state, and city taxes as applicable. Note that the right column calculates the expense percentage of total revenues. This is called a *common-sized income statement*. Although you have been rigorous in building up your statement, you can further validate it by comparing your common-sized income statement to the industry standards, which is where you start using the comparable method.

	Mon.	Tues.	Wed.	Thurs.	Fri.	Sat.	Sun.	Total
Store Hours	10:00–9:00	10:00–9:00	10:00–9:00	10:00–9:00	10:00–9:00	10:00–9:00	11:00–5:00	
Hours Open	11	11	11	11	11	11	6	72
Shift 1	9:30–1:30	9:30–1:30	9:30–1:30	9:30–1:30	9:30–1:30	9:30–1:30	10:00–2:00	
Shift 2	1:30–5:30	1:30–5:30	1:30–5:30	1:30–5:30	1:30–5:30	1:30–5:30	1:00–5:00	
Shift 3	5:30–9:30	5:30–9:30	5:30–9:30	5:30–9:30	5:30–9:30	5:30–9:30		
Shift 1 Hrs.	4	4	4	4	4	4	4	
Shift 2 Hrs.	4	4	4	4	4	4	4	
Shift 3 Hrs.	4	4	4	4	4	4	0	
Total Shift Hours	12	12	12	12	12	12	8	80
Staff Headcount								
Shift 1	2	2	1	2	1	4	3	
Shift 2	1	1	0	1	1	4	4	
Shift 3	1	1	1	2	4	4	0	
Total Staff	4	4	2	5	6	12	7	40
Total Hours Worked								
Shift 1	8	8	4	8	4	16	12	
Shift 2	4	4	0	4	4	16	16	
Shift 3	4	4	4	8	16	16	0	
	16	16	8	20	24	48	28	160
Mgr.	0	0	8	8	8	8	8	40
Asst. Mgr.	8	8	8	0	8	8	0	40

Total hourly employee hours/week = 160
Hourly rate $8/hour   8
Total wages per week $1,280
Total wages per year $66,560

■ Figure 8.6

Headcount table

Comparable Method

How can you tell whether your projections are reasonable? In the **comparable method,** you look at how your company compares to industry averages and benchmark companies. The first thing to do is gauge whether your revenue projections make sense and then see whether your cost structure is reasonable. Comparables help you validate your projections. For instance, a good metric for revenue in retail is sales per square foot. The bookstore is projecting sales of $1 million in 3,000 square feet, which equates to $351 per square foot. Secondary research into the average per bookstore[3] and also into what one or two specific bookstores achieve is a good place to start.[4] For example, $351 is in line with independent bookstores ($350/square foot), but higher than Barnes & Noble ($243/square foot).

The projections seem reasonable considering that you will be selling certain items like maps, which have a much higher ticket price than books, but there are a couple of caveats to this estimate. First, it is likely to take a new bookstore some time to achieve this level of sales. In other words, the income statement that has been derived might be more appropriate for the second or third year of operation. At that point, the bookstore will have built up a clientele and achieved some name recognition.

Second, you should run some scenario analyses. Does this business model still work if your bookstore only achieves Barnes & Noble's sales per square foot ($243)? Also run a few other scenarios related to higher foot traffic, recession, outbreak of war (sales of books

Total Revenues	$1,053,000	100%
Historical Books	607,500	
Videos	121,500	
Maps	135,000	
Ancillary Items	135,000	
Other	54,000	
Total COGS	**$587,250**	**55.8%**
Historical Books	364,500	
Videos	60,750	
Maps	67,500	
Ancillary Items	67,500	
Other	27,000	
Gross Profit	**$465,750**	**44.2%**
Operating Expenses		
Store Rent	90,000	
Manager Salary	60,000	
Assistant Manager	40,000	
Hourly Employees	66,560	
Benefits	19,987	
Bank Charges	10,530	
Marketing/Advertising	12,000	
Utilities	4,000	
Travel	1,000	
Dues	1,000	
Depreciation	10,000	
Misc.	4,000	
Total Operating Expenses	**$319,077**	**30.3%**
Earnings from Operations	**$146,673**	**13.9%**
Taxes	**$58,669**	**5.6%**
Net Earnings	**$88,004**	**8.4%**

Figure 8.7

Income statement

on Islam increased with September 11 and escalating tensions in the Middle East), and other contingencies. Having some validated metrics, such as sales per square foot, helps you run different scenarios and make sound decisions about whether to launch a venture in the first place, and then how to adjust your business model so that the venture has the greatest potential to succeed.

Other metrics that are easily obtainable for this type of establishment include *sales per customer* or *average ticket price*. Figure 8.3 shows expected sales of $2,925 per day from 75 unique store visitors. That translates into an average transaction per visitor of $39. However, not every visitor will buy; many people will just come in and browse. Figure 8.3 assumed that 75% of visitors would buy a book and a lower percentage would buy other items. If that percentage holds true, 56 people will actually purchase something each day. Thus, the average receipt is $52. This average ticket price is considerably higher than Barnes & Noble's rate of $27.

As with all your assumptions, you have to gauge whether a higher ticket price is reasonable. An entrepreneur might reason that the bookstore isn't discounting its books and is also selling higher priced ancillary goods. Run scenario analyses again to see whether your bookstore survives if its average ticket price is closer to Barnes & Noble's. In other words, see what happens to the model overall when you change one of the assumptions, the average selling price in this case.

After you're comfortable with the revenue estimate, you next need to validate the costs. The best way is to compare your common-sized income statement with the industry averages or some benchmark companies. It is unlikely that your income statement will exactly match the industry averages, but you need to be able to explain and understand the differences. Figure 8.8 looks at the common-sized income statement for your store and for Barnes & Noble. The first discrepancy appears in the COGS. Your store projects COGS of 56% of revenue, whereas Barnes & Noble is projecting 73%. Why would Barnes & Noble's COGS be so much higher? Upon further investigation, you find that Barnes & Noble includes occupancy costs like rent and utilities in COGS. If you add

	The History Shoppe		Barnes & Noble (in Millions)		(Fy 2002) Industry Average
Total Revenues	$1,053,000	100%	$4,871	100%	100%
Books	607,500				
Videos	121,500				
Maps	135,000				
Ancillary Items	135,000				
Other	54,000				
Total COGS	$587,250	55.8%	$3,557	73.0%	60.0%
Books	364,500				
Videos	60,750				
Maps	67,500				
Ancillary Items	67,500				
Other	27,000				
Gross Profit	$465,750	44.2%	$1,314	27.0%	40.0%
Operating Expenses					
Store Rent	90,000				
Manager Salary	60,000				
Assistant Manager	40,000				
Hourly Employees	66,560				
Benefits	19,987				
Bank Charges	10,530				
Marketing/Advertising	12,000				
Utilities	4,000				
Travel	1,000				
Dues	1,000				
Depreciation	10,000		$150		
Misc.	4,000				
Total Operating Expenses	$319,077	30.3%	$1,062	21.8%	37.5%
Earnings from Operations	$146,673	13.9%	$252	5.2%	2.5%
Taxes	$58,669	5.6%			
Net Earnings	$88,004	8.4%			

Figure 8.8

Comparable analysis

your store's $90,000 rent plus $4,000 in utilities into COGS, COGS becomes 65% of revenue, still lower. However, COGS of 65% is in line with the specialty retail industry rate of 67%.[5] The reasoning for this discrepancy is similar to that of the higher ticket price. Your specialty bookstore's COGS is likely lower than Barnes & Noble because it is not a discount book seller (meaning it earns higher margins on every book sold than Barnes & Noble). You also plan to sell other retail items that generate higher margins.

Since the gross profit margin is the inverse of COGS—revenue minus COGS—the explanation provided for COGS also holds for the gross margin. Barnes & Noble's gross margin is 27% versus 35% for The History Shoppe (with rent included in COGS).

When you compare operating expenses for the two companies, you can see that your bookstore is projecting operating expenses to be 30% of revenue versus 22% for Barnes & Noble. However, you must once again adjust for the occupancy expense, because you included occupancy in operating expenses whereas Barnes & Noble includes it in COGS. With that adjustment, your operating expenses are about 21% of revenue, almost the same as Barnes & Noble.

Based on the comparable analysis, it appears that your projections are reasonable. Your earnings from operations are higher (13.9%) than Barnes & Noble (5.2%) and the independent book store average (2.5%), but that may be explained by the higher gross margins and the fact that you haven't yet included any interest expenses. For example, if you use debt financing for any of your startup expenses, such as leasehold improvements, you will have an interest expense that would reduce your net income margin to be more in line with the comparable companies.

This exercise has primarily used benchmark companies, but industry averages also provide useful comparable information. The *Almanac of Business and Industrial Financial Ratios* published by Aspen Publishers, Inc., or *Industry Norms and Key Business Ratios* published by Dun and Bradstreet are excellent sources to use as starting points in building financial statements relevant to your industry. Specifically, these sources help entrepreneurs build income statements by providing industry averages for costs of goods sold, salary expenses, interest expenses, and other costs. Again, your firm will differ from these industry averages, but by going through scenario analyses and understanding your business model, you should be able to explain why your firm differs.

Building Integrated Financial Statements

Once you have a baseline income statement, the next step is to construct monthly income and cash flow statements for two years (followed by years 3 through 5 on a yearly basis), and a yearly balance sheet for all five years. Five years is standard for many business plans, because it usually takes new firms some time to build sales and operate efficiently. Five years also gives the entrepreneur a sense of whether her investment of time and energy will pay off. Can the business not only survive, but also provide the kind of financial return to make the opportunity costs of leaving an existing job worthwhile?

The income statement, cash flow, and balance sheet are the core statements for managing any business. Changes in one statement affect all others. Understanding how these changes affect your business can mean the difference between survival and failure. Many entrepreneurs will find their businesses on the verge of failure, even if they are profitable, because they fail to understand how the income statement is related to the cash flow and balance sheet. How is that possible, you might ask?

Entrepreneurs need to finance rapid growth. For example, a bookstore needs to buy inventory in advance of selling to its customers. The owner needs to ensure that he has enough books and other products on hand that he doesn't lose a sale because a customer is frustrated that the book isn't in stock. (Americans are notorious for wanting instant gratification.) Yet, having inventory on hand drains cash. If the bookstore expects sales of $500,000 in December, then it must have $280,000 worth of inventory at the end of November ($500,000 × 56%—the average COGS). How does the bookstore pay for this? Internal cash flow? Vendor financing? Equity? Having strong pro-forma financials helps the entrepreneur anticipate these needs far enough in advance to arrange the appropriate financing.

The earlier example illustrates why a new business wants to show the income statement and cash flow on a monthly basis for the first two years, the most vulnerable period in a new venture's life. It takes time to build up your clientele (during which you earn lower revenues), learn how to efficiently operate (during which you have higher costs), develop a track record so you can secure vendor financing (remember the cash flow implications), and understand seasonality (which will make demand vary). For instance, monthly projections allow the entrepreneur to anticipate and understand any seasonality that might happen in the business. In addition to the financing issue discussed previously, seasonality affects other key operations and decisions. For example, your bookstore will need to hire more salespeople during the holiday season. Integrated financials can help the entrepreneur plan for that hiring increase.

In sum, it is critical to show the first two years of pro-forma projections on a monthly basis because this is when a company is most vulnerable to failure. Monthly forecasts help you understand these issues and prepare for them. For years 3 through 5, yearly projections are sufficient because the further out one goes, the less accurate the projections become. Nevertheless, your longer-term projections communicate your vision of the upside potential of your opportunity. The exercise of going through the projection process is more important than the accuracy of the projections. The process helps you gain a deeper understanding of the business and whether you should pursue the opportunity or not.

The earlier example indicated how changes in one statement affect other statements. Figure 8.9[6] formally shows how the pro-forma financials are integrated. You can see that the income statement drives the balance sheet, which drives the cash flow statement (although the cash from financing and uses of cash from the cash flow statement feed back into the balance sheet). We'll briefly touch on how to move from our base income statement to a full set of financial pro-forma projections, but going into a step-by-step process is beyond the scope of this chapter.

Income Statement

The base income statement generated shows the level of operations that might be achievable in year 3 or 4. Thus, you need to make a number of adjustments to generate the other years. First, you need to create monthly statements for the first two years. That means you need to understand the seasonality of your business and the sales cycle. One mistake that many entrepreneurs make is showing revenues from the first day they launch the business, but remember, most new businesses incur expenses well in advance of generating revenue. In thinking about the bookstore, you would consider the business

EXHIBIT D-MASTER EXHIBIT
(Dollar amounts in thousands)

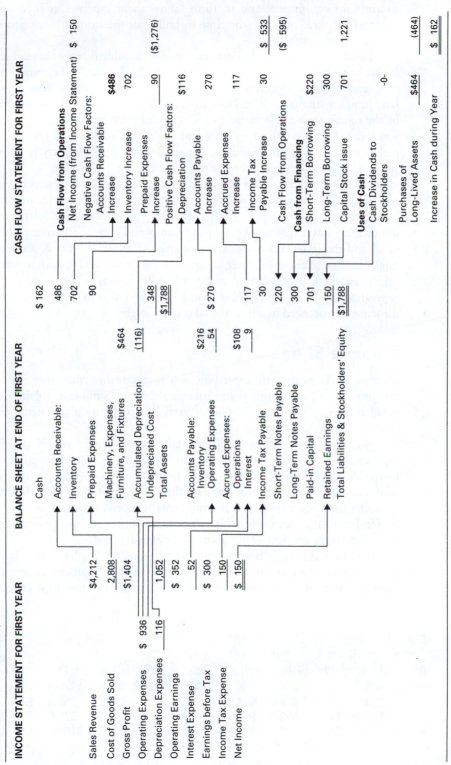

INCOME STATEMENT FOR FIRST YEAR

Sales Revenue	$4,212
Cost of Goods Sold	2,808
Gross Profit	$1,404
Operating Expenses	$ 936
Depreciation Expenses	116
	1,052
Operating Earnings	$ 352
Interest Expense	52
Earnings before Tax	$ 300
Income Tax Expense	150
Net Income	$ 150

BALANCE SHEET AT END OF FIRST YEAR

Cash	$ 162
Accounts Receivable:	
Inventory	486
Prepaid Expenses	702
	90
Machinery, Expenses, Furniture, and Fixtures	$464
Accumulated Depreciation	(116)
Undepreciated Cost	348
Total Assets	$1,788
Accounts Payable:	
Inventory	$216
Operating Expenses	54
	$ 270
Accrued Expenses:	
Operations	$108
Interest	9
Income Tax Payable	117
	30
Short-Term Notes Payable	220
Long-Term Notes Payable	300
Paid-in Capital	701
Retained Earnings	150
Total Liabilities & Stockholders' Equity	$1,788

CASH FLOW STATEMENT FOR FIRST YEAR

Cash Flow from Operations	
Net Income (from Income Statement)	$ 150
Negative Cash Flow Factors:	
Accounts Receivable Increase	**$486**
Inventory Increase	702
Prepaid Expenses Increase	90
	($1,276)
Positive Cash Flow Factors:	
Depreciation	$116
Accounts Payable Increase	270
Accrued Expenses Increase	117
Income Tax Payable Increase	30
	$ 533
Cash Flow from Operations	($ 595)
Cash from Financing	
Short-Term Borrowing	$220
Long-Term Borrowing	300
Capital Stock issue	701
	1,221
Uses of Cash	
Cash Dividends to Stockholders	-0-
Purchases of Long-Lived Assets	$464
	(464)
Increase in Cash during Year	$ 162

Figure 8.9

Interrelated financial statements[6]

launched soon after the first round of financing has closed. At this point, the entrepreneur can start spending money to establish the business. For instance, he might sign a lease, contract for equipment, and so forth. Show those expenses as incurred. Thus, show expenses for three months (the time to build out the store before opening) before you show your first revenue.

The next consideration in generating your monthly forecasts is seasonality. Revenues in retail are not evenly spread across the 12 months. Figure 8.10 estimates how sales might be spread for a retail operation. The make-or-break time is the holiday season, and you see sales jumping dramatically in November and December. Another important spike might be the tourist season (if you were to locate your store in Boston, demand might jump if you focused on Revolutionary War and colonial goods). Based on these projections, it makes sense to lease and build out the retail space in the January to March time frame when sales levels are expected to be low.

Another consideration is how long it will take your new business to build its clientele and ramp up its revenues. You are projecting sales of $350 per square foot once you hit your optimal operating position. In the first year of operation, that number might be significantly lower, say $200 per square foot, well below the Barnes & Noble average of $243 and the independent bookstore average of $350. In year 2, a reasonable estimate might be that average sales per square foot hit $250, and finally in year 3 you might hit the independent bookstore average of $350. And as you've seen, the business is not generating sales for the first three months of year 1 due to the time it takes to build out the store, so you need to adjust the sales accordingly.

Balance Sheet

The *balance sheet* can be the most difficult to integrate into your other financial statements. For pro-forma projections, yearly balance sheets are sufficient. Again, going into great detail is beyond the scope of this chapter, but there are a few items that often cause confusion.

First, will your business sell on credit? If so, it will record accounts receivable. Figure 8.9 shows how your sales from the income statement drive your accounts receivable on the balance sheet (some portion of those sales), which then drives an accounts receivable increase on the cash flow. While you would record the sale when the customer took possession, you may not actually receive payment until some point in the future. Recording the sale would have a positive impact on your profitability, but it would not affect your cash flow until the customer actually paid.

If your business is buying equipment, land, or a plant, or is adding leasehold improvements, you will have an asset of plant and equipment. A common error is to show this as a capital expense, meaning that it appears in full on your income statement

(000)												
Jan.	**Feb.**	**Mar.**	**Apr.**	**May**	**June**	**July**	**Aug.**	**Sept.**	**Oct.**	**Nov.**	**Dec.**	**Year**
3%	2%	3%	4%	6%	7%	9%	8%	5%	3%	10%	40%	100%
Year 1			$24.0	$36.0	$42.0	$54.0	$48.0	$30.0	$18.0	$60.0	$240.0	$552.0
Year 2 $22.5	$15.0	$22.5	$30.0	$45.0	$52.5	$67.5	$60.0	$37.5	$22.5	$75.0	$300.0	$750.0
Year 3 $31.5	$21.0	$31.5	$42.0	$63.0	$73.5	$94.5	$84.0	$52.5	$31.5	$105.0	$420.0	$1,050.0

Figure 8.10

Seasonality projections

the moment you contract for the work. This assumes you will fully use that equipment within the year (or whatever length your income statement covers). To accurately reflect the acquisition of the asset, instead show the full outflow of money as it occurs on your cash flow and then depreciate the cost per year of life of the asset on your income statement. You would also have an accumulated depreciation line item on your balance sheet showing how much of the asset has been used up. Referring back to Figure 8.5, you see the bookstore is projecting leasehold improvements of $100,000, which it expects to use up over 10 years ($10,000 per year or $833 per month).

Accounts payable acts in a similar manner to accounts receivable, except that it is a loan to your company from a supplier (see Figure 8.9). Once the new store is able to secure vendor financing on inventory, for example, it will show the COGS as it sells its books, but it may not have to pay the publisher until later (assuming that the book is a fairly fast moving item). So the expense would show up on your income statement but not on your cash flow—until you paid for it. Until then, it is held in accounts payable on the balance sheet.

The final problem area is retained earnings. Entrepreneurs know that the balance sheet should *balance*. A common error is to use the retained earnings line to make the balance sheet balance. Retained earnings is actually:

Previous Retained Earnings + Current Period Net Income

— Dividends Paid That Period

If you find that your balance sheet isn't balancing, the problem is often in how you have calculated accounts receivable or accounts payable. Balancing the balance sheet is the most frustrating aspect of building your financial pro-forma statements. Yet, hard-wiring the retained earnings will ultimately lead to other errors, so work through the balancing problem as diligently as possible.

Cash Flow Statement

If you have constructed your financial statements accurately, the **cash flow statement** identifies when and how much financing you need. You might want to leave the financing assumptions empty until after you see how much the cash flow statement implies you need (see Figure 8.11). One of the many benefits of this process is that it will help you determine exactly how much you need, so as to protect you from yielding too much equity or acquiring too much (or not enough) debt. The bookstore cash flow shows some major outlays as the store is gearing up for operation, such as inventory acquisition and equipment purchases. You can also see from the cash flow statement that the business is incurring some expenses prior to generating revenue ($17,000 listed as net earnings). This net earnings loss is reflected on the company's monthly income statement and is primarily attributable to wage expenses to hire and train staff.

You can see that in the first six months, the cash position hits a low of −$316,000. This is how much money you need to raise in order to launch the business. For a new venture, most of the money will likely be in the form of equity from the entrepreneur, friends, and family. However, the entrepreneur may be able to secure some debt financing against his equipment (which would act as collateral if the business should fail). In any event, once you recognize your financing needs, you can devise a strategy to raise the money necessary to start the business. To provide some buffer against poor estimates, you might raise $350,000. This amount would show up on both the cash flow and balance sheet.

	Month 1	Month 2	Month 3	Month 4	Month 5	Month 6
OPERATING ACTIVITIES						
Net Earnings	(17,000)	(12,882)	(2,244)	(7,079)	(1,277)	8,394
Depreciation	1,115	1,115	1,115	1,115	1,115	1,115
Working Capital Changes						
(Increase)/Decrease Accounts Receivable	0	(64)	(88)	40	(48)	(80)
(Increase)/Decrease Inventories	(104,562)	(19,605)	32,676	(39,211)	(65,351)	71,886
(Increase)/Decrease Other Current Assets	0	(230)	(316)	144	(172)	(287)
Increase/(Decrease) Accts Pay & Accrd Expenses	0	3,215	4,421	(2,010)	2,411	4,019
Increase/(Decrease) Other Current Liab	0	3,445	4,737	(2,153)	2,584	4,306
Net Cash Provided/(Used) by Operating Activities	(120,446)	(25,005)	40,301	(49,154)	(60,737)	89,354
INVESTING ACTIVITIES						
Property & Equipment	(101,000)	0	0	0	0	0
Other						
Net Cash Used in Investing Activities	(101,000)	0	0	0	0	0
FINANCING ACTIVITIES						
Increase/(Decrease) Short-Term Debt						0
Increase/(Decrease) Curr. Portion LTD						0
Increase/(Decrease) Long-Term Debt						0
Increase/(Decrease) Common Stock						0
Increase/(Decrease) Preferred Stock						0
Dividends Declared						0
Net Cash Provided/(Used) by Financing	0	0	0	0	0	0
INCREASE/(DECREASE) IN CASH	(221,446)	(25,005)	40,301	(49,154)	(60,737)	89,354
CASH AT BEGINNING OF PERIOD	0	(221,446)	(246,451)	(206,150)	(255,304)	(316,041)
CASH AT END OF PERIOD	(221,446)	(246,451)	(206,150)	(255,304)	(316,041)	(226,687)

Figure 8.11

Cash flow statement

Putting It All Together

Once you have completed the financial spreadsheets, write a two- to three-page explanation to precede them. Although you understand all the assumptions and comparables that went into building the financial forecast, the reader needs the background spelled out. Describing the financials is also a good exercise in articulation. If your reader understands the financials and believes the assumptions are valid, you have passed an important test. If not, work with the reader to understand her concerns. Continual iterations strengthen your financials and should give you further confidence in the viability of your business model.

This section of the planning process should include a description of the key drivers that affect your revenues and costs so that the reader can follow your pro-forma financials. This description is typically broken down into four main sections. First, the "overview" paragraph briefly introduces the business model.

The first subsection should discuss the income statement. Talk about the factors that drive revenue, such as store traffic, percentage of store visitors that buy, average ticket price, and so forth. It is also important to talk about seasonality and other factors that might cause uneven sales growth. Then discuss the expense categories, paying attention to the cost of goods sold and major operating expense categories, such as rent, interest expense, and so forth. Based on your description, the reader should be able to look at the actual financials and understand what is going on. The key focus here is to help the reader follow your financials; you don't need to provide the level of detail that an accountant might if he were auditing your company.

The next subsection should discuss the cash flow statement. Here you focus on major infusions of cash, such as equity investments and loan disbursements. It is also good to describe the nature of your accounts receivables and payables. How long, for instance, before your receivables convert to cash? If you are spending money on leasehold improvements, plant and equipment, and other items that can be depreciated, you should mention them here. Typically, the discussion of the cash flow statement is quite a bit shorter than the discussion of the income statement. The final subsection discusses the balance sheet. Here you would talk about major asset categories, such as the amount of inventory on hand and any liabilities that aren't clear from the previous discussion.

CONCLUSION □

Going through these exercises allows you to construct a realistic set of pro-forma financials. It's a challenge, but understanding your numbers "cold" enables you to articulate your business to all stakeholders, so you can build momentum toward the ultimate launch of your business. Just as we said in the last chapter that the business plan is a live document, so too are the financial statements a set of live documents. They are obsolete immediately after they come off the printer. As you start your launch process, you can further refine your numbers, putting in actual revenues and expenses as they occur, and adjusting projections based on current activity. Once the business is operating, the nature of your financial statements changes. They not only help you assess the viability of your business model; they'll also help you gauge actual performance and adjust your operations based on that experience.

Although most entrepreneurs tell us that drafting the financials induces some pain, they also concede that going through the process is gratifying and rewarding. They learn to master new management skills, build their business, and protect their investment. So dig in.

YOUR OPPORTUNITY JOURNAL

Reflection Point	Your Thoughts...
1. What are your revenue sources? How can you influence these revenues (what are your drivers)?	
2. Identify some companies that you can benchmark. What are their revenue sources? How do they drive revenue?	
3. Refine your projections. Who can you talk to that is knowledgeable about your business (customers, vendors, competitors)? What secondary sources can you find (Hoovers.com, RMA database)?	
4. Compare your common-sized financials to those of your benchmark company. Can you validate or explain differences between you and the benchmark company?	
5. Are there other metrics you can use (sales per employee or sales per square foot) to verify your projections?	
6. What happens to the viability of your business when you run some scenario analyses based on the different metrics you've identified?	

WEB EXERCISE

Look for some comparison metrics (the *Business Week* site is useful, e.g., http://www.businessweek.com/smallbiz/bizminer/bizminer.htm, but see if you can find others). How do your sales per employee figures match the benchmark reports? How does your pro-forma balance sheet match up to some of the presented ratios? Can you explain any differences?

NOTES

1 By minimum wage, we mean that the money the entrepreneur can take out of the business is less on an hourly basis than the minimum wage.

2 Tracy, John. *How to Read a Financial Report,* 6th Edition. Hoboken, NJ: John Wiley & Sons. 2004.

3 *1999 ABACUS Financial Study.*

4 Look for publicly traded companies on your favorite database, such as http://SEC.gov.

5 http://bizstats.com/otherretail.htm.

6 Figure 8.9 is a reprint of Exhibit D from *How to Read a Financial Report,* Second Edition, by John Tracy. New York: John Wiley & Sons, 1983.

P'kolino Financials

We revisit the P'kolino business plan in this chapter. Study the financial projections and evaluate how realistic you think they are.

These financials were prepared by Antonio Turco-Rivas and J. B. Schneider in support of their business. The original drafts were prepared in the Entrepreneur Intensity Track taught by Professor Andrew Zacharakis. © Copyright P'kolino and Babson College, 2005.

P'kolino™

Business Plan
May-2005

Prepared by:
J.B. Schneider &
Antonio Turco-Rivas N.

Contact Information:
Phone: (781) 497-0913
Email: jb@pkolino.com
          atrn@pkolino.com
Address:
600 West Cummings Park
Suite 5350
Woburn, MA 01801

Confidential Information
Business Plan - Dated May-2005
Woburn, Massachusetts – USA

9	Financial Plan

9.1 Basis of Presentation

This plan contains five-year projected financial information for our company. While management believes that the assumptions underlying the projections are reasonable, there can be no assurance that these results can be realized or that actual results will meet management expectations. It is important to notice that our first month of operations is expected to be April 2005, causing the holiday season to be reflected in the financial statement as the third quarter in our projections. Monthly financial statements for the first two years are available on request.

9.2 Income Statement Assumptions – Revenues

The number of tables sold each month is the main driver of revenues for P'kolino. This number is estimated based on the expected outcome of the marketing efforts the company has planned for each year. At the beginning the company will sell two different types of tables targeting the high-end segment of the market. However, at the beginning of the third year the company plans to introduce a third table that will target the mid segment.

For the Storage Unit, management assumes that 30% of those customers that purchase tables are likely to buy the Storage Unit as well. The Storage Unit is designed so that it holds up to 10 toy kits (three are offered as a bundled package with the Storage Unit).

Every time a new table is sold, a new customer has been gained. P'kolino projections assume that one out of every two customers will purchase one Toy Kit every 12 months for a period of 3 to 4 years. Gift purchases of the Toy Kits are also estimated as a percentage of the existing customer base. One out of every two existing customers will trigger (influence) one Toy Kit gift purchase every 12 months.

Accessories will enter the revenue stream at the 2nd year of operations. It is estimated that as the product line expands accessories will eventually represent up to 25% of our sales.

The numbers of new customers are expected to increase at an average rate of 35% for years 3,4 & 5 for products targeting the high-end segment and at 45% for those targeting the mid-segment of the market (as a benchmark Pottery Barn Kids sales increased 35% in 2004).

Exhibit 9-A
The Playroom Furniture Market

# Units	Year 1	Year 2	Year 3	Year 4	Year 5
Tables	**690**	**1,445**	**2,551**	**3,634**	**4,755**
Table A	449	939	1,268	1,712	2,311
Table B	242	506	683	922	1,244
Table C			600	1,000	1,200
Storage Unit	**228**	**477**	**824**	**1,169**	**1,533**
Toy Kits	**1,313**	**3,851**	**4,814**	**7,618**	**11,027**
Accessories	**0**	**9,925**	**15,606**	**21,068**	**28,442**

P'kolino will remain in the high-end segment of the market for its first 2 years of operations and has priced its products accordingly. All products are priced as a function of both their manufacturing costs and their marketing positioning strategies. At year 3 a $400 table with a 45% contribution margin will be introduced to the mid-segment.

Exhibit 9-B
Prices and Manufacturing Cost

Product	Selling Price	Manufacturing Cost	Contribution in US$	Contribution as % of Price
Table A	$650	$260	$390	60%
Table B	$1,200	$260	$940	78%
Table C	$300	$130	$170	57%
Storage Unit	$450	$140	$310	69%
Toy kit version 1	$30	$10	$20	67%
Toy kit version 2	$55	$26	$29	53%
Accessories	$60	$28	$32	53%

P'kolino will sell its products both online (direct) and through specialty retailers. Retailers are expected to markup our products by 50% (according to our primary research). Thus, our wholesale price will need to account for this markup. Management estimates that even though 80% (30% after year 2) of the units sold will be sold through retailers, only 23% of the revenue will come from this distribution channel. The percentage sold through retailers will drop over time as P'kolino gains brand recognition and further develops its direct distribution channel.

Exhibit 9-C
% of Revenues by Distribution Channel

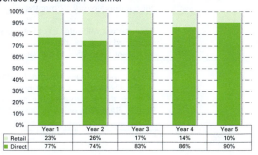

	Year 1	Year 2	Year 3	Year 4	Year 5
Retail	23%	26%	17%	14%	10%
Direct	77%	74%	83%	86%	90%

As stated earlier in this document the Toy kits and accessories are the main vehicles for generating recurrent revenue from existing customers.

Exhibit 9-D
Revenue Mix (% of revenue by type of product)

Revenue Mix	Year 1	Year 2	Year 3	Year 4	Year 5
Tables	79%	57%	54%	55%	54%
Storage	13%	9%	11%	11%	11%
Kits	8%	9%	6%	7%	8%
Accessories	0%	25%	28%	27%	27%

Revenues for P'kolino will increase significantly during the winter holiday season. As is the case in the toy industry, playroom products are seasonal and more than 50% of total revenues will be generated during this period. Summer will be the second best season because children are out of school and spending more time at home.

Exhibit 9-E
Seasonal Sales – Number of tables sold per month Year 1 & 2

Confidential Information
Business Plan - Dated May-2005
Woburn, Massachusetts – USA

Exhibit 9-F
Revenue Forecast

Revenue per year	Year 1	Year 2	Year 3	Year 4	Year 5
Tables	**$481,501**	**$1,008,361**	**$1,589,988**	**$2,274,038**	**$3,134,920**
Table A	$220,101	$460,937	$711,113	$976,358	$1,354,885
Table B	$261,400	$547,424	$698,876	$997,680	$1,420,035
Table C	$0	$0	$180,000	$300,000	$360,000
Storage Unit	**$79,871**	**$167,267**	**$334,359**	**$474,521**	**$656,146**
Toy Kits	**$50,772**	**$158,621**	**$189,781**	**$310,663**	**$462,848**
Accessories	**$0**	**$449,603**	**$807,891**	**$1,109,235**	**$1,539,278**
Total Revenues	**$612,145**	**$1,783,851**	**$2,922,020**	**$4,168,457**	**$5,793,191**
Revenue Growth		191%	64%	43%	39%

Exhibit 9-G
Revenue Monthly Forecast

Monthly Revenues	Year 1	Year 2	Year 3	Year 4	Year 5
Month 1	$0	$39,182	$64,182	$91,560	$127,247
Month 2	$0	$67,346	$110,316	$157,373	$218,712
Month 3	$0	$101,212	$165,789	$236,510	$328,694
Total 1st Quarter	$0	$207,741	$340,287	$485,443	$674,653
Month 4	$0	$124,420	$203,804	$290,740	$404,062
Month 5	$25,314	$29,350	$48,076	$68,584	$95,316
Month 6	$50,627	$30,775	$50,411	$71,915	$99,945
Total 2nd Quarter	$75,941	$184,545	$302,292	$431,240	$599,323
Month 7	$50,627	$127,270	$208,474	$297,402	$413,320
Month 8	$102,680	$366,132	$599,739	$855,567	$1,189,040
Month 9	$255,986	$729,413	$1,194,808	$1,704,473	$2,368,823
Total 3rd Quarter	$409,293	$1,222,815	$2,003,020	$2,857,442	$3,971,183
Month 10	$36,602	$57,750	$94,596	$134,948	$187,547
Month 11	$39,453	$39,327	$64,420	$91,899	$127,719
Month 12	$50,856	$71,674	$117,405	$167,485	$232,766
Total 4th Quarter	$126,911	$168,751	$276,421	$394,333	$548,032
Total for year	**$612,145**	**$1,783,851**	**$2,922,020**	**$4,168,457**	**$5,793,191**
Average Revenue					
by Month	$51,012	$148,654	$243,502	$347,371	$482,766
by Quarter	$153,036	$445,963	$730,505	$1,042,114	$1,448,298

Note: the Third quarter represents the holiday season.

9.3 Income Statement Assumptions – Cost of Sales

Our business model assumes that manufacturing of all P'kolino products will be outsourced to Brazil and then eventually to an Asian manufacturer. The average cost of sales will be 47% of revenues. Cost of sales is estimated based on manufactured units.

Exhibit 9-H
Cost of Sales

Manufacturing Costs	Year 1	Year 2	Year 3	Year 4	Year 5
Table A	$116,610	$244,205	$329,677	$445,064	$600,836
Table B	$62,790	$131,495	$177,518	$239,650	$323,527
Table C	$0	$0	$84,000	$140,000	$168,000
Storage Unit	$31,878	$66,759	$115,325	$163,668	$214,652
Kits	$25,818	$85,988	$95,251	$157,954	$237,232
Accessories	$0	$277,900	$436,968	$589,907	$796,374
Other	$29,193	$54,504	$200,357	$219,636	$245,602
Total COGS	**$266,289**	**$860,851**	**$1,439,096**	**$1,955,879**	**$2,586,223**

9.4 Income Statement Assumptions – Expenses

Expenses for P'kolino are centered on three main areas: 1) Sales and Marketing, 2) General Administration Expenses and 3) Research and Development.

For the first year, sales and marketing expenses are close to 20% of sales. Developing our website, generating initial marketing materials and a direct mail campaign are the main uses of these funds. Again after year 3, marketing efforts intensify as P'kolino makes an effort to enter the mid-segment of the market with a new product.

Over time, General and Administration expenses converge towards the industry average. However, P'kolino's business model calls for a lean organization that concentrates on sales, product development and marketing. Management will make every effort to outsource all areas of the business not directly related to the core competency of the company. By year 5, the company will have 10 employees. The company will open an office at a business incubator during its first and second year of operations. P'kolino will relocate to a new facility by the end of year 2.

Product development (or R&D) is central to the P'kolino business model. It will require 10% of revenues during the first and second year and 9% on average thereafter (the R&D for the first year has been partially funded and executed prior to starting operations). During years 1&2 the company will

Confidential Information
Business Plan - Dated May-2005
Woburn, Massachusetts – USA

develop a table for the mid-segment of the market as well as new Toy kits and accessories.

Other expenses such as legal expenses, insurance, etc. are estimated based on industry averages.

Exhibit 9-I
Projected Financial Statements

	Year 1	%	Year 2	%	Year 3	%	Year 4	%	Year 5	%
Revenues	$612,145	100%	$1,783,851	100%	$2,922,020	100%	$4,168,457	100%	$5,793,191	100%
Cost of Sales	$266,289	44%	$860,851	48%	$1,439,096	49%	$1,955,879	47%	$2,586,223	45%
Gross Profit	**$345,856**	**56%**	**$923,000**	**52%**	**$1,482,924**	**51%**	**$2,212,578**	**53%**	**$3,206,968**	**55%**
Expenses										
Sales & Marketing	**$121,379**	**20%**	**$354,768**	**20%**	**$559,581**	**19%**	**$861,467**	**21%**	**$1,180,662**	**20%**
Salaries & Benefits	40,250	7%	80,500	5%	242,932	8%	322,503	8%	335,403	6%
Advertising	15,000	2%	50,000	3%	60,000	2%	150,000	4%	300,000	5%
Direct Mail Campaign	20,000	3%	150,000	8%	150,000	5%	250,000	6%	350,000	6%
Free Kit	15,008	2%	31,429	2%	42,429	1%	57,279	1%	77,327	1%
Web Expenses Marketing	25,000	4%	25,000	1%	35,000	1%	40,000	1%	60,000	1%
Other Marketing Expenses	6,121	1%	17,839	1%	29,220	1%	41,685	1%	57,932	1%
General and Administration	**$103,333**	**17%**	**$201,583**	**11%**	**$369,867**	**13%**	**$424,276**	**10%**	**$531,254**	**9%**
Salaries & Benefits	90,000	15%	178,250	10%	319,534	11%	367,276	9%	449,587	8%
Depreciation	1,333	0%	3,333	0%	10,333	0%	17,000	0%	21,667	0%
Rent & Utilities	5,000	1%	10,000	1%	20,000	1%	20,000	0%	35,000	1%
Corporate Office	7,000	1%	10,000	1%	20,000	1%	20,000	0%	25,000	0%
Product Development (R&D)	**$61,000**	**10%**	**$227,324**	**13%**	**$288,017**	**10%**	**$318,938**	**8%**	**$450,095**	**8%**
Salaries & Benefits		0%	142,324	8%	148,017	5%	153,938	4%	160,095	3%
Testing	1,000	0%	5,000	0%	10,000	0%	15,000	0%	20,000	0%
Product Development	60,000	10%	80,000	4%	130,000	4%	150,000	4%	270,000	5%
Other Expenses	**$91,304**	**15%**	**$112,096**	**6%**	**$120,551**	**4%**	**$129,211**	**3%**	**$169,830**	**3%**
Legal	15,000	2%	20,000	1%	25,000	1%	25,000	1%	25,000	0%
Relocation		0%	10,000	1%		0%		0%		0%
Other	1,000	0%		0%		0%		0%		0%
Insurance	15,304	3%	44,596	2%	73,051	3%	104,211	2%	144,830	3%
Interest	60,000	10%	37,500	2%	22,500	1%		0%		0%
Total Expenses	**$377,016**	**62%**	**$895,771**	**50%**	**$1,338,016**	**46%**	**$1,733,892**	**42%**	**$2,331,841**	**40%**
Profit Before Taxes	**($31,160)**	**-5%**	**$27,229**	**2%**	**$144,908**	**5%**	**$478,686**	**11%**	**$875,127**	**15%**
Taxes		0%	5,446	0%	28,982	1%	95,737	2%	175,025	3%
Net Income	**($31,160)**	**-5%**	**$21,783**	**1%**	**$115,926**	**4%**	**$382,949**	**9%**	**$700,102**	**12%**

9.5 Balance Sheet Assumptions

P'kolino outsources manufacturing of their products allowing it to minimize investment on fixed assets. Inventory is assumed at 45 days (meaning 8 inventory turns per year, equal to the industry average according to Hoover's online database). Management believes it will be able to maintain this level due to its emphasis on direct distribution.

Accounts receivable will average 30 days due to expected receivables from sales to retailers. Direct sales will have limited receivables, occurring mostly by credit card.

Table designs will be considered intangible assets and supported by constant product development efforts.

Accounts payable will be 25 days during the first few years because vendors will require most of our purchases to be paid in advance. Over time, accounts payable will lengthen as we develop a credit history.

Exhibit 9-J
Projected Balance Sheet Statements

	Year 1	Year 2	Year 3	Year 4	Year 5
ASSETS					
Cash	$ 289,628	$ 133,388	$ 106,278	$ 338,241	$ 1,036,185
Accounts Receivable	$ 50,856	$ 71,674	$ 92,140	$ 131,444	$ 182,677
Inventory	$ 70,582	$ 91,338	$ 138,210	$ 197,167	$ 274,016
Total current assets	**$ 411,066**	**$ 298,400**	**$ 336,629**	**$ 666,852**	**$ 1,492,879**
Net fixed assets	$ 6,595	$ 18,476	$ 37,357	$ 44,571	$ 47,119
Fixed Assets	*$ 8,000*	*$ 24,000*	*$ 54,000*	*$ 79,000*	*$ 104,000*
Fixed Assets Acum. Deprec.	*$ 1,405*	*$ 5,524*	*$ 16,643*	*$ 34,429*	*$ 56,881*
Other assets	$ 6,103	$ 8,601	$ 11,057	$ 15,773	$ 21,921
Net Intangibles	$ 50,700	$ 50,700	$ 50,700	$ 50,700	$ 50,700
Patents + Intangibles	$ 50,700	$ 50,700	$ 50,700	$ 50,700	$ 50,700
Total assets	**$ 474,463**	**$ 374,177**	**$ 435,743**	**$ 777,897**	**$ 1,612,619**
LIABILITIES					
Accounts and trade notes payable	$ 42,719	$ 60,206	$ 77,398	$ 110,413	$ 153,449
Income Taxes payable	$ -	$ 5,446	$ 28,982	$ 95,737	$ 175,026
Other	$ 12,205	$ 17,202	$ 22,114	$ 31,547	$ 43,843
Total current liabilities	**$ 54,924**	**$ 82,854**	**$ 128,493**	**$ 237,697**	**$ 372,317**
Convertible LT debt	$ 400,000	$ 250,000	$ 150,000	$ -	$ -
Total liabilities	**$ 454,924**	**$ 332,854**	**$ 278,493**	**$ 237,697**	**$ 372,317**
	$ -	$ -	$ -	$ -	$ -
Paid-in capital	$ 50,700	$ 50,700	$ 50,700	$ 50,700	$ 50,700
Retained earnings	$ (31,161)	$ (9,377)	$ 106,550	$ 489,499	$ 1,189,602
Total liabilities and net worth	**$ 474,463**	**$ 374,177**	**$ 435,743**	**$ 777,897**	**$ 1,612,619**

9.6 Funding Assumptions

The company will fund its operations through equity and convertible long-term debt. Founders have issued $50.7K worth of equity. Proceeds will be used to pay for the product development of the initial product line. Additional funding will come in the form of long-term convertible debt (convertible into equity at the lender's discretion) for up to $400K over the next five years, at a 15% annual interest rate. Friends and family will be the primary investors initially.

Exhibit 9-K
Use of Funds (average)

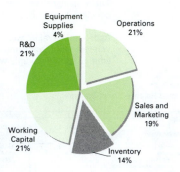

9.7 Cash Flow Assumptions

Investments will maintain positive cash flow the first 2 years. After this period, P'kolino estimates that it will generate enough cash from operations to repay the long-term debt and finance future growth.

Exhibit 9-M
Projected Cash Flow Statements

	Year 1	Year 2	Year 3	Year 4	Year 5
Net Income	$ (31,161)	$ 21,784	$ 115,927	$ 382,950	$ 700,102
Accounts receivable (increase)	$ (50,856)	$ (20,818)	$ (20,467)	$ (39,304)	$ (51,233)
Inventory (increase)	$ (70,582)	$ (20,755)	$ (46,873)	$ (58,956)	$ (76,849)
Depreciation	$ 1,405	$ 4,119	$ 11,119	$ 17,786	$ 22,452
Other Liabilities	$ 12,205	$ 4,996	$ 4,912	$ 9,433	$ 12,296
Accounts Payable	$ 42,719	$ 17,487	$ 17,192	$ 33,015	$ 43,036
Tax payable	$ -	$ 5,446	$ 23,536	$ 66,756	$ 79,288
Operating Cash Flow	$ (96,270)	$ 12,259	$ 105,346	$ 411,680	$ 729,092
Purchase of PPE	$ (8,000)	$ (16,000)	$ (30,000)	$ (25,000)	$ (25,000)
Other Assets	$ (6,103)	$ (2,498)	$ (2,456)	$ (4,716)	$ (6,148)
Change Intangibles	$ (50,700)	$ -	$ -	$ -	$ -
Cash from Investing	$ (64,803)	$ (18,498)	$ (32,456)	$ (29,716)	$ (31,148)
Convertible LT debt	$ 400,000	$ (150,000)	$ (100,000)	$ (150,000)	$ -
Issued Stock	$ 50,700	$ -	$ -	$ -	$ -
Cash from Finance	$ 450,700	$ (150,000)	$ (100,000)	$ (150,000)	$ -
Change in cash	$ 289,628	$ (156,240)	$ (27,110)	$ 231,963	$ 697,944
Cash Flow:	$ 289,628	$ 133,388	$ 106,278	$ 338,241	$ 1,036,185

9.8 Breakeven Analysis

Exhibit 9-N
Break-even vs. Revenues

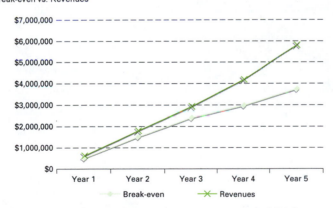

Preparation Questions

1. How do the common-sized income sheet ratios compare to industry standards? Can you explain the variances in a way that makes the projections seem sound?

2. How do the revenues per employee compare to industry standards? Again, can you explain the variances?

3. Do the financial projections accurately capture all the expenses that are implied in the written plan (refer back to previous chapter)?

4. Is the proposed financing sufficient to cover the company's cash flow needs? What happens if sales are not as high or quick to materialize as expected?

The 2006 Nobel Peace Prize was awarded to Professor Muhammad Yunus and the Grameen Bank, which he founded in 1983 to dispense tiny loans to Bangladeshi women who used the money to transform their lives by buying tools to start small businesses. (2004 Photo) (*Source*: Shafig. alam/AFP/Getty Images News and Sports Services)

CHAPTER 9

FINANCING ENTREPRENEURIAL VENTURES WORLDWIDE

A new business searching for capital has no track record to present to potential investors and lenders. All it has is a plan—sometimes written, sometimes not—that projects its future performance. It means that it is very difficult to raise debt financing from conventional banks because they require as many as three years of actual—not projected—financial statements and assets that adequately cover the loan. Hence, almost every new business raises its initial money from the founders themselves and what we call informal investors: family, friends, neighbors, work colleagues, and strangers; a few raise it from lending institutions, primarily banks; and a miniscule number raise it from venture capitalists, who are sometimes called *formal investors*. This chapter examines funding from entrepreneurs themselves, informal investors, and venture capitalists in the U.S. and throughout the

This chapter written by William D. Bygrave.

world. Chapter 10 will explain how to raise equity capital, and Chapter 11 will look at nonequity sources of financing, including banks.

Before we examine conventional means of financing startups in medium- and higher-income nations, we'll begin by looking at how many would-be entrepreneurs eking out subsistence livings in some of the most impoverished regions of the world are being financed by microcredit organizations.

Entrepreneurial Financing for the World's Poorest

"To 'make poverty history,' leaders in private, public, and civil-society organizations need to embrace entrepreneurship and innovation as antidotes to poverty. Wealth-substitution through aid must give way to wealth-creation through entrepreneurship."[1] But the challenge is, where do nascent entrepreneurs living in poverty get any money to start a microbusiness? In Africa, for instance, 600 million people live on less that $3 per day based on purchasing power parity. For China the number may be 400 million, and India 500 million.

La Maman Mole Motuke lived in a wrecked car in a suburb of Kinshasa, Zaire, with her four children. If she could find something to eat, she would feed two of her children; the next time she found something to eat, her other two children would eat. When organizers from a microcredit lending institution interviewed her, she said that she knew how to make chikwangue (manioc paste), and she only needed a few dollars to start production. After six months of training in marketing and production techniques, Maman Motuke got her first loan of U.S. $100 and bought production materials.

Today, Maman Motuke and her family no longer live in a broken-down car; they rent a house with two bedrooms and a living room. Her four children go to school consistently, eat regularly, and dress well. She currently is saving to buy some land in a suburb farther outside the city and hopes to build a house.[4]

Conventional banking is based on the principle that the more you have, the more you can borrow. It relies on collateral, which means that a bank loan must be adequately covered by assets of the business or its owner, or in many cases both. But half the world's population is very poor, so about 5 billion people are shut out of banks. For example, fewer than 10% of adults in many African countries have bank accounts. Even in Mexico the number is scarcely 20%.

Microfinancing

In 1976 in the village of Jobra, Bangladesh, Muhammad Yunus, an economist, started what today is the Grameen Bank. This was the beginning of the microfinance concept, which is best known for its application in rural areas of Bangladesh, but that has now spread throughout the world. Yunus believes that access to credit is a human right. According to him, "one that does not possess anything gets the highest priority in getting a loan." And he practices what he preaches. Even beggars can get loans from the Grameen Bank. They are not required to give up begging, but are encouraged to take up an additional income-generating activity, such as selling popular consumer items door to door or at the place of begging.[2] The bank provides larger loans, called *microenterprise loans,* for "fast-moving members." By the end of 2004, almost 300,000 Bangladeshis had taken microenterprise loans. The average loan was U.S. $344, and the biggest was U.S. $17,195 to purchase a truck. The loan recovery rate is almost 99%, which is remarkable because the bank relies entirely on personal trust and not collateral.[3]

Microfinancing is now available in many nations. It is generally agreed that it is a powerful tool in the fight to reduce poverty in poorer nations. The following is a microfinance success story from Mexico, excerpted from an article in *The Financial Times.*[5]

Oscar Javier Rivera Jimenez stands on the corrugated steel roof of his warehouse and surveys the urban wasteland around him. "We constructed all of this with the money from Compartamos," he says. "Before, there was nothing. We built it ourselves. That made it possible. And the help of God as well, which is the secret of everything." Compartamos is Latin America's biggest provider of microfinance—small loans aimed at budding entrepreneurs, targeted at areas of severe poverty.

Mr. Rivera, who set up his business six years ago in the municipality of Chimalhuacan, one of the poorest slums on the outskirts of Mexico City, is one of Compartamos' most successful clients. Starting at the age of 21 by delivering parts on a tricycle—much of the area lacks paved roads, while both water and electricity supplies are unreliable—he now controls an impressive warehouse, where builders can buy an array of different girders. He recently opened a second branch about a mile away. He now has nine employees, four from outside the family—showing that his brand of enthusiastic entrepreneurship might yet rescue the neighborhood.

Compartamos ("Let's share" in Spanish) started life as a nongovernmental organization, and gained its seed capital from multilateral funds. Now with more than 300,000 clients, its next plan is to convert itself into a bank, so that it can take in savings and also start to offer life insurance. Its portfolio grew by 58% last year, and Carlos Danel and Carlos Labarthe, its joint chief executives, intend to keep that growth going. By 2008, they aim to have one million clients. Compartamos average loan is for $330,[6] and as is typical of microcredit elsewhere in the world, only 0.6% of its loans are 30 or more days late.

Microcredit for the Poorest of the Poor

The Microcredit Summit Campaign was held in 1997. Its aim was "to reach 100 million of the world's poorest families, especially the women of those families, with credit for self-employment and other financial and business services by the year 2005." The Campaign defines the "poorest" people as those who are in the bottom half of those living below their nation's poverty line, or any of the 1.2 billion people in the world who live on less than $1 per day based on purchasing power parity. The Microcredit Summit Campaign Report 2004 provides the data shown in Figure 9.1.[7]

Women accounted for 82.5% of the total number of "poorest" clients. Assuming 5 persons per family, the 54.8 million poorest clients reached by the end of 2003 affected some 274 million other family members.[8] Figure 9.2 shows the relationship between the number of families living in absolute poverty in each region (living on under one dollar a day adjusted for purchasing power parity) and the number of poorest families reached in each region at the end of 2003.

In 2005—the International Year of Microcredit—the 1997 Microcredit Campaign came close to achieving its goal of reaching 100 million of the world's poorest families.

Year	Number of institutions reporting	Total number of clients reached	Number of 'poorest' clients reported
1997	618	13,478,797	7,600,000
1998	925	20,938,899	12,221,918
1999	1065	23,555,689	13,779,872
2000	1567	30,681,107	19,327,451
2001	2186	54,932,235	26,878,332
2002	2572	67,606,080	41,594,778
2003	2931	80,868,343	54,785,433

Figure 9.1

Growth in the implementation of microcredit, 1997–2003

	Asia (in millions)	Africa & Middle East (in millions)	Latin America & Caribbean (in millions)	Europe (in millions)
Number of Poorest Families	157.8	61.5	12.1	3.5
Number Reached by Microfinance	48.8	4.8	1.1	0.06
Percent Coverage	31%	7.8%	9.1%	1.7%

Source: Daley-Harris, S., *State of the Microcredit Summit Campaign Report 2004*, 2004, Microcredit Summit Campaign, www.microcreditsummit .org/pubs/reports/socr/2004/SOCR04.pdf.

■ **Figure 9.2**

Microfinancing by region 2003

Put another way, assuming 5 persons per family, microcredit reached 500 million, or 42% of the world's poorest persons.

In the following sections we will examine how entrepreneurs in all financial circumstances, from the poor in developing nations to the well-off in developed nations, raise money to start their new businesses.

Entrepreneurs and Informal Investors

Self-funding by entrepreneurs, along with funding from informal investors, is the lifeblood of an entrepreneurial society. Founders and informal investors are sometimes referred to as the **4 Fs:** founders, family, friends, and foolhardy investors. One of the most noteworthy findings of the Global Entrepreneurship Monitor (GEM) studies is the amount and extent of funding by the 4 Fs. The prevalence rate of informal investors among the adult population of all the GEM nations combined is 3.6%, and the total sum of money they provide to fund entrepreneurship is equal to 1.2% of the combined GDP of those nations. The entrepreneurs themselves provide 65.8% of the startup capital for their new ventures, so assuming that the remainder of the funding comes from informal investors, the funding from entrepreneurs and informal investors combined amounts to 3.5% of the GDP of all the GEM nations.

The informal investor prevalence rate among the GEM nations participating in the 2005 study is shown in Figure 9.3. Among the G7 nations, the United States has the highest prevalence rate (4.7%) and Japan has the lowest (0.9%). Those two nations also have the highest and lowest TEA (total entrepreneurial activity) rates, from which we might conclude that the prevalence rate for informal investors and the TEA rates among all nations are strongly correlated. However, it turns out that the correlation is not perfect. Brazil, for example, has a high TEA rate and a very low informal investor prevalence rate.

The annual amount of funding provided by informal investors as a percent of the GDP of the GEM 2005 nations is shown in Figure 9.4. The total amount of funding is the product of the number of informal investors and the average amount that each investor provides annually. Hence, a nation with a high prevalence rate and a high average amount per informal investor relative to its income per capita—New Zealand, for instance—ranks high in Figure 9.4. Norway, on the other hand, ranks low because, although it has a high prevalence rate, it has a low average amount per informal investor relative to its GDP. Of course, it is to be expected that in general the wealthier a nation, the higher the average amount per investor. Nonetheless, there is considerable variation,

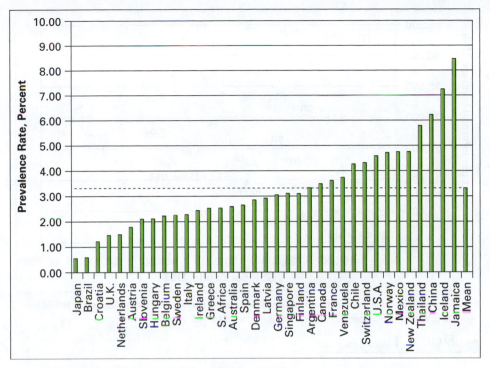

Figure   9.3

Informal investor prevalence rate, 2005

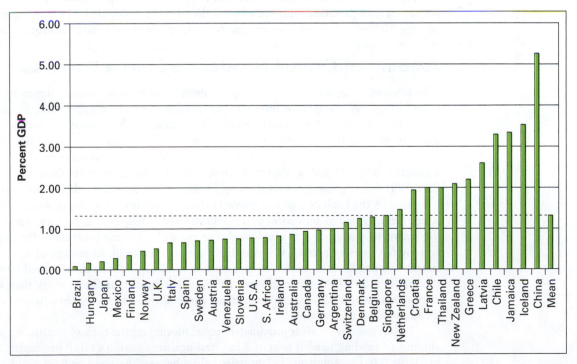

Figure   9.4

Annual informal investment percent GDP, 2005

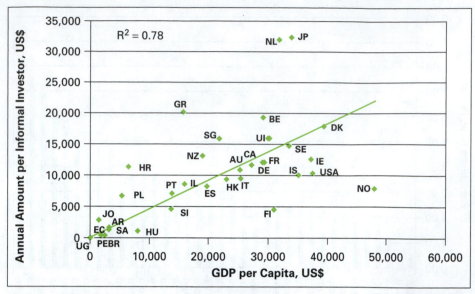

R² is the proportion of the variation that is explained by the trend line. An R² of 0.78 indicates that 78% of the variation in annual amount per informal investor is explained by GDP per capita.

Figure 9.5

Annual amount per informal investor vs. GDP per capita, U.S. $

as we can see in Figure 9.5, which compares the average amount per investor with GDP per capita. Informal investors in nations above the trend line provide more investment per capita than predicted, and those below the trend line provide less; for example, Japan and the Netherlands provide more, and Norway, Finland, and the United States less.

Amount of Capital Needed to Start a Business

The amount of capital that entrepreneurs need to start their ventures depends, among other things, on the type of business, the ambitions of the entrepreneur, the location of the business, and the country where it is started. In the United States, the average amount required to start a business is $62,594, with entrepreneurs providing 67.9% of the funding. For all the GEM nations combined, the average amount needed to start a business is $53,673 and, as expected, more is needed for an opportunity-pulled venture ($58,179) than a necessity-pushed one ($24,467). The amount needed to start a business is highest in the business services sector ($76,263) and lowest in the consumer-oriented sector ($39,594). The businesses that need the most startup capital are those created with the intent to grow and hire employees. For example, nascent businesses that expect to employ ten or more persons five years after they open require an average of $112,943 of startup money. Business started by men require more capital than those started by women ($65,010 vs. $33,201); a partial explanation is that women are more likely than men to start necessity-pushed businesses, which are more likely to be consumer-oriented and less likely to be business services.

To put nations on an approximately equal footing on the basis of wealth, we plot the amount of funding needed to start a business against a nation's GDP per capita, as seen in Figure 9.6. Entrepreneurs in countries falling below the trend line have a comparative advantage over entrepreneurs in countries above the trend, because it costs less to start a business relative to the income per capita in those countries, all other things being equal.

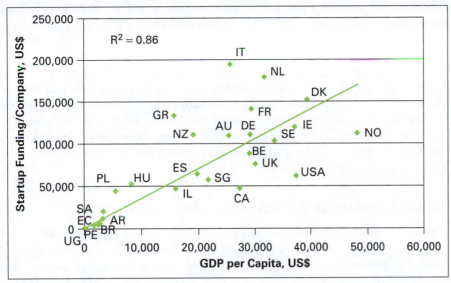

R^2 is the proportion of the variation that is explained by the trend line. An R^2 of 0.86 indicates that 86% of the variation in start-up funding per company is explained by the GDP per capita.

■ **Figure 9.6**

Startup funding per company vs. GDP per capita

This finding partially explains why the United States and Canada have the highest TEA rates among the G7 nations, and Italy the second-lowest rate. It might also explain to some extent why Norway has a higher TEA rate than its Scandinavian neighbors Sweden and Denmark.

Characteristics of Informal Investors

Entrepreneurs provide 65.8% of their startup capital; hence others, principally informal investors, provide the remaining 34.2%. Who are informal investors? We can categorize them as follows: close family and relatives of the entrepreneurs (49.4%) are first; next are friends and neighbors (26.4%); these are followed by other relatives (9.4%), work colleagues (7.9%), and strangers (6.9%), as shown in Figure 9.7. Strangers—the foolhardy investors among the 4 Fs—are usually called *business angels*.

Using GEM data for the United States, Bygrave and Reynolds[9] developed a model that predicted whether or not a person was an informal investor. They found that the

Relationship: Investor-Investee	Percent Total	Mean Amount Invested U.S. $	Median Payback Time	Median X Return
Close family	49.4%	23,190	2 years	1 x
Other relative	9.4%	12,345	2 years	1 x
Work colleague	7.9%	39,032	2 years	1 x
Friend, neighbor	26.4%	15,548	2 years	1 x
Stranger	6.9%	67,672	2–5 years	1.5 x
		24,202	2 years	1 x

■ **Figure 9.7**

Relationship of informal investor to investee

informal investor prevalence rate among entrepreneurs was 4.3 times the rate among nonentrepreneurs. With just one criterion, whether someone was an entrepreneur, their model correctly classified 86% of the entire population as being or not being informal investors. And with just two criteria, whether a person was an entrepreneur and that person's income, the model correctly identified an informal investor 56% of the time across the entire population, of whom slightly less than 5% were informal investors. Looked at another way, the model was 11 times better than a random choice at singling out an informal investor from the entire adult population. In general, this means that entrepreneurs in search of startup funding should target self-made entrepreneurs with high incomes. More specifically, they should first talk with the entrepreneurs among their close relatives, friends, and neighbors.

Financial Returns on Informal Investment

What financial return do informal investors expect? The median expected payback time, as you can see in Figure 9.7, is two years, and the median amount returned is one times the original investment. In other words, there is a negative or zero return on investment for half the informal investments. It seems that an informal investment in a relative's or a friend's new businesses is more often than not made for love, not money.

The amount invested by strangers is the highest. What's more, the median return expected by strangers is 1.5 times the original investment, compared with just 1 for relatives and friends. The most likely reason is that investments by strangers are made in a more detached and business-like manner than investments by relatives and friends.

There is a big variation in the times return expected by informal investors: 34% expect that they will not receive any of their investment back, whereas 5% expect to receive 20 or more times the original investment. Likewise, there is a big variation in the payback time: 17% expect to get their return in six months, whereas 2% expect to get it back in 20 years or longer.

Entrepreneurs are much more optimistic about the return on the money that they themselves put into their own ventures: 74% expect the payback time to be 2 years or sooner, and their median times return is 2, with 15% who expect 20 or more times on their original investment.

The expected **internal rate of return** or **IRR** (compound annual return on investment) is calculated from the expected payback time and the times return for informal investors and entrepreneurs who reported both (see Figure 9.8). The returns expected by entrepreneurs are almost the reverse of those expected by informal investors: 51% of informal investors expect a negative or zero return, and only 22% expect a return of 100% or more; by contrast, only 13% of entrepreneurs expect a negative or zero return, but a whopping 53% expect a return of 100% or more.

Supply and Demand for Startup Financing

Is the amount of funding sufficient to supply the external capital that entrepreneurs need to finance their new ventures? The average amount of an informal investment ($24,202) is more than the average amount of external financing that entrepreneurs need ($18,678). So for those entrepreneurs who are successful in raising money from informal investors, the amount on average more than meets their needs. But is there enough informal investment to supply all the nascent entrepreneurs in a given country?

The percentage of nascent businesses that could be funded with the available informal investment, assuming it all went to nascent businesses, is shown in Figure 9.9. Singapore has the highest percent of nascent businesses that could be funded, and Brazil the lowest. Of course, not all nascent businesses deserve to get funded. Without knowing the merits

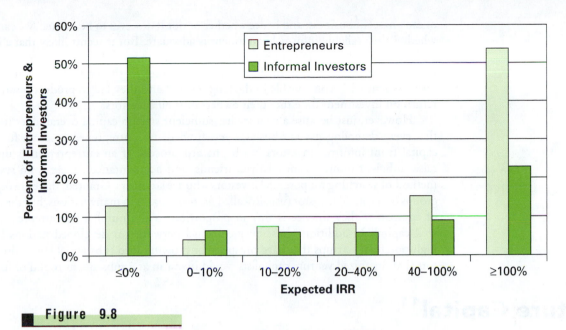

Figure 9.8

Expected IRR for entrepreneurs and informal investors

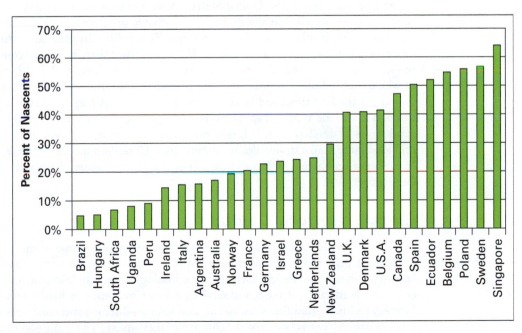

Figure 9.9

Percent of nascent businesses that could be funded by available informal investment

of each nascent business, and hence whether or not it deserves to be funded, we cannot say whether the available informal investment is adequate. But it seems likely that a country with enough informal investment to fund 40% or more of all its nascent entrepreneurs probably has sufficient informal investment because, in the end, the majority of new businesses never become viable in the long term,[10] and they fail to produce a satisfactory return on investment for either their owners or their investors.

However, just because a country has sufficient startup capital overall does not mean that every deserving nascent business gets funded. An entrepreneur's search for startup capital from informal investors is a haphazard process. If an entrepreneur is unable to raise sufficient money from relatives, friends, and acquaintances, there is no systematic method of searching for potential investors who are strangers. Granted, there are organized groups of informal investor (usually called *business angels*) in many nations, but the number of companies they finance is tiny in proportion to the number of entrepreneurs who seek capital. In addition, most business angel networks in developed nations look for high-potential startups that have prospects of growing into substantial enterprises of the sort that organized venture capitalists would invest in at a subsequent round of funding.

Venture Capital[11]

By far the rarest source of capital for nascent entrepreneurs is venture capital. In fact, nascent companies with venture capital in hand before they open their doors for business are so rare that even in the United States—which has almost two-thirds of the total of classic venture capital[12] in the entire world—far fewer than one in ten thousand new ventures get their initial financing from venture capitalists. In general, venture capital is invested in companies that are already in business, rather than in nascent companies with products or services that are still on paper. For example, out of 2,399 U.S. businesses in which $21 billion of venture capital was invested in 2004, only 799 received venture capital for the first time, and of those, very few were seed-stage companies. From 1970 through 2004, the venture capital industry invested $359.5 billion in 28,893 companies at all stages of development. It is estimated that over the same period, informal investors provided more than a trillion dollars to more than 10 million nascent and baby businesses. In every nation, there is far more informal than formal investment from venture capitalists (see Figure 9.10).

Classic Venture Capital

While classic venture capitalists finance very few companies, some of the ones that they do finance play a very important—many say a crucial—role in the development of knowledge-based industries, such as biotechnology; medical instruments and devices; computer hardware, software, and services; telecommunications hardware and software; Internet technology and services; electronics; semiconductors; and nanotechnology. Venture capitalists like to claim that the companies they invest in have the potential to change the way in which people work, live, and play. And indeed, an elite few have done just that worldwide; some famous examples are Intel, Apple, Microsoft, FedEx, Cisco, Genentech, Amazon, eBay, and Google.

It's not by chance that almost all the venture-capital backed companies with global brand names are American; rather, it is because the United States is the predominant nation with classic venture capital investments. In 2003, 74% of all the classic venture capital invested among the G7 nations was in the United States. The amount of classic venture capital as a percent of GDP for the GEM nations is shown in Figure 9.11. Israel,

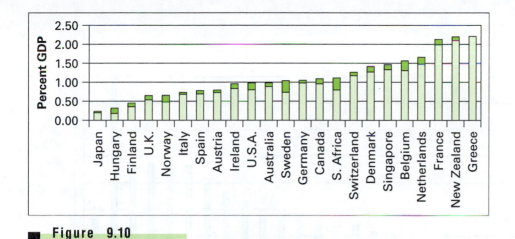

Figure 9.10

Informal investment and venture capital percent GDP, 2004

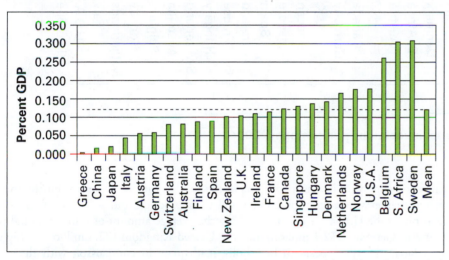

Israel (not shown) 1.25%

Figure 9.11

Classic venture capital investment percent GDP, 2004

which of all the GEM nations has a venture capital industry most like that in the U.S., has the highest amount of venture capital in proportion to its GDP (1.25%), while Japan has the lowest among the G7 nations.

While 74% of the classic venture capital invested in the G7 nations was in the United States, only 29% of the companies that received that investment were there, because the amount invested per company in the U.S. was $8.8 million compared with an average of $2.6 million per company in the other G7 nations. Figure 9.12 shows the amount invested per company for all the GEM nations, including the G7. It is hard to see how companies in Japan, for example, that received on average $537,000 of venture capital can hope to compete in the global market against companies in the U.S. that received $8.8 million. It is just as costly to operate a company in Japan as in the U.S., if not more

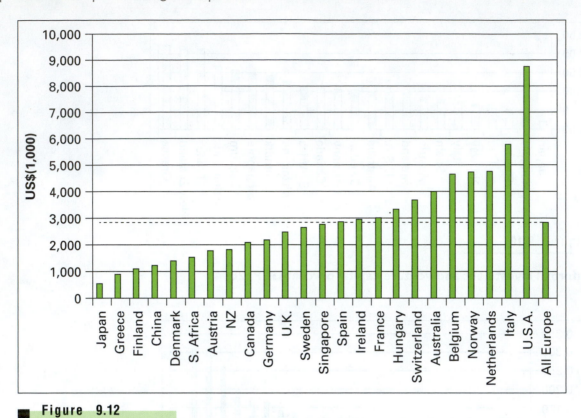

Figure 9.12

Classic venture capital investment per company, 2004

so. Entrepreneurs work just as long hours in the U.S. as they do in Japan. Furthermore, the home market where startups initially sell their products and services is more than twice as big in the U.S. as in Japan. Although the average amount of venture capital per company in Germany ($2.1 million) and the United Kingdom ($2.4 million) is higher than in Japan, it still appears to be wholly inadequate in comparison with the U.S. Since the main purpose of classic venture capital is to accelerate the commercialization of new products and services, U.S. companies have a very considerable advantage in the global market place. What's more, successful U.S. companies can build on their venture capital backing by subsequently raising very substantial financing with IPOs in the stock market.

American Free Enterprise Versus Government Sponsored Innovation

Google was developed entirely with money from the founders themselves, about $1 million from informal investors, $24 million from two venture capital firms, and $1.67 billion from its IPO. It is a classic example of American free enterprise at its best. Here is how the French and German governments were planning to create a European rival to Google in 2006—a decade after Google was founded in a dorm room by two 23-year-old Stanford graduate students.

A Franco-German Search Engine

In his 2006 New Year's speech, President Jacques Chirac said that France needed "to take up the global challenge posed by Google and Yahoo."[13] By then France and Germany had already started to develop a new search engine, Quaero ("I seek" in Latin). It was conceived in 2005 by Chirac and Gerhard Schröder, who was then the German Chancellor, as the Franco-German response to U.S. dominance in the search engine market.

Rather like the origin of Airbus Industrie in 1970 as a Franco-German challenge to Boeing's dominance of the global commercial aircraft market, Quaero is being developed by French and German companies backed with substantial government financing. In April 2006, Chirac announced that France's subsidy for Quaero was €90 million. The official estimate of the cost of developing Quaero is €450 million over five years,[14] but unofficial estimates put it much higher.[15]

Some industry experts are concerned that Quaero is driven more by national pride than the marketplace. They point out that Quaero's budget of €90 million ($115 million) per year for five years is dwarfed by Yahoo's $547 million and Google's $484 million annual R&D expenditure in 2005. They are concerned that by the time that Quaero is developed, the market will have moved on.

Ninety-one percent of the venture capital invested in the United States finances high-technology companies; by contrast only 29% of the venture capital invested in the other G7 nations, except Canada, is in high-technology companies. Seventy-three percent of the venture capital invested in high-technology companies at all stages from seed through buyouts in the G7 nations goes to companies in the U.S. But when the investment is narrowed down to only classic venture capital, the proportion invested in U.S. high-technology companies increases to an estimated 80%, with the U.S.'s share of classic venture capital invested in biotechnology at 81% and in computer hardware and software at 83%. When it comes to investment in all stages of consumer-related companies, the situation is reversed—only 13% of them in the U.S. and 87% in the other G7 nations.

Importance of Venture Capital in the U.S. Economy

One way of classifying young ventures is by their degree of innovation and their rate of growth[16] (see Figure 9.13). In the bottom left quadrant of the figure are companies that are not very innovative and grow comparatively slowly. They provide goods and services that are the core of the economy; for the most part they have lots of competitors and they grow at the same rate as the economy. In the upper left quadrant are companies that are innovative but not fast growing, because for one reason or another they are constrained—often because they are started and managed by entrepreneurs with limited ability. In the bottom right quadrant are companies that are not particularly innovative but that outpace the growth rate of many of their competitors because they are run by ambitious entrepreneurs with superior management skills. And in the top right quadrant are companies that are innovative and have superior management; among them are the superstar companies that attract media attention.

Informal investment goes to companies in all quadrants. In contrast, classic venture capital goes only to the companies in the uppermost corner of the glamorous quadrant. They are the companies with superstar potential to become leaders in their industries, and in a few instances to be central in the creation and development of a new industry segment. By and large, they are led by entrepreneurial teams with excellent management

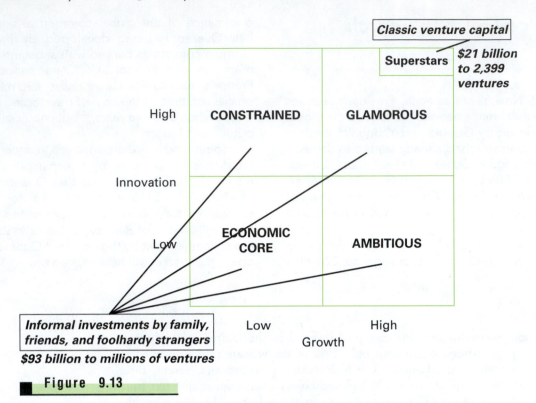

Classic venture capital

Superstars *$21 billion to 2,399 ventures*

High **CONSTRAINED** **GLAMOROUS**

Innovation

Low **ECONOMIC CORE** **AMBITIOUS**

Informal investments by family, friends, and foolhardy strangers
$93 billion to millions of ventures

Low   High
Growth

■ **Figure 9.13**

Financing entrepreneurial ventures in the U.S., 2004

skills. The companies are usually already up and running when the first venture capital is invested, although in a few rare instances venture capital is invested before the company is operational. Looked at another way, classic venture capital accelerates the growth rate of young, superstar companies; it seldom finances nascent entrepreneurs who are not yet in business. A relatively sophisticated subset of informal investors, business angels, invest

	2000	2003	2002–2003 Growth
Jobs	9.5 million	10.1 million	6.5%
Sales	$1.6 trillion	$1.8 trillion	1.6%

Top-5 States by Employment at Venture-Capital-Backed Companies Headquartered in the State in 2003
California 2,470,900
Texas 899,200
Massachusetts 712,300
Pennsylvania 604,000
Georgia 551,400

Source: National Venture Capital Association

■ **Figure 9.14**

Economic Benefits of Venture-Capital-Backed Companies

primarily in the glamorous companies, especially those with the potential to become superstars. Business angels are often entrepreneurs themselves, or former entrepreneurs who invest some of their wealth in seed and early-stage businesses. Angel investment frequently precedes formal venture capital.

If venture capital dried up in the United States, there would be no noticeable change in the number of companies being started because so few have venture capital in hand when they open their doors for business, whereas everyone has funding from one or more of the 4 Fs. But in the long term, the effect on the economy would be catastrophic, because venture-capital-backed companies generate a disproportionate number of good-paying jobs and create many of the new products and services. Those companies make a major contribution to the U.S. economy. For instance, by 2003, venture-capital-backed companies accounted for approximately 9.5% of jobs in the U.S. and 16% of its GDP (see Figure 9.14).

Venture-capital-backed companies in general outperformed other companies in job creation and sales growth between 2000 and 2003. For example, venture-backed-company sales grew by nearly 12%, compared with 6.5% for all U.S. companies. The computer software industry provides a strong example of the differential. Venture-backed computer software companies' sales increased 31%, compared with the growth rate of just 5% for the industry sector as a whole. The states with headquarters of venture-capital-backed companies earning the highest sales revenue were California, Texas, Massachusetts, Washington, and Pennsylvania.

Venture-capital-backed companies create jobs across the nation. California, Texas, Massachusetts, Pennsylvania, and Georgia led the nation by employment of venture-backed firms headquartered in their state in 2003. Venture-capital-backed companies headquartered in California alone were responsible for employing almost 2.5 million people nationwide in 2003 (see Figure 9.14).[17]

Venture-capital-backed companies, adjusted for size, spend over twice as much on R&D as other companies. In particular, small firms in the venture-dominated information technology and medical-related sectors are big spenders on R&D. Small firms—mainly venture-capital-backed ones—accounted for about 40% of the R&D spending in biotech in 2003, compared with 18% by large companies. Three of the top 10 U.S. spenders on R&D were venture-capital-backed companies: Microsoft, Cisco Systems, and Intel.

Mechanism of Venture Capital Investing

The formal venture capital industry was born in Massachusetts at the end of WWII when a group of investors inspired by General Georges Doriot, a legendary professor at the Harvard Business School, put together the first venture capital fund, American Research and Development. They did so because they were concerned that the commercial potential of technical advances made by scientists and engineers at MIT during WWII would be lost unless funding was available to commercialize them. The fledgling venture capital industry grew and evolved; eventually, the most common form of organization for U.S. venture capital funds became the limited partnership.

Henry Grossman/Time & Life Pictures/Getty Images News and Sports Services

Georges Doriot founded the venture capital industry when he started American Research and Development in Boston in 1946. His venture capital firm made many seed-stage investments of which the most famous was $70,000 for 77 percent of the startup equity of Digital Equipment Corporation (1979 photo)

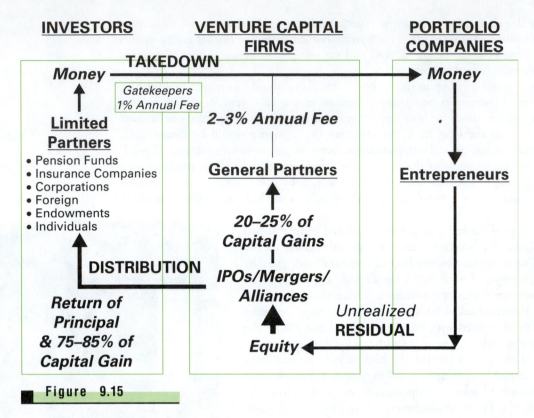

Figure 9.15

Flow of venture capital

The mechanism of venture capital investing is shown in Figure 9.15.[18] At the center of the process are the general partners of venture capital funds, which are limited partnerships with a ten-year life that is sometimes extended. The general partners of venture capital funds raise money from limited partners. In return for managing the partnership, the general partners receive an annual fee of 2% to 3% of the principal that has been paid into the fund. The general partners then invest money in portfolio companies in exchange for equity. If all goes well, the investment in the portfolio companies grows and the equity is eventually harvested, usually with an initial public offering (IPO) or a trade sale to a bigger company. The capital gain on the harvest is shared 80%-20% between the limited partners and the general partners once the limited partners have received back all the principal they put into the limited partnership. The general partners' share is called the *carried interest*, which is usually 20%. Sometimes gatekeepers (formally called *investment advisors*) are employed by limited partners to advise them on what venture capital funds they should invest in and to watch over an investment once it has been made. The fee for gatekeepers is approximately 1% of the capital invested.

In 2005 approximately 50% of the money invested by limited partners came from pension funds—both in the public and the private sectors—with the balance coming from endowments, foundations, insurance companies, banks, and individuals. As we've mentioned, each venture capital partnership (called a *venture capital fund*) has a ten-year life. If a venture capital fund is successful, measured by the financial return to the limited partners, the general partners usually raise another fund four to six years after the first fund. This, in essence, means that successful venture capital firms generally have two to four active funds at a time, since each fund has a life of ten years.

Kleiner Perkins Caufield and Byers:
A Legendary Venture Capital Firm

Eugene Kleiner and Tom Perkins formed their venture capital firm, then known as Kleiner Perkins, in 1972. Kleiner was one of the founders of Fairchild Semiconductor and Perkins was a rising star at Hewlett-Packard. It is probably the most successful venture capital firm ever. Today it is known as Kleiner Perkins Caufield and Byers. Headquartered on Sand Hill Road in the heart of Silicon Valley, since 1972 it has invested in more than 400 companies, among them AOL, Amazon, Compaq, Genentech, Intuit, LSI Logic, Netscape, Sun, and Google.

In 2004, KPC&B raised a $400 million fund, Kleiner Perkins Caufield & Byers XI. The limited partner investors in its 11th fund since 1972 are largely the same ones that have invested in KPC&B funds over the last 20 years or so. This family of funds had been so successful that it is virtually impossible for new limited partners to invest, because the general partners can raise all the money they need from the limited partners who invested in previous funds. The $400 million was to be invested by the general partners over three years in emerging growth companies in information technology, life sciences, and other fast-growing fields. The fund has six managing partners, including Brook Byers and John Doerr, and six partners.

Financial Returns on Venture Capital

A rule-of-thumb for a successful venture capital fund is that for every ten investments in its portfolio, two are big successes that produce excellent financial returns; two are outright failures in which the total investment is written off; three are walking wounded, which in venture capital jargon means that they are not successful enough to be harvested but are probably worth another round of venture capital to try and get them into harvestable condition; and three are living dead, meaning that they may be viable companies but have no prospect of growing big enough to produce a satisfactory return on the venture capital invested in them.

Approximately 3,000 of the 29,000 companies (almost 10%) financed with venture capital since 1970 have had IPOs.[19] Of the others that were harvested, mergers and acquisitions were the most common exit. In comparatively rare instances, the company's managers bought back the venture capitalist's investment.

The highest return on a venture capital investment is produced when the company has an initial public offering or is sold to or merged with another company (also called a *trade sale*) for a substantial capital gain. In general, however, trade sales do not produce nearly as big a capital gain as IPOs, because most trade sales are venture-capital-backed companies that aren't successful enough to have an IPO. For instance, one way of harvesting the walking wounded and living dead is to sell them to other companies for a modest capital gain, or in some cases a loss. The average post-IPO valuation of the 83 venture-capital-backed companies that went public in 2004 was $617.1 million,[20] compared with an average valuation of $83.5 million for those that were exited through mergers and acquisitions.[21] There were 333 mergers and acquisitions of venture-capital-backed companies in 2004, of which 181 disclosed their valuations.

The overall IRR to limited partners of classic venture capital funds, over the entire period since 1946 when the first fund was formed, has been in the mid-teens. But during those six decades there have been periods when the returns have been higher and/or lower. When the IPO market is booming, the returns on venture capital are high, and vice

Investment Horizon IRR Through June 30, 2005					
Fund Type	1 Years	3 Years	5 Years	10 Years	20 Years
Seed/Early Stage	2.1	−2.4	−10.5	48.8	20.2
Balanced Stages	11.7	7.6	−2.6	18.0	13.7
Later Stage	8.8	3.2	−6.8	14.1	13.8
All Funds	7.8	3.0	−6.3	25.8	16.0

Source: Venture Economics/NVCA[22]

Figure   9.16

Venture capital IRRs

versa. The returns of U.S. venture capital are shown in Figure 9.16. Over most of the 10- and 20-year horizons, seed/early-stage funds outperformed balanced and later-stage ones. This is what we might have expected, because the earlier the stage of investment the greater the risk, and hence the return should be higher to compensate for the risk. The seed/early-stage risk premium is spectacular for the 10-year horizon (48.8% versus 14.1% for later-stage funds) because the 10-year horizon includes the years 1999 and 2000, which was the peak of the Internet bubble, when year-to-year returns on all venture capital funds were 62.5% and 37.6%, with returns on seed/early-stage funds being much higher. However, the IRR for the 5-year horizon is −10.5% for seed/early-stage funds because it spans the aftermath of the bubble bursting, when the year-to-year returns on all venture capital were −32.4% in 2001 and −22% in 2002 for all venture capital.

The importance of the IPO market for venture capital is demonstrated in Figure 9.17, which shows the year-to-year IRRs of venture capital and the total amount of money

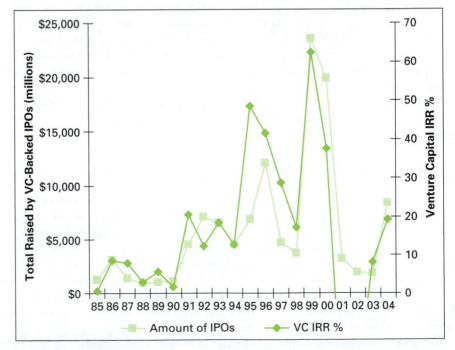

Figure   9.17

Venture capital year-to-year IRR and total raised by VC-backed IPOs

raised by IPOs of companies backed with venture capital. This shows a close correlation between the two lines—when the IPO market is thriving, as it was in 1999 and early 2000, the returns on venture capital are high. Not only do lucrative IPOs directly produce spectacular returns on venture capital invested in the companies going public, but they also indirectly raise the returns on acquisitions and mergers, because IPO market valuations tend to set the valuations of all private equity deals. For instance, in 2000 during the Internet bubble, the average valuation for a venture-capital-backed merger/acquisition was $338.4 million, but by 2002 following the burst of the bubble, the average valuation fell to $52.2 million.

Beginning in the second quarter of 2003, the number of venture-capital-backed IPOs and the amount raised in the offerings in the United States began an upward trend that built substantial momentum in 2004, when 83 venture-capital-backed companies had IPOs. Google's spectacular IPO in the third quarter of 2004 boosted the confidence of the venture capital industry. Some industry leaders expected that it would herald the start of a new cycle in venture capital investing with more money being invested in seed, startup, and early-stage businesses.

Venture Capital in Europe

Since the mid-1990s, venture capital grew rapidly, as most nations strived to emulate the impact that classic venture capital was having on the U.S. economy. It has happened before, at the end of the 1960s when the U.S. enjoyed a boom in classic venture capital, and again at the start of the 1980s as the rest of the world marveled at the success of the personal computer industry and the emerging biotech sector in the U.S. Unfortunately, in both instances it turned out to be a false dawn. Returns on classic venture capital outside the U.S. were—to say the least—disappointing, and classic venture capital floundered.

One of the principal reasons for the failure of classic venture capital in Europe at the start of the 1990s was the failure of the secondary markets after the general stock market crash of October 1987. The launch of the Unlisted Securities Market in London, the Second Marché in Lyon, the Marché Hors-Cote in Paris, the Mercato Restrito in Milan, and the Secondary Market in Brussels had been significant contributors and enabling factors for the introduction of venture capital in those European countries in the early 1980s, because they provided ready markets for floating IPOs of venture-capital-backed companies. Unfortunately, those European secondary markets, unlike the NASDAQ in the United States, did not recover, and so they faded, which left European venture capitalists without their favorite and most bountiful exit route from their investments: IPOs.[23]

In the late 1990s, markets for IPOs in Europe started to prosper, especially the AIM in the United Kingdom, but just as in the United States after 2001, it again became very difficult to float venture-capital-backed IPOs in Europe; consequently, classic venture capital returns fell and investments declined. Once more it demonstrated that classic venture capital cannot do well without a robust IPO market.

Factors Affecting Availability of Financing[24]

The three fundamental elements of an entrepreneurial society are an abundance of would-be entrepreneurs, plenty of market opportunities for new ventures, and sufficient resources—of which financing is a major component—for entrepreneurs to launch their new ventures. Numerous environmental and societal factors affect the three basic elements, and in combination with the basic elements they determine the degree of entrepreneurial activity in a region. We will now look at how financing correlates with entrepreneurial activity and the factors that affect the availability of financing. Because GEM includes many nations, we can see how informal investment and venture capital are related to environmental, societal, and governmental factors.

Total Entrepreneurial Activity and Informal Investing

The prevalence of informal investors correlates positively with the overall TEA index and three component TEA indices—opportunity, market expansion potential, and high job growth potential. And the amount of informal investment as a percent of GDP correlates positively with two TEA indices—necessity and high job growth potential. Those correlations are convincing evidence that nations with more informal investing have more entrepreneurial activity, but they do not separate cause from effect. Informal investing and entrepreneurship depend on each other: informal investment facilitates entrepreneurship, and entrepreneurship brings about a need for informal investment.

Factors Affecting Informal Investing

Money for informal investing comes from a person's after-tax income and savings, which more often than not are accumulated from after-tax income. Thus, it seems reasonable to hypothesize that the higher the rate of taxation, the less likely that a person will have discretionary money to invest and vice versa. In many nations, especially developed ones, the biggest taxes are social security, income taxes, indirect taxes such as sales tax on goods and services, and taxes on capital and property.

For all the GEM nations, the prevalence rate of informal investors is negatively correlated with social security taxes and with taxes on capital and property. For nations with an income of at least $5,000 per capita, the amount of informal investment per GDP correlates negatively with social security taxes, the highest marginal income tax rate, indirect taxes, and taxes on capital and property. Stated another way, nations with higher taxes on individuals have lower rates of informal investing. High tax rates inhibit informal investing.

Factors Affecting Classic Venture Capital

In contrast to informal investing, the amount of classic venture capital per GDP does not correlate with taxes on individuals or corporations. The explanation is that only a small proportion of classic venture capital comes from individuals and corporations. Far more comes from pension funds, which are essentially investing money that has been entrusted to them by others, and hence they are not directly affected by taxes nearly as much as individuals are.

The amount of classic venture capital per GDP correlates with the amount of informal investment per GDP. This occurs because almost all companies start out with informal investment; then if they show superstar potential, they attract classic venture capital. Thus vigorous informal investing paves the way for robust classic venture capital investing. So although there is no direct link between classic venture capital investment and taxation, there is an indirect link via informal investors, who are influenced by how much they pay in taxes.

As we pointed out earlier, there is a correlation between the returns on venture capital and the IPO market in the United States. In turn, this correlation means that the amount of venture capital provided by limited partners depends on the IPO market, because when the returns on venture capital are good, limited partners put more money into venture capital funds.

CONCLUSION

Financing is a necessary but not a sufficient ingredient for an entrepreneurial society. It goes hand in hand with entrepreneurs and opportunities in an environment that encourages entrepreneurship.

Grassroots financing from the entrepreneurs themselves and informal investors is a crucial ingredient for an entrepreneurial society. Close family members and friends and neighbors are by far the two biggest sources of informal capital for startups. Hence, entrepreneurs should look to family and friends for their initial seed capital to augment their own investments in their startups. Many entrepreneurs waste a lot of valuable time by prematurely seeking seed capital from business angels and even from formal venture capitalists—searches that come up empty-handed almost every time. Entrepreneurs must also understand that they themselves will have to put up about two-thirds of the initial capital needed to launch their ventures.

YOUR OPPORTUNITY JOURNAL

Reflection Point	Your Thoughts...
1. How much equity financing do you need to get your business launched? When do you need it?	
2. Where will you get your initial financing? How much money can you invest from your personal resources (savings, second mortgage, etc.)?	
3. Create a strategy for other equity financing. Build a list and rank order 4F funding sources. Estimate how much each of these investors might be able and willing to invest.	
4. Do you think your business has the potential to raise formal venture capital (high tech, high innovation, high-growth prospects, etc.)? If so, when might you be ready for VC? How much would you raise?	

WEB EXERCISE

What can you learn about equity financing on the Web? Search for some investor/entrepreneur matching sites (e.g., www.angelinvestmentnetwork.ca). Do you think these services are effective? Would they work for your business? What can you learn about venture capital on the Web? Look at www.pwcmoneytree.com/moneytree/index.jsp. What regions and sectors are receiving the most money? Which VC funds are the most active? Are they investing in your sector?

NOTES

1. Prahalad, C. K. Commentary: Aid Is Not the Answer. *The Wall Street Journal.* August 31, 2005, page A8.

2. Yunus, M. *Grameen Bank at a Glance.* Dhaka, Bangladesh: Grameen Bank. 2004.

3. www.microcreditsummit.org/involve/page1.htm.

4. Ibid.

5. Authers, John. Major Victories for Microfinance. *The Financial Times.* May 18, 2005.

6. www.accion.org/more about microfinance.

7. Daley-Harris, S. *State of the Microcredit Summit Campaign Report 2004.* Microcredit Summit Campaign. www.microcreditsummit.org/pubs/reports/socr/2004/SOCR04.pdf.

8. As of November 9, 2004, 6,321 institutions were members of the Microcredit Summit Campaign's 15 councils. Of that number, 3,844 institutions from 131 countries were members of the Microcredit Summit Council of Practitioners. Data in Figure 9.1 were collected from 2,931 institutions, which is 43% of the 6,321 institutions worldwide. Hence, the numbers in Fig. 9.1 underestimate the number of clients served throughout the world.

9. Bygrave, W. D. and Reynolds, P. D. Who finances startups in the U.S.A.? A comprehensive study of informal investors, 1999–2003. To be published in S. Zahra *et al.* (Eds.) *Frontiers of Entrepreneurship Research 2004*, Wellesley, MA: Babson College.

10. Business Success: Factors Leading to Surviving and Closing Successfully by Brian Headd, Center for Economic Studies, U.S. Bureau of the Census, Working Paper #CES-WP-01-01, January 2001. Advocacy-funded research by Richard J. Boden (Research Summary #204).

11. Venture capital data were obtained from the following sources: National Venture Capital Association Yearbooks, European Venture Capital Association Yearbooks, Australian Venture Capital Association, Canadian Venture Capital Association, IVC Research Center (Israel), and South African Venture Capital and Private Equity Association.

12. Classic venture capital is money invested in seed, early-, startup-, and expansion-stage companies.

13. Chrisafis, Angelique. Chirac unveils his grand plan to restore French pride. *The Guardian.* April 26, 2006.

14. Ibid.

15. O'Brien, Kevin J. Europeans weigh plan on Google challenge. *The International Herald Tribune.* January 18, 2006.

16. Kirchhoff, B. A. In Bygrave, W. D. (Editor), *The Portable MBA in Entrepreneurship*, p. 429. New York: John Wiley & Sons. 1994.

17. *Venture Impact 2004: Venture Capital Benefits to the US Economy.* National Venture Capital Association.

18. Bygrave, W. D. *Venture Capital Investing: A Resource Exchange Perspective.* Dissertation, Boston University. 1989.

19. National Venture Capital Association. www.nvca.com/def.html.

20. *National Venture Capital Association: Yearbook 2004.* New York: Thomson Venture Economics.

21. National Venture Capital Association. www.nvca.com/pdf/M&AQ42004 Final.pdf.

22. National Venture Capital Association. www.nvca.com/pdf/PerformanceQ42005final.pdf.

23. Peeters, J. B. A European Market for Entrepreneurial Companies. In William D. Bygrave, Michael Hay, and J. B. Petters (Eds.) *Realizing*

Investment Value. London: Financial Times/Pitman Publishing. 1994.

24 This is excerpted from a paper presented by William D. Bygrave at the Entrepreneurial Advantage of Nations symposium at the United Nations Headquarters, New York, April 29, 2003.

CASE

DayOne

In an uncharacteristic show of frustration, Andrew Zenoff nearly tossed the phone into its cradle on his desk when his latest funding lead—number 182—had decided not to invest. With the 2003 winter holiday season in full swing, the 38-year-old seasoned entrepreneur knew that his fund-raising efforts would now fall on deaf ears until after the New Year holiday.

Andrew stared out from the open office at a group of young mothers in the retail area—all cradling newborns—chatting with the nursing staff and with each other as they waited for the morning lactation class to begin.

> *Those new moms out there need us; that's why we're doing well despite a terrible location, a recession, and no money for advertising! So why can't I seem to convince investors what a great opportunity this is?! Am I—along with my staff and all of our satisfied customers—suffering from some sort of collective delusion?*

He closed his eyes, breathed deeply, and calmed down. After all, he quickly reminded himself, his San Francisco-based DayOne Center—a one-stop resource for new and expectant parents—was doing just fine as it approached its third year of operations. What Andrew and his team were being told, though, was that before funds would flow they would need to provide additional proof of concept—a second center, sited and scaled to match the DayOne business plan. The chicken-egg challenge, of course, was that they would need about a million dollars to build that proof. Andrew leaned back to consider his best options for moving forward.

My Brest Friend

A graduate of Babson College in Wellesley, Massachusetts, Andrew was no stranger to entrepreneurial mountain-climbing. For three years he had strived to build a national distribution channel for My Brest Friend, the most popular nursing pillow in a fragmented market. By 1996, he had secured an overseas manufacturer, office space in a San Francisco warehouse, and a few volume accounts that were yielding a decent—but far from satisfying—cash flow. He was still wrestling with the issue of how to educate the buyer about the advantages of his product when suddenly his venture had come under siege:

> *A nursing pillow company that was not doing well somehow thought that I had copied their design. There was no infringement, but they sued us anyway, and I decided to fight. The owner of this company was a woman with kids, and as the suit dragged on, my lawyers convinced me that if this thing went to trial, a jury might side with her, instead of a guy who has no kids and has never been married. If she won, they'd get an injunction against me and that would be the end of my business.*
>
> *That year I switched law firms three times, spent over $250,000 on legal fees, and ended up paying a settlement in the low six figures. I was emotionally drained, and nearly entirely out of cash, but I had managed to save my business.*

This case was prepared by Carl Hedberg under the direction of Professor William Bygrave.
© Copyright Babson College, 2004. Funding provided by the Frederic C. Hamilton Chair for Free Enterprise. All rights reserved.

A Question of Distribution

Following that painful settlement in the spring of 1997, Andrew set about to devise a more effective delivery model for his nursing pillow enterprise. He soon came to the realization that the solution he was looking for didn't exist:

> We definitely had the best product in the category. The problem was that people needed to be educated to that fact—either outright or through trusted word of mouth. The various channels I had worked with—big retailers, hospitals, Internet sites, catalog companies, lactation consultants—each offered only a certain facet of what a new parent needed, and so none of them had been really efficient at delivering my product to the marketplace. What it needed was a combination of education, retailing, and community.

Later that summer, Andrew got a call from one of his customers, Sallie Weld, Director of the Perinatal Center at the California Pacific Medical Center. An active promoter of My Brest Friend, Sallie had come to a frustrating juncture in her own career:

> During the mid to late 90s, I had spent a lot of time and energy setting up a new type of perinatal center. New moms were coming in asking for support and advice on various products—breast pumps in particular. When we started carrying pumps, that sort of opened up a Pandora's Box; now people wanted other products to go with the pumps. Andrew's pillow, for example, was the best on the market, so we started carrying that.
> And after a couple of years, this retail aspect of our childbirth and parenting education program began to turn a profit—and the minute it did, the hospital got greedy. They told us that we were not going to be able to hire more trained staff to handle the increased demand for our consults, and they said that all of our retailing profits would be channeled back into the general fund to support other departments. That was incredibly frustrating. I knew I was onto something, though, and I started a consulting business to help other perinatal centers. The problem was, they couldn't pay much for my services. That's when I decided to give Andrew a call.

They agreed to meet at Zim's Restaurant, an aging diner in the upscale Laurel Hill neighborhood of San Francisco. It was a meeting that would change their lives.

DayOne—Beginnings

In August of 1997, Sallie and Andrew met at Zim's for coffee and carrot juice, respectively. Sallie explained that no single service provider had ever been able to adequately serve the various needs of new moms:

> A hospital setting would seem to be the natural place to set up an educational support and product center for these women, but the bureaucracy just won't let that happen. There are also plenty of examples where nurses have tried to offer outside consulting services to new mothers, but while that's a great thought, they never seem to get very far without the business and retail component. And retailing without knowledgeable support is just products on a shelf.

After ninety minutes of brainstorming, the pieces suddenly fell into place. Andrew had found the unique distribution model he'd been searching for:

> I said to Sallie, 'Lets move these hybrid health-services retailing ideas into a private care center outside of the hospital—a retail center that could provide new and expecting

parents with everything they needed in one place. We'd be backing up the hospitals and supporting women at a critical and emotionally charged period in their lives.

This was like a lightning bolt of a vision for both of us, and at that moment we decided that we were going to build a national chain of these centers. That was the beginning of DayOne.

Having already built one business from scratch, Andrew noted that he wasn't surprised that it was months before they were ready to take a material step:

I had told Sallie that even though this sounded great, she shouldn't think about quitting her job at the hospital until I had a chance to lead us in an exercise to see if this business was a viable idea. I conducted a ton of focus groups, and every week Sallie and I would get together to talk about what I had learned—and what kind of center DayOne would be. After about nine months, in the summer of 1998, we decided, yes, this makes sense; let's do it.

Seed Funding

Andrew called investor Mark Anderssen, a shareholder and an active supporter of My Brest Friend. When Mark seemed receptive to the DayOne concept, Andrew paid him a visit:

I flew to Norway to meet with him in person. I was sure that after we opened up one of these, we'd be able to attract enough capital to start a chain. I figured that we would need about $300,000 to fund the next year and a half; writing the business plan and working on the build-out requirements so that when we were ready, we could move through the construction process quickly and get it opened. He said great, and put up about half the money to get us started.

As Sallie focused in on staffing requirements and retail offerings, Andrew began writing the plan, defining the target market (see Exhibit 9.1), designing the space, and looking for the right retail location: upscale, ground floor, easy parking, with excellent signage potential.

That summer, about a year after their momentous meeting of minds, the Zim's restaurant block fell to the wrecking ball to make way for a brand new office and retail complex. Andrew saw that the location was close to the hospitals, was in a vibrant retail area, had good stroller accessibility, and lots of parking. When the developer pointed out the street-level retail availability on the blueprints, Andrew saw that it was precisely where Zim's had been; DayOne would be growing up in the exact spot where Andrew and Sallie had had their first meeting.

Andrew secured the space with a sizable deposit, engaged the architects, and scheduled a contractor to handle the build-out. With their sights now set on an April 2000 Grand Opening, Sallie left her job to become DayOne's first paid employee. Everything was on schedule and proceeding as planned. Then, suddenly, nothing was.

Scrambling to Survive

In January, Andrew contacted his funding partner for the other half of the seed funding allocation. The investor, who had recently suffered some losses in high tech, explained that he would be unable to extend any more money. Andrew was in shock:

Things were already rolling along; I had architects working, Sallie and two assistants on payroll, a huge locked-in lease—and now, suddenly, with the bills mounting up, we were out of capital!

EXHIBIT 9.1 **Business Plan Excerpt: The Market**

The Center for New & Expectant Parents

The Market

According to the United States Department of Health and Human Services, women in the United States are having more children than at any time in almost thirty years. With four million births annually—more than half are first-time parents—the United States produces more than 2.2 million potential new customers each year. Indeed, the current baby boom is projected to continue until 2018. Spending an average of $8,100 on baby-related products and services during their baby's first year (excluding primary medical care), new parents represent more than $17.8 billion in annual purchasing power.

In recent years, the size of the juvenile products industry alone—i.e., products for babies 0–18 months—has grown to $16 billion annually. The company plans to reach the most commercially attractive part of this market—approximately 1,350,000 first-time parents each year with a college education and at least middle-income households. Additionally, the company expects to reach the market of more than 1,000,000 second-time parents annually, who comprise 25% of DayOne's target customer base.

The percentage of women in the United States who choose to breastfeed their babies continues to rise dramatically each year. According to a 2001 survey of 1.4 million mothers, the prevalence of breastfeeding in the United States is at the highest rate ever recorded, with 69.5% of new mothers now initiating breastfeeding, and 32% still breastfeeding at 6 months. (*Breastfeeding Continues to Increase into the New Millennium*, Pediatrics, Vol. 110, No. 6, Dec., 2002.) Moreover, 78.3% of college-educated mothers with household incomes of greater than $50,000 breastfeed versus a national average of 59.2%, and 59.2% of second-time mothers are breastfeeding.

As an ever-increasing number of studies confirm the advantages of breastfeeding for babies' immune systems and intellectual development, DayOne expects the incidence of breastfeeding to remain on the rise. Indeed, according to the United States Department of Health and Human Services, 75% of all first-time mothers will try to breastfeed their child compared to less than 50% only fifteen years ago.

More than two-thirds of breastfeeding women experience difficulty during breastfeeding and seek outside help. The majority of these problems surface after the brief hospital stay, when access to hospital-based lactation consulting programs is no longer available. Most mothers first turn to their pediatricians and OBGYNs, who are increasingly referring first-time mothers to lactation consultants because they lack the time and specific expertise. DayOne provides pediatricians, OBGYNs, and new mothers with a high-availability support solution.

There are numerous other market factors that favor DayOne's solution:

- Existing market is highly fragmented. In order to receive necessary services, products, and support, new and expectant parents must navigate between baby specialty stores, catalogs, Internet sites, hospitals, and independent childbirth educators and lactation consultants.

- Pregnant women and new mothers desire community for support, information, and the opportunity to share common experiences.

- Hospitals continue to downsize, reducing staffs and shortening the duration of maternity visits, forcing new mothers to rely on outside sources for needed support and services.

- Baby specialty stores continue to disappear off of the retail landscape in the face of big-box operators, reducing the personal touch that new parents seek.

Andrew had been pitching the DayOne vision to other investors all along, and that same week an individual came forward with a substantial amount of money to invest. Andrew explained that while the promise of cash got him motivated, he soon concluded that this wasn't just about the money:

> *This investor approached me and said that since I clearly understood the baby industry, he could get me a million and a half bucks for an Internet company. So I spent four weeks trying to figure out how I could do this on the Internet. Then I realized that even though I probably could come up with something, it wouldn't really provide new parents with what they needed. And so I went back to them and said that I can't do it; it's not in line with my values and my beliefs.*

Although he was now sure that the DayOne model wouldn't work as a Web business, Andrew saw that there still might be a way to leverage the red-hot Internet space to garner the funding he so desperately needed:

> *I met with a big online company that was doing baby-related things and told them that I thought their model had issues; first-time parents need to touch and feel and learn before they buy. I suggested that in order to survive long-term, they would need to partner with a bricks-and-mortar business like the kind we were building.*
>
> *Well, at the time their stock was worth several hundred million; those two guys told me that they were doing just fine and that they had no interest in what we were doing at DayOne. You know, a year later, they were out of business.*

DayOne centers were designed to be a key distribution channel for Brest Friend products, so Andrew aggressively leveraged resources at his wholesale venture in an effort to keep the flagship store on schedule. That had worked well for awhile, but ever since Andrew began working long hours to open DayOne, sales of his nursing pillows had fallen precipitously. It was now achingly clear that if this innovative distribution concept failed, My Brest Friend would be facing a long road back.

By March 2000, DayOne had amassed $200,000 in payables that Andrew couldn't begin to cover—at least not in the near term. Two architectural firms had already walked out on the project when they became aware that the startup was suffering from a severe funding gap. Andrew convinced the third one to come on board by pointing out that he himself wasn't drawing a salary, that his partner Sallie had resigned from a good job at the hospital to do this, and that they had already begun to interview and hire additional staff. This was real; they would find a way. That's just about the time that things began to get really ugly.

Nightmare on the Second Floor

By mid-March, DayOne had endured 45 days without cash, and Andrew had spoken with nearly 50 investors, without success. The landlord called. Construction, it seemed, was behind schedule—a fact which, under the circumstances, suited Andrew just fine. When the landlord requested a face-to-face meeting as soon as possible, Andrew was pretty sure that they guy wasn't calling him in to apologize a second time for the occupancy delay:

> *The landlord tells me that because of our financial position, they are not going to let us have a ground floor space; he's afraid that DayOne couldn't cover the rent. He says the only space they have for us is on the second floor—end of story. I said, "I don't know what to*

do; I don't have the money. I need to get out of this lease." He said, "Well, you're on the second floor, and you can't get out of the lease." Great; a lease for a top-floor space that I couldn't pay for.

Andrew returned the following day with a stronger argument:

I said look, you can't squeeze blood from a stone. And anyway, I am out of this lease because your building has taken so long to deliver that my investors have backed out! I told him that I can't honor the lease because he hadn't honored his deal. He didn't really respond to me, but we both knew that I was all done.

Andrew was trying to visualize how he was going to break this devastating news to his partner Sallie when he received an astounding call on his cell phone:

I had been pitching the business plan to everyone I could think of and hadn't gotten anywhere. All of a sudden here was an investor calling to say that he and three others were interested in putting up $150,000 apiece. $450,000 was about half of what I would need to open, and a lot less than the $1.5 million I was trying to raise as a first round. But it was a start; I pushed the "Go" button again.

I went back to the real estate guy and said, "You know, you're right; even if this is on the second floor, this is my space. I'll keep it." That's when he told me that he had already rented out half of our space to someone else. So, not only were we going to be way in back on the second floor with half the space we needed, we were now going to have to pay to completely reconstruct our architectural drawings.

Understanding that he was still a half a million dollars shy of what they would need to open the doors, Andrew continued to dole out just enough money to keep his various service providers on board. In June, the landlord informed him that the building was now ready for occupancy—meaning that the first $10,000 monthly rent payment was due. Andrew made sure to pay that bill on time, and in full.

Grand Opening

The construction business, like many trades, was a close-knit community of craftspeople and professionals. It was not surprising, then, that word was out on the slow-paying, under-funded project up on Laurel Hill that had already gone through three architectural firms and at least that many plan revisions. After a long search, Andrew located a contractor who apparently was not aware of DayOne's precarious financial situation. Along the way he had signed up another minor investor, so when construction began in August of 2000, DayOne had $480,000 on hand.

In late November—as the build-out neared completion—the contractor suddenly announced that he would not release the occupancy permits until he and his crew were paid in full for the work they had completed. Andrew recalled that it was another one of those pivotal moments:

I owed these guys something like $200,000, and I didn't have anything left. I just wanted to get to the opening party in January, because I felt that if we got enough people to come and enjoy it and get excited about what we were doing, we'd be able to raise the money we needed. I convinced the contractor to let us open, and at that party, two different guests pulled me aside and said that they wanted to invest. One woman wired me $50,000 the following Monday without so much as glancing at the business plan. I got another

$50,000 from a couple who had just had their baby. When we officially opened later that week, the contractor was paid in full, but we were again out of money.

As they had always planned to do, Andrew and Sallie called the area hospitals to let them know that DayOne was open for business and ready to serve. Andrew recalled that the response from the medical community took them completely by surprise:

One reason we thought we could make do with a second-floor location was because our plan had always been to drive traffic by being the type of place that medical professionals would want to send their patients. Instead, hospital directors were telling us that they considered us to be the competition, and that they were going to tell all the docs in San Francisco not to support our efforts in any way.

With no help from the hospitals, ineffective signage and cramped facilities (see Exhibit 9.2), and having no capital for marketing and advertising, Sallie and Andrew were faced with a harsh reality: either customers would love the experience enough to spread the word, or their business would quickly wither and die.

Delivering a Unique Customer Experience

DayOne immediately began attracting a base of young, mostly affluent, new and expectant moms seeking advice on everything from the latest baby carriers to sore nipples. Many signed up for the $99 annual membership on the spot to take advantage of discounts offered on programs and workshops (see Exhibit 9.3). Some dropped by out of curiosity or with specific questions for the professional staff. Sallie quickly established a ground rule that she felt struck a fair balance between the needs of these mothers and the need to advance the business:

When someone comes in with a question, we have a ten-minute rule. If your question is so involved that one of us cannot answer it in ten minutes, then you need to make an appointment, and we need to charge you.[1] Ideally these are people who are members, but many times, if they are not, we can convert them by giving them those ten minutes and maybe recommending some classes or products right there on the shelves that might be just what they were looking for. And they leave here thinking, wow, where else can I go where I can get that kind of knowledgeable service without having to be a member first?

Sallie noted that because of their customer-care orientation, she and her nursing staff were always looking out for ways to help—without first trying to calibrate whether a particular act of humanity or assistance would generate profits for the business. Pointing to a basic plastic and metal chair in the corner of her office, Sallie said that she wasn't surprised to see that simple kindness had its rewards:

Our favorite story is about that chair. We like new moms to be sitting up straight when they first start nursing—versus a rocking chair. I had one mom—not a member—who said every time she came in for a consult that the only way she could breast feed was in that type of chair. Every time she came in she said it, so finally I said, "Hey, why don't you take the chair home with you until you're feeling more comfortable with the whole process?" She looked at me and said, "Really?"

---

[1] Personal consulting service was offered at $89/hour, a competitive rate in the Greater Bay area.

EXHIBIT 9.2 Signage and Facility

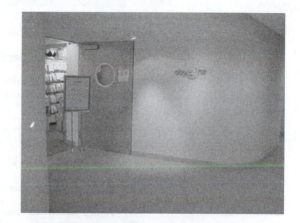

EXHIBIT 9.3 DayOne Membership Flyer

DayOne Membership

The Center For New & Expectant Parents

Why DayOne Membership?

A DayOne Membership provides a valuable opportunity for customers to save money, receive personalized attention, fully access our many resources, and connect with a community of new and expectant parents, seven days a week.

DayOne Membership Includes All of the Following:

- 40% Savings on DayOne Value Packages
- 30% Savings on Parent Groups
- 30% Savings on Workshops
- 25% Savings on Classes
- 20% Savings on Lactation Consultations
- Special Membership Prices on Selected Retail Items
- Unlimited Use of Resource Library
- Free Book & Video Rental
- Unlimited Use of Precision Baby Weigh Station
- Unlimited Use of Changing Stations
- In-Store Internet Access
- An Easy Way to Register for Classes & Purchase Products

DAY ONE MEMBERSHIP
Annual renewal fee $49   **$99**

Memberships are non-refundable

www.DayOneCenter.com • 3490 California St. San Francisco, CA 94118 • 415.440.DAY1 (3291)

So she took the chair home. The next day she became a member, she bought a breast pump from us instead of the one she was eyeing on eBay, and she went around telling all of her friends that we lent her that chair. She brought it back a few weeks later and has become one of our best customers.

What goes around comes around, and when we give a little bit, it's such a shock to them that they've gotten good service. I have this rule that if there's a mom hanging out in the rocking chair area, one of us goes over and asks if we could get her a glass of cold water.

I swear it's like you've just offered them a million dollars! They'll start to ask you questions, and it almost always turns into a sale. It's so funny—and a bit pathetic—that nobody ever thinks about these moms; everybody talks to, and about, the baby.

That's what we do differently. We make them feel good, knowing that if we take care of them, they'll take care of the baby. And all of that is definitely good for business.

Despite an encouraging level of customer interest and loyalty right from the start, the retailing side of the business continued to struggle. Andrew knew what the problem was:

The thing is, I am not a retailer. So everything we did early on was shooting from the hip. Sallie had some experience selling retail products at the hospital, but she was better on the service side. We had hired one retail buyer who lasted two months; didn't know what she was doing. Then another; same thing. The problem was, these people knew a lot about retailing, but we needed somebody who also understood the baby industry.

DayOne had begun to cover its operating expenses by the end of the summer of 2001, but the business was still in dire need of funding. As the capital markets continued to deteriorate that year, fund-raising became an even more arduous task than ever before. While the 9-11 terrorist attacks on the East Coast hurt retail sales and drove potential investors further underground, satisfied clients continued to drive new customers to the center.

In January 2002, the retail buyer that Andrew and Sallie had been searching for showed up on their doorstep. Ten-year retailing veteran Jennifer Morris had come over from The Right Start, the largest chain of specialty stores for infants and children in the U.S. She recounted how she was drawn to the new venture, and alluded to why her predecessors might have been overwhelmed by the task:

I found out about DayOne through working at The Right Start in San Francisco. I would either see a DayOne tote bag, or customers would tell me all about it. I started to investigate and found out that DayOne is not the kind of place you'd stumble on to. I was immediately attracted to the energy in this place; from the customers, the staff, the nurses, to the classes, and the workshops; everyone just really seemed to love it.

The biggest challenge for us is trying to be a one-stop shop. We have quite a few product categories (see Exhibit 9.4), and I buy from over 100 vendors—sometimes just one item from one vendor. A lot of those decisions are made by listening to our customers. If they come in with a terrific product, we can then go research that item and bring it in. We have no limits on that, really; we carry products from New Zealand, from Australia—from all over the world. If there's a great new product out there, we'll find it.

Sallie pointed out that in a similar way, she and the nursing staff were always looking for instructors and programs[2] that would distinguish DayOne as a premiere care center:

We search for the best and invite them to teach their classes here. More and more, though, the good ones come looking for us. We have started a lot of fresh and exciting workshops, but almost immediately other places in town copy what we're doing. Sometimes I wonder how long we can keep it fresh and exciting, but then again, that's what we thrive on.

The DayOne team began its second year of operations finding ways to trim overhead, enhance the customer experience, and refine the retail operations. To further this effort, Andrew tapped New York-based Stephen Cooper—an expert in retailing and finance—to serve as the company's Chief Operating Officer.

[2] In addition to a core of standard classes and support groups dealing with childbirth, breastfeeding, and exercise, the center offered other workshops such as Infant & Child CPR, Infant Massage, Musical Play, First Foods, and Practical First Aid & Safety.

EXHIBIT 9.4	Retail Product Offerings
Category	**Approximate Profit Margins**
Maternity Products	40%
Infant Clothing	54%
Nursing Clothes	52%
Breastfeeding Equip.	50%
Gifts	55%
Baby Accessories	47%
Infant Safety & Health	57%
Book Sales	42%
Toys	53%
Preemie Clothing	53%
Skin Care	47%
Hardgoods	44%
Bras	51%
Food & Beverages	10%

By early summer, the company—which in May had been honored with a "Best of SF" accolade (see Exhibit 9.5)—was signing up a steady stream of new members. Many of those clients were now being referred to the facility by local physicians who were quietly ignoring the sentiments of their hospital administrators. One such referral was Lisa Zoener, a new mom who said that she found out about DayOne from her obstetrician:

I have told lots of people about this place; it's definitely a word of mouth type of thing. My husband and I drop a ton of dough here on baby vitamins and other stuff. DayOne products are definitely higher priced than in other stores, but I'm already here for the classes—and a lot of us feel that buying DayOne products is a way to support what they're trying to do here. I don't find the second floor to be a problem—there is a parking garage right downstairs. It was full today, though.

Although he now had actual operating figures, a slew of customer testimonials, and an appropriate town picked out for the second DayOne, Andrew was still unable to raise the money he would need to proceed with those expansion plans. Then, in November, Andrew received a call that he was sure would change everything.

The Saudi Connection

Unknown to the DayOne staff, one of their very satisfied new moms was the daughter of a Saudi prince. Her father, Samir, was visiting from his home in London, and through her experience had learned a lot about what DayOne was doing. Andrew described their two-hour meeting at the center:

Samir said that he had an eye for businesses and that he thought what we were doing was brilliant. He said that he was the president of a multinational conglomerate out of London and Saudi Arabia; he wanted to fund our U.S. rollout and also help us export it to other countries.

EXHIBIT 9.5 | *SF Weekly* Best of 2002 Feature

Best Place to Go After You've Had a Baby

Day One

Your new baby has finally arrived. You're excited, anxious, sleep-deprived, and frankly a little concerned that medical professionals have let you leave the hospital with this newborn. You've forgotten everything you learned in parenting classes, and nothing you were told in childbirth class has happened the way they said it would. In short, you need support, reassurance, help, *something* ... and not from your mother-in-law. Look no more. Strap the little bundle into a carrier and get yourself to the knowledgeable, calm, and compassionate folks at Day One. As a business, the center is an odd mix: a retailer of higher-end baby tools and accessories, a lending library of books and tapes, the home of parenting classes, and a kind of lounge to hang out and nurse, chat, change diapers, or just get the heck out of your living room. As if all of that were not enough, Day One has medical scales to monitor your baby's weight and lactation consultants to help mother and baby get the hang of nursing. An annual membership is only $99, which also gets you a 5 percent discount on merchandise. The center is open seven days a week to fulfill its mission: "to provide new and expectant parents with a single-source, time-efficient solution for the essentials needed during this special and often challenging time of life." A brilliant idea that we're glad has finally arrived.

Details

Address: 3490 California (at Locust), Suite 203, 440-3291,

sfweekly.com | originally published: May 15, 2002

Andrew sent the prince on his way with a detailed business plan. Due diligence indicated that Samir was indeed who he said he was, so Andrew's excitement grew when the Saudi called a week later to say that he wanted to take it to the next level. That next step was having a colleague of his—a woman based in Arizona who had run four different billion dollar retail businesses—work as his eyes and ears to determine the best way to move the venture forward.

Ann Pearson, 60, a self-described workaholic and leading advisor to a separate $5 billion new venture fund, spent the entire day at the center and was thrilled with the concept. She explained that to move ahead, she and Andrew would need to build a business plan that would warrant her stamp of approval. Andrew recalled that that's when the real work began:

> For the next three months Ann was flying here every few weeks and Steve, our COO, was flying in from New York for three days at a time. She had us rewrite an entirely new business plan to sort of grind down to the nitty-gritty every aspect of the business so that she felt that she could put her stamp on it. We spent hundreds of hours, many tens of thousands of dollars. She was like this manic corporate raider-type, driving us really hard.

Along the way, Andrew had begun to notice that Ann didn't seem to have a high regard for his DayOne staff, and kept implying that before the business could begin its roll out, management changes would have to be discussed. It was bad enough when she suggested that Samir's daughter—a junior investment banker—might make a good choice for CFO, but when Ann began to infer that Andrew might not make the cut as CEO, he'd heard enough:

> *We had gotten into these heavy negotiations, and we had also started getting into huge fights. Ann ended up being an absolute animal; she wanted to drive everyone out of the business and take it over. But if you know me, I am not somebody who is going to get pushed around like that, and I wasn't going to sell out for anything. Then, all of a sudden, Samir calls and says that he's not interested anymore.*

It was nearly mid-spring of 2003 by the time Andrew turned away from that mirage—and several more months before the next major investor prospect would surface. The DayOne team now had a positive operating income for the center (see Exhibit 9.6), a detailed business plan with five-year pro-formas (see Exhibits 9.7–9.10), proven managerial performance, and, as always, a need for investment capital.

EXHIBIT 9.6	**DayOne Income Statement—San Francisco Actuals**		
	2001	**2002**	**2003**
Retail Sales			
Product Sales	$ 533,676	$ 687,492	$ 816,000
Memberships	55,566	62,774	76,050
Total Retail Sales	$ 589,242	$ 750,266	$ 892,050
Total Service Sales	181,761	222,947	272,000
TOTAL SALES	771,003	973,213	1,164,050
Total Cost of Retail Sales	288,569	346,213	434,627
Total Cost of Service Sales	196,144	156,680	190,624
TOTAL COST OF SALES	484,713	502,893	625,251
Gross Margin Retail Sales	300,673	404,053	457,423
Percent of Sales	51.0%	53.9%	51.3%
Gross Margin Service Sales	(14,383)	66,267	81,376
Percent of Sales	-1.9%	29.7%	29.9%
TOTAL GROSS MARGIN	286,290	470,320	538,799
Percent of Sales	37.1%	48.3%	46.3%
TOTAL CENTER EXPENSES	426,134	374,684	417,852
CENTER EBITDA	**(139,844)**	**95,636**	**120,947**
Percent of Sales	−18.1%	9.8%	10.4%

| EXHIBIT 9.7 | Five-Year Income Statement Projections—Roll Out |

	Year 1	Year 2	Year 3	Year 4	Year 5
Total Stores	2	6	14	26	42
New Stores	2	4	8	12	16
RETAIL SALES					
Product Sales	$ 1,904,000	$ 3,581,614	$ 10,713,896	$ 24,506,943	$ 46,011,931
Memberships	201,050	398,000	1,226,000	2,804,000	5,282,000
Total Retail Sales	2,105,050	3,979,614	11,939,896	27,310,943	51,293,931
Total Service Sales	647,000	1,250,800	3,713,000	8,470,000	15,882,000
TOTAL SALES	2,752,050	5,230,414	15,652,896	35,780,943	67,175,931
COST OF SALES					
Total Cost of Retail Sales	1,025,629	1,913,567	5,785,809	13,276,595	24,956,361
Total Cost of Service Sales	393,484	623,048	1,694,132	3,735,912	6,859,763
TOTAL COST OF SALES	1,419,113	2,536,615	7,479,941	17,012,507	31,816,124
GROSS MARGIN					
Gross Margin Retail Sales	1,079,421	2,066,047	6,154,087	14,034,348	26,337,570
Percent of Sales	51.3%	51.9%	51.5%	51.4%	51.3%
Gross Margin Service Sales	253,516	627,752	2,018,868	4,734,088	9,022,237
Percent of Sales	39.2%	50.2%	54.4%	55.9%	56.8%
TOTAL GROSS MARGIN	1,332,937	2,693,800	8,172,956	18,768,436	35,359,807
TOTAL CENTER EXPENSES	1,011,450	1,752,576	4,762,754	10,787,758	20,177,895
CENTER EBITDA	321,486	941,224	3,410,202	7,980,678	15,181,913

Prove It—Again

The DayOne plan called for opening 42 centers in five years, but so far the team found itself in a holding pattern around their flagship location. Andrew thought it ironic that by overcoming challenges and making compromises to get the first store open, they had developed a business that investors seemed unwilling to accept as a proof of concept:

> *We are now one of the most trusted brands in San Francisco. People love us. Investors are saying, well, this first center has done great for what it is, but your plan talks about a center that would be on the ground floor with street-side visibility, have support from the hospitals, and be in a bigger, more appropriate space. So because we are talking about a bigger center with bigger economics, they don't want to take the risks.*

EXHIBIT 9.8	Five-Year Cash Flow Projections—Roll Out				
	Year 1	Year 2	Year 3	Year 4	Year 5
Operating Activities					
Net Income	(974,692)	(592,920)	971,764	4,522,301	11,111,776
Adjustments for Non-Cash Items					
FFE					
Leasehold	102,857	308,571	720,000	1,337,143	2,160,000
Pre-Opening Costs	18,571	55,714	130,000	241,429	390,000
Product Promotions					
Total Adjustments for Non-Cash Items	121,429	364,286	850,000	1,578,571	2,550,000
Changes in Working Capital					
Current Assets					
Current Liabilities	(312,188)				
Net Changes in Working Capital	(312,188)				
Net Cash — Operating Activities	**(1,165,452)**	**(228,634)**	**1,821,764**	**6,100,873**	**13,661,776**
Investing Activities					
Investing Activities					
FFE					
Leasehold	(720,000)	(1,440,000)	(2,880,000)	(4,320,000)	(5,760,000)
Pre-Opening Costs	(130,000)	(260,000)	(520,000)	(780,000)	(1,040,000)
Inventory	(300,000)	(600,000)	(1,200,000)	(1,800,000)	(2,400,000)
Security Deposits	(120,000)	(240,000)	(160,000)	(240,000)	(320,000)
Net Cash — Investing Activities	**(1,270,000)**	**(2,540,000)**	**(4,760,000)**	**(7,140,000)**	**(9,520,000)**
Financing Activities					
Proceeds from Class B Unit Offering					
Founder Investment					
Payments on Notes Payable and LT Debt	(624,758)				
Common Stock Repurchases					
Proceeds from Exercised Stock Options					
Net Increase (Decrease) in Short-Term Debt					
Net Cash — Financing Activities	**(624,758)**				
Inc/(Dec) in Cash Equivalents	**(3,060,210)**	**(2,768,634)**	**(2,938,236)**	**(1,039,127)**	**4,141,776**
Cash and Equivalents Beginning Balance	7,232	(3,052,978)	(5,821,612)	(8,759,847)	(9,798,975)
Cash and Equivalents at Ending balance	(3,052,978)	(5,821,612)	(8,759,847)	(9,798,975)	(5,657,199)

Andrew estimated that he was going to need about $1.3 million to pay off current debt and open up a center that was more reflective of the business plan model (see Exhibit 9.11). That second DayOne would be sited in an affluent town about 35 miles to the south:

Palo Alto would be the next spot. It's in our back yard, and it's got the right demographics. It would be a bigger center, with more space, twice as many classrooms; twice the business, twice the sales.

EXHIBIT 9.9	Five-Year Balance Sheet Projections—Roll Out				

	Year 1	Year 2	Year 3	Year 4	Year 5
TOTAL STORES	2	6	14	26	42
NEW STORES	2	4	8	12	16
ASSETS					
Cash	$ (2,632,978)	$ (4,621,612)	$ (5,994,847)	$ (5,093,975)	$ 1,257,801
Other Current Assets	$ 25,316	$ 25,316	$ 25,316	$ 25,316	$ 25,316
Total Current Assets	(2,607,662)	(4,596,296)	(5,969,531)	(5,068,659)	1,283,117
Inventory	416,516	1,016,516	2,216,516	4,016,516	6,416,516
Fixed Assets					
Leasehold	1,352,424	2,792,424	5,672,424	9,992,424	15,752,424
Accumulated Depreciation	(102,857)	(411,429)	(1,131,429)	(2,468,571)	(4,628,571)
Net Leasehold	1,249,567	2,380,995	4,540,995	7,523,853	11,123,853
Security Deposit	172,000	412,000	572,000	812,000	1,132,000
Pre-opening Expenses	130,000	390,000	910,000	1,690,000	2,730,000
Accumulated Depreciation	(18,571)	(74,286)	(204,286)	(445,714)	(835,714)
Net Pre-Opening Expenses	111,429	315,714	705,714	1,244,286	1,894,286
Total Fixed Assets	1,532,995	3,108,710	5,818,710	9,580,138	14,150,138
TOTAL ASSETS	$ (658,150)	$ (471,070)	$ 2,065,694	$ 8,527,996	$ 21,849,772
LIABILITIES					
Short-Term Liabilities					
Trade Payables	—	—	—	—	—
Trade — Zenoff Products	—	—	—	—	—
Van — Note Payable	—	—	—	—	—
Other Payables	13,806	13,806	13,806	13,806	13,806
Total Current Liabilities	13,806	13,806	13,806	13,806	13,806
Long-Term Liabilities					
Accrued Compensation	—				
Notes Payable	—				
Total Long-Term Liabilities	—	—	—	—	—
TOTAL LIABILITIES	13,806	13,806	13,806	13,806	13,806
EQUITY					
Retained Earnings — Prior Year	(1,454,355)	(2,009,048)	(1,821,967)	714,797	7,177,099
Retained Earnings — Current Year	(554,692)	187,080	2,536,764	6,462,301	13,321,776
Additional Paid-in Capital	1,064,304	1,064,304	1,064,304	1,064,304	1,064,304
Partnership Earn/(Loss)	272,787	272,787	272,787	272,787	272,787
Total Equity	(671,957)	(484,876)	2,051,888	8,514,190	21,835,965
TOTAL LIABILITIES AND EQUITY	$ (658,151)	$ (471,070)	$ 2,065,694	$ 8,527,996	$ 21,849,771

EXHIBIT 9.10	Five-Year Corporate Salaries—Roll Out				
	Year 1	Year 2	Year 3	Year 4	Year 5
Executive					
CEO	175,000	175,000	200,000	200,000	200,000
Chairman			150,000	150,000	150,000
COO	150,000	175,000	200,000	200,000	200,000
CFO	75,000	100,000	125,000	150,000	150,000
Office and Finance					
Controller			90,000	90,000	90,000
Finance Clerk			40,000	40,000	40,000
IT Manager		85,000	85,000	85,000	85,000
Inventory Manager			85,000	85,000	85,000
Office Clerk	40,000	40,000	40,000	40,000	40,000
Office Clerk			40,000	40,000	40,000
Service					
Service Director	45,000	95,000	100,000	200,000	200,000
Service Manager				75,000	150,000
Service Assistant			40,000	80,000	80,000
Marketing					
Marketing Director		100,000	125,000	125,000	125,000
Marketing Assistant			45,000	80,000	80,000
Operations					
Operations Director			100,000	100,000	100,000
Operations Manager		60,000	60,000	120,000	180,000
Operations Assistant			40,000	40,000	40,000
Operations Assistant				40,000	40,000
Operations Assistant					40,000
Purchasing					
Buyer			60,000	60,000	120,000
Assistant Buyer			40,000	80,000	120,000
Total Salaries	485,000	830,000	1,665,000	2,090,000	2,410,000
Benefits Load (15%)	557,750	954,500	1,914,750	2,403,500	2,771,500
Increase (2%)		11,155	19,090	38,295	48,070
Total Corporate Payroll	1,042,750	1,795,655	3,598,840	4,531,795	5,229,570

Sallie noted that because of the rave reviews her group had received, some investors wondered aloud if that magic could be replicated in other centers:

> We have a great reputation in the community, and we set a tone here of warmth; we respect these women. Can we find as good a staff for Palo Alto, and can we train them well enough? Absolutely. Sure, it won't ever be what we have here, but it doesn't have to be to make the business work. I have no doubt that in every community we choose to locate in that we can find qualified, caring nurses who would love the chance to do what we are doing here.

EXHIBIT 9.11	Typical Center—Development Budget

PRE-OPENING COSTS

Store Build Out (~3,800 sq. ft)	418,000
6 Months Management Salary	110,000
Pre-Opening Expenses	65,000
Operations Consultant—Travel	10,000
Operations Consultant	30,000
Real Estate Acquisition	10,000
Inventory	155,000
Security Deposit	40,000
Miscellaneous	50,000
Total Pre-Opening Costs	888,000

CORPORATE OVERHEAD

Legal, Acctg, Other Prof Fee	15,000
Payroll and Benefits	225,000
FFE	10,000
Insurance	20,000
Utilities & Rent/Whse	12,000
Miscellaneous	20,000
Total Corporate Overhead	302,000
TOTAL CASH REQUIREMENTS	1,190,000

She paused, then added:

> *We hit bumps, and then we move on. And all the while we keep refining this model; the quality of our workshops, the way we work; it's all so much better than it was even one year ago. So it will happen; I'm sure of it—this struggle is for a reason. Andrew is big on that; it's all about the journey, not the destination.*

Moving Forward

Andrew checked his cash-on-hand balance. After three years he had still not taken a dime of salary, and yet he had to smile as he penned this particular company check. The cabinetry work at the facility had cost $85,000, and with this disbursement, Andrew would be making good on his promise to pay those guys—not quickly—but in full. There were plenty of others who were still waiting, but in time, they would be paid as well.

The phone rang, and on the other end was a young venture capitalist whose partner's pregnant wife had heard about DayOne from her sister's friend's pediatrician . . .

Preparation Questions

1. What more can the DayOne team do to build credibility and improve their chances of securing the capital they need to implement the business plan?

2. What other options might be considered for raising the funds needed to move the company ahead?

3. Imagine Andrew has approached you as a potential investor. Has DayOne proven the model yet? What are your concerns? Would you invest?

Jim Poss, founder of Seahorse Power Company, in Cincinnati with BigBelly® solar-powered trash compactor. The Cincinnati Ohio Parks Department unveiled its first 5 BigBelly® compactors on Earth Day, 2006. (*Source*: Courtesy James Poss)

RAISING MONEY FOR STARTING AND GROWING BUSINESSES

You've developed your business idea and written a business plan in which you have forecast how much money you'll need for your new venture. Now you're wondering where you will get the initial money to start your business and the follow-on capital to grow it. In this chapter we discuss the mechanics of raising money from investors including business angels, venture capitalists, and public stock markets. First we revisit the Jim Poss case, which you studied in Chapter 3, to examine how Jim scraped together the resources to start his business.

Jim Poss, Seahorse Power Company

During his second year of his MBA studies, Jim enrolled in Babson's Entrepreneurship Intensity Track, which is for students who want to develop a new venture that they will

This chapter written by William D. Bygrave.

run full time as soon as they graduate. Jim's first product, the BigBelly, is an automatic, compacting trash bin powered by solar energy. The innovative BigBelly dramatically cuts emptying frequency and waste handling costs, trash overflow, and litter at outdoor sites with high traffic and high trash volume. The BigBelly's target end users, such as municipalities and outdoor entertainment venues, face massive volumes of daily trash and very high collection costs. By the time he graduated in May 2003, Jim had a company, Seahorse Power Company (SPC), and a business plan, and he was developing a prototype.

While still in school, Jim won $1,500 of legal services at an investors' forum by Brown Rudnick Berlack Israels, LLP, a leading Boston law firm. Jim used this as part payment for the legal fees associated with his patent application. He invested $10,000 from his savings in SPC and was awarded $12,500 through the Babson Hatchery Program. He recruited two unpaid Olin College engineering students to help with the design, manufacture, and testing of the prototype. Jim then developed a partnership with Bob Treiber and his firm, Boston Engineering, from which he received a "ton of work" pro bono and free space in which to assemble and test the prototype. A Vail ski resort ordered a BigBelly and paid Jim the full purchase price ($6,000) in advance. In fact, he pre-sold nearly half the first production run, and there was a 50% down payment with each order.

Jim's parents invested $12,500. A business angel invested $12,500. Spire Corporation, a 30-year publicly traded solar energy company, invested $25,000. Jim won the Babson Business Plan Competition, which brought in $20,000 cash, which he shared among the team members—the first compensation they had ever received from the project. The award also brought in $40,000 of services and lots of publicity. Over the next year, Jim raised $250,000 with an "A" round of private investment from 17 individuals and companies, in amounts ranging from $12,500 to $50,000 with convertible debt. By the fall of 2005, SPC had sold about 100 BigBellys. In November 2005, Jim closed a round of equity financing.

Bootstrapping New Ventures

Jim Poss is a typical example of how an entrepreneur bootstraps a startup by scraping together resources, including financing, services, material, space, and labor. In Chapter 2 you read about how Steve Jobs and Stephen Wozniak at Apple and Sergey Brin and Larry Pate at Google raised their capital. Jobs and Wozniak developed their first computer, Apple I, in a parent's garage and funded it with $1,300 raised by selling Jobs's Volkswagen and Wozniak's calculator. They then found an angel investor, Armas Markkula, Jr., who had recently retired from Intel a wealthy man. Markkula personally invested $91,000 and secured a line of credit from Bank of America. Brin and Pate maxed out their credit cards to buy the terabyte of storage that they needed to start Google in Larry's dorm room. Then they raised $100,000 from Andy Bechtolsheim, one of the founders of Sun Microsystems, plus approximately $900,000 from family, friends, and acquaintances. Both Apple and Google subsequently raised venture capital and then went public.

There is a pattern in the initial funding of Seahorse Power Corporation, Apple, and Google that is repeated over and over again in almost every startup. The money comes from the 4Fs introduced in Chapter 9: First the founders themselves dip into their own pockets for the initial capital, next they turn to family, friends, and foolhardy investors (business angels). If their companies grow rapidly and show the potential to be superstars (see Figure 9.13 in Chapter 9), they raise venture capital and have an initial public offering (IPO) or are acquired by a bigger company.

The money from family and friends might be a loan or equity or a combination of both, but when it is raised from business angels, venture capitalists, or with an IPO, it will be equity. Before they raise money in exchange for equity, entrepreneurs must know the value of their companies, so they know how much equity they will have to give up. Before we discuss the mechanics of raising money, let's examine how to value a company.

Valuation

There are four basic ways of valuing a business:

- Earnings capitalization method
- Present value of future cash flows
- Market-comparable valuation
- Asset-based valuation

No single method is ideal, because the value of a business depends among other things on the following:

- Opportunity
- Risk
- Purchaser's financial resources
- Future strategies for the company
- Time horizon of the analysis
- Alternative investments
- Future harvest

The valuation of a small, privately held corporation is difficult and uncertain. It is not public, so its equity, unlike that of a public company, has very limited liquidity or probably none at all; hence, there is no way to place a value on its equity based on the share price of its stock. What's more, if it is an existing company rather than a startup, its accounting practices may be quirky. For instance, the principals' salaries may be set more by tax considerations than by market value. There may be unusual perquisites for the principals. The assets such as inventory, machinery, equipment, and real estate may be undervalued or overvalued. Goodwill is often worthless. There might be unusual liabilities or even unrecognized liabilities. Perhaps the principals have deferred compensation. Is it a subchapter S or limited liability corporation or a partnership? If so, tax considerations might dominate the accounting

When valuing any business, especially a startup company with no financial history, we must not let finance theory dominate over practical rule-of-thumb valuations. In practice, there is so much uncertainty and imprecision in the financial projections that elaborate computations are not justified; indeed, they can sometimes lead to a false sense of exactness.

The following sections describe the four methods to determine the valuation.

> *"The engine that drives enterprise is not thrift, but profit."*
> —*John Maynard Keynes*

Earnings Capitalization Valuation

We can compute the value of a company with the earnings capitalization method as follows:

$$\text{Company Value} = \text{Net Income}/\text{Capitalization Rate}$$

This method is precise when net income is steady and very predictable, but not useful when valuing a company, particularly a startup, whose net income is very uncertain. Even for an existing small business the method is fraught with problems; for example, should the net income be for the most recent year, or next year's expected income, or the average income for the last five years, or . . . ? Hence, we seldom use the earnings capitalization method for valuing small, privately held businesses.

Present Value of Future Cash Flows

The present value of a company is the present value of a the future free cash flows, plus the residual (terminal) value of the firm:

$$\mathbf{PV} = \sum_{t=1}^{N}(\mathrm{FCF_t})/(1+\mathrm{K})^{t} + (\mathrm{RV_N})/(1+\mathrm{K})^{N}$$

where K is the cost of capital, FCF_t is the free cash flow in year t, N is the number of years, and RV_N is the residual value in year N.

	Free Cash Flow
=	Operating Income
—	Interest
—	Taxes on Operating Income
+	Depreciation & Other Non-Cash Charges
—	Increase in Net Working Capital
—	Capital Expenditures (Replacement & Growth)
—	Principal Repayments

Free cash flow is cash in excess of what a firm needs to maintain its optimum rate of growth. A rapidly growing, high-potential firm will not generate any free cash flow in its first few years. In fact, entrepreneurs and investors want it to use excess cash to grow faster. Therefore, we determine the value of such a firm entirely by its residual value.

Market-Comparable Valuation (Multiple of Earnings)

This valuation method is the company's net income multiplied by a ratio of the market valuation to net income (P/E) of a comparable public company, or preferably the average for a number of similar public companies. Ideally, the comparable companies should be in the same industry segment as the company that we are valuing. If the company is private, we usually discount its valuation because its shares are not liquid.

$$\text{Total Equity Valuation} = \mathrm{NI} \times \mathrm{P/E}$$

For a public company, the total equity valuation is the same as the market capitalization. If we substitute net income per share (earnings per share or EPS) for total net income in this formula, we have the price per share instead of market capitalization.

Variations on this method use earnings before interest, taxes, depreciation, and amortization (EBITDA) multiplied by the price per share to EBITDA per share ratio of comparable companies, or simply the operating income (EBIT) multiplied by the price per share to EBIT per share ratio.

The NI × P/E method is the most common technique for valuing rapidly growing companies seeking investment from professional investors such as venture capitalists, or companies that are going public. For a fast-growing company with no free cash flow, NI × P/E is the same as the residual value, RV_N, in the equation in the previous section.

Asset-Based Valuation

There are three basic variations on the asset-based method:

- ▣ Modified (adjusted) book value
- ▣ Replacement value
- ▣ Liquidation value

Modified book value is appropriate for an established company that is stable or growing slowly. In this case, the value of the company is its book value, which is paid-in equity plus retained earnings, or looked at another way, assets minus liabilities. The problem with taking the book value on the existing balance sheet is that it assumes that accounting records accurately reflect the economic value of the assets and the liabilities. Unfortunately, the accounting of most businesses distorts the economic value of an organization—none more so than private, closely held companies. Hence, we must make adjustments to assets and liabilities before we can determine an accurate value. The major weakness of the modified book value is that it reflects the past instead of the future. It is static, not dynamic, because it is based on existing assets and liabilities rather than future earnings.

Replacement value is appropriate when someone is considering whether to set up a similar business from scratch or to buy an existing business.

Liquidation value is appropriate for a business that has ceased to be a going concern. It might be in bankruptcy, or it might simply be a business for sale that no one is willing to buy as a going concern. Just as the name implies, the valuation of the business is what someone is willing to pay for the assets.

Example of Market-Comparable Valuation

Here is a simplified illustration of market-comparable valuation, which is the most commonly used method for valuing a potential superstar company that is trying to raise venture capital:

> *Bug-Free Web Software (BFWS), a 12-month old Internet software company, has successfully beta-tested its product and is seeking $4 million of venture capital to go into full-scale production and distribution. BFWS is forecasting sales revenue of $50 million with net income of $5 million in 5 years. What percent of the equity will the venture capitalists require?*

To value this company and estimate the amount of equity that the venture capitalists will need to get their required rate of return (internal rate of return or IRR), we need the following:

1. Future earnings (NI)
2. Comparable price to earnings ratio (P/E)
3. Amount being invested (at time 0) (INV_0)
4. Risk-adjusted cost of capital (IRR)
5. Number of years before the investment will be harvested (N)

BFWS's financial projections forecast that the net income in five years will be $50 million; so NI is $5 million and N is 5 years. What is the P/E? The P/E will be the average for public companies that are comparable to BFWS. In general, P/E ratios are determined by the rate of growth of a company and of the industry segment the company is in. This is illustrated in Figure 10.1.

In the bottom left corner are companies in slow-growing industries; they grow at approximately the same rate as the industry—for example, automobile manufacturers. If the company is growing faster than the overall industry, its P/E should be higher

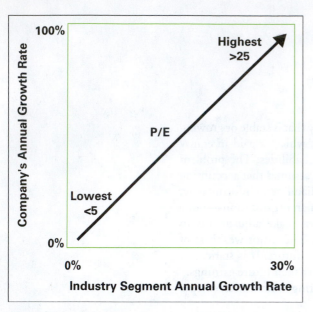

Figure 10.1

Price to earnings

than the industry average, and if it's growing slower, its P/E will be lower than average (of course, if a company is losing money, its NI is negative so it does not have a positive P/E ratio, in which case you might use a multiple of revenues). In the upper right corner are rapidly growing companies in high-growth industry segments, which is where BFWS expects to be. As we will see when we discuss venture capital later in this chapter, P/E ratios for superstar software/Internet companies in the top right corner are sometimes much higher than 25, but when valuing a very young company such as BFWS with no history of sales and income, venture capitalists will be conservative and use a P/E of approximately 20.

Using BFWS's financial projections, the future value of the company in five years will be as follows:

$$FV_5 = NI_5 \times (P/E)_5$$
$$FV_5 = NI_5 \times (P/E)_5 = \$5 \text{ million} \times 20 = \$100 \text{ million}$$

We now want to calculate the percent of the equity that the venture capitalists will need to get their required rate of return (IRR). The expected return depends on the risk involved. In general, the younger the company the greater is the risk. Figure 10.2 shows the expected IRR for the various stages of a company in which the investment is being made.

A *seed-stage* company is one with not much more than a concept; a *startup* company is one that is already in business and is developing a prototype but has not sold it in significant commercial quantities; a *first-stage* company has developed and market-tested a product and needs capital to initiate full-scale production. *Second-stage* and *third-stage/mezzanine* financing fuels growing companies; and *bridge* financing may be needed to support a company while it is between rounds of financing, often while it waits to go public.

BFWS has a prototype that has successfully passed its beta test and now wants to go into full-scale production, so it is classified as being at the startup stage where the expected IRR is 60%. Now we need to find out what percent of BFWS's equity the venture capitalists will need to meet a 60% return. Figure 10.3 show the percent of the equity needed to produce a return of 60% on a $4 million investment for various future values (from $20 million to $100 million) and holding periods (from 2 to 8 years).

The future value of BFWS is expected to be $100 million in 5 years; hence the venture capitalist will require 42% of BWFS's equity.

Company Stage	Expected Annual Return (IRR)
Seed	80%
Startup	60%
First-stage	50%
Second-stage	40%
Third-stage/Mezzanine	30%
Bridge	25%

Figure 10.2

Expected IRR of investors by stage of investment

Holding Period	Future Value, $million				
Years	20	40	60	80	100
2	51%	26%	17%	10%	10%
0	82%	41&	27%	20%	16%
4	NA	66%	44%	33%	26%
5	NA	NA	70%	52%	42%
6	NA	NA	NA	84%	67%
7	NA	NA	NA	NA	NA
8	NA	NA	NA	NA	NA

Figure 10.3

Percent of equity to produce a 60% IRR on a $4 million investment

The market-comparable valuation formula is as follows:

$$\text{Percent Equity} = \frac{\text{INV}_0 \times (1 + \text{IRR}/100)^N \times 100}{\text{NI}_N \times (\text{P/E})_N}$$

Applying this formula to BFWS:

$$\text{Percent Equity} = \frac{4,000,000 \times (1 + 60/100)^5 \times 100}{5,000,000 \times 20} = 42\%$$

There is a lot of uncertainty in this computation: Will BFWS achieve the net income it has forecast? If so, will it reach it in 5 years, or longer? Will the price to earnings ratio for comparable public companies be 20 or higher? Or will it be lower? Will the window for floating initial public offerings be open in 5 years, or will it be shut and delay BFWS's IPO? Any of these contingencies will affect the IRR when the venture capitalists harvest their investment in BFWS. Occasionally, a venture-capital-backed company does better than expected. However, more often than not it does not meet its financial forecast; thus, the actual IRR is usually less than expected.

Asset-Based Valuation Example

Most companies are ordinary rather than glamorous superstars. In this section we'll examine how to value an ordinary company that does not have the potential to attract venture capital or go public.

Suppose you want to become an entrepreneur by buying out an ordinary business—let's call it XYZ Corporation—that is well established in an industry that it growing about as fast as the overall economy and is an average performer. You will probably hope to buy it for its *modified book value*. The balance sheet for XYZ Corporation is shown in Figure 10.4. It lists the assets and liabilities as they are reported on the latest financial statements. The reported book value (total shareholder equity) is $5,159,000. In the second column are the adjustments that the accountants make to bring the assets and liabilities to actual market value; the footnotes explain the adjustments. The third column shows the restated numbers, which are the reported values (column 1) plus the adjustments (column 2). The restated book value is $6,309,000. That is probably what the seller will ask for the company.

Here are the critical questions the buyer should ask before buying an existing business:

- What is the growth rate of the industry?
- Is the company's growth rate above or below the industry average?

Assets	As Reported	Adjustments	Restated	Liabilities	As Reported	Adjustments	Restated
Cash	1,500		1,500				
Accounts Receivable (net) (1)	3,300	(100)	3,200	Capitalized Leases	500		500
Inventory (2)	3,419	450	3,869	Long-Term Debt	600		600
TOTAL CURRENT ASSETS	8,219	350	8,569	TOTAL LIABILITIES	4,860	100	4,960
Land and Buildings (3)	1,000	750	1,750				
Machinery & Equipment (4)	750	200	950	SHAREHOLDER EQUITY			
Other Assets (5)	50	(50)	0				
				Capital Stock	500		500
TOTAL ASSETS	10,019	1,250	11,269	Retained Earnings (7)	4,659	1,150	5,809
LIABILITIES							
Accounts Payable	1,700		1,700	TOTAL SHAREHOLDER EQUITY	5,159	1,150	6,309
Short-Term Debt	1,410		1,410				
Accruals (6)	650	100	750				
TOTAL CURRENT LIABILITIES	3,760	100	3,860	TOTAL LIABILITIES & SHAREHOLDER EQUITY	10,019	1,250	11,269

RESTATEMENT NOTES:

(1) Deduct $100 K for uncollectible receivables
(2) LIFO reserve adjustment of inventory to fair market value
(3) MAI appraisal of land & building reflect value of $950 K
(4) Machinery & equipment appraisal reflects current market value of $950 K
(5) Other assets were principally goodwill from expired patents — deduct
(6) Investigation found accruals unrecorded of an additional $100 K
(7) The net pre-tax effect of change in (1) through (6)

Figure 10.4

XYZ balance sheet adjusted to reflect fair market value of assets & liabilities ($'000)

- What adjustments need to be made to the income and cash flow statements and the balance sheet to reflect how the new owners will operate the business?
- How do the adjusted earnings and cash flows compare with industry averages?
- How does the balance sheet compare within industry averages (especially debt to equity)?
- How is the purchase being financed and how will that change the income, cash flow, and balance sheet?
- How will the new owner's strategies affect the company's future performance?

When these questions have been answered, the buyer should make five-year pro-forma financial statements and do some sensitivity analysis of the critical factors such as sales revenue, cost of sales, and interest and repayment of both the old debt the buyer takes over and any new debt added to help finance the purchase of the business.

Financing a New Venture

The first financing for your new business will come from you and your partners if you have any. It will be cash from your savings and probably from your credit card. According to the GEM study (see Chapter 1), the average amount of startup financing for a new business in the U.S. is approximately $70,000, of which about 70% is provided by the entrepreneurs themselves. Perhaps you will also contribute tangible assets such as intellectual capital, like software and patents, and hard assets such as computer equipment. As the company gets underway, you will also be contributing to your company financially by working very long hours for substantially less than the salary you could get working for someone else; 7-day work weeks and 12-hour days are not unusual for entrepreneurs starting up businesses.

Before you turn to family and friends for startup money, you should look at all the possibilities of getting funding from other external sources, just as Jim Poss did. Sources might include the following:

- Services at reduced rates (some accounting and laws firms offer reduced fees to startup companies as a way of getting new clients)
- Vendor financing (getting favorable payment terms from suppliers)
- Customer financing (getting down payments in advance of delivering goods or services)
- Reduced rent from a landlord (some landlords, such as Cummings Properties in Massachusetts,[2] offer entrepreneurs reduced rents or deferred rents for the first six months or perhaps a year)
- An incubator that offers rent and services below market rates
- Leased instead of purchased equipment
- Government programs such as the SBIR awards for technology companies

You probably should talk to a bank. But keep in mind that banks expect loans to be secured by assets, which include the assets of the business and its owner, or of someone else, such as a wealthy parent, who is willing to guarantee the loan with personal assets. The SBA guaranteed loan program is a possibility. In 2004 the SBA program provided approximately $50 million of loans per day to small businesses. However, even if you qualify for an SBA loan, you will have to guarantee the loan personally, and the bank granting the loan will expect that at least 25% of the startup financing will be owners' equity. This means that if you want to borrow $75,000 under the SBA program, you must have $25,000 invested in the company. The SBA figure of $50 million loaned per day is impressive, but most of that money goes to existing businesses rather than new companies.

Informal Investors

After you have exhausted all the other potential sources of financing, you should turn to informal investors for help with the initial funding of your new business. As you read in the preceding chapter, informal investors are by far the biggest source of startup financing after the entrepreneurs themselves. In the United States, informal investors provide in the region of $100 billion per year to startup and young businesses.[3] More than 50% of informal investment goes to a relative's business, 28.5% to a friend's or neighbor's, 6.1% to a work colleague's, and 9.4% to a stranger's.[4] In this section we will look at informal investors who are inexperienced when it comes to funding startup companies; in the next section we will look at an important subset of informal investors, business angels, who are more sophisticated.

Half of all informal investors in the United States expect to get their money back in two years or sooner, according to the GEM study. This suggests that they regard their money as a short-term loan instead of a long-term equity investment. We are using the term *investment* loosely in this context because it may be more like a loan rather than a formal investment. Whether it is a loan or an equity investment, the downside financial risk in the worst case is the same, because if the business fails, the informal investors will lose all their money. It is important to make clear to informal investors what the risks are. If you have a business plan you should give them a copy and ask them to read it. But assume that they probably will not read it thoroughly; hence, you should make sure you have discussed the risks with them. A guiding principle when dealing with family and friends is not to take their money unless they assure you they can afford to lose their entire investment without seriously hurting their standard of living. It may be tempting to borrow from relatives and friends because the interest rate is favorable and the terms of the loan are not as strict as they would be from a bank, but if things go wrong, your relationship might be seriously impaired, perhaps even ended.

How should you treat money that a relative or friend puts into your business in the early days? At the beginning the business has no operating experience and it is very uncertain what the outcome will be. Thus it is extremely difficult—maybe impossible—to place a valuation on the fledgling venture. It is probably better to treat money from friends and family as a loan rather than as an equity investment. As in any loan you should pay interest, but to conserve cash flow in the first year or two, make the interest payable in a lump sum at the end of the loan rather than in monthly installments. You should give the loan holders the option of converting the loan into equity during the life of the loan. In that way, they can share in the upside if your company turns to have star potential, with the possibility of substantial capital gains for the investors.

When you are dealing with relatively small amounts of money from relatives and friends, especially close family such as parents, brothers, and sisters, you may not need a formal loan agreement, particularly if you ask for money when you are under pressure because your business is out of cash. But at a minimum you should record the loan in writing, with perhaps nothing more than a letter or a note. If you want something more formal, CircleLending sets up loan agreements for small businesses with informal investors.[5] A documented loan agreement could be important if you subsequently start dealing with professional investors such as sophisticated business angels and venture capitalists.

Business Angels

In the previous chapter you saw that informal investors are most likely to be entrepreneurs. In the case of the funding of Apple, Google, Netscape, and many other companies not as famous, such as Seahorse Power, wealthy entrepreneurs play a key role in the funding of many new ventures. We call those types of informal investors **business angels.**

Business angels fund between 30 and 40 times as many entrepreneurial firms as does the formal venture capital industry, and they provide between $20 and $30 billion annually in the United States.[6,7] Angels invest in seed-stage and very early-stage companies that are not yet mature enough for formal venture capital, or that need financing in amounts too small to justify the venture capitalist's costs, including evaluation, due diligence, and legal fees.

We do not know how many wealthy persons are business angels, but we do know that SEC Rule 501 defines an "accredited investor" as a person with a net worth of at least $1 million, or annual income of at least $200,000 in the most recent two years, or combined income with a spouse of $300,000 during those years. According to Forrester Consulting, the number of households in the United States that fit that profile is approximately 630,000.[8] So that is the number of business angels qualified to invest in private offerings governed by SEC rules.

Angels on Broadway: The Color Purple[9]

The term *angel* was first used in a financial context to describe individual investors who put up money to produce new plays and musicals in the theater. Putting together a new theatrical production is not unlike starting up a high-potential business. It costs between $10 million and $12 million to produce a Broadway musical. Occasionally, a show is a gigantic success, for example, *Cats*, but more often than not it either fails or is mediocre. Seventy-five percent of Broadway shows fail.[10] It is said that you can make a killing on Broadway, but you can't make a living—in contrast to Wall Street, where you can make a steady living with an occasional killing.

The musical version of *The Color Purple* opened on Broadway in December 2005—eight years after producer, Scott Sanders, first recognized the opportunity of producing a musical stage version of Stephen Spielberg's 1985 movie, in which Oprah Winfrey was one of the stars. Oprah called it one of the greatest experiences of her life. After Sanders persuaded the author, Alice Walker, to allow him to produce a musical based on her 1982 Pulitzer Prize–winning novel, Walker wrote to Oprah in 1997 and asked her "to do a little angel work for the show." But there was no response from Oprah until July 2005.

In the meantime, Sanders had raised almost all the $11 million needed to put the show on Broadway. He put in some of his own money, then in 2002 he raised $2 million from AEG live—a strategic partner—with a commitment for another $2 million of follow-on investment. With the initial $2 million he produced a month-long trial run of *The Color Purple* in Atlanta to sold-out audiences and standing ovations in 2004. This attracted Roy Furman, a Wall Street financier and frequent Broadway angel, who had worked with Sanders in the past. Furman agreed to raise half the $11 million that Sanders needed and made a seven-figure investment himself. Furman took an active

Peter Kramer/Getty Images News and Sports Services

Author Alice Walker (L), Producer Scott Sanders, Oprah Winfrey and actor LaChanze at the curtain call for "The Color Purple" at the Broadway Theater on December 1, 2005, in New York City

interest in the production, attending rehearsals and management meetings. Then when the show was fully financed, Oprah called. She agreed to allow Sanders to put, ''Oprah Winfrey presents *The Color Purple*'' on the theater marquee. To make room for Oprah to invest $1 million, other investor's commitments were trimmed. Oprah also offered to feature a couple of songs from the musical on her hugely successful TV show. A book endorsement by Oprah almost guaranteed a place on the best-sellers list; Sanders and Furman hoped that by featuring *The Color Purple* on her show, Oprah would help to make it a Broadway hit.

Sanders and Furman estimated that if the average audience was 75% of full capacity in the 1,718-seat Broadway theatre, *The Color Purple* would pay back the original investment in 12 months. Five months after its opening, *The Color Purple* was grossing more than $1 million a week, making it one of the top five shows on Broadway. The show's backers should recoup their $11 million investment in less than a year.[11]

Searching for Business Angels

Most nascent entrepreneurs do not know anyone who is a business angel, so how should they search for one? The good news is that today there are ''formal'' angel groups, which are angels who have joined together to seek and invest in young companies. Most of them are wealthy entrepreneurs; some are still running their businesses, while others are retired. Angel investor groups have been around for many years, but they started to proliferate in the late 1990s when it seemed as if everyone was trying to make a fortune by getting in early on investments in Internet-related startups. Although many angels lost a lot of money on their investments when the Internet bubble burst, angel groups continued investing in seed- and early-stage companies, albeit at a much reduced rate.[12]

Angel groups have different ways of selecting potential companies to invest in. A few groups consider only opportunities that are referred to them, but most welcome unsolicited business plans from entrepreneurs. They evaluate the plans and invite the entrepreneurs with the most promising ones to make a presentation to the group at one of their periodic (usually monthly) meetings. A few of those presentations eventually result in investments by some of the angels in the group. Some groups charge the entrepreneurs a fee to make a presentation, and a few even require a fee when an entrepreneur submits a business plan. The size of each investment ranges from less than $100,000 to as much a $2 million, and in a few instances considerably more.

Important as angel groups have become, they comprise only a few thousand investors compared with hundreds of thousands of business angels who invest on their own. Hence, entrepreneurs are much more likely to raise money from angels who invest individually rather than in packs. Unfortunately, individual business angels are very hard to find. Searching for them requires extensive networking. But as Bill Wetzel, professor emeritus at the University of New Hampshire who pioneered research into angel investing, and who started the first angel investment network as the forerunner of ACE-Net (Angel Capital Investment Network),[13] says, ''Once you find one angel investor, you have probably found another half dozen.''

Consider how other entrepreneurs found business angels. Steve Jobs and Stephen Wozniak found Armas Markkula through an introduction by a venture capitalist who looked at Apple and decided it was too early for him to invest. Sergey Brin and Larry Pate were introduced to Andy Bechtolsheim by a Stanford University faculty member. Jim Poss worked for Spire Corporation and got to know Roger Little, founder and CEO of Spire Corporation and a leading expert on solar power; he met another of his angel investors at a wind energy conference sponsored by Brown Rudnick. When a leader in an industry related to the one the new company is entering becomes a business angel, it sends an important signal to other potential investors. For instance, once Andy Bechtolscheim had invested in Google, Brin and Pate soon put together $1 million of funding. And Jim Poss's parents said they would invest only if Roger Little invested.

Types of Business Angels

Business angels range from silent investors who sit back and wait patiently for results, to others who want to be involved in the operations of the company, as a part-time consultant or as a full-time partner. Richard Bendis classifies business angels in the following categories: Entrepreneurial, Corporate, Professional, Enthusiasts, and Micromanagers.[14]

Entrepreneurial Angels have started their own businesses and are looking to invest in new businesses. Some have realized substantial capital gains by taking their companies public or merging them with other companies. Others are still running their businesses full time and have sufficient income to be business angels. In general, entrepreneurial angels are the most valuable to the new venture because they are usually knowledgeable about the industry, and just as important, they have built substantial businesses from the ground up and so understand the challenges that entrepreneurs face. Hence, they can be invaluable advisors and mentors. Armas "Mike" Markkula is a famous example of a business angel who had made his fortune in two entrepreneurial companies, first Fairchild and then Intel. He had "retired" at the age of 38 when Steve Jobs and Stephen Wozniak were introduced to him. He invested in Apple; worked with Steve Jobs to write Apple's first business plan; secured a bank line of credit; helped raise venture capital; recruited Michael Scott, Apple's first president; and then became president himself from 1981 to 1983. According to Stephen Wozniak, "Steve [Jobs] and I get a lot of credit, but Mike Markkula was probably more responsible for our early success, and you never hear about him."[15]

Corporate angels are managers of larger corporations who invest from their savings and current income. Some are looking to invest in a startup and become part of the full-time management team. Corporate angels who have built their careers in big, multinational corporations can be a problem for a neophyte entrepreneur because they know a lot about managing companies with vast resources but have never worked in a small company with very limited resources. Here is an example of what might go wrong: A fish importing wholesaler was started and run by two young men. The company grew fast but it ran out of working capital. Two angels, one of them a marketing executive with a huge multinational food company, invested $500,000 on condition that the young company hire him as its marketing/sales vice president. Very soon there was a clash of cultures. The founders continued to work 12-hour days, while the new vice president was traveling first class and staying in fancy hotels when he made sales trips. Within a year, the business angels took control of the company. The two founders left, and a year later it closed its doors.

Professional Angels are doctors, dentists, lawyers, accountants, consultants, and even professors who have substantial savings and incomes and invest some of their money in startups. Generally, they are silent partners, although a few of them, especially consultants, expect to be retained by the company as paid advisers.

Enthusiast Angels are retired or semi-retired entrepreneurs and executives who are wealthy enough to invest in startups as a hobby. It is a way for them to stay involved in business without any day-to-day responsibilities. They are usually passive investors who invest relatively small amounts in several companies.

Micromanagement Angels are entrepreneurs who have been successful with their own companies and have strong views on how the companies they invest in should be run.

They want to be a director or a member of the board of advisors and get regular updates on the operations of the company. They do not hesitate to intervene in the running of the business if it does not perform as expected.

There is no ideal type of business angel. And in general, most entrepreneurs cannot pick and choose because it is so hard to find business angels who are prepared to invest. But just as a wise angel will carefully investigate the entrepreneur before investing, likewise a smart entrepreneur will find out as much as possible about a potential business angel. There is probably no better source of information than other entrepreneurs in whom the angel has previously invested. Ask the business angel whether he or she has invested in other entrepreneurs and whether you may talk with them.

Putting Together a Round of Angel Investment

If you're raising a round of investment from business angels, you'll need a lawyer knowledgeable in this area because there are various SEC rules that you need to comply with. The SEC Web site has a good brochure on private placements that you should read.[16] Most private placements by startup entrepreneurs are made under Regulation D, Rule 504 dealing with offerings up to $1 million; fewer are made under Rule 505 dealing with offerings up to $5 million. (There is a brief explanation of these in Chapter 12 on legal and tax issues.)

The first thing you'll want to do is place a value on your startup. Valuation of a seed-stage company is more art than science. It's also very subjective, with entrepreneurs placing a substantially higher value than business angels. Informed business angels will determine the value based on similar deals made by other angels and venture capital firms. The comparable-market valuation method will provide a back-of-the-envelope estimate to see whether the company has a chance of meeting the business angel's required return.

In general, business angels are satisfied with a lower return than venture capitalists because, unlike venture capitalists, they have only minimal operating costs and they do not have to pay themselves carried interest on any capital gains. You saw in Chapter 9 that venture capitalists charge as much as 3% per year on the money they invest, and on top of that they deduct carried interest of 20%—sometimes more—from the capital gain they pass on to their investors. So, to produce a return of 25% for their investors, venture capitalists need to get a return of 35% or more from their investment portfolio. According to Wainwright, business angels expect an IRR of 15% to 25%, with a payback time between 5 and 7 years.[17] An MIT study found that the business angels expected returns between 3:1 and 10:1 on their investments, and that actual returns ranged from losses on 32% of their investments to higher than 10:1 on 23%.[18] The same MIT study found that business angels were evenly split between preferring IPOs and acquisitions as their exit strategy; none preferred a buyback. In practice, 27% of business angel investments ended with an IPO, 35% with an acquisition, 5% with a buyback, and 32% were losses.

While financial returns are very important to business angels, they also invest for nonfinancial reasons including a desire to give back and mentor budding entrepreneurs, to be involved in startups without total immersion, to have fun, to be part of a network of other business angels, to stay abreast of new commercial developments, to be involved with the development of products and services that benefit society, and to invest in entrepreneurs without the pressure of being a full-time venture capitalist.[19]

Most angel investments are for preferred stock convertible into common stock on a 1 to 1 ratio. Preferred stock gives investors priority rights over founders' common stock, which relates to liquidation and voting. The potential problem with convertible preferred stock is that it sets a valuation on the stock at the first round. If that valuation turns out to be higher than the venture capitalist's valuation at the second round, negotiations between the venture capitalist and the entrepreneur will be difficult. The shortfall might even be a deal breaker.

Jim Poss placed a pre-money valuation of $2.5 million on Seahorse Power when he was raising his first round of funding from business angels. He raised $250,000, so the post-money valuation was $2.75 million. Investors would have owned 9.1% ($250,000/2,750,000 \times 100\%$) of the equity if Jim has issued stock. But instead of stock, he issued convertible debt. Some seed-stage companies that expect to get venture capital investment in later rounds of financing use convertible debt rather than convertible preferred stock. **Convertible debt** is a bridge loan that converts to equity at the next round of investment, assuming that it is an equity round. Convertible debt securities allow the next-round investors, who are usually venture capitalists, to set the value of the company and provide the first-round angel investors with a discount. Business angels would like to get a 30% discount, but actual discounts range from 10% to 30%. Convertible debt has the advantage over convertible preferred stock because it reduces or eliminates squabbling over the valuation between venture capitalists and the entrepreneur on behalf of the angels.[20]

The major conditions of a proposed deal are spelled out in a term sheet. Three examples of business angel term sheets are found in *Venture Support Systems Project: Angel Investors*.[21]

Venture Capital

In 2004, just 799 U.S. companies received venture capital for the first time, and most of those were not seed- or startup-stage companies. The reality is that a person has a better chance of winning $1 million or more in a lottery than getting seed- or startup-stage venture capital.[22] It is extremely rare that entrepreneurs have venture capital in hand when their new businesses begin operating.

Venture capital is almost always invested in companies that are already in business and have demonstrated the potential to become stars or, better yet, superstars in their industry. Venture capital accelerates the commercialization of new products and services; it seldom pays for the initial development of concepts. It is also important to keep in mind that the bulk of venture capital in the U.S. goes to high-technology-based companies. In 2004, for example, 60.3% of the 799 companies that received venture capital for the first time were in the information technology sector, 21.3% were in medical/life sciences, and only 18.4% were not high-technology companies.

Candidates for Venture Capital

Here, in order of importance, are the six top factors venture capitalists look at when evaluating a candidate for investment:[23]

1. Management team
2. Target market
3. Product/service
4. Competitive positioning
5. Financial returns
6. Business plan

Management Team. We've said that the crucial ingredients for entrepreneurial success are a superb entrepreneur with a first-rate management team and an excellent market opportunity. Entrepreneurs should have most of the startup team identified before they approach venture capitalists. If they are sufficiently impressed with the progress a startup company has made, venture capitalists will sometimes help recruit a key member of the team. They will even help recruit a new CEO if they have reservations about the lead entrepreneur's ability to build a rapidly growing company with the potential to go public. The best venture capitalists have extensive contacts with potential candidates for management positions in their portfolio companies.

"... there's plenty of technology, market opportunity, and venture capital, but too few great entrepreneurs and teams [in 2004]."[24]

— *John Doerr, legendary venture capitalist, Kleiner Perkins Caufield & Byers*

Target Market. The target market should be fragmented, accessible, and growing rapidly. The Internet triggered a stampede of venture capital investing in the late 1990s because it promised to become a huge market with many different segments; there were no dominant players in the new segments, and the segments were readily accessible to new entrants.

Product/Service. The product or service should be better than competing products and it should be protected with patents or copyrights. It does not have to be the first product in its market segment. For example, Google was not the first Web search engine; it simply was superior to the existing ones.

Competitive Positioning. There is no dominant competitor in the market niche. Distribution channels are open. And the company has an experienced marketing manager with expert knowledge of market segment. SolidWorks (the case associated with this chapter) positioned its CAD/CAM software in a niche where it was difficult for well-established competitors, especially Parametric Technology, to move into without cannibalizing their business models.

Financial Returns. The potential financial return is important, but classic venture capital does not depend on sophisticated financial computations. Venture capitalists have a rule of thumb for early- and expansion-stage companies—they will invest only if the company has the potential to return at least seven times their investment in five years. Or, in venture capital jargon "seven x" in five years. A 7x return in 5 years produces an IRR of 47.6%; a 10x return in 5 years produces an IRR of 58.5%.

Business Plan. Every entrepreneur seeking money from business angels or professional venture capitalists must have a competent written business plan. But no matter how good a business plan may be, it will not impress investors nearly as much as a product or service that is already being evaluated by customers. Too many entrepreneurs spend too much effort refining and polishing their business plans rather than implementing their businesses.

Ideal Candidates for Venture Capital

The *ideal* candidate for a first round of venture capital meets the following criteria:

- ◉ CEO/lead entrepreneur has significant management and entrepreneurial experience with demonstrated ability to manage a rapidly growing company in a fast-paced industry segment.
- ◉ Vice president of engineering is recognized as a star in the industry (if it is a technology-based business).
- ◉ Vice president of marketing has a proven track record.

- ◉ Some members of the top management team have worked together before.
- ◉ The product/service is better than its competitors.
- ◉ Intellectual capital such as patents and copyrights are protected.
- ◉ The market segment is fragmented, growing rapidly, and expected to be big.
- ◉ There are no dominant competitors.
- ◉ The company has satisfied customers.
- ◉ The company projects sales of $50 million in five years.
- ◉ The gross income margin is expected to be better than 60% with a net income margin better than 10%.
- ◉ The amount of investment is between $5 million and $10 million.
- ◉ The company has the potential to go public in 5 years.
- ◉ Potential return of 7× or higher.
- ◉ IRR of 60% or higher.

Actual Venture-Capital-Backed Companies

Venture-capital-backed companies that have IPOs are the cream of the crop, so by examining profiles of companies at the time they go public, we can see how the best companies measure up to the ideal. Figure 10.5 shows the results of a study of 122 venture-backed-companies that went public in the years 1994–1997,[25] when the stock market indices were rising, but before the Internet bubble (which ran from the end of 1997 to the beginning of 2001).

The management of those companies came close to the ideal. For instance, half of the top management teams had a combined 114 years of experience or more. Seventy-one percent of the companies had at least one founder with previous startup experience. And in about two-thirds of the companies, two or more founders had worked together before starting their present venture.

Market and operating performance at the time of the IPO was quite different among the industry segments (see Figure 10.5). The industry segments are in order of the maturity from left to right, with the Internet being the least mature and the semiconductor the most mature. Much of the difference between companies in the four industries is explained by the maturity of their industry segment. The Internet market segments were growing much faster than the semiconductor ones, as were the annual growth rate of sales revenue. There was a big difference between the characteristics of Internet and semiconductor companies.

Internet companies had the least sales revenue at the time of the IPO and the semiconductor companies the most. None of the four segments attained the ideal of at least $50 million in annual sales revenue. Not one of the industry segments met the net income margin of at least 10% prescribed for the ideal, but the Internet and software companies exceeded the gross margin requirement of at least 60%, whereas the hardware and semiconductor companies fell short. In all segments except the Internet, the annualized net income improved dramatically in the quarter before the IPO.

However, despite the shortcomings on sales revenue and net income, the venture capitalists met their hoped-for times return on the first round of venture capital in all industries except semiconductors. And their IRR handily topped their expectations. The median IRR for Internet companies was a whopping 507%, because they went public only 1 year after they received their first round of venture capital. In contrast, 5 years elapsed for semiconductor companies between the first round of venture capital and the IPO. So although the times return in the semiconductor segment was almost 5 compared with just over 7 in the Internet segment, the IRR in semiconductors was only 30.5%,

	Medians			
	Internet	Software	Hardware	Semiconductor
Marketing and Operations				
Market Growth Rate	135.7%	23.5%	37.5%	15.5%
Annual Sales Growth Trend (all years)	87.0%	54.3%	55.7%	24.7%
Sales Growth Trend (12 months)	93.3%	45.9%	54.3%	30.1%
Annualized Sales Revenue	$9,720,000	$23,396,000	$27,268,000	$39,940,000
Gross Margin	72.7%	75.6%	39.1%	42.2%
Profit Margin	−36.7%	3.4%	−0.5%	7.9%
Net Income (last year)	($2,414,530)	$308,000	($639,000)	$1,495,000
Net Income (last quarter annualized)	($3,462,921)	$1,644,000	$2,140,000	$3,226,000
R&D Ratio	27.0%	18.4%	14.5%	14.6%
# of Employees	124	134	92	213
Financial				
IRR	506.9%	124.8%	148.0%	30.5%
Times Return	7.16	6.67	10.71	4.94
Years from 1st VC investment to IPO	0.96	2.53	4.04	5.00
Time from Incorporation to IPO	5	8	7	11
Price/Share 1st Round of VC	$1.25	$1.50	$1.13	$2.79
IPO Price	$14	$12	$10	$11
P/E Ratio	70	54	32	26
Size of IPO	$34,000,000	$27,600,000	$22,320,000	$29,130,000
Market Capitalization after IPO	$163,488,290	$105,510,812	$89,244,768	$77,468,542

Figure 10.5

Venture-capital-backed public companies

because the longer an investment is held, the lower the IRR. The P/E ratios were 70 for the Internet companies that were profitable, 54 for software, 32 for hardware, and 26 for semiconductors. The difference in the P/E ratios mainly explains the differences in market capitalization among the different industry segments.

What does this mean for entrepreneurs who are seeking venture capital? First, there is not one set of ideal criteria for a company, but there are tendencies based on the industry sector. Second, the management team must be excellent. Third, the faster the growth of the industry and the growth of the company, the more likely it is to get the attention of venture capitalists. Fourth, entrepreneurs should focus on sales growth rather than profitability in the first few years, and then show a profitability spurt in the year before the IPO. Fifth, on average, companies are several years old before they get their first venture capital investment.

Dealing with Venture Capitalists

The first big challenge for an entrepreneur is reaching a venture capitalist. It is easy to get names and contact information for almost every venture capital firm; for example, *Pratt's Guide to Private Equity Sources* contains "over 4,400 listings that offer contact information, capital under management, recent investments and more, plus four indexes by company, personnel, investment stage, and industry preferences which enable users to hone their search and target the ideal firm with a minimum of effort. The Web-based product is continually updated and easy to search."[26] However, venture capital firms pay much more attention to entrepreneurs who are referred to them than to unsolicited business plans with a cover letter that arrive by mail. Entrepreneurs are referred to venture capitalists by accountants, lawyers, bankers, other entrepreneurs, consultants, professors, business angels, and anyone else in contact with venture capitalists. However, most of them are reluctant to recommend an entrepreneur to a venture capitalist unless they are confident that the entrepreneur is a good candidate for venture capital.

Entrepreneurs should be wary of "finders" who offer to raise venture capital for the entrepreneur. Most venture capitalists do not like dealing with finders because they charge the company a fee based on the amount of money raised—a fee that comes out of the money the venture capitalists invest in the company. What's more, it's the entrepreneur, not the finder, who has to deal with the venture capitalists.

If the entrepreneur is fortunate enough to find a venture capitalist who would like to learn more about the new business, a meeting will take place either at the company's or the venture capital firm's office. The first meeting is usually an informal discussion of the business with one of the partners of the venture capital firm. If the partner decides to pursue the opportunity, he or she will discuss it with more of the partners; if they like the opportunity, they will invite the entrepreneur to make a formal presentation to several partners in the firm. This meeting is the crucial one, so it is important to make as good a presentation as possible. Not only are the venture capital partners assessing the company and its product or service, they are also carefully scrutinizing the entrepreneur and other team members to see whether they have the right stuff to build a company that can go public.

If the venture capital partners like what they see and hear at this meeting, the firm will pursue the entrepreneur with the intent to invest and will begin its due diligence on the entrepreneur, other team members, and the company. Entrepreneurs who get to this stage will be evaluated as never before in their lives. It is not unusual for a venture capital firm to check dozens of references on the entrepreneur. Any suggestion of dubious conduct by the entrepreneur will be investigated. After all, the entrepreneur is asking the venture capital firm to trust him or her with several million dollars that in most cases is not secured by any collateral. All entrepreneurs should get a copy of their credit reports and be prepared to explain any delinquencies.

Entrepreneurs who get to this stage may be wondering whether the venture capital firm is the right one for them and be tempted to approach other venture capital firms to see what they might offer. But instead, conduct due diligence on the venture capital firm. Ask for a list of the entrepreneurs the firm has invested in and permission to speak with them. Here are some things to look for.

Value Added.
Value Added. The best venture capitalists bring more than money to their portfolio companies.[27] They bring what they call *value added*, which includes help with recruiting key members of management, strategic advice, industry contacts, and professional contacts such as accountants, lawyers, entrepreneurs, consultants, other venture capitalists, commercial bankers, and investment bankers.

Patience.
Patience. Some venture capital firms, especially newer ones with relatively inexperienced partners, are more likely to get impatient when a portfolio company fails to meet expectations. Studies of venture-capital-backed companies that have not yet gone public or been acquired find that approximately 50% to 60% of them have changed CEOs at some time after the first round of venture capital;[29,30] only 18% of those that have had IPOs have

---

VENTURE CAPITAL IS "RELATIONSHIP" CAPITAL

Brook Byers and Ray Lane talking about how Kleiner Perkins Caufield & Byers helps entrepreneurs.[28]

Brook Byers (referring to Kleiner Perkins Caufield & Byers' network): It's not keiretsu, it's relationship capital.

Ray Lane: Whether you call it a network, a Rolodex, keiretsu, or whatever, it is something that entrepreneurs crave, because they're looking for help. As Brook said, money is not a differentiator in our business, but they're looking for help. Either you have knowledge in their domain, and you can help them get from startup to a company that actually gets something in the market, or you help them scale through relationships. In this world, at least in the enterprise world, it helps to know somebody.

changed CEOs.[31] Another indication of lack of patience is a venture capital firm quick to invoke covenants in the investment agreement, which contains a couple of hundred pages. There are all manner of covenants in those agreements, and it is not unusual for a company to violate one or perhaps more. An experienced venture capitalist will usually waive a covenant unless the violation is so severe that it jeopardizes the viability of the company.

Deep Pockets. Will the firm have enough money to invest in follow-on rounds of venture capital if the company needs them? Venture capital firms that have been in business for a long time have established a reputation of producing good returns for their limited partners, so they are able to raise new funds from time to time. In contrast, a young venture capital firm with only one small fund without a proven track record of producing satisfactory returns for its limited partners will have difficulty raising a second fund.

Board of Directors. Does the venture capitalist sit on the board and regularly attend meetings? How often does the board meet? And how many boards does the venture capitalist serve on? A rule of thumb is that a venture capitalist should not be on more than half a dozen boards of portfolio companies.

Accessibility. Is the venture capitalist readily available when the entrepreneur needs advice? Conversely, does the venture capitalist interfere too much in the day-to-day running of the company?

Negotiating the Deal

The valuation of the company is probably the biggest issue to be negotiated. Generally, the entrepreneur's valuation is higher than the venture capitalist's. Entrepreneurs can make valuations of the company based on computations like the one earlier in this chapter for BFWS; they can also talk to other entrepreneurs who have recently received venture capital. In general, venture capitalists have more information about pricing than entrepreneurs, because they know the valuations of similar deals that have been recently completed, and those will be the basis for the valuation.

Let's return to BFWS. The entrepreneur's calculations show that the venture capital firm will be looking for 42% of the equity after it has put in its $4 million. Hence, the company will be worth $9.42 million ($4 million/0.42) after the money has been invested, or what is called the *post-money valuation*. The pre-money valuation is thus $5.42 million ($9.42 million − $4 million).

The venture capitalist knows that comparable deals have been valued at $4 million pre-money. So the venture capitalist needs 50% of the equity post-money. After negotiations, the entrepreneur and the venture capitalist settle for a pre-money valuation of $4.5 million for BFWS, which means that the venture capitalist will get 47.1% of the equity with a post-money valuation of $8.5 million, and the entrepreneurs and any angel investors who have already put money into BFWS will be left with 52.9%. The venture capitalists will expect that a pool of stock, about 15% of the issue, will be reserved for key employees who will be hired in the future.

The next step is for the venture capitalist to provide a *term sheet* listing the main conditions of the deal. (You can find samples on the Web.[32]) The term sheet will specify how much money the venture capital firm is investing, how much stock it is getting, a detailed listing of all the stock issued or reserved for stock options *before* the venture capital is invested—and *after*. The venture capitalists will in almost every case get convertible preferred stock. The rights of the preferred stock will be spelled out; they will include dividend provisions, liquidation preferences, conversion rights (usually one share of preferred stock converts to one share of common stock), antidilution provisions, voting rights, and protective provisions.

The term sheet will also have clauses covering information rights, such as a requirement for the company to supply timely unaudited quarterly and audited annual financial statements, board membership, a description of how the venture capital will be used, employment agreements, stock registration rights, and terms under which management can sell stock privately. It will also specify the date when the deal will close.

Term sheet provisions are subject to negotiation. But the sheet will contain a date and time when the venture capitalist's offer will expire unless the entrepreneur has accepted the offer in writing.

Follow-On Rounds of Venture Capital

It is quite likely that there will be subsequent rounds of venture capital. For instance, in 2004 there were 799 first-round venture capital financings and 1,706 follow-on financings in the United States. Let's see what might happen in a second-round of financing for BFWS.

Two years after the first round of venture capital, BFWS has met its milestones set out in its business plan, so the venture capitalists are happy. They had expected that the company would go public to raise more money, but the IPO window is closed (as it was in 2002 and 2003 after the Internet bubble burst, and investors lost their appetite for IPO stocks not only of Internet-related companies but of information technology companies in general). BFWS estimates it needs $6 million to stay on its rapid-growth trajectory for the next two years, when it hopes the IPO window will again be open.

When a company has met its milestones, its valuation has increased. It's not unusual for venture capitalists to agree to a valuation 3 times what it was at the first round. BFWS will be talking both to its present venture capitalists, who will be eager to invest in a second round, and to other venture capitalists so as to get more than one valuation. We'll assume the deal will be struck at a pre-money valuation 3 times the post-money valuation of the first round, or $25.5 million (3 × $8.5 million). The post-money valuation will be $31.5 million. So the venture capitalist will get an additional 19% of the stock for his $6 million investment at the second round of financing. If all goes well and the IPO window opens up during the next two years, BFWS expects to go public.

Harvesting Investments

When business angels or venture capitalists put money into a business, there has to be a way they can realize their investments at a future date. This is called the **exit** or **harvest** for the investor. There are three ways to exit an investment: an initial public offering, an acquisition, and a buyback of the investor's stock by the company itself. We've mentioned that most investors prefer an IPO because it produces the highest valuation in most cases, but not in every case. An acquisition is the second choice. And a buyback is a distant third because in almost every instance it produces a mediocre return.

One of the questions neophyte entrepreneurs seeking external equity financing most often ask is, "Can I buy back the investors' equity?" The answer is "In principle yes, but in practice it is extremely unlikely." Buybacks are rare because a successful and rapidly growing company needs all the cash it can get just to keep on its growth trajectory. It has no free cash to buy out its external investors. A firm doing a buyback is more likely to be one of the living dead for which an IPO or acquisition is not feasible, but somehow the company arranges a refinancing in which it buys back the stock owned by the original investors. Sometimes a venture capital agreement includes a redemption (buyback) clause that allows the venture capital firm to exit its investment by selling it back to the company at a premium if an IPO or acquisition does not occur within a specified time period.

Initial Public Offering

Only a miniscule number of companies raise money with a firm commitment IPO.[33] For example, in an average year, fewer than 100 venture-capital-backed companies have IPOs. When this is divided by the number of companies that raise venture capital each year, it turns out that only 10% of them ever go public. In 2004, 43% of all IPOs were by venture-capital-backed companies. Figure 10.6 shows the funding filters that most venture-capital-backed companies must pass through to get to an IPO.

Without doubt, initial public offerings are glamorous and generally yield the biggest returns for the pre-IPO investors, but in the long run they're not always satisfactory for the entrepreneurs and the management team, for a variety of reasons. Granted, many entrepreneurs such as Bill Gates (Microsoft), Larry Ellison (Oracle), Robert Noyce and Gordon More (Intel), and Bernie Marcus and Arthur Blank (Home Depot) took their companies public and never looked back, but that is not always the case.

Joey Crugnale took his small chain of brick-oven pizza restaurants, Bertucci's, public in 1991 at $13 per share. But he was unable to satisfy Wall Street's appetite for ever-increasing sales and earnings. By 1998 Bertucci's stock, which at one time peaked at $25, was languishing at $6. Crugnale decided that he wanted to take his company private

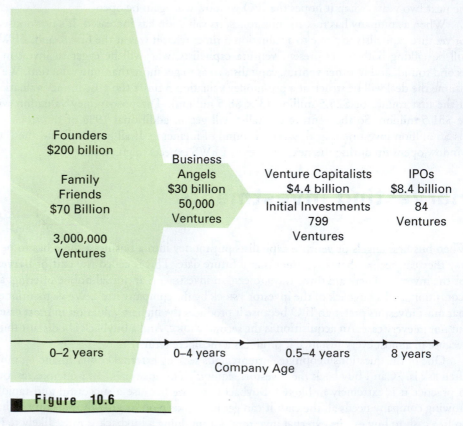

Figure 10.6

Financing filters: 3Fs to IPO based on 2004 data

so that he would be free from the continual scrutiny of investors. He made an offer to buy out the investors for $8 per share. He knew that once he proposed to buy back the company, there was a possibility other companies might bid for it, but he assumed that was very unlikely because he founded the company and he ran it. He soon found out his assumption was wrong. Quite unexpectedly, New England Restaurant Company handily topped his offer with a bid of $10.50 per share. Crugnale agonized over it but decided not to make a counteroffer. He walked away from Bertucci's a wealthy man at 46, but with a feeling of loss because he no longer was running the business he had built from scratch into a chain of 84 restaurants in 11 states and the District of Columbia. He sometimes regrets taking Bertucci's public instead of keeping the company private and building his personal wealth from the cash flow that his restaurants were generating.

Crugnale has subsequently started Cajun-Mexican, Latin-fish, and Italian restaurants—each one with several outlets—hoping to repeat his success with Bertucci's. So far it has eluded him. But he consoles himself with the knowledge that it took several years before Bertucci's was a hit. However, one thing he knows for sure is that his restaurants will not go public. "I have no investors, I own everything myself, so I don't have to answer to anybody . . . . There are no restrictions, and I like that freedom."[34]

Pros and Cons of an IPO

The following are the upsides of going public.

Financing. The principal reason for a public offering is to raise a substantial amount of money that does not have to be repaid. For example, the average amount of money raised by the 84 venture-capital-backed companies that floated initial public offerings in 2004 was $101.5 million. The average post-money valuation of the companies was $671.1 million. And on average, the companies sold 16.4% of their equity at the IPO.

Follow-On Financing. A public company can raise more capital by issuing additional stock in a secondary offering.

Realizing Prior Investments. Once a company is public, shareholders prior to the IPO know the value of their investment. What's more, their stock is liquid and can be sold on the stock market after the lockup period is over. The **lockup period** is a length of time after the IPO date (usually 180 days) when the prior shareholders are not permitted to sell any of their stock.

Prestige and Visibility. A public company is more visible and has more prestige. This sometimes helps the company with marketing and selling its products, outsourcing, hiring employees, and banking.

Compensation for Employees. Stock options presently held by employees or granted in the future have a known value.

Acquiring Other Companies. A public company can use its shares to acquire other companies.

And here are the downsides of going public.

High Expenses. Expenses associated with going public are substantial. They include legal and accounting fees, printing costs, and registration fees, which can range from $100,000 to $400,000 or more. Those expenses are not recoverable if the company does not actually go public, which happens to about half the companies that embark on the IPO process and fail to complete it. If the company does go public, the underwriter's commission takes approximately 7% of the money raised.

Public Fishbowl. When a company goes public, SEC regulations require that it disclose a great deal of information about itself that until then has been private and known only to insiders. That information includes compensation of officers and directors, employee stock option plans, significant contracts such as lease and consulting agreements, details about operations including business strategies, sales, cost of sales, gross profits, net income, debt, and future plans. The IPO prospectus and other documents that have to be filed with the SEC are in the public domain; they are a gold mine for competitors and others that want to pry into the company's affairs. At the peak of the Internet bubble in November 1999, Cobalt Networks went public; its market niche was inexpensive thin servers for small and mid-sized organizations. Before the IPO, the inexpensive thin-server market hadn't attracted much competition from big companies such as Dell, IBM, Hewlett-Packard, and Sun Microsystems. However, after Cobalt's spectacular IPO, they became aware that the niche was growing rapidly. Ten months later, Sun announced it was acquiring Cobalt.

Short-Term Time Horizon. After an IPO, shareholders and financial researchers expect ever-increasing performance quarter by quarter. This expectation forces management to focus on maximizing short-term performance rather than long-term goals.

Post-IPO Compliance Costs. To meet SEC regulations, a public company incurs accounting costs it never had when it was private. Those can amount to $100,000 or more annually.

Management's Time. After an IPO, the CEO and the CFO have to spend time on public relations with the research analysts, financial journalists, institutional investors, other stockholders, and market makers—so-called because they make a market for the company's stock. This is a distraction from their main job, which is running the company for optimal performance. Some public companies have executives whose main job is dealing with investor relations.

Takeover Target. A public company sometimes becomes the target of an unwelcome takeover by another company.

Employee Disenchantment. A rising stock price boosts the morale of employees with stock or stock options, but when it is sinking, it can be demoralizing—especially when an employee's options go "underwater" (the stock price falls below the options price). Underwater options can make it difficult to motivate and retain key employees.

The Process of Going Public

Before a company can have an IPO, it must file a registration statement with the SEC to ensure that the prospectus discloses everything the public needs to know before deciding whether to buy its shares. The IPO cannot go forward until the SEC has approved the registration statement. A delay sometimes wreaks havoc on a company's finances if the IPO window closes suddenly. When the Internet bubble burst, many CEOs who had anticipated using the proceeds from IPOs to finance their companies were unable to float public offerings. Some companies were sold at fire-sale prices, and others shut their doors with huge losses to private investors, especially venture capital firms.

Entrepreneurs with serious aspirations to take their companies public should be farsighted and run their companies from the beginning as if they will have a future IPO. In practice this means their accounting and law firms should be well-known national firms with lots of clients who have had IPOs. Of course this is more expensive than starting out with small, local firms, but it will pay off in the long run if there is an IPO or acquisition by a public company.

When a company decides it's time to go public, the first step is to select an investment banker. This is where professional advisers such as accounting firms, law firms, and venture capitalists are valuable. Studies have shown that companies backed by leading venture capital firms and taken public by leading underwriters have the highest market capitalizations.[35] Leading investment bankers are not shy. They aggressively pursue companies that they would like to take public. Banks compete for a company's IPO in what's called a *beauty contest* or *bake-off*. They present their credentials to the company's CEO and board of directors and place a preliminary valuation on the company using the market-comparable (NI × P/E) method. The company usually selects the underwriter that has had the most success with IPOs in the same industry during the previous few years. If the company selects more than one underwriter, the bank managing the IPO is the *lead underwriter*, and the other banks are called the *syndicate*.

As soon as the underwriter has been selected, the IPO process begins in earnest with an "all-hands" meeting in which the key players—including the lead underwriter, accounting and law firms, and company executives—decide what they will do and when. They then prepare the prospectus with all the information the SEC deems the public needs to know before investing. This document includes details of the offering, what the company plans to do with the proceeds, the company's financial history and its future strategy, information about company management, and the company's industry niche, especially its competition. Risks are spelled out in detail. The preliminary prospectus is colloquially called the *red herring* because on the front page is a notice printed in red stating that some information is subject to change, in particular the price per share and the number of shares to be offered. After filing the preliminary prospectus with the SEC, the company waits for the SEC, the NASD, and perhaps state securities organizations to review the documents for any omissions or problems that it must correct before the IPO can proceed. A *quiet period* lasts from the moment the company files the preliminary prospectus with the SEC until 25 days after the IPO. During this time the company is forbidden to distribute any information about itself that is not contained in its prospectus.

Once the preliminary prospectus has been approved, the lead underwriter and the CEO embark on a whirlwind tour of leading financial centers such as New York, San Francisco, Los Angeles, Chicago, Boston, and perhaps overseas centers such as London, Paris, Frankfurt, Hong Kong, and Tokyo. The purpose of the tour, or "road show," is to promote the upcoming IPO and gauge the level of interest from potential investors. During the road show and immediately after, the underwriter builds a book of investors who say they want to buy the stock. The underwriter and the company meet the day before the IPO and use the order book to set the price of the stock and the size of the offering. The more the stock is oversubscribed, the higher the price will be. The underwriter commits to deliver the agreed upon proceeds to the company regardless of whether it sells all the stock at the offering price. This commitment creates tension between the company pushing for a high price and the underwriter wanting to set a price that will enable it to sell all the stock at the offering price. Once the price had been set, the company distributes stock to the banks in the syndicate, who then allocate it to their clients.

The underwriter hopes the price at the end of the first day's trading will be about 15% higher than the offering price; this is known as the *first-day pop*. The number of shares in the offering multiplied by the pop is known as *money left on the table;* it is the additional amount of money the company would have received if the offering price had been the same as the first day's closing price. (Academic researchers refer to it as *under pricing*). During the Internet bubble, when the public's appetite for Internet-related stocks was insatiable, first-day pops of more than 100% were not unusual.

If the share price shoots up and stays there, some companies have a secondary public offering and raise more money, usually before the 180-day lockup expires and the market is flooded by insiders selling shares and depressing the price. Sycamore Networks, for example, raised $284 million at its IPO in October 1999. It had a first-day pop of almost 400%. About five months later, with the stock about 500% above its IPO price, it had a secondary offering and raised about $1.2 billion.

An IPO at the Peak of the Internet Bubble

Stephen DeWitt, the high-energy, 33-year-old CEO of Cobalt Networks, had just completed a 15-day, 4-country, 27-city, 61-presentation road show to pitch the IPO of the company. Now, on Wednesday morning, November 10, 1999, he was excited as he sipped coffee in a large conference room at the Wall Street offices of Goldman Sachs in New York City. All the investors he had met with were planning to participate, and in fact the offering was substantially oversubscribed. The offering of 5 million shares at an IPO price of $22 would raise just over $102 million after expenses and commissions. Those funds would be used to further strengthen international sales efforts and expand Cobalt's product line. Cobalt's objective was to become the leading global provider in the emerging market for flexible, low-cost Internet server appliances. The company had net revenues of $3.5 million in 1998, and $13.8 million for the first three quarters of 1999. Net losses were $10.5 million and $13.7 million for the same periods.

Five minutes after trading began, the stock was at $45 with no sell orders, and DeWitt stood before the monitors as the offering was placed in a 15-minute "penalty box"—1 of 2 mandatory cooling-off periods imposed to quell investor euphoria. Seven minutes out of the penalty box, transactions were suspended for the second and final time at $75 a share. Trading resumed and within 5 minutes the first sell order was received at $92 per share. The closing price at the end of the day was $139 a share, giving the company a market capitalization of just over $5 billion. At the end of the first day's trading, Cobalt Networks had the third-largest market capitalization of any IPO in NASDAQ's history.

BFWS Goes Public

Let's return to our example. Two years after raising its second round of venture capital, and five years after it was founded, the IPO window for software companies is open so BFWS decides to go public. It has exceeded its forecasts and has revenue of $75 million with net income of $8.33 million. Revenue is growing at 50% per year. It wants to raise $50 million gross with an IPO. Based on the prevailing industry P/E ratio of 30, the investment bank values the company post-IPO at $250 million ($8.33 million × 30). To raise $50 million, BFWS will have to sell 20% of its equity (50/250 × 100). That leaves the existing stock holders with 80% of the company.

Everyone should be happy with the return on their investments. At the IPO price, the $4 million of first-round venture capital is worth $64.8 million (16.2 × return and IRR of 100%), and the $6 million of second-round venture capital is worth $38.1 million (6.3 × return and IRR of 152%). The founders and the original investors hold stock worth $72.9 million, and the stock option pool is worth $24.3 million. The original founders and stockholders own 29.1% of BFWS, the venture capitalists own 41.1%, the stock option pool 9.7%, and the public 20%. And the company receives the proceeds of $50 million minus the underwriters 7% commission; that is $46.5 million.

Selling the Company

By far the most common way for investors to realize their investment, if a company has done well and chooses not to go public, is to sell the business to another company. A company is usually bought by a bigger company for strategic reasons, such as when a big pharmaceutical company buys out a young biotech company that has developed a promising drug but lacks the resources and experience to take it through the FDA approval process or market it once approved.

A Strategic Acquisition: LowerMyBills.com

Matt Coffin started LowerMyBills.com in 1999. His vision was to provide consumers with a free, one-stop Internet destination to obtain better deals on all their recurring monthly expenses including mortgages, utilities, automobile loans, insurance, and credit cards. LowerMyBills.com attracts customers for mortgage lenders and others by advertising on a wide variety of Web sites, including Yahoo!, AOL, and MSN. Consumers who click through on mortgage ads, for example, are taken to the LowerMyBills.com Web site, where they enter information relevant to the mortgage approval process. The Web site matches this against the lending criteria of the clients of LowerMyBills.com and passes qualifying leads on to several different lenders. The lenders contact the consumer, who can choose the most appropriate offer. LowerMyBills.com is paid for every lead it passes to a lender.

In the last quarter of 2001, LowerMyBills.com posted its first profit. By 2005, it had a leading position in the U.S. market. The company, based in Santa Monica, California, was financed with $12 million first from business angels and then venture capital firms. Coffin, who still owned 25% of the equity, commented:[36]

Courtesy Matt Coffin

Matt Coffin, Founder, LowerMyBills.com.

By 2004, I knew personally that I was way in the money, but I also knew that I had 99% of my net worth tied up in the business. Back when the Internet crashed, I had a bunch of friends that had started online companies that had gone up and come down fast. One guy who had turned down an offer for $700 million went bankrupt a year later.

Investment banks were calling me like crazy to say it was time for us to go public. We looked at the possibility of raising additional capital from new investors—recapitalize with new shareholders so that current stakeholders could get some liquidity. There was also the option of selling to a corporate buyer while staying on in some sort of earn-out arrangement.

The team hired an investment bank, gave nine presentations, and within short order had received eight offers from corporate buyers ranging from two to four hundred million dollars. Private equity firms that were interested in a partial buyout were putting forward valuations that averaged half of what the acquirers were offering. This decision was about a lot more than finance:

Every employee owns stock in this business, and they have worked really hard to get us to this point. We did need some sort of harvest, but I also knew that we still had a lot of growth ahead of us, and every option has its own set of risks and potential ramifications.

Coffin was in the enviable position of having a business that was growing rapidly in an industry segment that was expanding extremely fast. LowerMyBills.com had 176 employees. On a pro-forma basis, sales in the year ended March 31, 2005, were $120 million, with operating profit of $26 million. Clearly, the company could have gone public, but Coffin decided to explore being acquired by a strategic partner. In May 2005, LowerMyBills.com was acquired by Experian, a member of GUS, plc, the British retail and services group. Here are excerpts from a press release by GUS plc:

Acquisition of LowerMyBills.com by Experian[37]

GUS plc, the retail and business services group, today [May 5, 2005] announces that Experian has acquired 100% of the share capital of LowerMyBills.com, a leading online generator of mortgage and other loan application leads in the United States. LowerMyBills.com is complementary to Experian's existing direct-to-consumer activities and operates in large, fast-growing markets. The purchase price is $330 million, plus a maximum performance-related earn-out of $50 million over the next two years. Further strong growth in sales and profit is expected in the current financial year and beyond. The acquisition is being funded from GUS' existing banking facilities. The acquisition is expected comfortably to exceed GUS' financial target of generating a double-digit post-tax return on investment over time.

Experian is establishing leading positions in various markets in connecting consumers with companies via the Internet. Its strategy is to offer a wide range of products that assist consumers in managing the financial aspects of key life events such as moving house or buying a car. Experian enables consumers to find financial products and services that best suit their needs, while helping companies to find new customers quickly and effectively. As well as LowerMyBills.com, the newly-formed Experian Interactive operation includes Consumer Direct (selling credit reports, scores, and monitoring products to consumers) and MetaReward and Affiliate Fuel (both of which generate online leads for clients).

This acquisition is attractive because:

LowerMyBills.com operates in large, fast-growing markets. More than 20 million American households take out a new mortgage each year. In 2004, home lenders spent $22 billion on acquiring customers, an amount which has grown by over one-third in the last five years. Of the $22bn, about $1 billion is currently spent online and this is growing by about 30% a year. For example, Experian estimates that the percentage of mortgages originated online will treble between 2003 and 2008.

LowerMyBills.com has a strong market position. LowerMyBills.com is the most visited home loan service on the Internet. In a highly fragmented market, it is one of only two players of scale with its online leads generating more loans than any individual lending institution. It has strong relationships with more than 400 lenders, including five of the top ten mortgage providers in the United States.

Over time, LowerMyBills.com will benefit from the skills, expertise, and client relationships within Experian:

Consumer Direct, MetaReward, and LowerMyBills.com all work in the same Internet space and can share expertise and traffic. Combined, these businesses have more than 29 million visitors to their Web sites each month; and there are also benefits of LowerMyBills.com working more closely with Experian's Credit business. The introduction of Experian's modeling and analytical capabilities will allow it to improve the quality of leads passed to lenders. Experian will also be able to sell LowerMyBills.com's services to its existing financial services clients, where it has strong relationships.

Don Robert, Chief Executive Officer of Experian, commented:

"This acquisition represents a step-change in building Experian's direct-to-consumer activities. With LowerMyBills.com, we will now assist consumers in making the most cost-effective financial services decisions, while also providing our lender clients with

high-quality leads for new borrowers. The strategic fit could not be better and we are delighted to welcome the talented people of LowerMyBills.com to Experian."

Why Be Acquired?

The acquisition of LowerMyBills.com by Experian is a very good example of what the seller and the acquirer are seeking from a strategic acquisition. The following are the advantages and disadvantages of an acquisition from the perspective of the seller.

Management. By selling the company rather than going public, the managers can stay focused on what they do best—continue to build the company—rather then having to spend a lot of time on public relations with the financial community. Also, they probably will not be as driven by quarter-by-quarter results as they would be if the company were public. For example, LowerMyBills.com will have only a tiny effect on GUS's net income; it can probably focus on rapid sales growth rather than optimizing quarterly profits for the next few years.

Founder and CEO. Selling a company the entrepreneur has built from nothing into a thriving enterprise can be traumatic. Edward Marram (co-author of Chapter 14 of this book) sold his company, GeoCenter, in 2005. He said his head told him that it was the right thing to do, but his heart told him not to do it. After all, he was selling a company he started from nothing in 1975 and built into an organization with 1,100 employees. When a company is private, the CEO reports only to a board of directors, but when it is acquired he or she has to report to a boss; if the acquirer is a big company, that boss may report to a boss. It can be very frustrating for the CEO/founder who has been making all the important decisions to find that his or her ideas have to be approved by a hierarchy before they can be implemented.

Company. GUS has very deep pockets; it will be able to provide capital to LowerMyBills.com if it needs it.

Investors. Acquisitions are often paid for in cash rather than stock. Thus investors get cash immediately after the deal is completed, unlike in a public offering when pre-IPO investors have stock they cannot sell for 180 days and the risk that the stock will go down before they can sell it. Of course, if the company is bought with the acquirer's stock instead of cash, and if there are restrictions on the sale of the stock, there is still a risk that the stock price will go down before the investors can sell it.

Entrepreneur and Employees Stock. If it is a cash transaction, as it was in the LowerMyBills.com acquisition, the entrepreneurs and employees get cash immediately. The potential disadvantage is that they no longer hold stock, so they have no upside potential if the company continues to do well. True, there is usually an *earn-out,* which is additional compensation to be paid in a few years if the company meets targets specified at the time of the acquisition. In the case of LowerMyBills.com the earn-out is $50 million, compared with $330 million paid when the acquisition was completed. It is well worth getting the earn-out, but it is only 15.2% more, so it might not be enough to motivate key employees to stay.

Employment Agreement. Key employees will have an employment agreement that forbids them to compete with the company for a specific number of years—usually no more than two—if they leave. That will probably be the same agreement they had with the company before it was acquired. However, the CEO and top management will almost certainly be required to sign new noncompete agreements as part of their employment contracts with the acquirer.

Culture. Initially, the acquirer will not interfere in the management of the purchased company, but eventually it will probably want to put in its own management system and maybe its own executives in a few key positions. When it does that, there is a risk there will be a clash of cultures.

Expenses and Commissions. The expenses and investment banker's commission are substantially lower for an acquisition than for an IPO.

CONCLUSION

When an entrepreneur accepts money from a financially sophisticated investor such as a business angel or a venture capitalist, there has to be a future harvest when the investment can be realized. Generally that harvest occurs when the company is acquired; occasionally, it happens when the company goes public. The harvest is primarily for the investors rather than the entrepreneurs. If entrepreneurs are not careful, they can give would-be investors the impression that they themselves are planning to exit the company at the harvest. That is not what professional investors like to hear. They want to invest in entrepreneurs whose vision is to build a business and continue building it after the harvest, not in entrepreneurs who are in it to get rich quick. Remember that Bill Gates made almost all his huge fortune by the appreciation of Microsoft's stock after its IPO; so did Microsoft employees and investors who held on to their stock for many years after the IPO.

After a long negotiation between a Boston area entrepreneur and a venture capitalist for seed-stage financing of a medical device company, the venture capitalist asked the entrepreneur, "Where do you personally want to be in ten years' time?" The entrepreneur replied that he hoped he would have built a $200 million company that was the leader in its market niche and that he would still be the CEO. The venture capitalist immediately shook the entrepreneur's hand and said, "You have your money." The entrepreneur was very surprised because it seemed to him that the venture capitalist already knew about how big the company might become if things went well, so he asked what triggered the spontaneous decision to invest. The venture capitalist replied, "If you had said, 'retired to a house on the beach in Maine,' we would not have invested. We want entrepreneurs who are focused on building businesses for the long haul, rather than short-term personal wealth." The venture capitalists added, "Congratulations, you have just completed the most difficult selling job you will ever do. You have convinced a venture capitalist to invest in a seed-stage company."

YOUR OPPORTUNITY JOURNAL ☐

Reflection Point

1. How can you bootstrap your venture? What services can you get for free or at reduced rates? What equipment can you lease or buy used?

2. In the last chapter, you created a funding strategy. Now, think about how you will gain access to angels and VCs. Who can make introductions on your behalf?

3. What valuation method makes the most sense for you company? What comparable companies can you refer to as you prepare your valuation?

4. Imagine your harvest. What companies might likely acquire you? How can you prepare for that future acquisition?

5. Is there a possibility that your company could go public (high-growth industry)? What do you need to do to prepare for that?

Your Thoughts...

WEB EXERCISE ☐

Identify several companies that you can use as comparables in a valuation. What P/E ratios currently prevail across the companies? Can you explain the variance in P/Es? Which comparable company is yours most similar to? Where does the P/E fall in the range? Compute a valuation for your firm. What adjustments should you make?

NOTES ☐

[1] Keynes, John Maynard. *A Treatise on Money.* London: Macmillan and Co. 1933.

[2] Cummings Properties works with local colleges and universities to promote entrepreneurship. Cummings helps sponsor several local business plan competitions and also provides special rate packages for new businesses growing out of college programs. The following site has links to colleges with Cummings Properties sponsorship programs: www.cummings.com/how_to_lease_space.htm#entrep.

[3] Bygrave, W. D. and Reynolds, P. D. Who finances startups in the U.S.A.? A comprehensive study of informal investors, 1999–2003. In S. Zahra

et al. (Eds.) *Frontiers of Entrepreneurship Research 2004*, Wellesley, MA: Babson College.

4 Ibid.

5 CircleLending. www.circlelending.com. Although borrowing money from relatives, friends, and business associates is common, very little has been written about how to do it well. CircleLending, Inc. is a pioneering company that has developed a set of products and services to facilitate these transactions (see www.circlelending.com). Based in Waltham, Massachusetts, the company manages loans between relatives, friends, and other private parties in over 45 U.S. states, and offers information online you can use to get financing quickly. Generally, the process works like this:

1. Identify a lender and agree on financing terms, such as loan amount, interest rate, and term.

2. Formalize the loan with a legally binding document, such as a promissory note.

3. Create a system for repayment that is affordable for you and reassures your lender that the loan will eventually be repaid.

CircleLending has found a way to keep private loans on track by restructuring them if your business goes through difficult times along the way. Tracking the payments during a restructuring is critical in order to deduct the interest as a business expense. The company can also help you develop a credit rating for your business by reporting the performance of private loans to credit bureaus. By structuring your private financing in a business-like manner, you will be able to demonstrate to your investors that you are serious about your endeavor.

6 Wetzel. W. E. Jr. and Freear, J. Promoting informal venture capital in the United States: Reflections on the history of the Venture Capital

Network. 1994 In R.T. Harrison and C. M. Mason (Eds.), *Informal Venture Capital: Information, Networks and Public Policy*. Hemel-Hemstead, UK: Woodhead-Faulkner.

7 Osnabrugge, Mark Van, Robinson Robert J. *Angel Investing: Matching Startup Funds with Startup Companies—A Guide for Entrepreneurs, Individual Investors, and Venture Capitalists* Cambridge, MA: Harvard Business School. 2000.

8 Wainwright, F. Note on Angel Investing. Tuck School of Business at Dartmouth: Center for Private Equity and Entrepreneurship. Case # 5 001. 2005.

9 Excerpted from *Business Week*, November 21, 2005, pp. 105–112.

10 Seitz, Patrick. What's A Dream Team's DNA? Businesses could learn some team dynamics from Broadway, scientists. *Investor's Business Daily*, June 6, 2005.

11 "The Color Purple" Draws Diverse Crowd, New York, June 6, 2006. Associated Press. www.cbsnews.com/stories/2006/06/06/entertainment/printable 1689627.shtml.

12 As of the writing of this book, a comprehensive list of angel groups can be found at www.inc.com/articles/2001/09/23461.html.

13 http://activecapital.org/.

14 Cited in David R. Evanson and Art Berof, Heaven Sent. Seeking an angel investor? Here's how to find a match made in heaven. *Entrepreneur* magazine. January 1998.

15 www.failuremag.com/failure_interview.html.

16 www.sec.gov/info/smallbus/qasbsec.htm#eod6.

17 Wainwright, F. Note on Angel Investing. Tuck School of Business at Dartmouth: Center for Private Equity and Entrepreneurship. Case # 5 001.

18 *Venture Support Systems Project: Angel Investors*. Release 1.1. MIT

Entrepreneurship Center. February 2000.

19 Ibid.

20 Ibid.

21 Ibid.

22 www.lottery.state.mn.us/qanda.html#0.

23 Baccher, Jagdeep. Dissertation. University of Waterloo. 2000.

24 www.siliconbeat.com/entries/2004/11/13/qa_with_kleiner_perkins_caufield_byers.html.

25 Bygrave, W. D., Johnstone, G., Lewis, J., and Ullman, R. Venture Capitalists' Criteria for Selecting High-Tech Investments: Prescriptive Wisdom Compared with Actuality. *Frontiers of Entrepreneurship Research 1998*. Wellesley, MA: Babson College. www.babson.edu/entrep/fer/papers98/XX/XX_A/XX_A.html

26 *Pratt's Guide to Private Equity Sources,* 2004 Edition. Toby Walters (Editor). Publisher: Venture Economics. http://www.ventureeconomics.com/vec/publications.html

27 Rosenstein, J., Bruno, A. V., Bygrave, W. D. and Taylor, N. T. CEO Appraisal of Their Boards in Venture Capital Portfolios. *Journal of Business Venturing*, 8(2), 99–113. 1993.

28 http://www.siliconbeat.com/entries/2004/11/13/qa_with_kleiner_perkins_caufield_byers.html.

29 Rosenstein, J., Bruno, A. V., Bygrave, W. D., and Taylor, N. T. How Much Do CEOs Value the Advice of Venture Capitalists on Their Boards? *Frontiers of Entrepreneurship Research, 1990*. Wellesley, MA: Babson College. 1990.

30 Bygrave, W. D., Marram, E., and Scherzer, T. Boards of Directors of Venture-Capital-Backed Companies. Presented at Babson-Kauffman Entrepreneurship Research Conference, Boulder, Colorado, June 2002. Summary published in *Frontiers of Entrepreneurship 2002*. Wellesley, MA: Babson College.

31 Bygrave, W. D., Johnstone, G., Lewis, J., and Ullman, R. Venture Capitalists' Criteria for Selecting High-Tech Investments: Prescriptive Wisdom Compared with Actuality, *Frontiers of Entrepreneurship Research 1998*. Wellesley, MA: Babson College. www.babson.edu/entrep/fer/papers98/XX/XX_A/XX_A.html.

32 www.netpreneur.org/funding/anatomy_term_sheet.pdf.

33 In a firm commitment IPO, an underwriter guarantees to raise a certain amount of money for a company; in contrast, with a best efforts offering, an underwriter does its best to sell as many of the shares as it can at the offering price. Firm commitments are far superior to best efforts offerings. All IPOs that are listed on the NASDAQ, New York Stock Exchange, and the American Stock Exchange are firm commitment ones. The statistics given in this book refer to firm commitment offerings.

34 McGinn, Daniel. Reinventing Mr. Bertucci. January 18, 2004. www.boston.com/news/globe/magazine/articles/2004/01/18/reinventing_mr_bertucci?mode=PF.

35 Bygrave, W. D. and Timmons, J. *Venture Capital at the Crossroads*. Boston, MA: Harvard Business School Press. 1992.

36 *Matt Coffin*. A case study published by Babson College. 2006.

37 Excerpted from www.gusplc.com/gus/news/gusarchive/gus2005/2005-05-05/.

CASE

Jon Hirschtick's New Venture

August, 1994, 12 months after Jon Hirschtick left a great job to found a new venture in the software industry, SolidWorks, the deal was looking good. The seed capital discussions had shifted into high gear as soon as Michael Payne joined the SolidWorks team. After working on the deal for 9 months, Axel Bichara, the Atlas Venture vice president originating the project, finally got a syndicate excited about it: Atlas Venture, North Bridge Venture Capital Partners, and Burr, Egan, Deleage & Co. presented an offer sheet to SolidWorks two weeks after Michael was onboard.

This process was particularly interesting because Jon and Axel had worked together for most of the past eight years. They met at MIT in 1986 and cofounded Premise, Inc., a computer-aided design (CAD) software company, in 1987. After Premise was bought by Computervision, they joined that team as managers. Now, they sat on opposite sides of the table for Axel's first deal as the lead venture capitalist.

Jon and the other founders thought valuation and terms were fair, but the post-money[1] equity issue was unresolved. They had to decide how much money to raise. Did they want enough capital to support SolidWorks until it achieved a positive cash flow, or should they take less money and attempt to increase the entrepreneurial team's post-money equity?

If they took less money now, they could raise funds later, when SolidWorks might have a higher valuation. But they would be gambling on the success of the development team and the investment climate. If their product was in beta testing with high customer acceptance, raising more money would probably be fast and fun, but if they hit any development snags, the process could take a lot of time and yield a poor result.

Jon Hirschtick: 1962–1987

Jon grew up in Chicago in an entrepreneurial family. He fondly remembers helping with his father's part-time business by traveling to stamp collectors' shows across the Midwest. In high school, he was self-employed as a magician.

The entrepreneurial impulse continued during his undergraduate years. Jon recalls the Blackjack team he played with at MIT:

> *We raised money to get started. At the same time, we developed a probabilistic system for winning at Blackjack. The results were amazing! We tripled our money in the first six months, doubled it during the next six months, and doubled it again in the next six months. We produced a 900% annualized return. I learned a useful lesson: you really can know more than the next guy, and make money by applying that knowledge. We tackled Blackjack because people thought it was unbeatable; we studied it, and we won. The same principle applies to entrepreneurship. Opportunities often exist where popular opinion holds that they don't.*

Jon's introduction to CAD came from a college internship with Computervision during the summer of 1981. Computervision was one of the most successful startup companies to emerge during the 1970s. By the early 1980s, it dominated the CAD market.

This case was written by Dab D'Heilly and Tricia Jaekle under the direction of Professor William Bygrave. Funding provided by the Ewing Marion Kauffman Foundation and the Frederic C. Hamilton Chair for Free Enterprise Studies. © Copyright Babson College, 1995. All rights reserved.

[1] **Post-money valuation** is the value of a company's equity after additional money is invested.

After earning a master's degree in mechanical engineering (M.E.) at MIT, Jon managed the MIT CAD laboratory. He supervised student employees, coordinated research projects, and conducted tours for visitors.

Axel Bichara: 1963–1987

Axel was born in Berlin and attended a French high school. In 1986, while studying at the Technical University of Berlin for a master's degree in mechanical engineering, he won a scholarship to MIT. Axel had worked in a CAD research lab in Germany, so he selected the CAD laboratory for his work-study assignment at MIT.

Early CAD Software

CAD software traces its roots to 1969 when computers were first used by engineers to automate the production of drawings. CAD was used by architects, engineers, designers, and other planners to create various types of drawings and blueprints. Any company that designed and manufactured products (e.g., Ford, Sony, Black & Decker) was a prospective CAD software customer.

An Entrepreneurship Class: January 1987

Visitors to the MIT CAD lab often complained about problems that Jon knew he could solve. He enrolled in an entrepreneurship class to write a business plan for a CAD startup company, Premise, Inc. Jon described the decision to quit his job and start a company:

I once heard Mitch Kapor[2] use a game show metaphor to describe the entrepreneurial impulse. He said, "Part of the entrepreneurial instinct is to push the button before you know the answer and hope it will come to you before the buzzer." That's what happened for us: we didn't know how to start a company, or how to fund it, but Premise got rolling, and we came up with answers before we ran out of time.

Jon and Axel were surprised and delighted to find each other in the entrepreneurship class. They had worked together for the past month on a project at the CAD lab, and they decided to become partners in the first class session. Axel recalled:

It was a coincidence that we enrolled in the same class, but it was clear that we should work together. Jon had had the idea for a couple of months, and we started work on the product and the business plan immediately.

Axel took the master's exam at MIT in October 1987, and at Technical University of Berlin in July 1988. He was still a student at both universities when he and Jon started Premise. Axel graduated with highest honors from both institutions.

Premise, Inc.: 1987–1991

Premise went from concept to business plan to venture-capitalist-backed startup in less than six months. As Axel remembered:

---

[2] Mitchell Kapor founded Lotus Development Corporation.

The class deadline for the business plan was May 14. On June 1, we had our first meeting with venture capitalists, and by June 22, we had a handshake deal with Harvard Management Company for $1.5 m. We actually received an advance that week. It was much easier than it should have been, but the story's 100% true.

In the first quarter of 1989, Premise raised its second round of capital. Harvard Management and Kleiner Perkins Caufield & Byers combined to finance the product launch. The product shipped in May to very positive industry reviews, but sales were slow. Premise's software didn't solve a large mass-market problem. As Jon later recalled:

I've seen successful companies get started without talent, time, or money—but I've never seen a successful company without a market. Premise targeted a small market. I had a professor who said it all, "The only necessary and sufficient condition for a business is customers."

By the end of 1990, the partners had decided that the best way to harvest Premise was an industry buyout. They hired a Minneapolis investment banking firm to find a buyer. Wessels, Arnold & Henderson was considered one of the elite investment banking firms serving the CAD industry. Premise attracted top-level service providers because of the prestige of its venture capitalist partners. Jon explained:

Several bankers wanted to do the deal, and a big reason was because they wanted to work with our venture capitalists. We had top venture capitalists, and that opened all kinds of doors. This is often under-appreciated. I believe in shopping for venture capital partners.

Wessels, Arnold & Henderson were as good as their reputation. As Axel recalled:

We sold Premise to Computervision on 7 March 1991. Computervision bought us for our proprietary technology and engineering team. It was a good deal for both companies.

Computervision: 1991–1993

As part of the purchase agreement, Jon and Axel joined the management team at Computervision. They managed the integration of Premise's development team and product line for one year before Axel left to study business in Europe. Jon stayed on after Axel's departure.

Revenues for the Premise team's products grew 200% between 1991 and 1993, and perhaps as important as direct revenue, their technology was incorporated into some of Computervision's high-end products. In January 1993, Jon was promoted to director of product definition for another CAD product. He stayed in this position for eight months. After two years at Computervision, he was ready for new horizons. He resigned effective August 23, 1993. (See Exhibit 1 for excerpts from his letter of resignation.)

After a holiday in the Caribbean, Jon purchased new computer equipment, called business friends and associates, and began working on a business plan. He didn't have a clear product idea, but his market research suggested that the time was ripe for a new CAD startup.

CAD Software Market in the 1990s

By the 1990s, the hottest CAD software performed a function called solid modeling. Solid modeling produced three-dimensional computer objects that resembled the products

EXHIBIT 10.1	Excerpts from Hirschtick's Letter of Resignation from Computervision (CV)

This is my explanation for wanting to leave CV . . . The other day you asked me whether I was leaving because I was unhappy, or whether I really want to start another company. I strongly believe that it is because I really want to work on another entrepreneurial venture.* I want to try to build another company that achieves business value . . .

I am interested in leaving CV to pursue another entrepreneurial opportunity because I seek to:

1. Be a part of business strategy decision. I want to attend board meetings and create business plans, as I did at Premise.

2. Select, recruit, lead, and motivate team of outstanding people. I believe that one of my strengths is the ability to selected great people and form strong teams.

3. Represent a company with customers, press, investors, and analysts. I enjoy the challenge of selling and presenting to these groups.

4. Work on multidisciplinary problems: market analysis, strategy, product funding, distribution, and marketing. I am good at cross-functional problem-solving and deal-making.

5. Work in a fast-moving environment. I like to be in a place where decision can be made quickly, and individuals (not just me) are empowered to use their own judgment.

6. Work in a customer-driven and market-driven organization. I find technology and computer architecture interesting only as they directly relate to winning business. I want to focus on building products customers want to buy.

7. Have significant equity-based incentives. I thrive on calculated risks with large potential rewards.

8. Be recognized for having built business success. I measure "business success" by sales, profitability, and company valuation; I want to directly impact business success. Recognition will follow. I admit that this ego-need plays a part in my decision.

Summary

I've decided I want to work on an entrepreneurial venture . . . This is more a function of what I do best than any problems at CV . . . I don't have any delusions about an entrepreneurial company being any easier. I know first-hand that startup companies have at least as many obstacles as large established companies — but they are the obstacles I want.

---

*Underlines in original.

being built in almost every detail. It was primarily used for designing manufacturing tools and parts. Solid modeling was Solid Works' focus. The key benefits driving the boom in solid modeling were:

1. Relatively inexpensive CAD prototypes could be accurate enough to replace costly (labor, materials, tooling, etc.) physical prototypes.

2. The elimination of physical prototypes dramatically improved time-to-market.

3. More prototypes could be created and tested, so product quality was improved.

However, not all CAD software could manage solid modeling well enough to effectively replace physical prototypes.

Most vendors offered CAD software based on computer technology from the 1970s and 1980s. IBM, Computervision, Intergraph, and other traditional market leaders were losing market share because solid modeling required software architecture that worked poorly on older systems.

As one of the industry's newest competitors, Parametric Technology Corp. (PTC) was setting new benchmarks for state-of-the-art solid modeling software. (It was an eight-year-old company in 1994.) CAD was a mature and fragmented industry with many competitors, but PTC thrived because other companies tried to make older technology perform solid modeling functions.

Worldwide mechanical CAD software revenues were projected at $1.8 billion for 1995, with IBM expected to lead the category with sales of $388 million. PTC was growing over 50% annually and had the second highest sales, with $305 million in projected revenue. Industry analyst predicted 3% to 5% revenue growth per year, with annual unit volume projected to grow at 15%. The downward pressure on prices was squeezing margins, so many stock analysts thought that the market was becoming unattractive. However, PTC traded at a P/E between 21 and 40 in 1994.

Axel after Computervision: 1992–1994

After five year in the United States, Axel decided to attend an MBA program in Europe. From his experiences at Premise and Computervision, he had become intrigued with the art and science of business management and he was ready for a geographic change.

INSEAD was his choice. Located in Fontainebleau, an hour south of Paris, INSEAD was considered one of the top three business schools in Europe. the application process included two alumni interviews, and one of Axel's interviewers was Christopher Spray, the founder of Atlas venture's Boston office. Atlas Venture was a venture capital firm with offices in Europe and the United States. It had $250 million under management in 1994.

Since Axel had a three-month break before INSEAD started, Chris asked him to consult on a couple of Atlas Venture's projects. Axel found he enjoyed evaluating business proposals "from the other side of the table." He graduated in June 1993 and joined the Boston office of Atlas Venture as a vice president with responsibility for developing high-tech deals.

Axel reflected on the relationship between business school training and venture capital practice.

> I was qualified to become a venture capitalist because of my technical and entrepreneurial background; business school just rounded out my skill. you do not need a bunch of MBA courses to be a successful venture capitalist. Take finance, for example; I learned everything I needed from the core course. People without entrepreneurial experience who want to be venture capitalists should take as many entrepreneurship courses as possible.

John Founds SolidWorks: 1993–1994

Jon's business plan focused on CAD opportunities. He explained:

> I knew that this big market was going through major changes, with more changes to come. From an entrepreneur's perspective, I saw the right conditions for giving birth to a new business. I also knew I had the technical skills, industry credibility, and vision needed to make it happen. this was a pretty rare situation.

SolidWorks' product vision evolved slowly from Jon's personal research and from discussions was friends. He was careful to avoid using research that Computervision might

	Computer-Aided Drafting & Add-Ons	Production Solid Modeling
Low-end		
Windows	Autodesk	SolidWorks
~$5 K per station	Bentley	
VAR channel	CADKEY	
High-end		
UNIX	Application	PTC
~$20 K per station	CADAM	
Direct sales		

Figure 10.7

Competitive Positioning Grid

claim as proprietary. He was concerned about legal issues, because he would be designing software similar to what Computervision was trying to produce. Axel explained:

> Both Computervision and SolidWorks wanted to produce a quality solid modeling product. Solid modeling technology was still too difficult to learn and use. Only PTC's solid modeling software really worked well enough. The rest made nice drawings but could not replace physical prototypes for testing purposes.

There were only 50,000 licensed solid modeling terminals in the United States, and most of them belonged to PTC, but there were over 500,000 CAD terminals. There were two main reasons PTC did not have a larger market: (1) its products required very powerful computers, and (2) it took up to nine months of daily use to become proficient with PTC software. Solidworks' goal was to create solid modeling software that was easier to learn, and modeled real-world parts on less specialized hardware (see Figure 10.7).

This vision was not unique in the industry. Many CAD companies were developing solid modeling software, and the low-end market was wide open. SolidWorks' major advantage was its ability to use recent advances in software architecture and new hardware platforms—it wasn't tied to antique technology. Attracting talented developers was the top priority in this leading-edge strategy.

Teambuilding

Jon's wife, Melissa, enthusiastically supported his decision to resign from Computervision. Jon explained:

> Some spouses couldn't deal with a husband who quits a secure job to start a new company. Melissa never gave me a hard time about being an entrepreneur.

Jon described his priorities in October 1993 when he decided to launch SolidWorks.

> I knew I needed three things: good people, a good business plan, and a good proof-of-concept.[3] I needed a talented team that could set new industry benchmarks, but there was no way I could get those people without a persuasive prototype demonstration.

[3] **Proof-of-concept** is a term that refers to a computer program designed to illustrate a proposed project. Also referred to as a **prototype**, it is used for demonstration purposes and it is limited but functional in ideal circumstances.

The venture capitalists wanted a solid business plan, but that wouldn't be enough. They wanted a strong team. I needed fundable people who were also CAD masters. Venture capitalists couldn't understand most complex technologies well enough to be confident a high-tech business plan was really sound, so they looked at the team and placed their bets largely on that basis. If the proof-of-concept attracted the team, then the team and the business plan would attract the money. I needed a team that could create the vision and make venture capitalists believe it was real.

Jon worked on finding the team and developing the proof-of-concept concurrently, but the proof-of-concept was his first priority. He worked on it daily. In his search for cofounders, Jon talked to dozens of people; he even posted a notice on the Internet, but "none of those guys worked out."

Recruiting posed another dilemma—how to get people to work full-time without pay, while the company retained the right to their output? He resolved this problem by creating consulting agreements that gave SolidWorks ownership of employees' work and made salaries payable at the time of funding. As it turned out, this arrangement only lasted nine months. Jon described his approach to recruiting.

I always paid for the meal when I talked with someone about SolidWorks. I wanted them to feel confident about it, and that meant that I had to act with confidence. The deal I offered was: no salary, buy your own computer, work out of your house, and we're going to build a great company. I'd done it before, so people signed on.

Axel described Jon's management style as, "visionary, he's a talented motivator, and a strong leader."

Robert Zuffante: CAD Engineer/Consultant

A major development in 1993 was the addition of superstar consultant Bob Zuffante as manager of proof-of-concept development. Jon needed time to write the business plan and recruit his team. He had been working on the prototype for over a month when Bob took over development. Jon recalled the situation:

I hadn't seen him since we were students together at MIT, but when I thought about the skills I needed, my mental Rolodex came up with his name. I always thought about working with him again. We talked in late November, and about a month later, he began work on the prototype.

Bob knew Jon and Axel from MIT where he earned a master's degree in mechanical engineering. He had worked in the CAD industry for over ten years and had managed a successful consulting business. His arrival at SolidWorks allowed Jon to focus on other pressing issues.

Scott Harris: CAD Marketer

Scott Harris worked at Computervision for eleven years, where he managed development and marketing activities. Most notably, Scott was the founder and manager of Computervision's product design and definition group. He also managed the eleven-person solid modeling development group, and acted as technical liaison between Computervision's customers and R&D engineers.

Scott was let go by Computervision during a large-scale lay off. He was skeptical when John first told him about the SolidWorks vision, but he became a believer after seeing a proof-of-concept demonstration. Scott stopped looking for a job and started working full-time for SolidWorks almost immediately. Scott was impressed, "The prototype was the embodiment of a lot of the things I was thinking about. This was the way solid modeling should perform."

Scott started with SolidWorks about six weeks after Bob signed on. He became involved in the marketing sections of the business plan and in the product definition process. He ran focus groups, conducted demonstrations for potential customers, and analyzed the purchasing process. He kept the development team focused on customer needs—how did customers really use CAD software, and what did they need that current products lacked?

The Business Plan

When Bob came on in January, Jon turned to the business plan with a passion. The plan went through a number of versions as Jon and his advisors wrestled with key issues such as positioning, competitive strategy, and functionally. By the end of March, the plan was polished enough for Jon to show it to venture capitalists. Axel recalled:

> Jon and I decided that the business plan was ready to show in April, so I scheduled a presentation at Atlas. Jon gave the presentation to Barry [Barry Fidelman, Atlas general partner] and myself—market, team, and concept. Overall, Barry was encouraging, but not excited. He thought Jon's story was not crisp enough; he was looking for money to take on some very large companies; and the CAD market was not that attractive. It was a rocky start.

Initial Financing Attempts

In addition to negotiating with Atlas Venture, Jon met with other venture capital firms and rewrote the business plan several times. Axel described the rationale behind this process.

> If you talk to too many people and you do not make a good impression, it will be much harder to get funding, because the word on the street will be, "this deal will not fly." Meet with four or five venture capitalists at most, then revise the plan if you are not getting the right response. After each major revision, show it again to the lead venture partner.

While there were promising discussions with several venture capitalists, Atlas did not want to be the sole investor, and SolidWorks did not win support from other venture capitalists during the spring or summer.

Jon was contacted by an established CAD software company in May 1994. It wanted to acquire SolidWorks—essentially the development team and the prototype. The proposal was attractive; it included signing bonuses and stock. Scott recalled his excitement.

> This was a big shot in the arm. It meant that other industry insiders respected our vision and talent enough to put up their money and take the risk. This was like a cold bucket of Gatorade on a hot day.

Jon stopped seeking venture capital for about a month while he considered the buyout offer. If the offer was a boost to morale, the way the team rejected it was even more meaningful. Jon talked to each person (several other programmers had joined during the spring), and they were unanimous in wanting to continue toward their original goal. Affirming their commitment reinvigorated the team.

Turning Point: Michael Payne, CAD Company Founder

The most significant advance that summer began with a due diligence meeting set up by Atlas Venture. Atlas wanted the SolidWorks team to meet its agent, Michael Payne, who had recently resigned from PTC. Michael had confounded PTC, the number one company in CAD software, He was one of the most influential people in the industry.

Michael had grown up in London. He earned his bachelor's degree in electrical engineering from Southampton University and his master's degree in solid-state physics from the University of London. He came to the United States and worked many years for RCA designing computer chips. Michael continued his education at Pace University, where he earned an MBA. His senior CAD development experience began in the 1970s when he ran the CAD/CAM design lab at Prime Computer. He was subsequently recruited by Sam Geisberg, the visionary behind PTC. Michael recalled their first meeting in 1986: Sam had some kind of crazy prototype, and I said, "Hey, we can do something with that. This is what we should be working on."

PTC was founded in 1986 with Michael as vice president of development, and within five years the company had created a new set of CAD industry benchmarks. For FY 1993, PTC sales were $163 million, it earned a pre-tax profit margin over 40% and reached a market capitalization[4] of $1.9 billion. Michael's reputation as a development manager was outstanding. Remarkably, PTC had never missed a new product release date, and it released products every six months. This was considered a near-impossible feat in software development. He left PTC in April 1994 during a management dispute, about two months before the due diligence meeting with SolidWorks.

Jon had never met Michael, but knew by reputation that he was a tough character. The SolidWorks team was worried about two possibilities: that Michael would say they were on the wrong track, or that he might take their ideas back to PTC. Jon recalled the meeting.

> Bob and I were on one side of the table and Michael and Axel on the other. I decided to gamble on a dramatic entrance. Before we told him anything about SolidWorks, I asked Michael to show his cards. I asked him to tell us what he thought were the greatest opportunities in the CAD market. Michael mentioned many of the things we were targeting. I couldn't imagine a better way to start the meeting.
>
> We presented our plan and prototype. Michael asked us a lot of tough, confrontational questions. Afterwards, he told Atlas Venture, "These guys have a chance." Coming from him, that was high praise.

The due diligence meeting was also the beginning of a dialogue between Michael and Jon about joining SolidWorks. Over the next couple of months, Michael decided to join the team. Jon described the synergy between them.

> You almost couldn't ask for two people with more different styles, but we got along well because we were united in our philosophy and vision. We found that our stylistic differences were assets; they created more options for solving problems.

---

[4] **Market capitalization** is the value of the company established by the selling price of the stock times the number of shares outstanding.

Michael talked about his motivation for joining the SolidWorks team.

I couldn't go work for a big company because I didn't have any patience for petty politics. A startup was my only option. The larger the company, the more focused it would be on internal issues rather than on making a product that customers buy. Customers don't care about technique; they care about the benefits of the technology.

Jon focused on CAD features that I knew customers wanted, and he had a prototype demonstrating that he could do it. It was also quick and easier than what was on the market. Being able to develop it was another matter. They still had to build it. Implementation, that's where I would be useful. I told them, "Give me whatever title you want; I just want to run development."

Team Adjustments

Michael's arrival created an imbalance in the SolidWorks team, and it took time to sort it out. In fact, Michael didn't join the team until the last week in August. Jon described his thoughts about team cohesion.

When I decided to stat SolidWorks, I had three goals: (1) work with great people, (2) realize the vision of a new generation of software, and (3) make a lot of money.
    We didn't go looking for Michael Payne, but when he came along it was an easy decision. It can be hard to bring in strong players, but if those are your three goals, the decision falls out of the analysis rather naturally.
    Bob and I had to give up the reins in some areas so Michael could come onboard. We weren't looking for a top development manager because we thought we already had two. The change took some getting used to, but it was clearly the right thing to do.

Jon focused on team building, and Michael became the development manager. There were still big talent gaps, especially in sales and finance, but those positions could be filled when they were closer to the product launch. Michael was satisfied: "We didn't have a vast team, but you don't start out with a vast team, and we had a terrific nucleus."

September 1994

Atlas arranged for Jon to talk with venture firms interested in joining the investment syndicate. The team met with Jon Flint of Burr, Egan, Deleage & Co. and Rich D'Amore of North Bridge Venture Capital Partners. After completing their due diligence investigations, both firms joined the syndicate. Jon Hirschtick recalled the situation.

I was pleased that Jon Flint and Rich D'Amore decided to invest. I had met Jon many years earlier and thought very well of him. Rich also impressed me as a very knowledgeable investor. Both had excellent reputations and I looked forward to having them join our board.

An offer sheet was presented to SolidWorks two weeks after Michael officially joined the SolidWorks management team. Now the team had to decide how much money they really wanted. Michael's last venture, PTC, only needed one round of capital, and the team wanted to go for one round, too. SolidWorks' monthly cash burn rate was projected to average about $250,000 and they planned to launch the product in a year, so they needed $3 million for development. Sales and marketing would also need money; they

EXHIBIT 10.2	Pro Forma									
	1994		**1995**		**1996**		**1997**		**1998**	
Revenue	$	–	$	175,000	$	3,010,000	$	8,225,000	$	17,115,000
Cost of Sales	$	–	$	31,500	$	541,800	$	1,480,500	$	3,080,700
Sales & Marketing	$	71,919	$	765,920	$	1,930,000	$	3,030,000	$	5,822,500
R&D	$	605,544	$	1,126,208	$	1,350,000	$	1,500,000	$	2,050,000
G&A	$	185,954	$	445,175	$	650,000	$	800,000	$	1,050,000
Total Expenses	$	863,417	$	2,368,803	$	4,471,800	$	6,810,500	$	12,003,200
Operating Income	$	(863,417)	$	(2,193,803)	$	(1,461,800)	$	1,414,500	$	5,111,800
Margin Analysis										
Cost of Sales				18.0%		18.0%		18.0%		18.0%
Gross Profit				82,0%		82.0%		82.0%		82.0%
Sales & Marketing				437.7%		64.1%		36.8%		34.0%
R&D				643.5%		44.9%		18.2%		12.0%
G&A				254.4%		21.6%		9.7%		6.1%
Operating Income				−1253.6%		−48.6%		17.2%		29.9%

decided that $1 million should be enough to take them through the product launch to generating positive cash flow. To that total, they added a $500,000 safety margin. SolidWorks asked Atlas to put together an offer sheet based on raising $4.5 million.

SolidWorks received the offer sheet during the first week of September. It gave a $2.5 million pre-money valuation with a 15% post-money stock option pool.[5] (For SolidWorks' business plan proforma, see Exhibit 2.) These terms were fairly typical for a first-round deal, but the SolidWorks team didn't like what happened to their post-money equity when they ran the numbers.

Preparation Questions

1. Why has this deal attracted venture capital?
2. Can the founders optimize their personal financial returns and simultaneously ensure that SolidWorks has sufficient capital to optimize its chance of succeeding? What factors should the founders consider?
3. How can the syndicate optimize its potential return? What factors should it consider?
4. After you have answered questions 2 and 3, structure a deal that will serve the best interests of the founders, the company, and the venture capital firms.

---

[5] The pool of company stock reserved for rewarding employees in the future.

Babson College sophomore, Siamak Taghaddos started GotVMail in 2000 to provide emerging growth companies with professional phone answering service. Two years after his graduation *Business Week* named him one of the top 5 entrepreneurs in the U.S.A. under the age of 25. (*Source*: Courtesy Siamak Taghaddos)

DEBT AND OTHER FORMS OF FINANCING

Entrepreneurs at small, growing firms, unlike finance treasurers at most *Fortune* 500 companies, do not have easy access to a variety of inexpensive funding sources. In the entire world, only a handful of very large firms have access to funding sources such as asset-backed debt securitizations, A-1 commercial paper ratings, and below-prime lending rates. Most financial managers of small- to medium-sized firms are constantly concerned about meeting cash flow obligations to suppliers and employees and maintaining solid financial relationships with creditors and shareholders. Their problems are exacerbated by issues concerning manage growth, control, and survival. Moreover, the difficulty of attracting adequate funds exists even when firms are growing rapidly and bringing in profits.

This chapter describes various financing options for entrepreneurs and identifies potential financing pitfalls and solutions. We also discuss how these issues are influenced by the type of industry and the life cycle of the firm, and how to plan accordingly.

This chapter written by Joel Shulman.

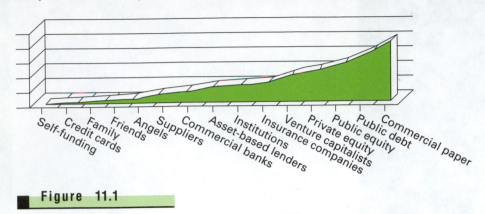

Figure 11.1

Sources of outside funding: Levels of funding and firm maturity

Getting Access to Funds—Start with Internal Sources

Entrepreneurs requiring initial startup capital, funds used for growth, and working capital generally seek funds from *internal* sources. Managers or owners of large, mature firms, in contrast, have access to profits from operations as well as funds from external sources. We distinguish internal from external funds because internal funding sources do not require external analysts or investors to independently appraise the worthiness of the capital investments before releasing funds. External investors and lenders also don't share the entrepreneur's vision, so they may view the potential risk/return trade-off in a different vein and demand a relatively certain return on their investment after the firm has an established financial track record.

Figure 11.1 shows a listing of funding sources and approximately when a firm would use each. In the embryonic stages of a firm's existence, as we've discussed, much of the funding comes from the entrepreneur's own pocket, including personal savings accounts, credit cards, home equity lines, and other assets such as personal computers, fax machines, in-home offices, furniture, and automobiles.

Soon after entrepreneurs begin tapping their personal fund sources, they may also solicit funds from relatives, friends, and banks. Entrepreneurs would generally prefer to use other people's money (OPM) rather than their own, because if their personal investment turns sour, they still have a nest egg to feed themselves and their families. The need to protect a nest egg may be particularly acute if the entrepreneur leaves a viable job to pursue an entrepreneurial dream on a full-time basis. The costs to the entrepreneur in this case include:

- The opportunity cost of income from the prior job
- The foregone interest on the initial investment
- The potential difficulty of being rehired by a former employer (or others) if the idea does not succeed

Add to this the embarrassment of having to beg for a new job while paying off old debts, and the prospective entrepreneur quickly realizes that the total cost of engaging in a new venture is very high. Family and friends may volunteer to fund the entrepreneur's project in the early stages and often will do so without a formal repayment schedule or specified interest cost. However, the funds are far from free. Total costs, including nonfinancial indirect costs—such as family pressure, internal monitoring, and strained relations—are probably extremely high. Moreover, family and friends make poor financial intermediaries since they have limited financial resources, different repayment expectations, and narrow loan diversification. This will contribute to the entrepreneur's desire to get outside funding from a traditional source as soon as possible. The question is, where can you go before a bank will give you money?

Start with Credit Cards and Home Equity Lines

Entrepreneurs who require an immediate infusion of cash often don't have the luxury of time to await the decision of a prospective equity investor or credit lender. They're prone to tapping their personal credit cards for business purchases or borrowing against a low-interest-bearing home equity line of credit. According to a Federal Reserve report,[1] at the end of 2005, consumers had personal credit outstanding of over $2,200 billion with approximately 1/3 applied to revolving credit (credit cards). Nonrevolving credit includes personal credit associated with loans for automobiles and vacations but does not include home equity lines. This credit, which is derived from commercial banks, finance companies, credit unions, and savings institutions, is for personal consumption. Presumably, entrepreneurs have applied some of it to their businesses. Many banks set up credit cards for either personal or business use. And "points" systems that provide credit toward frequent flyer miles or future purchases may give consumers an economic incentive to maximize their use of credit cards whether for personal or business purposes.

Home equity lines of credit (HELOC) are another important way in which consumers provide funding for their businesses. In mid-2004 there was approximately $500 billion in outstanding HELOCs, according to the Federal Deposit Insurance Corporation (FDIC). Although the majority of the funds (70%) went toward home improvements and debt consolidation, at least 2.5% went toward funding small businesses (LendingTree survey).[2] This means approximately $13+ billion of home equity lines of credit were reported to be directly applied to entrepreneurial businesses.

Sorry, I Only Fly First Class

In 1995, a college graduate and one of her friends started a Web design and technical consulting business in California. It began as a small, part-time venture with only a handful of clients. All the materials (computer, paper, office supplies, etc.) and the Web site were paid with credit card financing. The student's credit limit was only $5,000, but that was more than sufficient in the early stages as revenues were less than $20,000. By the third year, her revenues exceeded $100,000, but she still paid all nonpersonnel expenses with her credit card. In the third year her credit card limit was raised to $15,000. Over the years as the venture grew, many of the expenses, including media equipment, Web site, online Web advertising (Google ad words), and new computers were paid for with her credit card. She was careful to pay off any balances promptly in order to avoid steep interest rates, which approached 20% annually. Although the credit card was convenient to use, the primary motivation for using it in lieu of short-term bank financing was to accumulate frequent flyer miles. Some years she spent more than $200,000 on credit, which provided her with 200,000+ miles per year. By the time the entrepreneur sold her business to a competitor in 2004, she had generated over $3 million in revenues and designed more than 5,000 Web sites in 20 countries. In addition, she had generated close to one million frequent flyer miles, which she used with her family to travel the world free in first class. No debt other than credit card financing had ever been used.

Cash Conversion Cycle

One of the most important considerations in setting up a business is deciding when to pay the bills.

The business operating cycle for a traditional manufacturer begins with the purchase of raw materials and ends with collections from the customer. It includes three key components: the inventory cycle, the accounts receivable cycle, and the accounts payable cycle. The **inventory cycle** begins with the purchase of the raw materials, includes the work-in-process period, and ends with the sale of the finished goods. The **accounts receivable cycle** then begins with the sale and concludes with the collection of the receivable. During this operating cycle, the business generally receives some credit from suppliers.

The **accounts payable cycle** begins with the purchase of the raw materials or finished goods, but it ends with the payment to the supplier. The vast majority of organizations, particularly manufacturing operations, experience a gap between the time when they have to pay suppliers and when they receive payment from customers. This gap is known as the **cash conversion cycle (CCC).** For most companies the credit provided by suppliers ends long before the accounts receivables are paid. This means that as companies grow sales levels, they need to get external financing to fund working capital needs. One of the primary causes of bankruptcy is the inability to finance operations, shutting down potentially successful ventures.

Some companies generate payments from customers before they need to pay their suppliers. Their cash conversion cycle is negative, though from a cash flow perspective it is very positive. Your industry's typical cash conversion cycle is one of the most important things you should find out about your overall financing scheme. If you're fortunate enough to receive payments before providing the service or paying your supplier, it makes a big difference to your chances of success and growth.

Professor, Would You Like Me to Teach Class Today?

In 2000, a Babson College sophomore by the name of Siamak Taghaddos set up a new venture, GotVMail, that provided emerging growth companies with a professional phone answering service. Virtually all Taghaddos's sales were generated through an automated system that he created on the Internet. Customers paid upfront monthly fees ranging from $9.95 to $39.95 charged automatically to their credit cards. Taghaddos paid his own expenses a few weeks later. This negative cash conversion cycle enabled him to grow exponentially with little need for external capital (since he initially leased the equipment required for the service).

By his senior year Taghaddos was generating over $500,000 in revenues and out-earned all but a handful of his professors. Two years after his graduation he had revenues over $5 million and 20 employees and was named, along with his partner David Hauser, by *Business Week* as one of the top 5 entrepreneurs in the U.S. under the age of 25. Though this successful entrepreneur clearly generated the majority of his growth based on unique skill and marketing insight, had he not established a company with a negative cash conversion cycle, it's likely that his meteoric growth would have been constrained due to a severe cash crunch.

Working Capital: Getting Cash from Receivables and Inventories

The timing of receivables collection and payment of accounts payable are key determinants in whether a firm is cash rich or cash poor. For example, an increase in net working capital (that is, current assets minus current liabilities) doesn't necessarily translate into an increase in liquidity. One reason is that increases in net working capital often result from increases in operating assets, net of increases in operating liabilities. These operating assets, such as accounts receivable or inventory, are usually tied up in operations, and firms don't commonly liquidate them (prematurely) to pay bills, typically paying with liquid financial assets, such as cash and marketable securities, instead. Thus, we can use only liquid financial assets to assess a firm's liquidity.

Further, corporate insolvency usually results when the firm fails to service debt obligations or callable liabilities on time. We can estimate corporate liquidity fairly accurately by taking the difference between liquid financial assets and callable liabilities, referred to as the *net liquid balance*. Figure 11.2 shows how the net liquid balance is actually a part of net working capital. *Net working capital* is easy to calculate in one of two ways:

- ◉ Take the difference between current assets and current liabilities (as described earlier), or
- ◉ Take the difference between long-term liabilities, including equities, and long-term assets (such as fixed assets).

The first formula is often misinterpreted to be the difference between two liquid components, whereas the second definition suggests that the residual of long-term liabilities minus long-term assets is used to finance current assets, some of which may be liquid. The second definition also enables us to analyze the current assets and liabilities as consisting of both liquid financial/callable components and operating components.

Net working capital is actually the sum of the working capital requirements balance. This suggests that only a part of net working capital is liquid. Clearly, as a small firm grows, current operating assets will increase. If current operating liabilities don't increase at the same rate as the increase in current operating assets (which is true when an entrepreneur pays suppliers before receiving payment from customers), then the entrepreneur will find that the firm's net liquid balance will decrease (assuming the firm

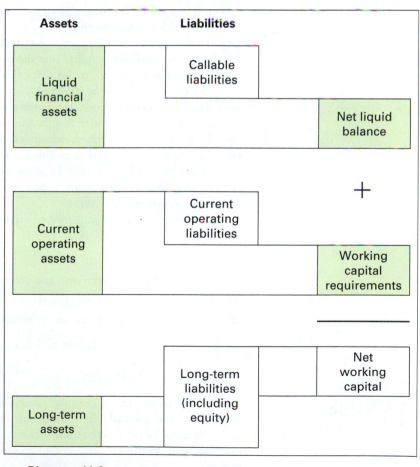

Figure 11.2

Integrative approach to working capital management

does not increase its long-term funding arrangements). This may be true even though the firm is generating paper profits. As long as the increase in working capital requirements *exceeds* the increase in profits (note that profits are included in the long-term liabilities part of Figure 11.2 due to increase in stockholders' equity), then the firm will find itself reducing its liquidity levels.

This highlights one of the fundamental weaknesses of the traditional liquidity ratios, such as the current ratio or quick ratio. These ratios include both liquid financial assets and operating assets in their formulas. Since operating assets are tied up in operations, including these assets in a liquidity ratio is not very useful from an ongoing-concern perspective. Note the difference between a liquidity perspective and a liquidation perspective. A **liquidation perspective** assumes that in the event of a crisis, the firm may sell assets off in order to meet financial obligations, while a **liquidity perspective** assumes the firm meets its financial obligations without impairing the viability of future operations. From an ongoing perspective, a new ratio—*net liquid balance* to *total assets*—may be more indicative of liquidity than either the current ratio or the quick ratio.

Using Accounts Receivable as Working Capital

Accounts receivable, that is, the money owed to the company as a result of sales made on credit for which payment has not yet been received, are a major element in working capital for most companies. And they are one of the reasons we can assert that *working capital* is not the same as *available cash,* and that the timing of short-term flows is vitally important.

If a company is selling a major part of its output on credit and giving 30 days' credit, its accounts receivable will be about equal to sales of 30 days, that is, to one-twelfth of its annual sales, if sales are reasonably stable over the year. And if the company's collection policies are so liberal or ineffective that in practice customers are paying on an average, say, 45 days after they are billed, accounts receivable are no less than one-eighth of annual sales. Investment in accounts receivable is a use of funds. The company has to finance the credit it is giving to its customers by allowing its money to be tied up in this way instead of being available for investment in productive uses. Therefore, accounts receivable, like cash, have an opportunity cost.

The magnitude of a company's accounts receivable obviously depends on a number of factors:

- ◉ The level and the pattern of sales
- ◉ The breakdown between cash and credit sales
- ◉ The nominal credit terms offered
- ◉ The way these credit terms are enforced through a collection policy

We'll discuss each of these factors in detail in the following sections.

The Sales Pattern

The basis of all receivables and collections is clearly *actual net sales,* that is, sales sold minus any returns. From actual sales come the assumptions about receipts from future cash sales and collections of future credit sales. These are the key inputs in forecasting cash flow, as discussed later in this chapter. Techniques for forecasting future sales fall into two broad groups:

- ◉ Techniques that use external or economic information
- ◉ Techniques based on internal or historical data from the company's own past sales

Most managers are more familiar with the techniques in the second group than they are with economic forecasting. The methods for forecasting from historical data range from the very simple (such as straightforward moving average) to fairly sophisticated models. For instance, variations on exponential smoothing make it possible to take into account both long-term trends in the company's sales and seasonal variations. Simply put, although the more sophisticated techniques are useful, no forecasting method based *only* on historical sales data is completely satisfactory. You cannot be sure that either total industry sales or the company's share of the sales will be the same as they have been; you must consider a variety of external factors.

Methods of forecasting environmental change also fall into two broad groups. One group is primarily concerned with *forecasting the future performance of the economy as a whole,* particularly future levels of the gross national product and the national income. These *GNP models,* as they are called, are highly complex, computer-based models. Their construction may be beyond the capabilities of most entrepreneurs, but you can easily purchase their output. The other group is more concerned with *forecasting sales for individual industries and products.* One way to do this is to identify economic time series to use as leading indicators to signal changes in the variable being forecast. Again, this technique is best wielded by an experienced economist with a computer. The important point for the entrepreneur is that forecasting techniques are becoming progressively less of an art and more of a science.

Cash Versus Credit Sales

The relative proportions of cash sales and credit sales may make an important difference to expected cash flows. Unfortunately, this is a variable over which most entrepreneurs have little control. For example, a company in retail sales can certainly take steps to increase its cash sales, either by banning credit entirely or by offering a discount on cash sales. But a company selling primarily to other corporate organizations—other manufacturing companies, wholesalers, distributors, or retail chains—has few cash sales. Its best hope is to set its credit terms to encourage prompt payment, but the sales will still be credit sales, not cash sales.

Okay, Now What Are You Going to Do?

In the mid-to-late 1980s a college senior by the name of Jeff Brown requested permission from his professor to miss class. It seems the student had to travel home and transfer cash receipts from the family business to an interest-bearing account before the weekend. He explained that if he did not transfer the money, his business would lose thousands of dollars of interest for the 2 days. When he began college, Brown's family owned one supermarket, but by the time he graduated the family business had expanded to 11 stores. Brown claimed he was the CEO and instrumental in the entire expansion. It wasn't until 2 months after graduation when Brown

fired his mother that his professor believed him (mom was losing lots of money trying to sell VCRs).

Brown explained that during his sophomore year he had negotiated new contracts with his suppliers enabling him to generate two weeks of payment float. Since his supermarkets were generating approximately $100,000 in cash receipts per day, the two weeks in payment delay generated approximately $1.4 million in excess cash. In each case, the student used the float to open a new supermarket. Thus, by the time he was a graduating senior the family business of 11 supermarkets had over $15 million in float (11 stores × $1.4 million float = $15.4 million). Since interest rates were at the time approximately 13%, the business generated approximately $2 million each year in interest float ($15.4 million × 13% = $2.002 million). It turned out that the float provided more profit to the family than selling groceries! About one year after Brown graduated from college, he sold his family business for millions. With his share of the proceeds he was financially secure and able to retire comfortably for the rest of his life. The only problem was that he was only 23 and didn't want to play golf every day with all the other retirees he knew in Florida.

Credit Policies

Credit policies boil down to two general questions:

- To whom should we give credit?
- How much credit should we give?

These two questions are closely interconnected. The business needs to evaluate most potential credit sales on their own merits, and this is costly and time consuming. In fact, the salaries and overhead of the credit analysts are likely to be the largest single item in the cost of giving credit to customers.

How much freedom a company has in setting the terms on which it will grant credit depends very much on its *competitive position*. For example, an organization in a monopolistic position has considerably more flexibility than one that faces aggressive competition. But real monopolies are rare. Most companies approach such a position only during very short periods, after they have introduced radically new products and before their competitors have had time to introduce similar ones. A company in such a position may be tempted to take advantage of it through product price, but it is unlikely to tighten up its credit policy as well. The advantage of restricting credit will be fairly short-lived, but the damage to customer relations could continue for a long time.

Nevertheless, economic factors do play an important part in credit policy. The key issue is *elasticity of demand* for the entrepreneur's product. (We assume that the credit terms are a component of the overall price as the customer sees it, and that customers will resist a reduction in credit, just as they will resist a price increase.) If demand for a product is *inelastic*—that is, if an increase in price or a restriction in the terms of credit will produce a relatively small drop in demand, with the result that net sales revenues actually increase—then there is some potential flexibility in the terms of sale. Even here, however, it will be the industry as a whole that enjoys this flexibility; individual companies will probably have to accept general industry practice. If demand for a product is *elastic,* on the other hand, there will be little room to change the terms of the sale, either at the company or industry level.

Finally, a company operating below full capacity or below its optimal output may well be tempted to offer unusually generous credit terms in order to stimulate demand. The key question then is whether the cost of the additional funds tied up in accounts receivable will be more than offset by the additional sales and reduced operating costs. Alternatively, a company working at full capacity, with its product back-ordered, is in a position to tighten up on its credit policies to reduce its investment in receivables.

Setting Credit Terms

The terms of credit include both the *length of time* given before payment is due and the *discount* given for prompt payment. Terms expressed as "2/10, net 30" mean that payment is due within 30 days (from the date of invoice) and that the payer can deduct 2% from the bill if he makes the payment in 10 or fewer days. Some companies, on the other hand, set their net terms as payment by the end of the month following the month in which the sale is invoiced. Obviously, this latter policy is considerably more generous than "net 30" and is likely to result in a much larger investment in receivables.

An entrepreneur's failure to take advantage of cash discounts available on its accounts payable may be a very expensive mistake, equivalent to borrowing short-term funds at 36%. Is it an equally serious mistake for a company to offer the same terms to its customers? The answer is that it depends on whether giving a cash discount really does speed up collections, and whether the *opportunity cost* of the funds that would otherwise have been locked up in receivables justifies the reduction in net sales revenues.

For example, assume that an entrepreneur's terms are 2/10, net 30 and that 25% of its customers actually take advantage of this discount. Annual sales are $36 million, of which $9 million are discounted, and the company recognizes profits when the sales are made. The discount's cost, therefore, is 2% of $9 million, or $180,000. Assuming that 25% of the customers pay in 10 days and the rest pay in 30, the average collection period (including both discount and nondiscount sales) is 25 days, giving average accounts receivable of $2.5 million, as shown in the following equation:

$$\$36,000,000/(360/25) = \$2,500,000$$

If the company did not give a discount, none of its customers would pay within 10 days and the average collection period would fall from 25 to 30. In that case average accounts receivable would be $3 million:

$$\$36,000,000/(360/30) = \$3,000,000$$

The question is, then, whether the added return the company makes on the $500,000 by which the discount policy has reduced the average accounts receivable exceeds $180,000, the cost of the discount policy. As this represents a return on investment of more than 36%, the answer is probably no.

A change in the net terms, however, is likely to make a greater difference to the average accounts receivable balance than giving or withholding a discount for prompt payment. Even if you give terms of 2/10, net 30, you can assume that a relatively small percentage of customers will take advantage of the discount. But if you change the net terms from 30 days to 45, doubtless a high percentage of customers *will* take advantage. Going back to the previous example and assuming that 25% of customers pay within 10 days and the rest at the end of 45 days, the average payment period now is approximately 36 days [(10 × 25) + (45 × .75)], and the average accounts receivable is $3.6 million, as shown:

$$\$36,000,000/(360/36) = \$3,600,000$$

In this example, we assumed that if the net terms are set at 30 or 45 days, everyone who does not take advantage of the discount for prompt payment will pay by the end of the net period. This is unrealistic. Many entrepreneurs and the companies they do business with make a practice of reducing their requirements for funds by paying all their bills late. True, the most commonly offered terms are 2/10, net 30, but a survey revealed that the actual experience of U.S. companies is that their average receivables run between 45 and 50 days. A company's accounts receivable depend not only on the terms of credit offered, but on how well those terms are enforced through the company's collection policy.

Collection Policies

Some of a company's accounts receivable will be paid some time after the theoretical time limit has expired. Others will never be paid at all and will have to be written off as bad debts. Neither of these variables is completely within the company's control, but both can be controlled to some extent.

The collection techniques of companies selling directly to the ultimate consumer are often highly standardized and even automated. The firms store master records of customers in computer data files and periodically search for overdue accounts. Each customer whose account has been outstanding for more than the net terms receives a series of increasingly stronger letters asking for payment. A system like this provides little opportunity to match the collection technique to the particular customer and situation. The average amount owed is probably small, however, and more individualized techniques are hard to justify in such circumstances.

When an entrepreneur's firm sells primarily in the industrial market and its customers are businesses, it will look at each individual case and determine how best to collect. If the other company is able to pay, the entrepreneur should rigorously attempt to secure payment before the situation becomes any worse. The methods include:

- Refusing any further supplies, or supplying only for cash
- Threatening legal action
- Actually undertaking legal proceedings, using a specialized collection agency

If the other company is already in serious financial trouble, however, an all-out collection attempt may simply force the customer into insolvency, followed by liquidation or reorganization. The wisest approach in this case may be to continue to give credit, or at least not to try to collect existing receivables, in the hope of keeping the other company in business. But if your company is one of a number of creditors, you gain nothing by being generous unless the other creditors are willing to do the same. Otherwise, you are simply subordinating your claims to those of others and increasing the chance that the debt will never be paid at all.

It's safe to say that collection procedures are expensive, and are justifiable *only when the expected results exceed the cost.* Collection operations are, in fact, an excellent demonstration of the economists' law of diminishing returns. For a given volume of overdue accounts, the first few thousand dollars spent on collection will probably produce worthwhile results. But further expenditure is likely to yield less and less return.

How much should you be willing to spend on collection? The answer depends on the reduction you expect in accounts receivable, and the return you'd expect if these additional funds were available for reinvestment in productive operations. Assume that you can reduce overdue accounts receivable $250,000 by hiring an assistant for $25,000. To cover the assistant's salary, you need to earn at least 10% return on the funds released from accounts receivable. This represents a fairly reasonable rate of return and should be attainable. However, consider all other nonwage costs of hiring an assistant, including FICA taxes, healthcare, and benefits, which could easily push the costs of the assistant up another $10,000, or 40%. Whenever you consider reducing excess receivables, examine the size and scope of the collection attempts and judge whether or not the costs justify the expenditure.

Setting Credit Limits for Individual Accounts

Another method of reducing overdue accounts and limiting bad debts is setting limits to the credit allowed on individual accounts. Again, as in collections, entrepreneurs need to distinguish between *sales to individual consumers* and *sales to corporate buyers.* An entrepreneur selling directly to consumers clearly cannot afford to undertake a thorough credit investigation of each one (unless the product being sold is a very expensive item, such as a boat or an automobile) and will set fairly arbitrary limits on the basis of limited information. But if the customers are business organizations, the setting of credit limits requires more thorough analysis, especially when the firm adds a new customer to its files and when it suspects an existing customer's circumstances have deteriorated.

Dun & Bradstreet publishes a reference book, revised every two months, that lists more than three million U.S. businesses and gives a credit rating for most of them. These ratings range from "high" to "limited" and include an estimate of the company's financial strength, usually based on net worth. If more detail is needed, Dun & Bradstreet and other agencies sell reports that include information about a company's principal officers, any past bankruptcies, and, most important, the company's credit history in relationship to its existing suppliers.

There are a number of other sources of information:

- Some industry associations operate credit advisory services for the benefit of their members.
- Companies selling directly to the consumer can get information from local credit bureaus.
- Commercial banks are also a useful source of credit information. An entrepreneur considering an extension of credit to a customer can ask her bank to carry out a credit investigation, which the bank will do by approaching the customer's bank for information about the customer.

You can cut short much of the work of appraising the creditworthiness of new customers by using external sources of information, but monitoring accounts receivable and deciding whether to increase credit limits or ban further credit is a continuing task for your own staff. The decisions are often difficult. No company likes to turn down orders. Once again, you face a trade-off: the potential profit on the sale versus the cost of financing increased receivables and the probability of bad debt. Since the cost of the latter far exceeds the cost of the former, most entrepreneurs are very careful about granting credit.

The two major determinants of the credit decision are the character of the individual creditor or management of the creditor firm, and the capacity of the firm to repay the loan. Entrepreneurs will find that the same simple set of guidelines they use in extending credit to customers is what banks use in extending credit to entrepreneurs. They're known as the Five Cs of credit:

- *Character* refers to the customer's integrity and willingness to repay the financial obligation.
- *Capacity* addresses the borrower's cash flow and ability to repay the debt from ongoing business operations.
- *Capital* is the borrower's financial net worth; consequently, a wealthy borrower may be a desirable customer even if her annual cash flows are relatively low.
- *Collateral* refers to the resale value of the product in the event repossession becomes necessary.
- *Conditions* refer to national or international economic, industrial, and firm-specific prospects during the time period of the credit.

The credit-granting decision is only part of the entrepreneur's concern. Another important task is monitoring accounts receivables balances. Since receivables tied up in operations may represent a large opportunity cost, either in lost investment returns or in greater borrowing balances, entrepreneurs are careful not to let the accounts receivable balances get too large.

Although the opportunity costs for accounts receivable may be quite large, the largest current asset balances are usually in inventories. As the entrepreneur's business grows, inventory balances rise, and resulting operating cash flows decline. You need to monitor both accounts receivable and inventories and keep the levels as low as possible without interfering with profitable sales. This is especially true if you have a shortage of capital or credit limitations.

Inventory

Inventory represents the most important current asset of most manufacturing and trading companies, yet money invested in inventory doesn't earn a return. In fact, it costs money to maintain inventories. Some inventory will be devalued or become a total loss because it deteriorates or becomes obsolete before it can be used or sold. These costs can easily add up to 20% or more annually of the inventory value. Since the money tied up in inventory might otherwise be invested profitably, the real costs plus the opportunity costs of carrying inventory may add up to 30%, 40%, or even more. As with accounts receivable, the dollar amount of inventory depends on when the entrepreneur chooses to recognize profit: Is it at the time of production or the time of sale? A strong argument can be made for valuing inventories at cost or market, whichever is lower. Given uncertainty about how much cash flow the inventory will actually generate, a conservative approach to valuation is best.

Entrepreneurs usually also want to keep inventory levels as low as possible, not only to reduce the inventory carry charges such as storage costs and insurance, but also to ensure that as little capital as possible is tied up in inventory.

But carrying too little inventory also incurs heavy costs. These include:

- The costs of too frequent reordering
- Loss of quantity discounts
- Loss of customer goodwill or plant efficiency due to items being unavailable when needed

You'll want to weigh these costs against those of carrying excessive inventory in order to be able to judge the optimal level of inventory.

The control of investment in inventories is particularly important to the *management of working capital.* Inventories are likely to represent your largest current investment and to be the least liquid of your current assets. Marketable securities can be turned into cash in a matter of hours, and most accounts receivable will usually be collected within the next 30 days. But three months' supply of inventory will take three months to turn into cash, if forecasts of demand or usage prove accurate. If your forecasts were optimistic, you might need even more time. The alternative—an immediate forced sale—is hardly attractive. You can sell marketable securities for their market value and sell, or factor, receivables for something like 80% of their face value. But inventories, other than some raw materials for which a ready market always exists, traditionally sell for little more than 10% of their acquisition cost in a forced sale. Thus, controlling a company's investment in inventory is of critical importance to managing your working capital.

Can I Buy Your Business with No Money Down?

In the mid-1990s, a couple of young East Coast entrepreneurs in their late 20s heard about an auction that a bankrupt international airline company was holding of its airplane parts inventory. Unknown to most consumers, until recently most major airline companies held their own parts inventory at each airport they served. This seemingly excessive inventory was needed since if an airplane was in need of a part, one company would not supply a competitor and the cost of delay might be astronomical (including meals, hotels, and airline transfers). Thus, each airline was forced to keep an extensive parts inventory for each type of plane in its fleet throughout the world.

With the advent of the major airline bankruptcy, the young entrepreneurs had an idea. What if they bought the available inventory at a discount and provided an independent airline parts company for all airlines? This new parts supplier company would save each of the airlines millions of dollars in idle parts inventories. The only problem was that the two entrepreneurs had no money to buy the inventory.

Fortunately, an asset-based lender thought the idea was terrific and decided to finance the entire inventory. However, the entrepreneurs would need to negotiate a very low purchase price. Fortunately for them, market conditions were poor for the airlines industry (have they ever been good?) and there were few other interested buyers.

The entrepreneurs were able to enter a multi-million dollar business with no money of their own. Within eighteen months they repaid the bank for the entire loan and still have enough parts inventory to last them at least a decade longer.

Sources of Short-Term Cash: More Payables, Less Receivables

Entrepreneurs usually don't have all the cash they need all the time. Very often, an entrepreneurial firm needs to build up its inventory, thus reducing cash levels. Or an entrepreneur's customers may place unusually large orders, thus increasing accounts receivable financing or reducing company cash levels. This section describes the many ways entrepreneurs obtain additional short-term cash to restore their cash balances to the required levels.

As a rule, entrepreneurs look for short-term cash at the lowest possible rates. For example, an entrepreneur faced with a cash shortage might look first to her company's suppliers because they extend credit to the company by collecting for goods and services after supplying them. The entrepreneur can enlarge this credit by paying bills more slowly—and also obtain additional cash by collecting from her customers more quickly.

Cash from Short-Term Bank Loans

Although supplier financing is convenient, it is often cheaper to pursue bank financing if possible. Entrepreneurs faced with a severe cash shortage may also try to convert into cash two of their working capital assets: accounts receivable and inventory. An entrepreneur may pledge her accounts receivable to a finance company in exchange for a loan, or she may sell them to a factoring company for cash. Similarly, an entrepreneur may pledge her inventory (often using a warehousing system) in exchange for a loan.

Cash from Trade Credit

Trade credit is one important and often low-cost source of cash. Nearly all entrepreneurs make use of trade credit to some degree by not paying suppliers immediately for goods and services. Instead, companies bill the entrepreneur, and the entrepreneur pays in 10 days, 30 days, or more. From the time the supplier first provides the goods or services to the time the customer finally pays for them, the supplier has, in effect, loaned the entrepreneur money. The sum of all these loans (bills) represents an entrepreneur's trade credit. By paying bills more slowly, an entrepreneur can increase the amount of these loans from his suppliers.

One way to take more time to pay bills (or stretch payables) is to stop taking discounts. For example, if your company normally takes advantage of all prompt-payment discounts, such as 2% for payment within 10 days, you can increase your company's cash by passing up the discount and paying the bill in the expected 30 days. Of course, this is an expensive source of cash. If you lose a 2% discount and have the use of the funds for 20 more days, you've paid approximately 36% interest (annual rate) for using the money.

In practice, though, the interest cost wouldn't really be 36%, because by foregoing discounts and aggressively stretching payables you wouldn't pay the bill in 30 days. Instead, you might try to pay in 60 days. Now, the equivalent interest rate is only about 15% (50 days' extra use of the money for 2%).

This brings up the subject of late payments. Many entrepreneurs don't consider 30 days (or any other stated terms) a real deadline. Instead, they try to determine the exact point at which further delay of payment will bring a penalty. For example, if a company pays too slowly, the supplier may take one of the following actions:

- ◉ Require payment in full on future orders
- ◉ Report the company to a credit bureau, which would damage the company's credit rating with all suppliers
- ◉ Bring legal action against the company

Many cash managers believe, however, that as long as they can pay company bills just before incurring any of these penalties, they maximize their company's cash at little or no cost. The *hidden costs* of this approach include such risks as damaged reputation, lower credit limit from suppliers, higher prices from suppliers to compensate for delayed payment, and the risk of exceeding the supplier's final deadline and incurring a penalty.

Customer Flips, Credit Crunch Flops

A rapidly growing 2-year-old medical devices company was paying its vendors in 60 days to conserve working capital. Its largest vendor was an electronics distributor that supplied 90% of the components used in the manufacture of its medical equipment. The distributor's sales rep made a routine visit to the company and casually asked about two unpaid invoices that were slightly more than 60 days old. The purchasing manager jokingly said, "I guess they didn't come out in the invoice draw last Friday!" "What's that?" asked the salesman. The purchasing manager continued facetiously, "Well, every Friday we put all the invoices older than 50 days in a bucket and draw them out one at a time until we have no more money left."

Less than an hour after the sales rep left, the distributor's accounts receivable manager called the CEO and founder of the medical device company and demanded that he pay all invoices that were 30 days

or older. The CEO explained that it was impossible, but that the two invoices that were slightly over 60 days would be paid immediately. The receivables manager was inflexible. He repeated his demand that all invoices 30 days or older be paid by the end of the day or he would put the company on COD terms.

The next morning when the purchasing manager tried to place an order with the electronics distributor, he was told that it would only be accepted on COD terms. The CEO of the company called the treasurer of the distributor and pleaded to get regular credit terms restored. But his pleas fell on deaf ears. The CEO immediately spoke with his purchasing manager and told him to set up a personal appointment with the sales manager of the next biggest electronics distributor in the metropolitan area. That same afternoon, they presented the sales manager with all the purchase orders that had been placed with their old distributor in the most recent 30-day period and asked him to give quotes for the same items. When the sales manager saw the size of the orders he immediately said, "I want your business." He offered 60-day payment terms; what's more, he added, "We will move you one and perhaps two price points lower, which will mean a savings of as much as 50% on some items." The CEO immediately placed a sizeable order and was extremely pleased to find that the total cost was 25% less than it would have been if it had gone to their old distributor.

The CEO told the purchasing agent to place no orders with the old distributor unless the item was unavailable elsewhere. One month later the old distributor's sales rep stopped by and asked whether business had suddenly slowed down because he had received almost no orders for several weeks. The purchasing agent took him out on the manufacturing floor and showed him that business was humming along. Then he showed him all the purchase orders—including prices—that the company had placed with his competitor. About 2 hours after the salesman left, the CEO received a phone call from the sales manager of the old distributor saying that he wanted to know what it would take to get his business back. The CEO told him how annoyed he had been with the harsh treatment he had received from the receivables manager and then the treasurer, but he said that he would consider splitting future orders if the old distributor would agree to 60-day terms, and move two price points on every item. The sale manager readily agreed and, without being asked, said he would assign the account to his best in-house telephone sales rep.

Cash Obtained by Negotiating with Suppliers

If an entrepreneur wants more credit and would like to stretch out her payables, very often she can negotiate with her suppliers for more generous credit terms, at least temporarily. If she and her supplier agree on longer credit terms (say 60 or 90 days), she can get the extra trade credits she needs without jeopardizing her supplier relations or credit ratings. One way suppliers compete is through credit terms, and you can use that fact to your advantage.

Some suppliers use generous terms of trade credit as a form of sales promotion that may well be more effective than an intensive advertising campaign or a high-pressure sales team. The credit may be a simple extension of the discount or net terms, or it may take a modified form such as an inventory loan.

Cash Available Because of Seasonal Business Credit Terms

If the entrepreneur is in a highly seasonal business, such as many types of retailers are, he will find large differences in credit terms in different seasons. For example, as a retailer, he might be very short of cash in the fall as he builds up inventory for the holiday selling season. Many suppliers will understand this and willingly will extend their normal 30-day terms.

Furthermore, some suppliers will offer exceedingly generous credit terms in order to smooth out their own manufacturing cycle. Consider a game manufacturer that sells half its annual production in the few months before Christmas. Rather than produce and ship most of the games in the late summer, this manufacturer would much rather spread out its production and shipping schedule over most of the year. To accomplish this, the manufacturer may offer seasonal dating to its retail store customers. **Seasonal dating** provides longer credit terms on orders placed in off-peak periods. For example, the game manufacturer might offer 120-day terms on May orders, 90-day terms on June orders, and so on. This will encourage customers to order early, and it will allow the game manufacturer to spread out production over more of the year.

Advantages of Trade Credit

Trade credit has two important advantages that justify its extensive use. The first advantage is convenience and ready availability; because it is not negotiated, it requires no great expenditure of executive time and no legal expenses. If a supplier accepts a company as a customer, it automatically extends the usual credit terms even though it may set the maximum line of credit low at first.

The second advantage (closely related to the first) is that the *credit available from this source automatically grows as the company grows.* Accounts payable are known as a spontaneous source of financing. As sales expand, production schedules increase, which in turn means that larger quantities of materials and supplies must be bought. In the absence of limits on credit, the additional credit becomes available automatically simply because the firm has placed orders for the extra material. Of course, if the manufacturing process is long and the company reaches the supplier's payment before selling the goods, it may need some additional source of credit. But the amount will be much less than if no trade credit had been available.

Cash Obtained by Tightening Up Accounts Receivable Collections

Rapidly growing accounts receivable tie up a company's money and can cause a cash squeeze. However, these same accounts receivable become cash when collected. Some techniques—such as lockboxes and wire transfers—enable firms to collect receivables quickly and regularly. But how can the firm increase the rate of collection temporarily during a cash shortage?

The most effective way is simply to *ask for the money.* If the entrepreneur just sends a bill every month and shows the amount past due, the customer may not feel a great pressure to pay quickly. But if the entrepreneur asks for the money, with a handwritten note on the statement of account, a phone call, or a formal letter, the customer will usually pay more quickly. Of course, more aggressive collection techniques also have costs, such as loss of customer goodwill, the scaring away of new customers, loss of old customers to more lenient suppliers, and the generation of industry rumors that the company is short of cash and may be a poor credit risk.

The entrepreneur can also *change his sales terms* to collect cash more quickly. Options include:

1. *Introduce, increase, or eliminate discounts.* A company can initiate a discount for prompt payment (for example, a 2% discount for payment within ten days). Similarly, a company with an existing discount may increase the discount (for example, increase discount from 1% to 2%). Finally, a company can eliminate the discount altogether and simply demand cash immediately or upon delivery (COD). Companies will have difficulty instituting these measures if competitors offer significantly more lenient credit terms.

2. *Emphasize cash sales.* Some entrepreneurs, particularly those selling directly to consumers, may be able to increase their percentage of cash sales.

3. *Accept credit cards.* Sales made on bank credit cards or on travel or entertainment cards are convertible within a couple of days into cash. The credit card companies charge 3% to 7% of the amount of the sale for this service.

Obtaining Bank Loans Through Accounts Receivable Financing

One approach to free up working capital funds is to convert accounts receivable into cash more quickly through aggressive collection techniques. However, if you fear aggressive collection may offend customers and cause them to take their business to competitors, you may decide to convert accounts receivable to cash through a financing company, using either pledging or factoring. The following sections describe both methods. In practice, finance companies and banks offer many variations on them.

Pledging

Pledging means using accounts receivable as collateral for a loan from a finance company or bank. The finance company then gives money to the borrower, and as the borrower's customers pay their bills, the borrower repays the loan to the finance company. With this form of accounts receivable financing, the borrower's customers are not notified that their bills are being used as collateral for a loan. Therefore, pledging is called *non-notification financing*. Furthermore, if customers do not pay their bills, the borrower (rather than the finance company) must absorb the loss. Thus, if the customer defaults, the lender has the right of recourse to the borrower.

A finance company will not usually lend the full face value of the accounts receivable pledged. In determining what fraction of the face value of receivables to lend, the finance company considers three factors:

1. The credit rating of the borrower's customers (because bills that may be paid slowly, or not at all, obviously do not make good collateral).
2. The quantity and dollar value of the accounts receivable (because a small number of large dollar-value receivable is easier to control).
3. The borrower's credit rating (because the finance company prefers having the loan repaid to taking possession of the collateral).

Typically, a company can borrow 75% to 90% of the face value of its accounts receivable if it has a good credit rating and its customers have excellent credit ratings. Companies with lower credit ratings can generally borrow 60% to 75% of the face value of their receivables. Pledging receivables is not a cheap source of credit. It's used mostly by smaller companies that have no other source of funds open to them.

Pledging with Notification

Another form of pledging is called **pledging with notification**, in which the borrower instructs its customers to pay their bills directly to the lender (often a bank). As checks from customers arrive, the bank deposits them in a special account and notifies the borrower that money has arrived. Here the lender controls the receivables more closely and does not have to worry that the borrower may collect pledged accounts receivable and then not notify it. The company loses under this system, however, because it must notify its customers that it has pledged its accounts receivable, which can reduce its credit rating.

Factoring

Factoring is selling accounts receivable at a discount to a finance company known as the *factor*. The factor takes over credit checking and collection. If the factor rejects a potential customer as an unacceptable credit risk, the company must either turn down the order or insist on cash payment.

Here's an example of how this process works. Suppose the W. Buygraves Inc. company (buyer) orders $10,000 worth of exotic wood and marble from the Saleman company (seller). The Saleman company calls its factor to report the order. The factor checks the credit rating of the Buygraves company and, if all is satisfactory, calls the Saleman company with an approval. The Saleman company then ships the goods and sends an invoice to the Buygraves company. The invoice instructs the Buygraves company to pay the factor. At the same time, the Saleman company sends a copy of the invoice to the factor, and the factor sends approximately 85% of the invoice amount ($8,500 in this case) to the Saleman company. The factor must now collect the $10,000 from Buygraves. When the factor actually collects the bill, it may send the Saleman company a small additional amount of money to recognize collections higher than the original estimates.

The fees that factors charge vary widely. They include:

- An interest charge, usually expressed on a daily basis for the time the bill is outstanding
- A collection fee, usually in the range of an additional 6% to 10% annual rate
- A credit checking charge, either a percentage of the invoice or a flat dollar amount

The factor keeps a hold-back amount (which is not immediately paid to the Saleman company) to more than cover these various fees and charges, deducts the total from the hold-back amount, and sends the remainder to the Saleman company.

Recourse

Factoring may be with or without recourse. In the preceding example, *factoring without recourse* means that if the Buygraves company doesn't pay its bill (it is a true deadbeat), the factor must absorb the loss. *Factoring with recourse,* on the other hand, means that if the Buygraves company doesn't pay the bill within a pre-negotiated time (for example, 90 days), the factor collects from the Saleman company. The Saleman company must then try to collect from the Buygraves company directly.

Naturally, a factor charges extra for factoring without recourse, typically 6% to 12% (on an annual basis) added to the interest rate it charges the Saleman company. For factoring without recourse, factors generally come out ahead because they minimize bad-debt expense by carefully checking each customer's credit. Nevertheless, the Saleman company might prefer factoring without recourse for two reasons:

- The Saleman company does not have to worry that any bills will be returned. In this way, factoring without recourse is a form of insurance.
- The factor expresses the extra charge for factoring without recourse as part of the daily interest rate. This daily interest rate may look very small.

Most factoring is done with notification. This means the customer company is notified and instructed to pay its bill directly to the factor. When factoring is without notification, the customer sends payment either directly to the supplier or to a post office box. In general, factoring is more expensive than pledging. On the other hand, factors provide services, such as credit checking and collection, that a company would otherwise have to carry out itself. For a small company, using a factor is often less expensive than providing the same services for itself.

Obtaining Loans Against Inventory

An entrepreneur's inventory is an asset that can serve as collateral for a loan, providing needed cash without jeopardizing access to the inventory. There are four basic ways to use inventory as security for a loan, depending on how closely the lender controls the physical inventory. These four ways are:

1. *Chattel mortgage,* in which specific inventory is used to secure the loan.

2. *Floating* (or *blanket*) *lien,* in which the loan is secured by all the borrower's inventory.

3. *Field warehousing,* in which the lender physically separates and guards the pledged inventory right on the borrower's premises.

4. *Public warehousing,* in which the lender transfers the pledged inventory to a separate warehouse.

We'll discuss each method in the following sections.

Chattel Mortgage

A **chattel** (or **property**) mortgage is a loan secured by specific assets. For example, a borrower might pledge 5,000 new refrigerators as collateral for a loan. To guarantee the lender's position as a secured creditor (in case of bankruptcy), a chattel mortgage must precisely describe the items pledged as collateral. In the case of the refrigerators, the loan agreement would include the serial numbers of the specific refrigerators pledged by the borrower. If the borrower sells some of these refrigerators or receives a new shipment of refrigerators, the chattel mortgage must be rewritten to include these changes specifically.

Because the chattel mortgage describes the collateral so specifically, it offers fairly high security to a lender. Lenders further reduce their risk by lending only a fraction of the estimated market value of the collateral. This fraction depends on how easily the assets can be transported and sold. In the case of refrigerators, which are easy to sell, a borrower might obtain as much as 90% of their wholesale cost. But a borrower with a highly specialized inventory, such as bulldozer scoops, might get 50% or less of their fair market value because the lender would have difficulty selling them to recover the money. Because chattel mortgages describe the collateral so specifically, lenders limit their use to high-value items.

Would You Like Some Shoes to Go with That Tie?

Some entrepreneurs are creating clever ways to finance their inventory and management practice. In the mid-1990s an MBA graduate by the name of Dana Katz was trying to figure out how he might best manage a shoe department in his men's clothing stores, Miltons. He was very good at selling men's suits but wasn't sure that he had the expertise to sell and stock men's shoes. Moreover, the casual look was already entering the marketplace and he wanted to conserve his cash for store renovations and other working capital needs. Since he had very large stores, space wasn't an issue. In fact, he had excess space due to declining demand in the marketplace.

Katz hit upon the idea of taking advantage of his seven prime real estate locations to subcontract space within his stores to a shoe merchant. Just like any retailer in a major mall location, the shoe merchant would pay a fixed rent for the space (based on square footage utilized) and staff and pay for the shoe department separately. The shoe department would pay a premium if sales exceeded a certain threshold.

In this manner, the clothier was able to increase sales and margins with no incremental investment in inventory or staffing. He was also able to keep the customers in the stores longer and possibly increase his sales in other ways. This is just one way that entrepreneurs use innovative ideas to manage their inventory levels.

Floating Lien

Instead of naming specific items of inventory to secure a loan, borrowers may pledge all their inventory. This is a **floating,** or **blanket, lien**. Because this arrangement doesn't describe specific items of inventory, it doesn't have to be rewritten each time the borrower sells an item from inventory or receives new items into inventory. However, this flexibility makes it extremely difficult for the lender to maintain the security for the loan. For example, the borrower might sell most of the inventory and not leave enough to secure the loan. For this reason, banks and finance companies will usually lend only a small fraction of the inventory's market value in writing a floating lien.

Field Warehousing

Field warehousing was invented to fully protect the lender's security. Under a field warehousing arrangement, the borrower designates a section of the premises, often a room or a specific area of the regular warehouse, for the use of the finance company. The finance company then locks and guards this field warehouse area and stores in it the actual inventory that the borrower is using as collateral. The finance company gives the borrower the agreed-on fraction of the fair market value of the inventory and receives in return a warehouse receipt, which gives the finance company title to the inventory.

Companies use field warehousing when the inventory is especially bulky or valuable, such as structural steel, bulk chemicals, or diamonds. Whenever the borrowing firm needs some of the inventory, it repays part of the loan, and the finance company releases part of the inventory. In this way, the finance company guarantees that there is sufficient collateral at all times to secure the loan.

Public Warehousing

Public warehousing is similar to field warehousing except that the actual inventory is moved to an independent warehouse away from the borrower's plant. As with field warehousing, the finance company releases inventory as the borrower repays the loan. Again, this ensures that the collateral is always sufficient to cover the loan. There are many variations of warehousing. For example, some bonded warehouses accept checks in payment for loans and then forward these checks to the finance company while releasing the appropriate amount of inventory to the borrower. If such an arrangement is acceptable to all parties, it helps the borrower regain title to the inventory more quickly.

Warehousing companies collect a service charge, usually a fixed amount plus 1% to 2% of the loan itself. This covers the cost of providing field warehousing facilities or of transferring inventory to a public warehouse. In addition, the warehouse company charges interest, usually 10% or more. Because of the high fixed costs of setting up a warehousing system, this form of financing is practical only for inventories larger than about $500,000.

Obtaining "Financing" from Customer Prepayments

Some companies are actually financed by their customers. This situation typically occurs on large, complex, long-term projects undertaken by defense contractors, building contractors, ship builders, and management consulting firms. These companies typically divide their large projects into a series of stages and require payment as they complete each stage. This significantly reduces the cash they require, compared to firms that finance an entire project themselves and receive payment on completion. In some companies, customers pay in advance for everything they buy. Many mail-order operations are financed this way.

Choosing the Right Mix of Short-Term Financing

The entrepreneur attempts to secure the required short-term funds at the lowest cost. The lowest cost usually results from some combination of trade credit, unsecured and secured bank loans, accounts receivable financing, and inventory financing. Though it is virtually impossible to evaluate every possible combination of short-term financing, entrepreneurs can use their experience and subjective opinion to put together a short-term financing package that will have a reasonable cost. At the same time, the entrepreneur must be aware of future requirements and the impact that using certain sources today may have on the availability of short-term funds in the future. In selecting the best financing package, the entrepreneur should consider the following factors:

- ◉ The firm's current situation and requirements
- ◉ The current and future costs of the alternatives
- ◉ The firm's future situation and requirements

For small firms, the options may be somewhat limited, and the total short-term financing package may be less important. On the other hand, larger firms may face myriad possibilities. Clearly, the short-term borrowing decision can become quite complex, but choosing the right combination of options can be of significant financial value to the entrepreneur's firm.

Traditional Bank Lending: Short-Term Bank Loans

After an entrepreneur has fully used her trade credit and collected her receivables as quickly as competitively possible, she may turn to a bank for a short-term loan. The most common bank loan is a *short-term, unsecured loan* made for 90 days. Standard variations include loans made for periods of 30 days to a year, and loans requiring collateral. Interest charges on these loans typically vary from the prime rate (the amount a bank charges its largest and financially strongest customers) to about 3% above prime.

Commercial banks are the most important suppliers of debt capital to small firms, supplying more than 80% of lending in the credit line market and more than 50% in other markets, such as commercial mortgages and vehicle, equipment, and other loans. In July 2004, the Federal Financial Institutions Examination Council (FFIEC) released data regarding the loan originations by 2,103 commercial banks and savings institutions to over 8 million small businesses. According to this data (which is estimated to represent approximately 91% of all small business loans), outstanding small business loans owed to commercial banks and other savings institutions amounted to approximately $279 billion.[3] But small firms are not just receiving loans from smaller, relationship-driven banks. Very large banks with assets of at least $10 billion are making a significant percentage of small loans of less then $100,000.[4]

Very often, an entrepreneur doesn't immediately need money but can forecast that she will have a definite need in, say, six months. The entrepreneur would not want to borrow the required money now and pay unnecessary interest for the next six months. Instead, she will formally apply to her bank for a *line of credit,* which is an assurance by the bank that, as long as the company remains financially healthy, the bank will lend the company money (up to a specified limit) whenever the company needs it. Banks usually review a company's credit line each year. A line of credit is not a guarantee that the bank will make a loan in the future. Instead, when the company actually needs the money, the bank will examine the company's current financial statements to make sure that actual results coincide with earlier plans.

Banks also grant *guaranteed lines of credit,* under which they guarantee to supply funds up to a specified limit, regardless of circumstances. This relieves the company of any worries that money may not be available when it's needed. Banks usually charge extra for this guarantee, typically 1% a year on the unused amount of the guaranteed line of credit. For example, if the bank guarantees a credit line of $1 million and the company borrows only $300,000, the company will have to pay a commitment fee of perhaps $7,000 for the $700,000 it did not borrow.

In return for granting lines of credit, banks usually require that an entrepreneur maintain a *compensating balance* (that is, keep a specified amount in its checking account without interest). For example, if an entrepreneur receives a $1 million line of credit with the requirement that she maintain a 15% compensating balance, the entrepreneur must keep at least $150,000 in her demand account with that bank all year. The bank, of course, does not have to pay interest on this demand account money, so the use of this money compensates it for standing ready to grant up to $1 million in loans for a year. Of course, when the bank actually makes loans, it charges the negotiated rate of interest.

Maturity of Loans

The most common time period, or maturity, for short-term bank loans is 90 days; however, an entrepreneur can negotiate maturities of 30 days to one year. Banks often prefer 90-day maturities, even when the entrepreneur will clearly need the money for longer than 90 days, because the three-month maturity gives the bank a chance to check the entrepreneur's financial statements regularly. If the entrepreneur's position has deteriorated, the bank may refuse to renew the loan and thus avoid a future loss.

Entrepreneurs, on the other hand, prefer maturities that closely match the time they expect to need the money. A longer maturity (rather than a series of short, constantly renewed loans) eliminates the possibility that the bank will refuse to extend a short-term loan because of a temporary weakness in the entrepreneur's operations.

Interest Rates

The rates of interest charged by commercial banks vary in two ways:

- The general level of interest rates varies over time.
- At any given time, different rates are charged to different borrowers.

The base rate for most commercial banks traditionally has been the *prime rate,* which is the rate commercial banks charge their very best business customers for short-term borrowing. This is the rate that makes the news every time it changes. Congress and the business community speculate about the prime's influence on economic activity because it is the baseline for loan pricing in most loan agreements.

Historically, the prime was a baseline for loan pricing; "prime plus two" or "2% above prime" was a normal statement of interest rate on many loan contracts. However, as the banking industry has begun to price its loans and services more aggressively, the prime is becoming less important and compensating balances less popular.

The current trend in loan pricing is *to price the loan at a rate above the marginal cost of funds* as typically reflected by the interest rates on certificates of deposit. The bank then adds an interest rate margin to the cost of funds, and the result is the rate charged to the borrower. This rate changes daily in line with the changes on money market rates offered by the bank. As liability management becomes more of a way of life for bankers, the pricing of loans will become a function of the amount of competition, both domestic and international, that the banker faces in securing loanable funds. As a result of this competition for corporate customers and enhanced competition from the commercial paper market, large, financially stable corporations are often able to borrow at a rate below prime.

The interest borrowers pay depends on several factors:

- ◉ The dollar amount of the loan
- ◉ The length of time involved
- ◉ The nominal annual rate of interest
- ◉ The repayment schedule
- ◉ The method used to calculate the interest

The various methods used to calculate interest are all variations of the simple interest calculation. *Simple interest* is calculated on the amount borrowed for the length of time the loan is outstanding. For example, if you borrow $1 million at 10% and repay in one payment at the end of one year, the simple interest is $1 million times 0.10, or $100,000. In the *add-in interest* method, the lender calculates interest on the full amount of the original principal and immediately adds it to the original principal, calculating payments by dividing principal plus interest by the number of payments to be made. If there is only one payment, this method is identical to simple interest. However, with two or more payments, this method results in an effective rate of interest greater than the nominal rate. Continuing with the previous example, if you repaid the $1 million loan in two six-month installments of $550,000 each, the effective rate is higher than 10% because you don't have the use of the funds for the entire year.

The *bank discount method* is common in short-term business loans. Generally, there are no immediate payments, and the life of the loan is usually one year or less. Interest is calculated on the amount of the loan, and the borrower receives the difference between the amount to be paid back and the amount of interest. In our example, the lender subtracts the interest amount of $100,000 from the $1 million, and you have the use of $900,000 for one year. If you divide the interest payment by the amount of money you actually used ($100,000 divided by $900,000), the effective rate is 11.1%.

If the loan were to require a compensating balance of 10%, you have the use of the loan amount less the compensating balance requirement. The effective rate of interest in this case would be 12.5% minus the interest amount of $100,000 divided by the funds available, which is $800,000 ($1,000,000 minus $100,000 interest and minus a compensating balance of $100,000). The effective interest cost on a *revolving credit* agreement includes both interest costs and the commitment fee. For example, assume the TBA Corporation has a $1 million revolving credit agreement with a bank. Interest on the borrowed funds is 10% per annum. TBA must pay a commitment fee of 1% on the unused portion of the credit line. If the firm borrows $500,000, the effective annual interest rate is 11% [(0.1 × $500,000) + (0.01 × $500,000) divided by $500,000].

Because many factors influence the effective rate of a loan, when evaluating borrowing costs, use only *the effective annual rate* as a standard of comparison to ensure that you compare the actual costs of borrowing.

Collateral

To reduce their risks in making loans, banks may require collateral from entrepreneurs. Collateral may be any asset that has value. If the entrepreneur does not repay the loan, the bank owns the collateral and may sell it to recover the amount of the loan.

Typical collateral includes both specific high-value items owned by the company (such as buildings, computer equipment, or large machinery) and all items of a particular type (such as all raw materials or all inventories). Banks use blanket liens as collateral when individual items are of low value, but the collective value of all items is large enough to serve as collateral.

The highest level of risk comes in making loans to small companies, so it's not surprising that a high proportion of loans made to small companies—probably 75%—are secured. Larger companies present less risk and have stronger bargaining positions; only about 30% of loans made to companies in this class are secured.

One aspect of protection that most banks require is *key person insurance* on the principal officers of the company taking out the loan. Because the repayment of the loan usually depends on the entrepreneur's or managers' running the company in a profitable manner, if something should happen to them, there may be some question about the safety of the loan. If the officer or officers die, the proceeds of the key person policy are paid to the bank in settlement of the loan.

When making loans to very small companies, banks often require that the owners and top managers personally sign for the loan. Then, if the company does not repay the loan, the bank can claim the signer's personal assets, such as houses, automobiles, and stock investments.

Applying for a Bank Loan

To maximize the chances of success in applying for a bank loan, make personal visits to the bank, and make quarterly delivery of income statements, balance sheets, and cash flow statements to sustain good relationships.

You'll need to conduct the actual process of obtaining bank credit (whether a line of credit or an actual loan) on a personal basis with the bank's loan officer. The loan officer will be interested in knowing the following information:

- How much money the company needs
- How the company will use this money
- How the company will repay the bank
- When the company will repay the bank

You should be able to fully answer these questions and support your response with past results and realistic forecasts.

Restrictive Covenants

Bank term loans are negotiated credit, granted after formal negotiations take place between borrower and lender. As part of the terms, the bank usually seeks to set various restrictions, or **covenants,** on the borrower's activities during the life of the loan. These restrictions are tailored to the individual borrower's situation and needs; thus, it is difficult to generalize about them. This section introduces some of the more widely used covenants and their implications. All are (at least to some degree) negotiable; it is wise for the financial executive to carefully review the loan contract and try to moderate any overly restrictive clause a bank may request.

The restrictive covenants in a loan agreement may be:

- *General provisions* found in most loan agreements and designed to force the borrower to preserve liquidity and limit cash outflows
- *Routine provisions* found in most loan agreements and normally not subject to modification during the loan period
- *Specific provisions* used according to the situation to achieve a desired total level of protection

Let's look at each in more detail.

General Provisions

The most common of all general provisions is a requirement relating to the *maintenance of working capital.* This may simply be a provision to keep net working capital at or above a specified level. Or, if the company is expected to grow fairly rapidly, the required working capital may be set on an increasing scale. For example, the bank may stipulate that working capital is to be maintained above $500,000 during the first twelve months of the loan, above $600,000 during the second, above $750,000 during the third, and so on. If the borrower's business is highly seasonal, the requirement for working capital may have to be modified to reflect these seasonal variations.

The provision covering working capital is often set in terms of the borrower's current ratio—current assets divided by current liabilities—which must be kept above, for example, 3 to 1 or 3.5 to 1. The actual figure is based on the bank's judgment and whatever is considered a safe figure for that particular industry. Working capital covenants are easy to understand and very widely used. Unfortunately, they are often of rather doubtful value. As we discussed earlier in this chapter, a company may have a large net working capital and still be short of cash.

Another widely used covenant is *a limit on the borrower's expenditures for capital investment.* The bank may have made the loan to provide the borrower with additional working capital and does not wish to see the funds sunk into capital equipment instead. The covenant may take the form of a simple dollar limit on the investment in capital equipment in any period. Or, the borrower may be allowed to invest up to, but not more than, the extent of the current depreciation expense. This provision may prove to be a serious restriction on a rapidly growing company. And clearly, any company will find such a covenant damaging if the maximum expenditure is set below the figure needed to maintain productive capacity at an adequate and competitive level.

Most term loan agreements include *covenants to prevent the borrower from selling or mortgaging capital assets without the lender's permission.* This may be extended to cover current assets other than the normal sale of finished goods, in which case the borrower is prohibited from factoring accounts receivable, selling any part of the raw-material inventory, or assigning inventory to a warehouse finance company without the bank's express permission.

Limitations on additional long-term debt are also common. The borrower is often theoretically forbidden to undertake any long-term debt during the life of the term loan, though in practice the bank usually allows new debt funds to be used in moderation as the company grows. The bank may extend the provision to prevent the borrower from entering into any long-term leases without authorization.

One type of covenant that clearly recognizes the importance of cash flows to a growing company is a *prohibition of or limit to the payment of cash dividends*. Again, if dividends are not completely prohibited, they may be either limited to a set dollar figure or based on a set percentage of net earnings. The latter approach is obviously the less restrictive.

Routine Provisions

The second category of restrictive covenants includes routine provisions found in most loan agreements that usually are not variable. The loan agreement ordinarily includes the following requirements:

- The borrower must furnish the bank with periodic financial statements and maintain adequate property insurance.

- The borrower agrees not to sell a significant portion of its assets. A provision forbidding the pledging of the borrower's assets is also included in most loan agreements. This provision is often termed a *negative pledge clause*.

- The borrower is restricted from entering into any new leasing agreements that might endanger the ability to pay the loan.

- The borrower is restricted from acquiring other firms unless prior approval has been obtained from the lender.

Specific Provisions

Finally, a number of restrictions relate more to the borrowing company's management than to its financial performance. For example:

- Key executives may be required to sign employment contracts or take out substantial life insurance.

- The bank may require the right to be consulted before any changes are made in the company's top management.

- Some covenants prevent increases in top management salaries or other compensation.

Restrictive covenants are very important in borrowing term loans. If any covenant is breached, the bank has the right to take legal action to recover its loan, probably forcing the company into insolvency. On the other hand, covenants may protect the borrowing company as well as the lender, in that their intention is to make it impossible for the borrower get into serious financial trouble without first infringing on one or more restrictions, thus giving the bank a right to step in and apply a guiding hand. A bank is very reluctant to force any client into liquidation.

Equipment Financing

Capital equipment is often financed by intermediate-term funds. These may be straight-forward term loans, usually secured by the equipment itself. Both banks and finance companies make equipment loans of this type. The nonbank companies charge considerably higher interest rates; they are used primarily by smaller companies that find themselves unable to qualify for bank term loans. As with other types of secured loans, the lender will evaluate the quality of the collateral and advance a percentage of the market value. In determining the repayment schedule, the lender ensures that the value of the equipment exceeds the loan balance. In addition, the loan repayment schedule is often made to coincide with the depreciation schedule of the equipment.

One further form of equipment financing is the *conditional sales contract*, which normally covers between two and five years. The buyer agrees to buy a piece of equipment by installment payments over a period of years. During this time the buyer has the use of the equipment, but the seller retains title until the payments have been completed. Companies unable to find credit from any other source may be able to buy equipment on these terms. The lender's risk is small because it can repossess the equipment at any time if the borrower misses an installment. Equipment distributors who sell equipment under conditional sales contracts often sell the contract to a bank or finance company, in which case the transaction becomes an interesting combination of equipment financing for the buyer and receivables financing for the seller.

The credit available under a conditional sales contract is less than the full purchase price of the equipment. Typically, the buyer is expected to make an immediate down payment of 25% to 33% of the full cash price, and only the balance is financed. The cost of the credit given may be quite high. Equipment that is highly specialized or subject to rapid obsolescence represents a greater risk to the lender than widely used standard equipment, and the interest charged on the sale of such specialized equipment to a small company may exceed 15% to 20%.

Obtaining Early Financing from External Sources

It's almost impossible for a brand-new company to get a conventional bank loan because it has no trading history and usually no assets to secure the loan. Even after a young company is up and running, it is still difficult to get a bank loan. Many entrepreneurs overlook the possibility of getting an SBA-guaranteed loan.

SBA-Guaranteed Loans[5]

SBA-guaranteed loans are available to small companies that have sought and been refused conventional financing loans from banks. SBA-guaranteed loans are made by banks, with the SBA guaranteeing 90% of a loan under $155,000 and up to 85% of a loan greater than that figure, up to a maximum of $750,000. Interest rates on SBA-guaranteed loans are negotiated between the borrower and bank, but they are subject to SBA maximums and generally cannot exceed 2.75% over the New York prime rate. The bank has to pay a one-time guarantee fee of 2% to 3% of the principal; that fee is usually passed on to the borrower.

To qualify for SBA loan assistance, a company must be operated for profit and fall within size standards. It cannot be a business engaged in the creation or distribution of ideas or opinions such as newspapers, magazines, and academic schools, or in speculation or investment in rental real estate. SBA-guaranteed loans can be used for the following purposes:

- Expand or renovate facilities
- Purchase machinery, equipment, fixtures, and leasehold improvements
- Finance receivables and augment working capital
- Refinance existing debt (for compelling credit reasons of benefit to the borrower)
- Provide seasonal lines of credit

- ◉ Construct commercial buildings
- ◉ Purchase land or buildings

Applying for an SBA Loan

The bank will require your company to have adequate paid-in equity, which usually means that the owners have invested sufficient money in the company that the debt to equity ratio will be no more than 3:1 after the loan. Put another way, if you are seeking a $75,000 loan, your paid-in equity must be at least $25,000. For a startup company, the bank will also expect that the paid-in equity will be cash. Another important condition is that everyone who owns 20% or more of the company must provide personal guarantees.

You'll have a better chance of getting a loan in a timely manner from a bank that processes lots of SBA loans rather than one that processes only a few. Visit the SBA Web site (www.sba.gov) and click on the state where your business is located. Then click on "(2006) Lender Ranking." This will produce a list of banks that have made at least one SBA-guaranteed loan in the most recent reporting period. For example, at the time of this writing, a Massachusetts entrepreneur could go to www.sba.gov, click on MA-Boston to go to the SBA Massachusetts site http://www.sba.gov/ma/, then click on "(2006) Lender Ranking" to get a list of banks that granted at least one SBA loan between 10/01/2005 and 08/31/2006. At the top of the list is Citizens Bank with 835 loans totaling $41.4 million; followed by Bank of America with 421 loans totaling $10.4 million; Sovereign Bank with 182 loans totaling $16.7 million; Capital One with 123 loans totaling $4.6 million; and TDBanknorth with 43 loans totaling $7.1 million. At the bottom of the rankings are banks that made only three or four loans in the same period.[6]

Once you've selected a bank:

- ◉ Prepare a current business balance sheet listing all assets, liabilities, and the net worth. Startup businesses should prepare an estimated balance sheet including the amount invested by the owner and others.

- ◉ Prepare a profit-and-loss statement for the current period and the most recent three fiscal years. Startup businesses should prepare a detailed projection of earnings and expenses for at least the first year of operation.

- ◉ Prepare a personal financial statement of the proprietor and each partner or stockholder owning 20% or more of the business.

- ◉ List collateral to be offered as security for the loan.

- ◉ List any existing liens.

- ◉ State the amount of the requested loan and the purposes for which it is intended.

If your loan request is refused, contact the local SBA office regarding other loans that may be available from the SBA.

Getting Traction with an SBA-Guaranteed Loan

Fred Curtis, Sr., founded Curtis Tractor Cab, Inc. in 1969 when he saw the opportunity to serve a niche market for the manufacture of after-market cab enclosures for small tractors. The company initially operated out of a small garage in Worcester, Massachusetts. Fred Curtis, Jr., started working full time at his father's company in 1991 at the age of 21 when total sales were approximately $1 million. Under his leadership, Curtis has made periodic capital investments and refinements to its manufacturing

Courtesy Fred Curtis, Jr.

Kubota cab manufactured by Curtis Industries. The Curtis family has designed, manufactured and distributed vehicle cab systems and snowplows for over 35 years.

systems, including the company's major expansion in 1995 when Curtis acquired and renovated its manufacturing facility using SBA's 504/Certified Development Loan Program. The project total was $1 million, with Banknorth Massachusetts providing the first mortgage and SBA the second mortgage. The loan enabled Curtis to manufacture its products from "soup to nuts" onsite and to significantly diversify its product line.

At the time the 504 project was approved, Curtis employed 62 people and generated revenues of $5.5 million; since then the number of employees has skyrocketed to 220 and revenues to $44 million—increases of 249% in the number of employees and 700% in revenues since 1995. Because of this phenomenal growth in revenues and numbers of jobs, Fred Curtis, Jr., was named the 2005 Massachusetts Small Business Person of the Year and placed third in SBA's national competition.[7]

Planning Cash Flow and Planning Profits

Although there is a relationship between them, cash flows are not the same as profit. **Profit** is an accounting concept designed to measure the overall performance of the company. It is a somewhat nebulous concept, open to variations in measurement techniques and accounting conventions, each of which produces somewhat different results, which are then open to different interpretations.

In contrast, **cash flows** are not always a direct measure of a company's performance. For example, take two opposite extremes: a young, profitable company sinking as many funds as it can get into a new venture, and an old unprofitable company heading for bankruptcy. The results in terms of cash flow are likely to be the same: *declining cash balances.* A company can earn a handsome profit and have a net cash outflow in the same month, if it pays for new capital equipment in that month. It can equally well show substantial loss and an increased cash balance in one month, if the results of new financing or the proceeds from the sale of substantial fixed assets are received in that month.

However, the concept of *cash* is not nebulous: Either the company has a certain amount of cash or it does not. And a lack of cash is critical. A company can sustain losses for a time without suffering, but a company that has no cash is insolvent and in imminent danger of bankruptcy, no matter what its profit picture may be.

Thus, many financial transactions that do not enter into the calculation of profit—such as buying new fixed assets, getting additional financing, and paying dividends—do enter into cash flows. Similarly, some transactions that enter into the determination of profit—notably, the deduction of depreciation and amortization of expenses—do not directly enter into cash flows (although there are cash flow benefits related to taxes), because they are noncash transactions with no effect on cash balances.

Many entrepreneurs and bankers are becoming increasingly interested in a concept called *free cash flow*. Free cash flow is equal to the firm's cash flow from operations minus investments in capital expenditures that are required to maintain the company's competitiveness. For example, a firm that has $1,500,000 in cash from operations that spends $2,000,000 in property, plant, and equipment has a *negative* free cash flow of $500,000 ($1,500,000−$2,000,000). This implies that the firm does not have surplus funds from operations, as it is in fact borrowing in order to maintain appropriate levels of capital investments.

Another term that is becoming more common is *pretax undedicated cash flow*. Undedicated cash flow is equal to free cash flow plus tax plus interest expense. Undedicated cash flow, or "raider" cash flow, is emerging as an important variable in appraising the investment attraction of engaging in leveraged buyouts, restructuring, and mergers of publicly owned companies. Prospective buyers (raiders) often add back interest and taxes so that they can get the broadest possible picture of the company's available cash. Then the investors determine how they could redirect the cash flows. Since the prospective buyers are going to be owners and not passive shareholders, they are more concerned about having control of the cash than about operating profits. Often, much of the operating cash flow is devoted to servicing debt after the transaction. As the firm begins to service the debt arrangement, the equity in the company automatically grows.

☐ CONCLUSION

Working capital is often misinterpreted as being synonymous with *firm liquidity*. In fact, only a part of net working capital is liquid; the balance of net working capital is tied up in firm operations. *Liquidity* is largely a function of a firm's growth and the timing of receipts and payments. In situations where payments are made to suppliers before customers pay, growth in sales generally results in lower liquidity.

Preparing a cash flow forecast assists entrepreneurs in assessing the timing and maturity of funding needs. With a cash forecast, the entrepreneur can more easily determine the type of funding to procure and the small, growing firm's ability to grow with available funds. This includes efficiencies in accounts receivable, inventories, payables, and accruals. To the extent that entrepreneurs can successfully negotiate with customers and suppliers, they will be able to manage future growth. However, small firms are rarely afforded the benefits associated with growth funded exclusively through internal cash generation. The more common occurrence includes external debt sources, leasing, cash innovations, and small firm/governmental programs. Such is the fate for the small business entrepreneur. Early growth stages offer large funding requirements and huge risks to those who can't meet payroll and supplier demands. However, once an entrepreneur has negotiated a level of external sources of funds, including bank financing, privately placed debt, leasing options, or other financing innovations, that entrepreneur has a better chance for long-term corporate survival.

YOUR OPPORTUNITY JOURNAL

Reflection Point	Your Thoughts...
1. What sources of capital do you have? Are you willing to take on a home equity loan? Use your personal credit cards? How much of a ''nest egg'' do you need to feel comfortable pursuing a new venture?	
2. What do you expect your cash conversion cycle to be? Is their a way to improve it? What A/R terms are common in your industry? How should you manage A/R?	
3. How much inventory does your business need to carry to avoid stockouts? What terms can you get on inventory (A/P)?	
4. Can you finance your A/R? What means (bank loans, factoring, etc.) are most available to you? Can you get loans on your inventory?	
5. What short-term loans are needed for your business (e.g., line of credit)? When will you be bank credit worthy?	

WEB EXERCISE

Visit the SBA Web site (www.sba.gov). The Web site has useful information on a number of startup issues. Take a look at the SBA loan programs. What steps do you need to undertake to qualify for these programs?

NOTES

[1] Excerpted from the Federal Reserve Web site: www.federalreserve.gov/releases/g19/current/default.htm.

[2] As reported in CNN-Money. http://money.cnn.com/2004/10/01/real_estate/financing/home_equity/.

[3] The FFIEC press release can be examined at www.ffiec.gov/hmcrpr/cra072604.htm.

[4] SBA. http://app1.sba.gov/faqs/faqindex.cfm?areaID=24.

[5] Excerpted from the SBA Web site: www.sba.gov.

[6] www.sba.gov/idc/groups/public/documents/ma_boston/ma_06loanvolume.pdf.

[7] Excerpted from the SBA Web site: http://www.sba.gov/ma/MA_SS2005_10.html.

CASE

BetterLiving Patio Rooms

April 1, 1998

John Esler thrived on recruiting good people to implement calculated business risks. Although he enjoyed the daily challenges involved in owning a business, some days were more satisfying than others. The first day of April, for example, was a bad day. He had a territory disagreement with Craft-Bilt that required immediate resolution, he had perplexing HR troubles, and production was half of what he had forecast, so his cash was flowing red.

John's company, Patio Rooms of America, Inc. (PRA), was the exclusive Craft-Bilt dealer of BetterLiving Patio Rooms for most of the state of Massachusetts. Craft-Bilt manufactured components for building BetterLiving Patio Rooms (see Figure 11.3). The key benefit of this product was that homeowners could spend time outside without being bothered by bugs or the weather—big problems for people in New England. John founded PRA as a BetterLiving Patio Rooms marketing and installation company in November, 1997.

Sales were vigorous, so a backlog of orders (and impatient customers) was growing. In the first 4 months of business, PRA sold 41 rooms worth $509,006 and had a 6-week installation backlog—and this for a "summer" business. John's comment was, "We had phenomenal sales in January and February. We proved that this business is not strictly seasonal."

John wanted to grow PRA—had to grow the company to support the infrastructure he was creating—but Craft-Bilt resisted selling him the adjacent Connecticut and New Hampshire territories, and upstate New York, Rhode Island, and Maine already had BetterLiving Patio Rooms dealers. Unfortunately, John was not rich enough, or successful

■ **Figure 11.3**

A BetterLiving Patio Room

Dan D'Heilly prepared this case under the supervision of Professor William Bygrave, Babson College, as a basis for class discussion rather than to illustrate either effective or ineffective handling of an administrative situation. Funding provided by the Ewing Marion Kauffman Foundation. Copyright © by Babson College

enough yet in Massachusetts to convince Craft-Bilt that he could manage another BetterLiving Patio Rooms territory.

Since Craft-Bilt was reluctant to commit immediately, John was trying to persuade Craft-Bilt to leave Connecticut and New Hampshire open until PRA was ready to expand, but Ross Lederer did not want to concede even that. Ross Lederer, the Craft-Bilt Director of Development, was not as receptive to PRA's growth plans as John would have liked. Ross was concerned that PRA could not properly service the additional territory soon enough, so he wanted to be unhindered when approached by qualified buyers. In fact, Ross began negotiating with a couple of Wharton Business School graduates for the Connecticut territory shortly after John asked for a right of first refusal.

On the human resource front, John also had serious challenges. PRA already had over a dozen employees, most building patio rooms. These employees were better paid than those in his previous businesses, but the operation was not building rooms fast enough. Craft-Bilt had told him that a 2-man crew would build 2 rooms a week, but PRA crews were only producing one room each week.

How would he persuade Craft-Bilt to give him a right of first refusal on the Connecticut and New Hampshire territories when PRA was not performing as projected? Were his goals unreasonable? Perhaps it was just that the company learning curve was steeper than he had hoped and he needed to be patient a little while longer. But maybe the problem was deeper: John had no background in construction, yet he was running a construction company . . . PRA had a sales backlog; now it had to construct rooms well enough to survive.

John Esler

Born and raised in Albany, New York, John first caught an entrepreneurial fever as a teenager. He had worked at the Saratoga racetrack selling tee shirts for a couple of summers and was promoted to supervisor after his junior year in high school. That summer, John found himself in charge when the owner of the business suddenly disappeared. John managed the operation for the next four years and paid his way through college with the profits. Upon graduating from SUNY Albany, John passed the business along to his brothers.

After college, John moved to New York City and worked for the Macy's department store as an associate buyer for two years. He found the work uninspiring, so he returned home to Albany. While looking for a job, John noticed that there was no valet service at an upscale restaurant that certainly would have offered it in New York City. He thought a valet service would make good money at this restaurant, so he approached the owner with a business proposition, and started Valet Parking, Inc. John turned one contract into a business, and managed the company for five years. It grew to $200,000 in annual revenue, and employed 30 people (almost all part-time), but he grew bored and sold it to a senior employee in 1990.

Then came SUBWAY sandwiches. John purchased an Albany SUBWAY store franchise in 1990, and over the next five years he opened four more stores. The businesses were successful, with two of his stores ranked in the top five SUBWAY stores for the region. However, it wasn't what he wanted longterm.

I set five-year goals, and when I grossed $1.5 million between the five stores, I definitely met my goals. But when it came time to set new goals, I didn't want to stay in that *business. I didn't like the employee equation, I didn't really like the restaurant business, I didn't particularly like the franchisor, and on top of all that, the margins were not very good. I decided to sell my stores and look for something better.*

The sale left him with a wider set of options. It was around this time that he met and married Jeannie Lawton, a doctoral psychology student. John became enthused with the idea of gaining more knowledge about his chosen profession. He wanted to develop more sophisticated business skills, to meet other entrepreneurs, and to pursue bigger business challenges with confidence.

John decided to get an MBA and selected the F.W. Olin Graduate School of Business at Babson College. Babson College is a business school on the outskirts of Boston with a one-year MBA degree and a renowned entrepreneurship program.

FranNet

While in school, John's studies included franchising, dealerships, and distributorships, and he wanted the advantages of business affiliation in his next venture. John started researching specific business opportunities, but had not found a compelling opportunity by the time he graduated in May 1997 (see Exhibit 11.1).

I was looking for growth potential—multiple units or a large territory. I told people, "I need a business that will be at least $5 million in five years. I already had the million dollar thrill." One of the things I got from Babson was, "What is your threshold?" How high can you set the bar? How much will you be satisfied with?

That summer, John took a three-week safari with his wife before getting to work identifying his next venture. Back from Africa, John decided to engage the services of business brokers. Eventually he found FranNet, a national network of franchise brokers who shared information about business affiliation opportunities. There were FranNet consultants selling franchises and dealerships nation-wide, and they operated much like realtors representing the sellers in a real estate transaction. The Boston branch was owned by Jack Kelt. Jack interviewed John then presented him with opportunities in the automotive, education, and food industries. John did not want to get back into the food business, and was not excited about the education industry, however, he thought the automotive industry had potential. After some research, John decided to meet with people at Cottman Transmission and AAMCO, both headquartered in Pennsylvania. Jack first heard of Craft-Bilt at this time, and suggested John visit while he was in Pennsylvania.

Meanwhile, John had also begun interviewing to get a job. What if finding a new venture took longer than expected? He and Jeannie were not independently wealthy. The negotiations for a position as a business development agent with Cedant, the largest franchisor in the world, went as far as getting an offer. John agonized over the decision, then accepted Cedant's offer.

FranNet had told me about Cottman Transmission and AAMCO, but I accepted a position at Cedant because they were pressuring me to make a decision. When I told them yes, they turned around and said it would take a week to get me an offer letter. Then they said there were still two other candidates they had to consider.

The week Cedant flip-flopped, John went to Philadelphia, as he recalled.

I was angry and booked a flight to Philadelphia to meet with Cottman and AAMCO. Craft-Bilt was also in Philly, I hadn't done any homework on them yet, so I only gave them three hours. I went out to dinner with the president and vice president for business development. First and foremost, I told myself, "I trust these people." I liked their openness and the look in their eyes.

I left Philadelphia knowing that I didn't like AAMCO or Cottman Transmission. With the auto shops, I didn't like the fact that everyone walked though the door upset. With patio rooms, you improve customers' lives. I liked that.

Ironically, Cedant called three days after John met with Craft-Bilt and made a firm offer for the job he had accepted the prior week. John turned them down without hesitation. After meeting with the people at Craft-Bilt, John was excited about building his own business. If his due diligence checked out, he would move forward. John returned to Boston and researched the BetterLiving Patio Rooms opportunity.

I proceeded to visit existing dealers. I traveled to Maine, Albany, Vermont, and Providence. These were older dealerships doing 20 to 50 rooms a year as a part of home remodeling businesses, and the dealers had nothing but praise for Craft-Bilt. I looked into the industry—no dominant player. I decided to negotiate an agreement. I thought, "If they can do this focusing on patios part-time, I should be able to focus full-time and really blow the doors off."

When John first discovered BetterLiving Patio Rooms, he was impressed by the people and the opportunity. Later the challenge came into sharper focus.

It hit me one day after I was well into the deal that BetterLiving Patio Rooms was, first and foremost, a construction play. I had thought of it more in terms of the opportunity: a great product with a great marketing concept supported by a great manufacturer in a fragmented market. It had growth, margins, almost everything I was looking for in a business.

Of course I had also wanted to know something about the business, but with my background, I didn't think this would be likely so I was not deterred by my inexperience in the construction trade (see Exhibit 11.1 for John Esler's resume). However, it has become clear to me that this is a monster challenge.

Patio Room Industry

More Americans own their own homes in 1997 than at any time in history, both by the percentage of households occupied by owners (about 65%) and in absolute terms.[1] The American home remodeling industry was $118.4 billion in 1997, an increase of 5% from 1996. Over 500,000 American households remodeled their homes each year to add sun space.[2] Analysts placed the size of the sun space market in the $6 billion range, putting sunrooms[3] at a little over 5% of the remodeling industry. The scale of market demand was confirmed in a 1991 home-owner survey where 31% reported that a sunroom was the single most desirable element in a new home, yet only 10% of the builders surveyed included this as a standard feature in their new construction developments.[4]

---

[1] U.S. Department of Census, telephone interview, August 1998.

[2] *Qualified Remodeler* magazine, September 1997.

[3] The term "sunrooms" is used for both 3-season and 4-season glass rooms. Patio rooms are 3-season rooms.

[4] *Professional Builder & Remodeler* magazine, 1991.

EXHIBIT 11.1 John Esler's Resume

JOHN K. ESLER
100 Otis Street ∗ Northboro, MA 01532
Telephone/Fax: 508-393-0400, Ext. 226 ∗ E-mail: jesler@patios.com

Background Summary

A results driven, high performance, entrepreneurial general manager and a sales/business development leader with an exceptional range of accomplishment based on key strengths in:

Leadership — The combination of analytical, interpersonal skills and emotional resilience gained through firing line experience to create a vision, engender dedication and hard work, and maximize team's talents to achieve outstanding performance.

Rapid Contribution — The learning skills, obsession with excellence and excitement for the task at hand to quickly contribute in new and rapidly evolving situations.

High Performance — Exceptional energy level, dedication, competitive drive and commitment to thrive on pressure and multiple challenges, and infuse the organization with the same level of performance.

Communications — Strong written and oral communicator with superior ability to negotiate and persuade.

General Management Perspective — Experience in a P&L position for a large company and ownership of a small business. Developed business planning, business strategy and implementation skills focused on creating profitable relationships with customers.

Entrepreneurial Management — Demonstrated ability to recognize opportunity, martial the necessary resources, create entrepreneurial organizations and achieve results.

Professional Experience

Subway Sandwiches, Albany, NY   **Principal/Owner**   **1990–1996**

Originated and operated 2 year-round and 3 seasonal locations that ranked as first and second volume locations in a 65-store market.

RH Macy and Company,   **Asst. Buyer,**
New York, NY   **Sportswear Dept.**   **1986–1989**

Promoted from Management Training program to Sales Manager to Assistant Buyer with responsibility for purchasing, inventory management and pricing for a $15 million product category.

Valet Services, Inc./   **Principal/Owner**   **1981–1995**
Saratoga Flats, Albany, NY

Founded and established two entrepreneurial businesses. Sold both as ongoing entities.

Education

F.W. Olin Graduate School of Business, Babson College   **1997**

Master of Business Administration — Entrepreneurial Studies and Marketing
Magna Cum Laude Honors, GPA: 3.7 Class Rank: 6, Class Size: 220

University of New York at Albany   **1985**

Bachelor of Arts, Dual Major — Finance/Economics

Outside Interests

National/American Hockey League — youngest ever to officiate at the professional level.

Enjoy golf, skiing, tennis, SCUBA diving and travel.

Other data on remodeling market demand was collected using the toll-free "Home-owner Remodeling Hotline" by NARI, the National Association for the Remodeling Industry. The public called this number to ask questions about remodeling. The statistics in Figure 11.4 demonstrate the extent of consumer interest in sunrooms. This is supported by Figure 11.5, a survey which shows sunroom projects were a more common project than either kitchens or bathrooms.

The sunroom industry could be thought of as comprising of four niches based on framing materials and usage: aluminum or wood, and 3-season or 4-season use. Patio room enclosures were defined as 3-season rooms. An industry trade group, the National Sunroom Association, estimated the patio room segment at about $1 billion in 1997. Consumers selected between styles based on budget, needs, and aesthetic considerations. Contractors using wood-framed construction accounted for the majority of patio room construction. Wood-frame enclosures took longer to construct and cost more than aluminum-frame rooms (the average selling price for a PRA room, $13,000, was about 70% less than an

Project Areas	Inquirers
Kitchens	47%
Bathrooms	46%
Other Interior	41%
Windows	39%
Room Additions	35%
Sunrooms	32%

Source: NARI Homeowner Remodeling Hotline, October 1997

Figure 11.4

Information Requests

Project	Rank
Windows/Doors	1
Siding	2
Whole-house	3
Other	4
Room Additions	5
Sunrooms	6
Kitchens	7
Roofing	8
Bathrooms	9
Outdoor Spaces	10

Source: Qualified Remodeler, September, 1997

Figure 11.5

Project Frequency

average wood-frame room). In addition, aluminum required less maintenance and lasted longer.

The patio room lifestyle cut across several socioeconomic classes. Purchasers of this product tended to come from the middle class, the upper portions of the lower socioeconomic class, and the lower portions of the upper socioeconomic class. In Pennsylvania, the BetterLiving Patio Rooms customer base had also been segmented by age, with baby boomers (ages 45–60) buying 60% of the patio rooms, younger couples (ages 30–45) buying 25%, and seniors the remaining 15% of the rooms. The prime patio room customer age was the largest part of the population (35–54) in Massachusetts.

John's experience was that customers purchase Betterliving Patio Rooms for a variety of reasons: lifestyle improvement, increased living space, value vs. the 4-season and wood alternatives, extended use of an existing deck, custom design vs. pre-fabricated alternatives, and protection from insects. John put it succinctly, "Our hottest markets are bug-infested! People need enclosures because of the mosquitoes."

Favorite patio room activities included private phone conversations, dinner "outside," bird-watching, and enjoying the evening sky. As an investment, the return on patio room additions was about the same as other home remodeling projects as shown in Figure 11.6.

There was no nationally dominant manufacturer in the aluminum patio room industry, and most manufacturers and dealers were privately held, so the industry size and growth rate were difficult to estimate. However, there were about a dozen aluminum frame manufacturers and the largest, Patio Enclosures, had revenue of $58 million in 1997. Patio Enclosures has had a compound annual growth rate over 10% since 1991.

Craft-Bilt

Founded in 1946, Craft-Bilt was located in Pennsylvania, an hour west of Philadelphia. This privately held family firm experienced a management succession in the late 1980s, when the founder Bud Stone died, and his son Andy rose from vice president to chairman and CEO. Andy recruited Ross Lederer, making him vice president and director of business development. Ross joined the team with carte blanche for growing the company.

Project	ROI
Minor Kitchen Remodel	102%
Bathroom	77%
Deck	73%
Siding	71%
Patio Room	70%
Home Office	69%
Windows	68%

Source: Today's Homeowner, February 1998

Figure 11.6

Remodeling ROI

Ross Lederer had experience in merchant banking and franchising. He had helped grow a restaurant chain to 300 units, then tried to buy it back from the franchisors. Unsuccessful in gaining control of the organization, Ross went looking for an opportunity to create a Fortune 1,000 company, and found Andy Stone with a similar vision. Together with Ross, Andy established a retail sales goal of $200 million for 2002. Privately held, Craft-Bilt declined to divulge annual sales numbers; however, an online company reporting service listed Craft-Bilt's 1992 wholesale revenues at $5 million. To achieve their goal, Craft-Bilt needed a revolutionary improvement in its dealership performance.

Historically, Craft-Bilt sold its patio rooms through small, established home remodeling contractor/dealers. Craft-Bilt paid for five-day training seminars for all dealership sales and installation personnel at corporate headquarters. The ten best BetterLiving Patio Rooms dealers usually sold over 100 rooms a year, but many sold less than a dozen. Meanwhile, the market leader, Patio Enclosures, had branches in Chicago, Cleveland, Philadelphia, Baltimore, and Washington D.C. which consistently installed 700 to 1,000 rooms a year. Patio Enclosures' offices were either owned and operated by the manufacturer (24 branches), or by franchisees (11 franchisees). These operations focused exclusively on selling patio rooms and two complementary products (casual furniture and window treatments).

In mid-1997, Craft-Bilt implemented a program offering world-class support for a new class of dealers known as Craft-Bilt Super Dealerships (CSDs). CSDs were created to focus on and dominate a patio room marketplace. Craft-Bilt developed new products and services to support the CSDs (e.g., "best in class" marketing, training, and dealer recruitment programs), and set a course for unprecedented growth.

Patio Rooms of America

John completed his due diligence and began negotiations. Andy and Ross were enthusiastic about John opening up the Boston territory, but John wanted a larger sphere, and made an offer for the Worcester and Springfield territories immediately. Ross was skeptical about John's request due to his lack of experience and financial depth. After discussions back and forth, John entered into exclusive dealership agreements with Craft-Bilt Manufacturing for three territories: Boston, Worcester, and Springfield, Massachusetts. John paid a $35,000 fee for the exclusive rights to the Boston territory. The Worcester and Springfield markets cost $10,000 each. John signed all three contracts in October 1997.

As someone who had financed five SUBWAY stores, he had a good idea what was involved. John was not too worried about raising $125,000 in bank debt because he had $75,000 in mutual funds for collateral, he was investing his own equity capital in the company, and he had a successful track record. His first stop was the bank that he worked with in Albany, as John recalled.

> Two days after I talked to him, my banker said, "You are approved. No problem." I was going to get $50,000 as a letter of credit for Craft-Bilt, and $75,000 in cash. They said it would take two weeks to do the paperwork.
>
> Two months later, I finally got a letter of commitment from the bank—after I had opened the business—and the deal fell through the same day I received the letter. Someone at the bank reviewed the deal and realized that some of my collateral was nonassignable! My folks could not use their retirement account for collateral. I should have looked into it, but I thought the banker would have known. So here I was in December, I owed

Craft-Bilt $30,000 for inventory already in my warehouse, and I had material worth another $20,000 on the way. I had to liquidate my mutual funds to pay the first bills.

The next day I called one of my contacts at Babson College, professor Joel Shulman, and he connected me with Tim Fahey of Middlesex Bank. They provided $125,000, collateralized by the assets of the company, and $35,000 of my cash. The $125,000 only yielded $40,000 in working capital, because Craft-Bilt demanded a $50,000 letter of credit (LC) in order to get 30-day terms on inventory. Without the LC, no terms. Bankers hate LCs; that's why Tim kept $35,000 against the $125,000. I wrote checks for all $40,000 the day I got the money.

John opened an office serving the Boston and Worcester territories on November 1, 1997. This territory included the entire state, north to New Hampshire and south to Rhode Island, beginning with Worcester county and moving east to the ocean. PRA established a 6,800 square-foot warehouse and office space in Northboro to serve as corporate headquarters.

John expected to install at least 850 rooms annually in these three territories within five years (see Figure 11.7). There were over 1.3 million owner-occupied homes in this area, and the 35–54 age group was the largest segment of the population (see Figure 11.8). When John Esler opened the Boston territory, PRA became one of the first CSDs. With PRA's mid-winter sales performance, it rapidly became a model CSD operation.

Territory	1998	1999	2000	2001	2002	2003
Boston	135	175	225	275	350	425
Worcester	31	50	100	150	175	200
Springfield		50	100	150	200	225
Rooms Sold	166	275	425	575	725	850

■ **Figure 11.7**

Patio Room Sales by Territory

(000s)	Pop	Personal Income	Home-owners	Homeowners Ages 35–54
Boston	4,011	$112,249,701	988	407
Springfield	666	13,664,970	164	68
Worcester	717	15,544,172	186	76

Sources: Markets in 1994 with Population by County—Regional Economic Information System CD (REIS); Household Size—Population Estimates Program, Population Division, U.S. Bureau of the Census August 21, 1997; Homeownership rates—U.S. Dept of Commerce, Economics and Statistics www.census.gov/hhes/www/homeown/source.html

■ **Figure 11.8**

Territory Demographics

We did some installations during the winter because most go on existing decks. The problem was doing the footings[5] in winter. We did not know what we were doing. It took a week with everyone pitching in to put up one room with new footings.

According to Craft-Bilt, this business should operate at about 37% COGS, 50% gross margins, and 15% net margins (see Exhibit 11.2 for the Income Statement). Overall, John expected that material costs would remain stable over time because prices for aluminum products were historically stable and Craft-Bilt had a track record of resisting price increases. The production labor costs should be controllable because of the modular process for installing rooms. Finally, the in-home sales transaction should continue to generate undiscounted sales. Startup inefficiencies had kept PRA's margins below these levels.

Team Building

John began putting his team together by networking. As he put it, "My most important function is selling the company to the people we need onboard." He found that two friends who lived in Albany were interested in helping to launch PRA. Ed Jackowski had known John at SUBWAY, where Ed was involved in selling franchises. Andy Constable was educated as an architect, skilled at carpentry, and had been in John's wedding party. Andy recommended another friend in Albany who was willing to move to Boston, also named Andy, Andy Malone, who was an architect by training, but a master carpenter by profession. With a nucleus in sales and production, John set up the warehouse in Northboro and began recruiting.

We're trying to build a company here. I am a good employer who treats employees like members of my family. That's why we provide medical and dental insurance, earlier than we can really afford it. I want everyone who works here to want PRA to be the last company they ever work for. It may sound corny, but I look for people with a good heart who can see that vision.

The results have been great so far. Low turnover and in each BetterLiving Patio Rooms training class, one of our people has finished number one. We have consistently attracted top-quality people.

Turnover was less than many firms in construction, and John believed that having founding principles was an important part of his success formula (see Figure 11.9). John explained how the third principle found a practical application.

These principles have to translate into little and big things. I bought a plunger after a toilet got clogged, and brought it to a sales meeting to illustrate the point. I said, "If the toilet gets clogged, I'll be the first one to grab the plunger. We shouldn't need to hire a janitor to clean up after us because if it is to be, it is up to me—and you."

By April, PRA had three people in sales (five including John and the sales manager), four in the media department (all but the manager were part-time), and four crews for a total eight installers and the production manager.

---

[5] *Footings* are the concrete foundation posts in the ground for supporting structural weight. Producing new footings is difficult when the ground is frozen, as it usually is in New England from December through February.

EXHIBIT 11.2	PRA Income Statement (continued on Exhibit 11.6)						
	Jan		**Feb**		**Mar**		**Total**
Rooms Installed	5		8		7		20
Recognized Sales	$71,571		$98,744		$81,657		$251,972
Average Selling Price	$12,599						
Cost of Construction							
Materials	28,317	40%	34,117	35%	37,444	46%	99,878
Field Installation	7,412	10%	9,854	10%	16,383	20%	33,648
Equipment & Trucks	5,650	8%	2,996	3%	6,138	8%	14,784
Permits	730	1%	550	1%	526	1%	1,806
Total CoC	42,109	59%	47,517	48%	60,491	74%	150,116
Gross Profit	29,462	41%	51,227	52%	21,166	26%	101,856
Sales & Marketing							
Sales Compensation	9,711	14%	11,656	12%	14,383	18%	35,750
Media Department	3,540	5%	3,691	4%	3,745	5%	10,976
Advertising	10,804	15%	3,992	4%	9,537	12%	24,334
Misc. Expenses	538	1%	1,712	2%	2,070	3%	4,320
Total Sales & Mkg.	24,594	34%	21,051	21%	29,735	36%	75,380
Indirect Operations							
Production Mgmt.	2,722	4%	4,000	4%	4,000	5%	10,722
Warehouse	244	0%	812	1%	476	1%	1,531
Awards	—		—		—		—
Indirect Oper. Exp.	2,966	4%	4,812	5%	4,476	5%	12,254
G & A							
Salaries	7,630	11%	4,167	4%	3,326	4%	15,123
Rent	3,883	5%	—	0%	3,883	5%	7,766
Telephone	2,922	4%	927	1%	2,639	3%	6,489
Insurance	3,199	4%	2,034	2%	3,191	4%	8,423
MIS	300	0%	774	1%	835	1%	1,909
Office Supplies	356	0%	250	0%	835	1%	1,440
Professional Fees	991	1%	2,138	2%	5,468	7%	8,597
Utilities	884	1%	1,502	2%	1,452	2%	3,837
Dues/Subscriptions	75	0%	85	0%	44	0%	204
Travel/Entertainment	1,602	2%	393	0%	644	1%	2,639
Bank Charges	30	0%	1,052	1%	—	0%	1,081
Total G&A	21,872	31%	13,321	13%	22,317	27%	57,509
TOTAL (non-CoC)	$91,540	128%	$86,701	88%	$118,130	145%	$296,372
EBIT	$(19,958)	-28%	$12,043	12%	$(36,473)	-45%	$(44,388)

An important part of John's team was his independent board of advisors. The board included world-class experts in several fields: manufacturer relationships, franchising, and entrepreneurship, construction, and one of John's classmates from Babson. These people met bi-monthly to review progress on the business.

Marketing

Compared to other firms selling patio rooms, John had a larger, more highly trained marketing team, and a more aggressive media program. PRA expected to spend 9% of projected gross sales on this program (an estimated $185,589) in year one of operations.[6]

Developed in part by Craft-Bilt, PRA's marketing mix relied heavily on television infomercial advertising (usually placed on cable stations). The 30-minute television infomercials were not run continuously due to the large number of leads produced by these programs. Media buys were made by Direct Results Marketing (DRM) as directed by PRA. Craft-Bilt hired Direct Results Marketing in Ohio to produce the infomercials, and the contract allowed DRM to place the ads and earn a 15% commission. To monitor variation from goal, PRA produced tracking sheets called Daily Marketing Reports (see Figure 11.10). The average cost for placement on a local cable station was $175 for a 30-minute spot, which produced an average of 12 names for $14.64 cost per name. PRA was the only market competitor using TV.

Craft-Bilt told us that the names to appointments ratio was 37%, appointment to close was 27%, so we could predict very closely what our sales would be. This was critical because we had to keep our salespeople busy and not keep our prospects waiting too long.

1. Practice integrity in everything that we do.
2. Value is always defined by the customer.
3. The Rule of the Ten Twos (10 words with 2 letters):
   "If it is to be, it is up to me."

■ Figure 11.9

PRA's Founding Principles

	Success Rate	Households
Names from TV	100%	100.0
Appointments Written*	33%	32.8
Appointments Issued**	76%	24.9
Demonstrations	91%	22.7
Sales Closed	28%	6.4
Installed Rooms	72%	4.2

Source: PRA Daily Marketing Reports

*This refers to the customer contact where an appointment is set.

**This refers to the confirmation call where each customer is contacted again the evening prior to the scheduled appointment.

■ Figure 11.10

Marketing Conversion Ratios

---

[6] Although expressed as percentage of sales, marketing expenditures were driven by lead requirements.

The key for using our capacity was to fill our day spots, because we knew that we could fill evenings and Saturdays. We were booking 18 appointments on Saturday, something like 60% of our business. There was a nice predictability to the revenue equation.

John planned to incorporate other marketing techniques later, but many traditional BetterLiving Patio Rooms dealers excluded TV from the marketing mix, so these other mediums were also proven to generate business.

The marketing process began when a prospective customer called for product information. The 800 number was fielded in Florida and faxed the next morning. The media department mailed literature after the faxes arrived. PRA planned to move some of these functions in-house at some point, as John explained.

| EXHIBIT 11.3 | PRA Sales and Installation Cycle |

- **Day 1:** TV ads generate calls to an 800 number answered in Orlando, Florida.

- **Day 2:** These leads are faxed to PRA the next morning and the PRA media supervisor sends out product literature to prospects.

- **Days 4–5:** The media department calls to answer questions and schedule in-home sales appointments. These calls are typically made in the morning or early evening when individuals can most often be reached at home.

- **Days 6–10:** The day before an appointment, media calls to confirm.

- **Days 7–11:** Scheduled appointments are conducted by the sales department. Initial job measurements are made as part of the sales demonstrations. PRA estimates that 65% of all sales are closed on the first visit to the home. A 33% deposit is the standard down payment.

- **Days 8–12:** John or the salesman begins work on obtaining customer financing if needed. Less than 50% of PRA customers seek financing.

- **Days 8–12:** The production manager receives work orders. He visits customers to confirm measurements, and fills out job order forms to purchase materials. Orders are placed once per week and materials are received within 10–14 days. Terms for material are net 30 days. Customers pay another 33% of the sales price prior to PRA ordering building materials.

- **Days 12–32:** Installations are scheduled to be completed 3–5 weeks from the close of the sale. During this time, the production manager obtains any building permits that may be necessary from the town. Additionally, any preparatory deck or foundation work is completed.

- **Days 33–46:** Patios are installed by PRA crews. Installation times range from 1 to 7 days, depending upon complexity and any complicating factors. The average installation time is running a little over 3 days. Upon job completion, the outstanding balance is collected.

- **Days 47–61:** Door hangings are placed on neighbors' doors and an open house is scheduled to be held in the newly installed patio room.

I would rather have developed print and television marketing expertise in-house; however, the Craft-Bilt turn-key system worked, and that was worth a lot. DRM knew the home remodeling direct response market, but we were as involved as we could be.

This marketing system created a sales interview virtually free from competition. Each lead was pre-qualified long before a salesperson arrived at the customer's home—the demonstration was at least the 5th contact with Betterliving Patio Rooms (see Exhibit 11.3). The PRA sales process involved no cold calling. As a result, PRA representatives were closing sales at a rate between 25% and 40%, and averaged 28% in March; they were required to achieve a minimum closing rate of 20% to remain employed by PRA. However, John was proud of the fact that this was not a high-pressure sale,

We explained the product and its benefits, then offered the same price sheets to everyone. Customers actually used our price sheets to design and price the room themselves. They could change the room to lower the price, and we offered a standard discount for "buying tonight," but we didn't haggle.

PRA received a 25–33% down payment at the time of sale. Two weeks later, before ordering materials from Craft-Bilt, PRA would bill for another third of the total. Then when the customer was satisfied with the installation, payment-in-full became due.

It was a long winter; I was down close to zero a couple of times. I didn't think of changing our payment terms until February. We were living on 25% down. Most customers accepted the new terms without blinking an eye. Our cash situation improved immediately.

Competition

Competition in the Massachusetts market was highly fragmented with small contractors accounting for the majority of patio room construction. These carpenters typically built fewer than ten wood-frame rooms per year. As John described it:

Our main competition was the conventional "stick build" addition, which takes over three weeks to build. However, we were 60% of the price and our rooms went up in 2 or 3 days. It was a fantastic advantage!

There were no other marketers using TV and representing competing manufacturers in New England. Companies in the Massachusetts market with an aluminum product similar to BetterLiving Patio Rooms included Texas-Aluminum (30 installations in 1997), Oasis Sunrooms (40 installations in 1997), and Four Seasons Patio Rooms (30 installations in 1997). These dealers were mostly contractors who specialized in home remodeling and built patio rooms as a product-line extension. Patio Enclosures was the only manufacturer with a comparable patio room marketing program. They had no branches in the Boston market.

At home shows, other aluminum patio room dealers offered direct competition; however home shows were a minor part of the PRA marketing plan. An estimated 15% of PRA's sales began with a referral in 1998, and John expected this percentage to increase with the growth of the installed base. The remaining 85% began with a TV infomercial. Almost all sales transactions occurred during in-home sales demonstrations. The intimate nature of the two-hour in-home presentation significantly reduced the threat of competitive challenge, as John explained.

People didn't usually shop around for patio rooms, unless they were at a home show. We went into the home as professional contractors—not salespeople. What we did in the home was warm and fuzzy. We talked about their dreams, about improving their quality of life, and two-thirds of our sales happened in the first meeting. You have got to love getting noncontested sales.

Production and Operations

PRA's operations were initially based on guidelines produced by Craft-Bilt. Craft-Bilt was in the process of creating a turn-key system for opening new territories. Craft-Bilt passed this system along by training owners, managers, installers, and salespeople at corporate headquarters. The training was supported afterwards by telephone consulting and regular on-site visits from key Craft-Bilt personnel.

The key position in the BetterLiving Patio Rooms system was the production manager. The production manager had to have construction experience, computer skills, and management talent. The production manager was responsible for all aspects of production. His human resource duties included hiring, training, and scheduling installers. His operations duties included coordinating the permit process, confirming sales measurements and job feasibility, ordering materials, managing inventory, and monitoring job costs. Hiring someone with this unique set of skills was a difficult challenge, as John recalled.

We blew our first production manager out of the water in two weeks. He had a lot of experience in construction management, and had even built patio rooms, so he seemed perfect. But after two weeks, he looked at me with fear in his eyes. For him, pulling 20 permits was like building 20 homes. He said, "I'm not your guy." I promoted a lead installer, John Leahy, and the whole team pitched in to make things work, but it continued to be a big problem area.

Another problem were the building permits, which were required for every job and issued by building inspectors. Unfortunately, every town had different requirements and inspectors, some with unexpected biases. For example, one inspector refused to let PRA build on a pre-existing concrete slab, in spite of the fact that he concurred that it was perfectly sound. Another wanted footings for the deck that were deeper than the footings for the house.

We wanted to be able sell a room today, measure it tomorrow, and get a permit the next day, but we learned in March that it never happens that fast. One reason is the plot plan. Homeowners don't have a plot plan, and nobody issues permits without one, so we have to get customers' land surveyed.

But the plot plan is just one of the hurdles to getting building permits. There seems to be no rhyme or reason to what gets approved. Building inspectors are prosecutor, judge, and jury all in one.

Once a permit was obtained, materials were ordered. With the BetterLiving Patio Rooms product, the most expensive parts of the room were custom-ordered by the job. In April, John speculated that PRA would never need to have more than $50,000 in inventory (see Exhibit 11.4).

After the building materials arrived, the job would be scheduled and installers assigned. Installers picked up building materials at the warehouse between 6:30 and

EXHIBIT 11.4	PRA Balance Sheet			
	Dec-97	**Jan-98**	**Feb-98**	**Mar-98**
Assets				
Checking/Savings	1,913	17,604	36,900	63,480
A/R	—	—	250	17,107
Inventory	3,197	37,989	16,300	34,759
Fixed Assets	—	2,874	4,666	7,802
Other Assets	37,125	37,125	37,125	37,125
Total Assets	**$ 42,235**	**$ 95,592**	**$ 95,241**	**$ 160,274**
Liabilities and Equity				
A/P	17,369	32,735	21,919	36,230
Loans from Related Parties	75,981	59,730	64,102	62,795
Notes Payable, Bank	—	74,000	73,700	73,025
Customer Deposits	4,649	4,849	(801)	88,496
Equity	(55,764)	(75,722)	(63,679)	(100,272)
Total Liabilities & Equity	**$ 42,235**	**$ 95,592**	**$ 95,241**	**$ 160,274**

7:30 AM, and returned between 4:30 and 6:30 PM. This produced more over-time than John had projected in his initial business plan. However, the larger problem was that jobs were not being done right the first time, or going up fast enough.

> The real challenge is in constructing rooms. You have to put rooms up fast and tight, or there is no profit. If a room takes too long, the profit gets killed by labor costs. If a room isn't done right, the profit gets killed by call-backs. I hate the sound of the phone ringing when it rains.

Problems on the job site were not always the fault of the installation team. PRA sold custom-built rooms. The installation guru at Craft-Bilt was on record saying, "50% of the rooms cannot be built as sold." It was the production manager's job to make sure he discovered these problems and resolved them before scheduling a crew for installation. John Leahy scheduled crews to build unbuildable rooms in March.

> I wanted to put up 20 rooms in March, but we only put up 5 because of permitting and construction problems. However, we sold 30 rooms, so we had $350,000 in sales and something like $75,000 in cash (see Exhibit 11.5). We expect to install 20 rooms in April because we are learning to be more efficient. If we can do jobs in 2–3 days instead of 4–5 days, we can start making money.

Often, making a room buildable meant extra expense, and John was displeased by how often customers were told that the price went up after the sale. Salesmen were not contractors, but ongoing training was essential because they needed to know what additional costs might arise when building a room. This was critical for all concerned because PRA salesmen were paid straight commission based on job profitability, so either they sold profitable jobs or starved.

Issues with Craft-Bilt in Early April

Although he was worried about construction and operations issues, John's biggest concerns involved Craft-Bilt. John did not accept the terms Craft-Bilt wanted to impose on the relationship, and saw potential problems awaiting down the road.

EXHIBIT 11.5	PRA Cash Flow Statement		
	Jan-98	**Feb-98**	**Mar-98**
Sales Collected	$75,946	$98,494	$64,800
Expenses:			
Cost of Construction	26,743	58,332	46,180
Sales and Marketing	24,594	21,051	29,735
Indirect Operating Exp.	2,966	4,812	4,476
General & Administrative	21,861	13,321	23,549
Total Expenses	**76,163**	**97,516**	**103,939**
Net Operating Cash Flow	**(217)**	**978**	**(39,139)**
(Inc)/Dec in Inventory	(14,793)	21,690	(18,459)
Inc/(Dec) in Cust. Deposits	200	(5,650)	89,297
Purchase of Fixed Assets	(2,874)	(1,792)	(3,137)
Loans from Related Parties	(16,251)	4,372	(1,307)
Loans from Bank	74,000	(300)	(675)
Net Cash Inflows/Outflows	**40,065**	**19,297**	**26,579**
Beginning Cash	(22,462)	17,603	36,901
Ending Cash	**$ 17,603**	**$ 36,901**	**$ 63,480**

I wrote a business plan focused on developing Boston in the two weeks after sales training, and realized that the whole nation was up for grabs. Either we got a bigger piece of the pie right away, or we would wish we had when we wanted to expand.

Craft-Bilt had never sold multiple BetterLiving Patio Rooms territories to a dealer before, but I sold them the vision of me as the Babson-educated super-entrepreneur. All Craft-Bilt upper management read my business plan. I went back to the table and got Worcester and Springfield.

Of course, they didn't believe we would actually implement the plan until they saw us doing it. We became a prototype dealer for BetterLiving Patio Rooms when we sold rooms all winter.

The biggest thing I missed in the dealership agreement was the way the letter of credit (LC) would work. I thought the $50,000 LC got me 30-day terms on inventory, but all it got me was terms on inventory worth $50,000. In effect, I got no terms. We're discussing this issue too. In the past, they were dealing with "hook and ladder" guys, so withholding credit made sense. However, when you've got CSDs, it makes no sense. I have an annual quota of 375 rooms beginning in year five, and seasonality creates a steep annual ramp-up, so why no terms? They say it would put the company at risk, but I don't buy it.

What do we want in our ongoing relationship with Craft-Bilt? We have a sales and marketing organization that can move home improvement products. We are developing a service delivery system. We are learning how to get our name in front of people and sell in the home. And we are learning how to deliver construction projects. Craft-Bilt offers us a quality product, but long term, there will have to be more value in it for us.

We have a great relationship now, but will they allow us to grow? We've talked about it, and they don't seem threatened, but they don't want to give me any more ground either. I want to open Connecticut and New Hampshire next year, but Ross is dragging his feet. I also want a right of first refusal for all other New England territories if any current dealers lose their regions. So far, Ross has not budged on these issues, yet he wants me to sign a

EXHIBIT 11.6 Pro-Forma Income Statement

	4/98	5/98	6/98	7/98	8/98	9/98	10/98	11/98	12/98	Totals
Rooms Installed	11	15	19	23	27	23	19	15	11	183
Total Sales	$142,340	$194,100	$245,860	$297,620	$349,380	$297,620	$245,860	$194,100	$142,340	$2,361,192
Cost of Construction										
Materials	52,666	71,817	90,968	110,119	129,271	110,119	90,968	71,817	52,666	$880,289
Field Installation	19,928	27,174	34,420	41,667	48,913	41,667	34,420	27,174	19,928	$328,939
Equipment	4,288	5,848	7,407	8,967	10,526	8,967	7,407	5,848	4,288	$78,330
Permits	621	847	1,073	1,299	1,525	1,299	1,073	847	621	$11,009
Total CoC	77,503	105,686	133,869	162,051	190,234	162,051	133,869	105,686	77,503	$1,298,568
Gross Profit	64,837	88,414	111,991	135,569	159,146	135,569	111,991	88,414	64,837	$1,062,624
Sales & Marketing										
Sales Comp.	14,234	19,410	24,586	29,762	34,938	29,762	24,586	19,410	14,234	$246,672
Media Dept.	2,847	3,882	4,917	5,952	6,988	5,952	4,917	3,882	2,847	$53,160
Advertising	6,405	8,735	11,064	13,393	15,722	13,393	11,064	8,735	6,405	$119,248
Misc.	805	1,097	1,390	1,682	1,975	1,682	1,390	1,097	805	$16,243
Total Marketing	24,291	33,124	41,957	50,790	59,623	50,790	41,957	33,124	24,291	$435,324
Indirect Operations										
Production Mgmt.	2,890	3,941	4,991	6,042	7,093	6,042	4,991	3,941	2,890	$53,543
Warehouse	300	409	518	627	736	627	518	409	300	$5,977
Total IO	3,190	4,350	5,510	6,669	7,829	6,669	5,510	4,350	3,190	$59,520
G & A										
Salaries	3,103	4,232	5,360	6,489	7,617	6,489	5,360	4,232	3,103	$61,109
Rent	2,570	3,505	4,440	5,374	6,309	5,374	4,440	3,505	2,570	$45,854
Telephone	1,607	2,191	2,776	3,360	3,944	3,360	2,776	2,191	1,607	$30,300
Insurance	2,413	3,290	4,168	5,045	5,923	5,045	4,168	3,290	2,413	$44,179
MIS	458	625	791	958	1,124	958	791	625	458	$8,696
Office Supplies	432	589	746	903	1,060	903	746	589	432	$7,341
Professional Fees	2,694	3,674	4,653	5,633	6,612	5,633	4,653	3,674	2,694	$48,516
Utilities	24	33	42	51	59	51	42	33	24	$4,195
Dues/Subscr.	131	178	226	273	321	273	226	178	131	$2,142
Travel/Ent.	489	666	844	1,022	1,200	1,022	844	666	489	$9,881
Bank Charges	45	61	77	94	110	94	77	61	45	$1,745
Total G&A	13,966	19,044	24,123	29,201	34,280	29,201	24,123	19,044	13,966	$264,457
TOTAL (non-CoC)	118,949	162,203	205,458	248,712	291,966	248,712	205,458	162,203	118,949	$2,057,869
EBIT	$23,391	$31,897	$40,402	$48,908	$57,414	$48,908	$40,402	$31,897	$23,391	$303,323

tighter non-compete. They have the power to limit the scope of this business to western Massachusetts. There is no way I am going to let that happen.

Preparation Questions

1. What do you think of Patio Rooms of America as an opportunity?
2. Evaluate John's efforts to date. As his advisor, what areas (e.g., finance, installations, recruiting) should he focus on? Short term? Long term?
3. Do you think that PRA will accomplish its income projection, Exhibit 11.6?
4. What recommendations would you make in those areas?

A Stock certificate is a document indicating legal ownership of shares of stock in a corporation. Stock certificates are made out to the shareholder or the brokerage firm, and identify the issuer, the number of shares, the par value, and the stock class. (Also known as a share certificate.) (*Source*: PhotoDisc/Getty Images, Inc.)

LEGAL AND TAX ISSUES

After college Deborah and Dave worked in the Information Technology division of a large corporation. In their five years there, the two friends had twice replaced all the desktop and laptop computers distributed to company employees with new machines. They understood the need to give their employees the best and most current computers, and to clean the drives of the old machines of sensitive information. But they didn't understand why, after all that effort, only a few were donated to local nonprofit organizations while the rest were simply disposed of. After all, the old machines might not be powerful enough to support the employees of a major corporation, but they certainly would have value to many smaller, less technologically oriented businesses. The problem, they were convinced, was the lack of any organized market for buyers and sellers of these machines to find each other.

This chapter written by Richard Mandel.

One night after work, the two budding entrepreneurs decided to establish their own company to develop and market a Web site where large companies could sell their "obsolete" computers to interested buyers, paying a small commission for the service. They could develop the Web site fairly quickly with their personal funds, but they would need significant bank and investor financing to fund the sophisticated marketing effort needed to bring their service to the attention of likely customers. Furthermore, although the two of them could probably perform all necessary tasks in the short run, they expected that additional programmers and sales professionals would be necessary in the long run. Both knew of fellow employees who would be perfect for these positions.

After discussing their idea with friends and business associates and drafting a business plan, Deborah and Dave were excited to learn that a prominent angel investor was interested in investing. They prepared to submit their resignations to their present employer.

Leaving Your Present Position

Many enthusiastic entrepreneurs are so excited about where they're going that they forget to consider where they've been. They're surprised to learn that there may be serious limitations imposed upon their freedom of action arising out of their former employment. Some of these limitations may be the result of agreements signed by the entrepreneur while employed in her former position. Others may be imposed as a matter of law, without any agreement or even knowledge on the part of the employee.

Corporate Opportunity

The **corporate opportunity** doctrine is an outgrowth of the traditional obligation of loyalty owed by an agent to a principal. In its most common form, it prohibits an officer or director of a corporation, a partner in a partnership, or persons in similar positions from identifying a business opportunity that would be valuable to his company and using that information for his own benefit or the benefit of a competitor.

Thus, a corporate director who discovers that one of the corporation's competitors may shortly be put on the market cannot raise money and purchase the competitive company himself. In order to discharge his legal obligation to the corporation of which he is a director, he would be required to disclose the opportunity to his board and allow the board to decide (without his participation) whether the corporation will make the purchase. Only after the corporation has been fully informed and decided *not* to take advantage of the opportunity may the director use that information for himself. Even then, as the new owner of a competitor, he would be required to resign his director position with the previous business.

The scope of this **duty of loyalty** is normally adjusted by the law to reflect the individual's position within the business. While the president and members of the board may be required to turn over knowledge of all opportunities that may be in any way related to the business of the company, lower-level employees probably have such an obligation only with regard to opportunities that are directly relevant to their positions. Thus, arguably, a sales manager may be required to inform her company of any sales opportunities she may encounter that are relevant to the company's products, but she may not be required to inform the company of a potential business acquisition.

Deborah and Dave must consider the corporate opportunity doctrine, since the opportunity to create a market for obsolete computers is directly relevant to one of their job responsibilities (replacing old employee computers with new ones). Yet both Deborah and Dave have positions low enough in the company hierarchy that their responsibilities in regard to corporate opportunities are probably very limited. The resale of old computers is likely very different from the business their present employer is in.

Recruitment of Fellow Employees

Another aspect of the duty of loyalty owed by an employee to an employer is the legal requirement that the employee not knowingly take action designed to harm the employer's business. This is, perhaps, pure common sense. We would not expect the law to countenance a paid salesperson's regularly recommending that customers patronize a competitor, nor would we expect the law to endorse an engineer's giving his best ideas to another company. Similarly, courts have held that it is a breach of the duty of loyalty to solicit and induce fellow employees to leave their jobs.

Once again, the likelihood that a court would enforce this obligation against an employee depends to some extent on the nature of the employee's activities and her position in the company. Neither Dave nor Deborah need fear reprisals for their having convinced each other to leave. Nor would there be much likelihood of liability if they convinced another employee to leave with them, especially if these conversations took place after working hours. However, if either of them worked in the Human Resources department where their job descriptions would include recruiting and retention of employees, this same activity might well expose them to liability. Further, if their plan included the wholesale resignations of a relatively large number of employees, such that the company's ability to continue to efficiently function might be compromised, a court might be more likely to intervene with an injunction or other relief. This would be especially true if the defendants' job descriptions included maintaining the efficient operation of the departments they were involved in destroying.

Proprietary Information

Yet another potential complication arising out of the present employment of Deborah and Dave is their possible use of information or technology belonging to their former employer. Such information need not be subject to formal patent or copyright protection to be protected from such use. Any information that the company has successfully kept confidential, and that is not otherwise known to outsiders, is likely to be protected by law as a trade secret. It may include inventions and technology, but also other valuable information such as customer lists, pricing strategies, and unique operating methods.

If Deborah had developed this computer resale concept as part of her job, that concept might well belong to the company and be unavailable to her and Dave as a new enterprise. Or if their current employer had compiled an extensive list of potential buyers of obsolete equipment, Deborah and Dave might be prohibited from marketing to that list. Of course, it is not enough for a concept or list to be developed by or for the company; the information must be unique and unknown to the industry at large, and the company must have taken steps to keep it that way. Thus, the company should label any physical manifestations of the information as "confidential," and should restrict its distribution to those who have either a legal or contractual obligation to keep such information private. If, on the other hand, the company had deliberately or carelessly allowed the distribution of the information to outsiders, it has likely lost the right to restrict its use.

Many companies require their employees to sign agreements that specifically spell out the employees' obligation to protect trade secrets. This has led some employees to believe that such an obligation must only attach to those who have signed such an agreement, leaving the remaining employees free to make whatever use of their employers' information they may choose. This is a misconception, however. The obligation to respect an employer's trade secrets and keep them confidential is imposed by law and is not dependent upon contract. Furthermore, it continues after the employment relationship has been terminated, for whatever reason, and indefinitely until the information makes its way into the public domain by other means.

Employers who require a confidentiality agreement from their employees generally do so as a method of making sure that their employees are aware of their responsibilities in this regard. After all, if an employee releases proprietary information to the outside, it is small comfort to the employer that it may have the right to sue said employee for damages. And a requirement that employees sign such agreements can be evidence that the employer has taken reasonable steps to keep its information confidential, thus making the information more likely to be deemed a trade secret.

Entrepreneur Indicted for Stealing Trade Secrets from Former Employer

The United States Attorney's Office for the Northern District of California announced that Trieu Lam, 44, of San José, California, was arraigned today [November 4, 2004] on an indictment charging him with one count of conspiracy to possess stolen trade secrets, and two counts of theft of trade secrets. Thanh Tran, aka David Tran, 45, of Milpitas, California, was charged in the same indictment with one count of conspiracy to possess stolen trade secrets. He was also arraigned today. An indictment simply contains allegations against an individual and, as with all defendants, Mr. Lam and Mr. Tran must be presumed innocent unless and until convicted.

According to the indictment, Mr. Lam was an employee at C&D Semiconductor Services Inc. (C&D) located in Milpitas, California, before starting his own company, More Technology Services Inc. (MTS) in San José. Mr. Lam and others allegedly used trade secrets stolen from C&D to produce and sell re-engineered and refurbished semiconductor equipment, called track systems, that apply photo-sensitive film to silicon wafers. Mr. Lam also allegedly recruited C&D employees, including Mr. Tran, to remove documentation and tooling from C&D, including drawings, assembly schematics, and similar equipment. Mr. Lam and MTS used these trade secrets to solicit business from C&D customers. The value of the trade secrets involved, as determined by the cost of their production, was alleged to be approximately $1.19M. FBI agents executed a search warrant at MTS in San José, California on November 6, 2002. C&D Semiconductor Services Inc. cooperated fully with the authorities in the investigation.

—Department of Justice, Northern District of California, November 4, 2004[1]

Fortunately for Deborah and Dave, they appear to have merely identified a need that is known generally to the industry, and have not begun to develop the specific software solution to the problem. And it does not appear that their employer has undertaken any organized effort to identify and list likely buyers of obsolete computers. On that set of facts, it is extremely doubtful that this new enterprise will make use of any information that legally belongs to Dave and Deborah's former employer.

However, it's equally likely that by the time Dave and Deborah have developed a business that meets this identified need, they will have created a body of proprietary information of their own. At that point they will be forced to turn their attention to protecting that information from use by competitors and end users who have failed to pay for the privilege.

A measure of protection can be had from the copyright laws, and, depending on the nature of their business process, from a patent. Both require disclosure of the information in exchange for the protection granted by the government and, thus, present the risk that others may engineer around the patent or reconfigure the software around the copyright.

In that case, Dave and Deborah will not likely have resources adequate to bring the necessary lawsuits to protect their rights. Thus, they may choose to forego statutory protection and protect their assets by a policy of nondisclosure as a trade secret, along with restrictive licensing agreements with the users of their Web site. (We discuss these issues and the relative advantages and risks of these various modes of intellectual property protection in Chapter 13.)

Noncompetition

Related to the obligation not to disclose proprietary information is the obligation not to compete with one's employer. Like most of the obligations we've already discussed, this duty is derived from the fiduciary relationship between employer and employee, specifically the duty of loyalty. How can we justify accepting a paycheck from our employer while we are simultaneously establishing, working for, or financing a competing business?

The law imposes this duty not to compete on all employees, officers, directors, and partners while their association with the employer remains in effect. Unlike the obligation to protect proprietary information, however, noncompete duty does not extend to the period after the termination of the relationship. To extend the obligation, the employer must obtain the employee's contractual promise. Thus, in the absence of a contract, as soon as Dave and Deborah quit their present jobs (but not before), they are free to go into direct competition with their former employer, so long as in doing so they do not use any of the employer's proprietary information.

We can analyze noncompetition agreements along many different dimensions, like the scope of the obligation. In an extreme case, an employee may have agreed not to engage in any activity that competes with any aspect of the business his former employer engaged in, or planned to engage in, at the time of the termination of the employee's association with the company. At the other end of the spectrum, the employee may have agreed only to refrain from soliciting any of his former employer's customers or (somewhat more restrictively) from dealing with any of the same, no matter who initiated the contact. We can also measure such agreements by the length of time they extend beyond the termination of employment and by their geographic scope.

Such measurements are important because, in the employment context, many states take the position that noncompete agreements contravene basic public policies, such as encouraging competition and allowing each individual to make the best use of his talents. A few such states actually refuse to enforce all noncompetition agreements. Most, however, purport to enforce only those deemed reasonable, recognizing the employer's interest in protecting its business and goodwill. Only those restrictions that prevent likely harm to the employer's legitimate interests will be enforced.

Thus, a medical practice that does business only with customers located within a 25-mile radius would not likely be able to enforce a noncompetition agreement that extends much beyond that geographic area. Furthermore, although a manufacturer may be able to enforce such an agreement against an officer, salesperson, or engineer who has either direct contact with customers or knowledge of the company's processes and products, it might not be able to enforce the same agreement against a bookkeeper whose departure would have little effect on the company's goodwill. Even the officer, salesperson, and engineer might be able to resist an agreement that purports to remain in effect beyond the time that the employer might reasonably need to protect its goodwill and business from the effects of new competition.

Another factor that may affect the enforceability of a noncompetition agreement is whether the employer agrees to continue part or all of the former employee's compensation during the noncompetition period. Similarly, a noncompetition agreement that might be unenforceable against an employee might nonetheless be enforceable against the seller of a business, or a major stockholder having his stock redeemed. Finally, some courts that find the scope or length of a noncompetition agreement objectionable nonetheless enforce it to the maximum extent they rule acceptable. Others take an all-or-nothing approach.

Since there is no indication Dave and Deborah have signed a noncompetition agreement, they would need only to resign from their current positions before taking any affirmative steps to establish a competitive enterprise. After their resignations, they would be under no further noncompetitive restrictions. Deborah and Dave's new business would probably not be deemed competitive with their present employer at all. Thus they may be able to begin this business at night and on weekends while remaining employed by their present employer, so long as the time devoted to the new business does not detract from their obligation to devote their full business time to their present jobs.

Sometimes companies are completely justified in taking action against former employees who have stolen trade secrets, but sometimes companies take legal action against former employees mainly to hinder them. If a former employee is starting a new business, lawsuits tie up the would-be entrepreneur in the legal process and may deter investors from putting money into the new venture. A well-heeled company knows that a costly protracted court battle will drain the limited resources of the former employee.

Within the first month or so following the initiation of legal action, the company will seek a temporary restraining order and file a civil lawsuit for injunctive relief and alleged damages; if it loses, it may file an appeal. A temporary restraining order or preliminary injunction essentially sidelines the would-be entrepreneur until the court battle is resolved.

Choosing an Attorney and an Accountant

Many people perceive engaging an attorney and an accountant as unnecessary expenses when beginning a new venture. However, the earlier you can consult these professionals, the more likely your business will avoid costly mistakes.

U.S. law does not officially recognize legal specialties. In practice, however, the U.S. legal profession has become highly specialized. Thus, most patent attorneys do very little else, and most good litigation attorneys concentrate on litigating. The representation of startups and small businesses has become a specialty as well.

Dave and Deborah would do well to ask their prospective attorney to describe her experience in representing small businesses and to supply some clients as references. An attorney experienced in the problems of startups will also be familiar with their unique cash-flow problems and may be willing to work out installment payments or other arrangements to avoid postponing essential early planning.

During the "Internet bubble" many attorneys adopted a policy of accepting equity in the new business as part of the fee arrangement, justifying it as the price of accepting the risk that their fee might not be paid if the business did not succeed. This arrangement led, in some cases, to dangerous conflicts of interest, as legal advice affected the value of the company's stock. After the Internet bubble burst, many law firms understandably discontinued the practice of taking equity as fees. Dave and Deborah will likely wish to avoid such an arrangement.

Many of the same considerations inform the choice of an accountant. Although the level of expertise in national and international accounting firms is unmatched, most have little experience with startups such as that proposed by Dave and Deborah, since their fee structures are inappropriate for the size of such businesses. Many local firms have all the skills necessary to serve the startup and can be sensitive to its cash-flow issues.

Engage the accountant as early as possible so he can establish the information management systems and recommend the computer software that will get your company's records off on the right track. This gives you the tools necessary to gauge the success of your efforts against budget before it is too late to adapt, and avoids the expensive and frustrating task of reconstructing the company's results from fragmented and missing records at the end of the year.

Choice of Legal Form

One of the first issues Deborah, Dave, and their professional advisors will confront, after weaving their way through the thicket of issues associated with leaving their current jobs, is what legal form they should choose to operate their new venture. Many choices are available.

The most basic business form is the **sole proprietorship,** owned and operated by one owner who is in total control. No new legal entity is created; the individual entrepreneur just goes into business, either alone or with employees, but without any co-owners. This entity will not be attractive to Deborah and Dave unless one of them chooses to forego ownership and act only as an employee.

The default mode for Dave and Deborah is the **general partnership.** This is the legal form that results when two or more persons go into business for profit, as co-owners, sharing profits and losses.

Another choice available to our entrepreneurs is the **corporation**. This form is created by state government, as a routine matter, upon the entrepreneurs' filing an application and paying a fee. It is a separate legal entity, with legal existence apart from its owners, the stockholders. Deborah and Dave might well choose to form a corporation, allocating its stock initially between them.

A variation of the corporate choice is the **subchapter S** or **small business corporation**. If a corporation passes a number of tests, it may elect to be treated as a subchapter S corporation, a designation that affects only its tax status. In all other respects, a subchapter S corporation is indistinguishable from all other corporations.

Another variation of the corporate form is the so-called **professional corporation**. This type of corporation is typically available only to businesses that render professional services, such as medical or legal practices, accountants, architects, social workers, and the like. It was originally created primarily to allow these professionals to take advantage of certain tax opportunities available only to corporations, without granting them the limited liability afforded by normal business corporations. Over time, however, many of the tax advantages formerly available only to corporations have been extended to sole proprietorships and partnerships, and some of the limited liability formerly associated with business corporations has been extended to professional corporations. Thus, the differences between these forms have narrowed considerably. In any case, Dave and Deborah will not be practicing a profession, so this business form will not be available to them.

Related to the professional corporation is the **limited liability partnership (LLP),** an entity that has become widely available over the last 15 years or so. The limited liability partnership is a general partnership that has elected, by filing documents with the state and paying a fee, to grant limited liability to its partners. This entity is thought to differ from other forms of limited liability entity in two ways: (1) as in a general partnership, all partners owe strict fiduciary obligations to each other, and (2) laws prohibiting mandatory retirement ages for employees may not apply to "partners" (as opposed to employees). These differences tend to appeal to those groups of practicing professionals who use to operate as general partnerships when there was no available way to limit personal exposure. Thus, law firms, accounting firms, and the like tend to elect this business form, but it is not widely used by other businesses, such as the one planned by Dave and Deborah.

Another possible legal form is a hybrid of the corporate and partnership forms, known as the **limited partnership.** Such a business would have one or more general partners who would conduct the business and take on personal risk, and one or more limited partners, who would act as passive investors (similar to stockholders with no other interest in the business). Since both Dave and Deborah intend to be actively involved in the business, neither would qualify as a limited partner. And as it is difficult to find many managers who would be willing to take on personal exposure for the risks of the business, this form of entity has over time faded into use in only a few niches such as venture capital funds and a number of hedge funds. In recent years, limited partnerships have come into use as an estate planning technique, but they are no longer attractive to most businesses.

An increasingly popular form of business entity is the **limited liability company (LLC).** These entities are owned by "members" who either manage the business themselves or appoint "managers" (either outsiders or a subset of the members) to run it for them. All members and managers have the benefit of limited liability (as they would in a corporation) and, in most cases, are taxed similarly to a subchapter S corporation without having to conform to the S corporation restrictions described later in this section.

Finally, a **nonprofit** (or **not-for-profit) entity** will typically take the form of a corporation or trust, and elect nonprofit status as a tax matter. Although many startups do not make a profit, nonprofit status is available only to certain types of activities, such as churches, educational institutions, social welfare organizations, and industry associations. If an organization so qualifies, its income is exempt from taxation (as long as it doesn't stray from its exempt purpose), and if certain additional tests are met, contributions to it may be tax deductible. Deborah and Dave might consider such status if their purpose were simply to collect obsolete machinery and donate it to charitable and educational entities, but since they plan to operate as a profit-making venture, distributing profits to themselves and investors, we need not further explore this option.

Although we can compare these forms of business on an almost endless list of factors, the most relevant include control issues, exposure to personal liability, tax factors, and administrative costs. We discuss these in detail in the following sections, and Figure 12.1 provides an overview of the issues and how they play out in each business form.

Control

Since there is only one principal in the sole proprietorship, he wields total control over all issues. In the general partnership, control is divided among the principals in accordance with their partnership agreement (which need not be written but should be, to encourage specificity). The parties may decide that all decisions must be made by unanimous vote, or they may adopt a majority standard (making their angel investor the swing vote). More likely, they may require unanimity for a stated group of significant decisions and allow a majority vote on others. In addition, Deborah and Dave may delegate authority for certain types of decisions to one or both the active partners.

Regardless of how power is allocated in the partnership agreement, each of the partners will have a free hand to contract with third parties, subject only to the consequences of the partner's breaching his agreement with the others. This is also true for the consequences of torts committed by any partner acting in the course of partnership business.

All of this applies equally to the limited liability partnership (since it is merely a general partnership that has elected liability protection). The looseness of the rules in general partnerships may well be enough to discourage Deborah and Dave from choosing the general partnership option.

A corporation, whether professional or business, and regardless of whether it has elected subchapter S status, is controlled by three levels of authority. Broadly speaking, the stockholders vote, in proportion to the number of shares they own, on the election

	Control	Liability	Taxation	Administrative Obligations
Sole proprietorship	Owner has complete control	Unlimited personal liability	Not a separate taxable entity	Only those applicable to all businesses
Partnership	Partners share control	Joint and several unlimited personal liability	Not a separate taxable entity	Only those applicable to all businesses
Corporation	Control distributed among shareholders, directors, and officers	Limited personal liability	Separate taxable entity unless subchapter S election	Some additional
Limited partnership	General partners control; limited partners do not	General partners: joint and several unlimited personal liability, limited partners: limited personal liability	Not a separate entity unless affirmatively chosen	Some additional
Limited liability company	Members share control or appoint managers	Limited personal liability	Not a separate entity unless affirmatively chosen	Some additional

Figure 12.1

Comparison of various business forms

of the board of directors, the sale or dissolution of the business, and amendments to the corporation's charter. In virtually all cases, these decisions are made either by the majority or two-thirds of the votes cast. Thus, if Dave, Deborah, and their investor each owned one-third of the issued stock, Dave and Deborah (if they voted together) could elect the entire board and sell the business over the objections of the investor. Unless agreed otherwise, the investor would not even be entitled to a minority position on the board. He would, however, be the swing vote should Deborah and Dave ever disagree, perhaps prompting them to consider nonvoting stock or some similar device for the investor.

The board of directors, in turn, makes all the long-term and significant policy decisions for the business, as well as electing the officers of the corporation. Votes are virtually always decided by majority. The officers, consisting of a president, treasurer, and secretary at a minimum, run the day-to-day business of the corporation, and are the only level of authority that can bind the corporation by contract or in tort. In this case, either Dave or Deborah would probably be president and the other, perhaps, executive vice president and treasurer, or CEO. It is not uncommon for the corporation's attorney to act as secretary, since the attorney presumably has the expertise to keep the corporate records of the company in an accurate manner. Deborah and Dave will likely convince their investor not to insist upon a title, thus eliminating his or here ability to deal with third parties on the corporation's behalf.

The limited partnership concentrates all control in the general partners, who exercise that control as set forth in the limited partnership agreement (just as such control is allocated in a general partnership agreement). Limited partners have virtually no control, unless the limited partnership agreement has granted them some influence over significant issues such as sale of the business or dissolution. Only the general partners have the apparent authority to bind the partnership in contract or tort with third parties.

The limited liability company can operate much like a general partnership. All members can share in control to the extent set forth in their agreement, known in most states as an *operating agreement.* However, members may choose to appoint one or more "managers" to control most of the day-to-day operations of the business. We might expect the three members to appoint Deborah and Dave as managers.

Based on control issues alone, therefore, Dave and Deborah would likely be leaning toward the limited partnership, limited liability company, or corporation. Their decision will, however, be greatly affected by considerations of personal liability.

Personal Liability

Should the business incur current liabilities beyond its ability to pay, must the individual owners risk personal bankruptcy to make up the difference? This unhappy result need not occur only as a result of poor management or bad business conditions. It could just as easily be brought about by an uninsured tort claim from a customer, or a victim of a delivery person's careless driving.

In both the partnership and the sole proprietorship, the business is not recognized as a legal entity separate from its owners. Thus the debts of the business are ultimately the debts of the owners if the business cannot pay. This unlimited liability is enough to recommend against these forms for virtually any business, with the exception perhaps of the one-person consulting firm, all of whose liability will be the direct result of the wrongdoing of its owner in any case.

If this unlimited liability is uncomfortable for Deborah and Dave, imagine what it would mean to an angel investor, such as the person interested in Dave and Deborah's business. The investor no doubt has significant assets to lose and will likely have only limited control over the business decisions that may generate liability. This risk is made even worse by the fact that all partnership liabilities are considered joint and several obligations of all partners. Thus, the investor will be responsible for full payment of all partnership liabilities if Deborah and Dave have no significant assets of their own.

But in trading away their influence over the operation of the business in a limited partnership, investors are granted limited liability for its debts. Thus, if the limited partnership cannot meet its obligations, an investor will lose his investment, but his personal assets will generally not be exposed to partnership creditors.

However, the general partners retain unlimited exposure. Dave and Deborah may believe they can afford to take this risk, especially if they currently have no significant assets, but that may not be the case when a later liability is incurred.

The answer lies in the corporation and the limited liability company, both of which afford limited liability to all owners. If the business ultimately becomes insolvent, its creditors will look only to business assets for payment; any shortfall will be absorbed by the unfortunate creditors. Such protection is also afforded to the owners of a limited liability partnership.

This solution is not quite as all-encompassing as it sounds. To begin with, creditors know these rules as well as the entrepreneurs do. Thus, large or sophisticated creditors, such as banks and other financial institutions, will insist upon personal guarantees from the owners of the business before extending credit. In addition, the law allows creditors to "pierce the corporate veil" and go after the owners of a failed corporation or LLC under certain conditions.

The first covers businesses that were initially underfunded or "thinly capitalized." A business should start out with a combination of capital and liability insurance adequate to cover the claims to which it might normally expect to be exposed. As long as the capital was there at the outset, and has not been depleted by dividends or other distributions to owners, causing insolvency, the protection of the separate entity survives even after the capital has been depleted by unsuccessful operation.

The second situation that may result in the piercing of the corporate (or LLC) veil is the failure of the owners to treat the corporation or limited liability company as an entity separate from themselves by:

- Failing to use *Inc.*, *Corp.*, *LLC*, or a similar legal indicator when dealing with third parties, or
- Commingling business and personal assets in a personal bank account or allowing unreimbursed personal use of corporate assets, or
- Failing to keep business and legal records and hold regular directors, stockholders, or members meetings.

Both the corporate and limited liability company forms should look rather attractive to Dave and Deborah. They should make no significant business decision, however, without a look at the tax consequences.

Taxation

Once again, the simplest of the business forms to understand in regard to taxation is the sole proprietorship. The financial results of the business are calculated, and the profit or loss appears on the tax return of the sole owner. She can eliminate much of the profit by taking it out of the business as salary, but that has no tax effect as it simply increases taxable wages in the exact amount that it lowers profit. The tax rate applied to any profit will be the maximum marginal rate to which the taxpayer is exposed by the combination of this profit and all other taxable income. A loss acts as a sort of tax shelter on the owner's return by offsetting an equal amount of other taxable income, if any.

Since a partnership is not recognized as a separate legal entity, it pays no taxes itself (although in many cases it is required to file an informational return). Its partners report its profit or loss, including any profit retained by the partnership and not distributed to the partners (resulting in "phantom income"). The percentage of profit or loss each partner reports is normally set forth in the partnership agreement by the partners themselves and must reflect a "substantial economic reality."

The limited partnership is taxed in exactly the same way as the partnership, with profit and loss allocated among *all* partners, both general and limited, in accordance with the limited partnership agreement. Since the business contemplated by Deborah and Dave is likely to lose money at the outset, the tax sheltering aspects of both the partnership and limited partnership may be attractive to the angel investor, who surely has other sources of income he would like to shelter.

Of the two, the limited partnership is preferable, since by accepting limited partner status, the investor can have his shelter without being exposed to personal liability. He may be tempted to request that the agreement allocate 99% of the losses to him, since he likely needs the shelter more than Deborah and Dave do. However, unless he is contributing 99% of the capital and will receive a similar percentage of profit (both operating and capital gain), such an allocation might run afoul of the "substantial economic reality" test without careful, professional tax planning.

A further obstacle to an investor's taking advantage of the possible tax shelter of early losses is presented by the passive loss rules of the Internal Revenue Code. Simply stated, if the investor is not "materially participating" in the business (which would by definition be the case if he were a limited partner), any losses distributable to him from the business could be used to offset income generated only by other passive activities (such as investments in other limited partnerships). The losses could not shelter income from salaries, interest, or dividends from traditional portfolio investments.

If the business were organized as a corporation, Dave and Deborah would doubtless be warned about *double taxation*. Double taxation arises when the corporation makes a profit, pays tax on it, and distributes the remainder to its stockholders as a dividend. The stockholders must then pay income tax on the dividend, allowing the same money to be taxed twice (although at a quite favorable, reduced dividend rate the second time).

In reality, however, double taxation is more a myth than a legitimate threat to the small business. In fact, in most cases, it presents an opportunity for significant economic savings. To begin with, most small corporations lower or even eliminate their profit by increasing deductible salaries and bonuses for their owners up to the limit deemed "unreasonable" by the Internal Revenue Service. The owners then pay only their own individual income tax on the money.

On the other hand, if it is necessary to retain some of these earnings, the corporation will normally pay income tax at a lower rate than the stockholders would have, since tax will be imposed at the lowest marginal corporate rate rather than the stockholders' highest rate. When the corporation is later sold, the stockholders will be taxed at favorable capital gain rates and the corporation will have had the use of the money in the meantime to create greater value. Thus, it is the rare small corporation that will actually pay double tax.

Furthermore, if the corporation meets certain eligibility requirements, it can elect, under subchapter S of the Internal Revenue Code, to be taxed essentially as if it were a partnership. Whatever profit or loss it may generate will appear on the tax returns of the stockholders in proportion to the shares of stock they own, and the corporation will file only an informational return. To take advantage of this option, the corporation must have 100 or fewer stockholders, all of whom must be individuals (with some exceptions) and either resident aliens or citizens of the United States. The corporation can have only one class of stock (with the exception of classes based solely on different voting rights) and is ineligible to participate in most multiple-entity corporate structures. Note that despite the name "small business corporations," there is no size limit on subchapter S eligibility.

The subchapter S election can be very useful in a number of circumstances. For example, if the business is expected to be profitable, and investors insist upon a share of those profits, Dave and Deborah could not otherwise avoid double taxation by increasing salaries and bonuses. Since an investor performs no services for the business, any compensation paid to him would automatically be deemed "unreasonable." But under subchapter S, since there is no corporate tax, a dividend to the stockholders would be taxed only at the stockholder level.

If the business were to become extremely successful, Deborah and Dave could reap the rewards without fear that their salaries might be attacked as "unreasonable," since, again, there are no corporate compensation deductions to disallow. An early subchapter S election can also avoid double taxation should the corporation eventually sell all its assets and distribute the proceeds to the stockholders in liquidation.

Furthermore, if the business is expecting losses in the short term, the investors might be able to use their share of the losses (determined by percentage of stock) as a shelter subject to the passive loss considerations described previously. Dave and Deborah could use their losses against the salary from their former jobs in the earlier part of the year, or against income earned by their spouses if they filed joint returns. However, they may find this advantage limited by another Internal Revenue Code rule that generally restricts the amount of loss usable by any owner to the amount of investment made by such owner.

On the other hand, Deborah and Dave will find that a subchapter S election (and for that matter, use of a limited liability company or limited liability partnership, all three of which are often referred to as *pass-through entities*) will make it difficult for them to receive tax-free employee benefits. Also, only the stockholders of a nonelecting corporation (or

C corporation) can exclude one-half of their capital gain upon sale of their stock after a five-year holding period. This latter benefit would be undercut anyway, for the most part, by the alternative minimum tax.

After having considered all of this, Deborah and Dave might wish to form a corporation, elect subchapter S treatment, and arrange their affairs such that when the angel investor contributes his investment, he can make as much use of short-term losses as could be supported by the "substantial economic reality" and "passive loss" rules. However, since profits and losses in an S corporation must be allocated in accordance with stock ownership, and only one class of stock is allowed, any disproportionate allocation of losses to the investor would have to be accompanied by a disproportionate allocation to him of later profits. More creative allocations of profit, loss, and control could be accomplished in a general or limited partnership, but one or more of the owners would have to accept exposure to unlimited liability in those entities.

Limited liability companies were designed for just this circumstance. If structured carefully, they afford the limited liability and "pass-through" tax treatment of the S corporation, while avoiding the S corporation's restrictive eligibility requirements. Freed from these restrictions, limited liability companies can use creative allocations of profit, loss, and control that would constitute prohibited multiple classes of stock in the S corporation context. However, since limited liability companies (as well as limited partnerships and limited liability partnerships) are required to calculate their income and loss in accordance with partnership tax rules (as opposed to S corporations, which use corporate tax rules), there may be some negative effects from this choice. For example, certain tax-free methods of selling the company may not be available to a limited liability company. On the other hand, in some circumstances involving significant company borrowings, partnership tax rules may allow greater losses to pass through to the owners who are eligible to make use of them.

At this point in the analysis, Dave and Deborah are probably still not sure of the solution. The limited liability company appears attractive since it shields all its owners from personal liability, and as managers, they might gain a measure of control of the company apart from the angel investor. The limited liability company would also allow them to allocate the maximum amount of short-term loss available under applicable tax rules to their investor, recognizing that Dave and Deborah's small initial investment would make any such losses useless to them. However, the angel investor may also have little ability to use these losses due to his lack of material participation in the business. Worse yet, the investor would certainly not be enthusiastic at the notion of "phantom income" when the company's financial performance turns positive. Perhaps a further investigation of the tax implications of initial investment will lead Deborah and Dave to an answer.

Initial Investment of the Founders

Left to their own devices, Dave and Deborah would likely arrange the issuance of their stock in the corporation for no tangible investment whatsoever. After all, they intend to look to angel investors for working capital in the short run, and their investment will be the services they intend to perform for the business in the future.

It is common to authorize stock with minimal par value (e.g., $0.01 per share) or even to authorize stock with no par value at all. The corporation then issues stock for whatever it believes to be its fair value. In addition, it has long been possible to issue stock in exchange for intangible assets such as past services rendered. However, although many proposals have been made to legitimize it, stock issuance for future services remains illegal under most corporate statutes.

This type of problem is minimized in limited liability companies and their cousins, such as limited partnerships and limited liability partnerships. In these business forms, tangible investments are reflected as credits to the member or partner's capital account, while service contributors normally are given no such credit. The company's creditors have no particular statutory protections analogous to par value or watered stock.

Of more practical concern, however, is the fact that any property (including stock or membership interests) transferred to an employee in exchange for the employee's services is considered taxable income under the Internal Revenue Code. Thus, even if it were possible to issue Deborah and Dave corporate stock in exchange for future services under corporate law, they would face an unexpected tax liability as a result.

The solution to all this in the corporate context may be to require Dave and Deborah to reach into their limited resources and contribute some minimal cash amount to the corporation in exchange for their stock. So long as the cash amount exceeds the par value (which will be minimal or nonexistent), this would avoid the corporate and tax problems associated with issuance for future services. In the LLC or partnership context, the Internal Revenue Service will, in most cases, value the ownership interest granted to the partner or member as equivalent to the amount credited to the capital account. Thus, as long as a noncontributing owner's capital account begins at zero and grows only to the extent of future profits, there will be no current taxation at the time of issuance. However, as noted earlier, if Deborah and Dave's minimal investment were the full extent of the business's initial capitalization, the limited liability protection (the "corporate veil") might well be in danger.

Of course, Deborah and Dave will have no reason to fear exposure to personal liability on this account, since, at approximately the same time that they will be making their minimal investment, the angel investor will be putting in the real money. However, since the angel investor will be paying substantially more for his stock than Deborah and Dave are paying for theirs, the Internal Revenue Service will likely take the position that they are getting a bargain in exchange for the services they are providing to their company. Thus once again, Dave and Deborah may be facing an unexpected income tax on the difference between the price per share of the angel's stock and the price of theirs.

One way to solve this problem is to postpone the angel's investment until Dave and Deborah can argue for an increase in the value of the corporation's stock. Aside from the essentially fictional nature of this approach, Deborah and Dave probably cannot wait that long. Instead, the parties must design a vehicle for the angel's investment sufficiently different from Dave and Deborah's interest to justify the higher price. This is taken care of in the LLC or partnership context by the difference in capital accounts. But the corporate context is a bit more complicated.

It may seem advisable to create some sort of senior security for the angel investor, such as preferred stock with a liquidation preference of approximately the amount he invested. Demonstrating the sometimes frustrating interrelated character of tax and corporate law, however, the issuance of preferred stock would render a corporation ineligible for subchapter S status, as it would then have more than one class of stock. The LLC and its cousins are not bound by any such restriction.

Another solution to this problem could lie in the utilization of debt securities. If the angel investor pays the same price per share for his stock as Deborah and Dave and injects the remainder of the investment in the form of a loan, Deborah and Dave will not face taxable compensation income and the business will retain the opportunity to benefit from subchapter S, if desired.

Investment as debt also affords the angel investor the potential for future nontaxable distributions from the company in the form of debt repayment, and he also gains priority as a creditor should the corporation be forced to liquidate. All the while, the investor protects participation in growth through the additional ownership of equity.

As with all benefits, it is possible to get too much of a good thing. Too high a ratio of debt to equity may expose all the owners to the accusation of thin capitalization, resulting in the piercing of the corporate (or LLC) veil. And abusively high debt/equity ratios or failure to respect debt formalities and repayment schedules might induce the Internal Revenue Service to reclassify the debt as equity, thus imposing many of the adverse tax results described earlier.

How does all this inform the choice of entity, then? Essentially, the pass-through form exposes the angel to potential "phantom income" if the company does well, while failing to provide practical use of losses on his personal return if the company loses money. On the other hand, preferred stock in a C corporation provides the liquidation, dividend, participation, and conversion privileges the angel investor desires without the risk of phantom income. And from Deborah and Dave's point of view, issuance of preferred stock to their investor has the benefit of solving their potential income tax problems without saddling them with restrictive repayment schedules or the risk of unintended personal liability. The parties will likely agree on the C corporation as the best choice of entity in this case.

Administrative Obligations

Upon entering business, Dave and Deborah should obtain an Internal Revenue Service federal identification number. On the state level, the business should obtain a sales and use tax registration number, both to facilitate reporting and collection of such taxes and to qualify for exemption from such taxes when it purchases items for resale. A nonprofit entity has 18 months to file for and secure nonprofit status from the Internal Revenue Service. Furthermore, all business entities will incur a certain amount of additional accounting expense, specifically for the calculation and reporting of taxable profit and loss.

Corporations, limited liability companies, limited liability partnerships, and limited partnerships, however, bring some additional administrative burden and expense. All four must file an annual report with the state government in addition to their tax return. This document usually reports only the business's current address, officers, directors, managers, general partners, and similar information, but is accompanied by an annual maintenance fee. The fee, in addition to any income tax that the state may levy, must be paid to avoid eventual involuntary dissolution by the state.

In addition, corporations are sometimes formed under the laws of one state while operating in another. In particular, the state of Delaware has a corporate law particularly sympathetic to management that has also been thoroughly interpreted by its long history of complex corporate litigation. Although these are questionable advantages in the context of a small business (where management and stockholders are generally the same people), Delaware does offer a method of calculating its fees that does not penalize a corporation for having a large number of authorized shares. This allows a corporation whose compensation strategy includes stock grants or stock options to use much larger numbers of shares in these grants, creating a psychological appearance of generosity that may not mathematically exist. Even corporations that have not adopted such a strategy often form in Delaware merely to share in an appearance of sophistication.

In all such cases, the corporation must not only pay initial and maintenance fees to the state of Delaware (or whichever state is chosen for formation) along with the costs of maintaining an address for service of process there, but must also pay initial and annual maintenance fees to qualify to do business in each state in which it actually operates. Many large, national concerns pay these fees in virtually all 50 states. Although Deborah and Dave could avoid these fees by operating as a partnership, they'll likely conclude that the advantages of the corporate or limited liability forms are worth the price. They would likely be well-advised, however, to form their entity in the same state as their operations in order to avoid duplicate fees. They can always reincorporate in Delaware in the future, generally just preceding a public offering.

Choosing a Name

The choice of a name for a business may seem at first to be a matter of personal taste, without many legal ramifications. However, since a business' name is ultimately the repository of its goodwill, the owner should choose a name that will not be confused with the name of another business.

Although partnerships and sole proprietorships need not do so, corporations, limited liability companies, limited liability partnerships, and limited partnerships obtain their existence by filing charters with the state. As part of this process, each state will check to see whether the name of the new entity is "confusingly similar" to the name of any other entity currently registered with that state. Some states will also deny the use of a name they deem misleading, even if it is not similar to the name of another entity. Selecting and protecting marks such as corporate and product names is covered in more detail in Chapter 13.

Once Deborah and Dave have chosen a name for their business and product, and elected the level of protection with which they are comfortable, they can turn their attention to the initial funding of their enterprise.

Stockholder and Operating Agreements

Deborah, Dave, and their investor's respective investments will normally be memorialized in an operating agreement in the case of an LLC, and a combination of a Stock Purchase Agreement, Charter Amendments, and Stockholders' Agreement in the case of a corporation. In the unlikely event that this business were a partnership or limited partnership, very similar provisions allocating equity interests and rights to distributions of profit and cash flow would appear in a Partnership Agreement. In all these cases, however, the parties would be well advised to go beyond these subjects and reach written agreement on a number of other potentially thorny issues at the outset of their relationship.

Negotiating Employment Terms

Dave and Deborah should reach agreement with the investor about their commitment to provide services and the level of compensation for doing so. It would be very unusual for Dave and Deborah to forego compensation solely to share the profits of the business with their investor. For one thing, what would they be living on in the interim? For another, the profits of the business are properly conceived of as the amount left over after payment of the expenses of the business—including reasonable compensation to its employees. Thus, Deborah and Dave should negotiate employment terms into the operating or stockholders agreement, setting forth their responsibilities, titles, compensation, and related issues.

This is especially important in this case, since each of the three stockholders may hold only a minority interest in the corporation (depending upon the voting rights given to the preferred stock). Both Dave and Deborah may wish to foreclose the possibility that the investor may ally with one of them and employ a majority of the shares to remove the other as a director, officer, or employee of the company. Given the lack of any market for the shares of this corporation, such a move would essentially destroy any value the shares had for the holder in the short run.

Although a concise description of each party's obligations and rewards is still advisable to avoid dispute, this negative scenario would be illegal in a partnership (in the absence of serious misconduct by the party being removed), since the majority partners would be violating the fiduciary duty of loyalty imposed upon each partner toward the others under partnership law. Although no such duty formally exists among stockholders in a corporation, many states (not including Delaware) have imported the fiduciary duties of partners to the relationship among the founders of a closely held corporation. Similar doctrines may be developed for LLCs. Thus, in many states, were Deborah to be removed without cause from her employment and corporate positions by Dave and the angel investor, she would have effective legal recourse even in the absence of a stockholders' agreement.

Disposition of Equity Interests

As for other items that might be covered in the agreement among Deborah, Dave, and the investor, many address the disposition of equity held by the owners under certain circumstances.

Transfer to Third Parties. To begin with, although sale of stock in a close corporation or LLC is made rather difficult by federal and state securities regulation and the lack of any market for the shares, transfers are still possible under the correct circumstances. To avoid that possibility, stockholder and operating agreements frequently require that any owner wishing to transfer equity to a third party must first offer it to the company and/or the other owners, who may purchase the equity, often at the lower of a formula price or the amount being offered by the third party.

Disposition of Equity on the Owner's Death. Stockholder and operating agreements should also address the disposition of each owner's equity upon death. Again, it is unlikely that each owner would be comfortable allowing the deceased owner's stock to fall into the hands of the deceased's spouse, children, or other heirs, although this may be more acceptable in the case of a pure investor. Moreover, should the business succeed over time, each owner's equity may well be worth a significant amount upon death. If so, the Internal Revenue Service will wish to impose an estate tax based on the equity's value, regardless of the fact that it is an illiquid asset. Under such circumstances, the owner's estate may wish to have the assurance that some or all of such equity will be converted to cash so the tax may be paid. If the agreement forbids free transfer of the equity during lifetime and requires that the equity be redeemed at death for a reasonable price, the agreement may well be accepted by the IRS as a persuasive indication of the equity's value, thus also avoiding an expensive and time-consuming valuation controversy.

Any redemption provision at the death of the owner, especially one that is mandatory at the instance of the estate, immediately raises the question of the availability of funds. Just when the business may be reeling from the effects of the loss of one of its most valuable employees, it may be expected to scrape together enough cash to buy out the deceased's ownership. To avoid this disastrous result, many of these arrangements are funded by life insurance policies on the lives of the owners. This would be in addition to any key person insurance held by the business for the purpose of recovering from the effects of the loss. In structuring such an arrangement, however, the parties should be aware of two quite different models.

The first, and more traditional model, is referred to as a *redemption agreement*. Under it, the business owns the policies and is obligated to purchase the equity upon death. The second model is referred to as a *cross-purchase agreement* and provides for each owner to own insurance on the others and to buy a proportional amount of the deceased's equity. Figure 12.2 illustrates the primary differences between the two forms of agreement.

The latter arrangement raises some serious mechanical problems, but may be quite advantageous if they can be overcome. To begin with, the cross-purchase agreement

	Effect on Tax Basis	Effect on Alternative Minimum Tax	Need for Adequate Corporate Surplus
Redemption agreement	No stepped-up basis	Risks accumulated current earnings preference for larger C corporations	Needs adequate surplus
Cross-purchase agreement	Stepped-up basis	No risk	Surplus is irrelevant

Figure 12.2

Comparison of stock redemption agreement and stock cross-purchase agreement

becomes quite complicated if there are more than a few stockholders, since each stockholder must own and maintain a policy on each of the others. There must be a mechanism (such as a form of trust or escrow agreement) to ensure that all these policies are kept in force and that the proceeds are actually used for their intended purpose. In addition, if the ages of the stockholders are materially different, certain owners will be paying higher premiums than others.

If these complications can be overcome, however, the cross-purchase agreement provides some significant benefits over the redemption agreement. Take, for example, a company in which each of three owners own one-third of the stock. If one of them were to die and the corporation purchased his stock, the remaining two would each own 50% of the corporation's stock, but their cost basis for a later sale would remain at the minimal consideration originally paid for their stock. In a cross-purchase arrangement, the remaining two would purchase the deceased owner's stock directly. This would still result in 50-50 ownership, but their cost basis for later sale would equal their original investment plus the amount of the insurance proceeds used to purchase the deceased owner's stock. Upon later sale of their stock or the company as a whole, the capital gain tax would be significantly lowered.

Another benefit of the cross-purchase agreement derives from the fact that although the receipt of life insurance proceeds is exempt from income taxation, it can result in a tax preference item for a C corporation. This would expose the corporation to the alternative minimum tax. This tax preference item does not apply to individuals, and is thus avoided by adopting the cross-purchase model. It can also be avoided by LLCs, S corporations, and certain smaller C corporations.

Lastly, the cross-purchase model eliminates the possibility that the company may not have sufficient retained earnings or surplus to fund a buyout upon the death of an owner. It would be highly ironic if the owner's life insurance merely funded an earnings deficit to the benefit of creditors and could not be used to buy his equity.

Disposition of Equity upon Termination of Employment. Stockholder and operating agreements normally also address disposition of equity upon events other than death. Repurchase of equity upon termination of employment can be very important for all parties. The former employee whose equity no longer represents an opportunity for employment would like the opportunity to cash in her investment. The company and other owners may resent the presence of an inactive owner who can capitalize on their later efforts. Thus, both operating and stockholder agreements will normally provide for repurchase of the interest of a stockholder or member who is no longer actively employed by the company. This, of course, applies only to stockholders or members whose efforts on behalf of the company were the basis of their participation in the first place. Such provisions would not apply to Dave and Deborah's angel investor, for example, since his participation was based entirely upon his investment.

This portion of the agreement presents a number of additional problems peculiar to the employee-owner. For example, the company cannot obtain insurance to cover an obligation to purchase equity upon termination of employment. Thus, it may encounter an obligation to purchase the equity of the former employee at a time when its cash position will not support such a purchase. Furthermore, in addition to the requirement of adequate surplus, courts uniformly prohibit repurchases that would render the company insolvent. Common solutions to these problems commit the company to an installment purchase of the affected equity over a period of years (with appropriate interest and security) or commit the remaining owners to make the purchase personally if the company is unable to do so for any reason.

Furthermore, these agreements frequently impose penalties upon the premature termination of a stockholder or member's employment. In our example, the angel investor is relying on the efforts of Dave and Deborah in making his investment, and Dave and Deborah are each relying on the other's efforts when entering this risky situation. Should either Deborah or Dave be entitled to a buyout at full fair market value if he or she simply decides to walk away from the venture? Often, these agreements contain so-called vesting provisions that require a specified period of service before repurchase will be made at full value. As an example, such a vesting provision might state that unless Dave had stayed with the venture for a year, all his equity would be forfeited upon his departure. After a year, one-quarter of his equity would be repurchased for full value, but the rest would be forfeited. Another 25% would vest at the end of each ensuing year.

Such provisions, in addition to providing incentive to remain with the company, have complicated tax implications as well. As discussed earlier, if an employee receives equity for less than fair market value, the discount would be considered taxable compensation. The Internal Revenue Code provides that compensation income with regard to unvested equity is not taxed until the stock is vested. But at that time, the amount of income is measured by the difference between the price paid for the equity and its value *at the time of vesting*. The only way to avoid this result is to file an election to pay the tax on the compensation income measured at the time of the purchase of the equity, even though the equity is not then vested. For Dave and Deborah, this provision acts as a trap. Although they have arranged the initial investments of the parties such that there is no compensation income at the time they purchased their stock, if it is not then fully vested, their taxable income will be measured at the end of each future year as portions of the stock vest. Thus, they must file the election to have their income measured at the time of purchase in order to avoid a tax disaster, even though there is then no income to measure. And contrary to what they might think, that election must be filed within 30 days of their receipt of the stock, not at the end of the year.

Distributions of Company Profits

Stockholder and operating agreements may also include numerous other provisions peculiar to the facts and circumstances of the particular business. Thus, pass-through entities often provide for mandatory distributions of profit to the members or stockholders at least in the amount of the tax obligation each will incur as a result of the profits of the business. Other agreements might include provisions to resolve voting deadlocks between owners, since otherwise a 50-50 split of voting stock might paralyze the company. Various types of arbitration provisions might avoid this problem.

Redemption Provisions

Further, some stockholder or operating agreements provide investors like Deborah and Dave's angel with the right to demand repurchase of his equity at some predetermined formula price at a designated future time, so he will not be forever locked into a minority investment in a closely held company. Conversely, some such agreements provide the company with the right to repurchase such equity at a predetermined price (usually including a premium) should the capital no longer be needed. Other agreements protect investors against being left behind if the founders sell their equity to third parties. The presence or absence of all these provisions depends, of course, on the relative negotiating strengths of the parties.

Legal and Tax Issues in Hiring Employees

From the beginning of this venture, Dave and Deborah have known that if they were successful, they would soon have to hire employees for both the software engineering and the marketing and sales functions. Thus, they need to consider some of the issues raised by the presence of employees.

Employees as Agents of the Company

Employees are agents of the company and, as such, are governed by many of the agency rules that already affect the relationships of partners to a partnership and officers to a corporation. Thus, employees have the duty of loyalty to the company and obligations to not compete, to respect confidentiality, and to account for their activities.

Yet, Deborah and Dave are probably more interested in the potential of their employees to affect the business' relationships with third parties, such as customers and suppliers. Here the rules of agency require that a distinction be drawn between obligations based on contractual liability and those resulting from noncontractual relationships such as tort actions. Figure 12.3 provides an overview of these relationships.

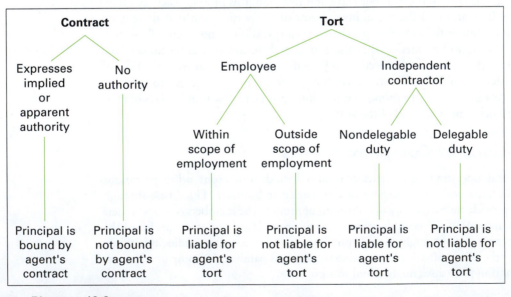

■ **Figure 12.3**

Power of employees/independent contractors to create contractual and tort liability for principals

Employees are authorized to bind their employers to contracts with third parties if such actions have either been expressly or impliedly authorized. Thus, if Dave and Deborah hire a sales manager and inform her that she has the authority to close any sale up to $50,000, she may wield that authority without further consultation with her principals. She also has the implied authority to do whatever is necessary to close such deals (such as sign a purchase order in the company's name, arrange delivery, and perhaps even alter some of the company's standard warranty terms).

However, the employee has authority that often extends beyond that expressly or impliedly given her. To illustrate this, suppose Dave and Deborah's sales manager decides to close a sale for $100,000. This goes beyond her express authority and is not within her implied authority since it was expressly prohibited. Yet, from the point of view of the customer, the company's sales manager appears to have the authority to close all sales transactions.

Unless the customer has been informed of the limitation imposed on the employee, he has no reason to think that anything is wrong. The law vindicates the customer in this situation by providing that the employee has apparent authority to conclude contracts within the scope of authority she appears to have due to actions of her employer. Since she was put into that position by her employer, and the employer has not informed the customer of the limits imposed on the employee, the employer is bound by the employee's actions.

Outside the contract arena, the employee's power to bind the employer is based on similar considerations. The employer, under the doctrine of respondent superior (or vicarious liability), is responsible for any actions of the employee occurring within the scope of her employment. Thus, if the sales manager causes a traffic accident on her way to a sales call, the employer is responsible for damages. This imposition of liability is not, in any way, based on the employer's fault. It is liability without fault imposed as a result of the economic judgment that employers are better able to spread losses among customers and insurance companies. Consistent with this approach, employers are normally not liable for the tort or criminal actions of employees *outside* the scope of their employment, such as actions occurring after hours or while the employee is pursuing his own interests. Furthermore, employers are normally not liable for the torts or criminal actions of agents who are not employees (so-called "independent contractors"), since they are more likely to be able to spread these costs among their own customers and insurers.

However, employers should not take this as an invitation to avoid all liability by wholesale hiring of independent contractors. To begin with, the labeling of a potential employee as an independent contractor is not necessarily binding by law. Courts will look at the level of control exerted by the employer and other related factors to make this determination. In addition, many activities of employers are considered nondelegable (such as disposal of hazardous waste). Employers cannot escape the consequences of such activities by hiding behind independent contractors.

Similarly, someone's status as an employee (or, for that matter, as an independent contractor) does not relieve him of responsibility for tortious or criminal acts. Notwithstanding any liability of the employer, the agent is always still jointly responsible for his own wrongful acts.

Employment Discrimination

In addition to these common-law considerations, there are, of course, a number of statutory rules of law that govern the employer-employee relationship. Perhaps the best known of these are the laws prohibiting employment discrimination. Title VII of the Civil Rights Act of 1964, the Age Discrimination in Employment Act, and laws protecting disabled and pregnant employees collectively prohibit employment discrimination on the basis of sex, race, national origin, religion, age, and disability. They do not prohibit discrimination on the basis of sexual orientation, although a number of state and local laws do.

Prohibited discrimination can occur not only in hiring, but also in promotion, firing, and conditions of employment. In fact, sexual discrimination has been found in cases of sexual harassment that simply created a so-called "hostile environment" for the employee.

These statutes are exceptions to the age-old common law concept of employment at will that allowed employers to hire and fire at their whim, for any reason or no reason at all. This rule is still in force in situations not covered by discrimination laws and, of course, not involving employment contracts. Notwithstanding that rule, however, courts in many states have carved out exceptions to employment at will for reasons of public policy, such as cases involving employees fired for refusing to perform illegal acts, or employees fired in bad faith to avoid paying commissions or other earned compensation to the employee. Furthermore, courts in some states have been willing to discover employment contracts hidden in employee manuals or personnel communications that employers may not have thought legally binding.

Other Employment Statutes

When they begin taking on employees other than themselves, Dave and Deborah will encounter a variety of other statutes that regulate the employment relationship and the workplace itself. For example, ERISA and the Internal Revenue Code closely regulate the form and amounts of any pension, profit-sharing, 401(k), or welfare plans that they may wish to maintain, generally prohibiting discrimination in favor of owners and highly paid employees. They will also find that OSHA and the regulations adopted under that act closely regulate safety and health conditions in the workplace, imposing heavy fines for violations. The Fair Labor Standards Act provides minimum wages and overtime pay for employees in nonexempt (generally nonexecutive) positions, as well as prohibiting child labor and other practices.

The corporation will find itself contributing to the Social Security system and an unemployment compensation fund for each of its employees, as well as withholding Social Security and income taxes from its employees' wages. The amount of their unemployment contribution may depend on the number of employees laid off over the years, causing Deborah and Dave to contest claims from employees who may have left voluntarily or been fired for cause.

In addition, the corporation will probably be required to carry workers' compensation insurance to cover claims under that system. Although the premiums may seem burdensome, workers' compensation is a welcome compromise of the interests of employers and employees. In exchange for avoiding the costs and uncertainties of litigation, employees were assured payment for job-related injuries but lost the opportunity to sue for increased amounts based on pain, suffering, and punitive damages. Employers gave up many common-law defenses that could be used against employees, but now avoid disastrously high jury judgments formerly available under common law.

Employment Agreements

The attraction of employment agreements comes, in the main, from their protection against firing without cause. Thus, a major item of negotiation will likely be the length of the contract. Courts have universally held that an employee cannot be forced to work for an employer against her will. Thus, an employment contract is essentially a one-way street. The employee is promised employment for a period of time, with accompanying salary, bonus, and incentive provisions, but she can leave the company at any time without consequence (unless legally enforceable consequences are specifically provided).

As a result, Dave and Deborah would be well-advised to avoid employment agreements whenever possible, and, if forced to grant one, at least to obtain some accompanying benefit for the company.

Such benefit usually comes in the form of the noncompetition and proprietary information covenants discussed at the beginning of this chapter. For example, a software engineer may promise, in exchange for a two-year employment agreement, not to work in the computer sales industry for a year after the termination of his employment. Yet, as mentioned earlier in the context of Dave and Deborah's former employment, proprietary information obligations exist quite apart from any employee agreement, and courts may refuse to enforce noncompetition provisions against the employee.

Equity Sharing

In addition to demanding job security, higher-level employees will frequently ask to participate in the company's success. A grant of stock might well upset the corporate balance of power and expectations of economic return among the major stockholders. A better solution might be an incentive bonus plan tied to the success of the company, or, more effectively, to the accomplishment of individual goals set for the employee.

If this is unacceptable to the employee, her return could be tied to the fortunes of the company by the use of phantom stock or stock appreciation rights (or similar devices in the context of an LLC) that simulate the effect of equity without involving actual equity ownership. These plans grant the employee bonuses equal to any distributions that would have been made to her if she had owned a certain number of shares while additionally rewarding her through payment of any increase in value such shares would have experienced. However, in certain cases it may be necessary to grant the employee stock in some form.

A direct grant of stock to an employee is considered a taxable event. The employee pays income tax on the difference between the value of the stock and the amount she paid for it, if any. However, the imposition of tax can be postponed if the stock is forfeitable, say, upon the employee's leaving the employ of the company before the passage of a designated period of time. No doubt Deborah and Dave would condition the grant of stock to any employee on her remaining employed for a substantial period, so this rule would apply.

The negative side of this rule, of course, is that when the stock is finally vested, the taxable income is measured by the difference between the amount paid, if any, and the value of the stock *at the time of vesting*. Worse yet, this tax will be payable before the employee has received any cash from this transaction. Cash will be available upon sale of the stock, but typically the employee will not wish to sell at this time, and there will be no market for stock in a closely held corporation in any case.

Stock Options. With stock, the employee is given the right to purchase stock in the corporation (or membership interests in an LLC) at a fixed price for a significant period of time. Thus, without investing any money, the employee can watch the value of this right increase as the value of the stock increases over the amount she would have to pay to purchase it.

Unfortunately, however, when the employee ultimately exercises the option and purchases the stock, the Internal Revenue Code requires recognition of income in the amount of the difference between the amount paid and the value of the stock at that time. Again, this occurs at a time when the employee has received no cash, and likely has little desire or ability to sell.

Recognizing this problem, Congress has provided more favorable tax treatment for an employee stock option that meets a number of requirements (although this treatment

Equity Grant	Date of Grant	Risk Removed	Sale of Equity
Vested equity	Ordinary income	Not applicable	Capital gain
Risk of forfeiture	No income	Ordinary income	Capital gain
Risk of forfeiture — Sec. 83(B) election	Ordinary income	No income	Capital gain
Stock Options	**Date of Grant**	**Date of Exercise**	**Sale of Stock**
Nonqualified stock option with readily ascertainable value	Ordinary income	No income	Capital gain
Nonqualified stock option with no ascertainable value	No income	Ordinary income	Capital gain
Incentive stock option (ISO)	No income	No income	Capital gain

■ **Figure 12.4**

Comparison of equity sharing methods

is, unfortunately, available only in the context of corporations). This is called an *incentive stock option (ISO).* Among other requirements,

- ◉ The ISO must be issued pursuant to a stock option plan approved by the corporation's stockholders;
- ◉ The exercise price must be the fair market value of the stock at the time of issuance;
- ◉ Each option cannot last more than 10 years, and no more than $100,000 of exercise price may become exercisable in any one year;
- ◉ And perhaps most significantly, the employee must hold on to any stock purchased pursuant to the option for the longer of one year after exercise or two years after the grant of the option.

If these requirements are met, unless she is subject to the alternative minimum tax, the employee is not taxed until she actually sells the stock acquired under the option (and has cash to pay tax). The income is then taxed at favorable long-term capital gain rates.

The corporation can still require the employee to sell such shares back to the corporation upon termination of employment. From the corporation's point of view, the only drawback is that it loses any deduction that would otherwise be available for compensation paid to employees. Dave and Deborah may find this plan to be an attractive way to grant the requested incentive to their key employees.

Figure 12.4 compares these various methods of sharing equity with employees.

Insurance

The expenses associated with beginning a business are not inconsiderable. As employees are added to the organization, Social Security, unemployment compensation, and other costs increase, and workers, cf. p. 498 compensation insurance is required by many states. But such insurance is not the only insurance that may be advisable to obtain.

Property Insurance

To begin with, Dave and Deborah should consider property insurance for any equipment or inventory that they may have on hand. In fact, should they ever obtain a loan for their business, the lender will likely take inventory and equipment as collateral and insist that it be insured (with the proceeds payable to the lender).

Liability Insurance

Deborah and Dave should also consider purchasing liability insurance to cover claims against their business for product liability and other possible tort claims. And although the corporate veil protects Deborah and Dave's personal assets against claims of undercapitalization, they no doubt hope that someday soon their business will have its own considerable net worth to protect. Automobile liability insurance is required by many states as a condition to register a car, and we have already discussed the dangers of tort liability caused by employees.

Key Person Life Insurance

We've discussed life insurance to cover stock redemptions under cross-purchase or redemption agreements. But also consider what would occur upon Dave's untimely death. Not only may Deborah or the corporation be required to repurchase his stock, but the operations of the corporation would likely grind to a standstill while it searched for someone to replace Dave. If the corporation owned additional life insurance on Dave's life, known as *key person insurance,* it would have funds to tide it over during this business slowdown as well as money to apply to the search for and compensation of Dave's successor.

Business Interruption Insurance

Business interruption insurance will, in many cases of catastrophic business shutdown, replace some of the company's cash flow. Such a policy is usually quite expensive, however, and may not be within the reach of a typical startup.

Group Life, Disability, and Health Insurance for Employees

As the company grows and adds employees, there will be increasing demand for insurance as employee benefits. Many corporations provide group life insurance and/or group disability insurance for employees. Recent changes in the tax law may make more affordable, high-deductible policies an appropriate choice.

The corporation may provide these three group policies tax-free and deduct the costs of premiums. The only exception to this favorable tax result is for partners in partnerships, members of LLCs, or significant shareholders of subchapter S corporations, all of whom must report these benefits as taxable income (although they may receive a corresponding deduction for a portion of the health insurance premiums). Thus, one additional positive aspect of the choice of a C corporation for Deborah and Dave is that any group life, disability, or health insurance provided to them by the corporation would be free of income tax.

Raising Money

Thoughts of future hirings will inevitably bring Deborah and Dave to consideration of another of the challenges they anticipated. Raising money from their potential investor (as well as probable future rounds of investors) involves another set of complex legal issues.

Legal Issues in the Sale of Securities to Investors

As an alternative to institutional lending, Deborah and Dave plan to turn to an outside investor. Although it will be difficult to attract venture capitalists to such a small startup, other sources of capital in the form of friends and family or local professionals and other individuals or entities with an interest in ground-floor investing may be available. Having chosen to take this route, it is crucial that they purge themselves of two common misconceptions.

Although most businesspeople are aware of the fact that both federal and state law regulates the offer and sale of securities, many believe that these statutes apply only to the offerings of large corporations. Small companies, they believe, are exempt from these acts. Unfortunately, this is one of the dangerous misconceptions held by many persons in the position of Deborah and Dave. In fact, these laws (specifically the federal Securities Act of 1933, the federal Securities Exchange Act of 1934, and states, so-called "Blue Sky" statutes) apply to all issuers and their principals.

Further, even those businesspeople who are aware of the reach of these acts believe that they only apply to issuers of equity securities, mainly stock. This, too, is a misconception. All these statutes apply to issuers of "securities," not just stock. Securities include, in addition to stock, most debt (other than very short-term loans or loans for very specific purposes such as real estate mortgages), options, warrants, LLC membership interests, and any other form of investment in which the investor buys into a common enterprise and relies on the efforts of others for the investment's success. Thus, such disparate items as orange groves, Hawaiian condominiums, and even worms have been held to be regulated securities under the circumstances of their respective cases.

The wide scope of these statutes led some to assert that they include the offering of franchise opportunities as well as stocks, bonds, and so on. Those offering franchises argued in return that the success of a franchisee was not normally determined solely by the efforts of the franchisor, but required significant effort on the part of the franchisee. This debate was rendered moot, however, by the adoption by the Federal Trade Commission of regulations requiring disclosure by franchisors of virtually the same range of information that would have been required under a securities registration statement. Many states have enacted similar franchise registration laws, requiring dual federal and state registration in most franchise offerings.

In general, then, the securities laws prohibit the offering of securities to the public without prior (and very expensive) registration with an appropriate government authority such as the federal Securities and Exchange Commission. They also punish fraudulent activities in connection with such offerings, including not only affirmatively false statements, but mere nondisclosure of material facts about the investment. Due to the complex and expensive nature of registration, these laws provide exceptions to the registration requirement in specific circumstances, but even these offerings are subject to the anti-fraud provisions of the laws. Thus, the challenge to our two entrepreneurs is to identify provisions in the securities laws that will offer them an exemption from registration, understanding that they must still provide sufficient disclosure to potential investors (in the form either of a so-called "offering circular" or, in appropriate circumstances, unlimited opportunity to perform due diligence) to avoid "anti-fraud" liability.

One such exemption contained in the Securities Act of 1933 is the so-called intra-state offering exemption. Based on the general principle that the federal government can constitutionally regulate only *interstate* commerce, the statute necessarily exempts offerings that are purely local. However, the scope of this exemption is relatively narrow. Not only must all persons who purchase the securities be residents of one state, all offerees must be residents there as well. Furthermore, the company offering the securities must be incorporated under the laws of that state (disqualifying many Delaware corporations) and have most of its assets and do most of its business there. Due to these restrictions, this exemption may be useful only in the case of the smallest of offerings. Besides, the exemption only excuses the offering from registration with the Securities and Exchange Commission. The state's securities laws may still require expensive and time-consuming state registration.

The more popular exemption from registration under the federal act is the so-called "private placement exemption," which excuses from registration transactions "not involving a public offering." The SEC has relied in part on this exemption to issue regulations designed to facilitate the raising of capital by small businesses in small offerings. Thus, as of this writing, Regulation D under the act exempts from registration any offering of under $1,000,000 of securities. Above that amount, the regulation requires increasing levels of disclosure (still short of full registration, however), and limits the number of offerees to 35 plus an unlimited number of so-called "accredited" investors. For these purposes, accredited investors are certain institutions, as well as individuals with net worth or annual income at levels that argue a need for less protection. Even apart from the regulation, however, issuers can argue under the statute that offerings made only to relatively sophisticated investors with prior relationships to the issuer, qualify as transactions "not involving a public offering."[2]

Of course, exemption from registration under the federal act does not grant exemption under state acts. In fact, offerings made to investors in a number of states require attention to the Blue Sky statutes of each such state. Fortunately, however, federal law has pre-empted state regulation in offerings beyond a certain size, and, even in the absence of pre-emption, virtually all state statutes contain similar exemptions for private placements, typically exempting offerings to 25 or fewer persons.

Thus, Dave and Deborah will likely be able to seek out the investment they will ultimately need without the necessity of registering with either the federal or state governments. However, it cannot be over-emphasized that they remain subject to the anti-fraud provisions of these acts. Thus, they will be well-advised to seek professional assistance in identifying the applicable statutory exemptions, drawing up a comprehensive offering circular for their offering if appropriate, and disclosing all that an investor would need to know about their company to make an intelligent investment decision.

CONCLUSION ☐

Considering all the legal and tax pitfalls described in this chapter, you may be tempted to ask whether Deborah, Dave, or any other entrepreneur would choose to go down the road of the startup if fully aware of the complications lying in wait. But not to be aware of these matters is to choose consciously to play the game without knowing the rules. These issues are there whether the entrepreneur prepares for them or not. Surely, Dave and Deborah are much more likely to succeed in their venture for having taken the time to become aware of the legal and tax issues facing the entrepreneur.

YOUR OPPORTUNITY JOURNAL	Reflection Point	Your Thoughts...

YOUR OPPORTUNITY JOURNAL

1. What fiduciary duty do you have with your current employer? Does your proposed new venture rely on proprietary information belonging to your previous employer? Are you materially interfering with your previous employer's business by recruiting away key employees?

2. When should you engage an attorney? What criteria will you use in your decision?

3. What legal form should you choose for your new company (sole proprietorship, corporation, etc.)? What criteria will you use in your decision?

4. What will you name your company? Have you registered your name with the state government? Are there other companies using the same or similar name (check the U.S. Patent and Trademark Office database)?

5. What provisions should you have in your shareholders' agreement? What kind of salary will you draw? When will you draw it? What provisions do you have for disposition of equity (e.g., death, termination, etc.)?

6. What type of equity sharing (if any) will you implement with your key employees?

7. What type of insurance is needed to protect your company? When will you secure this insurance?

WEB EXERCISE

Many Web sites offer legal form templates (e.g., shareholder agreements). Studying these templates helps you talk with your lawyer and can reduce your legal fees (time spent with lawyers), especially if you draft the documents and then have the lawyer approve them (rather than having your attorney draft the documents from scratch). Search out Web sites that offer legal templates.

1 www.cybercrime.gov/lamIndict.htm.

2 More information on private placements can be found on the SEC Web site at www.sec.gov/info/smallbus/qasbsec.htm#eod6.

NOTES ☐

CASE   # Cadence Design Systems and Avant! (A)

A NEST OF SOFTWARE SPIES?[1]
The Avant! trade-theft suit could begin to rein in Silicon Valley's freewheeling ways
Business Week, May 19, 1997
Peter Burrows in San Mateo, California

Cadence Design Systems CEO Joseph B. Costello traces his crusade against rival software maker Avant! Corp. to the day in 1994 when Vice President Gerald "Gerry" C. Hsu resigned. Four top employees had left to create Avant! three years before, so Costello wondered if Hsu planned to cross enemy lines, too. According to Costello, Hsu claimed merely to be taking time off at the beach—but was stone silent when asked if Avant! fit into his future plans. A few days later, Costello's suspicions proved correct when Hsu answered the phone at Avant! offices in Sunnyvale, California. "So is this the beach, Gerry?" Costello asked. Hsu declined to comment on the conversation.

Thus began what prosecutors now say was the most blatant case of trade-secret theft in the history of Silicon Valley. On April 11 [1997], Hsu and six other former Cadence officials were indicted on breathtaking charges: They allegedly had used stolen software to build a company with a market value that at one time exceeded $1 billion. The news sent Avant! stock down nearly 60% immediately after the arrests, to $9.81, though it has since bounced back up to $16.75. The defendants, who have all pleaded not guilty, each face up to seven years in prison and civil lawsuits.

"Over the Edge"

The tale that prosecutors tell is a sobering illustration of how far some executives will apparently go to gain a competitive edge. Many people are saying it also shows how little respect is accorded to other people's intellectual property these days in Silicon Valley, where the temptation to cut corners to get a product to market is acute. With engineers changing jobs like shirts, it's easy to look the other way when a new employee borrows ideas from a previous employer. And with Internet links and laptops, such heists are only a mouse-click away. "There's no clear border between right and wrong out here, and everyone goes a little over the edge at times," says Vincent F. Sollitto, CEO of San José-based Photon Dynamics Inc., a Cadence customer. "If Joe is right, this would make an example of someone who went over and didn't come back."

The Cadence story, if true, is also an object lesson in the difficulties software companies face trying to protect their intellectual assets. While trade-secret theft is rising by all accounts, busting the pilferers is expensive and time-consuming. It took pit-bull persistence by Costello, lucky breaks, and $10 million worth of lawyers and private investigators to get the case to this point. What's more, litigation is considered bad form in Silicon Valley, where the honorable way to win market share is through innovation. During the fight,

This case was prepared by Professor William Bygrave. Funding was provided by the Arthur M. Blank Center for Entrepreneurship. © Copyright Babson College, 2006. All rights reserved.

[1] Reprinted from the May 19, 1997 issue of *Business Week* by special permission, copyright © 1997 by McGraw-Hill Companies, Inc. www.businessweek.com/1997/20/b352792.htm.

Costello was lambasted in the media as a bully and his board, customers, and friends urged him to give up the chase. Says Costello, "When it's a solid-steel case, you have to do something about it. But there's so many things moving against you. It's uphill all the way."

Nimble Rival

Naturally, Avant! (pronounced Ah-VON-tee) sees things differently. Lawyers for the company insist it never received stolen software code and point out that the company even removed some suspicious code from its products to be sure it was clean. In written comments to *Business Week,* Avant! CEO Hsu suggests the conflict is more about personalities than felonies. "[Costello] seems intent on attacking me personally—particularly in the press. I can understand why he would prefer to talk about me instead of Cadence's . . . software products: Avant!'s are vastly superior to Cadence's tools, and chipmakers are voting with their pocketbooks," says Hsu.

Avant! backers claim Costello's crusade is little more than a dangerous vendetta against a small, nimble rival. If he succeeds, they say, it could have serious implications for startups, the lifeblood of Silicon Valley. In fact, Avant! claims Cadence is the one fighting dirty. It has countered Cadence's civil suit and seeks hundreds of millions of dollars to compensate for the company's swooning stock price. Among other things, Avant! claims Cadence employees have shorted Avant! stock and spread negative rumors to drive it out of business. Costello says these are diversionary tactics to take the focus off the evidence.

Sleaze Factor

Santa Clara (California) county prosecutors, who have heard both sides of the tale, believe Cadence's version. According to those prosecutors and court documents filed by Cadence in connection with its civil suit, this is no mere case of an employee grabbing a diskette or two on the way out the door. Rather, they allege that Hsu and the other indicted Avant! executives are guilty of a multiyear conspiracy to steal the "source code" to key Cadence "place-and-route" programs, used by microchip designers to arrange circuits on a slice of silicon. "We don't file unless there's a high sleaze factor," says District Attorney Julius Finkelstein. "We want people actually walking out the door with property, and that's what we got."

Ordinarily, place-and-route programs take years to develop. Not at Avant!. By stealing from Cadence on three separate occasions, prosecutors allege, Avant! was able to bring products to market with implausible speed. In the process, its sales soared from $39 million in 1994 to $106 million in 1996. In all, Costello figures Cadence has lost as much as $100 million in sales to Avant!.

According to Finkelstein, Avant! (then called ArcSys Inc.) from its very inception was built on stolen code. Avant! denies the charge. Finkelstein points to an electronic log found during a joint FBI and police raid on Avant!'s offices in December, 1995, that suggests Avant! founder Stephen Tzyh-Lih Wuu spent his final weeks as a Cadence research and development manager in 1991 copying a basic place-and-route program called Symbad. That, court documents say, is how Avant! was able to launch its first place-and-route offering, called ArcCell, in just two years—versus the six years it took Cadence to finish Symbad. Wuu says the 47,000 lines of code mentioned in his log were original work that he completed in 19 days. But Cadence disputes this claim, arguing that 100 lines is a normal day's work.

Prosecutors claim that in 1994, Avant! persuaded former Cadence engineer Mitsuru "Mitch" Igusa to commit the second theft. This time the target was allegedly a key enhancement to place-and-route software—a so-called area-based program that lets the computer do more of the grunt work in chip design. While Igusa never took a job at Avant!, prosecutors allege that indicted Avant! executive Shiaoli Huang paid him at least $15,000 for stealing Cadence code. The money allegedly came from a shell company Huang was administering called the Saurus Fund, which was set up by some of the indicted executives purportedly to fund future startups. [In 1995, Hsu asked the board of directors to reconsider hiring Igusa. The board refused to hire someone who was under criminal investigation, but the suggestion was made that while Avant! could not give financial help to Igusa, individuals could.[2]] Igusa now faces six felony counts for theft, stemming from a raid on his home in November, 1995, in which police found a hard drive full of Cadence source code, much of it stripped of the company's copyright notices.

Miracle Grow

Avant! says that the money it gave Igusa was for a potential startup project, and that the company never received stolen code from Igusa. For his part, Igusa has pled not guilty and could not be reached for comment. But once again, the speed with which the company released an area-based place-and-route program strikes at least one competitor as suspicious. About a year before Avant! released the product, Hsu allegedly approached rival Silicon Valley Research Inc. about a merger to bring in such technology—and was turned down. One Silicon Valley Research manager was shocked when Avant! later released the software: "They miraculously developed it overnight." Avant! Chief Financial Officer John Huyett declined to comment directly on the company's dealings with Silicon Valley Research but said that "Hsu has talked to just about everyone with something to offer in our industry."

The third theft allegedly occurred in January, 1995. According to prosecutors, on his next-to-last day at Cadence before leaving for Avant!, engineer Chin-Liang "Eric" Cheng copied a program he had written over the previous two years onto a file he named "byebye" and stored it on a backup tape. Called V-Size, the program lets designers figure how big a chip must be to handle a given number of circuits. While Avant! never marketed the product, it had planned to do so in 1996, according to documents seized by the FBI, which has been working with Santa Clara county prosecutors since 1994. Avant! denies any wrongdoing, and Cheng declined to comment.

Lucky Break

In retrospect, Costello finds it shocking how little loyalty his former employees appear to have had to the company. "The same people came into my house three times and stole some of my most valuable belongings. It's not right, and we can't live this way," he says.

By his own admission, Costello learned of the alleged thefts remarkably slowly. Originally, he wasn't alarmed when Avant!'s founders and other employees refused to sign

[2] *Cadence* vs. *Avant!* Case #E-61. Stanford University Graduate School of Business.

forms promising to respect Cadence's trade secrets. But he reconsidered after a surprising discovery in August, 1995. A Cadence engineer was on a routine visit to a customer when he happened to look at some of their Avant! software. He spotted a tiny flaw he had unintentionally written into a Cadence product years before—a misaligned edge of a rarely used screen that made it appear fuzzy. To confirm the engineer's hunch, Costello asked a customer to compare the two products. The results: 4,000 identical lines of code and even identical grammatical mistakes. Avant! denies that any theft took place.

Now armed with what he considered conclusive evidence that Avant! had ripped off Cadence code, Costello declared war. But even as his legal case was jelling, he found little support in tight-knit Silicon Valley. Industry reporters and customers alike accused him of using the courts to beat up on a feisty rival. A customer at chipmaker S3 Corp. sent him a heated e-mail message saying "this posturing in the courts is a waste of everyone's time," Costello recalls. Wall Street analysts urged him to stop mentioning the affair at financial meetings—it was detracting from their Avant! stock sales pitches. Through it all, customers continued to snap up Avant! software—usually without even investigating Costello's charges. "The thing that's mind-boggling is how people tried to dismiss it," says Costello. "It's like, 'So, they stole some things.'"

As the heat rose against Cadence in mid-1996, even personal friends and backers questioned Costello's judgment. Nervous about the expense and bad publicity, members of Cadence's board began to reconsider their support of the lawsuit. Says one Cadence manager, "Our board just didn't want to go to the mat." Friends and trusted advisers at Motorola Inc. and Siemens wrote off the issue, predicting that "you'll end up settling," Costello says. And as former Cadence colleague Prabhu Goel planned to sell his company, Frontline Design Automation Inc., to Avant! in late 1996, Costello couldn't even get Goel on the phone to discuss the ethical implications. Goel says he had made a "judgment call" that Hsu was innocent and didn't want to do anything that could scotch the deal.

Others questioned Costello's motives. After all, Avant! was winning away key customers, and Costello, a slick marketer, wasn't above playing dirty pool to hurt his rival's reputation, they said. Before the indictment, "I thought this could have been without cause—just two companies and two men fighting with each other," admits Walden C. Rhines, CEO of Mentor Graphics Corp. in Wilsonville, Oregon.

Now the indictments have given Costello at least partial vindication. But the story is hardly over. On April 30, a determined Hsu vowed at an industry conference to "take the offensive" against Cadence with an aggressive marketing and advertising campaign. "We are not going to stop until we win completely," said Hsu. Hsu went on to project that Avant! would quadruple in size by 2000. But for that to happen, he's going to have to keep himself and his executive team out of jail. Win or lose, Avant!'s tangle with Cadence has been a wake-up call to the rest of Silicon Valley.

Funding ArcSys/Avant!

Venture capital firms invested a total of $7.8 million in two rounds in ArcSys/Avant!. The venture capital firms were the following:

Advanced Technology Ventures

Amerindo Investment Advisors

August Capital

Newbury Ventures

Sutter Hill Ventures

In June 1995, ArcSys/Avant! raised $31 million with its IPO.

Board of Directors (1997)

Gerald C. Hsu, Chairman—Avant!

Eric A. Brill, Secretary

Y. Eric Cho—Avant!

Tench Coxe—Venture Capitalist, Sutter Hill Ventures

Charles St. Clair

The Case Against Avant!

How software maker Avant! allegedly stole trade secrets from rival Cadence—and got nabbed—resulting in one of the computer industry's biggest espionage prosecutions.

March, 1994: Gerry Hsu quits Cadence, reportedly telling CEO Joe Costello that he would probably leave high tech altogether. A few days later, Hsu emerges as CEO at competitor ArcSys, Avant!'s predecessor.

September, 1994: Key Cadence engineer Mitch Igusa quits. Subsequent investigation reveals that Igusa allegedly e-mailed four crucial files containing trade secrets to his home PC before leaving.

May, 1995: ArcSys, allegedly using stolen Cadence technology, goes public. Its market value quickly surpasses $1 billion.

August, 1995: Igusa is charged. Private investigators for Cadence discover an alleged "slush fund" set up by Avant! to pay him for his efforts.

December, 1995: FBI officers raid Avant!'s offices.

May, 1996: Cadence files for a preliminary injunction to prevent Avant! from selling possibly tainted software. In March, the injunction was denied, but the presiding judge suggested there was evidence that at least some Cadence code had been stolen.

April, 1997: Six Avant! managers are charged with trade-secret theft and conspiracy.

Fight to the Death

After six Avant! managers were charged in 1997 with conspiracy and theft of trade secrets from Cadence, Hsu responded by declaring war on his former employer. "He'd say, 'I'm going to fight this to the death. They don't know who they're dealing with,'" recalls one former executive.

Fight he did. On the legal front, Hsu assembled a defense dream team that included many of the Bay Area's top criminal lawyers. The attorneys ran scorched-earth campaign. Using a variety of tactics, the attorneys managed to get three judges in a row to leave the case. They also made three unsuccessful attempts to disqualify prosecutor Finkelstein. "The defense left no legal stone unturned," says Finkelstein.

Hsu also worked the public-relations angle. He launched an advertising campaign to turn public opinion. Avant! hired media consultant Mark Fabiani, who had helped the Clinton administration through the Whitewater scandal. That October, the company ran a full-page newspaper ad headed "The Ugly Truth," with a grotesquely morphed photo of Costello, claiming Cadence was using the courts to hurt a nimble competitor.

Then, in 1998, Hsu set up the Avant! Foundation, which bombarded Silicon Valley residents with syrupy radio ads offering to give away everything from college scholarships to free PCs for the elderly. According to state records, the Avant! Foundation spent almost $1.4 million promoting itself in 1999 and 2000, nearly twice what it had given away. Matt Lipschultz, the foundation's director of operations, said the promotions were necessary to find candidates for funding and that it was spending "more on programming."

Avant! and Six Executives Cop a Plea[3]

A long protracted legal battle ensued as Hsu and his partners in crime brazened it out. They proclaimed innocence and blamed their predicament on Cadence. They stalled the prosecution with a variety of tactics that stretched the law to the limits. But the prosecutors were persistent and they eventually got their day in court. Trial proceedings began May 14, 2001.

On May 22, 2001, Avant! and six current or former employees and/or directors entered pleas of no contest to conspiracy to misappropriate trade secrets, two counts of trade secret misappropriation, and a violation of California corporate securities law. In connection with the plea agreement, Avant! agreed to pay a fine of $27 million and to pay restitution in an amount to be determined by the court. On July 25, 2001, the court fixed the total restitution amount to be paid to Cadence at $195.4 million, any unpaid portion of which accrued interest at the statutory rate of 10% beginning July 25, 2001. In addition to the plea by Avant!, the individual defendants resolved the charges against them in the following manner:

— Gerald Hsu pleaded no contest to conspiracy to misappropriate trade secrets, failure to return stolen property, and a violation of California corporate securities law and agreed to pay a $2.7 million fine.

— Leigh Huang, Y.Z. Liao, and Eric Cho pleaded no contest to trade secret conspiracy and a violation of California corporate securities law. Huang, Liao, and Cho agreed to pay fines of $0.1 million, $2.7 million, and $0.1 million, respectively. Huang was sentenced to three years, probation. Liao and Cho were each sentenced to three years' probation and one year in county jail.

— Stephen Wuu pleaded no contest to trade secret misappropriation and a violation of California corporate securities law. Wuu agreed to pay a $2.7 million fine. Wuu was sentenced to two years in prison and three years' probation.

— Eric Cheng pleaded no contest to trade secret misappropriation. Cheng agreed to pay a $27,000 fine and was sentenced to three years' probation and 364 days in county jail. Effective July 25, 2001, Cheng resigned his position at Avant!.

— All charges were dismissed against former Avant! executive Mike Tsai.

---

[3] Excerpted from Synopsys 10K filing with the SEC. www.synopsys.com/corporate/invest/final18-K_73002.pdf.

— Mitch Igusa, who was never an Avant! employee, pleaded no contest. He was fined $27,000 and sentenced to one year in the county jail.

Joe Costello (Former Cadence CEO), May 2001[4]

Joe Costello in an interview with *Electronic News* hoped that the successful prosecution of the Avant! executives would encourage district attorneys throughout the country to pursue others who steal corporate trade secrets. He also hoped that companies would stand up and not put up with corporate theft.

He was still appalled at the number of companies that had turned a blind eye to Avant!'s behavior. Costello said, "That's the most interesting part of the story at this point: All of these people who told me to just drop it and go out and compete in the market . . . who told me they didn't want to hear it. I was there saying, 'Hey, none of that makes it right to steal!' "

"It really surprised me. I'd say 10% to 15% of the customers, people like T.J. Rodgers [Founder, President, and CEO, Cypress Semiconductor Corp.], said it's stolen property, and we won't buy it. Then another 10%, or 15%, these people just said they didn't care. And I'm not talking about low-level engineers; I'm talking high-up executives said this. I'd ask them, 'Would you buy a stolen car?' They were just brazen about it. Nearly 70% were in between the two. They'd say this is between you and Avant!."

Avant!'s admitting to three separate thefts of Cadence's property had Costello waiting to see how customers would respond. Now he would find out if they had been sincere when they previously vowed never to use Avant!'s software were it proven to have been stolen. He was not optimistic. One customer had just sent him an e-mail that more or less said that the crime did not bother him. "If that is how we feel about this, we have got a sickness in our high-tech society," Costello observed.

Maybe We Need Corporate Death Penalty[5]

Dan Gillmor is a noted American technology writer and former columnist for the *San José Mercury News*. He was so outraged by Avant!'s admission that it stole trade secrets that he posed a provocative question: "Should there be a corporate death penalty?" He continued, "It's worth asking that question in the wake of the stunning news Tuesday that Avant!, its chief executive, Gerald Hsu, and five current or former executives had copped [a plea] to criminal behavior. The bottom line was simple. These guys had created a computer-aided design company with software code they stole from the company several had recently left, Cadence Design Systems, and used the code to compete with their former employer."

Gillmor echoed the words of the district attorney that Avant!'s entire existence was a fraud, founded on criminal acts. He suggested that in a case as egregious as Avant!'s, "you have to ask whether the system would be improved with an ultimate corporate penalty—a sanction that would truly deter such misconduct."

---

[4] Excerpted from *Electronic News*, May 28, 2001.
www.reed-electronics.com/Electronicnews/index.asp?layout=articlePrint&articleID=CA83984.

[5] *San José Mercury News*, May 23, 2001.

The Avant! Saga: Does Crime Pay?[6]
The inside story of a company that stole software code
Business Week, September 3, 2001 By Peter Burrows in San Mateo, California

In early 1993, at a team-building exercise at the posh Claremont Hotel in Berkeley, California, executives from software maker Cadence Design Systems Inc. were asked to draw an image that described themselves. While many people pondered what to draw, division president Gerry Hsu—a talented artist, according to two attendees—quickly dashed off a picture of a big, powerful bird flying off into the distance, droppings falling all the way. "I always know where I'm going, and I get there very fast," he explained at the time, "but I tend to leave a trail of s___ behind me." Who could have predicted he would leave behind this much of it?

Since departing Cadence for Avant! Corp. in 1994, Hsu has transformed the tiny software boutique from a $2 million-a-year startup into a roaring profit machine that earned $70.9 million on sales of $358 million in 2000. But on May 22 [2001], Hsu and five top managers pleaded no contest to charges that they conspired to steal Cadence software. Now the company has been struggling to come up with enough cash to pay $195 million in additional criminal penalties. And the worst may be yet to come because Avant! is facing a potentially crippling civil suit by Cadence. From May 21 to August 22, the share price has tumbled from $18.55 to $7.55.

Criminal Origins

The Avant! case is probably the most dramatic tale of white-collar crime in the history of Silicon Valley. Hsu & Co. parlayed a product containing purloined code into a thriving 1,500-employee public company, with a gleaming, modern office complex in Fremont, California, and a highly visible charitable foundation that has blanketed the Bay Area with radio ads. "What makes the case unique is that you have a large, publicly traded company that was founded and built on stolen property," says Santa Clara County Deputy District Attorney Julius Finkelstein, the one-time computer-science graduate student who prosecuted the case.

That's bad enough. But in a month-long investigation, *Business Week* has learned that the problems at Avant! go beyond the issues raised in the criminal case. Hsu has been running the company almost as if it were his family business—seemingly without regard for many common tenets of corporate governance, according to more than a dozen former co-workers and customers. He pays CEO-level salaries to his son and a former flight attendant, though former employees say that both have limited business backgrounds. Under Hsu's watch, Avant! has also invested or made business deals with at least four other companies in which he has personal stakes. "To Gerry, every system is made to be manipulated. You push the line as far as it can go—hopefully without breaking it," says one associate.

Hsu, 56, declined repeated requests for interviews and did not respond to written questions. But in court, his lawyers have said that the software in question was unimportant and that the company made every effort to remove stolen code. As for questions of improper

---

[6] Reprinted from the September 3, 2001 issue of *Business Week* by special permission, copyright © 2001 by McGraw-Hill Companies, Inc. www.businessweek.com/magazine/content/01_36/b3747087.htm.

governance, Avant! executives say employees are paid appropriately, that all the deals with companies owned by Hsu have been negotiated at arm's length, and that the primary reason for Avant!'s success is its innovative engineering—a point echoed by others in the industry. "Avant! is a leading company with very strong products," says Bernd U. Braune, CEO of Get2chip Inc., a rival design software company. "Some individuals made some mistakes, and they are going to have to pay. But if someone says they were only successful because they stole some code, I think that's definitely wrong."

Avant! Cleans Up?

Avant! is also making an effort to clean up its image. On July 25, the company announced that Hsu would pass day-to-day control to former Chief Operating Officer Paul Lo, who would replace Hsu as president. Lo's first move: to issue a public apology. "Avant! Corp. is sorry for the events of the past," he wrote in a public letter. "We pledge to work hard to deserve the trust and support of our industry."

But few outside the company believe there has been any real change—and they point to Hsu as the main reason. Although he pled no contest to securities fraud, conspiracy to steal trade secrets, and failure to return stolen property, Hsu managed to avoid jail time, largely because there was no evidence that he directly participated in the thefts, according to Finkelstein. By contrast, co-conspirators Mitch Igusa, Eric Cheng, and Stephen Wuu were caught with Cadence code.

To alleviate the sting of the criminal proceeding, the board is paying Hsu's entire fine as well as all of his legal expenses. More important, he is remaining as the chairman of Avant!'s board and its chief strategist—roughly akin to Bill Gate's title and role at Microsoft Corp. Despite all the rogue behavior, fellow board members seem untroubled by Hsu's record. When the company announced his new role, it cited a mild heart attack as the reason, with no mention of the Cadence case. According to board member Daniel Taylor, a retired U.S. Forest Service park ranger, directors never considered asking Hsu to leave. "He's too precious," Taylor says.

In fact, the board will increase Hsu's $1.6 million salary by 5% a year through 2008, according to documents filed on July 25. That's five times more than Lo's $310,000 annual pay. The board is even trying to cement a continued role for Hsu with a new "poison pill." According to new employment contracts also unveiled on July 25, any decision by shareholders not to reelect Hsu as chairman would be deemed a "change in control." That, in turn, would allow many managers to cash out their options, thereby raising the cost of any hostile attempt to oust Hsu.

All of this conduct raises red flags with corporate governance experts. Despite conduct that would be completely unacceptable at most public companies, Hsu has skated through the Cadence debacle without any meaningful punishment. And though the stock has plummeted, most analysts believe Avant! will ultimately survive. "The Number 1 question is why they didn't fire the guy," says Nell Minow of the Corporate Library, a shareholder rights Web site. "There's something really, really wrong here."

Public Company or Sole Proprietorship?

Based on Hsu's assurances that the charges against him were bogus, investors ponied up $31 million in a June, 1995, initial public offering. Profits soared, and the share price zoomed from $13 to $45 by late July. Hsu cashed in on the company's success by embarking on a 13-company, $230 million acquisition spree, enabling Avant! to take on rivals Cadence and Synopsys Inc.

Even as a public company, though, Avant! was run almost like a sole proprietorship. According to several present and former employees, many family members have always been on the payroll. Hsu's son, John H. Hsu, is head of Avant!'s Asia operation, though he only received his master's degree in marketing from Loyola Marymount University in 1998. According to company documents, John was 27 as of July 27, and earned $209,996 in salary and a $778,629 bonus in 2000. "He's a nice kid, but he's extremely inexperienced," says one former executive. "He's a good softball player," says another. John Hsu did not respond to repeated requests for comment.

The second-highest-paid executive at the company is Noriko Ando, who earned $1.46 million in salary and bonuses in 2000. Previously a Japan Airlines flight attendant, Hsu hired her when he was at Cadence to help him arrange travel in Asia and coordinate meetings with executives from big Japanese customers, say several Cadence sources. Fiercely loyal to Hsu, she quickly rose through the ranks to become head of operations.

"She's good at doing what Gerry tells her to do," says a former Avant! executive, who adds that Ando's salary and power have become a source of bitter controversy within the company. "She doesn't know anything about technology," says another source. Ando declined to comment on her salary or qualifications. Since Lo became president, Ando and John Hsu have been moved to new positions, but there has been no change in their compensation, says a company spokesman.

So far, the board of directors has let Hsu get away with such actions. Of the six members other than Hsu, five have connections to Avant! insiders. Former park ranger Taylor is a friend of Hsu's sister. Also on the board are a venture capitalist in whose fund Avant! has invested $10 million, a former Avant! customer who now runs one of its distributors, and a former Avant! manager. The board has always been generous with Hsu. Thanks to a $2.8 million bonus in 2000, Hsu made twice as much as the CEOs of rivals Synopsys and Mentor Graphics Corp., although both of those companies are bigger than Avant!, and their stocks have performed much better. The company's general counsel, Clayton Parker, says, "Avant! is far and away the most profitable company in the [electronic design] industry. Perhaps it should be no surprise that the CEO is well compensated for that."

Hsu may get along well with the board, but he has had a harder time with outside auditors. In 2000, Avant! dismissed KPMG as its outside auditor. Not long afterward, the auditor filed a legally required document with the Securities and Exchange Commission in which it expressed concerns about fiscal years 1999 and 2000, including "incomplete and missing contract documentation," "inadequate internal communications in connection with recording revenue," and "lack of timely and accurate account reconciliations in a number of areas, including cash, unbilled accounts receivable, prepaid commissions, and investments in affiliates." KPMG won't comment further. While not necessarily an indication of fraud, says David F. Larcker, an accounting professor at the Wharton School, such a long list of grievances is unusual and indicates that KPMG may have believed its auditors were not getting sufficient information from the company. Avant! Finance Chief Viraj J. Patel denies any impropriety. "We're not cooking the books."

Critics say Hsu's history with the board and the KPMG incident are troubling, given Avant!'s history of making deals with other companies that Hsu has invested in. In 1997, for example, he, Ando, and a few others created a new Japan-based company called Maingate Electronics to distribute Avant! software. Hsu personally owns 50% of

Maingate, with the rest held by Ando and an investment fund in which other Avant! insiders are investors.

The Maingate deal is legal, to be sure. But it does create an opportunity for abuse. For example, Avant! has refused to disclose what price Hsu and other insiders paid for shares of Maingate recently bought back from Avant!. That raises a question of whether Hsu, with the support of the board, granted himself a low purchase price. And given Hsu's big stake in Maingate, it could be in his interest to pay Maingate overly cushy commissions—a potential means of shifting profits from U.S. shareholders to Maingate's owners. "The CEO should never be investing alongside the company," says Corporate Library's Minow. "That's just terrible. The temptation is too great to have the company prop up your investment."

Apparently, Maingate isn't an anomaly. When Avant! decided in 2000 to spin off its Taiwan operation into a new entity called Avant! Hi Tech Inc., Hsu ended up with a 5% share and his son John got 3%, making John the second-largest owner. Avant! would not say what price per share the Hsus paid for their stakes. And in 2000, Hsu invested $1 million of his own money in SMIC, a China-based startup that will build semiconductors on a contract basis. Later that year, Avant! committed $100 million. Since that corporate investment came in a later round of financing, the company could have paid a higher price per share. The company declined to provide detailed information on Maingate, Avant! Hi Tech, or SMIC.

Down but Not Out

Avant! still faces a civil suit filed by Cadence, which will probably seek damages of more than $1 billion but is likely to take at least another year before it's resolved. Some customers, worried about Avant!'s financial picture and angered by Hsu's prior insistence on his innocence, say they may look to newer design software companies with hotter technology. The biggest concern: that many of the top-notch engineers who believed Hsu's claims may now leave Avant! to escape the legal cloud.

But few people are willing to count Hsu out entirely. He's nothing if not a survivor. "Gerry's favorite book has always been Sun Tzu's *The Art of War*," says his old nemesis, former Cadence CEO Costello. "Well, the general is a little bit down and has lost a few battles. But he's still alive." No doubt. But if history is any guide, Hsu will simply regroup and prepare for the next fight.

Preparation Questions

1. What is your opinion of the behavior of the following actors:
   a. Joe Costello
   b. Gerry Hsu
   c. Former Cadence employees that went over to Avant!
   d. Customers and potential customers of Cadence and Avant!
   e. Avant!'s auditors

    f.   Avant!'s lawyers

    g.   The prosecutors

2. What is the responsibility of the venture capitalist(s) who funded ArcSys (Avant!)?

3. What is the responsibility of the underwriter who handled ArcSys/Avant!'s IPO?

4. Evaluate Avant!'s board of directors.

5. What should the board do now (September 2001)?

6. Should there be a corporate death penalty as Dan Gillmor proposed?

Anita Dembiczak came up with the idea of a plastic leaf bag configured to look like a giant Halloween style pumpkin when stuffed with leaves. Her initial application for a patent was rejected by a U.S. patent examiner. But a court of appeals overturned that decision and the patent was subsequently issued. (*Source*: Melissa King/iStockphoto)

INTELLECTUAL PROPERTY

Entrepreneurship and **intellectual property** (IP) go hand in hand. Intellectual property refers to creations of the mind, such as inventions; literary and artistic works; and symbols, names, images, and designs used in commerce. Business intellectual property includes patents, trade secrets, trademarks, and copyrights.

    Patents protect inventions so valuable that companies even base advertising campaigns around them. *Trade secrets* cover proprietary information, whether it's in the form of a recipe, a customer list, or a unique way of conducting business. *Trademarks* are key in differentiating a business's products and services from those of others, as well as in franchising arrangements. *Copyrights* protect authors' original creations including literary, musical, artistic, software, and other intellectual works.

This chapter written by Kirk Teska and Joseph S. Iandiorio.

Investors need to be assured not only that you've considered IP but also that you've implemented a plan to protect your company's crown jewels. And because IP protection costs money, you need to budget for and manage it.

In a survey we conducted, nearly 90% of venture capital firms in New England ranked IP as important or extremely important in making an investment decision.

There are few guarantees in the area of IP. Not every patent application is granted; a name you've chosen for your company might not be available or be registerable as a trademark for a variety of reasons; and not every noncompete agreement will pass muster in the courts. Sometimes entrepreneurs must take risks. To do that wisely, you'll want to understand the IP environment, which is slow to change in its legal underpinnings but continually being pushed to keep up with technological advances.

Even when it's successful, however, protecting IP is not the endgame. A patent, for example, doesn't generate revenue—it's just a document. A patent taken out for a great new idea is nothing unless people are willing to pay for that idea implemented in a product or service. Timing can play a crucial role in IP, just as it does in exploiting an entrepreneurial opportunity.

Finally, IP is everywhere. Just because your business isn't about technology, don't be mislead into thinking you won't ever face IP issues. Patents today cover nonengineering subject matter ranging from holders for floral bouquets to business methods; trademark law is invoked in Internet search engines, pop-up ads, and Web sites in general; and even users of another company's products, for example, can be sued for patent infringement.

The Basics: What Is Protectable and How Should It Be Protected?

When someone conceives a new idea or designs a new product or method, two of the first questions to arise are: Can I protect this? Can I keep competitors from copying this?

There are very practical reasons for protecting a new idea. Investors are loathe to put money into a venture that cannot establish a unique product niche. Stockholders will challenge a corporation's investment of its resources in a program that can be easily copied once it is introduced to the market. All the time, effort, and money you invest in perfecting a product, as well as advertising and promoting it, may be wasted if imitators can enter the market on your heels with a product just like yours. Moreover, the imitators can cut prices, because they have not incurred the startup expenses you had to endure to bring the idea from conception to a mass-producible, reliable, and appealing product or service.

The next question is: "Does my new product infringe the IP rights of anyone else?" Only by understanding the basics of IP can you answer that.

Once you have determined that your new idea, product, or method is eligible for one or more forms of IP protection—a *patent, trade secret, trademark*, or *copyright*—secure the rights as quickly as the budget allows. A single product can qualify for different forms of protection, each obtained in a different manner and providing a different set of rights. For example, consider a typical modern product—a microprocessor-based handheld device.

It bears the name of the manufacturer and a brand name and is accompanied by a user's manual. What is protectable, and how should you protect it? Where might others have IP that you must consider? The following sections provide information to help answer these questions.

Patents

Although there are actually three different kinds of patents, the kind you will usually seek to protect an invention is a **utility patent**. Think utility patent whenever you think "better, cheaper, faster." But don't confuse *invention* in the patent sense with "eureka"-type ideas. Most patents are simple combinations of well-known components. Consider the following examples.

In one case a patent allegedly protected the notion of a document scanner equipped with a USB (Universal Serial Bus) port. A USB is simply a connection between a computer and a peripheral device such as a scanner. The USB connection transfers data between the two and also allows the scanner to be powered from the computer. That way, with a USB connection, you don't have to plug the scanner into an electrical wall socket. Indeed, the scanner can even be powered by the computer's battery in the case of a portable computer. The "inventors" of this particular patent didn't invent either USB or the scanner. But when they decided to put the two together, they won a patent.

Consider also aerogel, listed in the *Guinness Book of World Records* as the world's lightest substance. A block of aerogel as big as you weighs less than a pound but can support a small car. Recently, numerous companies have been patenting new uses for aerogel—as insulation, in fuel cells, and as building structures, just to give a few examples. Engineers at those companies didn't invent aerogel—a Stanford University researcher discovered it in the early '30s. Still, the Patent Office will readily grant patents for new uses of aerogel.

Technically speaking, utility patents cover these classes of inventions.

- *Chemical inventions* that include new compounds, new methods of making old or new compounds, new methods of using old or new compounds, and new combinations of old compounds. Assays, biological materials and methods, drugs, foodstuffs, drug therapy, plastics, petroleum derivatives, synthetic materials, adhesives, pesticides, fertilizers, and feeds are all protectable.

- *General/mechanical inventions* include everything from gears and engines to tweezers and propellers, from zippers to Jacque Cousteau's scuba regulator. For example, complex textile-weaving machines, space capsule locks and seals, and diaper pins are all protectable.

- *Electrical inventions* include everything from lasers to light switches, from the smallest circuit details to overall system architectural concepts.

Computer software is also patentable in various forms.

- Application programs, such as the software that runs in a computer used to control a chemical-processing plant or a rubber-molding machine, are patentable.

- Software for running a cash management account at a brokerage house or bank is patentable.

- The microcode in a ROM that embodies the entire inventive notion of a new tachometer is patentable.

- Internal or operations programs that direct the handling of data in the computer's own operations are patentable.

Obtaining a Utility Patent

So there is no rule that patents cover only remarkable inventions. Instead, the basic requirement for a utility patent is that the idea be different in some way from what came before. Most importantly, patent protection can be broad: the owner of the patent has the right to exclude others from making, using, selling, offering for sale, or importing the patented invention during the term of the patent.

Historically the term of a U.S. patent was 17 years from the date of issue. Patents now have a term of 20 years from the date of filing. Patents already issued before June 8, 1995, maintain their 17-year term. Those patents issued after June 8, 1995, based on patent applications filed before June 8, 1995, have either 17 years from issuance or 20 years from filing, whichever is longer. On average, though, given that a patent application takes three years to process through the patent office, the patent term is usually about 17 years from the date the patent is granted.

The patenting effort begins when the inventor or inventors conceive of an invention. Typically a registered patent attorney acting on the inventor's behalf prepares a patent application and files it in the U.S. Patent and Trademark Office. From the date the application is filed there is a *patent pending*. There are no real legal rights associated with "patent pending." Full protection applies only if and when the Patent Office agrees that the invention is patentable and issues the patent. But with patent pending, a would-be competitor doesn't always know exactly what will be patented or when, and thus must proceed with caution in making the decision to offer the same or a similar product.

A common misconception is that software, Internet-based business ideas, and so-called "business methods" are not patentable. The truth is software has long been patentable. And, in 1998, the high patent court put to bed the notion that business methods were an exception to patentable subject matter when Signature Financial Group's patent for a mutual fund administration system was upheld as valid. Another well-known example is Amazon's "One-Click" Internet shopping patent (No. 5,960,411) litigated in 1999 against Barnes & Noble.

The patent application must contain a complete and understandable explanation of the invention. It doesn't have to be a nuts-and-bolts instruction manual. It is enough to convey the inventive concept so that a person "skilled in the art" can make and use the invention without undue experimentation. Further, the explanation must contain a full description of the best mode known by the inventor for carrying out the invention. For example, the inventor cannot use the second-best version or embodiment of the invention as an illustration for the patent application disclosure and keep secret the best embodiment. That could make the resulting patent invalid.

The *timing* of the filing is critical. In the United States, the patent application must be filed within one year of the first public disclosure, public use, sale, or even offer for sale of the product, or the filing will be barred and the opportunity to obtain a patent lost forever. This is known as the one-year period of grace. It may change in the future to a system in which there is no period of grace (then the application must be filed *before* any of these activities occur) to conform with the laws of most other countries. And if patent protection is beneficial in foreign countries, a patent application must be filed in the United States before any public activity occurs.

Market testing, exhibitions, or even use by the inventor himself can be a public use sufficient to activate the one-year period. One exception is a public use for experimental purposes. The test for whether a public use is an excepted experimental use is rigorous. The inventor must show that it was the operation and function of the invention that was being tested, not the appeal or marketability of the product employing the invention. Further, he should establish some evidence of the testing. For example, if samples were sent to potential customers for evaluation, it would be good to show that the customers returned filled-out evaluation forms and that the inventor considered and even made changes based on those evaluations.

A sale more than a year before the application will generally bar a patent even if the invention is embedded so deeply within a larger system that it could not ever be discovered. If the device containing the invention is sold, that is enough. The idea is that an inventor should be given only one year in which to file her patent application after she has begun to commercially exploit or to attempt to commercially exploit her invention. Thus, for an invention embodied in a production machine installed in a locked, secure room, the one-year period for filing a patent application begins the first time a device produced by that machine is sold, even though the machine may never be known to or seen by anyone other than the inventor. And it is not just an actual sale that triggers the one-year period: an offer for sale is sometimes enough, even if the sale is never consummated.

Criteria for Obtaining a Utility Patent

A patent "application" is not a form to be filled out. Instead, each patent application is unique, although the form of all patents contains the same three basic sections:

- ◉ Drawings showing an embodiment of the invention,
- ◉ A written description of the invention referring to the drawings akin to an engineering specification, and
- ◉ One or more **claims**—hybrid legal and technical language that "captures" the invention in words.

The definition of the patented invention—the protected property—is not what you disclose in the drawings or specification portion of the application; this is only a description of one or more specific embodiments or versions of the invention. Instead, the coverage of the patent is defined by the third part of the application, the legal claims.

To qualify the invention for a patent, the claims must describe something both novel and unobvious. *Novelty* is a relatively easy standard to define: if a single earlier patent, publication, or product shows the entire claimed invention, the invention is not novel and no patent will be issued. *Obviousness* is somewhat more difficult to grasp and, worse, the test for obviousness is fairly subjective: Are the differences between the invention and all prior knowledge (including patents, publications, and products) such that the invention would have been obvious to a person having ordinary skill in the art? If so, the invention is not patentable even if it is novel.

Consider an example of what "novelty" and "unobvious" mean in the area of patentability. Suppose a person is struggling to screw a wood screw into hard wood, and he realizes the problem is that he cannot supply enough twisting force with the blade of the screwdriver in the slot in the head of the screw. So he gets the bright idea of making the slot a little deeper, so that the screwdriver blade can bite a little deeper and confront more surface area of the slot, thus applying more force to turn the screw. This is a good idea, but it creates another problem. The deeper slot extends much closer to the sides of the screw head. There is less support, and fatigue lines develop that eventually cause the screw head to crack. The inventor then gets the idea to use a new screwdriver with two shorter, crossed blades, which will give increased surface-area contact with two crossed slots in the head of the screw.

But a problem still exists. Although the twin blades do not require such deep slots, there are now twice as many slots, and the screw head is seriously weakened. Now the inventor sees another path: keep the double-blade configuration, but chop off the corners, so that the slots need not extend out so close to the edge of the new screw head.

The result: he has invented the Phillips head screwdriver, for use with a Phillips head screw. Certainly the invention is "novel": no one else had made that design before. It is

also "unobvious" and thus patentable. The addition of the second blade and elimination of the corners has resulted in a wholly new screwdriver concept. The concept is patentable.

Now suppose another party, seeing the patent issued on this double-blade Phillips head, comes up with an improvement of her own. Her invention is to use three crossed blades (cutting the head of the screw into six equal areas), with their corners removed. This design may not be patentable. Certainly it is novel, but is it unobvious? Not likely. Once the first inventor has originated the idea of increasing the number of blades and eliminating corners, it may be obvious to simply add more blades. Even so, patents still regularly issue today for new screw heads and even more mundane items such as the shape of the arbor hole in a circular saw blade.

Drafting the Patent Claims

Once you have decided that a patentable invention exists, you must protect it with properly drafted patent claims. It is the claims that the U.S. Patent and Trademark Office examiner analyzes and accepts or rejects in considering the issuance of the patent; it is the claims that determine whether someone has infringed a patent; and it is the claims that define the patented property.

Claims, then, are clearly the most important part of a patent. It is no good to have claims that cover the invention and yet do not protect your product or process from being copied by competitors. Does this sound contradictory? Study the following example and you will understand.

Suppose an entrepreneur meets with a patent attorney and shows the attorney a new invention for carrying beverages on the slopes while skiing. The invention eliminates the risk of smashing glass, denting metal, or squashing a wineskin, and it also eliminates the need to carry any extra equipment: It's a hollow ski pole. The ski pole has a shaft, a chamber, and a handle. The handle has a threaded hole opening into the hollow shaft. Partway down the inside of the hollow shaft is a plastic liner that creates a chamber for holding liquids; this plastic liner is sealed to the shaft. The chamber is closed by a threaded plug. The entrepreneur wants to patent this invention, and so he assists the patent attorney in writing a description of the ski pole. They write the following claim:

"A hollow ski pole for carrying liquids, comprising:

- a hollow shaft,
- a plastic liner inside the shaft to define a chamber for containing liquid,
- a handle on the shaft,
- a threaded hole in the handle that opens into the chamber, and
- a threaded plug for sealing the threaded hole."

The patent application is filed. The U.S. Patent and Trademark Office examines the application and three years later issues the patent with that claim. The inventor is happy: the claim describes exactly what the entrepreneur markets and sells. But not for long, because a competitor comes out with a similar hollow ski pole that doesn't use a liner. The competitor simply welds a piece of metal across the inside of the shaft to make a sealed chamber. The competitor has avoided infringing the patent because there is no liner

---

Obviousness is a somewhat subjective determination, but many ideas have ultimately been deemed patentable even though they were originally rejected as obvious by an examiner of the United States Patent and Trademark Office. In one notable case, Anita Dembiczak came up with the idea of a plastic leaf bag configured to look like a giant Halloween style pumpkin when stuffed with leaves. The United States Patent and Trademark Office essentially concluded that since leaf bags were well known and pumpkins drawn on paper lunch sacks were also well known, the idea of a pumpkin leaf bag was obvious and therefore not patentable. Not so, said the Court of Appeals for the Federal Circuit: the Patent Office failed to prove there was any motivation to combine the idea of a Halloween pumpkin with a leaf bag. As a result, the patent for the leaf bag pumpkin was issued. Obviousness rejections are to be expected from the Patent Office.

June 23, 1964   J. S. KILBY   3,138,743

MINIATURIZED ELECTRONIC CIRCUITS

Filed Feb. 6, 1959   4 Sheets—Sheet 1

Courtesy US Patent Office

INVENTOR

Jack S. Kilby

BY

Stevens, Davis, Miller & Mosher

ATTORNEYS

Jack Kilby invented the integrated circuit in 1958, filed a patent application in 1959, and the patent (#3138743) was issued on June 13, 1964. This invention triggered the digital revolution that is at the core of every electronic device that we use today. Jack Kilby was awarded the physics Nobel Prize in 2000. Here is the first page of figures in Kilby's patent. You can research this and any other patent by visiting the US Patent Office Web site.

that was one of the requirements of the patented claim. Still another competitor replaces the threaded plug with an upscale mahogany cork. Again the patent is not infringed because there is no threaded plug as required by the claim. Patent claims are akin to requirements, and a competitor who can sell a competing product without meeting *all* the claim requirements doesn't infringe the patent.

You can avoid this problem by exploring the various ways in which you can build your product before you file the patent application. You may need input from sales, marketing, engineering, and production people as well as from the inventor. After a thorough study, a better claim might emerge as follows:

"A hollow ski pole for carrying liquids, comprising:

- a hollow shaft,
- a chamber in the hollow shaft for containing a liquid,
- a handle on the shaft having a hole opening into the chamber, and
- a closure for the hole in the handle."

Now the liner and a threaded plug are not required. This claim, then, would likely be good enough to keep competitors at bay. There is a limit to how broadly you can word the claim, however. Eventually, if it becomes broader and broader and does not specify the ski pole or hollow shaft, it may apply to a bottle or a pot with a cover, and the patent will not be obtainable—it is not new. Careful claim drafting is thus critical.

If you don't remember anything else about patents remember this: it's the claims that matter.

Provisional Patent Applications

A new type of patent application, referred to as a **provisional,** is now available. People like provisionals because they don't have to include patent claims—indeed, a paper, specification, or report can be filed as a provisional. Be careful, though. In one case, a product embodying an invention was sold in the spring of 1996, a provisional application was filed in the spring of 1997 for the product, and a full patent application was filed in the fall of 1997. But, the provisional failed to adequately describe the invention actually claimed in the full patent application. The result? The patent was held invalid because the provisional failed to provide the necessary disclosure. When the patent owner sued a competitor for patent infringement, a court found the resulting patent claims contained detailed information not present in the provisional patent application. As a result, the patent was invalidated and the competitor was free to use the patented invention.

Provisionals have found favor because they are typically less expensive than full patent applications and allow companies to advertise "patent pending." In 2002, over 80,000 provisional patent applications had been filed. But, as this case proves, provisionals are only as good as the details they contain. If you don't actually draft the legal claims for the invention, you should at least envision them to ensure that the provisional application adequately supports the claims you file later in the full utility application.

Design Patents

Another type of patent is the **design patent**. Hockey uniforms, ladies' dresses, computer housings, automobile bodies, buildings, shoes, and game boards are all protectable with design patents. But this type of patent covers only the *appearance* of the product, not the idea, underlying concept, or functionality of the product. What you see is what you get. Design patents are generally less expensive than utility patents but typically also offer far less protection.

Managing Patent Costs

Patents are expensive: plan on spending between $8,000 to $15,000 to prepare and file a patent application and between $4,000 and $6,000 to **prosecute** the patent application. Prosecution is what occurs in the two to three years following filing of the application as you attempt to convince the Patent Office that the invention is worthy of a patent in the face of inevitable rejections. Foreign patents can cost $5,000 to $10,000 per country in filing fees alone. But, you have to put these costs in perspective. Consider the price of a mold for a plastic part, for example, or the cost of a marketing study undertaken by a consultant. Because of the potential value of a patent, the cost of filing is often well worth it. If, for example, Gillette's patent for the three-bladed Mach3 razor can really be used to stop all competitors from introducing razors with three or more blades, the cost of the Gillette patent and even the cost of patent litigation (typically $1 million or more) is well worth the protection afforded, especially given the enormous cost of Gillette's advertising campaigns surrounding the Mach3 razor.

On the other hand, some patents may not have enough potential value to provide a return on the investment. Consider a patent for aerogel used as an insulative liner in deep-sea oil-well piping. If other insulating materials work as well or almost as well, the patent might not be worth the cost—unless it is worth something to advertise "the only deep-sea oil-well piping with aerogel!"

The problem is, at the time the patenting decision must be made, the value of the patent might be hard to measure. Big companies regularly file for numerous patents and have a yearly IP budget in the millions of dollars. Entrepreneurial companies cannot typically afford those costs and thus must be particularly adept at planning and managing patents and other IP, all the while remembering the deadlines and that the value of a given patent is measured by its claims.

Finally, don't forget to make sure your new product or service doesn't infringe someone else's patent. In our survey of venture capitalists, 63% had experienced IP lawsuits against companies they had funded.

In 2005, for the twelfth consecutive year, IBM was granted more U.S. patents than any other company. It earned 2,941 patents—1,113 more than the second-ranked company, Canon Kabushiki Kaisha. It was the eighth consecutive year that IBM received more than 2,000 U.S. patents; it was the only company ever to have received more than 2,000 patents in one year. Approximately 50% of IBM's patents were related to software.

Trade Secrets

One benefit of trade secrets is they can cover everything patents cover, and much more. A **trade secret** is defined as knowledge, which may include business knowledge or technical knowledge, that is kept secret for the purpose of gaining an advantage in business over one's competitors. Customer lists, sources of supplies of scarce materials, or sources of supplies with faster delivery or lower prices may be trade secrets. Certainly, secret processes, formulas, recipes, techniques, manufacturing know-how, advertising schemes, marketing programs, and business plans are all protectable.

Another benefit of trade secrets is there is no standard of invention to meet, as there is with a patent. If the idea is new in this context, if it is secret with respect to this particular industry or product, then it can be protected as a trade secret. Also unlike the case for patents, trademarks, and copyrights, there is no formal government procedure for obtaining trade secret protection. Protection is established by the nature of the secret and the effort to keep it secret.

Finally, a trade secret can be protected eternally against disclosure by all those who have received it in confidence and from all who would obtain it by theft for as long as the knowledge or information is kept secret.

The key disadvantage of trade secrets is that, unlike the case with patents, there is no protection against discovery by fair means, such as accidental disclosure, independent inventions, and reverse engineering. Many important inventions, such as the laser and the airplane, were developed more or less simultaneously by different persons. Trade secret protection would not permit the first inventor to prevent the second and subsequent inventors from exploiting the invention as a patent would.

This example illustrates the distinction between patents and trade secrets. A woman designed a novel keyholder and immediately filed a patent application. It was a simple design and could be easily copied. While the patent was still pending, she licensed it to a manufacturer for a 5% royalty, with the agreement that if the patent didn't issue in 5 years, the royalty would drop to $2\frac{1}{2}$%. The patent was never issued, and the royalty was dropped to $2\frac{1}{2}$%. Over the next 14 years, on sales of $7 million, the manufacturer's edge eroded as others freely copied the design. The manufacturer repudiated the royalty contract on the ground that it required payment forever for the small jump that the manufacturer got on its competitors, whereas the patent, had it issued, would have allowed only 17 years of exclusivity. The court held the manufacturer to its requirement to pay. The ruling allowed the inventor to receive $2\frac{1}{2}$% royalty for as long as the manufacturer continued to sell the keyholder. Had the patent been issued, royalties would have lasted only 17 years!

But don't be misled into thinking trade secrets are a fallback position to patents or that they offer "free protection." Consider the feature of the Windows program that allows you to open two files at the same time, display them on the screen, and drag content from one into the other. Nice feature, but it cannot be a trade secret. Why not? Because you and everyone else can see the feature in operation every time you use it. Microsoft even advertises it. It's not a secret. Any competitor of Windows can write code that affords the same functionality. Microsoft's exact code that carries out that functionality is secret, to be sure, but even that is not "free" protection when you consider the overhead costs Microsoft incurs to ensure the code is always kept under wraps and that its numerous employees and consultants are subject to secrecy agreements.

Many companies use both approaches, filing a patent application and during its pendency keeping the invention secret. When the patent is ready to be issued, the company reevaluates its position. If the competition is close, they let the patent issue. If not, they abandon the patent application and rely on trade secret protection. But, following a change in law, patent applications are now published 18 months after their earliest filing date, voiding trade secret protection unless the filer takes active steps to prevent publication (such as an agreement not to file an application for the invention in any foreign country).

Despite the problems with trade secrets, some have been appraised at a value of many millions of dollars, and some are virtually priceless. For example, the formula for Coca-Cola is one of the best-kept trade secrets in the world. Known as "Merchandise 7X," it has been tightly guarded since it was invented over 100 years ago. It is known by only two persons within the Coca-Cola Company and is kept in a security vault at the Trust Company Bank in Atlanta, Georgia, which can be opened only by a resolution from the company's board of directors. The company refuses to allow the identities of those who know the formula to be disclosed, or to allow the two to fly on the same airplane. The company elected to forego producing Coca-Cola in India, a potential market of 550 million people, because the Indian government requires the company to disclose the secret formula as a condition for doing business there. While some of the mystique surrounding the Coca-Cola formula may be marketing hype, it is beyond dispute that the company possesses trade secrets that are carefully safeguarded and extremely valuable.

Secrecy is essential to establishing trade secret rights; without it there is no trade secret property. There are four primary steps for ensuring secrecy.

1. Negotiate confidential disclosure agreements with all employees, agents, consultants, suppliers, and anyone else who will be exposed to the secret information. The agreement should bind them not to use or disclose the information without permission.

2. Take security precautions to keep third parties from entering the premises where the trade secrets are used. Sturdy locks, perimeter fences, guards, badges, visitor sign-in books, escorts, and designated off-limits areas are just some of the ways that a trade secret owner can exercise control over the area containing the secrets.

3. Stamp specific documents containing the trade secrets with a confidentiality legend and keep them in a secure place with limited access, such as a safe, locked drawer, or cabinet.

4. Make sure all employees, consultants, and others who are concerned with, have access to, or have knowledge about the trade secrets understand that they are trade secrets, and make sure they recognize the value to the company of this information and the requirement for secrecy.

Trade secret owners rarely do all these things, but they must do enough so that a person who misappropriates the secrets cannot reasonably excuse his conduct by saying that he didn't know or that no precautions were ever taken to indicate that something was a trade secret. This is important because, unlike patents, trade secret protection provides no "deed" to the property.

Since there is no formal protection procedure, the necessary steps for establishing a trade secret are often not taken seriously until a lawsuit is brought by the owner against someone who has misappropriated them. In each specific case the owner must show that the precautions taken were adequate. Those precautions can incur significant overhead costs, especially as the number of secrets, employees, and consultants grow.

Trade secret misappropriations generally fall into one of two classes: someone who has a confidential relationship with the owner violates the duty of confidentiality, or someone under no duty of confidentiality uses improper means to discover the secret.

Trade secret theft issues frequently arise with respect to the conduct of ex-employees. Certainly, a good employee will learn a lot about the business during her employment. And some of that learning she will take with her as experience when she leaves. We cannot prevent that. The question is, did she simply arrive smart and leave smarter, or did she take certain information that was exclusively the company's?

For example, in one case a company that had been making widgets for the government for many years did not get its annual contract renewal. When the company questioned the loss of the contract, it discovered that a competitor was supplying widgets of equal quality at a lower price. Upon investigation, the company determined that the competitor was located in the same town, that the competitor's widgets were uncannily identical in every dimension, and that the competitor was owned by an ex-employee of the company who had left over a year before. Amicable approaches failed, and a lawsuit was instituted during which the company discovered that the ex-employee had copied its detailed engineering drawings to make the widgets. This eliminated all engineering and design costs and enabled the competitor to sell the widgets to the government at a much lower price.

But the ex-employee had not stolen anything. It seems the man knew that every year his ex-employer reissued important engineering drawings that had become torn and tattered or that needed updating, and threw out the old ones. The ex-employee testified that while driving by one day, he had seen the old drawings sticking out of the dumpster. He drove in, took them out of the dumpster, put the ones he wanted in his car, and chucked the rest back. That's how he got a widget with identical dimensions. The court held him liable for misappropriation of trade secrets. He had trespassed to obtain the drawings, and he had learned of the ex-employer's practice of disposing of old drawings while an employee with a duty of confidentiality to the company. The court granted an injunction preventing the ex-employee from selling widgets for a period of months equal to the jump he got by not having to develop his own engineering drawings.

But what if the ex-employee had not trespassed to obtain the drawings from the trash? What if he had waited for the trash collector to remove them and then asked whether he could look over the trash? Or what if he had gone to the dump and picked the drawings out of the mud? When does the owner part with ownership of trade secret materials it has discarded?

In summary, trade secrets can be valuable but they are not a form of "free protection," nor is protection available for secrets that can be discovered. Still, in a survey, venture capitalists ranked trade secrets as at least as important as patents when they make an investment decision in a startup company.

Bruno Vincent/Getty Images News and Sports Services

Managing director of Apple Corps, Neil Aspinall leaves the Royal Courts of Justice during a break for lunch on March 29, 2006, in London. The Beatles' record label Apple Corps sued Apple Computer over use of the Apple name and logo in the music business, which they claimed was in breach of a 1991 agreement.

Trademarks

Trademarks are the stuff of advertising. Technically speaking, trademark protection is obtainable for any word, symbol, or combination thereof that is used on goods to indicate their source. Any word—even common words such as "look," "life," and "apple"—can become a trademark, so long as the word is not used descriptively. "Apple" for fruit salad might not be protectable, but Apple for computers certainly is and so too is Apple for a record company. Interestingly, the Beatles' company, Apple Corps, which owns the trademark Apple in the context of recorded music, unsuccessfully sued Apple Computer on the grounds that the Apple iPod, which downloads and plays recorded music, infringes on the Beatles' trademark.[1] It was expected that Apple Corps would appeal the ruling, which was made by a British judge in May 2006.

Common forms such as geometric shapes (circles, triangles, squares), natural shapes (trees, animals, humans), combinations of shapes, and colors may also be protected. Even the single color pink has been protected as a trademark for building insulation. Three-dimensional shapes such as bottle and container shapes and building features (for example, McDonald's golden arches) can serve as trademarks.

While people generally only speak of trademarks, that term also encompasses other types of marks. A trademark is for products. A **service mark** is a word or symbol or combination used in connection with the offering and provision of services. Blue Cross/Blue Shield, Prudential Insurance, and McDonald's are service marks for health insurance services, general insurance services, and restaurant services, respectively. McDonald's is a service mark (fast-food restaurant services) and also a trademark (the McDonald's brand Big Mac hamburger).

If you use any such name or feature to identify and distinguish your products, then think trademark protection. Ownership of a trademark allows you to exclude others from using a similar mark on similar goods that would be likely to confuse consumers as to the source of the goods. This right applies for the duration of ownership of the mark—that is, as long as the owner uses the mark.

Trademarks can be more valuable to some companies than patents and trade secrets combined. Consider the sudden appearance and abrupt increase in the worth of trademarks such as Cuisinart, Häagen-Dazs, and Ben & Jerry's. Consider also the increased value that a trademark name such as IBM, Microsoft, or GE brings to even a brand-new product. But don't be misled—trademarks and service marks protect the *names* of products and services, not the products and services themselves.

You can establish a trademark, unlike a patent, without any formal governmental procedure. You acquire ownership of a trademark simply by being the first to use the mark on the goods sold in commerce. It remains your property as long as you keep using it. And keep using it you must, because nonuse for a period of three years or more may constitute abandonment.

The mark should not be too descriptive of the goods on which you use it, and it is best to select a mark that is arbitrary and fanciful with respect to the goods. The reason is that every marketer, including a competitor, has the right to use a descriptive term to refer to its goods. Therefore, no one can secure exclusive rights to descriptive marks.

A trademark owner should also take care to prevent the mark from becoming generic, as happened to Aspirin, Cellophane, Linoleum, and other product names. Thus, it is not proper to refer to, for example, a *xerox*—the correct form of description is a Xerox brand photocopier.

If a name is too descriptive, you cannot register it and competitors may freely use it as is or in a slightly modified form. The more descriptive the mark, the less advertising required to inform consumers what the product is for. But so descriptive a mark enjoys a much lower level of protection.

On the other hand, a highly protectable arbitrary mark (Exxon, Kodak) requires significant expenditures in advertising dollars in order to inform consumers what the product or service associated with the mark actually is. Pick trademarks that are suggestive enough to adequately inform consumers but are not too descriptive. Examples of marks held to be too descriptive include "Beer Nuts," "Chap-Stick," "Vision Center" (for an optical clinic), "Professional Portfolio System" (stock valuations), "5 Minute" (glue that sets in five minutes), "Body Soap" (body shampoo), "Consumer Electronics Monthly," "Light Beer," and "Shredded Wheat." The trademark *Windows* itself has more than once been the subject of legal action in which evidence existed that "windows" was descriptive before Microsoft adopted it.

It is wise to research a proposed new mark to be sure the mark is *clear* before you use it; that is, verify that no one else is already using or has registered the same or a similar mark on the same or similar products. It's confusing to customers and expensive to change a mark and undertake the costs of all new printing, advertising, and promotional materials when you later discover that your mark has previously been used by another company. Moreover, in a due diligence study, either at the time someone invests in your entrepreneurial company, when you make a public offering, or during a sale or merger, you can be sure a trademark search will be conducted. It would be unfortunate, for example, if you've been incorporated in one state for five years under a company name used earlier by another company in another state. If you plan to enter foreign markets, make sure your mark does not mean something unintended in a foreign language.

Registering a Mark

Although trademarks don't have to be registered, there are significant benefits that make it worthwhile. You can register in individual states, or you can obtain a federal registration. A state registration applies only in the particular state that granted the registration and requires only use of the mark in that state. A federal registration applies to all 50 states, but to qualify you must use the mark in interstate or foreign commerce. A distinct advantage of federal registration is that even if you initially use a mark only locally, say in New England, you can establish federal protection in all 50 states. Without a federal registration, you may later be blocked from using your mark in other states if a later user of the same mark, without knowledge of your use of the mark, federally registers it.

Also, you can file an application to register a mark that is not yet in use. After the U.S. Patent and Trademark Office examines the application and determines that the mark is registerable, you must show actual use within six months. The six-month period can be extended if good cause is shown for non-use. Nevertheless, before registration, even before actual use, the mere filing of the application establishes greater rights over others who actually used the mark earlier but did not file an application for registration.

A typical search and registration costs between $1,000 and $3,000 per mark. Given these fairly low costs, entrepreneurial companies regularly seek federal registration for all trade and service marks. Do a search to increase the odds your registration will be successful, since the Trademark Office primarily evaluates two things: is the mark too descriptive, and is it too similar to another already registered mark? If the answer to both these questions is "no," the registration is typically issued about a year after you file the trademark application.

Ownership of a Mark

Be careful with your trademark properties. You cannot simply sell a trademark by itself or transfer it like a desk, car, patent, or copyright. You must sell it together with the business or goodwill associated with the mark, or the mark will be considered abandoned. Further, if you license a mark for use with a product or service, provide for quality control of that product or service. That is, require the licensee to maintain specific quality levels for products or services with which it uses the mark. Exercise that control through periodic inspection, testing, or other monitoring that will ensure that the licensee's product quality is up to a prescribed level.

Claiming ownership of a mark can be an important business decision. When Cuisinart started selling its food processors, it promoted them vigorously under the trademark *Cuisinart*. A good part of the business' success was due to the fact that the machines were sturdily made by a quality-conscious French company, Robot Coupe, that had been making the machines for many years before they became popular among U.S. consumers under the mark Cuisinart. When price competition reared its head, Cuisinart found cheaper sources. Robot Coupe owned no patents and had no other protection. Cuisinart began selling brand X under the name Cuisinart, and a wild fight ensued through the courts and across the pages of major newspapers in the United States, but to no avail. The whole market had been created under the name Cuisinart, and Cuisinart had the right to apply its name to any machine made anywhere by anyone it chose.

Robot Coupe, whose machine had helped create the demand for food processors, was left holding its chopper.

Copyright

Copyrights cover all manner of *writings*, and the term writings is very broadly interpreted. It includes books, advertisements, brochures, spec sheets, catalogs, manuals, parts lists, promotional materials, packaging and decorative graphics, jewelry, fabric designs, photographs, pictures, film and video presentations, audio recordings, architectural designs, and software.

Exact copying is not always required in order to engage in infringement. For example, you can infringe a book without copying every word; the theme may be protected (even though upon successive generalizations the theme will devolve to one of seven nonprotectable basic plots). One example exists in the software area, where using the teachings of a book to write a program has resulted in copyright infringement of the book by the computer program. In another case, a program was infringed by another program even though the second program was written in an entirely different language and for an entirely different computer. Copyright, then, can sometimes be a good source of protection, but be careful: it doesn't generally protect engineering, inventions, marketing or advertising ideas, or business plans. The good news is that a copyright registration is easy to obtain, protection lasts a long time, and it is inexpensive (typically less than $500). But, unless your business is related to some form of the arts (music, movies, books, photography) or software, copyright usually only offers very limited protection because ideas and functionality are not generally protected by copyright.

Copyright registration is not compulsory, but it bestows a few valuable benefits. If the copyright owner has registered the copyright, special damages can be recovered. This can be a real advantage in copyright cases where actual damages can be difficult and expensive to prove or actual damages are limited.

Registration simply requires filling out the proper form and mailing it to the Copyright Office with the proper fee and copies of the work to be registered. Accommodations are made for filing valuable or difficult deposit copies; for example, deposits for large computer programs may consist of only the first and last 25 pages. Further, if the program contains trade secrets, there is a provision for obscuring those areas from the deposit since the Copyright Office's records are public. The Copyright Office doesn't really check to make sure the material is copyrightable; provided the form is filled out correctly, the copyright office will stamp it and you have a registration.

Summing Up

Now consider the question posed at the beginning of this chapter: What parts of a handheld microprocessor-based product are protectable, and how can you protect them? You can cover the circuitry, the programming of the microprocessor, and the overall architecture and functionality of the product by patents and/or trade secrets. All the other software resident in the device could be protected by patent too, and you could protect that same software and the screen displays by copyright. You protect the user's manual for the product by copyright. The company name and the product name could be trademarks. The business and marketing studies and plans surrounding the product's introduction could be trade secrets—at least until the product is formally released. Sources of supplies,

	Patents	**Trade Secrets**	**Trademarks**	**Copyright**
Subject Matter	Inventions and innovation, i.e., new products, features, and functionality	Only what can be kept secret	Names of companies, their products and services	Works of authorship, i.e., the arts and software
Cost	Expensive: $10–20K per patent per country	Depends on the volume of those secrets and the number of employees and consultants; definitely not "free"	Moderate: $1–3K per mark	Inexpensive: less than $500
Government Review	Yes — extensive and mandatory	No	Yes — moderate and optional but a good idea	Yes — but it is a rubber stamp
Term of Protection	On average, 17 years from issuance	Potentially forever — as long as the secret is kept secret	Potentially forever, as long as the mark is used	Long time — 100 years
How Long to Achieve Protection	A fairly long time: 3–5 years	Immediately	Immediate — when the mark is used; registration takes about a year	Immediate, and registration takes only about a month
Pros	Can provide very broad protection even when an infringer didn't know about your patent	No government review; protects things not protectable by patents	Cost is moderate and the odds of achieving a registration can be determined beforehand	Inexpensive and immediate
Cons	Value is commensurate with the claims; high level of government scrutiny; strict time requirements	Cannot be used if the "secret" really isn't; others have the right to discover the secret on their own	Only protects names — not the products or the services themselves	Outside of software and the arts, copyright usually doesn't offer extensive protection

Figure 13.1

IP considerations

lists of customers and ideas for later versions of the product could also be trade secrets. Figure 13.1 summarizes a few key aspects of the different avenues of IP protection.

International Protection for Intellectual Property

Obtaining protection for patents, trademarks, and copyrights in the United States alone is no longer sufficient in the modern arena of international competition and global markets. International protection often needs to be extensive and can be quite expensive, but there are ways to reduce and postpone the expense in some cases. You will want to consider protection in countries where you intend to market the new product or where competitors may be poised to manufacture your product.

A patent in one country does not protect the product in any other country: You must protect a novel product or method by a separate patent in each country. In addition, different countries have different conditions that you must meet to obtain any patent protection. The first and most important restriction is the *time limit* within which you must file an application to obtain a patent in a country or else forever lose your right to do so.

Patent Filing Deadlines

Not all countries are the same with respect to filing deadlines. There is no period of grace in any other country but the United States, and each country has a slightly different view of what constitutes making an invention public. In Japan, for example, public use before the filing of an application bars a patent only if the public use occurred in Japan; in France, any public knowledge of the invention *anywhere* bars the patent.

Thus, whereas the United States allows a business one full year to test market its new product (see the earlier discussion), most other countries require that the patent application be filed *before any public disclosure,* that is, before the owner can begin to determine whether the new product will be even a modest success. Meeting this requirement is not inexpensive, especially when the U.S. dollar is down against the currencies of other major countries.

How to Extend Patent Filing Deadlines

However, there are ways around having to file immediately in all foreign countries. If you file in the United States and then file in another country within one year of that date, the U.S. filing date applies as the filing date for that country. In this way, by filing one application for the invention in the United States, you can preserve your initial U.S. filing date for up to one year and then immediately make the invention public by advertising, published articles, and sales. If within one year the product appears to be a success, you can then file in selected foreign countries, even though the prior public use of the invention would ordinarily bar your filing in those countries. You can even delay up to 20 or even 30 months before incurring the costs of filing in individual countries.

Thus, by filing a special Patent Cooperation Treaty (PCT) patent application in a specially designated PCT office within one year of your U.S. filing, and by designating certain countries, you can preserve your right to file in those countries without further expense for 20 or 30 months after the U.S. filing date. That will provide an additional 8 or 18 months for test marketing the product. This does introduce the extra cost of the PCT application filing, but if you are considering filing in, say, six or more countries, it may be well worth the cost for three reasons.

- It delays the outflow of cash that you may not presently have or may require for other urgent needs.

- It provides for a uniform examination of the patent application.

- If the product proves insufficiently successful, you can decide not to file in any of the countries designated under the PCT and save the cost of all six national application filings.

Another cost-saving feature of international patent practice is the **European Patent Convention** (EPC), which is compatible with a PCT filing and which enables you to file a single European patent application and designate any one or more of the European countries in which you wish the patent to issue.

A number of international treaties affect trademark rights and copyrights as well. A "European" trademark registration is now available, for example, known as a Community Trade Mark (CTM). A single registration will cover the entire European Union (EU)—with the benefit of a single filing, you obtain plenary protection. However, there are certain drawbacks. For example, a single user in any country of the EU could block registration everywhere, and cost considerations make a CTM filing uneconomical unless you seek trademarks in at least three countries. Registration is also now possible simultaneously in the U.S. and other foreign countries via a treaty known as the Madrid Protocol.

Let's now take yet another look at the handheld microprocessor-based product. You filed two U.S. patent applications last week and you did it before anything was made public about the product. The product introduction will occur in a few weeks. You now have nearly a year to file your foreign PCT patent application at a cost of $3,000 to $5,000. It will then be a year and a half after that before you have to file in the specific countries, at a cost between $3,000 and $10,000 per country. But it is not too early to begin planning now. Where will you sell the product? Where will your competitors be located? Also, do you need trademark registrations in any of these countries?

Licensing and Technology Transfer

Sometimes the so-called "boilerplate" provisions of a license or other technology agreement can come back to haunt one or both the parties. A court held that the contractual language "jurisdiction for any and all disputes arising out of or in connection with this agreement is California" was *permissive* rather than mandatory, allowing the defaulting company to file suit in a location remote from the licensor. In other cases, courts have found inconsistencies between various boilerplate provisions, placing important contractual rights in jeopardy. Even the contractual boilerplate is important. Draft it carefully with legal advice and think it through.

Large and small businesses regularly "license out" their intellectual property and also "license in" the intellectual property of others. A **license** is simply a special form of contract or agreement. Each party promises to do or pay something in return for the other party doing or paying something. Contracts that deal with the transfer of technology, or more broadly, intellectual property—patents, trade secrets, know-how, copyrights, and trademarks—are generally called licenses. The licensed property can be anything from the right to use Mickey Mouse on a tee shirt or make copies of the movie *Star Wars*, to the right to operate under the McDonald's name, to manufacture or sell a patented product (such as a handheld microprocessor-based product), or to reproduce, use, or sell a piece of software. Software licenses are just one of the many types of licenses. The basic considerations are the same as for any other license, but specific clauses and language are tailored to the software environment.

Common Concerns and Clauses

The term *license* typically refers to a number of different types of contracts covering intellectual property, including primarily an assignment, an exclusive license, and a nonexclusive license. We'll use this broad reference in this section. An **assignment** actually is an outright sale of the property. Title passes from the owner, the assignor, to the buyer, the assignee.

A license is more like a rental or lease. The owner of the property, the licensor, retains *ownership*; the buyer, the licensee, receives the *right to operate* under the property, be it a patent, trade secret, know-how, copyright, or trademark. An **exclusive license** gives the licensee the sole and exclusive right to operate under the licensed property to the exclusion of everyone else, sometimes even the licensor. A **nonexclusive license**, in contrast, permits the licensee to operate under the licensed property but without any guarantee of exclusivity. The licensor can try to find more licensees and license them, there may be others who are already licensed, and the licensor can also operate under the property.

By definition, an assignment is exclusive since the assignee acquires full right and title to the property. Many licensees prefer an assignment or exclusive license, because they want a clear playing field with no competitors in order to maximize their revenue from the property and justify the license cost. Licensees, though, generally pay more for an exclusive than a nonexclusive license.

Besides the nonexclusive versus exclusive consideration in licensing, there are a lot of other considerations and possibilities. Here are just a few.

- Can the licensee sublicense or transfer the license?
- How long does the license last?

- What happens if there is a dispute concerning the license? Where and how it is settled?
- Are there any guarantees or warranties?
- What happens if improvements are made by the licensee to the property licensed?
- What happens if either the licensee or licensor goes bankrupt?

No consideration in a license, however, is more important than defining the property being licensed.

Defining the Property Being Licensed

Take great care to clearly define the property being licensed. For example, consider the following questions.

- Is it more than one patent, just one patent, or only a part of one patent?
- Is it just the trademark, or the entire corporate image—names, advertising, and promotional scheme and graphics?
- If it concerns copyright, does it cover just the right to copy a book or other printed material in the same print form, or does it include any of the following rights?
  - Translation into another language
  - Adaptation for stage, screen, or video
  - Creation of derivative works
  - Merchandising its characters and events on tee shirts and toys
- If it involves know-how or trade secrets, where are they defined?

Licensees must be sure they are getting what they want and need, and a licensor must make clear the limits of the grant. In a software license, if the grant is only to use the software, not to modify it or merge it with other software, that must be expressly stated.

Limitations on Licenses

A license may have numerous different limitations, including time, the unit quantity, and the dollar value of products or services sold. The license can also be limited geographically. Field-of-use limitations are quite common, too. This limitation restricts the licensee to exploiting the licensed property only in a designated field or market.

Assigning Value to a License

Perhaps the most universal concern in negotiating a license is how to assign a dollar value to intellectual property. First, determine what it cost to acquire or build that property. For example, all the following are hard costs that go into creating a property.

- The research and development cost of coming up with a new invention
- The design cost of coming up with a new trademark or copyrighted work
- The cost of commercializing the invention
- The cost of advertising and promoting the trademark or copyrighted work
- Incidental costs, such as legal costs, engineering costs, and accounting costs

Second, determine how this intellectual property affects the profitability of the product or the business. Can you charge more because the product has a famous name or because of the new features the invention has bestowed on the product? Can you cut your costs because of the new technology of the invention? If so, determine dollar values for those advantages.

You might also determine how much the intellectual property increases gross revenues, whether by opening new markets or acquiring a greater percentage of established markets. Convert all these figures into dollar amounts for valuation.

Royalty Rates

A "typical" royalty rate for a nonexclusive license to a patent, trade secret, or know-how is universally stated to be 5% but that rule is breached as often as it's honored. Nonexclusive license royalty rates in patent licenses can be 10%, 20%, 25%, or even higher. Exclusive license royalty rates tend to be higher because the licensee receives total exclusivity and the licensor is at risk if the licensee does not perform. Exclusive licensors generally demand initial payments for the same reason. In determining a reasonable royalty as a damage award in an infringement suit, courts have considered the following factors.

- The remaining life of the patent
- The advantages and unique characteristics of the patented device over other, prior devices
- Evidence of substantial customer preference for products made under the patent
- Lack of acceptable noninfringing substitutes
- The extent of the infringer's use of the patent
- The alleged profit the infringer made that is credited to the patent

Negotiating License Agreements

In any commercial agreement in which the consideration promised by one party to the other is a percentage of profits or receipts or is a royalty on goods sold, there is nearly always an implied promise of diligent, careful performance and good faith. But licensors generally seek some way to ensure that the licensee will use its best efforts to exploit the property and maximize the licensor's income. One approach is simply to add a clause in which the licensee promises to use its "best efforts." Another approach is to compel certain achievements by the licensee. The license may require a minimum investment in promotion and development of the property, which may be expressed in dollars, human labor hours, or even specific stated goals of performance or sales. Or you can use the simpler approach of a minimum royalty: The licensee pays a certain minimum dollar amount in running royalties annually, whether or not the licensee's sales actually support those royalties—not a pleasant condition for the licensee, but one that provides a lot of peace of mind for the licensor.

Perhaps the best assurance of performance is a competent, enthusiastic licensee. A little preliminary investigation of the licensee (in terms of net worth, credit rating, experience, reputation, manufacturing/sales capability, and prior successes/failures) can assuage a lot of fears and eliminate risky licensees. A *reverter clause*, which evicts the licensee and returns control to the licensor in the event of unmet goals, is the ultimate protection. Often the licensor's greatest concern is that the licensee might now or later sell one or more competing products, leading to a plain conflict of interest. A *noncompetition clause* can prevent this, but antitrust dangers are raised by such clauses, and licensees do not like this constraint on their freedom. Other approaches are safer, such as specified minimum performance levels.

Confidential disclosure clauses are necessary in nearly all license agreements, especially those involving trade secrets, know-how, and patent applications. Such clauses are necessary to protect not only the property that is the subject of the license, but also all the technical, business, financial, marketing, and other information the parties will learn about each other during the license term, and even during negotiations before the license is executed.

Foreign Licenses

The clauses and concerns mentioned pertain generally to all licenses, domestic U.S. as well as foreign. In addition, there are other clauses more peculiarly suited to foreign agreements because of the somewhat different treatment of intellectual property in each country. You can limit the manufacture and use of the product related to the patent, trade secret, or know-how to the United States but permit sales worldwide. You'll define payment in terms of the currency to be used and stipulate who will pay any taxes or transfer charges. The parties must provide for government approval of the transfer of royalties and repatriation of capital.

A license agreement is a special form of contract in which each party promises to do something in exchange for promises by the other party. It is based on a business understanding between the parties and common sense applied to the attainment of business goals. But it is more complex than a normal contract because of the uniqueness of its subject matter, intellectual property—patents, trademarks, copyrights, trade secrets, and know-how. These properties require special action for their creation and maintenance, and great care is necessary in licensing such properties to maximize their returns and prevent their loss.

Software Protection

Protection for computer software has been the subject of debate for many years. There has always been strong opposition to the awarding of patents for inventions embodied in or involving software. Still, software is now commonly patented. Trade secret protection is available, but only if you keep the software secret, and the Copyright Office has a procedure whereby you can register software copyrights and specifically preserve trade secrets contained in the software.

Patents for Software

Broad patent protection is available for software. The scope of patent protection extends beyond the coding or routines, beyond the structure and organization, beyond the user interface and menus of the program, to the broad underlying concept of an algorithm. All manner of software is protectable by patent regardless of how it is perceived—as controlling industrial equipment or processes, as effecting data processes, or as operating the computer itself.

For example, software implementation of steps normally performed mentally may be patentable subject matter. In one case the software implementation of a system that, upon the occurrence of preset conditions, automatically transferred a customer's funds among a brokerage security account, several money funds, and a Visa/checking account was held to be patentable subject matter. Also, a software method of translating from one language to another (Russian to English) was found to be protectable.

Software "law" is really a collection of many different federal and state laws: patent law broadly protecting the functionality of the software; copyright law protecting the code itself, and, to a limited extent, the structure of the code; trademark law protecting the commercial name given the software; trade secret law (in some cases); contract law for licenses associated with the software (click-wrap licenses, shrink-wrap licenses, user agreements, development agreements, and other software agreements); tort law (you want to disclaim warranties in all licenses); and even criminal law. The Digital Millennium Copyright Act further defines what is and what is not permissible in the area of reverse engineering and breaking access protection schemes implemented in software.

Many patents have been issued on software. Here are some examples:

- The "one-click" Amazon patent
- A system for registering attendees at trade shows and conventions
- A securities brokerage cash management system
- An automated securities trading system
- An insurance investment program for funding a future liability
- Software for managing an auto loan
- Software for optimization of industrial resource allocation
- Software for automatically determining and isolating differences between text files (word processing)
- Software for returning to a specified point in a document (word processing)
- Software for determining premiums for insurance against specific weather conditions

Software specific to the operation of the computer itself is patentable, too. For example, patents have been issued on:

- Software for converting a source program to an object program
- Programs that translate from one programming language to another
- A cursor control for a pull-down menu bar
- Software that displays images in windows on the video display
- A computer display with windowing capability

One useful approach to exposing copiers is to include a short routine that does nothing. Then, if a competitor copies the program as is or even codes it in another language, it will be easier to prove infringement if the "do-nothing" routine ends up in the competitor's product. A company desiring to develop a software program that competes with an existing product should employ so-called "clean-room" techniques, wherein the company's programmers are given functional specifications but have no access to the competitor's program or code.

The software may be composed of old routines as long as they are assembled in a different way and produce a different result, for it is well established in patent law that a combination of old parts is patentable if the resulting whole is new. Indeed, as we've seen, most inventions are a new assembly of well-known parts or steps.

Software Copyrights

Copyright protection is applicable to software, though not as broad as patent protection. All forms of computer programs are protectable by copyright—from source code to machine code. And it makes no difference whether the program is an operating system or an applications program: No distinction is made concerning the copyrightability of programs that directly interact with the computer user and those that, unseen, manage the computer system internally. Protection is also afforded microcode or microprograms that are buried in a microprocessor, and even programs embedded in a silicon chip.

Software Trade Secret Protection

You can also protect software through a trade secret approach, separately or in conjunction with patent and copyright protection. Normally, all information disclosed in a published copyrighted work is in the public domain. However, the U.S. Copyright Office fully recognizes the compatibility of copyright and trade secret protection, and its rules provide special filing procedures to protect trade secrets in copyrighted software.

The Internet

Internet activity is placing new pressures on intellectual property practice. Uploading and downloading of copyrighted material on the Internet can be copyright infringement. Copyright infringement has also been found in some cases against bulletin board operators and administrators who have received and stored such material.

Domain names are taking on some of the characteristics of trademarks. Further, there have been some instances where a party has incorporated a well-known name or mark of another in his own domain name, resulting in infringement. And there is now a domain name dispute-resolution system offering trademark owners a less expensive alternative to court when pursuing cybersquatters. Web pages can be fraught with IP issues. Google, for example, was sued by Geico because when a user typed in "Geico" using the Google search engine, Geico's competitors were listed as sponsors. Adware, spyware, pop-up ads, links, and other features of Web sites are regularly litigated but often with unpredictable results. Dual-use software—software that has both legitimate purposes but can also be used to download or traffic in protected content—can also raise IP issues. Licensing via the Internet using so-called "click-wrap" agreements can be problematic if not in accordance with general contract law precepts. Finally, the dust has yet to settle on the question whether a company located in one state can be sued in a distant state merely on account of the company's Web site.

IP Agreements

When you think of protecting a new idea or product, your thoughts probably turn to patents, trade secrets, and copyrights. But the game can be won or lost long before you have the opportunity to establish one of those forms of protection. That's why a fundamental form of protection—confidential disclosure agreements, employment contracts, and consultant contracts—is so important. Whether or not an idea or product is protectable by an exclusive statutory right such as a patent or copyright, before you obtain such protection *keep the basic information confidential* in order to prevent public use or disclosure, which can result in the loss of rights and inspire others to seek statutory rights before you.

Confidential disclosure agreements, employment agreements, and consultant agreements have some things in common. They define the obligations of the parties during the critical early stages of development of a new concept, product, or process. Entrepreneurs often overlook them until it's too late, after the relationship is well underway and a problem has arisen. One of the worst things that can happen in due diligence is to discover a programmer hired by the company as an independent consultant never signed over his copyright in the company's flagship product. For proper protection of the business, work out agreements with employees, consultants, and in some cases suppliers and customers to keep secret all important information of the business and to assign to the business all rights to that information.

Many people think that only technical information can be protected. This is not so. All of the following can be protectable information:

- ◉ Ideas for new products or product lines
- ◉ A new advertising or marketing program
- ◉ A new trademark idea

- ▣ The identity of a critical supplier
- ▣ A refinancing plan

And all these can be even more valuable than the technical matters when it comes to establishing an edge over the competition and gaining a greater market share.

Employment contracts, consultant contracts, and confidential disclosure agreements all should be put in writing and signed before the relationship begins, before any work is done, before any critical information is exposed, and before any money changes hands. A business must not be in such a rush to get on with the project that it ends up without full ownership of the very thing it paid for. And the employees, consultants, or other parties must not be so anxious to get the work that they fail to understand clearly at the outset what they are giving up in undertaking this relationship.

Preparing Employment Contracts

Employment contracts must be fair to both parties and should be signed by all employees, at least those who may be exposed to confidential company matters or may contribute ideas or inventions to the business. They should also be short and readable if they are ever to be effectively enforced.

Employment contracts, like all agreements, must have considerations flowing both ways. If I agree to paint your house for $5,000, my consideration to you is the painting of your house. Your consideration to me is the $5,000. In an employment contract, the consideration from the employee includes all promises to keep secrets secret and to assign all ideas and inventions to the business; the consideration from the business is to employ the employee. Thus, it is best to present these contracts to the prospective employee well before she begins work.

After the job has begun, the consideration will be the employee's "continued" employment, and that sounds a bit threatening. Although "continued" employment is certainly proper consideration, in construing these contracts courts can easily see that the employer usually has the superior bargaining position, and so they generally like to know that when the contract was offered for signature, the employee had a fair opportunity to decline without suffering severe hardship. It is not a good idea to present the employment contract in a packet of pension, hospitalization, and other forms to be signed the day the employee shows up to begin work after having moved the entire family across the country in order to take the job.

Transfer of Employee Rights to Company Innovations

One of the most important clauses in an employment contract is the agreement by the employee to transfer to the company the entire right, title, and interest in and to all ideas, innovations, and creations. These include designs, developments, inventions, improvements, trade secrets, discoveries, writings, and other works, including software, databases, and other computer-related products and processes. The transfer is required whether or not these items are patentable or copyrightable. They should be assigned to the company if they were made, conceived, or first reduced to practice by the employee. This obligation should hold whether the employee was working alone or with others, and whether or not the work was done during normal working hours or on the company premises. So long as the work is within the scope of the company's business, research, or investigation, or it resulted from or is suggested by any of the work performed for the company, its ownership is required to be assigned to the company.

This clause should not seek to compel transfer of ownership for everything an employee does even if it has no relationship to the company's business. For example, an engineer employed to design phased-array radar for an electronics company may invent a new horseshoe or write a book on the history of steeplechase racing. An attempt to compel assignment of ownership of such works under an employment agreement could be seen as overreaching and unenforceable. The same may be true of a clause that seeks to vest in the employer ownership of inventions, innovations, or other works made for a period of time after employment ends or before employment begins.

Ancillary to this transfer or assignment clause is the agreement of the employee to promptly disclose the inventions, innovations, and works to the company or to any person designated by the company, and to assist in obtaining protection for the company, including patents and copyrights in all countries designated by the company. The employee at this point also agrees to execute:

- Patent applications and copyright applications
- Assignments of issued patents and copyright registrations
- Any other documents necessary to perfect the various properties and vest their ownership clearly in the company

If these activities are called for after the employee has left the company, she is still obligated to comply but must be paid for time and expenses.

How Employee Moonlighting Might Compromise Confidentiality

Another important concern is **moonlighting.** While a company that sells CAD/CAM workstations doesn't care if its programmers drive fish delivery trucks on their own time, there are extremely sensitive situations that the company as well as the employee must take care to avoid. In one case, a CAD/CAM company discovered huge telephone charges for various lengthy periods from 3:00 PM to 8:00 PM on most days of the week, including Saturdays and Sundays. The company challenged the telephone bill and found that the calls were indeed made from the company's own phones to a major computer manufacturer many miles away. The computer manufacturer claimed ignorance. But after a lengthy investigation it was discovered that an employee of the company had been hired on a consulting basis by a middle manager at the manufacturer to develop a software system. The employee had been doing his consulting for the computer manufacturer over the telephone lines from his computer terminal while sitting at his desk in his company office. The employee was not shortchanging the company as far as hours were concerned; he was working long hours to make up for his moonlighting, and the software he was developing was not in the company's CAD/CAM area. But the revelation was chilling. The mere awareness that an information line existed between this giant computer manufacturer and the company, and what might have transpired over that line, haunted the company's officers and managers for some time afterward.

> Be careful if employees use so-called "open source" code. Such code is indeed open but it's not free. Often, the originator of the code requires that any patents relating to products containing any open source code in it be freely licensed to all. In due diligence, one question that might be asked of your company is "Was any open source code used in your products?" Expect a frown by the investors if the answer is "yes."

To prevent this, the employee should agree in the employment contract that during employment by the company there will be no engagement in any employment or activity in which the company is now or may later become involved, nor will there be moonlighting on the company's time or using the company's equipment or facilities.

Noncompetition Clauses

A closely related notion is a **noncompetition provision** whereby the employee agrees not to compete during his employment by the company and for some period after leaving the company's employ. This is a more sensitive area. It may be perfectly understandable that a company does not want its key salesperson, an officer, a manager, or the head of marketing or engineering to move to a new job with a competitor and have the inside track on his ex-employer's best customers, new product plans, manufacturing techniques, or new marketing program. But the courts do not like to prevent a person from earning a livelihood. They do not compel a lifelong radar engineer, for example, to turn down a job with a competitor in the same field and instead take a job designing cellular phones.

Courts in different jurisdictions take different approaches to noncompetes. In New Hampshire, for example, an ex-employee cannot be prohibited from soliciting *all* the employers' customers. Instead, solicitation is prohibited only to the customers the ex-employee had contact with during his employ. In contrast, neighboring Massachusetts may uphold noncompete agreements that prohibit solicitation of all the company's customers irrespective of whether the ex-employee had contact with them. That being said, Massachusetts's courts have completely invalidated noncompetes when, for example, the employee changed jobs within the company and was not required to execute a new noncompete.

However, the higher up and the more important a person is in the operation of the company, the greater the probability that that person will be prevented from competing if the employment agreement provides for it. Officers, directors, founders, majority stockholders, and other key personnel have had such provisions enforced against them, but even then the scope of the exclusion must be fair and reasonable in terms of both time and geography. A few months, a year, or even two years could be acceptable, depending on how fast the technology and market is moving. Worldwide exclusion might be acceptable for a salesperson who sells transport planes. In the restaurant business, a few miles might be all that is necessary. A contract that seeks to extend the exclusion beyond what's fair will not be enforced. In general, courts will very carefully scrutinize noncompete agreements.

One way to ensure that an ex-employee does not compete is to allow the company to employ the person on a consultant basis over some designated period of time. In this way the employee's involvement in critical information areas can gradually be phased out, so that by the time the employee is free to go to a competitor there is no longer a threat to the company, and at the same time the employee has been fairly compensated.

Bear in mind, however, that even if ex-employees are free to compete, they are not free to take with them (in their memories or in recorded form) any trade secrets or any information confidential or proprietary to the company, or to use it or disclose it in any way. To reinforce this, the employment contract should provide that the employee will not, during employment by the company or at any time thereafter, disclose to others or use for her own benefit or for the benefit of others any trade secrets or any confidential or proprietary information pertaining to any businesses of the company—technical, commercial, financial, sales, marketing, or otherwise. The restriction could also protect such information pertaining to the business of any of the company's clients, customers, consultants, licensees, affiliates, and the like.

Along with this, the employment contract should provide that all documents, records, models, electronic storage devices, prototypes, and other tangible items representing or embodying company property or information are the sole and exclusive property of the company and must be surrendered to the company no later than the termination of employment, or at any earlier time upon request of the company. This is an important provision for both the employer and employee to understand. In some states, the law imposes serious criminal sanctions and fines for the removal of tangible trade secret property.

Preventing Employee Raiding

Another potential area of conflict is employee raiding, the hiring away of employees by an ex-employee who is now employed by a competitor or who has founded a competing business. This is a particularly sensitive situation when the ex-employee holds a position of high trust and confidence and was looked up to by the employees she is now attempting to hire. And it is particularly damaging when the employees being recruited are critical to operations, because of either their expertise or their sheer numbers. In all circumstances such an outflow of employees is threatening, because of the potential loss to a competitor of trade secrets and know-how. You can address this with a clause prohibiting an employee, during her employment period and for some period thereafter, from hiring away fellow employees for a competing enterprise.

Employee Ownership of Copyright

One of the most hazardous areas of ownership is the title to copyrights. If a copyrighted work is created or authored by an employee, the company automatically owns the copyright. But the employee must be a bona fide employee. If a dispute arises over ownership between the company and the author, the courts will seek to determine whether the author was provided a full work week, benefits, withholdings, unemployment insurance, worker's compensation, and an office or workspace. If the author was anything less than a full employee, the copyright for the work belongs to the person, not to the company.

This means that if the company hires a part-time employee, a consultant, a friend, or a moonlighter, when the nonemployee completes the software system that will revolutionize the industry and bring income cascading to the enterprise, the employee, not the company, will own the copyright. The company will own the embodiment of the system that the employee developed for the company, but the employee will own the right to reproduce, copy, and sell the system over and over again. It has happened. A company that spent hundreds of thousands of dollars to develop a software system owned the finished product but not the copyright in the product. The nonemployee owned the copyright and had the right to reproduce the product without limit and sell it to those who most desire it—typically the company's competitors and customers.

This is a chilling scenario but one that is easy to avoid with a little forethought. Simply get it in writing. Before any work starts, payment changes hands, or plans are revealed, *have the proposed author sign a written agreement* specifying that, whether or not the author is subsequently held to be an employee or a nonemployee, all right, title, and interest in any copyrightable material is assigned to the company. The lack of such a clear understanding in writing can wreck great dreams, ruin friendships and partnerships, and hamstring businesses to the point of insolvency while the parties fight over who owns the bunny rabbit, the book, the software, the poster, or the videotape on how to be a successful entrepreneur.

Rights of Prior Employees

Here is another issue to consider under employment contracts. When a new employee is to be hired, obtain a copy of the employment contract with the last employer or the last few employers to determine whether this employee is free to work for your company now in the capacity he seeks. Prior employers have rights, too, that can conflict, rightly or wrongly, with the employee's new employment.

Consultant Contracts

Consultant contracts should contain provisions similar to those in an employment contract, along with some additional ones. A consultant agreement should clearly define the task for which you've hired the consultant—for example, to research a new area; analyze or solve a problem; design or redesign a product; set up a production line; or assist in marketing, sales, management, technical, or financial matters. The agreement should show:

- Why the consultant was hired
- What the consultant is expected to do
- What the consultant may be exposed to in the way of company trade secrets and confidential and proprietary information
- What the consultant is expected to assign to the company in the way of innovations, inventions, patents, and copyrights

A company hiring a consultant wants to own the result of whatever the consultant was hired to do, just as in the case of an employee. But a consultant's stock in trade is her expertise and ability to solve problems swiftly and elegantly in a specific subject area. Draw sharp lines around what the consultant will and will not assign to give both of you peace of mind.

Consulting relationships by their nature can expose each of the parties to a great deal of the other party's trade secrets and confidential and proprietary information. The company can protect itself with clear identification of the pertinent information and by employing the usual safeguards for trade secrets. It also must limit disclosure to the consultant to what is necessary to do the job, and also limit the consultant's freedom to use the information in work for others and to disseminate it. Consultants must protect themselves in the same way to prevent the client company from misappropriating their special knowledge, problem-solving approaches, and analytical techniques.

An often overlooked area is the ownership of notes, memos, and failed avenues of investigation. False starts and failures can be as important as the solution, especially to competitors. Related to this is the question of the ownership of the raw data. Raw data may be extremely valuable in its own right, but it can also be a way to easily reconstruct the end result of the consultant's work, like a market survey.

Confidential Disclosure Agreements

Whenever you are going to reveal an idea, information, an invention, or any knowledge of peculiar value, have the receiving party sign a **confidential disclosure agreement** (aka a *nondisclosure agreement*) for your protection. The disclosure may be necessary for any of the following reasons:

- To interest a manufacturer in taking a license to make and sell a new product
- To hire a consultant to advise in a certain area
- To permit a supplier to give an accurate bid

◉ To allow a customer to determine whether or not she wants a product or wants a product modified

Disclosure agreements are important not only to protect the knowledge or information itself, but also to preserve valuable related rights such as *domestic and foreign patent rights*. These agreements should be short and to the point.

Basically, the recipient should agree to keep confidential all information disclosed. *Information* in this context means all trade secrets and all proprietary and confidential information, whether tangible or intangible, oral or written, and of whatever nature (for example, technical, sales, marketing, advertising, promotional, merchandising, financial, or commercial).

The recipient should agree to receive all such information in confidence and not to use or disclose it without your express written consent. Make it clear that no secrecy obligation is incurred for any information proven in the public domain.

Limit the receiver to disclosing the information to only those of its employees who need to know in order to carry out the purposes of the agreement and who have obligations of secrecy and confidentiality to the receiver. Further, the receiver should agree that all its employees to whom any information is communicated are obligated under written employment agreements to keep the information secret. The receiver should also represent that he will exercise the same standard of care in safeguarding this information as he does for his own, and in no event less than *a reasonable standard of care*. This latter phrase is necessary because some businesses have no standard of care or a very sloppy attitude toward even their own important information.

Provide for the return of all tangible embodiments of the confidentially disclosed information, including drawings, blueprints, designs, parameters of design, monographs, specifications, flow charts, sketches, descriptions, and data. You can also include a provision preventing the receiving party from entering a competing business or introducing a competing product or service in the area of the disclosed information. The receiver can request a time limit, after which she is free to disclose or use the information. Such a time period could extend from a few months to a number of years, depending on the life cycle of the information, tendency to copy, competitive lead time, and other factors present in a particular industry. Strong, clear language will establish that no license or any other right, express or implied, to the information is given by the agreement.

While such confidential disclosure agreements between the discloser and receiver are the ideal, they are not always obtainable. The receiver may argue that no such agreement is necessary, saying in effect, "Trust me." Or the receiver may flatly refuse on the grounds that it is against her policy. Some large corporations turn the tables and demand that the discloser of information sign the company's own standard *nonconfidential* disclosure agreement before the disclosure of any information.

Under a nonconfidential disclosure agreement, often referred to as an *idea submission agreement,* the discloser gives up all rights to the information except as covered by a U.S. patent or copyright. Outside those protections, the receiver is free to use, disclose, or do whatever he wishes with the information. This is not due simply to arrogance or orneriness. A large corporation has many departments and divisions where research and development of new ideas is occurring unknown to other areas of the corporation. In addition, in a number of cases courts have held corporations liable for misappropriation of ideas and information when no written agreement existed, and even where a *nonconfidential* disclosure agreement purported to free the receiver from any restriction against dissemination and use of the idea.

If you cannot reach agreement or if the receiver makes a counteroffer of a non-confidential disclosure agreement, you must decide whether to keep the idea under the mattress or take a chance on the honesty of the receiver. In the latter case you are wise to reduce the initial disclosure to a minimum, in order to cut your losses should a careless or unscrupulous receiver make public or misappropriate the idea.

A middle ground that courts have recognized is an implied confidential relationship evidenced by the actions of the parties. In one case, a letter soliciting a receiver's interest in a particular field and indicating that the matter was confidential resulted in a face-to-face meeting between the discloser and receiver, where the full idea was revealed. Later, when the receiver came out with a product using the idea, the discloser sued and won. The letter set up a confidential relationship that the receiver did not reject, but rather accepted by meeting with the discloser and accepting the idea without any comment or exclusion. The letter was not signed by the receiver, but it bound the company nevertheless under the totality of the circumstances.

These basic forms of protection—employment contracts, consultant contracts, and confidential disclosure agreements—need not be complex or lengthy, but they are essential at the earliest stages of idea generation to protect and preserve for the business some of its most valuable and critical property.

CONCLUSION

Consider now again the hypothetical handheld microprocessor-based product. Suppose you need a supply agreement for the microprocessor itself, a consultant to write the software, and a manufacturing house to deliver the main circuit board to you for final assembly. A license to a patent covering a component you want to incorporate in the product is required, and you also need a designer to develop your Web site that will advertise the product for sale. Confidentiality concerns probably exist with respect to all the resulting agreements, as do ownership and noncompetition issues.

Time passes and the product is an unqualified success. Have any of your ex-employees, suppliers, consultants, or vendors begun competing unfairly? With your own IP—patents, copyrights, trademarks, and trade secrets—in place, you have a good chance at protecting your market share. And, with your written agreements clearly spelling out the ownership, noncompetition, and confidentiality issues, you further protect your valuable IP.

Or, did you rely on the wrong form of IP protection, or forget to address IP ownership issues and/or the IP of others? Did your provisional patent application lack sufficient details? Did you fail to meet a deadline imposed by law, cut out certain types of protection because of budget constraints, or fail to conduct the necessary searches to make sure, for example, your trademark was clear? Now, not only might the people you once trusted compete, others too might start eroding your market share, or, worse, levy a charge of IP infringement against you.

One premise of this book is that entrepreneurship can be taught. IP, being synonymous with entrepreneurship, too can be learned. IP doesn't guarantee product sales or the success of a new service but, without it, the entrepreneur has little chance of fending off the inevitable competition.

Reflection Point

1. Does your business have IP? If not, why not? What is your strategy to protect your IP?

2. Does your new venture potentially infringe on anybody else's IP?

3. Do you have IP that can be patented? When will you file (remember that you have to file within one year of initial public disclosure in the U.S., and prior to any disclosure in many other countries)?

4. What "trade secrets" underlie your business? How do you plan to protect these secrets?

5. Will you trademark your company name or symbol? What about your product name? Will you use copyright protection at all?

6. Do you need to seek international IP protection? When and how?

Your Thoughts...

YOUR OPPORTUNITY JOURNAL

☐

Use the U.S. Patent Office searchable database (www.uspto.gov/patft/index.html) to look at issued patents and published applications in the area of your interest. How many patents have been filed? How are the applications written? Is this something you can do on your own or do you need a lawyer's assistance?

WEB EXERCISE

☐

[1] http://news.com.com/Beatles+judge+finds+iTunes+nothing+to+get+hung+about/2100-1027_3-6069490.html.

NOTES

☐

CASE

Cadence Design Systems and Avant! (B)

Avant! Pays Fines and Legal Costs of Six Current and Former Employees August 2001[1]

In connection with the plea agreement, Avant! agreed to pay a fine of $27.0 million and to pay restitution in an amount to be determined by the court. On July 25, 2001, the court fixed the total restitution amount to be paid to Cadence at $195.4 million, any unpaid portion of which accrued interest at the statutory rate of 10% beginning July 25, 2001. Avant! recognized the resulting expense of $222.4 million in the second quarter of 2001. During the third quarter of 2001, Avant! paid the $27.0 million fine and made restitution payments to Cadence totaling $170.0 million. Avant! made a final payment of $26.5 million to Cadence on October 3, 2001, to conclude payment of the restitution owed to Cadence. These payments included $1.1 million of interest.

As part of the settlement, Avant! agreed to indemnify all of the current and former Avant! employees named in Exhibit 13.1, with the exception of Mr. Cheng, for the fines assessed against them, and indemnify them for the taxes levied as a result of this indemnification. Avant! recognized the resulting expense of $14.1 million in the second quarter of 2001. Under the applicable law, Avant! was authorized to pay the defense expenses and fines of its officers, directors, and employees if the Avant! board found that "the person acted in good faith and in a manner the person reasonably believed to be in or not opposed to the best interests of the corporation, and, with respect to any criminal action or proceeding, had no reasonable cause to believe the person's conduct was unlawful." The Avant! board, having determined that these criteria were met, paid, or agreed to pay, the amounts shown in Exhibit 13.1 in litigation expenses and fines for the listed individuals in connection with the Santa Clara criminal action.

EXHIBIT 13.1			
Name	**Fines(1)**		**Litigation and Related Expenses(1)**
Gerald C. Hsu	$	2,700,000	$ 518,019
Stephen Wuu	$	2,700,000	$ 1,813,009
Y.Z. Liao	$	2,700,000	$ 1,044,457
Eric Cho	$	100,000	$ 617,685
Leigh Huang	$	100,000	$ 866,765
Eric Cheng		—	$ 1,410,100(2)
Michael Tsai		—	$ 502,402

(1) Amounts do not include amounts to indemnify each of the individuals for any actual tax liability attributable to amounts received from or paid on their behalf by Avant!.

(2) Amounts include litigation expenses related to both the Santa Clara criminal action and the Avant!/Cadence litigation.

This case was prepared by Professor William Bygrave. Funding was provided by the Arthur M. Blank Center for Entrepreneurship. © Copyright Babson College, 2006, All rights reserved.

[1] Excerpted from Synopsys 10K filing with the SEC. www.synopsys.com/corporate/invest/final8-K_73002.pdf.

On July 25, 2001, Eric Cheng, Y.Z. Liao, and Stephen Wuu resigned from Avant!. Eric Cho, Leigh Huang, and Mike Tsai were former Avant! employees.

All told, Avant! engaged 10 high-powered law firms and paid them $30 million; in contrast, the government case was initially led by Finklestein on his own; later, he was joined by two associates.

Securities Class Action Claims (March–April 2001)[2]

On December 15, 1995, Paul Margetis and Helen Margetis field a securities fraud class action complaint against Avant! in the United States District Court for the Northern District of California. This lawsuit alleged securities laws violations, including omissions and/or misrepresentations of material facts related to the events and transactions which are the subject of the claims contained in Cadence's civil lawsuit against Avant!. In addition, on May 30, 1997, Joanne Hoffman field a securities fraud class action in the United States District Court for the Northern District of California on behalf of purchasers of Avant!'s stock between March 29, 1996 and April 11, 1997, the date of the filing of a criminal complaint against Avant! and six of its employees and/or directors. The plaintiffs alleged that Avant! and its officers misled the market as to the likelihood of the criminal indictment and as to the validity of the Cadence allegations.

In March 2001, Avant! reached agreement with counsel for the plaintiff classes in both securities actions for a voluntary resolution of the cases. Under that agreement, Avant! paid a total of $47.5 million in exchange for dismissal of the actions and a release of claims by members of the classes. The District Court entered an order on June 22, 2001, that gave final approval to the settlement and dismissed the litigation with prejudice. Avant! paid the full settlement amount of $47.5 million in April 2001. Avant! recognized the settlement as an expense in the fourth quarter of 2000.

Synopsys to Acquire Avant!, December 2001[3]

Mountain View, California—An acquisition that promises to fundamentally alter the EDA landscape unfolded Monday (Dec. 3) as Synopsys Inc. announced its intent to purchase Avant! Corp. Valued at $830 million at current stock prices, the acquisition is by far the largest in EDA history—and likely the riskiest from a legal and financial point of view.

If successfully completed, the acquisition will give Synopsys most of the IC design flow for "power users," and could possibly unseat Cadence as the EDA market revenue leader. But Synopsys will inherit a civil lawsuit in which Cadence is seeking up to a billion dollars from Avant!, and so far, Cadence is showing no inclination to settle.

"The bottom line is that this merger is a bold move that instantly puts us in the leadership position in IC design automation," said Aart de Geus, chief executive officer

[2] Ibid.

[3] *EE Times*, December 3, 2001. www.eet.com/story/OEG20011203S0077.

of Synopsys. "It instantly brings the best front- and back-end design tools together under a single roof."

The acquisition will bring to an end the most controversial chapter in EDA history —the long-running criminal and civil prosecution for source-code theft. Gerry Hsu, the former Avant! president and CEO who pled "no contest" to several criminal charges this spring, will not join Synopsys but will probably receive a payment of around $40 million. [As it turned out, actual payment to Hsu was $43 million; it was part of the $177 million in severance and other payments made by Synopsys to Avant! employees and board members.[4]]

"This merger opens up a new chapter in the history of the EDA industry," said Paul Lo, president of Avant!. "Two acknowledged leaders are joining forces to become what we believe will soon be the preeminent supplier in the EDA business."

Cadence and Avant! Settle Lawsuit, November 2002[5]

Chip-design software maker Cadence Design Systems agreed to settle its civil lawsuit against rival Avant! for $265 million, closing the chapter on a long-running case that centered on stolen trade secrets.

Under the terms of the settlement, the two companies and individuals named in the suit have agreed to dismiss all pending claims and counterclaims, which date back to 1994. In addition, they agreed to enter into reciprocal licenses covering the intellectual property at the heart of the lawsuit.

The money Avant! must pay in this latest civil settlement is in addition to the amount it was ordered to pay in the criminal case, bringing its total payments to more than $460 million.

Synopsys, a large chip-design software maker that purchased Avant! in June [2002], will pay the money out of an insurance policy from Illinois National Insurance Company, a policy it bought upon completion of the acquisition. Under the terms of the settlement, Cadence will accept $265 million in two installments; $20 million will be paid on or before November 22, and $245 million will be paid on or before December 16.

When it acquired Avant! Synopsys took out an insurance policy to limit its financial exposure in any future settlement of Cadence's civil lawsuit against Avant!. Synopsys paid a one-time $85 million premium for the policy with a $250 million deductible. If the settlement was above the $250 million deductible, Illinois National would pay the additional amount up to a maximum of $500 million (i.e., a total settlement of $750 million). Hence if the settlement was less than $335 million ($250 million deductible plus $85 million premium), Illinois National would make a profit. As the settlement was for $265 million, Illinois National made a profit of $70 million on the policy. So the settlement cost Synopsys $335 million ($265 million

---

[4] Cadence vs. Avant! Case #E-61. Stanford University Graduate School of Business.

[5] CNET News.com, November 14, 2002. http:/news.zdnet.com/2100-9595_22-965890.html.

settlement minus $15 million from Illinois National plus $85 million premium for the policy).

Synopsys's total cost of acquiring Avant! was approximately $1.25 billion.[6]

Preparation Question

1. What could Cadence have done to better protect its intellectual property?

[6] Synopsys faces unusual acquisition costs." *The Wall Street Journal.* June 5, 2002.

(*Source*: Courtesy Yankee Candle Co.)

ENTREPRENEURIAL GROWTH

While entrepreneurship begins with an opportunity, sustainable success comes from creating an organization that can execute on that opportunity. But as organizations start to gain more sales and customers, managing growth becomes a critical challenge that if not handled appropriately can lead to venture failure.

Why do entrepreneurs fail to manage growth? Often they have limited time and resources to spend on organization building. They're constantly fighting fires in the business's day-to-day operations or they're chasing too many opportunities, leaving little time for planning. Entrepreneurs without organizational or business skills may retreat into something they do know and are more comfortable doing, like product development. They may hire salespeople or engineers to handle sales and technical support before bringing in someone with organizational and business skills. But eventually growth overwhelms the operation. In order to survive and continue to grow, entrepreneurs need to pay attention to the requirements of a firm in its growth phase. They cannot neglect the planning and preparation required for long-term success.

Many believe that entrepreneurial skills and managerial skills are mutually exclusive and operate at different phases of the firm's life. Entrepreneurial skills *are* critical during the venture's launch, while managerial skills become increasingly important thereafter.

This chapter written by Donna J. Kelley and Edward P. Marram.

CHAPTER 14

➤ The objectives of any entrepreneur wishing to create a sustainable enterprise should include building an efficiently operating organization while developing an organization-wide entrepreneurial capability.

Yet the organization will need to retain its entrepreneurial spirit as it grows. It can't function over the long term by simply managing what it has previously created. Customer needs inevitably change. Competitors eventually offer superior products or services. Economic conditions, politics, technology, and a variety of other external shifts will create a constantly changing opportunity set that leads to new possibilities while rendering old opportunities obsolete.

It's no wonder that half the businesses started today will not be around in eight years. And far fewer firms will continue to grow and stay profitable—as few as one in seven.[1] What distinguishes those firms that not only survive, but thrive? Entrepreneurs and leaders who build an efficient operating organization while maintaining the organization's entrepreneurial ability.

Making the Transition from Startup to Growth

During startup, the business opportunity is taking shape, but as yet there are no significant sales. The founders are acquiring resources and organizing initial operations—and they do everything. At the other end, in the mature stage and beyond, the business must deal with the problems of a well-established organization. Systems and structures can become entrenched and the culture can impede efforts to grow further, leading to decline. In this chapter we look at how entrepreneurs operate once they've started and, we assume, their companies have reached a point of initial success with their opportunity. The primary task beyond this startup stage is to create a professional organization capable of managing its current growth, while setting the stage for continued entrepreneurship to ensure the organization can sustain growth as it matures and avoid decline.

The chapter is organized around four driving forces in the growth stages: leadership, the opportunity domain, resources and capabilities, and execution. Before we get to this discussion, let's review a key decision every entrepreneur must consider beyond startup: whether to sell, maintain, or grow the venture.

Looking Forward: The Choice to Grow, or Not, . . . or Sell

Figure 14.1 presents post-startup options for an entrepreneurial business. Each option presents at least two alternatives for the founder.

If a new venture is successful in generating sales, entrepreneurs can reap capital gains by finding a suitable buyer. If the entrepreneur decides to sell the business, she may stay with the acquiring company, or leave and either seek other employment, or start another company. The first situation is perhaps the most common; the entrepreneur sells to reap a capital gain, but stays on with the organization for several years to help in the transition. Jon Hirschtick, the founder of SolidWorks (the case we covered in Chapter 10) sold his company to Dassault Systemes of France in 1997 and remained with the company for five years. The buyer wants the entrepreneur to stay, in order to reduce risk.

A typical acquisition might give the entrepreneur one-third of the price in cash, one-third in the acquiring company's stock (vested over the term of an employment contract), and one-third in an earn-out which is tied to the performance of the acquired company. If the acquired company meets certain milestones, the entrepreneur earns the full amount of the earn-out. If it falters, the entrepreneur's earn-out is at risk. Thus, the entrepreneur has an incentive to work hard after the acquisition takes place.

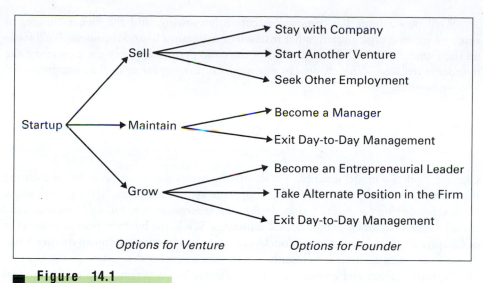

Figure 14.1

Post-startup options

If a company is publicly traded, on the other hand, it is easier for the entrepreneur to sell and leave. Jim Clark, who co-founded Silicon Graphics in 1981, sold his remaining interest in the company in 1994 and left. He subsequently went on to cofound Netscape with Marc Andreessen. When selling a business, the founders often have contractual agreements to consider, like restrictions on their activities if they exit; for example, noncompete clauses may place limitations on their next venture. If you sell your business, the acquirer will prohibit you from starting a new, directly competing business.

When maintaining a business, the entrepreneur is faced with two basic choices. He can continue to lead the organization or exit day-to-day operations. For example, he can bring in someone else to lead the organization and himself take another position, as Don Mitchell did. Mitchell founded MicroE, a manufacturer of optical encoders for the computer industry, in 1994. Five years later, after raising $5.7 million in venture capital and leading the company to sales of over $11 million, he decided to bring in an outside CEO. He recruited Ray Sansouci, a 52-year-old Harvard MBA with international experience in automation technologies, to take over as CEO, while he—Mitchell—stayed on as CTO. With Sonsouci at the helm, the company continued on its rapid growth path—sales nearly doubled the next year—and Mitchell was free to focus on what he loved and did best.[2]

While our focus is on growing a business, it's true that many entrepreneurs choose to operate lifestyle businesses that pay enough salary for them to have a comfortable lifestyle, with less risk and complexity. These firms usually aren't large or successful enough to be sold, and the entrepreneurs don't have the desire to grow the business. One of the authors of this chapter, for example, was working with an ergonomics consulting company that hired her to grow the business. They explored a number of options, but growth would mean hiring more employees and moving out of the founder's basement. The founder decided he preferred the flexibility, lower risk, and greater control associated with staying small. After two engineers who had worked with him part-time finished college and moved on to other jobs, he maintained the business as a one-person operation, outsourcing any additional expertise, and keeping his commute to "a walk downstairs." What this example illustrates is that the decision to grow (or not) is multifaceted. It should take into account not only the ability to grow (the company could capture more customers if it were larger), but the desires of the entrepreneur.

We'll now assume the company is currently growing, and the owner chooses to sustain a growing organization rather than sell or maintain a lifestyle business. We'll focus on the founder as CEO, although most of the concepts also apply in the case where the founder is replaced. We next present our model of driving forces in the entrepreneurial firm's growth stages.

A Model of Driving Forces of Growth

Chapter 2 offers a model describing three driving forces that must be in balance during the startup process: the entrepreneur, the opportunity, and resources. In the growth stage, these three driving forces shift to *leadership, the opportunity domain*, and *organizational resources and capabilities,* as Figure 14.2 illustrates. While the business plan is at the core of Chapter 2's model, the growth model has *execution* as its core and fourth driving force. These forces must all come into balance and remain so during the growth phase.

Both the startup and growth models are affected by uncertainty and environmental conditions. Whether at startup or in its growth phase, an organization is unable to predict many events, such as a competitor introducing a superior product soon after launch, or customers adopting a product much more slowly than anticipated. Environmental conditions, such as economic cycles, the regulatory environment, and technological change can also affect a venture's viability and success. In all phases of its life, the organization will need to balance the driving forces amid conditions it cannot control.

Stakeholders have the largest impact on a firm's growth potential. **Stakeholders** are those having a stake in the venture's success, like investors, customers, suppliers, and employees. As a new venture grows, it accumulates a range of insiders and outsiders who become increasingly dependent on the firm and exert heavy influence on its decisions. The organization will need to balance the current needs of these stakeholders with its need to think about how to sustain itself over the long term.

When Kodak, for example, announced in 2004 that it would stop selling film-based cameras and switch to digital photography, it reduced its workforce and threatened its long-standing relationship with Walgreen drugstores, which relied heavily on sales of Kodak film cameras. The announcement also angered Kodak's stockholders, who thought

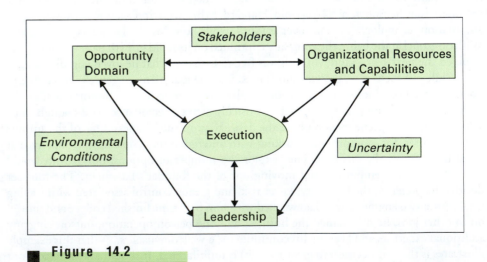

Figure 14.2

Driving forces of growth

that milking the core business would provide them with higher dividends. Kodak, however, foresaw the end of film and knew it needed to make a huge commitment that couldn't wait and couldn't be accomplished by appeasing stakeholders who had more to gain from business as usual. By the end of 2004, Kodak had shipped nearly five million digital cameras and passed Sony as the leading U.S. digital camera vendor.

The Growth Process

Figure 14.3 shows the challenges associated with the four driving forces outlined in Figure 14.2, and the key imperatives the firm needs to address to achieve overall balance among the forces.[3] The table differentiates between a venture's early and later growth stages. This distinction is important, because the problems facing a company at an early stage of growth are different from those it faces later, and therefore the decisions and solutions will change. By knowing where the organization stands in the life cycle, an entrepreneur can tell which problems are normal and which require special attention. For example, while an entrepreneur needs to focus her firm's strategy during early growth, she will need to look toward expansion in later growth stages.

Execution

The growth model has execution at its core. Execution depends on the other components in the model—leadership, the opportunity domain, and organizational resources and capabilities—but it has the most direct link to profits. The startup is commonly loosely managed, with few controls, very little performance assessment, and a lack of responsibility for outcomes. It often puts an emphasis on sales over profits, with chasing a new customer taking priority over considering the costs of serving that customer, for example. Growth will soon overwhelm operations, however, leaving the company capable only of reacting to inventory outages, overdue collections, diminishing cash flows, and delivery restrictions by suppliers. In addition, uncontrolled growth can lead to poor coordination between activities such as sales and inventory planning.

Without an adequate system of controls, the company can't optimize its decision making and prevent the waste of resources. One startup, for example, had a printing and paper supplier that charged the company more than three times the normal price for copy paper. The owner of the printing business told an employee (who later relayed the remark to the owners of the startup), "They're too caught up in their own growth to notice."

With only so many hours in the day and so many days in a week, it is hard to step back, develop, and implement new processes, hire and train people, and ensure everything functions adequately. Yet these control tasks are essential to creating an organization that can continue to thrive and grow. Therefore, your most critical first task in transitioning beyond startup is to create an efficient operation. This will eventually overlap with your efforts to sustain an entrepreneurial organization, but the firm will first need to catch up to its burgeoning growth—then it can set the stage for creating new sources of growth in the future. The key objectives for a control system should be to institute controls, track performance, and manage cash.

Instituting Controls

Your first **control system** in early growth should be relatively simple. The organization should quickly and easily be able to get it up and running and train people to use it.

	Early Growth		Later Growth	
	Challenges	**Key Imperatives**	**Challenges**	**Key Imperatives**
Execution	Emphasis on sales over profits. Reactive orientation (fighting fires). Rapid growth overwhelms operations. Inadequate systems and planning leads to inefficiency, poor control, and quality problems. Informal communication and processes create confusion and lack of accountability.	Develop basic systems to manage cash, control receivables, inventory, and payables. Develop simple budgets and metrics to track performance and expenditures.	Profit orientation can constrain later growth. Organization outgrows initial systems and planning structure. Difficulties with coordination and control as decentralization increases.	Upgrade and formalize systems for control and planning for the longer term/future — before they are needed. Proactive planning replaces reactive approach. Maintain balance between control and creativity; ensure processes don't constrain innovation.
Opportunity Domain	Tendency to over-commit, pursue many diverse opportunities. Lack of clear strategy for how the venture competes.	Develop a focused strategy that leverages the company's unique value. Maintain the consistency of this strategy with all company activities (such as product development, marketing, operations).	Original opportunity domain may provide fewer opportunities for growth. Competitive pressures and changes in the market may threaten current businesses.	Establish competitive uniqueness and move beyond "one-product" orientation. Expansion into the periphery with products and markets. Also, develop strategy for future that provides new momentum and long-run effectiveness. Anticipate/respond to changes in industry/market environment.
Organizational Resources and Capabilities	Financial and human resources constrained as rapidly expanding sales require more people and financing. Generalized skills increasingly incapable of handling increased complexity.	Get profitability and cash flow in check. Tap early financing sources. Hire people with specialized expertise. Protect intellectual property.	Insufficient resources for growth.	Maintain bootstrap mentality. Manage cash for internal growth resources. Secure growth financing.
Leadership	Company outgrows entrepreneur's abilities. Entrepreneur unable to delegate. Internally promoted managers often lack adequate skills.	Start the process of delegating responsibility to others. Promote/hire functional managers/supervisory-level managers. Invest in management training.	Management lacks the managerial sophistication required for the increasing size and complexity of a growing organization. Inadequate communication throughout organization. Tensions between professional management and entrepreneur, between new and old managers and employees.	Recruit key professional management talent. Build fully functioning Board of Directors. Ensure leadership team shares in strategic planning and preserves entrepreneurial capability. Create decentralized reporting structure.

■ Figure **14.3**

Challenges and key imperatives for managing growth

With a simple system, there's less that can go wrong, and as employees and managers get accustomed to control practices, you can upgrade the systems later to handle a larger and more complex organization. You can also implement the systems stepwise—for example, by starting with components having the greatest gap between actual and desired performance, or with those that are easiest to put in place and therefore will have immediate impact.

An effective control system includes the following (all of which were covered in detail in Chapter 11):

- Accounts receivables and collections policies
- An inventory management system
- Account payables policies
- Assessment of performance and expenditures
- Metrics to track trends in cash, receivables, inventory, payables, expenditures, and performance

Managing costs requires both making decisions about expenditures and instituting controls that monitor spending. A growing firm's selling and administrative costs often expand rapidly with its escalation in sales. This expenditure is often appropriate, because you need marketing to generate sales and administrative overhead to support the burgeoning organization. Yet you do need to monitor these areas to determine effectiveness and detect overspending. For example, certain advertising approaches may be more effective than others, or they may work in one region but not another.

As the company begins to sell more and more products in multiple markets, you will want to analyze its performance in different product or market segments, along with how effectively it is spending its resources. You need to understand what each product costs and whether you are truly making a profit. All the costs going into each product are those costs, both variable and fixed, that would disappear if the product were discontinued. After you cover these, the remainder contributes toward company overhead and generating profits.

You can also develop performance metrics to aid in decisions about investments and expenditures. Performance measures in an early-stage company are designed less for evaluating actual outcomes against a plan (as they would be in a more stable established organization) than to help in entrepreneurial decision making. As the company's operations expand, managers can develop metrics to help them answer the following questions:

- Which products or markets generate the highest revenues and margins?
- Which customers or customer groups are reliable accounts (make timely payments, are at low risk of default)?
- How effective are our expenditures in areas such as marketing and sales, and does this differ across markets?

Tracking Performance

How do you determine what's good or bad when examining key metrics? For some financial ratios, published sources can provide industry averages for comparison. Entrepreneurial firms, however, often adopt policies that differ from those of more stable established firms, such as spending on marketing while building brand awareness. Thus it may be more useful to look at trends in metrics over time; for example, an increase in your collection period for receivables could indicate a relaxing in collection efforts, or a decrease in inventory turns could indicate you are at increasing risk of stock-outs. If you see significant changes and they are not the result of policy shifts in your firm, look for causes and consider making adjustments in policy.

One key point is to make performance measures as simple and inexpensive to track as possible, while providing information that helps you make better decisions. One very successful consulting firm had simple but useful measures. The entrepreneur tracked performance through his "B-Report." The B-Report was a simple Excel spread sheet, with each consultant occupying a row, and columns representing every week of the year. If consultants expected to bill in a given week, they put a "B" in the column. If they did not, they left it blank. If the entrepreneur did not see a lot of B's, he knew he had a problem.

The company can also develop simple budgeting practices to estimate cash and inventory needs, schedule production, determine staffing requirements, and set sales and profitability goals. It should upgrade and formalize these controls, metrics, and budgets as it moves toward later growth. But more importantly, these tools should evolve to provide the best information possible in aiding the company's decision making. The value they provide should more than justify the time and effort spent to develop and maintain them.

> Performance measures for a growing organization should be as simple and inexpensive to track as possible, while providing information leading to better decision making.

There may be times when it's appropriate to slow the pursuit of new growth in order to give the company room to improve its ability to manage growth. Joel Kolen, president of Empress International Ltd., a seafood distributor, emphasizes that:

By taking a break from growth and putting in controls such as those at a large company, an entrepreneur can ease the growth transition and ensure that the qualities that helped build the company don't get lost in the rush to fill new orders. [4]

Managing the Cash Cycle

The **cash cycle** shows the amount of time that passes between cash outlays and cash inflows during the company's sales process. It also shows the relationship between three key measures: days in payables, days in inventory, and days sales are outstanding. Let's use Albercan Drilling Supply to illustrate the cash cycle, and how better controls can conserve resources. Albercan's sole business was the sale of drill pipes and collars to drilling contractors in the local area. In 2004, as the company was growing, it seemed to be in a constant need for cash. At the same time, its bankers were hesitant to extend more credit. A review of the key measures in Figure 14.4 shows that all have increased substantially in two years, more than doubling the cash conversion period.

As Figure 14.5 illustrates, the cash conversion period extends from the time of cash outlay (to suppliers) to cash inflow (from customers). Looking at this diagram, you can imagine how an increase in sales would actually decrease cash inflows in the short term. The company would need to borrow money to cover the costs associated with this increase in sales until cash comes in 98 days later. In the meantime, as it makes additional sales, the company would need to cover these costs. When cash finally comes in, the company would likely need that cash for more inventory!

Another problem revealed in this analysis is the length of time Albercan takes to pay suppliers. If typical payment terms are 30 days (whereas Albercan is paying in 58 days),

Albercan Drilling Supply	2002	2003	2004	Increase 2002–2004
Days sales outstanding	39	45	53	37%
Days in inventory	44	86	98	122%
Days in payables	36	38	53	48%
Cash conversion period	47	92	98	108%

Figure 14.4

Albercan cash conversion analysis

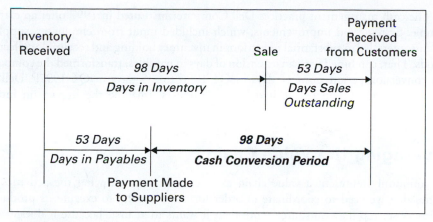

Figure 14.5

Cash conversion period for Albercan: 2004

the company may be testing its relationship with suppliers. This could lead them to refuse to ship additional product until Albercan pays past invoices, or in the worse case, they might refuse to do business with the company.

The easy solution would be to borrow from a bank or other debt source, preferably a revolving line of credit that allows the company to draw funds as needed and pay back when it receives cash. These are short-term loans designed to cover shortfalls such as this. Borrowing can get expensive, though, so why not think about reducing the average cash conversion period? This is much more difficult, but it instills a sense of resource parsimony that boosts a company's efficiency. What if Albercan can reduce its days in inventory to 60 and its days sales outstanding to 40? We'll also assume Albercan needs to reduce days in payables to 45. This all leaves a cash conversion period of 55 days, as Figure 14.6 below shows. Not only will that reduce the period of time the company would need to borrow, but it would reduce the average amount needed, because cash comes in more quickly and is therefore available for more inventory.

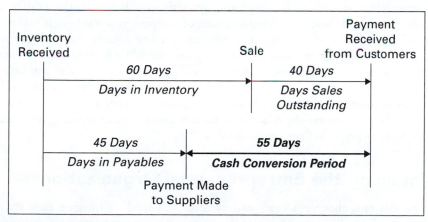

Figure 14.6

Adjusted cash conversion period for Albercan: 2004

The cash management practices Dell Computer instituted in 1997 offer an extreme example. Systems and improvements, which included input from employees, suppliers, and customers, led to substantial reductions in inventory holding and receivable collections periods. That, combined with an extension of days in payables, transformed the company's cash conversion period from 40 days in Q4 1996 to −5 days in Q4 1997![5] Dell was basically getting cash in before it delivered products. Imagine the impact on interest expenses.

Leveraging the Value Chain

We commonly represent a value chain as a series of steps showing the activities and entities that we need to coordinate in order for the company to execute its product or service. A startup may outsource more than it wants to at first, because it doesn't have the resources or capabilities to do everything in-house. Often it designs a product with as many off-the-shelf parts as possible to minimize design and tooling charges. On the other hand, the firm may need to take on some value chain activities because there is no reliable or ready source for them; this is particularly true for new products or services for which there is little infrastructure. Or value chain players may not cooperate, leaving the company to, for example, sell its product direct rather than create channel conflict for distributors who deal with more stable older companies.

As the company grows, you should decide which value chain positions are capable of creating the most value, and for which you can establish unique advantage. For example, the founders of Paratek,[6] a small computer peripheral startup, initially thought they would build what they could themselves, including wiring their own circuit boards. It didn't take them long to realize it would take them about half a day to build one board, when it could be done in minutes—and more reliably—by a board house. As they worked with their suppliers and gained experience with the product, they eventually had their suppliers take on more and more steps. The board house, for example, would build and test the boards, then ship them directly to the housing manufacturer, which would then install the boards into the housing. Eventually, the company only needed to insert a drive mechanism, test the completed unit, add any accessories to the order, and ship the product. This enabled it to run a leaner operation that focused on product development and the coordination of value chain activities, many of which were performed quicker, cheaper, and more reliably by others than the firm could do in-house.

Outsourcing can enable a growing company to focus on those activities it can perform particularly well, and those underlying its source of competitive advantage. It makes sense to outsource those activities other companies can do more reliably and less expensively, like the board house just mentioned. But recognize that while moving activities outside reduces the steps the firm performs in-house, it will also reduce the control you have over those activities, and often consume substantial time just for managing the relationship. The firm will therefore need to weigh some considerations, such as how it will maintain quality and how responsive the value chain partner needs to be in reducing or increasing production in response to fluctuations in sales.

Maintaining the Entrepreneurial Organization

With all this talk about efficiency and controls, it's hard to imagine how anything entrepreneurial can happen. That is sadly the case with many companies. A history of success creates preferences for recreating the past rather than building toward the future. Efficiency in current operations often does not accommodate new initiatives, like those requiring different sales channels or different value chain partners. Customers want the company to improve the products they know best, rather than be forced to change their behavior and endure the switching costs of adapting to a new product.

How, then, can a well-run organization maintain the ability to create new businesses? It's primarily a combination of the remaining driving forces of the growth model: how leadership views and manages its opportunity domain and the organization's people and resources.

Opportunity Domain

While a startup is focused on shaping an opportunity and bringing it to life, as the organization grows, its leadership needs to define a strategic arena that guides decisions on how it competes in its industry and creates value for its targeted markets. An organization defines this arena through a balance of the unique capabilities it builds and its ability to differentiate itself in its competitive environment. This balance then guides decisions about how the company markets and sells its products, and which opportunities it pursues in expanding its business.

The impact of Stonyfield Farm's strategic focus can be seen in many aspects of its business. Stonyfield positioned itself as producing high-end yogurt products with quality, natural ingredients. It first sold its product through natural food and specialty stores, building a plant to better control its supply of hormone-free milk. The firm's marketing consisted of developing awareness and word of mouth by educating consumers about the quality of the product, promoting the company's social and environmental mission, and building a loyal following through plant tours, newsletters, and other customer relationship–focused programs. Stonyfield introduced new yogurt flavors, low-fat yogurt, and frozen yogurt. Its strategic focus shaped its distribution, manufacturing, marketing, and product development activities.

Courtesy Stonyfield Form

Gary Hirshberg, founder of Stonyfield Farm.

A focused strategy in early growth helps guide the firm through the maze of opportunities that materialize once it experiences initial success. All too often, a startup chases diverse opportunities, without defining what it can do distinctly well. During early growth, define your firm's core focus and develop capabilities around this, spending your limited resources and time close to this core, just as Stonyfield focused on building awareness of its unique brand and strengthening this brand with new yogurt flavors.

In later growth, your company has established its competitive uniqueness and can now leverage this, while training a strategic eye on the future. It may continue to extend its advantage in its current position by, for example, upgrading its products. Over time, however, opportunities will eventually diminish in a particular product space, and you will need to combine incremental extensions with expansion into the periphery. A company may create a next-generation product that includes improvements and new features for existing customers, while exploring new products and new markets. A restaurant chain can start offering Sunday brunch to its customers, for example, or it can launch a catering business.

Pay attention, however, to new developments in the industry and market environment. These may determine where you should best focus your strategic efforts at specific points in time. For instance, you may emphasize a current product to gain maximum returns before competition comes in. Or you may seek new ground if the market is becoming crowded by large competitors or if a technology foundation is becoming obsolete.

Yankee Candle Company illustrates how a company can expand over time within an existing product/market space and into the periphery. The company traces its origins to young Michael Kittredge's home operation, which soon expanded to an old paper mill. The company grew its sales of candles through gift shops and expanded into the international market through distributors. It started selling online and through catalogs. The company also opened its own retail stores, including a flagship store in South Deerfield, Massachusetts, which serves as a tourist destination, with a candle museum,

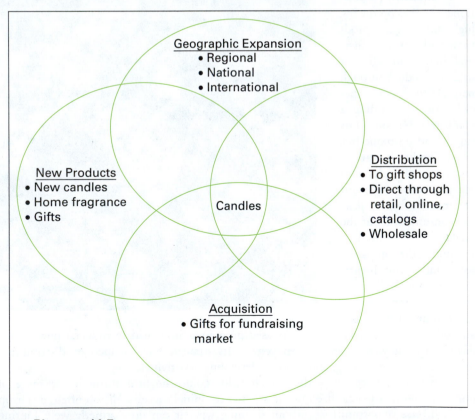

■ **Figure 14.7**

Yankee Candle's opportunity domain

a restaurant, and sales of toys, gifts, home accessories, and other products, along with candles of all shapes and sizes.

While this expansion continued, the company entered the home fragrance market with products such as electric home fragrancers, room sprays, potpourri, and bath care products. The primary target audience was still women ranging in age from 20 to 60. But the company started to test new markets through it acquisition of GBI Marketing, a distributor of selected gift products (including Yankee Candle products) to fundraising organizations.

As Figure 14.7 on page 566 shows, Yankee Candle has taken a multipronged approach to expanding its business: geographic expansion, new products, new distribution methods, and acquisition. There is a common logic surrounding all these methods, extending from core elements relating to its original product: candles. You've probably encountered small, single-operation candle shops. The Yankee Candle example shows how a seemingly slow-growth business can become a high-potential venture.

As a company grows, it may experience stagnating growth in its core business but see little opportunity for expansion into the periphery. It may need to make drastic shifts in its business. As Channing Bete's experience illustrates (see box), however, the company should make these forays outside the periphery carefully.

A Cautionary Note on Expanding Through Acquisitions: The Channing Bete Setback

Channing Bete enjoyed years of success with its information pamphlets providing advice on a range of topics, from managing diabetes to handling bullies. The company had a broad range of customers that included schools, hospitals, and government agencies. With its acquisition of Developmental Research Programs, Channing Bete set the stage for expanding from its single business of publishing printed information to a consulting operation focused on helping youth steer clear of drug use, delinquency, and pregnancy.

A few years later, revenues from the largest division of the acquired business fell 21.4% and the division was shut down. A customer commented that Channing Bete's contributions to the business were little more than cosmetic but increased costs substantially. Losses spread to the core business, and the company fired one-fifth of its work force. Tension mounted within the company as changes were imposed, such as replacing "flextime" with a 9-to-5 workday, even while the company touted its family-friendly culture. One former employee commented that the company got in over its head; it put a great deal of money and energy into the acquisition, neglecting lines of business that had been profitable.

Adapted from "Bete Consulting Bet Falls Short: Move Brings Losses, Firings, Retrenchment," by Sunshine Dewitt. *Daily Hampshire Gazette*. July 18, 2005. Vol. 219, No. 271, pp. A1 and D1.
Reprinted with the permission of the *Daily Hampshire Gazette*. All Rights Reserved.

Acquisitions can provide inroads into new businesses for a company, but this undertaking requires an underlying logic. While Channing Bete attempted to move from publishing to consulting, Yankee Candle was already in the gift market when it made its acquisition. The central precept is the connection between organizational resources and capabilities, and the opportunity domain, as illustrated in Figure 14.2. The growing organization should not consider external opportunities that simply appear attractive unless it has some particular ability to pursue them better than competitors.

Obviously, a company cannot be driven only by opportunities that leverage current capabilities. Expansion opportunities will stretch these capabilities, and the company may choose to build new ones over time. Think about how this likely happened for Yankee Candle. The company can experiment or partner to reduce risk. It can adopt an options strategy, spreading exploratory resources across multiple business options with the logic that a few, as yet unknown, will warrant more substantial commitments. The company can also stage its investments, as venture capitalists do, investing a minimal amount in a new business opportunity and tying further investment to the achievement of milestones or the reduction of uncertainty. These practices minimize impact on the organization until more is known.

The one uncertainty entrepreneurs can count on, however, is change. You will need to anticipate, respond to, and even sometimes drive change. Professor Richard Osborne examined 26 privately held firms, all of which experienced initial success. Six of these firms were able to sustain growth beyond the entrepreneurial phase, while the rest saw their growth stalled. Factors such as inadequate resources, poor managerial capabilities of the entrepreneur, and bureaucracy were minor factors in the growth stall, according to this research. The main factor was the inability to perceive and respond to changing opportunities and conditions in their environment.[7]

The growing company therefore needs to be responsive to impending environmental shifts, maintaining its ability to transform its strategy and establish a new source of uniqueness in a changed environment. Crunch Fitness, for example, enjoyed tremendous success in the late 1980s as a startup in the competitive aerobics studio market in New York City by offering innovative aerobics classes, creating a unique brand image and employing creative marketing techniques. While other aerobic studios fell victim to the decline of the aerobics craze and the emergence of multi-activity health clubs in the mid-1990s, Crunch shifted its strategy by transforming to a full-service facility while maintaining the uniqueness it was founded on.

As your company grows, its strategic planning efforts will benefit from the input of others inside and outside the company with critical knowledge that can influence the company's direction. Customers, particularly lead users, can provide information about market needs. Specialist employees who are close to markets and technologies can identify future opportunities. The firm can institute a function that gathers and monitors outside information, and examines external trends and opportunities.

Organizational Resources and Capabilities

> A bootstrap mentality does not end once the company is launched and successful; it is a lasting orientation toward maximizing value from resource parsimony.

Efforts to finance growth internally go hand in hand with controls. By improving its cash flow, your growing company can better avert a cash crisis and avoid being at the mercy of reluctant or expensive lenders or investors. You may even be able to self-finance some of its future growth, reducing reliance on more expensive sources of funding. The key lesson is this: A bootstrap mentality does not apply just to starting a company; it is a lasting orientation that maximizes returns through resource parsimony.

Obtaining Financial Resources for the Growing Company

Shortening operating cash cycles and increasing margins are vital for conserving cash. They essentially represent costless financing. The rapidly growing organization, however, will likely need to tap additional sources to finance its growth. Not only will you need financing to support accelerating sales, but new policies, such as granting customer payment terms or taking on bulk orders, as well as investments in new products or services, will create a drain on cash.

Despite its success and future prospects, however, a company early in its growth cycle may have only certain options available. For example, a bank would not typically extend credit to a firm with little operating history and fluctuating sales. But as we discussed in Chapter 11, a supplier who is motivated to make a sale and gain a loyal, growing customer might. After a company has been established for a year, a bank might be willing to loan monies against a portion of its receivables, the founders' good credit, or with signed guarantees, perhaps requiring loan covenants to maintain certain numbers or ratios.

It's therefore useful to think in terms of stages when financing growth. Sources closed to the firm earlier in its life may open up later. Undertake periodic surveys of the firm's current financing options, and consider any changes that may open up new and cheaper financing sources. In this way, you may recognize new opportunities for refinancing at lower rates.

As we covered in Chapters 9, 10, and 11, sources of financing for early growth include:

- Investment from key management
- Founder loans
- Family and friends
- Angel investors
- Venture capital
- Loans on assets, such as receivables, inventory, and equipment
- Equipment leases
- Credit cards

As the company moves into later growth and undertakes expansion efforts, such as selling internationally or launching new products or services, it will need financing from sources more appropriate for higher-risk and longer-term investment. Banks typically will not loan substantial funds, unsecured, for riskier expansion efforts that won't generate returns for quite some time. The firm will likely need to rely on equity sources.

But there are other ways to finance future growth. Look to strategic partners who may provide more favorable financing terms. You may also decide to expand by franchising. Take the risks of these financing modes into consideration: for example, potential customers who compete with your strategic partner may view a relationship with you as too risky because your partner has some control over your firm, or has greater access to information that could unfavorably affect the customer. Determine your resource needs by your firm's range of value chain activities. Reducing activities to those considered core to the business, and achieving better coordination throughout the chain, can reduce your resource requirements and risk, as we detailed in the execution section.

Intangible Resources and Capabilities

Resources at startup include people, but the focus is on acquiring capital, since the key human resource is the founder or founding team. As the company grows, it accumulates capital, to be sure, and fixed assets. But it also builds intangible assets. These are resources such as the proprietary knowledge underlying its products and services, and the skills of the organization's people. You should have addressed intellectual property considerations early on, before early growth—even before starting the business. But this should also be an ongoing process requiring continual legal advice and subsequent actions to protect technologies, processes, and creative work through trade secrets, copyrights, trademarks, and patents (see Chapter 13).

Starting in early growth, you'll need to develop or hire people with specialized skills. Generalist skills are important at startup: everyone should be able to pitch in and help with shipping, inventory control, marketing, and so forth. As volume increases and the business becomes more complex, it becomes harder to maintain efficiency and effectiveness with generalist skills. Now you will need to hire specialists in areas such as marketing, inventory management, accounting and finance, and logistics.

An organization also develops capabilities which define what it is good at. These are processes that coordinate and integrate the organization's tangible and intangible resources to create unique sources of value. Just like inventory and equipment, they lead to revenues for a company. Think about businesses or organizations that are familiar to you, and what they do best. McDonald's has efficient processes to deliver fast, low-priced meals. Dell Computer can deliver a custom computer quickly and inexpensively. These transactions translate to capabilities. Now think about whether these organizations would be good at doing something totally different in their industry. Could McDonald's open a high-end restaurant? Could Dell invent its own computer products? Probably not so easily. But there are opportunities to expand into the periphery with their capabilities. For example, McDonald's began to offer salads in an attempt to attract more health conscious, but also convenience-minded and price-conscious, eaters.

Your capabilities need to be consistent with your firm's strategic focus. As the opportunity domain section of this chapter reveals, organizations define their strategy both through detecting where the opportunities are for unique advantages in the external competitive environment, and through building and leveraging a set of unique capabilities. McDonald's needs to have processes that optimize efficiency and cut costs out of its operations. Dell needs to have capabilities for sourcing and integrating multiple components into customized computer systems that meet the needs of its customers. Think again about the capabilities Stonyfield Farm or Yankee Candle needed as they started and expanded their businesses.

Sustained growth in a changing environment requires constant attention to identifying what the company does best and matching that with the potential for unique value in the competitive environment. Your company may be good at user-friendly innovations. If it does this better than rivals and users are willing to pay a premium for that, then leverage it—ensuring the right people and systems are in place to maximize the value you can gain from this capability.

Meanwhile, you need to monitor the uniqueness and value of its capabilities over time. If competitors duplicate this ability, or customers shift toward more technically complex solutions, reassess what your company does best. Renew key capabilities periodically. A research study of telecommunications and computer startups found that high levels of innovativeness at founding did not translate to higher growth seven, eight, or nine years out. And simply forming alliances didn't help. But those building internal technology capabilities beyond founding were more likely to achieve a higher level of sustained growth.[8]

Leadership

Figure 14.8 summarizes some key differences between entrepreneurs, managers, and entrepreneurial leaders. The entrepreneurial leader plays a distinct role, critical for sustaining a growing organization.

Entrepreneur	Manager	Entrepreneurial Leader
Locates new ideas	Maintains current operations	Leverages core business while exploring new opportunities
Starts a business	Implements the business	Starts businesses within an ongoing organization
Opportunity driven	Resource driven	Capability and opportunity driven; leverages capabilities and builds new ones to expand opportunity domain
Establishes and implements a vision	Plans, organizes, staffs, controls	Establishes a vision and empowers others to carry it out
Builds an organization around the opportunity	Enhances efficiency of organization	Maintains entrepreneurial ability as organization grows; ensures culture, structure, systems are conducive to entrepreneurship; removes barriers
Leads and inspires others	Supervises and monitors others	Develops and guides entrepreneurial individuals; bridges between individuals and groups with diverse expertise and orientation
Orchestrates change in the competitive environment	Maintains consistency and predictability	Orchestrates change in both the organizational and competitive environment

Figure 14.8

The entrepreneur vs. manager vs. entrepreneurial leader

Starting the Delegation Process

The entrepreneur typically starts out doing everything. She answers phones, ships product, designs advertisements—in essence, performing just about all the activities needed to ensure the organization gets product sold and out the door. But sometime in early growth the organization will outgrow her ability to keep up. She will have neither the time nor the expertise to deal with the range of challenges a burgeoning business presents. The following are symptoms revealing that the organization has outgrown the entrepreneur's capacity.

- The volume of decisions multiplies. The entrepreneur is working harder but accomplishing less.
- Decisions become more difficult to make: more complex and specialized. The entrepreneur increasingly wonders whether she has made the right decision.
- Everyone is still pitching in and doing everything, but more and more, something critical slips by or mistakes occur.
- If the entrepreneur is not directly involved in the task, no progress can happen.

Starting in early growth, the entrepreneur must delegate responsibilities to others in the organization. The process of delegation is mapped out in Figure 14.9.

As Figure 14.9 shows, the entrepreneur starts out assigning specific tasks to others. As delegation proceeds, she passes responsibility for achieving objectives to specialists, then managers, without needing to understand or know about the underlying mechanics. Then, the setting of objectives moves to others: experienced managers and teams close to the activity. This process enables the entrepreneur to spend less time on the day-to-day details of everything and focus on what she does best, while those most qualified make

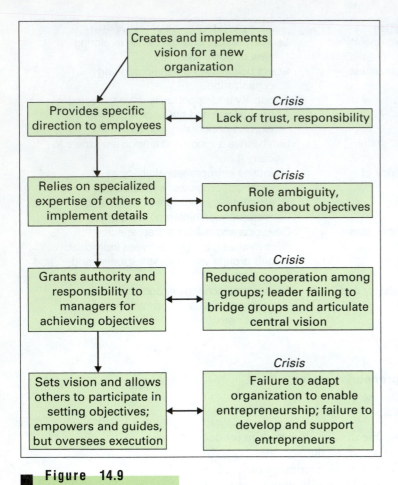

Figure 14.9

Transition from entrepreneur to entrepreneurial leader

decisions. At the same time, the entrepreneur needs to oversee execution by providing guidance to managers and using metrics to evaluate progress, but she may need to step in when necessary, particularly when initiatives meet with resistance.

Delegation, while necessary for surviving the entrepreneurial growth phase, is typically difficult for the entrepreneur to accomplish. She may continue to attempt to do everything herself, but she's increasingly unable to do so. Faced with these challenges, the entrepreneur may revert back to what she does best, ignoring tasks she has neither the comfort level nor the capability to deal with. A technical entrepreneur may retreat to developing new products, while ignoring the company's inability to pay bills on time. What's bad is not the entrepreneur doing what she does best—it's having no one pay attention to the company's most critical problems.

Employees may not have a problem with the lack of delegation, because they may prefer that the entrepreneur make decisions which they can then carry out. Then they don't need to take responsibility for outcomes. On the other hand, in allowing employees to take responsibility for decisions, the entrepreneur also needs to let them make mistakes and learn from them, circumstances neither the employees nor the entrepreneur may feel comfortable with. The entrepreneur cannot continue to be the "go-to" guy, however, when the volume of decisions mushrooms and she becomes increasingly less qualified to provide direction in many areas.

As the entrepreneur delegates, she will need to put in place managers who can be responsible for executing in specialized areas. Then, in her leadership role, she must develop the ability to inspire people with a range of expertise to organize, communicate, collaborate—and be creative in both running an efficient operation and pursuing entrepreneurial ideas.

First-Level Management

In early growth, the first set of supervisors can come from within. In some sense, they deserve to be promoted because they have been with the company since its early days and have contributed to its success. They were willing to chip in whenever and wherever needed, they have worked closely with you, the entrepreneur, and they therefore understand your vision and the purpose of the organization. They may also have the respect of their peers.

Assess whether these people have the potential to become managers, however, and whether they can develop their abilities through training and experience. There are a few things you should do: (1) set expectations up front, including setting personal performance goals; (2) providing coaching, mentoring, and training; and (3) periodically assess behavior and performance. But developing managers takes time. If the venture is late forming its management structure and is therefore playing catch up, if internal and external conditions are rapidly changing, or if the learning gap between current employees and needed management is too wide, then allowing managers to learn on the job is too risky. You will need to hire from the outside.

Hiring from the outside has its own hazards, because the workers, particularly those who have been there from the beginning, may not respect these outsiders. First act as a broker between the employees and management during this transition. This includes advising the new manager and recognizing the cooperation and contributions of employees. The latter can mean acknowledging accomplishments through personal contact or making these visible around the organization. In addition, you (and your managers) can ensure employees have a satisfactory career path by promoting them and moving them into jobs in which they increasingly feel engaged and challenged.

Where possible, employ a mix of externally hired managers and internally promoted managers. Again, broker between these internal and external managers during the transition by setting expectations, advising and coaching, and monitoring behavior. By achieving cooperation among internal and external managers, you're more likely to accomplish broad cooperation across the organization. Also reinforce the authority of your new managers, whether they originate from the inside or the outside. For example, route to them employees who have always gone directly to you.

From Delegation to Decentralization

What starts as a process of delegation in early growth evolves into a decentralized reporting structure as the organization approaches later growth. As functions become more specialized and the product and service offering broadens, responsibility and decision making are best left to those with the expertise and day-to-day involvement in specific areas.

A decentralized structure can also aid communication flow throughout the organization, which increasingly becomes challenged as the organization grows. While closeness to the entrepreneur in early stages helps everyone understand her vision and the organization's objectives, the complexity and changes a growing organization experiences can create confusion about direction and purpose. Communication and understanding need to happen between the members of the management team, who then ensure consistent information flow throughout their areas.

Professional Management and Boards

In later growth, the organization needs to ensure it has a leadership team in place: professional managers who share in the organization's strategic planning process and have the capability to balance the need for efficient operations with the benefits of maintaining its entrepreneurial edge. Once the organization has created control systems, a management structure, and a strategic focus, it needs to look toward its future. This job becomes increasingly complex and requires those with experience and track records. Employees who have been promoted into managerial positions are not likely to be qualified for the organization's top levels. Consequently, professional managers typically come from the outside.

With the introduction of a leadership team, the organization itself becomes more professional. This is a major change, even more so than the shift from startup to early growth. Some employees will leave, but others will make this transition. The practices you put in place to integrate managers and employees and insiders and outsiders during early growth will be critical to your introduction of a professional management team.

By carefully selecting members of the board of directors, you can provide alternative perspectives and depth and breadth of experience. The board should include experts from outside the firm who can become key participants in the strategic planning process. What's important for the firm is a proactive, rather than reactive, approach to seeking ways to extend and build value. The composition of the company's board of directors will typically undergo changes as the firm emerges from its startup phase. Initially, the board may be informal—occupied by those unlikely to have high-level experience, but able to provide support to the entrepreneur in her early endeavors. In early growth, boards typically evolve to include those able to provide operational guidance, for example, retired bankers, investors, and lawyers.

As the company professionalizes, the board should be more useful for strategic purposes, with members having a broader and visionary view of the market and industry, for example, other CEOs, industry experts, and senior executives in related businesses. While many investors require representation on the board of directors, avoid stakeholders who can control the firm for their benefit through board positions, such as suppliers, customers, and the company's lenders.

Supplement the skill and experience of the company's leadership and board of directors with the skill and experience of advisory boards and consultants. For example, you may assemble a group of technology experts from universities, government labs, and corporations to examine industry technological trends, or you may bring in a marketing consulting firm to determine tactics for expanding into overseas markets.

Coordinating the Driving Forces

The driving forces model shows a link between the three elements: organizational resources and capabilities, opportunity domain, and leadership. And at the core of this is execution: ensuring the most efficient and effective coordination of these activities in a way that enhances the organization's profitability. Capabilities and the opportunity domain interact: capabilities define where the company can best play, and opportunities extend capabilities. Leadership maps out a particular opportunity domain with its strategic focus and modifies this focus over time, as the industry and market environment changes and the company seeks future growth. Leadership also ensures its capabilities and opportunity domain are in balance. But as the organization grows, a key concern for its leaders is how to manage its people and maintain its entrepreneurial capabilities, as the next section illustrates.

Leading People; Developing Entrepreneurs

The most common "people mistakes" an entrepreneurial firm makes are preparing people inadequately and maintaining the wrong people as the organization grows. Early in the business's life, organization members do their jobs and pitch in wherever needed. It is more important for the lean team to maintain the flexibility and broad skills needed to accomplish a lot with a little. Early in the game, it is not yet apparent these employees lack the skills needed to scale up the organization. It is difficult to think about training to develop future skills when growth is consuming everyone's time.

As the need for specialists and managers arises, the tasks you expect of some employees may exceed their abilities, and you may need to place them in other roles, or even fire them if necessary. Other employees may be able to rise up to the challenges presented and assume these new functions and responsibilities. The process of adapting to these new roles takes time, however. The company will often need to do some hiring from the outside. You will have to deal with reduced motivation from setbacks or crises at the same time that employees struggle with adapting to new employees and higher-level managers coming from the outside, both of whom lack the shared experiences gained through the organization's history.

The second tier of employees, beyond the founding group, is often said to be more like 9-to-5ers who tend to view working there as a job. But in most companies, there are entrepreneurs in the mix. While we often think that ideas come from anywhere or that anyone can be creative if given a chance, the reality is that some people don't have the stomach for ambiguity and risk. And in many companies, the entrepreneur remains the sole entrepreneurial engine.

Our research on corporate entrepreneurship suggests the organization's leaders need to:

- Identify those exhibiting passion for entrepreneurship
- Develop their ability to work under conditions of high ambiguity
- Ensure they have the inclination and credibility to convince others in the organization to contribute and commit to their projects
- Facilitate, support, and guide their efforts while also providing them with sufficient freedom and empowerment
- Recognize their contribution to the company's innovation and growth ambitions.
- View failure as a risk associated with entrepreneurship and an opportunity for learning, therefore ensuring that well-intentioned failures are not punished

We suspect these practices are also critical in smaller organizations. One study reports that human resource practices like training and development distinguish high-growth firms from more slowly growing ones.[9]

CONCLUSION

Starting a business is a risky endeavor, but staying in business can be just as challenging. As the entrepreneurial firm grows beyond founding, it needs to ensure its organization is capable of managing growth. We have outlined a driving forces model that integrates leadership, opportunity domain, and resources and capabilities—and has execution at the core. The entrepreneur should understand and anticipate the challenges associated with building and managing a growing organization at different stages, and prepare the organization to execute effectively at each point, as well as set the stage for a healthy future.

These efforts, however, must not distance the company from its entrepreneurial roots. Growing companies struggle not just with such concerns as having fewer resources than big companies, but also with coordinating an increasingly bigger and more complex business. The team must work to prevent the organization from becoming a bureaucracy that inhibits entrepreneurship. They must continually foster entrepreneurial actions even when this is their biggest challenge. They have to consciously work on preserving and maintaining their entrepreneurial spirit, and if they lose it, they have to rejuvenate the company and rekindle entrepreneurship before it's too late.

☐ **YOUR OPPORTUNITY JOURNAL**

Reflection Point	**Your Thoughts...**

1. What are your personal growth objectives for your venture? Is a ''lifestyle'' business going to meet your personal goals? Or a high-potential venture?

2. What will your role within the company be at various stages of growth? Do you want to remain the CEO? Are you more interested in another aspect, say CTO?

3. What skills will you need to develop as the company grows to satisfactorily fulfill the roles you aspire to? Which of these skills can you learn on the job? Which skills might need further education or other outside development?

4. What kind of controls can you establish early in your venture's life? How will these help you manage cash and other key components of your business?

5. What aspects of your business should you keep in-house and which should you outsource? How do you protect your competitive advantage?

6. What is your strategic focus for early growth? How do you leverage what you do really well? What are some possible peripheral growth opportunities for later in your venture's life?

7. What are your organization's key resources and capabilities? What should they be in the future? How do you build toward those resources and capabilities?

8. What is your leadership plan? When and which responsibilities will you delegate? How will you promote people in your organization? When might you need to go outside to hire?

Identify three companies that have experienced successful, rapid growth in your industry. Study their Web sites and search for articles about the companies. Can you discern their strategic focuses early in their growth cycles? What are the core areas that they are leveraging? How do their growth strategies change later in their lives? What are some peripheral markets/customers they are going for? Have they grown by acquisition? How has that worked out?

NOTES ☐

1 Zook, C., and Allen, J. *The Facts About Growth*. New York: Bain Company. 1999.

2 Hedberg, Carl, and Marram, Edward. Micro E Systems Case. Babson College. 2004.

3 Additional resources on growth stages can be found in the following references:
- Adizes, Ichak. *Managing Corporate Lifecycles*. Prentice Hall Press: Paramus, NJ. 1999.
- Churchill, Neil C. The Six Key Phases of Company Growth. In S. Birley and D. Muzyka, *Mastering Enterprise*. Pitman Publishing: London. 1997.
- Flamholtz, Eric G., and Randle, Yvonne. *Growing Pains: Transitioning from an Entrepreneurship to a Professionally Managed Firm*. San Francisco: Jossey-Bass. 2000.
- Greiner, Larry E. Evolution and Revolution as Organizations Grow. Harvard Business Review. 76(3), p. 55–63, 1998.
- Harper, Stephen C. *The McGraw-Hill Guide to Managing Growth in Your Emerging Business*. New York: McGraw-Hill. 1995.

4 Kolen, Joel, and Jaffe, Susan Biddle. Knowing When to Take a Breather: Controlling Company Growth. *Nation's Business*. 83(11), 6.

5 Dell Computer Corporation, company Web site, April 2003.

6 Paratek is a disguised name.

7 Osborne, Richard L. Second Phase Entrepreneurship: Breaking Through the Growth Wall. *Business Horizons*. 37(1), p. 80–86, 1994.

8 Kelley, Donna, and Nakosteen, Robert. Technology Resources, Alliances and Sustained Growth in New, Technology-Based Firms. *IEEE Transactions on Engineering Management*. 52(3). 2005.

9 Barringer, B., Jones, F., and Neubaum, D. A Quantitative Content Analysis of the Characteristics of Rapid-Growth Firms and Their Founders. *Journal of Business Venturing*. 20, 663–687. 2005.

□   *CASE*   **Nancy's Coffee**

As the busy president of the $7 million Nancy's Coffee Café chain, Beth Wood-Leidt wasn't able to visit each of their thirty suburban coffee shops as much as she would have liked. Whenever she did journey out as she was doing today, it was with a passion for building brand and enhancing profitability.

Beth approached one of her more challenging locations—in a mall in central New York—and surveyed the space with a practiced eye.

> *. . . that front table needs a wipe . . . the display shelves are dusty . . . the OneCard holder is hidden behind the tip jar . . . isn't it too early in the day to be out of plain bagels? . . .*

She warmly greeted the staff she knew, introduced herself to new faces, and ordered a cappuccino from a slightly nervous young hire at the counter. As the teenager set about to whip up the best coffee drink of her brief career, Beth took the manager aside to offer a quick rundown on areas for improvement.

Beth was just finishing up with her quality assessment when her cell phone buzzed with a call from a former corporate colleague in whom she had often confided about the challenges of running a retail business. Beth took a sip of her frothy brew, winked her approval to the relieved girl who had brewed it, and headed out into the mall to chat. When her friend noted that Beth sounded tired, the 40-year-old CEO closed her eyes and nodded into the phone:

> *Gosh, I am tired! Remember about a year ago I started saying that I wanted to figure out where this business was going? Well, I'm still asking the same questions like, how can we attract the capital we would need to grow faster; what is the best exit strategy to shoot for; and what is the best way to enhance the value of what we are building?*
>
> *Sure, we'll add another two more stores this year, but that's just not doing it for me. It's early winter, 2003—and that means I've been running this thing now for over ten years. And, as you know, the story hasn't really changed; we're still too small to be acquired, not valuable enough to be worth selling outright, and yet the business is large enough to need someone thinking about it almost all the time; yes, that would be me. We've hit a long plateau here; it's past time to make some critical decisions.*

From Nuts to Beans

In 1973, Nancy Wood—then a 36-year-old mother of three and married to Sandy Wood—founded a mall-kiosk business to sell dried fruit and nuts. When demand for that fare appeared to be softening, she began the search for a more viable product line. After connecting with master coffee roaster Irwin White at a fancy-food trade show in 1978, she decided to turn her lifelong passion for great coffee into a new business. Nancy's eldest daughter, Beth, recalled that the concept was a bit ahead of its time:

> *My mother took her kiosks and slowly began to convert them over to coffee bars she had named the Coffee Collection. She started introducing Kenyan and Columbian coffees, but people responded "no way; there is Folgers, and there's Maxwell House, and Dunkin' Donuts." It was a very strange thing to many people who were being asked to pay a whole*

This case was prepared by Carl Hedberg under the direction of Professor Edward Marram, with assistance from Les Charm. © Copyright Babson College, 2004. Funding provided by the Ewing Marion Kauffman Foundation. All rights reserved.

dollar for a single cup of coffee—or told they could grind their own fresh-roasted beans at home. They looked at my Mom like she was nuts. In those days it was very much about educating the consumer.

By the late 1980s, Nancy's son Carter and her daughter Roxanne had joined the venture full-time. While Beth had been contributing to the effort by periodically reviewing the aggregate financials for her mother, she had never taken much interest in the enterprise. So it was, with her mother's blessing and encouragement, that Beth earned her BS at Babson College in Wellesley, Massachusetts, and soon began a rewarding management career in consumer product marketing. Newly married, Beth happily immersed herself in the busy corporate world of high-profile projects and after-hours brainstorming sessions—first with PepsiCo, and later, with Johnson & Johnson:

I loved the work. I had a good salary, a 401(k), stock options, bonus check, company car, great suits; I was loving life.

Then suddenly, everything changed! Nancy died of cancer at the age of 56.

Beth Enters the Family Business

In 1993, Beth took a leave of absence from J&J to return home and help sort through the heartache and turmoil that followed her mother's death. Sandy Wood had inherited his wife's business, but made it clear that if his kids were not interested in keeping the small chain going, then he would either try to sell the sites or liquidate the assets.

Operating on the assumption that Beth would be returning to her corporate job once they had closed the doors on her mother's enterprise, Beth carefully examined the financials and visited each of the seven locations to estimate what they might be worth. In the course of that investigation, Beth realized that her mother had developed a solid business model within a largely untapped niche—suburban shopping malls—and she was drawn to the possibilities. Beth's husband, Bill, recalled that when Beth asked him to join her in the venture, it didn't take much convincing:

I was running a division of Bell Atlantic in Pennsylvania at the time. Beth and I had worked together much earlier in our lives; I had really enjoyed that. I have always figured that if two married people were meant to work together, it was Beth and I. We get along very well, and we both know our own place in the sandbox.

One of the issues that we discussed was that one of our egos would have to get checked at the door. I was a leader where I was working before, but I understood that this was Beth's family's business, and that she was now going to be the face of The Coffee Collection, now named Nancy's Coffee.

With equal amounts of sadness, trepidation, and excitement, Beth informed J&J that she would not be returning. Her father was pleased, and said that he would divest his interest in the business by annually gifting equal shares to his three children. It was understood by all that Beth would be the new CEO of Nancy's Coffee.

The Specialty Coffee Industry

The Green Dragon, a Boston coffeehouse founded in 1697, became the clandestine headquarters of the American revolution. It was there, in 1773, that the Boston Tea Party was planned as a protest against the tea taxes being levied by King George on his colonies. By the time the British and the colonists had settled accounts, coffee had become the hot beverage of choice in America.

Throughout the nineteenth century in the United States, neighborhood coffeehouses proliferated, and home-roasting coffee became a common practice. The industrial revolution, however, fostered a demand for quicker, cheaper, and easier caffeine solutions. With the advent of vacuum packaging and modern transportation, it became possible for a roaster on one side of the country to sell to a retailer on the other side. As with many other food products, quality was compromised to accommodate mass production and efficient distribution. By the 1940s, the coffeehouses had disappeared, and Americans had been sold on the idea that fresh coffee went "woosh" when the can was opened. In 1950, William Rosenberg founded Dunkin' Donuts in Quincy, Massachusetts. While his donut shop took pride in serving what they called the "World's Best Coffee," it would be twenty more years before U.S. consumers could purchase a truly high-end cup.

In the early 1970s, a small cadre of coffee aficionados began to offer a unique brew made from hand-picked beans, fresh-roasted in small batches. Peets, founded on the West Coast by legendary coffee idealist Alfred Peet, quickly set the standard for superb coffee. In Seattle, Gordon Bowker, Jerry Baldwin, and Zev Siegl, named their coffee shop business Starbucks, after the coffee-loving first mate in *Moby Dick*. On the East Coast, George Howell was building his chain of Coffee Connection shops in the Boston area. New Yorker Irwin White began making a name for himself supplying fresh-roasted grounds to some of the finest restaurants in Manhattan. San Franciscan coffee broker Erna Knutsen coined the term *Specialty Coffee*, and in 1985 helped to found the SCAA (Specialty Coffee Association of America).

SCAA membership grew steadily as these coffee pioneers—Nancy Wood included—developed dynamic, profitable business models by proactively educating American consumers about fine coffee. By the time Beth took the helm of her mother's business in 1993—the same year that Starbucks had gone public—upscale consumers had developed a real taste for an excellent brew.

Growth under the Radar Screen

Beth and her management team undertook an aggressive search for retail space. To facilitate that process, they worked almost exclusively with the regional mall management companies that had been doing business with their mother for years. Beth explained they chose this path partly as a way of dodging a direct confrontation with the powerhouse sweeping in from the west:

> Starbucks had clearly stated that as they came east they were going to do cities like Philadelphia, Boston, D.C., and Manhattan in a big way. We really didn't know how to play in that kind of shark tank, so we figured that we'd let Starbucks have that, and play the suburban card. And at the time, that was low-hanging fruit.

Even so, Beth was up against Starbucks almost immediately. One of her first meetings after coming on board concerned a regional mall lease that Starbucks had been considering for a while. During that meeting Beth suddenly realized how happy she was to be free of the inefficiency, multilayered bureaucracies that characterized much of corporate America:

There were two leases on the table: a Starbucks lease, and one for Nancy's Coffee. The mall representative said that the Starbucks lawyers had had the lease for six months—but she was willing to wait. I said, "Look, do you want Starbucks, or do you want a leased space?" When she said, "A leased space," I said, "Give me the pen." That lease is up next year, and I still haven't gotten around to reading it.

Beth noted that Starbucks wasn't the only coffee vendor shying away from space in enclosed malls:

Establishing your brand in mall locations is not, quite frankly, a strategy for the faint of heart. Managing a mall shop is a difficult business, and it costs a lot of money. That worked for us in a way, since newcomers would get scared off by the idea of paying something like $100,000 a year in rent, when they could be paying $2,000 a month for a Main Street space in "Anytown, USA."

The team had learned through their mother's experience, however, that these pricey mall locations offered an advantage that few suburban in-town settings could match: a captive base.

The Captive Audience

Throughout the 1990s, Nancy's Coffee and its suburban-model competitors like Peets and Caribou had the luxury of being able to choose locations where no other specialty coffee shops were operating. Beth explained that this monopolistic positioning was especially advantageous in a setting with high overhead and two distinct customer groups:

Our bread-and-butter customer is the mall employee—the three to five hundred people who come to the mall every day to work. If you can get them to try, you can get them to repeat.

Then, obviously, we have our transient customers, the shoppers. We have squarely positioned ourselves to cater to stroller moms—mothers with time on their hands and kids to entertain. They come to the mall for something to do; they may not always buy, but they always have to eat. So we have lots of cookies, apple juice, and bagels on hand for the little ones, which helps us get the mom for her cappuccino.

In January 2002, in a move to foster a loyal base of customers, Nancy's contracted with Paytronix, a nascent venture that had developed a swipe-card with both payment and loyalty program capabilities. Beth noted that the OneCard system (see Exhibit 14.1) went well beyond the paper cards used by a variety of food-retailers to encourage repeat business:

This is like an electronic punch card that also functions as a debit card—either by putting in a cash balance or by prepaying for product. For example, we have this one guy—an eyeglass store manager at a mall in New Hampshire—who shells out $150 on the first of each month to buy the 85 cappuccinos he knows he's going to drink over the next thirty days. We get his money upfront, and he gets our $3 drink for less than $2.

If you can get mall employees to buy a OneCard membership for a dollar a year, they're going to come to you every day, since for every nine drinks they get one free—they can even get a jumbo mocha in exchange for nine basic coffees. That's a drink that we sell for four dollars; free to them, and my cost is about seventy-five cents.

The OneCard is really a nice competitive advantage. We just had a Starbucks open in Buffalo, one floor below us. Our staff was nervous, but I didn't understand why. I told

EXHIBIT 14.1   **The OneCard**

The OneCard Concept

The OneCard is a true technological innovation never before utilized in a restaurant/retail environment. You can use the card to gather "loyalty points" toward free purchases, or, by storing money on the card, you can enjoy fast and easy payments—like having a Mobil SpeedPass for the best coffee products anywhere! The OneCard, which is activated at the time of purchase, can be used for instant discounts on the Web or at our fine cafes.

Two Membership Levels

Standard

- Nancy's Bonus Program (In Store): Beverages (Buy 9/1 Free), Lite Fare (Buy 5/1 Free), Bulk Coffee (Buy 9 lbs./ 1 lb. Free)
- Free beverage of your choice with OneCard Web Registration
- OneCard Standard Annual Membership: $1.00

Premium

- Nancy's Bonus Program (In Store): Beverages (Buy 9/1 Free), Lite Fare (Buy 5/1 Free), Bulk Coffee (Buy 9 1bs./ 1 lb. Free)
- Free beverage of your choice with OneCard Web Registration
- Free beverage of your choice every month for 1 year ($60.00 value)
- Nancy's SpeedPay (stored value)
- Monthly discounts & promotions
- OneCard Premium Annual Membership: $15.00

> them that with the OneCard, you already have all of your mall employees in your pocket. It worked; that Starbucks kiosk is struggling.

By late 2003, Nancy's Coffee shops could be found in over thirty locations from Boston west to Niagara Falls, and from Nashua, New Hampshire, south to New Jersey (see Exhibit 14.2). Three of the stores had been acquired from the owner of a four-chain enterprise who had come to the stark realization that running coffee shops was not going to be the road to riches that he had once imagined it would be. Beth recalled that they were able to make significant improvements in the stores they took under management:

EXHIBIT 14.2   Locations

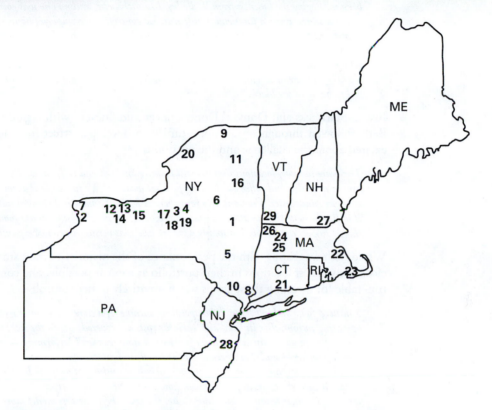

New York

Albany
1 Crossgates Mall

Buffalo
2 Walden Galleria

Clay (to be closed 01/04)
3 Great Northern Mall

DeWitt
4 Shoppingtown Mall

Middletown
5 Galleria @ Crystal Run

New Hartford
6 Sangertown Square Mall

Niagara Falls
7 Niagara Factory Outlet

West Nyack
8 Palisades Center Mall

Plattsburgh
9 Champlain Centré North

Poughkeepsie
10 Poughkeepsie Galleria

Queensbury
11 Aviation Mall

Rochester (4)
12 Frontier Field (Seasonal)
13 Irondequoit Mall
14 Marketplace Mall
15 Eastview Mall

Saratoga Springs
16 Wilton Mall

Syracuse (3)
17 Carousel Center
18 Carousel Center (Kiosk)
19 Center Armory

Watertown
20 Salmon Run Mall

Connecticut
Madison
21 RJ Café; RJ Julia Bookstore

Massachusetts
Boston
22 Copley Place (to be closed 02/04)

Dartmouth
23 Dartmouth Mall

Holyoke (2)
24 Holyoke Mall @ Ingleside
25 1st & 2nd Level

Lanesboro
26 Berkshire Mall

New Hampshire
Nashua
27 Pheasant Lane Mall

New Jersey
Freehold
28 Freehold Raceway Mall

Vermont
Manchster
29 4943 Main Street

> *When we acquired Café Coffee, their gross margins were running in the low 30s. They had been managing the business from Wellesley, Massachusetts, and no one was going out to visit the stores. From a financial standpoint, we controlled the employee hours and monitored the food costs. That helped to drive their gross margins closer to 50%. Operationally, we kept some of their people, but not all. We put some of our own people in who had much different operational standards than the Café Coffee people. At one store, we saw an increase in customer count, and in 6 months that store went from being in the red to being in the black.*

Just as Starbucks and Dunkin' Donuts never said "never" with regard to mall locations, Beth followed through on an opportunity to develop a street-front location. She was excited about the challenge and the possibilities:

> *There are so many locations that are still looking for high-end coffee bars. The question is, are we as a high-end coffee bar looking for that location? We just opened a store on the street in Manchester, Vermont. My rent there is $1,800 a month. I think it will work, but it will take some time to attract a customer base. If we can find some more good towns like that, I suspect that we will probably do more like that versus more mall expansions.*

While Beth was happy with the performance of the majority of their stores, she sought to close the weakest locations in their portfolio as soon as possible. She commented that the timetable for divesting those shops was not entirely in her control:

> *You need to be making 15 to 20% operating income. If a store can't make 15% in operating income after its fixed and variable costs are covered—then the store needs to be closed. But in our business, you can't just close a store that isn't performing—even one that is losing money—and that's because of the leases we have to sign.*
>
> *These management companies finance their malls using not only the building as collateral, but the leases as proof of cash flow and their ability to repay the debt. If they were to give their tenants a kick-out clause, it makes their business model more risky and harder to leverage for borrowing. That's why they insist on five, seven and ten year leases.*
>
> *I have a couple of locations I'd like to close tomorrow, but it would mean paying a termination fee—and leaving all my investment behind in terms of property, plant, and equipment. You can be sure that the day those leases expire—those stores will be gone.*

Managing the Organization

Before his death in 1999, Sandy Wood completed the gifting of the business to his children—all as shares, except for the first distribution, when Roxanne and Carter had received a cash equivalent in lieu of stock. Beth now had a slightly larger stock position which left her to direct the company's future:

> *My brother said that after 15 years, it was time for him to go work for somebody else. So I suggested that Roxanne and I buy his stock and split it evenly. I own 51 percent of the business and my sister owns 49 percent. Our bylaws are very clear the control rests with the majority ownership. It is now my responsibility to set the business on a strategic path for growth.*

Beth had discovered that "living and dying by every single decision every single day" fired her up in ways that her corporate job could not. Now a mother of an eight- and a five-year-old, she reflected that running the show had given her the freedom to craft a working environment that was far more response to the rhythm of life:

I know that I never would have had children if I had stayed in corporate America. Now my time is much more my own than it ever was. I may work longer hours than I did in corporate, but if I want to leave at two o'clock to go watch my daughter in a French play, I can do that. This path has helped me to get more balance.

I take the position that as long as you get your work done, it makes no difference to me how you configure those hours. When I had my first child, my bookkeeper's baby was due three months later. So we set up a nursery in my office and hired someone to watch over the babies.

Right now I have four key people out on maternity leave! The other day one of my managers said to me that these are people who watched me. have two children without skipping a beat—that I have allowed them to be moms and to be professionals at the same time. It's great to have that kind of impact.

The Nancy's Coffee business was supported by a six-person staff at the home office in Madison, Connecticut. Roxanne oversaw the purchase and delivery of goods like fresh-roasted coffee, display-shelf merchandise, and branded paper supplies—all drop-shipped to the individual stores by the various vendors. Perishables such as dairy, breads, and confections were procured at the store level.

In addition to the administrative team, the organization fielded a number of experienced supervisors to oversee training, quality, and recruitment. While the company had enjoyed years of loyal service from many of these senior managers (see Exhibit 14.3), Beth had discovered early on that it wasn't long-term staff that she had to worry about:

EXHIBIT 14.3 Management Structure; Years of Service

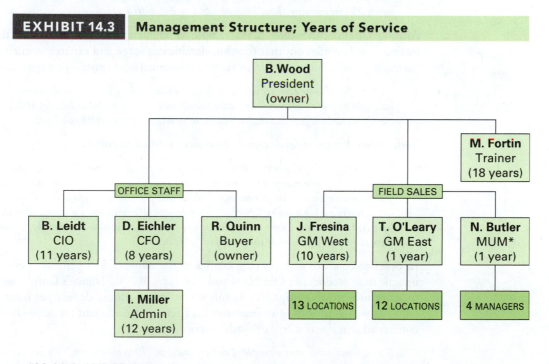

*Multiple Unit Manager

The retail employee population is the reason that a lot of people franchise—they don't want to manage those headaches. And you will hear me say every week that, boy, if I didn't have employees, I'd have no problems!

The Revolving Door

In 1997, as Beth prepared to file over 1,500 W-2 forms for 250 positions at the company, she realized that the company needed to make a fundamental change:

> *Our employee turnover that year was 700% . It was staggering. We did some analysis and saw that the under-18 kids were just a revolving door. I had this kid Chaz leave his keys on the register and walk out—he left the store wide open with nobody there. I held his final pay check because I wanted to find out why he did that. When he finally did call, he swore up and down at me for not mailing his check to him right away. At that point I'd had enough; we were done with those people.*
>
> *So we stopped hiring under-18 workers by taking advantage of a Department of Labor crackdown on minors working in food service operations. An espresso machine, for example, is considered high-pressure steam equipment—and minors were not permitted to operate it—so we started saying that because of that and other restrictions, we could only hire people over the age of 18.*
>
> *Last year my turnover was 200%—all of it at the 18-to 24-year-old range. By lowering that churn, we were doing less training and hiring. That cut our labor cost a full point; it's now running about 28% of sales (see Exhibit 14.4).*

Although Beth acknowledged that employee challenges were inherent in the retailing business, she pointed out that the considerable challenge and expense of hiring, training, managing, and retaining viable workers was lessened when employees got involved:

> *We have found some families who were interested in working for us, and we hired their kids, and their kids' husbands and their friends and cousins, and that has sort of helped us create an employee population that has, in some locations, been relatively loyal.*

Beth added that the motivations of new-hires seemed to correlate with age:

> *With young people, it's always, "what are you gonna pay me?" They don't really care about the job security. But once people hit their 30s and early 40s, they want to know that they will have some job security, for example, "What role position can I play, and if I perform, will you give me job security?" Nothing is for certain, of course, but I do think that we have created a culture where employees know I won't walk in, demand their keys, and tell them to get out. That sort of thing happens a lot in retail.*

In order to compete with starting salaries in the range of $10 per hour being offered by upscale mall vendors like Old Navy and The Gap, in 2001 Nancy's Coffee began to allow its workforce to accept tips. While this was a way of adding dollars per hour to the base pay—as well as providing an incentive for friendly and efficient service—Beth remained concerned that it was a very difficult practice to oversee:

> *If a customer hands over a couple of dollars and says, "Keep the change," it's just too easy to drop everything in the tip cup and not ring up the sale. That happens a lot, and there are very few point-of-sale systems for cash-based businesses that can keep theft to a minimum. I wish everybody could pay with plastic, because even though I'd be paying 3% to the card companies, I would know the money is coming to me at the end of the day.*

EXHIBIT 14.4	Statements of Income and Retained Earnings (Fiscal Year Ending 09/30)					
	2003	%	2002	%	2001	%
Sales	6,972,553	100.0	7,443,429	100.0	7,387,620	100.0
Cost of Goods Sold						
Beginning Inventory	128,620	1.8	115,343	1.5	82,027	1.1
Purchases	1,936,778	27.8	2,068,914	27.8	2,047,361	27.7
Direct Labor	1,930,639	27.7	2,062,481	27.7	2,107,349	28.5
Payroll Taxes	187,892	2.7	196,906	2.6	197,524	2.7
Supplies	20,697	0.3	33,008	0.4	31,234	0.4
Less Ending Inventory	(154,884)	(2.2)	(128,620)	(1.7)	(115,343)	(1.6)
Total Cost of Goods Sold	4,049,742	58.1	4,348,032	58.4	4,350,152	58.9
Gross Profit	2,922,811	41.9	3,095,397	41.6	3,037,468	41.1
General & Administration Expenses						
Rent; Retail Outlets	1,913,196	27.4	2,059,796	27.7	1,981,514	26.8
Other G & A	725,722	10.4	765,214	10.3	853,747	11.6
Total G & A Expenses	2,638,918	37.8	2,825,010	38.0	2,835,261	38.4
Income from Operations	283,893	4.1	270,387	3.6	202,207	2.7
Other Expense						
Interest Expense	80,427	1.2	97,534	1.3	105,571	1.4
Misc. Expense	–	–	19,818	0.3	–	–
Loss on Disposal of PPE (from Store Closings)	253,828	3.6	272,286	3.7	133,541	1.8
Total Other Expense	334,255	4.8	389,638	5.2	239,112	3.2
Profit (Loss) Before Recovery of Income Taxes	(50,362)	(0.7)	(119,251)	(1.6)	(36,905)	(0.5)
Recovery of Income Taxes	43,973	0.6	12,705	0.2	6,572	0.1
Net Profit (Loss)	(6,389)	(0.1)	(106,546)	(1.4)	(30,333)	(0.4)
Retained Earnings						
Beginning	602,507		709,054		739,387	
Ending	596,118		602,508		709,054	
Number of Stores	30		30		32	

Beth concluded that the primary advantage of the tip program was that it pushed up wages by as much as $10 per hour over the base salary during the frenzied winter shopping season. The prospect of that extra compensation was enough to virtually eliminate employee turnover during the fiscal quarter that had the largest impact on the bottom line.

Financial Management

In the early days, Beth used to review the company financials with the aim of providing her mother with a general assessment of aggregate performance. As CEO, Beth was shocked at the lax financial management that she uncovered when she attended to the details. At the same time, she was thrilled about how fast she'd be able to make a real difference:

> When I first arrived at Nancy's nobody in the organization could read a financial statement. Store managers were spending like crazy drunks—buying bagels for a dollar and selling them for 99 cents. I have brought about a complete shift from my Mom's approach—from thinking that financials were something that accountants (and daughters) took care of—to running this thing like a real business.
>
> Store managers are now accountable for their bottom line, and they are very cost conscious because of it. I had to educate them on how to read a profit and loss statement, and I made that skill part of their review. They know that they need to negotiate the price on everything they buy, and they understand that their cost of goods can't exceed 30%. That means that if they are planning to sell a napoleon for $1.99, then they know that they can't pay more than 60 cents for it.

The company had attempted to design a program that would link these required skills to a performance reward, but Beth noted that it had not worked out:

> We tried to do a performance bonus that was based on our three key numbers for evaluation: sales, labor, and net operating income. Almost nobody received the bonus because in order for the curve to work, we had to set the bar really high. Those people who did earn bonuses didn't seem to value it very much; they still wanted their raise at the end of the year as part of their performance evaluation. The mindset wasn't right the first time we tried it; we will regularly revisit that opportunity.

With regard to justifying her passion for developing stringent systems and standards, Beth referred to the ominous weather forecast:

> It's the beginning of the Christmas season, and if we get the 20 inches of snow throughout the Northeast like they're predicting, our overall sales this weekend will be cut by at least a third; just because of one poorly timed snowstorm! There are so many factors—like the weather—that I've discovered I just can't control, so as a result you have to over-control the things you can have an influence over.

Pointing out a significant decrease in accounts payable in her cash flow statement (see Exhibit 14.5), Beth explained that she had recently initiated a move designed to lower prices, generate more volume, and become more competitive:

> When we were smaller, I was buying the very top end of the six grades of coffee that our roaster offers. The people we attracted years ago were extremely discerning, but we had so few of them. As the market has matured, and more players have come into the marketplace, people's perception of coffee quality had been diluted. I decided that it would be okay to dial back a little on our quality a bit, and I think that is working out for us.

Beth was now satisfied that she had created the financial and managerial groundwork that could support an aggressive expansion. The challenge was that despite the great strides the company had made toward sustainable profitability, Nancy's current funding source was highly reluctant to fuel the aggressive expansion effort that Beth was anxious to undertake.

Fueling Growth

Cash flow from operations, plus long-term debt borrowings, generated an annual investment pool of between $400,000 and $500,000 (see Exhibit 14.5). Maintenance and

EXHIBIT 14.5	Cash Flow Statements (Fiscal Year Ending 09/30)		
	2003	**2002**	**2001**
Cash Flows from Operating Activities			
Net Loss	(6,389)	(106,546)	(30,333)
Adjustments to Reconcile Net Loss to Net Cash			
Provided by Operating Activities			
Amortization and Depreciation	204,589	258,294	245,366
Deferred Income Taxes	(4,000)	(14,000)	(12,000)
Loss on Disposal of Property, Plant, and Equipment	253,828	272,286	133,541
Changes in Operating Assets and Liabilities			
Increase in Inventory	(26,264)	(13,277)	(33,316)
Decrease in Prepaid Expenses	–	5,621	26,086
Decrease in Accounts Payable, Accrued Expenses	15,347	(142,673)	(100,290)
Net Cash Provided by Operating Activities	437,111	259,705	229,054
Cash Flows from Investing Activities			
Purchase of Property, Plant, and Equipment	(274,539)	(144,918)	(196,796)
Increase in Deposits	(289)	(1,322)	(4,790)
Increase in Intangible Assets	783	(1,724)	(2,950)
Net Cash Used by Investing Activities	(274,045)	(147,964)	(204,536)
Cash Flows from Financing Activities			
Principal Payments on Long-Term Borrowings	(291,023)	(314,760)	(473,161)
Proceeds from Long-Term Debt	239,857	236,000	292,996
Principal Payments Under Capital Lease Obligations	(59,567)	(48,503)	(32,879)
Proceeds from Loans Payable; Officers and Related Party	–	223,100	476,780
Payment on Loans Payable; Officers and Related Party	(188,781)	(162,002)	(290,778)
Net Cash Used by Financing Activities	(299,514)	(66,165)	(27,042)
Net Increase (Decrease) in Cash	(66,448)	(45,576)	(2,524)
Cash; Beginning	91,053	45,477	48,001
Cash; Ending	24,605	91,053	45,477

upgrade expenses on existing stores were running about $200,000, leaving enough capital to open two new stores at an average build-out cost of $150,000 each. While this dynamic had enabled Nancy's to grow to nearly thirty stores, Beth explained that from a financial standpoint, the business was not ready for sale:

> There's not enough money in it for me to give this up right now. At this point we'd be looking at a million and a half, maybe two million for the whole thing. I've got a $350,000 bank debt, and a bit more than that in outstanding payables. At the end of the day my sister and I might split about a million dollars. I just think that I've worked too hard for nearly eleven years for a half a million bucks.

Beth figured that to reach a size worthy of harvest, they would need to add fifteen to twenty more stores to the chain—at a growth clip of five to seven stores per year. Beth referred to recent balance sheets (see Exhibit 14.6) as she discussed the weaknesses of their existing leverage arrangements:

EXHIBIT 14.6 Balance Sheets (Fiscal Year Ending 09/30)

ASSETS	30-Sep-03	30-Sep-02	30-Sep-01
Current Assets			
Cash	24,605	91,053	45,477
Inventory	154,884	128,620	115,343
Prepaid Expenses			5,621
Total Current Assets	179,489	219,673	166,441
Property, Plant, and Equipment			
Automobiles & Trucks	102,390	98,698	110,781
Equipment	1,092,449	975,312	1,060,069
Furniture & Fixtures	365,585	404,093	410,021
Leasehold Improvements	2,116,370	2,385,453	2,674,878
Total PPE	3,676,794	3,863,556	4,255,749
Less Accumulated Depreciation	(1,703,669)	(1,737,308)	(1,785,909)
PPE; Net	1,973,125	2,126,248	2,469,840
Other Assets			
Intangibles; Net	26,071	26,854	29,232
Deposits	14,269	13,980	12,658
Deferred Income Taxes	42,000	38,000	24,000
Total Other Assets	82,340	78,834	65,890
Total Assets	2,234,954	2,424,755	2,702,171

LIABILITIES	30-Sep-03	30-Sep-02	30-Sep-01
Current Liabilities			
Notes Payable; Demand	150,000	150,000	150,000
Current Portion of Notes Payable	199,604	273,182	338,241
Accounts Payable	384,342	371,139	515,799
Current Portion; Capital Lease Obligations	54,857	55,350	44,540
Accrued Taxes and Expenses	117,644	115,500	113,513
Notes and Loans Payable; Officers	180,932	97,992	97,992
Loans Payable; Shareholders	50,625	38,526	35,929
Total Current Liabilities	1,138,004	1,101,689	1,296,014
Long-Term Liabilities			
Notes Payable	245,968	223,556	237,257
Capital Lease Obligations	87,164	115,482	136,827
Notes and Loans Payable; Officers	–	228,695	131,668
Loans Payable; Shareholders	137,700	122,825	161,351
Total Long-Term Liabilities	470,832	690,558	667,103
Total Liabilities	1,608,836	1,792,247	1,963,117
Stockholders' Equity			
Capital Stock	30,000	30,000	30,000
Retained Earnings	596,118	602,508	709,054
Total Stockholders' Equity	626,118	632,508	739,054
Total Liabilities and Stockholders' Equity	2,234,954	2,424,755	2,702,171

My bank has been great to me. I have a million-dollar line of credit, but because I'm a cash flow customer—without some big building to give them as collateral—they keep me on short leash. We sign 10-year leases at our locations, but the bank is unwilling to go beyond 36 months on debt repayment. That doesn't work for us. What we need to do is raise a million dollars, pay off our bank debt, and use the remaining capital either to open new stores or acquire some more independent shops that are in good locations but are struggling financially. If our bank will give us the terms we need, then we'd love to continue to pass our millions through them—if not, we'll have to go elsewhere.

Beth was working with an advisor to develop a proposal for a million-dollar loan with a ten-year term. They planned to give her current institution a one-month lead time on the idea. If those bankers wouldn't offer more liberal terms, then the plan was to find a lender—or an individual—who would. While she preferred to raise the funds as long-term debt rather than give up equity, Beth was open to the idea of bringing on board a moneyed partner in exchange for a piece of the business—as long as she could maintain her majority position. Failing that course, Beth reflected on what seemed to her as a viable, but less attractive, option:

I figure that I could always cut back to ten stores and three million dollars in sales. In that case we'd have no headquarters—bookkeeping, purchasing, tech support—all of that goes away and I'd run the thing from my home with some senior people to cover the stores. But I think if I did that, I would probably open another business and do something else in addition to that. That's why I want to explore the growth path first. If we can't grow or get acquired, then the ten-store idea is a retrenching position that I could fall back to.

Ever since her business management initiatives had begun to yield sustained profitability, Beth had been considering franchising as a way to leverage those systems, along with the Nancy's brand name and the interesting story behind it:

I have thought about the franchise route a lot, and I have considered bringing someone on board to help me explore that opportunity. You can certainly get growth faster and cheaper by franchising, but there are trade-offs. Franchising for me is a struggle between control and lack of control; influence and lack of influence.

One aspect that I'm not too excited about, for example, is that as a franchise organization, all of my personal and business finances would be out there for all to see. Right now, as a small business owner with everything privately held, I have a lot of flexibility. If I stepped into the role of managing franchisees, they would hold me financially accountable for every step that I made; I'm not so sure that is a stress that I need right now.

I also like the culture that we have been able to create. From Niagara Falls to Boston, we have built a culture that feels like the same company. That is often not the case with franchises.

In an effort to leave no stone unturned, Beth had arranged a meeting with senior managers at Starbucks. She explained that while her instincts had probably been correct, she probably should have guessed the outcome:

Strategically my idea to have them acquire us made a lot of sense. They are not in enclosed shopping malls, they are really not having great success in New England because their coffee is too dark-roasted for most people, and they don't sell flavored coffee—which is 65% of what we sell. Their response was, "We like your business and we think it's interesting, but we don't do malls." As one of my business advisors said, you can't force an acquisition down somebody's throat; when they have a board meeting and they decide that they are going to go out and buy a small chain in our region, then we'll probably be the one they call first.

Moving Target

Beth took another sip of her warm cappuccino, thinking that it was about time to wrap up her cell chat and get back to the tasks at hand. Thanking her friend for the call and encouraging words, Beth added:

> *Don't get me wrong—you know I love this business. I just think that I have to make some fundamental decisions about where we should go—either an exit strategy, or a more aggressive growth strategy. Should we cut back to ten of our best stores and run it as a side venture? Or maybe franchise, or locate some equity partner and open new stores until we become a more attractive acquisition target? I don't have the answers, but I can tell you that the questions are sure keeping me up at night! Good thing I know where to get a great cup of coffee, huh?*

Preparation Questions

1. Based on your analysis of the case, what course of action would you recommend to Nancy going forward?

2. Imaging that you are Beth's current banker. You have reviewed her request for a $1 million expansion loan with a ten-year term. If you don't offer the loan, she takes her business elsewhere. What will you tell her?

3. How much equity might Beth be asked to give up in exchange for the $1 million she seeks to expand the business. If you could, would you become her equity partner? What kind of arrangement would you suggest?

4. Discuss this business venture from a lifestyle point of view. Would you be drawn to a venture such as this one? Why or why not?

GLOSSARY

Accredited Investor: Under the Securities Act of 1933, a company that offers or sells its securities must register the securities with the SEC or find an exemption from the registration requirements. The Act provides companies with a number of exemptions. For some of the exemptions, such as rules 505 and 506 of Regulation D, a company may sell its securities to what are known as "accredited investors."

The federal securities laws define the term **accredited investor** in Rule 501 of Regulation D as:

1. a bank, insurance company, registered investment company, business development company, or small business investment company; an employee benefit plan, within the meaning of the Employee Retirement Income Security Act, if a bank, insurance company, or registered investment adviser makes the investment decisions, or if the plan has total assets in excess of $5 million;

2. a charitable organization, corporation, or partnership with assets exceeding $5 million;

3. a director, executive officer, or general partner of the company selling the securities;

4. a business in which all the equity owners are accredited investors;

5. a natural person who has individual net worth, or joint net worth with the person's spouse, that exceeds $1 million at the time of the purchase;

6. a natural person with income exceeding $200,000 in each of the two most recent years or joint income with a spouse exceeding $300,000 for those years and a reasonable expectation of the same income level in the current year; or

7. a trust with assets in excess of $5 million, not formed to acquire the securities offered, whose purchases a sophisticated person makes.

Acquisition: Acquiring control of a corporation, called a target, by stock purchase or exchange, either hostile or friendly; also called **takeover**.

Agency theory: A branch of economics dealing with the behavior of principals (for example, owners) and their agents (for example, managers).

All-hands meeting: A meeting of managers, lawyers, accountants, and investment bankers that sets the timetable and tasks to be accomplished prior to an initial public offering.

American Stock Exchange (Amex): Stock exchange located in New York, listing companies that are generally smaller and younger than those on the much larger New York Stock Exchange.

Angel: An individual who invests in private companies. The term business angel is sometimes reserved for sophisticated angel investors who invest sizeable sums in private companies. *(See informal investor.)*

Anglo-Saxon capitalism: So-called Anglo-Saxon capitalism (also Anglo-Saxon finance) is largely practiced in English speaking countries such as the United Kingdom and the United States). It is a capitalist macroeconomic model in which levels of regulation and taxes are low. In addition, Anglo-Saxon economies generally are more "liberal" and free-market oriented than other capitalist economies in the world. Another major difference between Anglo-Saxon and non-Anglo-Saxon countries is the legal system, which is based on case-law rather than civil code law.

Antidilution (of ownership): The right of an investor to maintain the same percentage of ownership of a company's common stock in the event that the company issues more stock. *(See dilution.)*

Asked: The price level at which sellers offer securities to buyers.

ASP (Application Service Provider): An ASP deploys, hosts, and manages access to a packaged software application for multiple parties from a centrally managed facility. The applications are delivered over networks on a subscription basis.

Asset acquisition: Means of affecting a buyout by purchase of certain desired assets rather than shares of the target company.

Asset-based valuation: This method considers the fair market value of fixed assets and equipment, and inventory. It is most appropriate for asset intensive businesses such as retail and manufacturing companies.

Audited financial statements: A company's financial statements prepared and certified by a certified public accounting firm that is totally independent of the company.

Babson College: Babson College, located in Wellesley, Massachusetts, is recognized internationally for its entrepreneurial leadership in a changing global environment. Babson grants BS, MBA, and custom MS and MBA degrees, and has a school of executive education. The Arthur M. Blank Center for Entrepreneurship was dedicated in 1998, and provides a dynamic home for Babson's world-famous entrepreneurship program.

Backlog: The sales that have been made but not fulfilled due to lack of inventory to finalize the sale.

Bake-off: When a private company compares offers from different investment banks to take it public.

Balance sheet: Summary statement of a company's financial position at a given point in time. It summarizes the accounting value of the assets, liabilities, preferred stock, common stock, and retained earnings. Assets = Liabilities + Preferred stock + Common stock + Retained earnings. *(See pro forma statements.)*

Basis point: One-hundredth of a percent (0.01%), typically used in expressing yield differentials ($1.50\% - 1.15\% = 0.35\%$, or 35 basis points). *(See yield.)*

Bear: A person who expects prices to fall.

Bear market: A period of generally falling prices and pessimistic attitudes.

Best efforts offering: The underwriter makes its best efforts to sell as much as it can of the shares at the offering price. Hence, unlike a firm commitment offering the company offering its shares is not guaranteed a definite amount of money by the underwriter.

Beauty contest: When investment banks make their best offers to take a company public.

Bid: The price level at which buyers offer to acquire securities from sellers.

Big Board: *See New York Stock Exchange.*

Blue sky: Refers to laws that safeguard investors from being misled by unscrupulous promoters of companies with little or no substance.

Book value (of an asset): The accounting value of an asset as shown on a balance sheet is the cost of the asset minus its accumulated depreciation. It is not necessarily identical to its market value.

Book value (of a company): The common stock equity shown on the balance sheet. It is equal to total assets minus liabilities and preferred stock (synonymous with net worth and owners' equity).

Bootstrap: To build a business out of nothing, with minimal outside capital.

Bottom-up forecasting: Forecasting your income sheet revenue and expenses based upon a typical day and then multiplying those forecasts by the number of days in the period (i.e., month, quarter, or year).

Brain-writing: Similar to brainstorming, but the process is done with written versus oral communication. Ideas are presented and participants add their thoughts in writing. The key is to build on the idea rather than argue why the idea can't work.

Break-even point: The sales volume at which a company's net sales revenue just equals its costs. A commonly used approximate formula for the break-even point is Sales revenue = Total fixed costs/Gross margin.

Bridge financing: Short-term finance that is expected to be repaid relatively quickly. It usually bridges a short-term financing need. For example, it provides cash needed before an expected stock flotation.

Burn rate: The negative, real-time cash flow from a company's operations, usually computed monthly.

Business Angel: *See angel.*

Business model: The way in which a business makes a profit. As an example, here is IBM's definition of its business model: "IBM sells services, hardware and software. These offerings are bolstered by IBM's research and development capabilities. If a customer requires financing, IBM can provide that too." Southwest Airlines' business model is to provide inexpensive fares by keeping costs low through being more efficient than its major competitors.

Business plan: Document prepared by entrepreneurs, possibly in conjunction with their professional advisors, detailing the past, present, and intended future of the company. It contains a thorough analysis of the managerial, physical, labor, product, and financial resources of the company, plus the background of the company, its previous trading record, and its market position. The business plan contains detailed profit, balance sheet, and cash flow projections for two years ahead, and less detailed information for the following three years. The business plan crystallizes and focuses the management team's ideas. It explains their strategies, sets objectives, and is used to monitor their subsequent performance.

Buyback: A corporation's repurchase of stock that it has previously issued; for example, a company buys its stock back from a venture capital firm that has previously been issued stock in return for money invested in the company.

Call: A contract allowing the issuer of a security to buy back that security from the purchaser at an agreed-upon price during a specific period of time.

Capital gain: The amount by which the selling price of an asset (for example, common stock) exceeds the seller's initial purchase price.

Capitalization rate: The discount rate, K, used to determine the present value of a stream of future earnings. $PV = $ (Normalized earnings after taxes)$/(K/100)$, where PV is the present value of the firm and K is the firm's cost of capital.

Carried interest: A venture capital firm's share of the profit earned by a fund. In the United States, the carried interest (carry) is typically 20% of the profit after investors' principal has been repaid.

Cash flow: The difference between the company's cash receipts and its cash payments in a given period.

Cash-flow statement: A summary of a company's cash flow over a period of time. *(See pro forma statements.)*

Channel coverage: The product distribution strategy in regards to how many channels to use. It can be intensive (multiple channels), selective (a subset of channels), or exclusive (one channel).

Chattel (or property) mortgage: A loan secured by specific assets.

Classic venture capital: Money invested privately in seed-, startup-, expansion-, and late-stage companies by venture capital firms. The term "classic" is used to distinguish from money invested privately in acquisitions, buyouts, mergers, and reorganizations.

Collateral: An asset pledged as security for a loan.

Common stock: Shares of ownership, or equity, in a corporation.

Common-sized income statement: Converting the income statement into percentages with total revenue equaling 100% and all other lines a percentage of total revenue.

Comparable: Using existing industry or company financials to forecast your own venture's financials.

Compensating balance: A bank requires a customer to maintain a certain level of demand deposits that do not bear interest. The interest forgone by the customer on the compensating balance recompenses the bank for services provided, credit lines, and loans.

Conversion ratio: The number of shares of common stock that may be received in exchange for each share of a convertible security.

Convertible debt: A loan that can be exchanged for equity.

Convertible security: Preferred stock that is convertible into common stock according to a specified ratio at the security holder's option.

Corporation: A business form that is an entity legally separate from its owners. Its important features include limited liability, easy transfer of ownership, and unlimited life.

Cost of capital: The required rate of return of various types of financing. The overall cost of capital is a weighted average of the individual required rates of returns (costs).

Cost of debt capital: The interest rate charged by a company's lenders.

Cost of equity capital: The rate of return on investment required by the company's common shareholders (colloquially called the hurdle rate).

Cost of goods sold: The direct cost of the product sold. For a retail business, the cost of all goods sold in a given period equals the inventory at the beginning of the period plus the cost of goods purchased during that period minus the inventory at the end of the period.

Cost of preferred stock: The rate of return on investment required by the company's preferred shareholders.

Covenant: A restriction on a borrower imposed by a lender. For example, it could be a requirement placed on a company to achieve and maintain specified targets such as levels of cash flow, balance sheet ratios, or specified capital expenditure levels in order to retain financing facilities.

Cumulative dividend provision: A requirement that unpaid dividends on preferred stock accumulate and have to be paid before a dividend is paid on common stock.

Current ratio: Current assets/Current liabilities. This ratio indicates a company's ability to cover its current liabilities with its current assets.

Customer relationship management (CRM): Systems designed to compile and manage data about customers.

Customer value proposition (CVP): The difference between total customer benefits and total customer costs, which are both monetary and non-monetary.

Deal flow: The rate at which new investment propositions come to funding institutions.

Debenture: A document containing an acknowledgment of indebtedness on the part of a company, usually secured by a charge on the company's assets.

Debt service: Payments of principal and interest required on a debt over a given period.

Deep pockets: Refers to an investor who has substantial financial resources.

Default: The nonperformance of a stated obligation. The nonpayment by the issuer of interest or principal on a bond or the nonperformance of a covenant.

Deferred payment: A debt that has been incurred and will be repaid at some future date.

Depreciation: The systematic allocation of the cost of an asset over a period of time for financial reporting and tax purposes.

Dilution (of ownership): When a new stock issue results in a decrease in the preissue owners' percentage of the common stock.

Discounted cash flow (DCF): Method of evaluating investments by adjusting the cash flows for the time value of money. In the decision to invest in a project, all future cash flows expected from that investment are discounted back to their present value at the time the investment is made. The discount rate is whatever rate of return the investor requires. In theory, if the present value of the future cash flows is greater than the money being invested, the investment should be made. *(See discount rate, internal rate of return, net present value, and present value.)*

Discount rate (capitalization rate): Rate of return used to convert future values to present values. *(See capitalization rate, internal rate of return, and rate of return.)*

DJIA: Dow Jones Industrial Average. The Dow Jones Industrial Average is a price-weighted average of 30 significant stocks traded on the New York Stock Exchange and the NASDAQ. The DJIA was invented by Charles Dow back in 1896. Often referred to as "the Dow," the DJIA is the oldest and single most watched index in the world. The DJIA includes companies like General Electric, Disney, Exxon, and Microsoft.

Doriot, General Georges: Founder of the modern venture capital industry, Harvard Business School professor, and one of the creators of INSEAD.

Double jeopardy: The case where an entrepreneur's main source of income and most of her/his net worth depend on her/his business.

Due diligence: The process of investigation by investors into a potential investee's management team, resources, and trading performance. This includes rigorous testing of the business plan assumptions and the verification of material facts (such as existing accounts).

Dun & Bradstreet (D&B): The biggest credit-reporting agency in the United States.

Early-stage financing: This category includes seed-stage, startup-stage, and first-stage financing.

Earnings: This is synonymous with income and profit.

Earnings before interest and taxes (EBIT): *See operating income.*

Earnings before interest, taxes, depreciation, and amortization (EBITDA): Often referred to as cash flow. It removes non-cash charges, such as depreciation and amortization, to get a clearer view of the cash-flow-generating ability of a company.

Earning-capitalization valuation: This values a company by capitalizing its earnings. Company value = Net income/Capitalization rate.

Earnings per share (EPS): A company's net income divided by the number of common shares issued and outstanding.

Earn-out: A common contract provision when a company is sold or acquired. The founders will earn a portion of the sales price over time based upon continuing performance of the new venture.

Elasticity of demand: The percentage change in the quantity of a good demanded divided by the percentage change in the price of that good. When the elasticity is greater than 1, the demand is said to be elastic, and when it is less than 1, it is inelastic. In the short term, the demand for nonessential goods (for example, airline travel) is usually elastic, and the demand for essentials (for example, electricity) is usually inelastic.

Employee stock ownership plan (ESOP): A trust established to acquire shares in a company for subsequent allocation to employees over a period of time. Several possibilities are available for structuring the operation of an ESOP. Essentially, either the company makes payments to the trust, which the trust uses to purchase shares; or the trust, having previously borrowed to acquire shares, may use the payments from the company to repay loans. The latter form is referred to as a leveraged ESOP and may be used as a means of providing part of the funding required to affect a buyout. A particular advantage of an ESOP is the possibility of tax relief for the contributions made by the company to the trust and on the cost of borrowing in those cases where the trust purchases shares in advance.

Employment agreement: An agreement whereby senior managers contract to remain with the company for a specified period. For the investing institutions, such an agreement provides some measure of security that the company's performance will not be adversely affected by the unexpected departure of key managers.

Equity: *See owners' equity.*

Equity kicker (or warrant): An option or instrument linked to the provision of other types of funding, particularly mezzanine finance, which enables the provider to obtain an equity stake and hence a share in capital gains. In this way, providers of subordinated debt can be compensated for the higher risk they incur.

EU: The European Union, originally included the following countries: the Netherlands, Sweden, Finland, Denmark, Germany, Belgium, Luxembourg, the United Kingdom, Ireland, France, Austria, Portugal, Spain, Italy, and Greece. Since May 1. 2004, the following countries also belong to the EU: Cyprus, Estonia, Hungary, Latvia, Lithuania, Malta, Poland, Slovakia, Slovenia, and the Czech Republic.

Exit: The means by which investors in a company realize all or part of their investment. *(See harvest.)*

Expansion financing: Working capital for the initial expansion of a company that is producing and shipping products and has growing accounts receivable and inventories.

Factoring: A means of enhancing the cash flow of a business. A factoring company pays to the firm a certain proportion of the value of the firm's trade debts and then receives the cash as the trade debtors settle their accounts. Invoice discounting is a similar procedure.

FAQ: Frequently asked questions—a computer text file that contains answers to common questions about a topic.

FASB (Financial Accounting Standards Board): A private sector board (industry) that establishes financial accounting and reporting standards.

Filing: Documents, including the prospectus, filed with the SEC for approval before an IPO.

Financing flows: Cash flows generated by debt and equity financing.

Finder: A person or firm that attempts to raise funding for a private company.

Firm commitment offering: The underwriter guarantees to raise a certain amount of money for the company and other selling stockholders at the IPO.

First-round financing: The first investment made by external investors.

First-stage financing: Financing to initiate full manufacturing and sales.

Five Cs of credit: The five crucial elements for obtaining credit are character (borrower's integrity), capacity (sufficient cash flow to service the debt), capital (borrower's net worth), collateral (assets to secure the debt), and conditions (of the borrowing company, its industry, and the general economy).

Fixed and floating charges: Claims on assets pledged as security for debt. Fixed charges cover specific fixed assets, and floating charges relate to all or part of a company's assets.

Floating lien: A general lien against a group of assets, such as accounts receivable or inventory, without the assets being specifically identified.

Flotation: A method of raising equity financing by selling shares on a stock market, and often allowing management and institutions to realize some of their investment at the same time. *(See initial public offering.)*

Follow-on financing: A second or subsequent round of funding for a company.

Founder shares: Shares that the founders issue to themselves in exchange for their "sweat equity;" meaning that the founders do not buy their shares for a nominal amount of cash. Founder shares are typically issued prior to the first round of financing.

Four Fs: Founders, family, friends, and foolhardy person who invest in a person's private business, generally a startup. *(See informal investor and angel.)*

Franchising: An organizational form in which a firm (the franchisor) with a market-tested business package centered on a product or service enters into a continuing contractual relationship with franchisees operating under the franchisor's trade name to produce or market goods or services according to a format specified by the franchisor.

Free cash flow: Cash flow in excess of that required to fund all projects that have a positive net present value when discounted at the relevant cost of capital. Conflicts of interest between shareholders and managers may arise when the organization generates free cash flow. Shareholders may desire higher dividends, but managers may wish to invest in projects providing a return below the cost of capital. *(See cost of capital and net present value.)*

Future value: The value at a future date of a present amount of money. $FV_t = PV \times (1 + K/100)^t$, where FV, is the future value, PV is the present value, K is the percentage annual rate of return, and t is the number of years. For example, an investment of \$100,000 must have a future value of \$384,160 after four years to produce a rate of return of 40%, which is the kind of return that an investor in an early-stage company expects to earn. *(See net present value, present value, and rate of return.)*

Gatekeeper: Colloquial term for a person or firm that advises clients on investments in venture capital funds; formally called an investment advisor.

G7: Group of Seven Countries—Canada, France, Germany, Italy, Japan, United Kingdom and USA—that meet to discuss issues covering macroeconomic management, international trade, international finances, relations with developing countries, and other global issues. They are sometimes joined by Russia, making the co-called G8.

GDP (Gross Domestic Product): The total market value of goods and services produced by workers and capital within a country's borders during a specific period, which is generally a calendar year.

Gearing: British term of leverage. *(See leverage.)*

GEM (Global Entrepreneurship Monitor): An annual study of entrepreneurial activity within different countries.

General partner: A partner with unlimited legal responsibility for the debts and liabilities of a partnership.

Going concern: This assumes that the company will continue as an operating business as opposed to going out of business and liquidating its assets.

Golden handcuffs: A combination of rewards and penalties given to key managers to dissuade them from leaving the company. Examples are high salaries, paid on a deferred basis while employment is maintained, and stock options.

Goodwill: The difference between the purchase price of a company and the net value of its assets purchased.

Gross margin: Gross profit as a percentage of net sales revenue.

Gross profit (gross income, gross earnings): Net sales revenue minus the direct cost of the products sold.

Guarantee: An undertaking to prove that a debt or obligation of another will be paid or performed. It may relate either to a specific debt or to a series of transactions such as a guarantee of a bank overdraft. For example, entrepreneurs are often required to provide personal guarantees for loans borrowed by their companies.

Guerilla marketing: Unique, low cost marketing methods to capture attention in a crowded marketplace.

Harvest: The realization of the value of an investment. *(See exit.)*

Headcount: The number of employees within a company at a particular point in time.

High-potential venture: A company started with the intent of growing quickly to annual sales of at least \$30-50 million in five years. It has the potential to have a firm-commitment IPO.

Hurdle rate: The minimum rate of return that is acceptable to investors. *(See return on investment.)*

Income statement: A summary of a company's revenues, expenses, and profits over a specified period of time. *(See pro forma statements.)*

Informal investor: An individual who puts money into a private company—usually a startup or a small business. Informal investments range from micro loans from family members to sizable equity purchases by sophisticated business angels.

Initial public offering (IPO): Process by which a company raises money, and gets listed on a stock market. *(See flotation.)*

Intellectual property (IP): Knowledge that a company possesses and considers proprietary. IP can be protected through patents, trademarks, etc.

Interest cover: The extent to which periodic interest commitments on borrowings are exceeded by periodic profits. It is the ratio of profits before the deduction of interest and taxes to interest payments. The ratio may also be expressed as the cash flow from operations divided by the amount of interest payable.

Internal locus of control: Persons with an internal locus of control see themselves as responsible for the outcomes of their own actions. These individuals often believe that they control their destiny.

Internal rate of return (IRR): The discount rate that equates the present value of the future net cash flows from an investment with the project's cash outflows. It is a means of expressing the percentage rate of return projected on a proposed investment. For an investment in a company, the calculation takes account of cash invested, cash receipts from dividend payments and redemptions, percentage of equity held, expected date of payments, realization of the investment and capitalization at that point, and possible further financing requirements. The calculation will frequently be quoted in a range depending on sensitivity analysis. *(See discount rate, present value, future value, and rate of return.)*

Inventory: Finished goods, work in process of manufacture, and raw materials owned by a company.

Investment bank: A financial institution engaged in the issue of new securities, including management and underwriting of issues as well as securities trading and distribution.

Investment flows: Cash flows associated with purchase and sales of both fixed assets and business interests.

IPO: *See initial public offering.*

IRR: *See internal rate of return.*

ISP: Internet Service Provider—a company that provides direct connections to the Internet for computer users.

Junior debt: Loan ranking after senior debt or secured debt for payment in the event of a default.

Junk bonds: A variety of high-yield, unsecured bonds tradable on a secondary market and not considered to be of investment quality by credit-rating agencies. High yield normally indicates higher risk.

Key person insurance: Additional security provided to financial backers of a company through the purchase of insurance on the lives of key managers who are seen as crucial to the future of the company. Should one or more of those key executives die prematurely, the financial backers would receive the insurance payment.

Key success factors (KSFs): The attributes that customers use to distinguish between competing products or services. KSFs go beyond just product attributes, and may include brand and other intangibles.

Lead investor: In syndicated deals, normally the investor who originates, structures, and subsequently plays the major monitoring role.

Lead underwriter: The head of a syndicate of financial firms that are sponsoring an initial public offering of securities or a secondary offering of securities.

Lead venture capital firm: The head of a syndicate of venture capital firms that is investing privately in a company.

Lemons and plums: Bad deals and good deals, respectively.

Leverage: The amount of debt in a company's financing structure, which may be expressed as a percentage of the total financing or as a ratio of debt to equity. The various quasi-equity (preference-type shares) and quasi-debt (mezzanine debt) instruments used to fund later-stage companies means that great care is required in calculating and interpreting leverage or gearing ratios.

Leveraged buyout (LBO): Acquisition of a company by an investor group, an investor, or an investment/LBO partnership, with a significant amount of debt (usually at least 70% of the total capitalization) and with plans to repay the debt with funds generated from the acquired company's operations or from asset sales. LBOs are frequently financed in part with junk bonds.

Lien: A legal claim on certain assets that are used to secure a loan.

Limited liability company: A company owned by "members," who either manage the business themselves or appoint "managers" to run it for them. All members and managers have the benefit of limited liability, and, in most cases, are taxed in the same way as a subchapter S corporation without having to conform to the S corporation restrictions.

Limited partnership: A business organization with one or more **general partners,** who manage the business and assume legal debts and obligations, and one or more **limited partners,** who are liable only to the extent of their investments. Limited partners also enjoy rights to the partnership's cash flow, but are not liable for company obligations.

Line of credit (with a bank): An arrangement between a bank and a customer specifying the maximum amount of unsecured debt the customer can owe the bank at a given point in time.

Line of credit (with a vendor): A limit set by the seller on the amount that a purchaser can buy on credit.

Liquidation value (of an asset): The amount of money that can be realized from the sale of an asset sold separately from its operating organization.

Liquidation value (of a company): The market value of the assets minus the liabilities that must be paid of a company that is liquidating.

Liquidity: The ability of an asset to be converted to cash as quickly as possible and without any price discount.

Listing: Acceptance of a security for trading on an organized stock exchange. Hence, a stock traded on the New York Stock Exchange is said to be listed on the NYSE.

Living dead: Venture capital jargon for a company that has no prospect of being harvested with a public offering or an acquisition; hence, the venture capital firm cannot realize its investment in the company.

Liquidation value: The total amount that could be realized from selling the business' individual assets, after satisfying all of the business' liabilities.

Loan note: A form of vendor finance or deferred payment. The purchaser (borrower) may agree to make payments to the holder of the loan note at specified future dates. The holder may be able to obtain cash at an earlier date by selling at a discount to a financing institution that will collect on maturity.

Lock-up period: An interval during which an investment may not be sold. In the case of an IPO, employees may not sell their shares for a period of time determined by the underwriter and usually lasting 180 days.

Locus of control: The perception of the factors responsible for the outcome of an event. Individuals with an internal locus of control believe their actions caused the outcome. Conversely, individuals with an external locus of control believe the outcome was determined by outside forces.

Management buy in (MBI): The transfer of ownership of an entity to a new set of owners in which new managers coming into the entity are a significant element.

Management buyout (MBO): The transfer of ownership of an entity to a new set of owners in which the existing management and employees are a significant element.

Market capitalization: The total value at market prices of the securities in issue for a company, a stock market, or a sector of a stock market, calculated by multiplying the number of shares issued by the market price per share.

Market-comparable valuation: The value of a private company based of the valuation of similar public companies.

Marketing: An organizational function and a set of processes for creating, communicating, and delivering value to customers and for managing customer relationships in ways that benefit the organization and its stakeholders.[1]

Merger: The combining of two or more entities into one, through a purchase acquisition or a pooling of interests.

Mezzanine financing: Strictly, any form of financing instrument between ordinary shares and senior debt. The forms range from senior mezzanine debt, which may simply carry an interest rate above that for senior secured debt, to junior mezzanine debt, which may carry rights to subscribe for equity but no regular interest payment.

Microcredit: Tiny loans to entrepreneurs too poor to qualify for traditional bank loans. In developing countries especially, microcredit enables very poor people to engage in self-employment projects that generate income.

Microfinancing: Same as microcredit.

Modified book value: Valuation of a business in which all assets and liabilities (including off-balance sheet, intangible, and contingent) are adjusted to their fair market values.

Money left on the table: The difference between the price at the end of the first day's trading and the initial offering price, multiplied by the number of shares in the offering.

Multiple: The amount of money realized from the sale of an investment divided by the amount of money originally invested.

Murphy's Law: What can go wrong, will go wrong. An unexpected setback will happen at the most inconvenient moment.

National Association of Securities Dealers Automated Quotation (NASDAQ): An electronic system for trading stocks. It is owned and operated by The Nasdaq Stock Market, Inc.

Necessity entrepreneurship: A business started out of necessity by an entrepreneur who cannot find a better source of income through employment.

NGO: Non-Governmental Organization.

Net Assets: Assets less liabilities.

Net income (net earnings, net profit): A company's final income after all expenses and taxes have been deducted from all revenues. It is also known as the bottom line.

Net income margin: Net income as a percentage of net sales revenue. In a typical year an average US company has a net income margin of about 5%.

Net liquid value: Liquid financial assets minus callable liabilities.

Net present value: The present value of an investment's future net cash flows minus the initial investment. In theory, if the net present value is greater than 0, an investment should be made. For example, an investor is asked to invest $100,000 in a company that is expanding. He expects a rate of return of 30%. The company offers to pay him back $300,000 after four years. The present value of $300,000 at a rate of return of 30% is $105,038. Thus, the net present value of the investment is $5,038, so the investment should be made. *(See free cash flow, future value, present value, and rate of return.)*

Net profit: *See net income.*

Net surplus: Total revenue minus total cost and expenses in a non-profit organization; equivalent to net income in a for-profit enterprise.

Net worth: *See book value.*

New York Stock Exchange (NYSE): The largest stock exchange in the world, located in New York. Also known as the Big Board.

NPO: Non-Profit Organization; also Not-for-profit Organization.

OECD: The Organization for Economic Cooperation and Development comprises Australia, Austria, Belgium, Canada, Czech Republic, Denmark, Finland, France, Germany, Greece, Hungary, Iceland, Ireland, Italy, Republic of Korea, Japan, Luxembourg, Mexico, the Netherlands, New Zealand, Norway, Poland, Portugal, Spain, Sweden, Switzerland, Turkey, UK, and United States.

Offering circular: *See prospectus.*

Olin College: Starting in the late 1980's, the National Science Foundation and the engineering community at-large started calling for reform in engineering education. In order to serve the needs of the growing global economy, it was clear that engineers needed to have business and entrepreneurship skills, creativity, and an understanding of the social, political, and economic contexts of engineering. The F.W. Olin Foundation decided the best way to maximize its impact was to help create a college that could address these emerging needs. Olin College was chartered in 1997 and took its first freshman class in 2002. It is located adjacent to Babson College.

Operating cash flows: Cash flows directly generated by a company's operations. The cash flow from operating activity equals net income plus depreciation minus increase in accounts receivable minus increase in inventories plus increase in accounts payable plus increase in accruals.

(See financing flows and investment flows.)

Operating income: Earnings (profit) before deduction of interest payments and income taxes, abbreviated to EBIT. It measures a company's earning power from its ongoing operations. It is of particular concern to a company's lenders, such as banks, because operating income demonstrates the ability of a company to earn sufficient income to pay the interest on its debt. *(See times interest earned.)*

Opportunity: An idea that has commercial viability and that provides the entrepreneur and company the potential to earn attractive margins and a return on their investment.

Opportunity entrepreneurship: The pursuit of a new venture because it is deemed as better than remaining in one's current job or other jobs that might be available.

Options: See stock option plan.

Out of cash (OOC): A common problem with entrepreneurial companies. The OOC time period is cash on hand divided by the burn rate.

Over the counter (OTC): The purchase and sale of financial instruments not conducted on a stock exchange such as the New York Stock Exchange or the American Stock Exchange. The largest OTC market is the NASDAQ.

Owners' equity: Common stock plus retained earnings. *(See book value of a company.)*

Pain point: A potential customer's problem that a business can relieve with its product or service.

Paid-in capital: Par value per share times the number of shares issued. Additional paid-in capital is the price paid in excess of par value times the number of shares issued.

Partnership: Legal form of a business in which two or more persons are co-owners, sharing profits and losses.

Par value: Nominal price placed on a share of common stock.

Patent: Granted by the government, patents protect unique devices (or combinations of components integrated into a device) and processes.

Penetration pricing: Pricing your product at a relatively lower price to gain high market share, but with lower margins.

Piggy-back registration rights: The right to register unregistered stock in the event of a company having a public stock offering.

Pledging: The use of a company's accounts receivable as security (collateral) for a short-term loan.

---

[1] American Marketing Association, 2004; http://www.marketingpower.com/content21257.php

Pop (first day): Percentage increase in the price of a stock at the end of the first day's trading over the initial offering price.

Positioning: A company's offering on certain product attributes—the ones customers care about most—relative to competitive offerings.

Portfolio: Collection of investments. For example, the portfolio of a venture capital fund comprises all its investments.

Post-money valuation: The value of a company immediately after a round of additional money is invested.

Pratt's Guide to Private Equity Sources: Annual sourcebook for private equity, especially venture capital.

Preemptive rights: The rights of shareholders to maintain their percentage ownership of a company by purchasing a proportionate number of shares of any new issue of common stock. *(See antidilution, dilution, and pro rata interest.)*

Preferred stock (Preference shares): A class of shares that incorporate the right to a fixed dividend and usually a prior claim on assets, in preference to ordinary shares, in the event of a liquidation. Cumulative preference shares provide an entitlement to a cumulative dividend if, in any year, the preference dividend is unpaid due to insufficient profits being earned. Preference shares are usually redeemable at specific dates.

Pre-money valuation: The value of a company's equity before additional money is invested.

Preliminary prospectus: The initial document published by an underwriter of a new issue of stock to be given to prospective investors. It is understood that the document will be modified significantly before the final prospectus is published; also called a red herring.

Prepayment: A payment on a loan made prior to the original due date.

Present value (PV): The current value of a given future cash flow stream, FV_t, after t years, discounted at a rate of return of K% is $PV = FV_t/(1 + K/100^t)$. For example, if an investor expects a rate of return of 60% on an investment in a seed-stage company, and she believes that her investment will be worth $750,000 after five years, then the present value of her investment is $71,526. *(See discount rate, future value, net present value, and rate of return.)*

Present value of future cash flows (valuation): Present value is today's value of a future payment, or stream of payments, discounted at some appropriate compound interest, or discount rate; also called time value of money.

The present value of company is the present value of the future free cash flows plus the residual (terminal) value of the firm:

$$PV = \sum_{t=1}^{N}(FCF_t)/(1+K)^t + (RV_N)/(1+K)^N$$

Where K is the cost of capital; FCF_t is the free cash flow in year t; N is the number of years; and RV_N is the residual value in year N.

Free Cash Flow
= Operating Income
− Interest
− Taxes on Operating Income
+ Depreciation & Other Non-Cash Charges
− Increase in Net Working Capital
− Capital Expenditures (Replacement & Growth)
− Principal Repayments

Prevalence rate: The percentage of a population participating in a particular activity.

Price discrimination: A strategy where different customer segments are charged different prices.

Price-earnings ratio (P/E ratio): The ratio of the market value of a firm's equity to its after-tax profits (may be calculated from price per share and earnings per share).

Price points: Product pricing in standardized or fixed points.

Price promotion: Discounts from the base price for a short period to attain specific goals such as introducing a product to new customers.

Price skimming: The strategy of pricing your product high to generate high margins, but recognizing that you'll gain limited market share because prices are relatively high.

Primary data: Market research collected specifically for a particular purpose through focus groups, surveys, or experiments.

Primary target audience (PTA): A group of potential customers identified by demographic and psychographic data that will be the focus of the company's early marketing and sales efforts.

Prime rate: Short-term interest rate charged by a bank to its largest, most credit-worthy customers.

Private placement: The direct sales of securities to a small number of investors *(See Regulation D.)*

Product life cycle: A stage model of a product's life, including introduction, growth, maturity, and decline; a similar concept to the S-curve lifecycle for an industry.

Profit: Synonymous with income and earnings.

Pro forma statements: Projected financial statements: income and cash-flow statements and balance sheets. For a startup company, it is usual to make pro forma statements monthly for the first two years and annually for the next three years.

Pro rata interest: The right granted the investor to maintain the same percentage ownership in the event of future financings. *(See antidilution and dilution.)*

Prospectus: A document giving a description of a securities issue, including a complete statement of the terms of the issue and a description of the issuer, as well as its historical financial statements. Also referred to as an offering circular. *(See red herring.)*

Psychographics: Information that categorizes customers based upon their personality, psychological traits, lifestyles, values, and social group membership. It helps to understand what motivates customers to act in the ways they do, and is important because members of a specific demographic category can have dramatically different psychographic profiles. Marketing strictly based on demographic information will be ineffective because it ignores these differences.

Purchasing Power Parity (PPP): A method of measuring the relative purchasing power of different countries' currencies over the same types of goods and services. Because goods and services may cost more in one country than in another, PPP allows us to make more accurate comparisons of standards of living across countries. PPP estimates use price comparisons of comparable items, but, since not all items can be matched exactly across countries and time, the estimates are not always "robust."

Put: A contract allowing the holder to sell a given number of securities back to the issuer of the contract at a fixed price for a given period of time.

Quiet period: The period starting when an issuer hires an underwriter and ending 25 days after the security begins trading, during which the issuer cannot comment publicly on the offering, due to SEC rules.

R^2 (R-Square): The fraction of variation in the dependent variable that is explained by variation in the independent variable. A high value indicates a strong relationship between the two variables.

Rate of return: The annual return on an investment. If a sum of money, PV, is invested and after t years that investment is worth FV_t the return on investment K = $[(FV/PV)^{1/t} − 1] \times 100\%$. For example, if $100 is invested originally, and one year later $108 is paid back to the investor, the annual rate of return is 8%.

Realization: *See exit and harvest.*

Redeemable shares: Shares that may be redeemable at the option of the company, or the shareholder, or both.

Red herring: Preliminary prospectus circulated by underwriters to gauge investor interest in a planned offering. A legend in red ink on its cover indicates that the registration has not yet become effective and is still being reviewed by the SEC.

Registration statement: A carefully worded and organized document, including a prospectus, filed with the SEC before an IPO.

Regulation D: An SEC regulation that governs private placement exemption.

Reserve(s): Non-profit organization's equivalent of owners' equity in a for-profit company.

Residual value: Market capitalization of a company at a specific time.

Revenue drivers: Elements within a business model that can be influenced to increase revenue, such as price, quantity purchased, awareness of product, availability, and so forth.

Retained earnings: The part of net income retained in the company and not distributed to stockholders.

Return on investment (ROI): The annual income that an investment earns.

Roll-up: A strategy to consolidate a fragmented industry. The primary examples are Wal-Mart, Home Depot, and Staples.

Running returns: Periodic returns, such as interest and dividends, from an investment (in contrast to a one-time capital gain).

Road show: A series of meetings with potential investors and brokers, conducted by a company and its underwriter, prior to a securities offering, especially an IPO.

SBA: Small Business Administration.

SBDC: Small Business Development Centers (supported by the SBA).

SBI: Small Business Institutes, run by universities and colleges with SBA support.

SBIC: Small Business Investments Companies.

SBIR: Small Business Innovation Research Program.

S-curve: A model of new market product adoption. It illustrates market emergence, rapid growth, stability, and decline.

Schumpeter, Joseph A.: Moravian-born economist whose book *The Theory of Economic Development,* written in Vienna in 1912, introduced the modern theory of entrepreneurship, in which the entrepreneur plays the central role in economic development by destroying the static equilibrium of the existing economy. Excellent modern examples are the roles played by Steve Jobs, Bill Gates, and Dan Bricklin in creating the microcomputer industry in the late 1970s. By the beginning of the 1990s, microcomputers (personal computers) were the principal force shaping the computer industry, and the old companies manufacturing mainframe and minicomputers, which dominated the computer industry until the mid-1980s, were in distress, ranging from outright bankruptcy to record-breaking losses.

SCORE: Service Core of Retired Executives, sponsored by the SBA to provide consulting to small businesses.

Secondary data: Market research that is gathered from already published sources, like an industry association study or census report.

Second-round financing: The introduction of further funding by the original investors or new investors to enable the company to grow or deal with unexpected problems. Each round of financing tends to cover the next period of growth.

Second-stage financing: Financing to fuel the growth of an early stage company.

Secondary offering: The sale of stock by an issuer or underwriter after a company's securities have already begun trading publicly.

Secondary target market (STA): See primary target audience. A group of potential customers identified by demographic and psychographic data that will be a secondary or alternative focus of the company's early marketing and sales efforts.

Securities and Exchange Commission (SEC): Regulatory body for investor protection in the United States, created by the Securities Exchange Act of 1934. The supervision of dealers is delegated to the self-regulatory bodies of the stock exchanges and NASD under the provisions of the Maloney Act of 1938.

Seed financing: A relatively small amount of money provided to prove a concept; it may involve product development and market research but rarely involves the initial marketing of a product.

Seed-stage company: A company that doesn't have much more than a concept.

Sensitivity analysis: Examination of how the projected performance of the business varies with changes in the key assumptions on which the forecasts are based.

Short-term security: Generally, an obligation maturing in less than one year.

Slotting fees: The fees that a product manufacturer pays a retail outlet to place products in its warehouse and then ultimately in the retail store.

Small business: The SBA defines most small businesses as ones with 500 or fewer employees; but there are exceptions. Details can be found at http://www.sba.gov/size/sizetable2002.pdf.

Social capital: Networks, norms, and trust that facilitates coordination and cooperation between people for mutual benefit.

Social entrepreneur: Someone who develops social innovation through entrepreneurial solutions. A social entrepreneur recognizes a social problem or need, comes up with a solution, and creates an organization to pursue it.

Social model: This term is often applied to the economic systems of nations where there is high welfare protection including restrictions on employer's rights to hire and fire employees, generous unemployment benefits, and mandated work weeks (e.g., 35 hour maximum in France). The social models are especially strong in France and Germany.

Sole proprietorship: A business form with one owner who is responsible for all the firm's liabilities.

Startup company: A company that is already in business and is developing a prototype but has not sold it in significant commercial quantities.

Startup financing: Funding provided to companies for use in product development and initial marketing. Companies may be in the process of being organized or may have been in business a short time (one year or less), but have not sold their product commercially. Generally, such firms have assembled the key management, prepared a business plan, made market studies, and completed other preliminary tasks.

Stock option plan: A plan designed to motivate employees, especially key ones, by placing a portion of the common stock of the company under option at a fixed price to defined employees. The option may then be exercised by the employees at a future date. Stock options are often introduced as part of the remuneration package of senior executives.

Stock-out: Demand for a product exceeds the inventory that a company has on hand. Stock-outs may lead to lost sales as customers seek other options.

Strategic acquisition: When a company buys another company to get access to a product or service that complements its existing business.

Subchapter S corporation: A small business corporation in which the owners personally pay the corporation's income taxes.

Subordinated debt: Loans that may be unsecured or, more commonly, secured by secondary charges that rank after senior debt for repayment in the event of default. Also referred to as junior debt or mezzanine debt.

Sweat equity: Equity acquired by the management team at favorable terms reflecting the value to the business of the managers' past and future efforts.

Syndicate: A group of investors that act together when investing in a company.

TEA Indices (Total Entrepreneurial Activity Indices): The percent of the adult population that is participating in a specific type of entrepreneurship. For example, the TEA (Overall) Index is the percent of the adult population that is in the process of starting a new business or has a business less than 42 months old.

Tertiary Target Audience (TTA): See primary target audience. A group of potential customers identified by demographic and psychographic data that will **not** be the focus of the company's early marketing and sales efforts.

Term loan: Debt originally scheduled to be repaid in more than one year, but usually in 10 years or less.

Term sheet: Summary of the principal conditions for a proposed investment in a company by a venture capital firm.

Third-stage financing: Funding to fuel the growth of an early stage company.

Times interest earned: Earnings before interest and taxes, divided by interest (**EBIT/I**). The higher this ratio, the more secure the loan on which interest is paid. It is a basic measure of the creditworthiness of a company.

Top-down forecasting: Determining projected revenues by estimating what a certain percentage of market share translates into in terms of revenues. This method is highly suspect and bottom-up and comparable projections tend to be better.

Trade promotion: Price promotions offered to retailers to induce them to carry your product.

Trade sale: This is the sale of a business to another company, often, but not always, in a similar line of business.

Trade secret: Knowledge that is kept secret for the purpose of gaining an advantage in business over one's competitors.

Trademarks: Protection obtainable for any word, symbol, or combination thereof that is used on goods to indicate their source.

Triggering event: An incident that prompts a person to take steps to start a new venture.

Underpricing: The difference between the closing price on the first day of trading and the initial offering price of a stock.

Underwater stock options: When the price of a stock is lower than the exercise price of a stock option. *(See stock option.)*

Underwrite: An arrangement under which investment banks each agree to buy a certain amount of securities of a new issue on a given date and at a given price, thereby assuring the issuer of the full proceeds of the financing.

Underwriter: An institution engaged in the business of underwriting securities issues.

Underwriting fee: The share of the gross spread of a new issue accruing to members of the underwriting group after the expenses of the issue have been paid.

Unsecured loans: Debt that is not backed by a pledge of specific assets.

Valuation (of a company): The market value of a company. *(See market capitalization.)*

Value-added (by investors): Many venture capital firms claim that they add more than money to investee companies. They call it value-added, which includes strategic advice on such matters as hiring key employees, marketing, production, control, and financing.

Value proposition: The value of a business' products and services to its customers.

Venture capitalist: A financial institution specializing in the provision of equity and other forms of long-term capital to enterprises, usually to firms with a limited track record but with the expectation of substantial growth. The venture capitalist may provide both funding and varying degrees of managerial and technical expertise. Venture capital has traditionally been associated with startups; however, venture capitalists have increasingly participated in later-stage projects.

Vesting period: The time period before shares are owned unconditionally by an employee who is sold stock with the stipulation that he must continue to work for the company selling him the shares. If his employment terminates before the end of that period, the company has the right to buy back the shares at the same price at which it originally sold them to him.

Visible venture capital (formal venture capital): The organized venture capital industry consisting of formal firms, in contrast to invisible venture capital or informal venture capital.

Vulture capital: A derogatory term for venture capital.

Waiver: Consent granted by an investor or lender to permit an investor or borrower to be in default on a covenant.

Walking wounded: Venture capital jargon for a company that is not successful enough to be harvested with an IPO or acquisition, but might be worth another round of investment to try to get it into harvestable condition.

Warrant: An option to purchase common stock at a specified price. *(See equity kicker.)*

Warranty: A statement of fact or opinion concerning the condition of a company. The inclusion of warranties in an investment agreement gives the investor a claim against the company if it subsequently becomes apparent that the company's condition was not as stated at the time of the investment.

Yield: Annualized rate of return on a security.

COMPANY INDEX

NAME INDEX

SUBJECT INDEX